ENDING ON THE RIGHT NOTE

Reviews 2010-2016

Stan Metzger

These reviews by Stan Metzger (1947-2016) first appeared on Seen and Heard International, MusicWeb International's review site for concerts, operas and ballet, and are reprinted with their kind permission. The reviews are published here in reverse order by date, as they appear on the site.

On the cover: *String Musicians* (1568) by Jost Amman

Printed in the United States of America

♫ *Two E-flat Symphonies: A Study in Contrasts*

The Philadelphia Orchestra, Yannick Nézet-Séguin (conductor), Carnegie Hall, New York, 26.1.2016

Haydn: Symphony No. 103 in E-flat major, "Drumroll"
Bruckner: Symphony No. 4 in E-flat major, "Romantic"

The works in this performance do have a commonality, but more in theory than in actual practice. They share an E-flat major key and the traditional four movements of fast, slow, minuet (Scherzo) and a quick finale. The Haydn is the penultimate "London" symphony, as well as the penultimate of his 104 symphonies. It's only recently that his earlier, and in many ways more interesting, symphonies have come into their own. These earlier works, starting with the "Morning," "Noon" and "Night" (6, 7, 8) through the "Sturm und Drang" (40s-50s), were daring and experimental. There are occasionally performances of some of the named symphonies ("Bear," "Hunt," "Chicken") or works that have a story behind them, such as the "Farewell" symphony where the players leave as each of the orchestral section parts ends. The later symphonies tend to be tighter structurally but also less daring. It was these late pieces that made it easy to tag Haydn with a "Papa" appellation as a stodgy purveyor of straitlaced music.

With the arrival of the early music movement, specialist groups wanted to rethink Haydn performance practice in terms both of the size of the orchestra and the sounds of the instruments. Now that many of the assumptions of the early music movement have been absorbed by most conductors, we don't have to feel judgmental when a standard orchestra plays a Haydn symphony. Adjustments can be made in terms of changing orchestral section size. Although not all the string players here were consistently vibrato-less, the concertmaster, David Lee, was and set an example of how music of this time should be played.

Nézet-Séguin had barely reached the podium when a brief booming sound came from the stage. I thought maybe the timpanist was still tuning his drums, or perhaps the notorious rumblings that have plagued the hall from the adjacent subway had finally reached their limit. But then the conductor feigned surprise, smiled and continued with the performance. I was doubly surprised, knowing that Haydn had marked the tremolo *pp*.

It's nothing new to speak of how unusual Bruckner's music is and how strongly listeners either love him or hate him. Most who "understand" him also understand why others don't. Like so many influential artists, he forces you to approach his music in a new and different way, and it is a difficult way. Unlike Mahler, to whom he is often compared, Bruckner's thematic motifs come to the forefront and then just fade away as quickly as they appear. Sometimes they show up again later, but themes are never developed as in the traditional sonata form. The overall construction of his symphonies, within each movement and between movements, often feels unbalanced and incomplete. Yet in many ways Bruckner's musical genius was ahead of its time, still working within the tonal system but using that system to suspend tonal resolution: blocks of notes rise from soft to loud, then at the critical moments dissolve instead of resolve. This leaves the listener unsatisfied but hungry for more, until the movement or symphony is resolved by a true cadence. It's like riding a wave, satisfied with the current wave but always expecting the next one.

When Bruckner is played the way he should be played, there are moments of sheer beauty. The music shimmers and glistens. It is a yearning for something not easy to define, something that goes beyond the bold unresolved crescendos. At this performance, Nézet-Séguin dampened and dulled moments when sharp accents were needed. The monumental crescendos at their highest peaks were at times a bit too jagged and raw. Some brief woodwind solos were buried by the strings, but the strings did a fine job sustaining the symphony's underlying pulse, mainly through long stretches of tremolos. There was no lack of technical confidence on the part of the instrumentalists (aside from a few rough spots from the horns), and the orchestra seemed both passionate about the music and committed to their leader.

♪ *Marc-André Hamelin: Imperturbable as Ever*
Marc-André Hamelin (piano), Carnegie Hall, New York, 20.1.2016

Mozart: Piano Sonata in C major
Busoni: "Giga, bolero e variazione" (after Mozart) from *An die Jugend*
Ravel: *Gaspard de la nuit*
Hamelin: *Pavane Variée* (New York Premiere)
Liszt: Piano Sonata in B minor

I make a habit of trying to catch all of Marc-André Hamelin's recitals in New York. Surprisingly, this concert was only his third solo event in the main hall at Carnegie Hall. His first appearance was in 1985 as a contestant (and winner) of the Carnegie Hall International American Music Competition for Pianists. The second time was in 1988. Another 15 or so visits have seen him as part of a group or as pianist in a concerto. His recitals are always occasions to catch up with his widening musical interests and, of course, to see which impossibly difficult works he has chosen with which to awe the audience. Unlike many touring artists, he rarely plays the same concert twice. Not to denigrate the status of Angela Hewitt or Andras Schiff, but their seasonal recitals are set programs performed at every stop on their tours. Hamelin may play a Medtner or Scriaban sonata in New York. But rest assured that the next day in Boston, he might play the same composers but often different works. One can only imagine how much repertory he has internalized as he never performs with a score in front of him.

My interest in him grew out of his recording of Godowsky's transformations of the Chopin *Études*, which created the odd title "Studies on the Studies of Chopin." These pieces are not simply transcriptions but rather reworkings that gain effect through their increased difficulty. Hamelin is at his peak in these recordings, accepting every challenge Godowski put in his score, and then some. Most amazing are those that were written for one hand—Chopin's original *Études* are difficult enough to perform with two.

The concert opened with Mozart's Piano Sonata in C major, the sonic opposite of what one expects from Hamelin. Mozart himself called this piece "sonata facile." But nothing by Mozart is really easy and getting to the heart of the music cannot be done by overpowering it. There are big pianists who can temper their style and get lovely results. Sokolov is one: a bear of a man, capable of the most delicate and lyrical Mozart. Hamelin, not surprisingly, excels at Haydn, with several albums recorded. Haydn can tolerate big gestures: Hamelin plays Haydn sensibly and is always in touch with the composer's humor. With Mozart, Hamelin gets the sonata's big picture but not the heart of the work which is in the details.

Much of the delight in Ravel's *Gaspard de la Nuit* comes from sounds never produced before on the piano: the gleaming and glistening glissandos of "Ondine"; the relentless repetition of B-flat chords representing the tolling of bells before the gallows in "Gibet"; and "Scarbo," one of the most challenging pieces of music ever written. Aiming to portray goblins and dwarfs, the music becomes progressively gnarly, with dissonances made up from appoggiaturas that remain unresolved and groups of arpeggiated seventh and ninth chords. Hamelin reveled in the work's technical demands, playing some of the most difficult chords as fast as humanly possible.

A gap in my musical knowledge was a piece that I came to through Busoni's transcription of it: Mozart's "Eine Kleine Gigue." Busoni must have been attracted to this work by its modern sensibility, so modern, in fact, that he barely changed the first and second binary sections, merely transposing everything down an octave. The variations occur only after the bolero, a slightly disguised rendering of the fandango from Mozart's *Marriage of Figaro*. The only uniquely Busoni-style material is the melding of both sources. It sounded very modern, and Hamelin accomplished this by avoiding legato, emphasizing a détaché styling instead. One need only listen to the transitional "12 tone row" of the first movement of Mozart's "Jupiter" symphony, written a few years earlier, to realize what Mozart was capable of envisioning about the future of music.

Hamelin's own composition, *Pavane Variée*, opens on a 16th-century dance tune that is heard once but then is varied with such heavy Lisztian chords and use of the pedals that we only get a sense of the direction in which Hamelin is taking us. It's certainly a piece that deserves a more thorough listening before judging its worth.

For many, including me, the Liszt piano sonata that concluded the program is his masterpiece. Liszt wrote an immense amount of music; recording his entire piano output consumes just under a hundred CDs. Much of this is bombast, and there are volumes and volumes of transcriptions, which are the work of a craftsman. Because he didn't possess the genius of Beethoven, Liszt settled for transcribing all of Beethoven's symphonies for piano.

This sonata is different. Even the term sonata barely describes what is really a fantasia on the order of Schuman's Fantasia, Op.17. Although the score has tempo markings which signify a new section, it would be hard to call them end-of-movement signifiers. There is also little of the classical sonata form in either the individual sections or in their relation to one another.

The piece is arduous, to say the least, and I've heard it attempted by young, extremely talented performers who nail the very difficult technical aspects. But that is only part of the whole: once you get past the tough passages, you have to rethink the score. This is an ideal work for Hamelin's mind and body. He doesn't need to be concerned with playing the notes, and that allows him the freedom to be more sensitive to the work's emotional content. There are enough *ppp* and *fff* for him to display the range of colors throughout the dynamic palette.

Seemingly unfazed by this massive effort, Hamelin performed three encores which were no child's play. The last and most familiar work was the final prelude from Debussy's Book 2 of *Préludes*. What could be a more appropriate end to a concert of fireworks than *feux d'artifice*.

♫ *Biondi and Europa Galante Reveal Diary from a Vivaldi Star Pupil*

Chiara's Diary: A Life at the Pieta Orphanage in Venice, 1730—1770: Europa Galante, Fabio Biondi (conductor, violin, viola d'amore), Zankel Hall, Carnegie Hall, New York, 16.1.2016

Porta: Sinfonia in D major for Strings and Continuo
Vivaldi: Sinfonia in G major for Strings and Continuo
Porpora: Sinfonia in G major for Two Violins and Continuo
Martinelli: Concerto for Violin in E major
Vivaldi: Concerto in D major for Violin, Strings and Continuo
Martinelli: Concerto in D major for Viola d'amore and Strings
Bernasconi: Sinfonia in D major for Strings
Perotti: Grave for Violin and Organ in G minor
Bernasconi: Sinfonia in D major for Strings
Latilla: Sinfonia in G major

Like his French counterpart, William Christie, Fabio Biondi rarely fails in any project he undertakes. One can attend a concert or purchase a recording by him confident that the performance will be of the highest quality. On stage there is minimal posturing: even Biondi's occasional dips and twists are restrained. The preparation for this concert and its earlier recording are exemplary, and Biondi's involvement is thorough.

Just about any program notes on Vivaldi will mention his role as director of the all-female orchestra of Venice's Ospedale della Pietà. While little is known about the training of these young women, the discovery of a diary belonging to one of the most talented musicians, Chiara, offers some first-hand information on the musical life within the cloisters. Not much has been revealed about the personal writings of Chiara, who lived her entire life in the sanctuary, but there is enough to gather that Chiara was deeply attached to Vivaldi and, as evinced by some of the music written for her by the Red Priest, her admiration was reciprocated.

Whether or not there is something in the Italian sensibility that wants to make stories or projects out of rediscovered manuscripts, Biondi here has done here what Cecilia Bartoli has been doing for decades. Her rediscoveries of music hidden or previously lost have resulted not just in recordings and recitals but in packages, thoroughly researched and documented: music written in Rome during the ban on opera at the turn of the 18th century; the "sacrifices" of castrati; the mysterious life of the composer and political operative, Agostino Steffani.

Biondi's take on Chiara is nowhere near as exciting. Chiara's diary connects her with composers of the day, most of whom were successors to Vivaldi. Her cadenzas further link her to specific works. One would have hoped that real discoveries might have come from this, perhaps composers writing on the level of Vivaldi. Unfortunately, this is not the case: Vivaldi's music stands out from his successors. Because she lived through most of the 18th century (1718-1791), Chiara saw music change from the complex works of the late Baroque through the Rococo to the Classical (Galante). In fact, after Vivaldi's death in 1741 no great Italian composers appeared on the scene, and when they did appear, composers such as Rossini and Verdi flourished, but elsewhere than in Venice.

Biondi and his superb ensemble did their best to put some life into the weaker pieces. At times he made gestures to the group to rev them up, but they were doing fine. He resisted speeding up tempi which is always an easy way of grabbing the audience and also a way of overcoming the inherent weakness of a piece of music. Oddly, the first encore contained the most potent and heartfelt moments of the concert: the second movement from another piece that Vivaldi wrote for Chiara, the Concerto in B-flat Major. If there was any doubt about Vivaldi's feeling toward Chiara, just listen to this movement.

As a reward to the audience for sitting through nearly two hours of mainly serviceable music, Biondi and his group then ripped through a wildly virtuosic rendition of the first movement of "Winter" from *The Four Seasons*.

♫ Harpsichordist Jory Vinikour's Rewarding Recital Spans the Baroque Era

Jory Vinikour (harpsichord), Weill Recital Hall, Carnegie Hall, New York, 10.12.2015

Bull: "Lord Lumley's Pavan and Galliard," "The King's Hunt"
Bach: Partita No.3 in A minor
Scarlatti: 4 Sonatas in D major
Couperin: Suite in C major
Rameau: Suite in A minor from *Nouvelles suites de pièces de clavecin*

Before this concert, I was not familiar with either Jory Vinikour or his recordings. This speaks both to my ignorance and to the situation of harpsichordists performing in the States today. The drain of American musical talent to Europe and elsewhere continues as it has for the last century, although success abroad often leads singers and musicians back to the States with coveted prizes traded in for coveted positions or roles.

The situation with harpsichordists is more serious. Not that anyone would have expected William Christie to always stay stateside, but he left Buffalo for Paris, never to look back. He toured for 10 years as a harpsichordist before founding the still pre-eminent early music group, Les Arts Florissants. The late Alan Curtis did for Italy what Christie did for France. Similarly, Scott Ross, the most brilliant and prolific harpsichord of this era, left Maine for Europe, his talents recognized there and his eccentricities ignored. Ross's legacy includes the first recording of Scarlatti's complete 555 sonatas on 34 CDs. Jory Vinikour moved to Paris in 1990.

Even though the performance took place in the smallest of Carnegie Hall's theaters, Weill Recital Hall, the fact that it was a sold-out event proves there is more than enough interest in early keyboard music to justify more concerts like this one. Vinikour chose a varied program, from the beginning of the Baroque era and the music of John Bull through Scarlatti in and around the middle Baroque, back a bit to the earlier Baroque and ending with a Rameau Suite.

The opening music by John Bull immediately put the audience into a faraway past as successfully as any play by Shakespeare, who was born just two years after Bull. If the music sounded like it came from a lute, it did and it didn't. Most harpsichords have lute stops which work very well in making the instrument sound like the plucking of a lute.

The Bach suite that followed is a big jump, some 25 years. By this time the improvisational style of the Toccatas, Fantasies and Preludes was beginning to seem old-fashioned. Bach was known in his time as a virtuoso organist, while the larger body of his works was considered old-fashioned. Because all of Bach's instrumental suites were emulations of dance movements, there would be no need to specify a tempo, certainly for his contemporaries. Vinikour took the Allemande at an undanceable pace, but since there was no dancing in the aisles, it was perfectly acceptable. The same is true of the repeats. Bach specifies repeats of the binary A-B sections. It is not often done, but Vinikour took the repeats on the A section but not the B. Both Glenn Gould in his Bach and Ross in his Scarlatti toe the line and take the repeats, but do occasionally drop them on the B section. Sometimes it's clear why, at other times not.

Considering the amount, quality and variety of Scarlatti's output, too much praise cannot be given to Scott Ross who continued his Scarlatti project through to his terminal illness at the age of 38. Like running a four-minute mile, thought an impossibility, once a complete set was achieved, it became not quite commonplace but still doable. Since Ross's set there have about a half-dozen others, either completed or soon to be. The pieces selected here are examples of the pairing of sonatas that Ralph Kirkpatrick used in establishing Scarlatti's method of composing. I'm not sure why this performance hierarchy reversed the order in both pairs. This is very difficult music, and there were mis-hits on some of the crosshand jumps, particularly at the end of K. 120, made even more impossible by the speed at which it was taken.

Louis Couperin's Suite in C major is most interesting for his non-measured first movement Prélude that reflects what improvised music of the time would sound like. It's coded in such a way as to give the player a guideline, but not much more. A careful reading, as was done here, produces a sense of spontaneity that strongly contrasts with the more rigidly set dances that follow. The concluding Passacaille is a set of variations on a repeating bass. More commonly known as a chaconne, it combines a hypnotic rhythm with a continuous repetition. Rameau used it often in his operas as a closing dance. Vinikour gave this movement a well-measured interpretation.

Rameau's music is like no other of the period. The opening Allemande is the right tempo and meter, yet it is laughable to even imagine someone dancing to it. As François Couperin did in his later books, Rameau began giving titles to his "pièces." Here, in "Les trois mains," through the use of crosshands and overlapping, he produces the effect of three hands playing. Vinikour grasped the humor inherent in much of Rameau's music with the sudden short descending runs leading to the cadences in "Les trois mains." The concluding variations of the Gavotte were a fitting climax to a well-played and well-selected program.

♫ *Baroque Chamber Music Performed as if at Home*

Baroque Collection: Chamber Music Society of Lincoln Center, Alice Tully Hall, Lincoln Center, New York, 8.12.2015

Boismortier: Sonata in E minor for Flute and Violin
C. P. E. Bach: Sonata in B minor for Flute, Violin and Continuo
Vivaldi: Sonata in A minor for Cello and Continuo
Couperin: *La Parnasse, ou L'Apothéose de Corelli* for 2 Violins and Continuo
Böddecker: Sonata in D minor for Violin and Continuo from *Sacra partitura*
Corelli: Sonata in A major for Violin and Continuo
Telemann: Trio in A minor for Flute, Violin and Continuo
Reali: *La Folia* for Two Violins, Cello and Continuo

There was something especially homey and warm surrounding this particular performance: familiar faces on stage; an elderly crowd, many of whom knew each other; well-mannered (except for one cell phone at the very conclusion of a work); and a tempered applauding of the excellent performance and performers. Indeed, much of the program consisted of works written for use in the comfort of the bourgeois living-room: amateur musicians playing for themselves or for friends and family. The title pages of these published scores often had as a selling point the fact that multiple combinations of instruments could be accommodated. A trio like the Boismortier played here might state on the score's cover that it could be for violin and flute or two flutes or two violins. Boismortier said about his Op. 34 sonatas in four parts that any combination of "transverse flutes, violins or other instruments" would do, even going so far as to imply that in dire need a recorder (the most common amateur's instrument) could be substituted.

Boismortier is one of many under-appreciated composers of the Baroque. He was no great innovator, but he was capable of writing charming pieces. His music is rustic, often sounding as if were written for a musette or hurdy-gurdy, instruments for which he did in fact compose. I would have liked a little more levity in the playing and a better dynamic match-up of the two instruments: the flute dominated the violin here. All the pieces were played on modern instruments in a traditional 20th-century manner, and I wondered why at least some of the vibrato wasn't held back.

The second eldest son of the great Johann Sebastian Bach, C. P. E. Bach was the brightest and most successful of the Bach boys. His public and sacred works reveal little of his capabilities, but his more personal pieces, like the hundred or so sonatas for clavichord and small instrumental groups, were composed for himself. This piece was written in 1731 when he was a student, and it seems to look back to his father's more structured writing. I say "seems" because the version played is the 1747 revision; the original 1731 work is not extant. Then there's the density of the writing. In C. P. E.'s middle and later years, the bass line became simpler—so schoolbook simple, in fact, that his bass lines in many sonatas and trios almost seem as if they were overreacting to J. S. Bach's heavy and melodic bass lines. Again, the performance was sterling in spite of the thick varnish that an historical performance would have avoided.

Virtuosity and affect are key words for the Vivaldi cello sonata RV 43. This sonata is unusual in that it is in four movements, two of which are Largo, just about as slow as you can go. Add to this a performance in the key of A minor and you have as much seriousness as Vivaldi produced. If there needed to be a best-moment-in-concert vote, I would nominate the sonata's second Largo. Efe Baltacigil took his time drawing each poignant note from his instrument.

The set of programmatic movements by Couperin, "La Parnasse de Corelli," is a most unusual work and difficult to categorize. Although the piece is infrequently performed, when it is done, often the text for each section is read aloud. This makes for a more formal production, but is truer in spirit than when there is no text at all. The "lyrics," unlike in Vivaldi's *Four Seasons* where references to birds or storms are easy for a composer to emulate, are more abstract. Some works of the Baroque are fine in modern attire, but I don't think so here. Instrumental coloring depends on using an appropriate instrument. Virtuosity aside (praise again to members and here especially to the Kavafian sisters), this work demands a lighter and looser touch than it received.

Böddeckker is one of the composers who flourished during a time when substantial changes were in the works. This sonata, completed around 1650, was an early work for violin and continuo. It's complex and difficult to perform, but Bella Hristova's performance was outstanding. Showing little strain, she handled the torturous passages admirably. The work must have been a shock to the composer's contemporaries, who would have to face even more difficult music during the 1660s with Biber, Schmelzer and Pandolphi all trying to one-up each other in *stylus phantasticus*.

Corelli's sonata is the only work on the program in a major key. Here his distinctive style is a move away from the wildness of the early Baroque to the more refined middle Baroque. His influence was a major force on musical style, and his school ultimately triumphed in the long battle between the Italian and French schools. Although his sonatas followed a style called "church style," there is no religiosity here. Only virtuosity remained, most significantly in Ani Kafavian's blazing final movement.

Telemann's production was enormous: hundreds of works in every and all formats and styles of the day. He is the ideal composer for anyone looking for a work to perform with any unique combination of instruments. Have three violins handy, no problem; violin and oboe, got that; two horns, yes indeed. You couldn't possibly have one for three horns and violin? Sure do. Here we had a trio sonata, performed enthusiastically and needing just a little less vibrato on Ani Kafavian's part for it to be nearly perfect.

La Folia, in some form, dates back well before its first publication in the mid-1650s. A number of composers wrote variations on its theme: Lully, Marais, J. S. Bach, C. P. E. Bach, Liszt and Grieg to name a few. Like its sibling, the chaconne, the unique rhythms of *La Folia* are awe-inspiring, catchy and jaunting. It's the kind of musical warhorse that gives a performer the freedom do what he or she does best, and musical directives are at the whim of the instrumentalist. Here, a speeding up of the tempo to an insane pace ended an imaginative concert.

♫ *Bronfman Plays Prokofiev with an Intensity Beyond the Ordinary*
Yefim Bronfman (pian0), Zankel Hall, Carnegie Hall, New York, 13.11.2015

Prokofiev: Piano Sonata No. 1 in F minor, Piano Sonata No. 2 in D minor, Piano Sonata No. 3 in A minor,
Piano Sonata No. 4 in C minor

Encores:
Chopin: Etude in F major
Schumann: Romanze from *Faschingsschwank aus Wien*

I avoid reading other critics' articles on a musical event that I'm in the process of reviewing, but the headline of Vivian Schweitzer's piece in *The New York Times*, "Seemingly Channeling a Mix of Rage and Grief," caught my eye. As she notes, this concert had a level of intensity beyond the ordinary. I felt the atmosphere in the hall change as the executive director of Carnegie Hall, Clive Gillinson, walked on to the stage. He asked for a moment of silence for the victims of the Paris terrorist attack, which was still unfolding at the time. I'm not even sure that everyone was yet aware of the event, but the audience responded with total silence. Gillinson walked off the stage and Yefim Bronfman entered, bowed quickly, sat down at the piano and ripped into Sergei Prokofiev's Sonata No. 1.

We still hear complaints that "modern music" is difficult, unpleasantly atonal and dissonant. One would think Prokofiev would be part of the modernists' post-WWI rebellion against the confines of 19th-century musical rigors, but looking back now, how "modern" was he when all his sonatas and concerti have standard key signatures. His works were still centered around pre-20th-century musical modalities, and his first sonata could have been written by Liszt. The toccata-like opening brings up a romantic, lyrical, catchy theme that dominates the rest of the piece. There are few signs of the future Prokofiev here; the 16-year-old (!) pianist was working out his relationship to the past, testing out what he could do with the material he had mastered. The older Prokofiev would never have let a sentimental theme like this one appear without mocking it. Bronfman added muscle to this youthful work with an intensity that would have rendered other pianists' hands limp.

A more mature Prokofiev makes an appearance in Sonata No. 2. Almost from the start, at the tempo change to *pùi misso*, Prokofiev brings out twittering birds reminiscent of the "Ballet of the Unhatched Chicks" from Mussorgsky's *Pictures at an Exhibition*. He follows with a lyric theme that starts off normally but quickly goes off balance and becomes asymmetrical. He accomplishes this by repeating the same theme but with two notes changed, one going up, one down. The sonata's slow Andante was sensitively played, and the Vivace was fleetingly dispatched.

If the one-movement Sonata No. 3 was an attempt by Prokofiev to see if he could outdo his earlier one-movement Sonata No. 1, then he succeeded. The opening sounds like a continuation of the second sonata's final Vivace movement, slightly slower but marked "tempesto." All kinds of shifts occur here, sudden changes of tempo, meter and rhythm. The pianist is required to play agitato, feroce and percipitato, as well as dolce and con effetto, and Bronfman was certainly feroce.

The Sonata No. 4 was written during the same time period as No. 3, and it returns to three movements. This is the calmest and most reflective of the works on the program. Although the first movement is marked allegro, it is usually done more slowly because Prokofiev asks for it to be played "molto sustenuto," meaning sustained or drawn out. This is followed by an Andante. The last movement makes up for the two slower ones with a classic Prokofiev off-beat, wobbly, over-the-speed-limit run that stops dead in its tracks.

The encores were showstoppers themselves: the Chopin lithe and graceful, the Schumann dark and pensive.

♪ Suzuki Broadens his Horizons from Bach to Handel and Vivaldi to Great Effect

Bach Collegium Japan, Masaaki Suzuki (conductor, organ, harpsichord), Joanne Lunn (soprano), Zankel Hall, Carnegie Hall, New York, 6.11.2015

Bach: Brandenburg Concerto No. 2 in F major
Vivaldi: Concerto in C major for Recorder, Strings and Continuo
Handel: Gloria in B-flat major
Bach: Flute Sonata in E minor

Vivaldi: Concerto in C major for Oboe, Strings and Continuo
Bach: Cantata No. 51, "Jauchzet Gott in allen Landen"

Masaaki Suzuki has been visiting New York for several years now, often to mentor and conduct Juilliard415, the Historical Performance student group. For some of Bach's larger works, he has combined forces with Yale's early music instrumental and vocal programs. As founder and director of the Bach Collegium Japan, Suzuki's greatest achievement has been to record the complete secular cantatas of Bach: an accomplishment reserved for only a handful of conductors. As an instrumentalist, he has played and recorded most of Bach's keyboard works. When he is not playing Bach, he has pretty much kept within the German Baroque, performing works by Bach's predecessors such as Schutz and Buxtehude.

Some of the music on this program is not often performed, and the works that are more familiar benefited from a fresh approach. The Vivaldi Concerto for Recorder, usually played on the flautino, has been a staple ending for several of the Italian groups visiting New York. It's a showcase for Giovanni Antonini and his group, Il Giardino Armonico: the conductor ends many of his programs dipping and dancing, awaiting the wide-eyed audience's applause and bravi. Andreas Böhlen, when performing it here, upped the ante by not only matching Antonini's speed but also taking the da capo of the final movement and ornamenting every measure. Surely this is something that any virtuoso flautino player could have done when performing it with her fellow students at the girls' orphanage where Vivaldi taught. But delightful as it may have been, the time has come to put this concerto out to pasture.

The Brandenburgs are a linchpin for many baroque groups' programs. If only one is chosen, the decision is often determined by the technical abilities of the concertino group. The Third focuses on the violin and viola, the Fifth on a harpsichordist with the ability to play the dazzling first movement cadenza and the Second on the difficult trumpet part. I won't go into the history of the still-ongoing controversies as to which instrument Bach had intended for the Second; his only notation on the manuscript was a "tromba in F". Did he mean really mean a "tromba" (trumpet) or "corno" (horn) or was it a "corno di caccia" (hunting horn) or a "tromba piccolo"? Maybe it was a tiny, high-pitched clarion trumpet. Or it could just be a trumpet in F. Playing the part with any of these is supremely difficult, and I think Bach would have been happy with any instrument that was able to hit the notes most of the time.

I always sit on the edge of my seat when the Second opens, anticipating a sour note coming from the brass section, and sometimes I don't relax till the work ends. Guy Ferber struggled a bit in the first measures but came through with barely a nick. Even though I began to trust him midway in the first movement, his playing so teetered on the razor's edge that I never fully relaxed. But he did a fine job, and every bravo he received was earned.

A very sensitive and delicate performance of one of Bach's flute sonatas continued the program after the intermission. It's not often that speed is sacrificed so that the listener can actually dwell in the music, but it was so with Kiyomi Suga's rendition. Suga was no slouch either, as demonstrated by her virtuosic skills in the last movement Allegro.

One of the two vocal works brought Joanne Lunn on stage is the recently discovered Gloria in B-flat, thought to be by Handel. There are still holdouts who doubt its authenticity, and I can see why. Although it has some striking moments, it has none of the spark and levity that one finds in other works from Handel's first years in Rome, such as his series of Italian cantatas. These works had to be disguised as sacred music due to a ban by the powers that be. Handel had no great difficulties with writing music in Rome: sacred music will have a very different libretto, but music is abstract and cannot be made into anything other than itself. One cannot hear music from this period and state categorically that it is sacred or profane.

Joanne Lunn had the right voice to cover the required range in the *Gloria*. There were some melismas that seemed to go on forever, and Lunn was in control of all of them, all of the time. In the joyful Cantata BWV 51, trumpet and voice vied but never drowned each other out. Suzuki got the balance just right.

♫ *Telemann: Baroque Composer, Renaissance Man*
Juilliard Baroque, Sandra Miller (flute), Monica Huggett (violin), Dominic Teresi (bassoon), Sarah Cunningham (viola da gamba), Avi Stein (harpsichord), Paul Hall, Juilliard School of Music, Lincoln Center, New York, 2.11.2015

Telemann: Quartet in E minor from *Six Quatuors ou Trios*; Fantasia No. 6 for Solo Violin in E minor from *Fantasias*; Trio No. 2 for Viola da gamba, Harpsichord and Basso continuo in G major from *Essercizii musici*; Concerto Primo in G major from *Quadri*; Sonata for Violin, Bassoon and Basso continuo in F major; Fantasia No. 10 for Solo Traverso in F-sharp minor; Concerto for Flute, Gamba and Bassoon in B minor; Quartet in A minor from *Six Quatuors ou Trios*

It's difficult to write about Telemann without mentioning his prodigious output: 45 Passions and over 1,700 cantatas and, in the secular realm, some 50 operas, more than 600 orchestral suites and hundreds of works for various chamber music combinations. Bach by comparison wrote a mere 300 cantatas, five Passions, no operas and four orchestral suites. To be fair, Telemann was born four years before Bach, and lived and continued to write music for another 17 years after Bach's death.

He was also a novelist, poet and entrepreneur who exercised total control over all aspects of publishing his scores, including engraving. He wrote three autobiographies and was an avid collector of exotic plants. He claimed to be an autodidact and taught himself to play the flute, oboe, viola da gamba, double bass, trombone and keyboard. Well-traveled, he incorporated into his works the influences of French and Italian music as well as ethnic music from Poland, Spain and other countries.

Although Telemann's music has certainly not been neglected, there is still a tremendous amount to be prepared for performance. The more we hear, the more we realize how good his music really is. Several CD labels are committed to recording the voluminous genres of instrumental and vocal music he produced. One of them, the German company *cpo*, has been regularly releasing his violin concerti, wind concerti and cantatas. They have a long way to go.

Telemann's music is distinctive and well-constructed. He was no Vivaldi, churning out music as fast as his pen could write and using the same formulas over and over. The most interesting pieces on this concert's program were those for unaccompanied flute and unaccompanied violin, both of which belong to sets of 12 Fantasias each. It might have been interesting if one from the set of 36 Fantasias for keyboard had also been selected: the program would then have included one piece from each solo instrument set. While none of the violin Fantasias compare to Bach's solo sonatas and partitas for violin, they are all, at a minimum, charming. Usually the bassoon is there just to support the basso continuo, so it was good to see and hear the bassoon up front in one of the sonatas and in one of the concerti. This was especially the case because it was played so well by Dominic Teresi. Sarah Cunningham's da gamba playing in the Trio in G was also most enjoyable, bringing to mind the da gamba sonatas of Telemann's godson, C. P. E. Bach.

The pieces played here succeeded in demonstrating a broad cross section of the chamber music Telemann wrote. The instrumentalists, all faculty members of the Historical Performance program, excelled in every piece.

♫ *Andras Schiff Reaches the End of Last Three Sonatas by Four Classical Composers*
Sir Andras Schiff (piano), Carnegie Hall, New York, 30.10.2015

Haydn: Piano Sonata in E-flat major
Beethoven: Piano Sonata No. 32 in C minor
Mozart: Piano Sonata in D major
Schubert: Piano Sonata in B-flat major

Encores:
Schumann: Variations for Piano on an Original Theme
Bach: Aria from *Goldberg Variations*

Looking back at my earlier reviews, I see Sir Andras Schiff's name appearing in more programs than I would have expected. Aside from his frequent visits as soloist, Schiff has also appeared as an accompanist to outstanding performers and as a conductor from the podium and the piano. His real love is keyboard music from the early Baroque through the middle of the 19th century. Whether it's his Scarlatti in the 1970s, Bach in the 1980s or Schubert in the 1990s, there is a reliability and consistency that vary little with time.

It might be hard to believe that at one time Schiff was a controversial figure, but his recording of the *Goldberg Variations* in the 1980s, while nowhere as radical as that of Glenn Gould, riled some critics for its fast tempi and his *détaché* style. It is still one of the great Goldbergs. As Gould did 25 years after his first *Goldberg Variations*, Schiff re-recorded his 20 years later; but both versions are less interesting than their forebears.

This evening's performance was the third recital in a cycle that highlighted the antepenultimate, penultimate and final piano sonatas by Haydn, Mozart, Beethoven and Schubert. It is an interesting framework, but really makes sense for works that were not only last sonatas but were final works as well, as is the case with Schubert. Mozart's final keyboard sonata was written two years before he died. He would still compose his clarinet concerto, *Così fan tutte* , *Die Zauberflöte, La Clemenza di Tito* and, of course, the *Requiem.* Beethoven had not yet written his *Missa Solemnis,* let alone the Ninth Symphony and last quartets. Haydn lived another 15 years after writing his final sonata and had quartets and symphonies as well as the *Creation* to come. It might be said that the finality of these "last works" are less about the end of life than the end of interest on the part of patrons paying composers to write sonatas, or publishers selling unplayable scores to students and amateurs.

The Haydn that opened the concert suited Schiff well, and he played crisply and brightly, helped by a fine sounding-Steinway, possibly Schiff's own; at one time he hauled his Bosendorfer with him on concert tours. There was never any melding of notes, aided by his minimal use of the pedals which allows the clarity needed to delineate each musical line. This is life affirming music, very much the opposite of what we think of as final.

Going the rounds of our circumscribed music critics' world is the appellation "anti-Lang Lang," as applied to the performance style of a pianist like Schiff. He presents a calm and easy-going demeanor: no hands flying in the air, no bouncing off his stool, the most passionate music deriving its effect from his stillness. Nothing perturbed him. At the close of the Haydn sonata, before he had even finished playing, a bravo broke the silence. Schiff just shrugged his shoulders and smiled.

He breezed through the Beethoven without showing any signs of how difficult a piece it is to play. In this regard he is very much like the virtuoso's virtuoso, Marc-André Hamelin, whose approach to music is surprisingly similar in its lack of affectation and the just plain joy of playing music.

Mozart's last sonata looks both forward and back: forward to music of greater dissonance and more intricacy and back to Bach in its contrapuntal complexity. I might have wanted a little more flare in the first and last movements, but one could do worse than an approach that draws out the gracefulness and elegance inherent in Mozart's music.

Schubert's last sonatas are the only ones that really speak to finality here. These dark-hued works are filled with lovely lyrical melodies that, like the song cycles, get darker and colder as they progress. The penultimate Sonata in A major has an Andantino that must be the saddest music ever written. Schiff took the opening movement of the B-flat major Sonata at a livelier pace than most pianists. But he put us on guard with the ominous trill that rumbles up from the depths

handful of musicians.

What really seems to have made a difference and will continue to do so in the future are the students of Juilliard whose training makes them true professionals. This particular performance stood on a level that matches any other professional group I've seen or heard. Granted, the conductor was the eminent William Christie, who at the end of the concert told the audience that due to travel delays he shortchanged the students, not giving them the time he would have normally spent preparing them for this program. He too seemed moved by the quality of the players. The students may have started off the evening a little wooly, but that cleared up quickly. They also ended a little raggedy, perhaps unprepared for Christie's unexpected upbeat and the driven tempo of the "Réjouissance" from Bach's fourth orchestral suite, played as quickly as I've ever heard it. I also had a sense that the encore, "Tendre Amour" from *Les Indes Galantes,* had received very little practice time. Although it's slow enough in tempo to be sight-read, it could have used some Christie magic. If the encore seemed to end on an unresolved cadence, it did. What in fact was played was only the long introduction to a number that would be sung by a chorus.

It is difficult to single out individual members of the orchestra for praise, but I was close enough to the proscenium to observe the string playing. As I've written elsewhere, the group's concertmaster, Augusta McKay Lodge, stands out as the real thing, a true virtuoso.

The next Christie-led concert was with his own group, Les Arts Florissants. It has been mentioned elsewhere that Christie has not recently been as active in bringing out new material to perform as in the past. But striding up to the podium for this production and for the earlier one with Juilliard, he showed an impressive level of energy, to say the least. Christie is a charismatic conductor, and he handled his group with deftness, including hand gestures to draw the instrumental groups to the forefront and wonderful facial expressions and grimaces as well.

Theodora, Handel's penultimate oratorio, shares an emotional connection with other composers' late works. Mozart's *Clemenza di Tito,* Beethoven's late quartets and piano sonatas, Strauss's last songs: all have a sense of other-worldliness. Although Handel lived ten years after the completion of *Theodora*, his output was minimal: one oratorio, *Jephtha,* an organ concerto and some revisions and pastiches were all he composed before he lost his vision two years after *Theodora*'s dismal failure. There are other bleak Handel oratorios based on stories from the Bible, but none are so consistently dark as *Theodora*. Handel's instrumentation, the absence of tympani and the very limited use of trumpets and horns are telling signs that there will be far fewer fanfares or regal pomp than one is used to from him. It's hard to find another Handel work that contains so many consistently slow movements. From the middle of Act I, after the rallying cries of the evangelical Valens to his subjects, there are only three arias marked Andante or faster; the other 24 or so arias are predominantly Largos and Adagios.

An astute businessman, Handel was willing to change arias to satisfy the whims of his singers, or to revise parts of his operas to better appeal to the customers. One would have to assume that with *Theodora*, as with *Messiah*, monetary gain played second fiddle to a personal and spiritual need.

Like *Messiah*, *Theodora* was written in a burst of creativity in barely a month. Handel considered it more highly than *Messiah* and opined, a contemporary noted, that the chorus "He Saw the Lovely Youth" was far beyond *Messiah*'s "Hallelujah Chorus." Granted, there were external circumstances for *Theodora*'s fiasco: an earthquake had driven his wealthy patrons from London and out to their country estates. But Handel must have known that a story that ends with the cruel and torturous death of the innocent heroine and hero would have little appeal to his audience. Add to this almost three hours of mostly slow music neither acted nor costumed, plus a minimal number of catchy tunes (and even those, such as the gruesome aria "Racks, Gibbets, Sword And Fire," not likely to be sung in the shower), and it's easy to see why *Theodora* closed after only three performances.

As for the soloists, there is little to complain about and much to praise. It is difficult to give them a fair and just hearing if one has seen live or on DVD the brilliant staging and cast from Peter Sellars' 1996 Glyndebourne production. Lorraine Hunt Lieberson's heart-wrenching Irene in the Sellars is the be-all and end-all of this role. Stephanie d'Oustrac, who goes back 20 years with Christie, never had a very big voice, but in a relatively small venue like Alice Tully she managed to fill the role and the hall convincingly. Philippe Jaroussky's voice has at times been almost piercingly sharp, but he seems to have lost some of that edge and gained a warmer, more rounded tone. Katherine Watson could not stand up to Dawn Upshaw's' Theodora, but she gave a solid reading of the martyred heroine. The male singers, with more dramatic material than their female counterparts, gave strong performances but failed to delineate one character from the other. This may have been due in part to Thomas Morell's rather weak libretto.

It was nice to see the hall nearly filled, and with a younger audience. One could understand, but not condone, that some listeners left early, eager to go off to watch the World Series or, inspired by this opera's gruesomeness, join in on a Halloween party or parade.

♫ Hewitt Reaches a Touchstone of Western Music

Angela Hewitt (piano), Kaufmann Concert Hall, 92nd Street Y, New York, 29.10.2015

Bach: *The Art of Fugue*; Chorale Prelude, "Vor deinen Thron tret Ich hiermit"

Any performance of Bach's still-mysterious touchstone of Western music, *The Art of Fugue*, must by the work's nature be a compromise. Played as written it would be endless, pages and pages and almost all in the same meter and key, without any guidance as to how fast or slow a given contrapunctus (a short piece that uses some type of counterpoint) would be. It is really in the hands of the artist to more or less improvise what feels appropriate. We do know that if Bach were to have played this music on a harpsichord, he would only have been able to minimally vary dynamics. We'll never know if Bach would have approved of the decisions that must be taken to make the work palatable, or even if he saw it simply as a pedagogical tool like his *Inventions* or *The Well-Tempered Clavier.*

There have been a number of attempts to reign in *The Art of Fugue* by adding a second keyboard, transcribing it for quartet, or playing it on an organ (which has the advantage of producing another voice from the foot pedals). Considering how popular Bach's *Goldberg Variations* became, could the same happen here? Probably not, but if it were to happen, Angela Hewitt would be in the forefront.

She gave a short introduction to the work, mentioning several passages that many think cannot be played with two hands. The most notorious example is Contrapunctus 11, which Hewitt called "torturous," and the 13th, which cannot be played with just 10 fingers. (At some point Bach realized this and revised it for two keyboards.) Hewitt solves this problem, stating elsewhere, that "by adding lightness and agility, a few broken leaps and on the piano some judicious use of the pedal." Whatever she did, she managed to execute the impossible.

The AOF is one of a kind, and performances of it cannot easily be compared to other recitals or, for that matter, Hewitt's own body of works. This isn't the Bach of the Brandenbergs, *St. Matthew Passion,* or *Goldberg Variations.* There is little of Bach's rhythmic verve and fluidity of execution. But this is music that won't yield to a lighter touch: fire needed to be added and it was. Crescendo, fortissimo, and legato were there, not in the score but in Hewitt's head and hands.

As was to be expected from her previous projects such as *The Well-Tempered Clavier*, she has thoroughly mastered her subject, and it showed with every Contrapunctus and Canon, all of which were well thought through. Tempos were moderate, probably the best way to play as we don't really know what Bach would expect. It could be debated whether Hewitt's codas had to be so dramatic, but there is little room in these dense pieces to add drama, and most of the time they were welcome.

Hewitt played her own Fazioli piano, which looks beautiful and sounds it as well. Its clean-pitched tone makes the Steinway seem appropriate for works of the 19th and 20th centuries but less so for Classical and Baroque pieces.

At the close of the concert, Hewitt was drained and pale after a cathartic experience that, given the audience's response, she clearly had shared with each of us.

♫ *Nelsons Proves his Talent in Russian Music*

Nadezhda Serdyuk (mezzo-soprano), Boston Symphony Orchestra, Andris Nelsons (conductor), Tanglewood Festival Chorus, James Bagwell (chorus conductor), Carnegie Hall, New York, 22.10.2015

Prokofiev: *Alexander Nevsky*, Cantata
Rachmaninoff: *Symphonic Dances*

Sergei Eisenstein, the director of the film *Alexander Nevsky*, for which Prokofiev wrote the music, was under tremendous pressure from the Russian propaganda office to finish a film meant to mobilize the Russian populace for the impending invasion by the Axis powers. He felt at the time that it would be "impossible to find and reproduce that wonderful inner synchronization of plastic and musical images, that is, to achieve that in which lies the secret of audio-visual impression….This is where the magician Sergei Prokofiev came to the rescue."

Magician, he was, collaborating with the cinematic giant, Eisenstein, to produce what is arguably the greatest piece of background (foreground?) music ever written. Their collaborative relationship was one of true respect, trust and dedication to the film's importance for their country's survival. Any lover of this masterpiece of both film and music can hear the music if silently viewing the film, and can visualize the images if hearing the music alone. I grew up listening to Fritz Reiner's recording with the Chicago Symphony, and when I finally got to see the film, it was as if the music went from black and white to Technicolor.

Prokofiev knew he had outdone himself, and he later revised the music to make it more palatable. This mainly meant cutting some of the long sequences. The battle scenes, powerful as they are, go on for almost 30 minutes, and without the visual support would have weakened the tightness of the music.

The performance by the Boston Symphony Orchestra under its new conductor, Andris Nelsons, was a showpiece: raw and raucous, at times ("The Crusades in Psov" and "The Battle on the Ice"); languishing ("Song of Alexander Nevsky"); and poignant ("The Field of the Dead"). I don't know Russian, but the chorus must have been trained well enough to be understood, as the Russians next to me smiled, laughed or repeated the words coming from the chorus. Nadezhda Serdyuk gave the poignant "Field of the Dead" the proper gravitas.

The Rachmaninoff *Symphonic Dances* that followed the Prokofiev, not unexpectedly, was anticlimactic. The work is another showpiece, and Nelsons pushed it in both dynamics and tempo. The result was pleasantly bombastic, as I find much of Rachmaninoff.

♫*An Elektra to Remember*
Boston Symphony Orchestra, Andris Nelsons (conductor), Tanglewood Festival Chorus, James Bagwell (chorus conductor), Carnegie Hall, New York, 21.10.2015

Richard Strauss, *Elektra*
Concert Version

We all know that this opera begins in medias res, that Elektra's father has already been killed. Angry at everything, she knows that she has lost or will lose her family, that she will soon be rootless. She is beyond good and evil and meanders upon the stage knowing that her time will soon be up. Elektra's tragic pains are existential in nature: she is alienated and has alienated most of her family and friends. Obsessed with her father's death, Elektra is determined to take revenge, even if it means murdering her mother. This is one complicated character, and it takes someone special to take on the extraordinary part. Strauss himself is quoted as saying: "The title role must above all be given to the highest and most dramatic soprano that can be found."

There have been great Elektras who have built their characters over many years, but few like Christine Goerke, who was only "discovered" a few years ago in the role of the Dyer's Wife in Strauss's *Die Frau Ohne Schatten*. Having previously played the role of Chrysothemis, Goerke has clearly now absorbed Elektra and made it her own. The fact that this was a concert version cut both ways. On the plus side was Carnegie Hall, where the famous acoustics gave to one's ears the equivalent of what 3D glasses give the eyes. On the minus side, with the orchestra and chorus sharing the stage, often Goerke didn't quite know what to do with herself, having only the small passages between orchestral sections in which to pace and to negotiate her belle-of-the-ball dress. Her voice was so pure that it betrayed her character: how could a woman with this angelic voice hurt anyone? And how could anyone perform a role which demands 90 minutes of nonstop and challenging singing.

So large a force was Goerke that when some of the singers took their bows, I barely remembered what they had sung. It was as if they had hardly appeared at all. Gun-Brit Barkmin never really convinced me that she was a homebody who believes things will go back to normal, her torments will end. Jane Henschel was more convincing as Elektra's heartless mother; her ability to produce creepy cackling sounds as she laughed her way off stage does make one believe she was capable of killing her husband. The men had much less to sing, and although you know who they are, they don't have enough time to clearly differentiate their roles.

With regard to the orchestra, there's not much more that I can say but "Wow." All the orchestral members excelled. The brass, particularly the four Wagner tubas, made the entire theater shake. Much of the passion and precise playing that came from the orchestra was due to Andris Nelsons' superb shaping of the orchestral groups. It's good to know that the BSO will be in the hands of a dynamo who, so far, seems to understand exactly what this orchestra needs to keep its deserved reputation intact.

I don't remember when I've heard such long ovations.

♫ Masaaki Suzuki Conducts All-Bach Program: What More Can One Ask?
Juilliard415, Yale Schola Cantorum, Masaaki Suzuki (conductor), Peter J. Sharp Theater, Juilliard School of Music, Lincoln Center, New York, 15.10.2015

Bach: Sinfonia from Cantata "Am Abend aber desselbigen Sabbats"; Mass in A major; Brandenburg Concerto No. 3 in G major; Mass in G minor

Looking at a copy of the manuscript of the cantata whose Sinfonia opened this concert, I was reminded that what came out of Bach's mind and onto the paper went way beyond what anyone else has accomplished. Perhaps Bach could claim, as Vivaldi did, that he could write a concerto as fast as his pen was able to scrawl across a page. But much of Vivaldi's music rearranges the same notes and adds a few more, and the 3-minute egg is done. Bach's music never cuts corners, is never less than complex, never varies in quality: his late works are not terribly different from the first. The notes on the page continue to flow with ease from measure to measure.

The Sinfonia that opens this concert sounds very much like a triple concerto. Bach, as did most other composers of the period, borrowed from his own library as well as those of others. Several cantatas have opening instrumental or choral movements borrowed from extant works, such as the Brandenburgs or Orchestral Suites. This sinfonia has some glorious music: at one point, each of the soloists hands back and forth a melody, transforming a few notes into something so incredibly moving. The three instrumentalists played smoothly and with great assurance, keeping up admirably with the fast pace that Suzuki took: a pace slightly faster than his recorded performance.

The fact that Bach actually wrote Masses other than the Mass in B minor may come as a surprise to many. We are familiar with other vocal forms in addition to the cantatas, such as the Oratorios, Passions and Motets. Why these Masses are so obscure is beyond me. If much of the content has been taken from other compositions, it's the same case as in other, more popular, works of Bach: the *Christmas Oratorio* and arias from both Passions contain musical derivatives (called parodies) yet are still part of the standard Bach repertory. The Kyrie of the Mass in A major is about the most upbeat beginning of a Mass until Haydn started writing.

The opening chorus of the Mass in G minor is particularly lovely with the canonic entrances of the four vocal ranges and the slow, almost dance-like swaying. It contains several arias borrowed from earlier works, but even if somewhat familiar to the listener, they gain a new freshness in this different context.

As for the performance of the third Brandenburg, I will go out on a limb and state that it comes very close to being the best version that I can remember hearing. The instrumentalists played with passionate bravura. The last movement, done at a record-setting pace, never sounded strained or forced. All the string players were more than simply virtuosic, but the splendid Augusta McKay Lodge has to be singled out as an exceptional violinist.

In a performance a few days ago by the group Baroque Incorporated (which includes many Juilliard Historical Performance graduates), I commented on the risks of performing choral parts with one person per part. Here, with the Yale Scola Cantorum, there were no such worries. They sang with tremendous vitality, never wavering under the guidance of Suzuki, one of the few conductors to have recorded all the Bach cantatas. In whatever short period of time he had to rehearse these students, he drew from them a quality of sound certainly near, if not equal to, the instrumentalists and chorus of his Bach Collegium Japan.

There are other groups in the city performing Bach's vocal music, some with Juilliard members, but to have one of the great masters of Bach on stage with one the best choruses and the top student orchestra in its field is to feel that, yes, we have made progress towards a better world.

Note: In a review that I wrote several years back, I started with following comment:
Congratulations! But to whom and why so soon? Because my first prize goes not to the music and musicians, but to the "Notes on the Program" written by Robert Mealy. They are an example of how all program notes should be written: clear, concise and to the point.

Change Mr. Mealy's name to Melanie Williams, and you have an apt description of the program notes to this concert. Thoroughly researched and well-written, they don't look down at the reader nor oversimplify what are rather complex details. A star goes to Ms. Williams and another to her mentors at Juilliard.

♫ *Schubert's Cycles Given Distinctive and Distinguished Readings*
Mark Padmore (tenor), Kristian Bezuidenhout (fortepiano), Alice Tully Hall, Lincoln Center, New York, 14.10.2015, 15.10.2015, 17.10.2015

Schubert: *Die schöne Müllerin*; *Schwanengesang*; *Winterreise*
Beethoven: *An die ferne Geliebte*

Few concerts leave a listener in such a trance that upon exiting the theatre one feels like the doppelganger of Schubert's song: one of you is outside, the other is still inside. This feeling of *Innigkeit* was felt after each of these three concerts but was strongest with the richest set of songs, *Winterreise*. To converse about anything other than what was experienced seemed pointless. At some time during the first hour after *Winterreise* ended, my friend wondered if we had recovered enough to change the topic. The effect, though, lingered for days.

Although independent song cycles themselves, *Die schöne Müllerin* and *Winterreise* share many similarities. The texts for both were written by the same author, Wilhelm Müller (no relation to the schöne Müllerin!); both focus on unrequited love and its power to destroy; both are somewhat ambiguous as to whether their anti-heroes have indeed taken their lives. *Die schöne Müllerin* is considerably less severe than *Winterreise*: there is a brightness to the former that is absent in the latter. *DSM* is a poem of day, *W* is one of night.

It's always unfortunate when, after much anticipation, a scheduled performer is unable to appear. It is even more unfortunate that in the case of Paul Lewis, originally announced to accompany Mark Padmore, the reason was a freak accident: Mr. Lewis was attacked by seagulls and knocked to the ground, injuring his hand badly enough to require surgery. One expected the concert to be canceled, but there was enough time to bring in another accompanist, one with whom Mr. Padmore has played and recorded. Kristian Bezuidenhout, a specialist in early music practice, replaced Lewis and went beyond that by changing from a piano to his preferred instrument, the fortepiano. The result was a significant and pleasing difference in coloring and tonal balance. The instrument itself is beautiful, a copy by Maine's R. J. Regier of a Graf fortepiano built in Vienna in the 1820s. Some of the moments when the pianist plays loudly enough to overpower the voice will never be a problem with the quieter fortepiano: its sound is on a more human scale than present-day grand pianos. In Schubert's time, the fortepiano, which had been around since the 1720s, was still common; but not long after Schubert's death, it lost favor to the newer pianos as we know them.

There have been an amazing number of recitals and an equally impressive number of recordings of the songs performed here. Without simplifying the complexity of each vocalist who attempts them, they seem to fall into two categories: in the style of Dietrich Fischer-Dieskau, and not in the style of Fischer-Dieskau. Listening to him is a trip back in time: the clarity of line is there, but listeners today have ultimately judged him lacking in warmth, empathy and understanding. Those who choose not to follow his vocal journey tend to be more in tune with the characters described in the cycles: two young, overly sensitive men, quiet externally but in turmoil inside. Nowhere in Fischer-Dieskau's renditions does one ever believe that his is the voice of either youth. The current group of vocalists who, for lack of a better term, are historically informed, singers who sing instead of disclaim, emote rather than scream, include Padmore, Ian Bostridge, Florian Boesch and Christoph Pregardien.

Empathy and ultimately sympathy were the basic feelings that flowed from Padmore's recitals. Even in the more dramatic moments, one felt the fragility of these characters. They were no crazier than the scores of men who killed themselves after over-identifying with the young Werther.

The accord between the musicians was palpable: both played as if they had been doing this for years. There were several instances where the music that emanated from the keyboard was unworldly and perhaps closer to the sounds that Schubert heard in his mind. The most potent examples of this are songs from *Schwanengesang*: "Der Atlas," "Die Stadt" and "Der Doppleganger."

Padmore's voice never wavered at either end of his vocal range. His voice has an identifiable sweetness that belies his ability to show pain or strong emotions. It came as a shock that he could put as much power as he did into some of the songs and do so without losing his distinct voice. My head still echoes with the roiling words "Dein is mein Herz" from *Die schöne Müllerin*'s "Ungeduld." One cannot but be impressed at Padmore's ease and confidence. Not once did he stop for a sip of water, his voice never faltering even at the end of these monumental cycles.

♪ *Bach, Bach's Cousin and Telemann Mourn*
New York Baroque Incorporated, Monica Huggett (violin, viola), Grace Rainey Rogers Auditorium, Metropolitan Museum of Art, New York, 9.9.2015

J. S. Bach: Brandenburg Concerto No. 6
Telemann: Trauer Kantate, "Du aber, Daniel, gehe hin"
Johann Christoph Bach: "Ach, dass ich Wassers gnug hätte"
J. S. Bach: "Gottes Zeit ist die allerbeste Zeit" ("Actus Tragicus")

There was a time when a common complaint among New York music-goers was the absence here of a permanent Baroque orchestra. Boston has the Boston Baroque and the Baroque Early Music Festival. There's the Philharmonia Baroque Orchestra in San Francisco, Music of the Baroque in Chicago and Cleveland's Apollo's Fire. Europe had Baroque orchestras as early as the 1970s, if not before. By the year 2000, there were, and still are, one or more groups in most major European cities.

New York has had a number of groups that came and went. The groundbreaking New York Pro Musica was started in the 1950s and specialized in pre-Baroque music; it continued until the director's death in 1966. Even with Andrew Parrott as director, the New York Collegium Musicum couldn't make a go of it and shut down in 2010.

It has taken some time, but we are now seeing a number of groups of various sizes committed to playing Baroque music on Baroque instruments. Not surprisingly, the source of many of these groups in New York and elsewhere has been Juilliard's Historical Performance department. Now in its seventh year, the program has gained a reputation that has spread around the world, with invitations to the student orchestra to perform in local and foreign venues.

This concert by the young players of New York Baroque Incorporated with guest director Monica Huggett (currently artistic advisor to Juilliard) shows these musicians are both technically proficient and as serious and professional as any early music group. The program was untitled, but the main theme was mourning and death. This was a brave choice since the common perception of Baroque music, if there is one, is that it is for light listening: music such as Vivaldi's *Four Seasons* or Albinoni's "Adagio" (actually not by Albinoni, but by a spurious mid-20th-century composer). But death was at the core of Bach's and much of Telemann's music. Bach wrote at the end of most of his completed scores the words "Soli deo gloria" ("Only for the Glory of God"). In a recent article in *The New Yorker*, Alex Ross opens with these words: "Johann Sebastian Bach lost both of his parents when he was nine and watched ten of his children die young. He was, in other words, well acquainted with death, and may have been uncommonly sensitive to the emotional chaos that it engenders."

The selection of the sixth Brandenberg was also a wise choice. Although this concerto (as well as the others) is in a major key, the choice of only dark-hued instruments gives the work a minor-key feel. The effect of this work is the same regardless of whether the viola da gambas are replaced by celli, or whether the violas are some variant of the da gamba family, not the modern violas of the string section. These dark colors were heightened by the contrapuntal complexities of the work.

Playing this concerto with one voice per part allows every line to be heard: OVPP relies on just one person to carry the musical moment. Monica Huggett and the others offered fine playing, but Kyle Miller as the second violist, although technically capable of playing his part, failed to articulate clearly and loudly enough to be an equal to Ms. Huggett.

The recorder players, Priscilla Herreid and Luke Conklin, were sensitive to the rocking lyricism of the opening sinfonia of Bach's 106th Cantata. As good as all the instrumentalists were, the vocalists also impressed with their technical skills and their presentation. Soprano Sara MacKimmie has the pure sound that is a requisite for the vocal music of the Baroque. The highpoint was the disconsolate Lamento by J. S. Bach's older cousin Johann Christoph Bach, "Ach, dass ich Wassers gnug hätte," sung to perfection by alto Sara Coudin.

♫ *Carnegie Hall's 125th Anniversary Gala Opening: NY Philharmonic and Tchaikovsky Reunited*
Evgeny Kissin (piano), New York Philharmonic Orchestra, Alan Gilbert (conductor), Carnegie Hall, New York, 7.10.2015

Magnus Lindberg: *Vivo* (2015; World Premiere, co-commissioned by Carnegie Hall)
Tchaikovsky: Piano Concerto No. 1 in B-flat minor
Ravel: *Daphnis et Chloé*, Suite No. 2

For the opening night gala of Carnegie Hall's 125th season, it was appropriate that the New York Philharmonic Orchestra, whose home is in Lincoln Center, trekked across town to perform. It was in Carnegie Hall that the NYPO gave the inaugural concert in 1891, and they were also the house orchestra before taking up residence in Avery Fisher (now David Geffen) Hall. Fittingly, they chose a work by Tchaikovsky who, along with William Damrosch, opened the official first season here.

It was an eclectic audience that included some 250 benefactors. The days before had been rife with rumors and innuendos about upper management machinations, and there was some conversation around the hall, but if there was an undercurrent of political intrigue, I never felt it. Probably more diverting were the logistical problems inherent in seating late-arriving, elegantly dressed patrons, which left Gilbert and the NYPO waiting until a solution could be found.

Patriotism has obviously made a comeback: the orchestra opened with a rousing rendition of "The Star Spangled Banner." The audience stood up and, in traditional ballpark fashion, cheered at its end. Fortunately, we did not have to sit through a soloist reaching beyond his or her vocal capabilities.

Vivo, the commissioned piece by Magnus Lindberg, had the elements of a fanfare or overture and was performed by an orchestra heavy on brass and percussion. Bongos, crotales, cymbals, bells—all added to the dense blocks of sound that alternated with lighter (but never light) passages. Some moments brought to mind Mahler finales: an unrepressed Mahler, not afraid to turn the volume up. Other moments had me thinking that somehow Copland's "Fanfare for the Common Man" had reared its head, still alive but angrier and more discordant.

What was noticeable in this piece and in the works that followed was how good the NYPO sounded in Carnegie Hall, with a vibrancy not usually heard in their Lincoln Center home. They might have been the Berlin Philharmonic: the brass buffed to a shine, the strings playing sumptuously and the winds clear and clean.

If only timbre were sufficient to please the listener, Tchaikovsky's Piano Concerto No. 1 might provide a tolerable half hour of music. Kiril Gerstein makes a convincing argument that the posthumously published edition (definitive in our time) was not the composer's final say. For instance, the bombastic opening chords are a sound world apart from the earlier edition in which they are arpeggiated. Given the popularity of the work and its unending presence in documentaries about the Moscow and Van Cliburn competitions, it was good to hear Kissin use a just and measured approach, reigning back from piano pounding. Gilbert, as well, kept much of the orchestra frenzy-free. The short solo passages for cello and clarinet were elegantly dispatched.

Ravel's heavily programmatic *Daphnis et Chloé* showed the orchestra at its best. Although Ravel's score carries his descriptions of which images the listener should be visualizing, it is best to close one's eyes and just listen to his opulent music. Ravel was one of the century's great orchestrators, able to bring color and light to every measure. Gilbert's performance here was full-bodied, the orchestra totally responsive to his gestures. It takes years for a conductor to reach the point where the members of an orchestra know exactly what is expected of them. Gilbert's announced departure after the next season will be a loss for all involved.

♫ *Juilliard Baroque Celebrates C. P. E. Bach's 300th + 1 Birthday*
Juilliard Baroque: Sandra Miller (flute), Cynthia Roberts (violin), Robert Mealy (violin and viola), Phoebe Carrai (cello), Peter Sykes (clavichord and harpsichord), Paul Hall, Juilliard School of Music, Lincoln Center, New York, 12.9.2015

C. P. E Bach: Trio Sonata for Flute, Violin, and Basso continuo in A major; Rondo for Clavichord in A minor; Trio Sonata for two Violins and Basso continuo in C minor, "Sanguineus und Melancholicus"; Fantasia for violin and clavichord in F-sharp minor; Sonata for Flute and Basso continuo in G major, "Hamburger Sonata"; Quartet for Flute, Viola, and Obbligato keyboard in D major

A pleasant corollary for me to a new musical season is the opening performance by the faculty members of the Historical Performance Program at the Juilliard. This will be the school's seventh year, and with each year its professional reputation and recognition have grown, resulting in invitations from as close as Boston and as far away as England and Japan.

The first event of the Fall 2015 season was a performance by Juilliard Baroque devoted to the music of C. P. E. Bach. The concert came too late to mark CPE's 2014 tercentennial year which generated much interest in Europe but little in the States. The anniversary did give some of the record companies an opportunity to dig down into their libraries and reissue multi-volume sets of his music at a discounted price. There were also several major projects that aimed at completion by 2014. The most important was the publication by the Packard Humanities Institute of Bach's entire opus. To make his works more readily available, the volumes have been reasonably priced; they've also been digitized and are available for free downloading.

Another important project comes from keyboardist Miklos Spanyi. Spanyi aimed at, but has not yet completed, the recording of all the keyboard sonatas. There are 30 volumes so far, mostly played on the clavichord, but there are at least ten more albums to go. His 26-volume piano concerto cycle, which he started in 1998, was completed this year. Ana-Marija Markovina has done the nearly impossible job of completing 27 volumes of keyboard music in roughly a year and a half.

The inevitable question that arises—or should arise—whenever a clavichord appears on a stage is, "Am I close enough to hear it?" Tonight was no different from other clavichord recitals that I've attended. How much you hear depends upon how close you are to the stage, how good (or bad) the acoustics are and how good your hearing is. I've had similar experiences with clavichord recitals, and have several times been frustrated with the lack of audibility. The Rondo for Clavichord is rife with dynamic markings that suddenly go from loud to soft. I'm sure the composer himself might have appreciated a modern piano with its ability to articulate and to be fully responsive to the player's touch.

Peter Sykes' clavichord was not as soft as others I've heard, and the acoustics of the theater are pretty good, so the fortes were audible, but when the pianissimos came the effect was lost. I was a few rows in from the stage, but I imagine no one in the back of the auditorium heard much of anything. For CPE the clavichord was an instrument on which to accomplish two things: mundanely, to write music for sale for an instrument that was readily available; and spiritually, to write music for personal use or for an intimate group of friends and family. Sykes performed the Rondo with appropriate *Emfingdunen*, a word that has come to be associated not simply with emotions but also a stronger, passionate state, referred to later as *Innigskeit* or the "inner world."

The unusual Fantasia is better known in its original form without the violin *obligatto*. Why CPE added the violin is beyond me; the keyboard part certainly stands well enough alone as one of CPE's many improvisatory pieces. Robert Mealy wisely took a cautious approach, seeming hesitant about sounding any louder for fear of drowning out the substantive keyboard part.

Not all of CPE's instrumental pieces are melancholic. The Trio for flute, violin and bc was given a perfect reading. Sandra Miller was impeccable on Baroque flute and Cynthia Roberts responded to the flute's conversation with stylish ease. CPE had a humorous side too: he never completes the cadence at the end of the first movement, leaving the players and listeners up in the air.

The Trio for two violins and bc, subtitled *Sanguineus und Melancholicus*, is a most unusual composition, a shortened version of the struggle between two opposite humors. (Would Bach have known Handel's *L'Allegro, il Penseroso ed il Moderato*, a pastoral oratorio presented similarly as a conversation between sanguine and melancholic characters?) Like his father, CPE was not a man of the theater and had no interest in opera; this was about the only form of music that he did not conquer. Songs and choral works came naturally to him, but unlike Telemann, his godfather, he never ventured into the burgeoning musical world of opera. This piece of program music was his attempt to prove that one can express ideas through the abstract without visual cues. It's not a very convincing argument given the amount of textual detail he felt was needed to explain the emotions each violinist was expressing.

The instrumentalists gave a convincing argument that CPE's music, like his father's, was mainly serious and deeply felt but with moments of delightful abandon. His heart, though, was in the keyboard, and in his solo pieces and concerti we find this composer's unjustly neglected accomplishments which are slowly being reevaluated.

♫ *Mostly Mozart Festival Ends with Haydn's Beginning*

Mostly Mozart Festival Finale: Concert Chorale of New York, James Bagwell (director), Mostly Mozart Festival Orchestra, Louis Langrée (conductor), Sarah Tynan (soprano), Thomas Cooley (tenor), John Relyea (bass), Avery Fisher Hall, Lincoln Center, New York, 21.8.2015

Haydn: *The Creation*

We often think of Haydn as a dilettante, a composer sweet enough to bear the appellation "Papa," and much of his music does reinforce this image. There are, of course, exceptions: those symphonies written during the Sturm und Drang period (1760–1780), often easily spotted by titles such as *Lamentatione, Trauer* or *La Passione*; the use of minor keys (in only 11 symphonies out of 104); or his Masses and his one-of-a-kind "Seven Last Words of Jesus at the Cross." But he was, after all, an employee at the service of royalty (granted, enlightened royalty), and he was expected to write music of a kind. He was no Beethoven or Mozart, neither of whom would have tolerated being treated as a servant, consigned, as it were, to eating with the staff.

Even after leaving the Esterhazy estate for London, where he was afforded a compositional carte blanche from his numerous London admirers and patrons, he remained conservative, never progressing as far as he might have in his final symphonies. As popular as these works are, they suffer from a rigidity and a simplicity that was meant to please rather than to enlighten. Few of his operas are familiar, for good reason; Beethoven knew opera was not his strength and wrote only one, but Haydn produced over a dozen. When Haydn did make small leaps into the unknown, it was often under the influence of another composer or style. This can be seen in the stylistic changes he made to his symphonies during the Sturm und Drang period and in the quartets influenced by Mozart. It is hard not to see the influence of Handel in Haydn's oratorios, *The Creation* and *The Seasons*. Handel had written many sacred oratorios, based on biblical stories of Deborah, Saul and Theodora, before tackling "The Messiah," but Haydn went straight to the top of the pile with the story of the Creation.

The overture, entitled "The Representation of Chaos," has its share of the chaotic, with dissonance most prominently heard from the brass. The score also calls for two clarinets; although the clarinet had been around for some time, it had not been used prominently in orchestral works of the period. Here Haydn uses them for their timbre. When the clarinet appears, as it does in a glissando during the overture, it feels anachronistic. Langrée used all the given resources to the full. The overture was performed at a considerable clip, and the fortes were appropriately forceful. It was clear this was not going to be a tempered performance, as several others that I've seen have been. Langrée made no attempt to hide dissonances, treated in some productions as if they were mistakes. Somehow everything cohered, being both precise and clean, which is not easy to accomplish in a work that is meant to be the essence of the chaotic.

Yet as the oratorio continued, the whole began to seem as if it were going to be less than its parts. From movement to movement, individual solos, choruses and recitatives were more than technically correct, but lacked distinctiveness. Yes, every member excelled, with particular praise due to the male soloists who replaced the originally announced singers, but there was an overall lack of variety. When a conductor has already brought us to pseudo-climaxes several times, there are not many places he can go at the close of a section or at the finale. There were times when the music had such a sense of finality that one felt the oratorio must be over.

A specific example was the chorus and soloists together singing a text that clearly was meant to refer back to Handel's *Messiah*: "The lord is great and great his might. The glory lasts forever and for evermore." The expected effect would have been more potent had some of the earlier choruses been more tempered. Certainly we don't want to go back to an old-world plodding performance à la Handel oratorios of the 19th and early 20th centuries, but the conductor's job is to understand a work's construction and overall effect. Large works, whether a Passion by Bach or a symphony by Mahler, don't stand up when the conductor does not have a vision of the whole and focuses only on the parts.

The instrumentalists and vocal soloists excelled in every way. They were clear and fluent, able to hold their own amid the full volume of the orchestra. How lucky it was to have two of the three soloists replaced by singers who never once sounded unprepared. These vocalists were appearing at the Mostly Mozart Festival for the first time, and one must give credit to Langrée who kept everything moving. Sarah Tynan's voice soared and shone through the density of the music, carrying even the highest notes clearly to the rafters.

Alto Erin Kemp appeared near the end in what must be the shortest soloist role in music, with only a half dozen measures to deliver during the final vocal tutti—and she did them very nicely.

♫ *More Mozart but Not "Mostly Mozart" and Across the River*
Manhattan Symphonie, Gregory Singer (conductor, violin), Mark Peskanov (violin), Gregory Durozel (violin), Kyungha Ko (violin), Alexander Mishnaevski (viola), Bargemusic, Fulton Ferry Landing, Brooklyn, New York, 1.8.2015

Vivaldi: Concerto for 4 Violins and Orchestra in B minor
Mozart: Concerto for Violin and Orchestra No. 3 in G major; Sinfonia
Concertante for Violin, Viola and Orchestra

If there was ever an unusual venue for a concert, it must be the barge floating in the East River in the shadows of the Brooklyn Bridge. Moored to the dock, it seems to be a spruced-up version of the working barges that go up and down the river separating Brooklyn from Manhattan. It did have a more genteel history, carrying as it did bags of coffee to Lake Erie, which were then shipped west by rail. Getting to the barge takes you first to a subway station whose only exit is through a small tube that makes you think of Alice's rabbit hole, but going up and out, instead of down and in. The walk to the concert hall from the station goes through an area called "Dumbo," not named after Walt Disney's cartoon but an acronym of "Down Under the Manhattan Bridge Overpass." The barge is docked by the Brooklyn Bridge Park, which on this weekend evening was filled with families seeking to cool off and lining up for pizza and ice cream.

The sign on the gangplank suggested that the concert-goer hold tightly to the railing, as it is known to sway in bad weather. Inside the barge is a perfectly respectable concert hall holding about 220. The walls are acoustically tiled and somewhat soundproof, a necessity in a public park, but they couldn't completely block the beat from woofers outside. It was disturbing to everyone except the musicians, well inured, I'm sure, to extraneous sounds. The river was calm this night, but like on an airplane, pockets of disturbance occur unexpectedly, and river currents occasionally rocked the boat.

I was attracted to the performance by all three concerti, but especially by the Sinfonia Concertante. Not that this work is never played, but to my mind, it is never played enough. A friend and ex-pianist in his 80s, who lived in London and was an avid concert-goer, once asked me if I had ever heard this piece, since he had recently heard it for the first time. I immediately bought him my favorite recording with George Szell and soloists of the Cleveland Orchestra. I couldn't imagine him leaving this earth without having become familiar with it.

The overall sound of the smallish orchestra was thin, but this was a minor sacrifice compared to what was gained by the clarity given to the solo lines. It was key here for the soloists to provide the exuberance and richness that is usually provided by a larger orchestra. Both Mark Peskanov and Alexander Mishnaevski did just that, exuding tremendous warmth when needed, and passion in the heartfelt second movement (an amazing show of maturity for the-23 year-old composer). In those instances where there is a back and forth between the two instruments, like a handing off of the baton to the next runner in a relay race, it must be done, and was done, seamlessly. The listener should not hear any transitions at these moments, should not be aware of the point where the two instruments meet and the second takes over.

It takes a brave musician to tackle some of Vivaldi's virtuoso violin concerti. Add three more soloists, as in the Concerto for 4 Violins, and you have four times as many chances of making a mistake. There might have been some slight slips in intonation, and the Allegro Vivace tempo may have been intentionally slowed so that all the soloists were able to play at the same speed, but it would seem that Vivaldi himself had done something similar. A count of the measures in the first movement allocated to each violin goes from 29 for the first to 22 for the second, 17 for the third and 12 for the fourth. The second movement is an odd mix of chords similar to the transition between the first and last movement of Bach's Third Brandenburg; and a series of repeated phrases varies very slightly harmonically, as Philip Glass would do *ad nauseum* 250 years later.

Mozart's Violin Concerto No. 3 is the first of the great concerti he wrote for the violin in the autumn of 1775 at the age of 18. Peskanov played it effortlessly here, conversing with the four non-string instruments: two oboes and two horns. The cadenza that Peskanov used had elements of lightheartedness and humor, unlike the rather stodgy ones by Ysaye and Kriesler. The second movement is all sweetness and light and leads to the rambunctious Presto finale. The coda ends the work on the quietest of notes, repeating an early cadence which leads the listener to expect a reentry by the violin. This surprising ending may not work as effectively as Haydn's more demonstrative ending of his "Farewell" Symphony, but it confused so many in the audience that Peskanov had to gesture that the concert was, indeed, over.

♪ *Not Mostly Mozart but All Mozart in Opening Concert of Festival*

Mostly Mozart Festival 1: (Repeat of Tuesday Concert), Emanuel Ax (piano), Erin Morley (soprano), Mostly Mozart Festival Orchestra, Louis Langrée (conductor), Avery Fisher Hall, Lincoln Center, New York, 29.7.2015

Mozart: Overture to *Der Schauspieldirektor* ("The Impresario"); Piano Concerto No. 14 in E-flat major (with Mozart's cadenza); "Vorrei spiegarvi, oh Dio!"; "No, che non sei capace"; Symphony No. 34 in C major

Although this year's Mostly Mozart Festival has its share of non-Mozart events and composers, it is a nod to its history that the opening concert was all-Mozart. The main non-Mozart events this year are the premier of composer-in-residence George Benjamin's opera, *Written on Skin*; and the Festival's closing concert, Haydn's *Creation*. In previous years, a composer was often highlighted, such as Beethoven, Schubert or Haydn. Some years a theme was used to distinguish one Festival from another. The 2012 theme, for example, revolved around composers whose works were influenced by or featured bird songs. Loudly played in the lobby, the tweets and chirps became obnoxious when mid-Festival they began to accompany you to the restrooms. In the past few years the Festival's opening concerts have been what they should be: mostly Mozart.

This year the Festival is presenting a particularly fine array of Mozart's works, a smorgasbord of the varied styles in which he was proficient. Mozart was just about the last composer to totally master all the musical forms available to him. Beethoven and Schubert missed the mark with their failed operas. Chopin was uncomfortable in writing for any instrument other than the piano. Schumann and Brahms too had difficulties writing vocal music for the opera although they were both profound composers of lieder.

This appreciation of the breadth and depth of Mozart's music is why the Festival has survived long enough to celebrate next year its 50th season.

The overture to "The Impresario" is as lithe and effervescent as any of Mozart's opera overtures and similar in its goodwill and humor to *The Marriage of Figaro*, completed in the same year. This five-minute piece, written nearly in sonata-form, is followed by *singspielen* and four arias; and the whole work almost could have been added to the program finishing as it does in under a half-hour. If it had been continued there would have been an additional advantage: having Erin Morley, who starred last year in "The Impresario" at the Santa Fe Opera.

Emanuel Ax has always been disarmingly self-effacing, and his performance here captured the calmness of what is often considered the first of the Mozart's great piano concerti. I would agree if a caveat were given noting the aberrational maturity of the Concerto No. 9, as sophisticated a concerto as any of the later ones but written seven years earlier.

Nothing was rushed. Mozart knew the anticipation that was created by delaying the piano's entrance, and he used it to great effect here. Once Ax joined the group, he created a central focus, leaving the orchestra as no more than an accompaniment. This was fine for Langrée who was content to follow Ax and produce big sounds only when needed. There was nothing earth-shattering, but there needn't be. Mozart had more than enough opportunities to excite and surprise, and that he does.

Unusually, Ax returned to the stage after several curtain calls to perform an encore, a tender rendition of Schumann's first *Fantasiestücke*, Op.12.

Depending on how you slant it, Mozart wrote between 25 and 50 concert arias: a large body of works, many simply orphans taken out of his operas because they did not suit the singer. In many cases, the reason they did not suit the singers was due to their stratospheric highs and equally deep lows. This was certainly the case in these two arias written for Mozart's sister-in-law, Alyoshia. With notes reaching well above high C and dropping down several octaves, Erin Morley made a tremendous effort but was shrill on top and barely audible on the bottom.

The 34th Symphony is unusual for late Mozart in that it is only three movements. Although he began writing a Minuet for it, he completed only the first 14 measures which Langrée performed half-humorously. At the sudden end to this fragment, Langrée gave a quick explanation, turned around and zipped through the final Allegro vivace at a tempo considerably faster than the opening Allegro vivace.

To be able to say that this opening concert held its own against the first season nearly a half century ago would be a presumptuous leap in memory, but that the music still pleases is a tribute to both Mozart and Mostly Mozart.

♪*American Premier of Vivaldi's Catone in Utica at Glimmerglass:*

Singers Galore

Glimmerglass Festival Orchestra, Ryan Brown (conductor), Alice Busch Opera Theater, Glimmerglass, New York, 18.7.2015

Vivaldi: *Catone in Utica*

For years I confused Glimmerglass with Glyndebourne. I would attend performances at the New York City Opera that were new productions and notice in the *Playbill* that the NYCO had been working jointly with Glimmerglass (or Glyndebourne) on creating them. In fact, there were more than 20 joint productions between the NYCO and Glimmerglass. Baroque opera thrived in New York during the nine years that Paul Kellogg ran the NYCO; before that, Kellogg had been with Glimmerglass during three of its most important decades.

In preparation for attending this first American production of Vivaldi's *Catone in Utica*, I went through the opera's history and found Act I such a mishmash of lost, replaced or borrowed music that I had to lay out the opening act on a spreadsheet according to the source of each aria. In the two complete versions that were available to me (a third version exists but is prohibitively expensive), each had its own way of accounting for the missing arias. One version, from a 2001 performance by Jean-Claude Malgoire, filled out Act I with borrowings from other Vivaldi operas. Another edition (the one used at Glimmerglass, by the late conductor and Baroque scholar Alan Curtis) replaces the lost Act I with music adapted by Alessandro Ciccolini. It also includes one aria from *Rosmira Fidele*, thought to have been originally in *Catone in Utica*.

Reconstruction is pretty much the norm with Vivaldi: only 11 of the 30 or more operas that have been unearthed are complete. But there is no real reason to skip scenes or whole acts just because they are incomplete. If that attitude were taken towards the wonderful Vivaldi operas (really pastiches) *Bajazet*, *Montezuma* and *Andromeda Liberata*, it would be a great loss. It's better to hear plugged-in, borrowed arias from other Vivaldi operas than to have nothing at all. Ciccolini, in fact, made very workman-like additions to the missing arias in *Catone*; he also took two arias from the unperformed Act I and used them for the added suicide scenes.

In the end, my spreadsheet was not needed as Act I was not to be performed. We were told before the start by conductor Ryan Brown that Act I had nothing much to say and could be summed up in a few short texts projected on scrims. We were also informed that there would not be the happy ending Vivaldi wanted in place of librettist Metastasio's tragic finale.

Gone are the days when an orchestra is belittled for attempting to play Baroque-era operas on non-period instruments. But one does expect an effort to at least emulate the sound by lessening vibrato. This should be particularly true of Ryan Brown whose specialty is Baroque opera. Throwing in a theorbo just doesn't do it. The end result was a performance that lacked the spirit of Vivaldi. From the first notes of the overture, a sinfonia taken from Vivaldi's *L'Olimpiade*, the tonal color was bland.

As it should be, the singers were the stars of the show, and smart choices were made in the selection of voices. This is not easy music, and the production people wisely chose professionals for the elaborate arias, particularly those with serpentine melismas and cadenzas. Among the students in the cast, Eric Jurenas excelled as the unwanted suitor, Arbace. Thomas Michael Allen as Cato did not have enough vocal material to show his strengths but brilliantly acted the role of Cato. Sarah Mesko blew me away with the aria "Come invano il mare irato," running through two octaves as if it was child's play.

I last saw countertenor John Holiday in 2013 as Radamisto in a student production at the Juilliard School, and what I said then could be applied here: "His rich, natural, unforced voice never sounded false, and the ease with which he expressed all kinds of emotions was first-rate. His voice was equally impressive in arias that required dramatic strength, such as the show-stopping 'Vile! Se mi dai vita' with its long and difficult melissmas [read 'Se mai senti spirarti sul volto lieve' in *Catone*]."

Ryan Brown kept the da capo structures that were standard for the era. Many people find the A-B-A form difficult to sit through, and this is particularly true with Handel's long arias. But Vivaldi's arias are quick and tidy and give the vocalist opportunity to improvise in the repeats.

Note: There has not been much mention of the recent and sudden death of the great reviver of Italian Baroque opera, Alan Curtis. With his group "Il Complesso Barocco" he reconstructed many Baroque operas, including Vivaldi's *Catone in Utica*. Curtis and his counterpart in France, William Christie, are American-trained harpsichordists who became residents of two musically rich countries, and both have done much to revive early music. His absence is a grave loss to the music world.

♪ *Faculty Pianists Make the Grade*
Faculty Gala, PianoSummer, Julien J. Studley Theater, SUNY New Paltz, New Paltz, NY, 11.7.2015

Vladimir Feltsman
Bach: Partita No. 1 in B-flat major

Paul Ostrovsky
Beethoven: *Andante Favori* in F major; *Rondo alla ingharese quasi un capriccio*

Susan Starr
Chopin: Nocturne in B-flat minor; From Études, Op. 25, No. 1 in A-flat major, *Sostenuto*; No.2 in F minor, *Presto*

Robert Roux
Brahms: From *Klavierstücke*: No. 1. Intermezzo in A minor; No. 2. Intermezzo in A major; No. 6. Intermezzo in E-flat minor

Robert Hamilton
Bartók: *Improvisations on Hungarian Peasant Songs*

Alexander Korsantia
Ravel: *La Valse* (arranged by Korsantia)

It has been six years since I last attended a recital at the annual "PianoSummer" Festival held on the campus of SUNY New Paltz. Created by Vladimir Feltsman, this is a forum for skilled young pianists to immerse themselves in practice under the tutelage of renowned teachers. It has quietly continued as a yearly event, and although not as well-known as the nearby festivals at Caramoor, Bard College and Glimmerglass, it has thrived and is now in its 20th year. The Festival includes master classes by visiting artists, student recitals, weekly artist recitals and a piano competition, the winner of which performs in a final gala as soloist in a to-be-determined concerto.

This opening public concert of the Festival was a recital by the faculty members. Not that anyone would question the authority of the staff, but it certainly set an example for the students of what their mentors have accomplished. The entire faculty (except for Phillip Kawin, who was ill) played their own idiosyncratic samples with both élan and panache. Their chosen repertoire was in nearly chronological order from Bach to Bartók; only in the penultimate and final works were the composers' birth dates out of order.

The concert opened with Feltsman's performance of Bach's first Partita for keyboard. Tastes in music seem to change so rapidly that at times they go right past one. Even the most hardened purist (read defender) of historically informed performance would have a hard time finding a pianist taking an urtext score at face value. Keyboardists on piano or harpsichord have come around to the realization that the old contest between the two Bach specialists of the middle years of the past century, Roslyn Tureck and Glenn Gould, clearly has been won by the latter. Listening to Tureck's readings of the great keyboard works of Bach, I find her playing almost comically rigid, stiff and inflexible. Repeats were always taken, and never varied by even the most basic ornamentation; tempos were conservative and rhythms hardly dance-like. Glenn Gould saw Bach as a constantly evolving composer who undoubtedly never performed the same piece twice. To say that Gould's journey to Russia in 1957 (documented in *Glenn Gould: The Russian Journey*) made a strong impression on the pianists and their students in the great Russian conservatories would be an understatement. It took a longer time for Western countries to follow suit, weighed down as they were by the conservative pianists of the day.

Feltsman's performance of the first Partita was no mirror image of Gould: never quite as *détaché* as Gould, freer than Gould about ornamentation and the taking or skipping of repeats. His tempi, though, were very close to Gould's, as was his use of arpeggiated chords and ritardandos at the close of each movement. In the context of the other works on the program that take advantage of the modern piano's extra octaves, one sees how much of Bach's keyboard music was constrained by the limited range of the harpsichord and early pianofortes. Feltsman's playing, particularly in those passages requiring hand over hand execution or those where the intervals are tighter, created a kind of kinetic energy that is inherent in Bach's circumscribed keyboard compositions.

Next, Paul Ostrovsky played two short pieces by Beethoven. Many of Beethoven's minor pieces have gained in popularity through their titles: somehow, sticking a name on a composer's otherwise nameless piece immediately raises the perceived worth of that composition. This is also true of works which are untitled but carry with them a story, whether apocryphal or true. It doesn't make a difference if the title came from the composer or from someone else. In the pieces played here, *Andante Favori* purportedly was named by Beethoven; the "Rage over a Lost Penny" was titled by Diabelli who published it after Beethoven's death and likely sold more copies by giving the piece a human face. Ostrovsky was a bit choppy in the Adagio, but improved enough to bring sprightliness to the otherwise bombastic "capriccio."

Susan Starr gave a heartfelt performance of Chopin's B-flat minor Nocturne. Published in 1833, it was the first of Chopin's 21 pieces in this form to be printed. It's not often played, and there are surprisingly few recordings. Perhaps it suffered from comparison to the really first nocturnes, those of the Irish composer John Field. As late as the beginning of the 20th century, its lack of popularity was noted with surprise by one critic who called it "one of the most elegiac of Nocturnes...for some reason neglected." Ms. Starr succeeded in capturing the work's melancholy. Her control of the keyboard was also apparent in the first two of the Op. 25 Etudes.

There is a long hiatus between Chopin's early Nocturnes of 1833 and Brahms' piano pieces of 1893, and we see in the later works the beginning of the end of the Romantic era. These short pieces are complex, and it can be difficult for an audience to see through the density of even their most lyrical moments. The entire keyboard is played, down to its lowest notes. The very Brahmsian stylistic marks abound here: hemiolas, diminished seventh chords, vague or abrupt modulations, often to faraway keys. Robert Roux had control of these disparate elements at all times and, admirably, his playing never sounded studied.

We are fully in the 20th Century with Bartók's *Improvisations on Hungarian Peasant Songs*. Bartók wrote volumes of piano music based on his collections of his country's indigenous folk music; the set that Robert Hamilton chose to play falls into the third part of Bartók's own classification of how he incorporated the songs into his scores. This music is more Bartók the modernist than Bartók the musical archaeologist. He himself stated that whatever use he made of folk tunes was to be "only regarded as a kind of motto." In fact, much of the enjoyment of these dense, convoluted works comes from trying to catch the "hidden tunes," only clear to me in the last two pieces.

Alexander Korsantia's arrangement of Ravel's orchestral "La Valse" **had** to be the final work even if Ravel was born six years after Bartók. This arrangement, Lisztian in its demonic power, required tremendous technical skills and, surely, un-tuned a piano already in need of adjustment in its upper octave. If Ravel were still alive, his immodesty and vanity would surely have suffered a blow. Korsantia has written a reversed transcription of Ravel's orchestral powerhouse, *La Valse*, and done it on a level that equals, if not surpasses, Ravel's transcription for orchestra of Mussorgsky's *Pictures at an Exhibition*, originally written for piano.

All in all, this was an auspicious opening concert that more than bodes well for the rest of the series.

♫ *Carnegie Hall's Before Bach Series Finale Highlighted by Sir John Gardiner*

English Baroque Soloists, The Monteverdi Choir, Sir John Eliot Gardiner (conductor), Carnegie Hall, New York

Monteverdi: *Vespro della Beata Vergine*, 30.4.2015
Orfeo, 1.5.2015

The highlight of Carnegie Hall's Before Bach series has to have been the finale: two evenings devoted to Monteverdi with Sir John Eliot Gardiner, the English Baroque Soloists and The Monteverdi Choir. Both concerts were sold out, or nearly so. This speaks to both the charisma of Gardiner and to the taste of New Yorkers. Classical music, we are told, is moribund, of interest only to the old and gray, but there were plenty of young people in attendance. After both concerts there were standing ovations, and the enthusiastic applause went on and on.

It was even more impressive that the audience was so tuned in to the music because the works are far from your typical fare. This was music outside the usual Baroque-to-21st-century repertory. Carnegie might fill a house just by mentioning Bach, Beethoven or Mozart. But here we had two nights of uncompromising music, nearly two hours each without intermission, with works written 400 years ago and 75 years before Bach was born. There are no catchy tunes, and some of the instruments are ones that many have never seen or even heard. And what vocal sounds these singers produced, ranging from recitative secco to roulades, and filled with challenging ornaments and melismas.

Precision is the keyword for Gardiner's playing style. This is a man whose 620-page study, *Bach: Music in the Castle of Heaven*, is as detailed as any scholar's lifetime work. With musical direction as well, Gardiner leaves nothing out, nothing is unstudied, and he is peerless in his control of all the forces at hand. More of an effort was required to keep things together in *L'Orfeo* then in *Vespro*, which had no acting or dancing. *Vespro* is church music, *L'Orfeo* is theater music

This precision also applies to the logistics of how and where Gardiner placed the instrumentalists and the soloists. During the echo stanzas in *L'Orfeo*'s "Questi i campi di Tracia, e questo è il loco," the respondent sang from a back balcony. As individuals moved to the forefront or to join other groups, each reached his or her goal at precisely the right time by walking at a slow, studied pace. Although Gardiner is known to be a difficult conductor in terms of rehearsing, he clearly and equitably managed to give every member of the choir a turn either as soloist or as part of a small ensemble.

But logistics must come naturally to Gardiner, who conquered a logistical nightmare in his project to perform and record 198 Bach cantatas at different churches in 50 cities and 13 countries around the world. Having completed 22 discs for Deutsche Grammophon, he asked them to finance a pilgrimage in which he would record the cantatas to mark the 250th anniversary of Bach's death. DGG refused, but Gardiner managed to make the financial arrangements and go ahead. He recorded them for his own label, Soli deo Gloria, named after Bach's inscription near his signature on most of his works.

If the second evening's concert version of *L'Orfeo* did not completely succeed, that is only in comparison to the first night's *VDBV*, which was truly phenomenal. Well-versed in performance practices of the period, all the singers and instrumentalists excelled. There was no lack of variety here, given Monteverdi's inclusion of so many forms or practices: recitatives, motets, chants and modal music, at times contrapunctal and harmonic, and at other times sharply dissonant. Gardiner followed the constraints and liberties that Monteverdi himself took to bring music into the Baroque era.

Vespro was an evening of pure music but, obviously, it didn't reveal Monteverdi's talent as a dramatist. *L'Orfeo*, done here in semi-concert style, gave a taste of what a full Monteverdi opera production delivers. In 1999, Trisha Brown offered a production at the Brooklyn Academy of Music and it was a rare staging, filled with wonderful costumes and clever effects. But Gardiner's *L'Orfeo*, with its stylized choreography, particularly the slow walking with arms stiffly held or hands awkwardly lifted, reminded me of another Orpheus tale: Gluck's *Orphée et Eurydice*, staged by Robert Wilson and conducted by Sir John himself, where the same walking style was used.

One has to give credit to the young singers from the choir who took up the difficult task of acting out the opera in a less-than-inviting stage setup, working splendidly in the restricted space carved out for them around and between the musicians.

♫ *Bezuidenhout Reveals Little-Known Influences on Bach*
Kristian Bezuidenhout (harpsichord), Weill Recital Hall, Carnegie Hall, New York, 23.4.2015

Weckmann: Toccata in E minor, No. 1
Purcell: Prelude from Suite in G minor; Almand from Suite in G minor; Rondeau Minuet from *The Gordian Knot Unty'd*; Round O from *Abdelazer, or The Moor's Revenge*; Ground in C minor
Muffat: Passacaglia from *Apparatus musico-organisticus*
Couperin: Prelude in C major
Ritter: Suite in C minor
Couperin: Passacaille in C major
Froberger: Tombeau in C minor

Kristian Bezuidenhout's performances as soloist and as conductor have always reflected a refined, at times even fragile, sensibility, but one that is tempered by a firm intellectual rigor. This particular program, part of the Before Bach series currently running at Carnegie Hall, demonstrated the range of composers whose works were influential in creating Bach's unique musical sensibility. As at previous concerts, Bezuidenhout gave a brief informal talk about the pieces to follow. Many might be aware of the impact that Buxtehude and Vivaldi had on Bach, but few would be familiar with the scores of several of the composers included here.

Most of the pieces flowed easily from one to the next, each one highlighting another aspect of Bach's musical inheritance. Bezuidenhout opened with a piece by Mattias Weckmann, a competitor for musical positions with Froberger, who later became his friend. Weckmann most likely learned the toccata form from Froberger, who wrote two sets of them in the mid-17th century. The toccata is usually a showpiece with sudden fast runs, striking chords and arpeggios, but in Bezuidenhout's hands it was more thoughtful than virtuosic, due perhaps to the thinness of its harmonic texture. The catchy, jumpy, fugue-like middle section leads to a final improvisatory closing.

The Prelude from the G minor Suite by Purcell seemed like a continuation of the toccata we had just heard. The "Round O" from *Abdelazer* will be familiar to many: it forms the basis of Britten's *A Young Person's Guide to the Orchestra*. Purcell's Ground in C minor led to Muffat's "Passacaglia." What are a Ground and a Passacaglia? You might also throw in a chaconne, rhythmically different but structurally the same. In fact, they are basically alike: all are built on a repeating motif in the bass that continues without change from the beginning to end.

Because of the bare notation in Louis Couperin's Prelude, much freedom is given to the performer. There is so much freedom to improvise that it might be hard to believe when listening to different performers that they are playing the same piece. Bezuidenhout held to a dignified tempo and avoided heavy ornamentation which would have belied the work's poignant nature.

Very little keyboard music by Christian Ritter still exists, but if the little suite played here is representative, we've lost a lot. Bezuidenhout took the opening Allemande almost as slowly as the suite's Sarabande, and to good effect. The work's title, "On the departure of Charles XI, King of Sweden," underscores the music's mournfulness.

Froberger was a follower of the "stylus fantasticus," a style of playing that emphasizes the freedom to improvise, as in the toccatas discussed above. The "stylus fantasticus" went even further in the direction of improvisation, allowing dissonance and the relegation of melodies. It can also be seen as the high point of Baroque style, which aimed to be ornate, elaborate, complex and intense.

The final work, Bach's Partita No.4, is in the key of D major but has two movements, the Allemande and the Sarabande that, as played here by Bezuidenhout, seemed to be in a minor key, a natural continuation of the earlier heartfelt works. I'm quite familiar with this Partita, having played it (not well) on an out-of-tune piano in the graduate-school lounge almost every day for a year. Bezuidenhout's sterling performance made me feel like I was hearing it for the first time.

♪ *Caldara Masterpiece Resurrected*
American Classical Orchestra and Chorus, Thomas Crawford (conductor), Church of Saint Mary the Virgin, New York, 21.4.2014

Handel: Chandos Anthem No. 10, "The Lord is my light"
Torelli: Concerto for Trumpet and Strings in D major
Allegri: *Misere mei, Deus*
Caldara: *Maddalena ai piedi di Cristo*

In the program notes, musical director and conductor Thomas Crawford replaces the traditional explication of *Maddalena* with a "personal commentary" that begins with the question, "Where's Tony nowadays?" Tony is Antonio Caldara, the 18th-century composer whose prolific output was barely enough to meet the demands of the public for his vocal works. He wrote music in every form, with over 90 operas and 40 oratorios to his name. Based upon their popularity today, one would expect Vivaldi to have died a wealthy man and Caldara a pauper, instead of the other way around. (Can you imagine how much Vivaldi might have drawn on royalties from his *Four Seasons* alone?)

Mr. Crawford bemoans the fact that Caldara has not made his way to New York. This is not entirely accurate: there has been the infrequent stray song appearing in vocal recitals, one going as far back as 1905, but no work of substance has been performed. If we are going through a reevaluation and revival of Caldara's music, it might be in part because of a recording by René Jacobs of *Maddalena*. Jacobs' performance shows Caldara in his best light, featuring now-familiar names such as Maria Cristina Kier, Bernada Fink and countertenor Andreas Scholl as Celestial Love.

Crawford then asks why a work like the *Messiah*, a lesser masterpiece by any standard, is so popular. Actually, Handel himself was puzzled by this. When asked what his favorite work was, he replied *Theodora*, an oratorio as visceral as anything Handel wrote and now rarely performed. To my mind there is an endless list of composers whose names will never appear on anyone's ten-composers-to-listen-to-before-I-depart roster. My short list, in addition to Caldara, would include Chistoph Graupner, whose solo keyboard music and cantatas have only recently been recorded; Sylvius Leopold Weiss, the composer of charming music written solely for the lute; and Niccolò Jommelli, born the same year as Gluck, whose reform operas he complements and occasionally surpasses.

Often the revival of a previously unheralded composer coincides with a performer or performance that hooks enough of an audience to make them want to hear more. Classic examples are Mendelssohn's resurrection of Bach's vocal works and Glenn Gould's revival of Bach's keyboard pieces. It's unlikely that early in the sonata and appears again towards the end, each iterance followed by an unusually long silence that does not bode well for what follows. By the end of the movement we were part of Schubert and Schiff's Weltschmerz, not to be released until the applause that started, correctly this time, by the pianist lifting his hands off the keyboard.

The musicology of the "Last Sonatas" project may not be the most rigorous, but an artist like Schiff has no need to convince us of the worthiness of any project he decides to bring before the public.

♫ *William Christie Conducts Juilliard415 and Les Arts Florissants with Results that Amaze*

Juilliard415, William Christie (conductor), Alice Tully Hall, Lincoln Center, New York, 29.10.2015

Handel: Concerto Grosso in F major
Rameau: Suite from *Les Indes Galantes*
Handel: Concerto Grosso in G minor
Bach: Orchestral Suite No. 4 in D major

Chorus and Orchestra of Les Arts Florissants, William Christie (director and conductor), Alice Tully Hall, Lincoln Center, New York, 31.10.2015

Handel: *Theodora*
Concert Version

This is the sixth year that I have attended and reviewed concerts and operas put on by the Juilliard Historical Performance program. Quite a few of their graduates have begun to enliven the New York Early Music world, helping New York build a reputation that has eluded it when compared to cities such as Boston, Portland and San Francisco. We had a number of Early Music groups, going back to the 1950's with Noah Greenberg and New York Pro Musica, but their demise after 14 years left the city with just a few groups whose reliability and performance depth varied from year to year with the vagaries of the financial world.

So how is it different now? For one thing, students and graduates are more willing to perform in less-than-ideal venues. Concerts in old warehouses have become *de rigeur*: the latest is a theater in Brooklyn that had previously been a sawdust factory. And as the cliché goes, it's the music that is important. It would be nice to have larger orchestras and choruses, or even an extra instrument or two for the basso continuos, let alone costumes and settings for a full-blown opera. But there's enough Baroque music out there that six to a dozen musicians could play. It helps, certainly, if a group supports the theory that much early instrumental and vocal music was performed with one part per voice or musical line. There have been a number of successful productions of works like the *Messiah* and the Mass in B Minor, as well as Bach's cantatas, done with only a

Vivaldi would have been so popular if he had never written the ubiquitous *Four Seasons.*

Whether Caldara will ever get the attention he deserves is impossible to answer. Suffice it to say that Crawford gave an admirable reading of this undeservedly neglected work. There were so many memorable moments that I'll only mention a few. In addition to "Per il mar del pianto mio," a moving aria by Magdalena, there's "Pompe inutili," reminiscent of Bach's great cello obbligato arias from his cantatas; and "La mia virtude," the concluding aria of Part I, a complex duo which is comparable to those written by any better-known composers of the time.

Although it is often stated in playbills that a given vocalist will be singing or has sung in a Baroque style, more often than not this is ersatz. Vibrato may be second nature to most singers, but few really reach a level in which "whiteness" and warmth coexist. This was not the case here: all were well-versed in baroque singing style. Guest soloist Hana Blažíková had a remarkably pure voice, but so did Solange Merdinian and, even if less potent, Marcy Richardson did too. Abigail Fischer's rich mezzo only lacked the heft needed to carry through to the back of the Church. The men's roles were slighter, but Martin Coyle as Jesus had a strong presence.

The only misjudgment—one that had little impact on the quality of the performance—was the decision to squeeze the entire opera into the second half of the concert; the Jacobs performance runs slightly over two hours. This was accomplished by ignoring the da capo marks that appear at the end of most of the arias. Even without the repeats of the "A" sections, it still ran too long to prevent numerous audience members from leaving early.

Given the performance of *Misere mei, Deus* by Allegri, whom the program note calls "a one-hit wonder," you could see why Crawford wanted to squeeze this little gem into the program. The work is scored for two choirs, but it took a bit of time to realize that the choir in the front of the church was complemented by one in the back balcony. Most striking were the piercing high Cs that came near the end of each of the back choir's refrains. This mixture of modal chant with the tonal style of the day leaves one awed and chilled by its beauty.

One of Torelli's many trumpet concerti served as a treat between pieces. John Thiessen, the excellent Baroque trumpeter, played his valveless instrument as if it were no different than today's keyed trumpets. In fact, it is an impossibly difficult instrument to master, and Thiessen deserves much praise for making it seem so easy.

In comparison with the exceptional quality of the Caldara, the opening Chandos Anthem was less interesting. These choral works were written during Handel's stay at Chandos, a large estate outside London, where for two years he was the resident composer. Unfortunately, he had limited access to both voices and instruments and, hence, in this anthem there is the strange absence of the viola. Handel borrowed many arias written for earlier works, which gives these anthems a feeling of being a pastiche. Here in the 10th Anthem, for example, he borrows the music for "They are brought down and fall'n" from the much earlier

41

aria in the Italian cantata *Lucrezia*, "Alla salma."

My thanks to all for the hard work that must have been gone into putting this exceptional program together.

♫ *Jordi Savall Plays Music of the French Baroque with Élan and Joie de Vivre*

Principal players of Le Concert des Nations: Jordi Savall (director and bass viol), Marc Hantaï (flute), Pierre Hantaï (harpsichord), Manfredo Kraemer (violin), Philippe Pierlot (bass viol), Zankel Hall, Carnegie Hall, New York, 16.4.2015

Anon.: *Concert donné à Louis XIII en 1627* (selected by André Danican Philidor)
Sainte-Colombe: Concert No. 44 à deux violes esgales, "Tombeau les Regrets"
Lully: Selections from *Le bourgeois gentilhomme*
Couperin: Prélude from *Deuxième concert royal*
Muzette from *Troisième concert royal*; Chaconne légère from *Troisième concert royal*
Marais: "Sonnerie de Ste-Geneviève du Mont-de-Paris"
Rameau: *Pièces de clavecin en concerts*, Cinquième concert
Forqueray: "La du Vaucel"
Leclair: Sonata in D major

There was a time not long ago when the only music ever heard from the French Baroque period was the opening theme for *Masterpiece Theater*. This fanfare-rondeau by Jean-Joseph Mouret epitomized what was thought to be the music of that time: pompous, stiff, overblown. Why would one waste time listening to music written by the bewigged Lully, Couperin, Marais or other effete dandies, the servants of equally decadent royalty? Like peeling an onion, at the core was nothing; or so it seemed to many.

There had always been an interest in composers such as Bach and Handel, but with the availability of recorded music, it didn't take much time for listeners to tire of the same works recorded over and over again. This was true as well for live concerts and music heard on the radio. But those who were young in the 1960s and 1970s questioned all areas of the arts, pushing the boundaries of what was acceptable music both in terms of what was chosen and of how it was played. Music of Bach's time and before was brought into focus; emphasis was given to the way music was being played so that it reflected as closely as possible the style in which the music was first performed; and iconoclastic conductors and performers appeared and were cultivated.

Before this, when works by Bach, Handel and earlier composers were performed, it was done with the assumption that the modern orchestra would "improve" this music by using instruments technically designed to hit a high note with as much ease as possible. Why would anyone in his right mind want to play a valveless trumpet with notes produced by shaping one's lips when valved trumpets are available. Poor Bach, had he only the resources that Stokowski had, he too might have transcribed his organ music for a large orchestra and pumped up the dramatic moments as Beethoven or Mahler would have done. If the

Messiah was to be made palatable, a huge chorus and orchestra were required. Most of the music before Bach was thought to be of interest only to specialists and scholars; swaths of scores were sitting in libraries gathering dust.

The music world was clearly ready for a change. Glenn Gould appeared on the scene not to dig up unknown music from the past, but to free existing scores from the confines of scholars' desks. The question then became, if Bach's music can be as exciting as Gould's performances make it, what else is out there that hasn't been heard or has been heard but in the wrong way. Nicolas Harnoncourt discovered that Bach's cantatas, played with instruments of the period and featuring the voices of young church choristers, contain some of the most glorious music ever written. Other discoveries by the iconoclasts followed: Ralph Kirkpatrick's revival of Domenico Scarlatti, William Christie's performances of Marc-Antoine Charpentier and Jean-Philippe Rameau. This brings us around to Jordi Savall and Le Concert des Nations.

Savall is one of earliest and most respected proponents of music before Bach, favoring works that make use of his preferred instrument, the bass viol. The performance here ranged from anonymous pieces for a concert given to royalty in 1627 to a sonata by Jean-Marie Leclair composed a century later. While I knew that the entire Concert des Nations couldn't fit on the stage at Zankel Hall, I was a bit surprised to see only five chairs on-stage. Given the fact that some of the music requires additional instruments, much color was lost. Both the selections from *Le bourgeois gentilhomme* and the *Concert donné à Louis XIII en 1627* require winds and percussion. In fact, the latter's complete title is *Concert donné à Louis XIII en 1627 par les 24 Violons et les 12 Grands hautbois*. It might be prohibitive to bring in that many instrumentalists for this one event, but not having even one voice per part is the opposite of what would be expected of an early music group.

It's worth noting that regardless of instruments left out, the five artists here are independent, highly regarded musicians, and each showed himself in the best light. Pierre Hantaï is considered one of Europe's top harpsichordists, with a long list of praised recordings. For most of the concert Hantaï played as a continuo member, but in Rameau's *Pièces de clavecin* he is one of the soloists, and some repositioning of the instrument should have taken place for it to be heard more clearly. Manfredo Kraemer was head of a respected, if oddly named, early music chamber group called The Rare Fruits Council. Marc Hantaï and Philippe Pierlot (not to be confused with Philippe Pierlot, son of the famous oboist Pierre Pierlot) are also well-respected soloists. Kraemer's playing stood out above the others, but he also had much more music to play.

♫ *Purcell: Accomplished Beyond His Years*
Les Violons du Roi, La Chapelle de Québec, Richard Egarr (conductor), Carnegie Hall, New York, 12.4.2015

Purcell: Excerpts from *The Fairy Queen* and *King Arthur*; *Dido and Aeneas*

This concert is part of the Before Bach series currently being presented at

Carnegie Hall. Although Henry Purcell, born in 1659, falls within the parameters that define the series, he was much ahead of his contemporaries, combining his own unique talents with a thorough understanding of music from Italy and France. He brought English music out of the age of modality and into the future, where tonality was to blossom in the music of Handel. Like Mozart and Schubert, who also died at a too-early age, Purcell was a musical genius whose compositions flowed effortlessly. Listening to his music leaves one in awe of his ability to create melody upon melody. As a previous age had its genius in the form of Shakespeare, late-17th-century England had its genius in the form of Purcell.

The first half of this program consisted of excerpts from two semi-operas, *The Fairy Queen* and *King Arthur*. I was at first somewhat taken aback with the quality of the sound that the orchestra produced. The last production of *The Fairy Queen* that I attended, in a small theater downtown, had one voice per part for the instrumental backup and a chorus that consisted solely of cast members. That orchestra produced a perfect reading of the music, both rustic and intimate. The acoustics of the Stern/Perelman Hall proved bottom heavy, with the highs getting lost somewhere above the 2000 seats. Even with moderation in the use of vibrato, at times I couldn't help but think of Mantovani, so lush were the strings.

The vocalists were on the mark, highlighted by the brief appearances of Stefanie True as the First Nymph in the aria "How happy the lovers" from *King Arthur* and the Second Woman in *Dido and Aeneas*. She has the wherewithal to project her voice in a way that overcame the tricky acoustics of the hall. To my ears, she was the only soloist whose voice had the right color: the color we have come to expect from vocalists singing music of the Baroque period.

Richard Egarr has been an all-around musician this season, as soloist and director/conductor of the Academy of Ancient Music and now as guest conductor of the Canadian Les Violons du Roi. And that just accounts for his musical presence in NYC. In this concert he conducted from a harpsichord, providing the sole keyboard support for the basso continuo (although there were also the standard archlute, bass and Baroque guitar). It's not unusual in a concert of this sort for the conductor to be part of the continuo, and it is done by many keyboardists turned conductors such as William Christie, Christophe Rousset and Trevor Pinnock. The logistics of leading the group while playing an instrument required Egarr to jump up and down, which was particularly detrimental to several initial upbeats. After a few notes, the group pulled together, but there was some confusion for a few of the members of the orchestra who were not quite ready to begin.

Dorothea Röschmann has long been an advocate of early music, her rich voice a staple in revivals of Baroque operas by Telemann, Keiser and Alessandro Scarlatti. She had no difficulty internalizing the emotions expressed in the heartfelt texts and melodies, particularly in the two dirge-like arias, "O let me weep" from the *Fairy Queen* and, of course, "When I am laid to rest" from *Dido and Aeneas*. It is hard for me to say this without sounding churlish, but the great performances of "Dido's Lament" have been by soloists with less "operatic" voices. Topping my list would be Lorraine Hunt Lieberman's account with Nicholas McGegan and the Philharmonia Baroque Orchestra.

♫ *Pavel Kolesnikov: Technically Adept, But Lacking Heft*
Pavel Kolesnikov (piano), Zankel Hall, Carnegie Hall, New York, 24.3.2015

Mozart: *Fantasy* in C minor
Schumann: *Fantasie* in C major
Scriabin: *Vers la flamme*; Piano Sonata No 4 in F-sharp major
Beethoven: Piano Sonata No. 32 in C minor

There is a little-known 1961 documentary entitled *Susan Starr: Portrait of a Pianist* which follows the travails of Ms. Starr in the days leading up to and including her performance as a finalist in the Dimitri Mitropoulos Competition. Three young soloists perform their set pieces, and it doesn't take long to tell who will be the gold, silver and bronze medalists. All three were pretty much on the same level technically, but charisma and charm tipped the judges in favor of one of the competitors, the soon-to-be-famous Agustín Anievas; a muscular presentation by Marta Pariente landed the silver. Ms. Starr (suffering as well with a bad cold) just didn't have it that night, but she did go on to win the silver prize in the more prestigious Tchaikovsky Competition in 1962. Both Starr and Pavel Kolesnikov, who competed in the 2012 Tchaikovsky, had the misfortune of going up against known talents: Starr against Ashkenazy and Ogden, and Kolesnikov against Daniil Trifanov.

There is no doubt that Kolesnikov has mastered the piano beyond what one might expect any protégé to achieve. His fingers negotiate the keyboard as if it were the easiest and most natural thing to do, and he manages tricky cross-hand and hand-over-hand playing without any sign of strain. He showed no fear in the difficult sections of the Schumann *Fantasie*. In Scriabin's *Vers la flame*, dynamic markings were followed as written, and the Sonata No. 4 was played flawlessly. Both pieces, though, lacked the intensity and spirituality that are inherent in every work by this eccentric composer.

It has been said over and over how Mozart piano sonatas are rarely played by an accomplished pianist who can do justice to his genius. Andras Schiff recently showed himself to be a rare decoder of Mozart's music. Playing the "Beginner's" sonata, K. 545, Schiff drew out hidden voices, managed to find its inner seriousness and came close to convincing me that, simple as it sounds, it really is a "late" work sharing the maturity of the other late works on that program. Kolesnikov found nothing personal in Mozart's very personal music. Every note was played exactly as written, four-square. With so many opportunities to make the music his own and with so much room to do this, Kolesnikov followed the straight and narrow. The many sudden shifts in dynamics yielded no surprises; segues between parts were simply rests rather than dramatic suspensions. To (mis)quote a song from the 1960s, "He played all the notes and sang all the words but never quite learned the song."

Schumann's *Fantasie* in C major is one of the great works of the Romantic era. It is to Schumann what the Sonata in B minor is to Liszt. The *Fantasie* is filled with raw emotion and almost asks to be played wildly, but Kolesnikov failed to communicate the work's tragic nature.

Most artists realize that certain works in the repertory should not be taken casually, that they reveal themselves only after years of exposure. Casals waited ten years before he felt he could do justice to the Bach Suites for Cello. Beethoven's final piano sonata might not have been the right one to choose, but I will say that Kolesnikov almost pulled it off. The late sonatas are experimental works that have no precedents and, as a result, they allow a wider range of discretion. Technical prowess can go a longer way than in most of the other Beethoven sonatas, and that was the case here. Perhaps it was because this was the last piece on the program, but Kolesnikov loosened up a bit. It wasn't the deepest interpretation, but it did cast a brighter light than the previous pieces had.

Not every talented musician has to emulate a Trifanov, who may be too revealing of his emotional state, but now that Kolesnikov has the skills required to play anything he chooses, his choices should be more deeply thought out.

♪ *Variations Galore! Bradley Brookshire Plays Buxtehude and Bach*
Bradley Brookshire (harpsichord), The Church of the Epiphany, New York, 25.3.2015

Buxtehude: *Partite diverse sopra l'aria "La Capricciosa"*
Bach: *Goldberg Variations*

Bradley Brookshire was the replacement for the originally scheduled harpsichordist, Giuseppe Schinaia, whose tour was cancelled due to a hand injury. Announcing that he might not have made the right decision in choosing the *Goldberg Variations*, Mr. Brookshire said, almost under his breath, that he was playing them because he loved them.

A telling number is the one that appears on amazon when you look up recordings of "Bach Goldberg Variations": 870 results. This is a far-out total because reprints, special editions and MP3 versions make up a large part of it. Nonetheless, it's indicative of the work's ubiquity. How strange to think that it was mostly neglected until the 1955 recording by Glenn Gould became a best-selling album.

Given the *GV*'s popularity, it shouldn't be surprising that some interpretations are more "creative" than performances of other works. The *GV* has been transcribed for string trio, harmonica, Moog synthesizer and harp. It has been turned into a loving parody in performances by Uri Caine. And liberties abound. Glenn Gould's chosen tempi in his first recording were considered either too fast or too slow. He takes no repeats and finishes in 55 minutes. How slow does he go? The infamous Variation No. 25 is so slow that it takes up almost a quarter of the entire performance.

Brookshire began the *GV* in the very common early Baroque keyboard practice of opening a suite with an improvised, loose and frilly prelude. It could be entitled toccata, fantasie or capriccio as well since they are all basically the same: an invitation to the performer to feel free to do what he wants. Bach did not use these terms or, for that matter, tempo markings except for a few in the final variations. Not that Brookshire needed permission, but he did posit the idea that the slow tempo of a sarabande allowed for improvisation, and that the aria was in fact a sarabande. He did this before each binary segment. As he went along, he imaginatively ornamented the repeats but never improvised, as he did in the opening statement.

There was a freeness to the performance that was quite winning. This was a reading that was the complete opposite of the rigid, mechanical playing of Wanda Landowska on her heavy-handed Pleyel. It also was far from the overdrive tempi of Gould. Variety abounded with frequent use of the stops and the couplers to the second manual to give some of the variations special coloring.

An intermission split the *GV* into two sections, but the second part had to be cut short because of time restraints. Brookshire would be able to complete the variations if he dropped the repeats and, sadly, he had to ignore the da capos in the score (although he did do some). It was clear that his enthusiasm as well as the enthusiasm of the audience, particularly those who shouted "Do the repeats," was dampened. Many have played the *GV* with or without repeats but few with Brookshire's imagination and brilliance. I must have 25 versions of the *GV*, but if Brookshire recorded his performance I would happily place it near the top of the pile.

Buxtehude, whose small but sparkling keyboard works fit on three CDs, is a composer who is, unfortunately, overlooked. The delightful variations on the aria "la Capricciosa" give a strong impression of being the source of Bach's *GV*. Brookshire's free style of playing was well-suited to the music of the man Bach admired, and who is to be thanked for providing Bach with the groundwork to write his own monumental set of variations.

♫ *Vivaldi, Vivaldi, Vivaldi, Not Vivaldi, Vivaldi…*
Avi Avital (mandolin), Anna Fusek (Recorder), Venice Baroque Orchestra, Zankel Hall, Carnegie Hall, New York, 11.3.2015

Vivaldi: Concerto in C major; Concerto in D minor; Concerto in D major for Lute
Marcello: Concerto in G major
Vivaldi: Concerto in G major for Two Mandolins (arr. for mandolin and recorder by Avi Avital)
Geminiani: Concerto Grosso in D minor (after Corelli's Violin Sonata, "Folia")
Vivaldi: Concerto in C major for Mandolin
Paisiello: Concerto in E-flat major for Mandolin
Vivaldi: Concerto in G minor, "L'estate"

Encores:
Trad. (Bulgarian): "Bucimis"

In a review of the Venice Baroque Orchestra's concert two years ago, I commented positively on their "wildness": in spite of the liberties they took with the scores, the performance was redeemed by a "sparkling freshness" and "the enthusiasm of all of its members." Nothing played at this concert could be described any differently. But this was not a simple repeat of the previous one. Aside from the Geminiani concerto, there was no duplication, but there was a game-changing loss and addition. The loss was the founding director, Andreas Marcon, and the gain was mandolin player Avi Avital.

Even though Marcon as director did not strictly conduct—he played the harpsichord standing up, quickly giving signals when he could—he restrained the group's tendency to overplay. I thought that as the performance here progressed, their playing got looser. This was less of a problem when Avital joined them; the ensemble receded into the background as Avital became the center of attention. One might have expected Avital to show off, as many young super-stars do, and perhaps he did in the past, but this instrumentalist is 37 and not the 25 or so that he appears. His technique is impeccable, and he refrains from overly dramatic gestures. His transcriptions from lute and violin avoid the temptation to produce anything other than an accurate reproduction of the solo instrument. At its best, I felt that I was listening to the original, unadulterated score, the only difference being the work's instrumentation.

The music chosen for the program was a mix of the familiar and the little known. The Geminiani sonata did not stand up as well here as at other performances I've heard. The important basso continuo line was drowned out by the strings, which resulted in a set of variations that sounded somewhat unfocussed.

Benedetto Marcello's Concerto would likely still be covered in dust if Bach hadn't taken his Oboe Concerto in D minor and transcribed it for solo keyboard. (Bach did the same with several Vivaldi concerti.)

First violin Gianpiero Zanocco was in a difficult chair, replacing the virtuoso Giuliano Carmignola as well as substituting for Marcon, and he should be congratulated for his stamina. Cellist Daniele Bovo kept up with Zanocco in the give-and-take segments, and he too should be commended. Anna Fusek gets two rounds of applause, both for her violin playing and for her command of the sopranino recorder and flautino.

♫ Sir András Schiff: Late Works by Masters of the Classical Period
Sir András Schiff (piano), Carnegie Hall, New York

10.2.2015
Haydn: Piano Sonata in C major
Beethoven: Piano Sonata No. 30 in E major
Mozart: Piano Sonata in C major
Schubert: Piano Sonata in C minor

12.3.2015
Mozart: Piano Sonata in B-flat major
Beethoven: Piano Sonata No. 31 in A-flat major
Haydn: Piano Sonata in D major
Schubert: Piano Sonata in A major

Is it necessary to give a concert or a series of concerts a name to explain or summarize the reasons why a given work was chosen? Often there's no reason at all. At other times, titles may just state a fact, such as "20th-Century Music from Darmstadt" or "Bach and Sons." There might be links that are discovered after a program has been created—sometimes believable, sometimes less so. In an interview with Alan Gilbert about the connection between disparate pieces already chosen for a program, Gilbert dug deep and came up with the comment that they are all dark.

The project that Sir András Schiff is currently touring is called "The Last Sonatas." This heading might have heft if he chose to play a single composer's final compositions. Performances of the last three Beethoven sonatas, for example, are commonplace, and the same holds true for Mozart's last three symphonies. But Schiff has not programmed these works as individual concerts, one for each composer; rather, he is performing the four composers' antepenultimate, penultimate and final sonatas in three recitals.

Setting them together implies that there is something special about these works, that they present something final. Are they unusual in and of themselves? Are there any connections between them stylistically or otherwise? Do they sound like last works? The final three Schubert sonatas were written the year he died and do have a sense of finality about them, but Beethoven's last three were composed seven years before his death, before his *Missa Solemnis*, Ninth Symphony and final quartets. Haydn wrote Masses, major string quartets and *The Creation* after his final sonatas. There is nothing in Mozart's last sonatas, written two years before his death, that betrays the melancholic undertows of his last piano concerto, the otherworldliness of his clarinet concerto or the doom of the *Requiem*.

Schiff may not have been successful in making connections between these composers' late works, but it mattered little given the remarkable attention to detail he afforded each work on the two-night program. The opening Haydn sonata created the ambience for the rest of the concert, one of geniality, calmness and reserve. Even Schiff's most sensitive probing of the Beethoven and Schubert sonatas never sounded overwrought. His technique didn't press too hard; he kept his cool and took his time. This particular sonata received a similar reading, bouncing hands and all, from Jeremy Denk, but Schiff had the edge with a better piano and acoustics.

The least "final-sounding" piece, Mozart's so-called "Beginners' Sonata," was imaginatively performed. Normally it's played straight on with little rubato or rhythmic flexibility, but Schiff approached the work not simply but subtly, slightly adjusting the tempo, bringing out the melodic lines in the left hand or increasing and decreasing volume in the repeats. There was even a Baroque-like cadenza added to the final Rondo.

Schiff's performance of Beethoven's Sonata No. 30 was tightly controlled, not a bad approach to a work of such wildness. This may not have been the most *innigster* performance, but it was in character with the rest of the concert and totally convincing.

His Schubert was something else. Having recorded all of the sonatas for Decca in the mid-1990s, Schiff has lived with the music long enough to have them all under his fingers, and he knows how to exert the exact pressure to achieve the sound he wants from each note. The Sonata in C minor of the first concert was filled with subtle nuances like stretched-out fermatas, and big and sudden volume changes that come as surprises even when one knows they are about to occur.

The second recital followed consistently upon the first. The Mozart here, considerably more complex than the piece from the previous night, was played in a way that revealed among other things its hidden counterpoint. The Haydn was another far-from-final-sounding sonata, not much more than a trifle of two brief movements, perhaps never completed because it wasn't up to Haydn's high standard: his abbreviated version of an unfinished sonata.

The Beethoven Sonata No. 31, although more challenging than the 30th, gave Schiff no great difficulties. The dense, multi-voiced final fugue, sounding at times like a piano transcription of the *Grosse Fuge,* was dispatched with alacrity and aplomb.

I leave the best for last. Schubert's Sonata in A major, a great piece of music yet hampered, I've always thought, by repetitive iterations and Schubert's inherent weakness in composing satisfying development sections in classical sonata form. Granted, Schiff took liberties in following Schubert's markings, but the result was one of those too-rare epiphanies that had me saying, "Now I know why I have devoted so much of my life to music." The Andantino, always moving but seemingly weak structurally, came through as some of the saddest and most heart-breaking music ever written. The closing Rondo was a study in contrasts, spanning the musical and emotional spectrums from despair to ecstasy.

Each concert ended with three encores: some familiar impromptu and impromptu-like works of Schubert and two Bagatelles from Beethoven's Opus 126. Schiff played the No. 4 with its jazzy syncopations and the No. 6 which begins with a coda and ends with the same chords. Both were packed with such energy that he seemed refueled to easily replay the entire concert.

♫ *Handel's Semele in Chinese Temple Built 450 Years Ago: Watch Out for Donkeys and Dragons*

Canadian Opera Company, Christopher Moulds (conductor), Brooklyn Academy of Music, Brooklyn, New York, 4.3.2015

Handel: *Semele*

What do a 17-ton, 450-year-old Chinese temple; a film about its history and deconstruction; a donkey with a very strong libido and an instrument that proves it; Buddhist monks with a penchant for what Norman O. Brown called "polymorphous perversity"; a Tibetan throat singer; two 350-pound sumo wrestlers who engage in a real fight; a huge bed atop a corner of the temple roof upon which a mammoth blow-up doll droops; a sinuous Chinese dragon puppet; and, yes, a funeral procession in which mourners hum "The Internationale" have in common?

They are all part of the production of Handel's oratorio/opera *Semele* taking place at the Brooklyn Academy of Music. BAM has never been the Metropolitan Opera, and happily it continues the high standard of presenting new and controversial events. (Just look at the Met season for 2015-2016: two 20th-century "modern" operas—*Lulu* and *Elektra*—and none, not one, that predates Mozart.) Stagings of Baroque opera and dance over the years have always been imaginative and often provocative re-creations, so I doubt there was much shocking of the bourgeoisie here. The copulating rabbits in Purcell's *The Fairy Queen* took the edge off any orgies emulated in *Semele*.

This mixed media production is directed by Zhang Huan, a controversial performance artist in his first foray into opera. He recently commented about how he felt a strong connection with *Semele* and its dramatic (operatic) possibilities, and as odd and off-beat as the staging was, it worked. Why? For one thing, there are no directions given in the libretto as to how it should be staged. According to Christopher Hogwood, Handel stated that *Semele* was "written after the manner of an oratorio," and it was originally performed in concert style with the chorus on stage and no acting. However, William Congreve, the librettist, thought he was writing for an opera, and the storyline is better suited for a dramatic presentation. No one can say that one staging has more authority than another since there is no standard against which to judge. This and other Baroque operas often have a feeling of being arbitrary: scenes appear that have little connection to the ongoing story. The scene here with Somnus, for example, may have been meant to serve as a comic interlude; but in Baroque opera, often anything goes.

Yet the performance, despite brilliant costumes and a striking set, was curiously lackluster. The quality of the music itself comes nowhere near Handel's later oratorio, *Theodora*, which he considered his greatest work. It is possible that Handel shortchanged *Semele* by rushing it, completing the entire piece in about a month. It was the first work he was able to produce after recovering from a "palsy" that had prevented him from writing for several weeks; by comparison, *Theodora* took twice as long to complete.

Much of the humor was sophomoric or built on sexual activity, and the cast played up these actions. In most cases it was fine, but one of Handel's greatest arias, "Where'er You Walk," suffered from the distraction of pairs of chorus members faux-fornicating in the background. It's hard to focus on the vocalist when soft-porn is going on.

The soloists were all good, with no real star outshining the others. The great countertenor Lawrence Zazzo had only a small number of arias to sing as

Athamas, and he handled believably the requisite touching and groping that persisted throughout most of the opera. Although everyone sang well, particularly Jane Archibald as Semele and Hilary Summers as Ino, Semele's sister, and Juno, I found Colin Ainsworth's voice exceptionally warm and sweet, giving a positive spin to the role of Jupiter. This was a Jupiter made human, a believable person as opposed to the threatening, all-powerful Thunder-Thrower. The orchestra and conductor were adequate, but it would have added more color to the music and reduced some of the dullness of the many da capo arias if this had been a Baroque music band instead.

There was one major decision, mentioned in the playbill, that colored or rather darkened the whole performance. Zhang Huan has stated that he intentionally ends the play unhappily. I've complained elsewhere that the happy endings of many serious or tragic operas contradict the whole direction of where the piece was going. Zhang stops, logically, where he should: after the singers finish their lament for the dead Semele and hum "The Internationale." Handel, on the other hand, closes with the chorus singing:

Happy, happy shall we be,
Free from care, from sorrow free.
Guiltless pleasures we'll enjoy,
Virtuous love will never cloy;
All that's good and just we'll prove,
And Bacchus crown the joys of love.

Not a very appropriate ending for a play whose heroine who has just been burned to death.

♫ Gluck's Iphigénie en Aulide: Professional Performance in Student Production
Soloists and Singers from The Metropolitan Opera's Lindemann Young Artist Development Program and Juilliard Opera, Juilliard415, Janet Glover (conductor), Peter Jay Sharp Theater, Juilliard School of Music, Lincoln Center, New York, 10.2.2015

Gluck: *Iphigénie en Aulide*
Concert Version

It's interesting that C. W. Gluck, known mostly as the composer of *Orphée et Euridice* and a handful of other operas, actually wrote almost 40 of them. Over the last five years, the Metropolitan Opera has performed only two of his works, *Orphée et Euridice* and *Iphigénie en Tauride*, both in 2011. Known as a reformist, Gluck followed his own rules in the operas he wrote, and today it seems like the rules were more influential than the music itself. His reaction was a natural one in a transition period that was turning away from the elaborate excesses of the Baroque era towards a simplified "classic" style. Both Mozart and Haydn learned much from Gluck, but they went well beyond it in a short time. You can see Gluck's influence on Mozart's early operas such as *Mitradate, re di Ponto* and *Il sogno di Scipione.*

Iphigénie en Aulide both exemplifies and negates the reforms urged by Gluck. The old Handel da capo arias were replaced with arias that flowed from one to another, melissmas were left to a minimum, and the recitativo secco was replaced by ariosos backed by an orchestra and not a basso continuo. Embellishments and improvisatory ornamentation were forbidden.

A Gluck opera may not have recitativo secco, but that doesn't prevent the work from ending up as an "opera secco." Although *Iphigénie en Aulide* doesn't use da capos to merely repeat the first sections, the singer often repeats words that would have been used in da capo sections. Gluck touted seriousness of purpose, realism and truth, rather than the unbelievable reversals of Baroque opera. Yet what could be more artificial, unrealistic or just plain unbelievable than the goddess Diane coming down to earth to tell the suffering protagonists that she was just kidding, and they can now get married and live happily ever after.

The vocalists in this production were so good that the lines blurred between professional and student, between those who were from the Met program and those who are at Juilliard. As far as I could tell, they all performed captivatingly at or near the top of the spectrum. A key to the success of this production for me, aside from the glorious voices, was that from my seat it was possible to see and be affected by the artists' excellent acting skills and their ability to reflect convincingly every emotional color. During the few moments when the plot and action bordered on the bathetic, the performers were able to pull it off. If there was anyone who excelled, if even slightly, in performance and vocal skills, it would be Ying Fang as Iphigénie. There were moments when I thought I was listening to the young Magdalena Kocena: few compliments could be better than that. It is a shame that Liz Redpath, who sang so beautifully last year in Handel's *La resurrezione* had only one aria at the end of the final act.

Jane Glover has had a long history with Gluck; she has conducted at least five different operas and here she was impeccable. Juilliard415 stayed right with Glover and were well-synced throughout this superb performance.

♪ *Well-Tempered, Yes. Well Played, Well…*
Richard Egarr, Weill Recital Hall, Carnegie Hall, New York, 9.2.2015

Bach: French Suite No. 5 in G major; Partita No. 6 in E minor; Partita No. 1 in B-flat major
Handel: Suite No. 3 in D minor

The radical assumptions of the Historically Informed Performance (HIP) movement have long been absorbed by the traditional musicians and organizations who were initially the most opposed to anything deemed "authentic." There are fewer zealous proponents of this approach to early music, and fewer negative reactions from the generally conservative public. Established orchestras and conductors no longer feel threatened by these "new" rules.

Neither group can claim victory. Those who thought that they could discover, through careful readings of early scores, how Bach's music was played and how it sounded, now realize there are no definitive answers. Musicians and conductors alike accept the fact they cannot play Vivaldi with the same size orchestra that would play a Mahler symphony. The Metropolitan Opera picked up on City Opera's successful productions of Handel and Rameau operas and even commissioned a pastiche of a Baroque opera. The audience no longer giggles when a woman plays the role of Julius Caesar, or a man dressed in military garb opens his mouth and notes come out in the tessitura of a contralto.

The performance by Richard Egarr of keyboard works by Bach and Handel and his commentaries before playing them brought these and other issues to mind. Egarr spoke about numerology and cryptography in Bach's scores. These topics, although around for centuries, became grist for the early music mill. In his inexhaustible *Bach in the Castle of Heaven*, John Gardner mentions that Bach's own cousin was aware of the use of the Bach name as either musical notes or as numbers. Egarr also brought up the cryptography on the title page of *The Well-Tempered Clavier*. Bradley Lehman decodes the decorations at the top of the page as a secret message meant to define the solution to both temperament and correct tuning pitch. Before the Web but during the Internet's incipiency, BBSs (bulletin boards) were the way to communicate in chat rooms. One of them, The Bach Forum, was a podium for Lehman and others, and many issues that needed to be addressed were done so there.

In his 2007 recording of *The Well-Tempered Clavier*, Egarr took Lehman's theories to heart and tuned his harpsichord accordingly. The results were impressive. Key signatures that pretty much sounded the same due to modern-day equal and even tuning took on individual colors. So much so that, with enough practice, even those not gifted with perfect pitch could hear the difference between B-flat major and G major as easily as most people hear the difference between major and minor keys.

The ambience and acoustics of the Weill Recital Hall were nearly ideal for the instrument played, and it was a pleasant recital. Egarr's enthusiasm carried over to the audience; oddly though, the performance felt rushed and unpracticed. Egarr has recorded all the works on the program, so one is able to compare the studio performance to this live one. There were a considerable number of mistakes and occasional struggles with maneuvering cross-handed measures. The most noticeable was in the Gigue of Bach's first Partita, where Egarr's hands both floundered. In addition, his decisions as to which sections of the binary movements should be repeated were arbitrary: at one point he didn't play the "b" section at all (in the same movement mentioned above). The use of the second manual and stops seemed arbitrary as well. In one movement of the French Suite, instead of the repeat of the b section, he only played its final measures.

He did provide additional ornaments as are normally applied to the second repeat of each section. Many were lovely and accomplished what they were meant to do: vary what was played rather than rigidly repeating the same notes. The question then arises as to how much or how little additional ornamentation is called for. The answer: enough to not impinge upon the structure of the work or its melodic line. Egarr was moderately discreet in most of the repeats, but the sarabandes, because their tempi are slow, suffered from an over-application of ornamentation to the detriment of the musical flow.

♪ *Muti and Chicago Symphony Orchestra Take on Two Russian Heavyweights*

Alisa Kolosova (mezzo-soprano), Sergey Skorokhodov (tenor), Chicago Symphony Orchestra and Chorus, Riccardo Muti (conductor), Duain Wolfe (chorus director), Carnegie Hall, New York, 1.2.2015

Scriabin: Symphony No. 1 in E major
Prokofiev: *Alexander Nevsky*

In 2008 *Gramophone* ranked the Chicago Symphony as the sixth greatest orchestra in the world and the best in the US. Although Muti didn't become the orchestra's leader until 2010, I doubt that their position would have dropped, to judge by the excellence of the performance here. Muti is a conductor who flourishes with music on the grand scale. He directed La Scala for almost 20 years, and he brought an opera-style conducting to this program. It was an accomplishment just to fit the orchestra and chorus on the stage of Carnegie Hall.

Both of these works fall into the category of cantata. We often think of cantatas, like most of those written by Bach, as sacred works; while there are references to the Divine in Scriabin's choral text in the last movement, the religion he praises is an aesthetic god named "Art." In the Prokofiev, Alexander Nevsky's god is his Russian homeland.

Muti has been an advocate of Scriabin since he recorded the Symphony No. 1 in 1986; his recordings of the three symphonies are considered the best available. No. 1 was not a success when it premiered in 1900, although it did have a run of performances later in Scriabin's life. The overall structure of the piece and the music itself don't quite cohere, and it makes one question why he wrote it. Perhaps it was some form of grandiosity: after all, not many composers would or could write a composition that ends like Beethoven's 9th with its famous choral movement. This attempt to imitate Beethoven is a particularly pretentious gesture considering it is Scriabin's first symphony; Brahms wouldn't write his first until he was 43, fearing he might be compared to Beethoven and found wanting. In addition, one can also hear derivations from Wagner in Scriabin's *Liebestod*-like suspensions, and from Liszt's repeating phrases in *Les Préludes*.

Muti and the orchestra were clearly committed to this work and produced a powerhouse performance as if it really were Beethoven's Ninth. The chorus came through strongly, even though much of the text (Scriabin's own) is doggerel. The brass, in particular, was bright and crisp, and it added to the orchestral coloring. The finale with its build-up to the stirring coda is hard not to like. If only the music itself were more inspired, this could have been an exceptional performance.

Prokofiev's *Alexander Nevsky* brought me to this concert, and I was not disappointed. It was written as the score to Sergei Eisenstein's classic 1938 movie, and there is little subtlety in this film which depicts Russian peasants pushing back Swedish crusaders in the 13ᵗʰ century. The movie closely reflected the contemporary political situation and was meant to inspire its audience to prepare themselves for an onslaught by the Germans. Prokofiev's music reinforces this propaganda, but it's too good to just be background to a film. He ensured that his score would be remembered by creating a separate suite and publishing it as Op. 78.

I was also attracted to this performance by the fact that I grew up on the great recording of *Alexander Nevsky* made in 1959 by the Chicago Symphony under Fritz Reiner with mezzo Rosalind Elias. Muti too gave a ravishing performance, from the opening massive rumblings through its potent choruses and joyous songs of victory. While Alisa Kolosova cannot match Elias in the ethereal aria "The field of the dead," she was able to convey mournful feelings as a Russian woman who nurses the wounded after the battle.

♫ *Savall, Juilliard415 and the Charms of Nature*
Amid the Charms of Nature: Juilliard415, Elizabeth Blumenstock (concertmaster), Jordi Savall (director), Alice Tully Hall, Lincoln Center, New York, 31.1.2015

Leclair: Overture to *Scylla and Glaucus*
Marais: From *Alcyone*: March pour les Matelots, Tempeste
Telemann: "Hamburger Ebb und Fluth"
Rameau: Orages, tonnerres et tremblementes de terre
Handel: Suite from *Water Music*

Encore:
Rameau: Final Contredanse from *Les Boréades*

Jordi Savall's visits to Juilliard are eagerly awaited annual events that have been enhanced by his imaginative program choices. Last year he covered music of Shakespeare's time. This year, appropriately enough in a city digging out from under a few inches of snow that caused street and public transportation closures, Savall chose "program" music: music depicting storms, thunder and earthquakes. Music appreciation classes introduce children to classical music by asking them to listen and then describe what they hear. But as we refine our musical tastes, we learn that music itself cannot tell a story. Where is the sound of water in Handel's *Water Music*? Who could distinguish between Telemann's "Ebb" and his "Fluth" without a program telling us this is what we are meant to hear. Similarly, the flute or piccolo can imitate the song of a bird; but if there's no melody, all one hears are notes from a high-pitched instrument.

There is nothing connected to inclement weather in the overture to Leclair's sole opera, *Scylla and Glaucus*, although there is later in the work. This grossly under-appreciated opera is filled with magical music. Written in 1746, it falls just short of the classical era and blends inherited Baroque opera with the developing "reform" operas of Gluck. The arias are filled with catchy tunes, charming interludes, dances and choral accompaniment. Leclair knew he had a hit with this overture. Not only does he repeat it two more times in the opera, he later transcribed it as the opening work in his Opus 13 set of *Ouvertures et Sonates en Trio*. It is a classic model of the French *ouverture* with its broad, stately pace and the use of dotted and double-dotted notes. The middle section is a short fugue leading to a recapitulation of the opening section. Savall took the first part of the overture a little slowly, and although it coalesced, it verged on the edge of losing its structure.

Marin Marais, for those whose memories are short, was the young man in the film *Tous les matins du monde* who comes to learn at the feet of the great viola da gambist, Sainte Colombe. Marais' opera *Alcyone* is another water-related work. The "March pour les Matelots" played here is an abbreviated version of the march in the opera which has alternating repetitions of the theme by soloists and chorus. The piece entitled "Tempeste" incorporates some of the stock instruments used for sound effects, including the wind machine. Whether it's a tempest or a thunderstorm or just heat lightening really doesn't matter: this is exciting music, played here with much enthusiasm. There was demanding instrumental material, and the student orchestra played as well as one would expect from any professional group.

The Overture-Suite "Hamburger Ebb und Fluth" is really no different in content and style from dozens of other pieces that Telemann wrote during his long life. Standard dance names like "gavotte" are given to the individual movements, but so too are programmatic titles such as "Naiads at play." There was much variety, and Savall was able by subtle gestures to bring out the contrasts and create the particular spirit of each movement.

Rameau was a great colorist with the ability to create small and unique musical sound worlds. Others had composed tempests, winds and storms, but none were as powerful as Rameau's. He knew what to do with woodwinds and brass to let them rage beyond the more traditional imitations. Since each Rameau movement is strongly defined, it is possible to set up a suite of movements from different compositions and make them work as an entity. Marc Minkowski created a CD playlist and sampler of Rameau's interludes entitled "Une symphonie imaginaire," and Savall did something similar here: he chose one to three movements from four different operas.

In the final piece, a Suite from Handel's *Water Music*, the addition to the orchestra of brass added a brilliance to a program that up to this point had felt dark. From the opening salvos of the near-perfect brass, it was clear we were hearing music substantially more interesting than the previous works. The orchestra performed this piece, which for many in the audience has become hackneyed through overplaying, with a vigor and a physicality not seen in the evening's earlier works.

This was a well-played concert which is to be praised even more highly for having been rehearsed in a shorter time than usual due to the weather.

♪ *Alexandre Tharaud: Better with Baroque*
Alexandre Tharaud (piano), Zankel Hall, Carnegie Hall, New York, 26.01.2015

Mozart: Piano Sonata in A major
Couperin: Selections from *Pièces de clavecin*
Schubert: 16 German Dances
Beethoven: Piano Sonata No. 31 in A-flat major

Encores:
Bach: Prelude in B minor (arr. Siloti)
Scarlatti: Sonata in D minor

I owe an apology to a colleague for questioning his description of Alexandre Tharaud as "the astonishing Baroque pianist." It seemed to me that one might call Glenn Gould or Rosalyn Tureck "Baroque pianists," but Tharaud? His latest disk consists of music by Haydn and Mozart and, before that, there was a CD of short pieces that might be presented as encores. Bach is there, but so are Chopin, Grieg, Fauré and Scriabin. Going back one more is a CD that includes "The man I love."

But despite this repertory, far from anything that can be called Baroque, I've changed my mind about the appellation "Baroque pianist." I did so because I think that this is the style of music he plays best. He seemed more comfortable and more assured in the Couperin, and in the obsessively eccentric encore by Scarlatti. His Mozart on the whole was very broadly played, with more rubato than needed and a very un-classical looseness. At times he followed Gould in some of his quirkiness, such as bringing out melodic lines in the left hand covering the real melody in the right; or changing legatos not quite to staccato but certainly *détaché*. Granted, he comes nowhere near the comical hurdy-gurdy playing of Mozart by Gould, who admitted that he hated Mozart's music.

Most Baroque composers could not easily protect their works from hacks and plagiarists, and they themselves hacked and plagiarized others. Bach borrowed music from Vivaldi and Marcello, Vivaldi from Broschi and Hasse, Handel from Scarlatti and Telemann. But Couperin was different. Working within and protected by the court of Louis XIV, he had little fear of his music being published without his authorization. As he wrote in the preface of Book 3 of his *Pièces de Clavecin*: "I am always surprised to hear of people who have learned them without heeding my instructions…. My pieces must be executed as I have marked them, and they will never make an impression on persons of real taste unless one observes to the letter all that I have marked without any additions or deletions." Few pianists can take the music of Couperin and successfully replicate his idiosyncratic style. What might he have thought of the Steinways of Tharaud and the Faziolis of Angela Hewitt?

Tharaud has the sensitivity to—and ability to recreate—a sound world that neither demeans the sometimes overwrought ornamentation, nor enlarges music that is soft-spoken and fragile. While there are debates as to what the titles of these pieces mean, many are inside jokes, *pièces de caractères,* including one entitled "*Le Couperin,*" clearly the first auditory "selfie" to be created. Some pieces were more successful here than others. The often-played "*Les barricades mistérieuses*" and "*Les ombres errantes*" generally worked well, given the ability of the piano to dampen and sustain the notes, thus coming closer than a harpsichord can to create a feeling of mystery or visions of roving shadows. Tharaud did the best he could on a piano with "Le triomphante" which, with the right stops on a multi-manual harpsichord, can approximate trumpet fanfares.

No piano except, perhaps, a toy one can replicate the ethereal sounds of *Le Carillon de Cithère,* whose chiming silvery notes can be best approximated by the harpsichord.

Schubert's 16 German dances are slight throwaways that, given Tharaud's proclivity towards short pieces, were well characterized and charmingly played. Tharaud's cameo in the French film "*Amour*" had him playing Beethoven's self-described *Bagatelles.* But there is a big leap between bagatelles and Beethoven's penultimate sonata, and it was less than successful. The fast movements have little softness in them, and strong-armed chords alone cannot support the music around them. Only in the Adagio did Tharaud capture some of the poignancy and heartache of this transcendent music.

Was it a second wind that had Tharaud give his some of best playing of the evening in Bach's Prelude in B minor (a slightly different arrangement of the 10th prelude from the *WTC* Book 1). Even better was Scarlatti's sonata, with its runs and repetitions of 16th notes played six to a measure at an allegro pace for most of the work, turning into increasingly more dissonant clusters as the binary iterations progressed. Unfortunately, the audience applause could not coax Tharaud out for a third (perhaps another Scarlatti?) encore.

♪ *Beethoven Down-Dated for the 19th Century*

Chloe Fedor (violin), Juilliard415, Monica Huggett (director and violin), Peter J Sharp Theater, Juilliard School of Music, New York, 18.1.2015

Beethoven: Overture to *Die Geshöpfe des Prometheus*; Romance in F major for Violin and Orchestra; Symphony No. 4 in B-flat major

It was wise that the Juilliard School chose the name "Historical Performance" for a department title. If they had named it the "Early Music" or "Music Before 1800" department, they may have run into some difficulty scheduling this all-Beethoven concert on period instruments. A school that offers "Historically Informed Performances" is not constrained by periods or centuries. Music that has stylistic elements not commonly applied today can be referred to as HIP; it needn't be an original instruments group if the musicians understand that they will be emulating HIP.

So when does the HIP period end? It ends when the modern orchestra comes into being. But the period can also be extended when the director of a group feels that a particular composer will benefit from the HIP approach.

Here Monica Huggett has joined a number of HIP conductors who have moved into the 19th century to apply their stylistic techniques. I can't imagine Ms. Huggett directing Juilliard415 in a Bruckner symphony; yet Bruckner symphonies have been conducted by inveterate HIPsters such as Sir John Gardiner and Sir Roger Norrington with no damage to their continued forays into earlier music. Both have done complete Beethoven symphony cycles, which puts Ms. Huggett in good company. The big conceptual issue with the Beethoven symphonies, particularly for HIP players, is the question of tempi. Beethoven had marked very clearly in his symphonies what the metronomic tempo should be. This has not been an issue for modern-day conductors because it was thought that these numbers couldn't be right. The fast movements would be unplayable at the tempo indicated, so many editors simply elided them from the scores. If they were in the score they were summarily ignored by the conductor. Norrington proved that these tempos were playable, but the end result was odd to say the least. The most current research, based on the recent discovery of the metronome that Beethoven purportedly used, indicates that the device very likely was not working properly: an off-beat (!) but convenient solution, until another surprise is discovered.

Ms. Huggett took a moderate pacing for all the works on the program, beginning with Beethoven's overture to the ballet *The Creatures of Prometheus*. The most salient feature of this program was its orchestral coloring. Every note played was so fresh and so much richer in timbre than its modern day counterparts. The opening two chords, played by the entire orchestra, produced a sound that would be hard to describe and impossible to duplicate. Each orchestral group had its chance to be highlighted. The woodwinds were particularly vibrant: the instruments' voices were clear and distinct. Every detail meant to be heard was heard. Perhaps the playing was a bit scruffy and raw, but that seemed to add to its charm and warmth.

The Romance that followed, one of two that Beethoven wrote, is usually viewed as a precursor of the Violin Concerto, and in particular its slow middle movement. Here violinist Chloe Fedor offered a different interpretation, one that was totally convincing yet bravely very un-Beethovian. In her unhurried pace it turned into a fragile and delicate song, made all the purer by being vibrato-less.

The Fourth Symphony shared some of the positive adjectives used above, but was unwieldy and shapeless at times. This symphony, as any other by Beethoven, consists of pieces that need to be picked up and put together to end in some structure. It's no easy thing to do, and here the roughness worked to the piece's disadvantage. The Fourth is by far the least frequently played Beethoven symphony, and nothing here disproved the reasons why.

♫ *William Christie and Juilliard415 Breathe Life into Handel's Resurrezione*
Soloists and Juilliard415, William Christie (conductor), Alice Tully, Hall, Lincoln Center, New York 8.12.2014

Handel's most productive stay in Rome, which he visited several times, was in 1707-1708. His oratorios *Il trionfo del Tempo e dell Disiganno* and *La resurrezione* were written in Rome at the tail end of the papal ban on staged productions, which started in 1698 and ended in 1710. Going underground has always been the way repressed groups keep the flames lit. The resistance to this papal ban came from the last group one would have expected: the Cardinals living in Rome. Several of the wealthiest Cardinals as well as the secular Marquis Rispoli avoided gaudy stage productions but had no difficulty mounting "sacred" musical events. It seemed sufficient just to call a work a cantata or oratorio to get around the ban. Handel wrote about 80 of these works, but there is nothing in them that comes even close to the word "sacred" as it is used to describe Bach's cantatas. No "Weinen, Klagen, Sorgen, Zagen" here. Instead we have "Delirio Amoroso" or "'n' alma inamorata." Handel's texts were often from Greek mythology and did not suppress any of the more earthly themes. He did write some real operas during his stay, but they were performed in other Italian cities such as Florence and Naples.

La resurrezione is the exception: it does in fact have a sacred text, one appropriate to Easter, covering as it does the period after Jesus is crucified and following Maria Maddalena and Maria Cleofe through the Resurrection. It's just as well that Handel didn't try to develop an opera out of his material; its thin plot couldn't support the weak text. We get no real differentiation or development of the characters as we do in a much later Handel oratorio, *Theodora*.

From a musical point of view, Handel's compositional skills were in full use even at the early age of 22. From the very beginning of *La Resurrezione*, we are in the hands of an accomplished composer. The early measures of the overture contain conversations that require brief but difficult solo work from the violin and cello. This was tough going for the orchestra members, but Christie wasn't going to slow down. The opening aria, "Disserratevi," sung by Liv Redpath, is filled with runs up and down the scale, and then asks the soprano to hold a high A for several measures. The passages where the oboe doubled the soprano's florid melismas demanded great technique on the part of both the soprano and oboist David Dickey. Aside from a little jitteriness, both showed they had it. Redpath's clear and smooth voice needs only a little more depth and maturity, and she should be ready for anything that is asked of her.

Reminiscent of the character of Polyphemus in Handel's *Acis and Galatea*, baritone Elliott Carlton Hines provided the proper depth for Lucifer who is dispatched to Hades but not until he has expressed his anger at heaven in a well-honed and somber "Ahi, abborito nome." Avery Amereau's distinctive mezzo in "Piangete, si Piangete" expressed her lamentation in words and song that could have come from a Bach Passion. Nathan Haller impressed with a touching "Caro figlio," a precursor to Handel's more famous "Cara," "Cara Sposa" from *Rinaldo*. Mary Feminear sang exceptionally well throughout, and especially in a heartfelt "Ferma l'ali."

William Christie still seems unable to do any wrong. The early nervousness of the musicians faded away mostly, I suspect, through the unconditional approval and acceptance of the conductor. I hope the recent financial cuts made by the French cities that have supported Christie as well as Minkowski will think twice about what they could lose. These groups should be given the same certainty and status as the French government gives to the upkeep and support of buildings that have historical importance. The musicians are a national treasure as well.

♩ *Rossini's Guglielmo Tell: Grand Opera Even in Concert Version*
Teatro Regio Torino Orchestra and Chorus, Gianandrea Noseda (director and conductor), Claudio Fenoglio (chorus master), Carnegie Hall, New York, 7.12.2014

Rossini, *Guglielmo Tell*
Concert Version, translated into Italian from French

Rossini's *Guglielmo Tell* is a bear of a work. So much has been written about and provoked by this grand opera: its importance as a precursor of Verdi's operas, its connection to Rossini's decision to end his career as a composer of operas, the political debates on its incendiary topics. Whenever it is performed, *Guglielmo Tell* is touted as a rare production, a first-time-performed-here or first-ever "Complete" version. Granted, it's not *Carmen,* but it's not *Bianca e Falliero* (a minor Rossini opera) either. In recent years there have been productions in San Francisco, Munich, Pesaro, Amsterdam, Geneva, Cardiff and Wichita.

Many reasons have been posited as to why there have been fewer performances of an opera that is generally considered Rossini's greatest work. The four-hours of *Guglielmo Tell* are often mentioned, but this has never been a real issue with Wagner's four-hour-plus *Die Meistersinger* or the even longer *Rienzi*. Detractors talk about the text's complexity. What operas plots aren't complex? Handel's *Tamerlano*? Beethoven's *Fidelio*? It might not seem an issue now but Rossini's reputation was strongly based on his comic operas: operas that were subtitled various combinations of *farcia, giocoso, melodramma, commedia* and *buffo*. Would an audience come to a serious dramatic opera written by a composer of fun operas?

The opera's performance history, its successes and failures, were also dependent upon the times. Its main topic is one that it is politically sensitive to this day: the rights of people to bear arms against a tyrannical leader or an occupying country. In this particular scenario, it is Switzerland rebelling against the Austrian occupation. In periods of political repression, *Guglielmo Tell* had few performances. It was considered inflammatory by the powers that be. When the political climate favored separatist policies, there was more freedom to stage revivals.

The score for *Guglielmo Tell*, both vocally and instrumentally, is tremendously demanding, and Noseda made no attempts to minimize the difficulties. It was clear that the orchestra had been drilled to reach such a high level of playing. Noseda's ambition has been to make the Torino Orchestra a world class ensemble and, after seven years, this is exactly what they have become.

The famous overture was driven forcefully to its conclusion with no sense of the final section having the long hackneyed history that makes it the darling of inappropriate usage. There had been much anticipation preceding the performance. Perhaps some of it was the realization that this time when the overture ended, it would have been just what it was meant to be: the opening to the performance that followed.

The singers were all solid and to say that is no light compliment. John Osborn in the role of Arnoldo sang a glorious "Corriam! Voliam!" and "Troncar suoi," both with a gaggle of high Cs. Luca Salsi sang a heartbreaking "Resta immobile." Although not appearing until the second act and having only a few arias to sing, Angela Meade as Mathilde sang on a different level: one that was more potent than any of the other vocalists.

There is little flexibility in a concert version as to where to go when not singing. In most that I've seen, soloists sit on chairs on both sides of the stage. Here they walked off the stage when not performing. It might have been less distracting had they remained.

♫ *Preposterous! An Opera Based on Charles Rosen's The Classical Style*

Jeremy Denk (piano), The Knights, Robert Spano (conductor), Zankel Hall, Carnegie Hall, New York, 4.12.2014

Mozart: Rondo in F major; Sonata in C minor
Steven Stucky/Jeremy Denk: *The Classical Style: An Opera (of Sorts)*
NY Premiere, co-commissioned by Carnegie Hall

In a musical season plagued by such issues as budget cutting, pared-down productions, bankrupt symphony orchestras and labor disputes, and marked by performances of works that were unusually dark, like *Der Winterreise, The St. Matthew Passion* and Mahler's 2nd, a good dose of clever silliness would be more than welcome. And it did arrive, in the form of an opera (of sorts) written by Steven Stucky and Jeremy Denk.

The seed of this work occurred to Denk as he recovered over a whiskey: the previous night he had dined with the esteemed musicologist and pianist Charles Rosen. Both loquacious and curmudgeonly, Rosen was known for his expansive knowledge which he used to great effect on all who dared question his facts. He was a pianist capable of dashing off Bach and Mozart or Schoenberg and Elliot Carter with equal understanding and sympathy. His major study, *The Classical Style*, is not for the musical dabbler. (Looking at it now, I'm amazed that I actually read it, but I was 15 years younger and brighter then). Filled with musical fragments, the book draws the reader's attention to the very essence of Haydn, Mozart and Beethoven. But everywhere in the book there is also a stepping back from the minutia, to broadly assess the music and its humanity as well. Here is a classic example of Rosen's style: "The pretension of Haydn's symphonies to a simplicity that appears to come from Nature itself is no mask but the true claim of a style whose command over the whole range of technique is so great that it can ingenuously afford to disdain the outward appearance of high art." It may be a long and convoluted sentence, but it concludes with a truth that would be difficult to dispute.

The first part of the concert was a finely attuned, straight-up performance by Jeremy Denk of Mozart's Rondo K. 494 and Sonata K.457. The Rondo is slightly odd in that the returning main theme is never played exactly the same way. Traditionally, the rondo form consists of an opening section that is followed by a new section that should return to an exact repeat of the opening before going on to the next new section. Marked Allegretto, the piece was taken on the slow side, darkening its overall color. Not much was needed on the part of Denk to continue this gloomy approach in K. 457. One of only two sonatas written in the minor key, this work comes about as close to what would be Beethoven's style as any written by Mozart. Denk, as with all the performances of his that I've seen, had the music in his fingers. His mastery over everything technical is so thorough that it seems his only task is to add his personal stamp to what his fingers do by themselves.

This short recital gave the audience an early intermission as the stage was set up for *The Classical Style*. After a short overture by Steven Stucky in his own musical language, the opera opens on the three composers covered in Rosen's book, Haydn, Mozart and Beethoven, who are in heaven whiling away their time. What the audience more or less "gets" from what follows is dependent on one's knowledge of music.

The opening "complaint" (in the literary sense as a protest against some misfortune) by Haydn is that although he was the mentor of Mozart and Beethoven, he has been largely and unfairly ignored over the centuries. Meanwhile, Mozart is writing to petition the producers of the movie *Amadeus* for compensation for the right to use his name; and Beethoven, sullen and depressed, sits at a table too absorbed in thought to care what is happening around him. It is with Mozart's aria that Stucky begins to integrate other music into the score. Many of the references are to *Don Giovanni*, as several of its characters make cameo appearances. Bits of *The Magic Flute, The Abduction from the Seraglio* and Beethoven's *Ninth* seamlessly waft through the score. Mozart also complains about "too many notes," repeating these words in an aria many times. This conceit works on two levels. The first is the quote itself: the story, apocryphal or not, is that Emperor Joseph II complained to Mozart at a rehearsal of *The Abduction from the Seraglio,* that there were "too many notes, my dear Mozart." On another level, Mozart is tired of hearing this cliché (and I've used it here again).

Perhaps the wittiest aria is the parody of "Madamina, il catalogo è questo" (also known as the "Catalog Aria") from *Don Giovanni*. Denk replaces Leporello's list by country of Don Giovanni's romantic conquests with facetious numbers relating to performances of Beethoven's Ninth Symphony: "In America alone, 403 performances of the Ninth Symphony and about the same number of interminable pre-concert lectures, 137 pretentious program notes . . . 1800 standing ovations, and 5,000 people who think Beethoven was a dog."

In addition to the three composers, there are three anthropomorphic concepts, Tonic, Dominant and Sub-Dominant. A basic understanding of harmony helps one understand (and laugh at) the references made to and by these characters. For example, with an oblique reference to the *Wizard of Oz,* the character Dominant sings an introductory arioso, "If Only I Could Resolve." At the Bar (ahem!), Tristan Chord walks in on them and states, using the forging metaphor from Wagner's *Das Rheingold,* that "out of the darkness I forged myself a chord . . . so ambiguous, so unresolvable." The orchestra at this point chimes in with a parody of Wagner's "Prelude and Liebestod" from *Tristan and Isolde.* There are many inside jokes here involving drifting seventh chords, tonal ambiguities and broken harmonic rules. (At a rehearsal, the conductor Robert Spano started laughing so hard while conducting this scene that the orchestra had to take a break until he recovered himself).

In the role of Tristan Chord, Kim Josephson presented himself as a slightly seedy character with an eye patch and a smoker's cough. Tristan Chord cleverly gives a frightening glimpse into the future when all rules are broken and the reign of the standard chords ends. Josephson was marvelous both in this role and as the Charles Rosen character, whom he eerily resembled.

The acting and singing were delightful. Jennifer Zelman performed the trouser role of Mozart with comic bravura, and Peabody Southwell as Subdominant was appropriately sensual. Robert Spano did a fine job with the convoluted score. The audience at sold-out Zankel Hall thoroughly enjoyed the performance, as was evident by their generous applause.

♫ *Haïm, Dessay and Dumaux in Selections from Handel's Guilio Cesare*

Le Concert d'Astrée, Emmanuelle Haïm (conductor), Alice Tully Hall, Lincoln Center, New York, 30.11.2014

Handel: Selections from *Giulio Cesare in Egitto*; Suite in G major, from *Water Music*

Encore:
"Kind Health Descends on Downy Wings"

Natalie Dessay has not had it easy. A series of operations on her vocal chords caused her to drop out of a number of performances. Several years ago, she fell on stage during opening night at the Met while singing the title role in *Lucia di Lammermoor* (to generally mixed reviews). On another opening night at the Met, she was indisposed, and she was not able to sing the role of Cleopatra in *Giulio Cesare in Egitto* on the night that I reviewed it. She recently announced that she will no longer do staged operas but will continue to perform recitals such as the one reviewed here.

It is tricky to assume that an actor or actress is over- or underplaying a part due to personal reasons. Coming on stage at one point, funereally, with her head down, Ms. Dessay gave the impression that she wanted to be anywhere else except where she was now. There was a listlessness about both her singing and acting. At one point during an aria, she took the conductor's hand, as if she needed encouragement. Her singing was accurate enough, but lacked depth. In the high range, she bordered on being shrill. It also struck me as a bit odd that she needed a score for a role she has done on stage many times before in full productions.

Christophe Dumaux, who has played the role of Tolomeo in the David McVicar production, had the opportunity here to switch from the bad guy to the title character, Giulio Cesare. He did so with a rich and flexible voice that took him up and down registers without any slips. He should be thanked too for the unscored, freely improvised ornamentations he added to the da capo sections of many arias. This spiced up the sometimes dull repeats that are often a complaint made about Handel's aria style.

Emmanuelle Haïm exhibited authority and decisiveness in her conducting. It was good to hear her take the overture at a sensible tempo, as it is often rushed in other productions. The piece is unusual in that it starts off as a French overture with a stately opening that is repeated. It then segues into a fugue based on a short motif, but instead of repeating the opening as a French overture does, it goes into a minuet. Although Ms. Haïm did at times signal the flutes and oboes to bring out their colors, they tended to recede quickly into the background. Her style of conducting seemed less like William Christie, under whom she played keyboard for many years, than that of another expatriate from Les Arts Florissants, Christophe Rousset.

Haïm and the orchestra did a fine job with a suite from *Water Music* used as a non-vocal musical interlude. I was curious why she had flutist Sébastien Marq come to the front of the stage as soloist in music that doesn't call for one, but it became clear that he was there to embellish the repeats, which he did imaginatively on both the Baroque flute and piccolo.

After the audience's final applause brought back the conductor and soloists, they performed a lovely rendition of the duet "Kind Health Descends on Downy Wings" from Handel's *Ode for the Birthday of Queen Anne*.

♫ Six Characters and a Turk in Search of an Author

Soloists, Juilliard Orchestra and Chorus, Speranza Scappucci (conductor and continuo), Peter Jay Sharp Theater, Juilliard School of Music, Lincoln Center, New York, 22.11.2014

Rossini: *Il Turco in Italia*

Images of Gioachino Rossini (1792-1868) portray a rotund, self-satisfied, perhaps curmudgeonly bon-vivant. But these portraits are not of the man as he looked in his productive years. He famously stopped writing operas at the age of 38 and never returned to that form again. *Il Turco in Italia* was his 13th opera, composed in

1814 when he was not much older than most of the musicians and vocalists who took part in the Juilliard production. He retired from composing in 1829, one year after the death of Schubert and two years after the death of Beethoven. *Guillaume Tell*, his final opera, had opened and was a tremendous success, but due to the political climate in Italy at the time, he had difficulties getting it produced. It doesn't seem so odd then, knowing Mozart and Schubert had died young and Rossini had 39 operas under his belt, that he needed to move on. And he did.

For various reasons, some artistic, some political and some moral, *Il Turco in Italia* was not a success when it first opened in 1815. It was periodically revived but never caught the public's eye until the 1950s. It's a shame that it was rarely performed for it is quite witty, and more complex in a modern way than its simple plot line would suggest. The character of the playwright is one reason for this complexity. When we first meet him, he is having problems coming up with a satisfying plot. But once he realizes that there is material for a new play going on around him, we see that he is now in three different worlds: his life outside the play looking in, as do we, the audience; the play that is on stage now, in which he is a character; and the future play which will be acted from the script he distributes at the end. As the opera progresses, the playwright revises, edits and adds scenes based on what other characters are doing, even going so far as to influence them so they act in ways that suit his sense of what will work in the new play. Although he himself is an actor in the play, he is oblivious to their concerns and solely interested in his work in progress.

The role of the playwright was sung by baritone Szymon Komasa, whose acting, singing skills and acerbic wit kept the action going. He was really the main character, and he kept the balance admirably among his multiple roles.

Rossini added the unneeded character of Don Narciso to the libretto as an opportunity for a great tenor who happened to be in town at the time to show off his vocal abilities. Rossini wrote three arias for this role, the last of which, "Tu seconda il mio disegno," demands a voice that reaches so high it will stop the show for applause, and this was the case here with Joseph Dennis.

The character of Selim was sung by the only non-student in the production, Michael Sumuel, who handled with panache the complex character of a Turkish prince who has to prove his masculinity and justify the harem at his palace. Kara Sainz took on the role of Zaida, a former member of the Prince's harem. She has managed to escape the Prince's clutches but still loves and fears him. Sainz's voice was pure and well rounded, but she was somewhat awkward in this role. In other productions, Zaida is almost an equal to the cunning Fiorilla, but here she doesn't quite convince.

Tenor Nathan Haller as Albazar did not have much opportunity to sing: he had just one aria in Act II. I do remember him singing well in another production during William Christie's visit to New York. Geronio, the guileless husband of Fiorilla, was played broadly by Daniel Miroslaw in a role that is typical of the cuckolded husband in a *commedia del'arte* play. His nervous character was well reflected by his voice.

Maria Callas brought the role of Fiorilla (and this opera) to the modern public. It is a demanding role that requires much coloratura singing and energetic acting and clearly suits a diva. Hyesang Park exhibited all these qualities. With nearly perfect intonation (a few slips here and there) and a strong comic sense, she was an ideal Fiorilla: alluring, egotistical, but ultimately shallow and weak without a man to support her.

After the overture, an opera orchestra should drop into the background and stand out only when the composer wants their presence known. Conductor Speranza Scappucci drew the best from the students. The overture featured French horns and trumpets which were bright and crisp. She handled the classic Rossini crescendos brilliantly, never going overboard, or speeding through them or turning them into background cartoon music.

The staging and sets were moved to 1960 and fit comfortably in the realm of the libretto's story-line. The inn and the arrival of the gypsies were replaced by a spa (Terme) and spa employees. The main set, with lounge chairs around a pool, accommodated most of the action. A sliding wall allowed some of the space to be semi-enclosed for private tête-a-têtes; and it opened upon the water, serving as entrance and exit to the dock where the Prince's yacht was anchored.

With reasonably priced tickets, good acoustics and a relatively small theater (which was sold out), these Juilliard productions help to fill the space left by the demise of so many small opera companies in New York.

♫ Denk Interweaves Schubert and Janáček in Stimulating Recital
Jeremy Denk (piano), 92nd Street Y, New York, 15.11.2014

Haydn: Piano Sonata in C major
Janáček: Movements from *On an Overgrown Path*, alternating with
Schubert: Movements from *Ländler, Moments musicaux; Ländler and Écossaises; Grazer Galopp*
Mozart: Rondo in A minor
Schumann: *Carnaval*

Sometimes the connections between works on a program are opaque. There was an interview recently with Alan Gilbert who was asked why three specific pieces were programmed that week. His answer was something to the effect that they all have dark moments in them, which is like saying they are connected to each other because all are scores written with musical notation. Sometimes a musician is so determined to make connections that the performance is actually destructive to the music. A recent recital by Jonathan Biss was very similar to the one performed here; but Denk interspersed Janáček and Schubert and made his point about connections without destroying the works. Biss's recital interspersed movements from Janáček's *On an Overgrown Path* with movements from Schumann's *Fantasiestücke*, which made for a mildly interesting didactic experiment in deconstruction, but not a particularly satisfying evening of music.

The Schubert pieces are all miniatures unto themselves, and the Janáček pieces were not meant to be played as a whole (as were the *Fantasiestücke* of

Schumann). *On an Overgrown Path* was written over a period of 12 years, and it is clear that, at least in the first book, there was no design or overall structure. Both Janáček and Schubert were exposed to dance and folk music, which is really what most of these pieces are. Although we think of Janáček as modern (he died in 1928), he was born just 26 years after Schubert's death. Denk certainly proved his point about the clear connections between these two seemingly disparate composers. There were several times when I wasn't quite sure if what Denk was playing was by Janáček or Schubert.

Watching Denk perform is an experience in itself. He is the rare musician who has so totally absorbed the music he plays that it appears they are one and the same. There were times when the music seemed innate to Denk, like someone who has been driving for so many hours over the years that the car almost drives itself. It may look like he's on auto-pilot, but that doesn't do justice to the amount of work Denk must have done to reach this level of proficiency. I can only think of one living pianist to whom he can be compared, and that would be Marc-André Hamelin. Nothing humanly possible to perform is beyond the abilities of these two pianists. Interestingly, Hamelin has just come out with a CD featuring Schumann's *Kinderszenen* and *Waldszenen* plus *On an Overgrown Path, Book I*.

Denk's performance of Schumann's *Carnaval* was a dream filled with surprises. Not since recordings by Claudio Arrau have I heard these pieces played with such sensitivity to every nuance. The series of fast tempi, from "Reconnaissance" to "Marche des Davidsbündler," was simply dazzling. So immersed was Denk in the music that he never seemed to come up for air.

The concert opened with a brisk and witty interpretation of Haydn's Piano Sonata in C major, and Denk's hands bounced off the keyboard. The Adagio may have been taken too slowly and mined too preciously for emotional content. This could also be said of the Mozart Rondo in A minor, which is so beautiful that it didn't need to be squeezed. Left by itself, it would have been sufficient to reveal a sublime sadness.

Responding to the ovations, Denk proceeded to play two encores: the first was a movement from *Davidsbündler*, but the second was quite a surprise. The last piece one might have expected to hear as an encore to this program was a work by Charles Ives, in this case the "Alcotts" movement from *Concord Sonata*. Granted, it was not one of the big movements from this monster of piano music, but nonetheless it was a surprise ending to a concert filled with other surprises, both big and little.

♫ *Juilliard415 in Diverse Program of the Italian Baroque*

La Stravaganza: Music of the Italian Baroque, Robert Mealy (violin and director), Eric Jurenas (countertenor), Soloists, Juilliard415, Alice Tully Hall, Lincoln Center, New York, 14.11.2014

Handel: Overture from *Agrippina*
Corelli: Concerto grosso in D major
Vivaldi: *Amor, hai vinto*; Concerto for Two Violins and Two Cellos in D major;

Concerto for Two Flutes in C major; Overture from *L'Olimpiade*
Veracini: Overture No. 6 in G minor
Vivaldi: *Cessate, omai cessate*

The Historical Performance Program students at this concert seemed to me younger but even more accomplished than their predecessors. Who would have thought five or so years ago that this continually changing student group would appear in Augsburg and Munich, and be good enough to perform as professionals under such conductors as Nicolas McGegan, William Christie and Masaaki Suzuki? Granted, there was not quite the rock-solid tightness that comes with learning and lots of time together, and not every student exhibited brilliant technical abilities. But having seen what time in this program can do, I would expect continued growth and maturity.

The concert opened with Handel's brilliant Overture to *Agrippina*, starting off with as good an imitation of the classic Lully overture as there is: filled with dotted rhythms, giving emphasis to the oboe and with a stately pacing. Normally, there would be a fugal middle section and then a return to the opening tempo, but Handel goes off on his own with a middle section that is Italianate in style with emphasis on the strings, even giving the first violin a solo. The overture ends after a scurrying downward slide of notes to a sudden almost comically long silence before an oboe solo leads to the last notes. This was not an easy piece to play, and the students stuck together, handling the breakneck speed as if all were virtuosi.

Countertenor Eric Jurenas sang two cantatas by Vivaldi, both well suited for his vocal range. The training for this kind of voice is a demanding one, and it is impressive to see and hear someone so young with such talent. The challenging melismas that Vivaldi wrote to emphasize words in the text—for example the "a" at the end of "ondo urtando và" (rolling waves), or the last syllable in "mi torno à respirar" (breathing again)—were accurately sung with warmth and solid intonation.

Many Vivaldi concerti were written for unusual combinations of instruments. Some of these combinations are within the traditional Italian repertory: 2 violins or 2 flutes or violin and cello. Some are sui generis: 2 violins and 2 cellos, 2 hunting trombones, oboes and bassoon or, my favorite, 3 violins, oboe, 2 recorders, 2 viole all'inglese, chalumeau, 2 cellos, 2 harpsichords, 2 trumpets and strings. Why such crazy combinations? Vivaldi's concerti were written for the girls at the Oespedale della Pietà. If the best musicians available were 2 violinists and 3 horn players, they became the soloists in Vivaldi's new concerto.

The concerto for 2 violins and 2 celli was enthusiastically played and fun to watch as each theme was, like a hot potato, thrown to the next instrumentalist. Vivaldi was capable of writing these concerti in the time it took to put ink to paper. But there had to be shortcuts, and a major one (which is true for both concerti here) is that the orchestral accompaniment consists mostly of doubling the soloists. The double flute concerto was equally delightful, with soloists who played with fluid ease and were able to bring out a darker, richer color that cannot be duplicated on a modern flute.

The Overture to *L'Olimpiade*, like most of Vivaldi's overtures, is really a sinfonia, a three-movement work, usually fast-slow-fast, that has nothing to do with the opera that follows. Many of the more recently discovered operas are missing overtures, so it's not unusual to hear the same overture leading two or three different operas.

My thought on the well-played Veracini overture was that it is pleasant enough but should make us thankful for the many more substantial composers of the period.

I look forward to future concerts and opportunities to see these talented, already mature players evolve.

♫*Aimard Plays Bach: Well-Tempered and Well Played*
Pierre-Laurent Aimard (piano), Carnegie Hall, New York, 13.11.2014

J. S. Bach: *The Well-Tempered Clavier, Book I*

The documentary *Pianomania: In Search of the Perfect Sound* follows the peregrinations of Stefan Knüpfer, the piano-tuner's piano tuner as he prepares instruments for the likes of Lang, Alfred Brendel and Pierre-Laurent Aimard. A year before Aimard recorded the *Art of the Fugue* for Deutsche Grammophon, he was already obsessing about the kind of sound he wanted his piano to produce. At one point, the ever-patient Knüpfer asks Aimard, "Do you want a big sound," and stretches out his arms; "or a little one," and puts two fingers together, as if to say "itsy bitsy." Aimard smiles and replies, "I want both." At one point, Knüpfer even takes the piano apart to accommodate a request by Aimard for an adjustment in sound.

I'm not sure if the piano Aimard was using here was, in fact, that special Steinway, but I was impressed with the sound and the ever-changing tonal colors that that he was able to draw from it. If I had closed my eyes, I would have said that Aimard (or Knüpfer) had gotten around the Steinway monopoly on the Carnegie Hall stage. Instead, I would have assumed they had replaced it with a Fazioli or the Bösendorfer Imperial: both instruments are capable of a light silvery tone not normally heard on the Steinway.

Aimard, a strong advocate of modern music, has played and recorded works by Elliot Carter, Messaien, Ligeti and Boulez. His recordings of the Ligeti *Études* and Messaien's *Vingt regards sur l'enfant-Jésus* are the standard against which all others are judged. So I wondered what stylistic influences, if any, he might reveal. Listening to the opening prelude, played matter-of-factly as if by a first-year student, I worried about what would come for the next two hours. I needn't have: every prelude and every fugue had been thoroughly thought through. Not all were executed in a style that would please each listener, but there was something for everyone. There was not the muscle of Richter's *WTC* or the mad rushes of Glenn Gould, the studied rigidity of Rosalyn Tureck, the crisp, cool playing of Angela Hewitt or the appealing Glenn-Gouldish Andras Schiff, but there seemed to be some of all these pianists in his fingers.

After the intermission, the theater, which may have been 90% filled at the start, lost perhaps 20% of that audience. This is not background music, and it was never meant to be performed as a complete work. Many of the pieces are pedantic in nature. The opening of the 7th Prelude could have been filched from Bach's *Two-Part Inventions*, another work Bach used for pedagogical purposes. I realized, too, that Aimard must be impervious to such rudeness and laziness on the part of the audience.

Aimard isn't as strict as Schiff, who avoids all use of the pedal, and his foot stayed on the sustain pedal, but it was used sparingly. As a rule, he paused between pieces, but in some instances, as between the 11th and 12th, he sped up in the final measures and went straight into the next prelude. I loved the way he took the syncopations in the 13th Prelude, giving the two-note motif a little turn in its dynamics as if he wanted to imitate a hiccup. And then there was the sheer upbeat joy of the 15th Prelude and Fugue in G major.

I guess every performer wants the final cadences of the last work in the program to be outstanding, dramatic, memorable. But Bach never thought of this work as one requiring anything special for the ending because he didn't imagine it being played as a whole. Aimard went a little too far in slowing down the final measures, holding on dramatically well past the time for the notes to decay, and another good 30 seconds before lifting his hands from the keyboard and allowing the audience to applaud. (Interestingly, he leaves the 30 seconds of silence on his recording of this work as well.)

Those who left before the second half of the program missed out on a far more upbeat group of preludes and fugues than in the first part. Played well, as they were here by Aimard, these piano exercises prove to be lovely miniatures filled with wit and charm.

♫ *No More Surtitles! Who Cares What Schubert's Poets Wrote?*
Matthias Goerne (baritone), Markus Hinterhäuser (piano), White Light Festival, Alice Tully Hall, Lincoln Center, New York, 11.11.2014

Schubert: *Winterreise*

This is the ninth review of *Winterreise* published this year at Seen and Heard. What is it about this work of infinite sadness that calls out to singers, and to listeners who fill venues to hear it? We've had *Winterreise*s that encompass all kinds of approaches: one highlights "estrangement and repressed bitterness" and another "could not have been stronger"; one expresses "palpable sincerity" while another is "uncommonly forlorn." This Lincoln Center performance was strikingly different from any of the previous ones. The philosophical underpinning took priority over the music and ultimately produced a dissatisfying evening that failed to convince either musically or philosophically.

Video artist William Kentridge posits in his writing in *Playbill* and in his lecture at the University of Chicago that because we don't understand every word that comes from a singer on stage we should instead "listen to the image." Stating that he is in a "precarious terrain: a celebration of incomprehension," Kentridge wants to "redeem that [incomprehension] with the imaginative gain this lack produces." He decries singers of Schubert who want the words they sing to be understood, and makes fun of Fisher-Dieskau for his perfect diction, nylon pants and cardigan sweaters, stating that in the 1970s he would have been considered "retro-hipster cool." His model for the ideal Schubertian singer is Charles Panzera, a baritone who flourished during the first half of the twentieth century. I suspect Kentridge admires Panzera's Schubert because his recordings on scratchy old 78s and LPs make it difficult to understand the words. And isn't incomprehension the goal?

I was disappointed that there weren't any surtitles, but the reason soon became clear. This was intentional and part of Kentridge's video concept: the lack of surtitles leaves all but the most erudite listener at a loss for words, and that loss is what he desires. The average listener, confused enough without words for Schubert's 24 songs, becomes totally confounded by images that have little to do with the song cycle.

In point of fact, Kentridge intentionally chooses to frame images that go against the sound and the text itself. He claims that he was "not finding (nor looking for) illustrations of the songs," but seeking instead a connection that is "rhythmic, textual, iconic." It seems to me that the best connection would be images that represent what the song is trying to convey rhythmically, textually and iconically. In Schubert's "Auf dem Fluss" and "Wasserflut," Kentridge may feel that there is a stronger connection to images of a bathroom shower than to one of floods, but on any level wouldn't images of streams and floods be as close as one could get to connecting rhythmically, textually and iconically? He praises the distances between images and music so that those in which there are great disparities are like "a letter from another world, but there is always distancing." Yet there are songs here where images perfectly match the music, such as the notes on a pianola roll that represent the tears in "Gefrorne Tränen."

Kentridge is from Johannesburg, a far cry from Vienna, and his videos include texts about unrest in his homeland and silhouettes of South Africans playing games indigenous to the region. But what does a parade of women carrying baskets on their heads or a hanging tree where bodies fall like apples have to do with an organ-grinder in the final song, "Die Leiermann"?

Several years back I saw a joint collaboration between William Christie's group and Robyn Orlin in a production of Handel's *L'Allegro, il Penseroso ed il Moderato*. Coincidently, she too pushed the accompanying videos with images from South Africa, and there was often little connection between the images and the words. This was tolerable because the singers were great and most of the images were innocuous. In contrast to Kentridge, who rationalizes why he prefers not to synchronize the music with images, Orlin's dancers were in synch with the singers and orchestra.

What Kentridge is really doing here is sabotaging the musical recital with images. In his lecture, he theorizes three possible ways they can reflect the music being played. The first is what he calls the "emotional" connection: sad music is accompanied by sad images. The second is grammatical: the images respond to (are in sync with) the music, as in Disney's *Fantasia*. But it is the third that interests him the most, and that is using "sound to change what we see and what we then see will change what we hear." We give precedence to the image so that it affects our hearing the music.

Kentridge's subtitle of a section in his lecture "Listening to the Image" says it all: "Who Needs Words." It is a grand presumption to grant power to images as a way of distorting text and music. Shouldn't we concern ourselves with the words of Bach's *St. Matthew Passion* or Purcell's *Dido and Aeneas*?

Matthias Goerne held well to the music, giving some attention to the visuals and expressing convincing emotions when called for. Markus Hinterhäuser played conservatively, if sometimes stiffly, but never went very far to enhance Goerne's more emotional songs.

Finally, why is credit given to Greta Goiris for costume design unless Mr. Goerne's brown suit qualifies as a costume.

♫*Academy of Ancient Music: Iconic Early Music Group Continues to Thrive Under Richard Egarr*

Academy of Ancient Music, Richard Egarr (director and harpsichord), Zankel Hall, Carnegie Hall, New York, 7.11.2014

J. S. Bach: Orchestral Suite No. 4 in D major; Orchestral Suite No. 2 in B minor; Orchestral Suite No. 1 in C major; Orchestral Suite No. 3 in D major

It would be hard to overstate the impact on early music practice that Christopher Hogwood and the Academy of Ancient Music had when they released their initial recordings of what eventually became the complete Mozart Symphonies. In the early 1970s, there were a number of groups playing, to varying degrees, in an early music style. Some, like I Musici, performed as a Baroque band but played on new instruments. Concentus Musicus Wien and the Leonhardt-Consort used Baroque instruments or copies of them in their recording of the complete Bach Cantatas.

The Bach Cantata series might have been a little abstruse to appeal to many concert goers and record buyers, particularly the first ones which came out as LPs with the complete scores enclosed. The series took 18 years to complete and now exists in a boxed set of 60 CDs. By comparison, the AAM Mozart series required only 19 CDs and seven years to complete.

What Hogwood and the AAM did was to set the standard for how to get as close as possible to what music might have sounded like to a composer of early music. Scholarly research was done so that where possible every symphony was traced back to its original source; and attempts were made to replicate the number of instruments and of players in the first performance. The result of this practice was music that was fresh, clear and clean.

The number of early music specialists who were part of the AAM and went out on their own is stunning. Just the list of conductors who formed their own Baroque groups is impressive: Simon Standage, Roy Goodman, Monica Huggett, John Holloway, Nicholas McGegan, David Woodcock and Simon Preston among them.

Richard Egarr, the current director and conductor of the AAM, continues the Hogwood tradition. In his brief remarks before the concert, Egarr prepared the audience for the sounds to follow. By lowering the pitch and using one voice per part (OVPP), the music would sound softer and darker than what one expects when hearing these suites, and it did indeed.

The Bach Orchestral Suites are cousins to the Brandenbergs, though it's not surprising that they are rarely performed as a set. The latest research has shown that they were not all written in the 1720s and composed as a whole; two came later, the Third Suite ca. 1731 and the Second in 1738-39. The ordering of the pieces for this performance was clearly done for aesthetic reasons, at least in the choice of the Third to end the program. The Third has most of the players onstage and also uses the brass to great effect, going out with a flourish.

Although there is variety in the Suites' dance movements, they can start sounding the same. This wasn't a problem here. Each movement had its own coloring, enhanced by the fact that with a small ensemble no one instrument can overpower the soloist. Egarr, playing from the keyboard (as support for the basso continuo), kept a moderate pace throughout and was clearly well-attuned to the Suites' nuances.

Pavlo Beznosiuk, a Baroque violin virtuoso in own right, added tasteful ornamentation to a number of the da capo iterations, noticeably in the doubles in the Menuet and Passepied of the First Suite, as well as the da capos of the famous Air from the Third Suite. Bassoonist Ursula Leveaux did an unusually good job supporting the bass line, and in her solo parts as well. The three oboists, Frank de Bruine, Lars Henricksson and Gail Hennessy, had some intonation problems and an occasional slip-up getting back from the da capos, but overall they were impressive.

I listened again to a performance of the Suites recorded in the early 1960s, which was my introduction to the works. There certainly was some good playing, but without the dotted rhythms, vibrato-less strings and easement of four-square playing. Today we accept historically informed performance (HIP) as the norm for most early music, and even non-Baroque orchestras concede to some of the tenets discussed here. We should be thankful for the work done by Hogwood and the AAM in mentoring a whole generation of musicians who have promulgated an approach that has brought back to life music that might otherwise never have been heard.

♫Bezuidenhout and Juilliard415 Perform Music that Never Shouts
Juilliard415, Kristian Bezuidenhout (director and fortepiano), Alice Tully Hall, Lincoln Center, New York, 30.10.2014

J. C. Bach: Sinfonia in G major

W. F. Bach: Sinfonia in D minor
Mozart: Piano Concerto in F major; Rondo in A minor; Piano Concerto in E-flat major ("Jenamy")

Kristian Bezuidenhout is not known to me as a conductor or, more accurately, a "director" as stated in the program notes. In an interview with a Baroque violinist a while back, I casually conflated "conductor" with "director" and "leader," only to be told in no uncertain terms that conductor is a very different position, one that requires years of training and practice. She felt her role was more that of a first violinist or concertmaster in a chamber ensemble assuring that all the players start on the right beat. Given the fact that Bezuidenhout was the soloist in two piano concerti and was required to provide *continuo* for the other two, there was very little "conducting" that he could really do here. The playing by the Juilliard415 members has blossomed over the last few years and can now match any other "headless" orchestra measure for measure.

The program opened with the weakest piece of the evening, a sinfonia by Bach's youngest son, Johann Christian. Italy was the country to go to if you had any interest in the newest musical styles, and he was the only Bach to be exposed directly to the popular Italian style, an elegant and *galante* musical language. Most of his music is pleasant enough but has little substance. Perhaps it was nervousness (for the director as well as the students) that made the playing of this sinfonia seem a bit muddled. If it was meant to be a warm-up, then it did its job. From here on, the playing was top-notch, enthusiastic and professional on all levels. The opening two works share a name but little else. As with many terms in music, one has to intuit what the composer meant when he entitled a piece "sinfonia." J. S. Bach used it to describe the overture-like instrumental opening to many of his cantatas, but Italian composers of the period used sinfonia in its defined sense as simply a congregation of players.

The Adagio opening of W. F. Bach's Sinfonia is almost pastoral in timbre with the Baroque flutes giving it much of its color. This bucolic music though is dampened by the key of D minor which darkens the music, creating a sense of foreboding. The listener expects something dramatic to come. The sudden switch from the Adagio to the Fugue was meant to surprise, and it did. The orchestra adeptly handled the complex fugue (modeled so clearly after W. F.'s father's fugues for organ) and, particularly in the *stretti,* kept the inner voices clearly discernable.

Attention shifted to the soloist in the two Mozart piano concerti. The fortepiano on stage was modeled after one by the Viennese keyboard maker Johann Schantz from c.1800 that was admired by Haydn for its delicacy and light touch. The heart of what makes performers and listeners so passionate about historically informed performances was clearly demonstrated in the playing of these concerti. The music is put back in the context of where it belongs. It is the equivalent of being in Mozart's home where you might say," So this is how he lived." Here one could say, "So this is what he heard."

It was a joy to watch Bezuidenhout's fingers flying over the keyboard. I specifically use the word "over" because it seemed like he wasn't touching the keys. I can only think of two very different performers with a similar lightness of touch: Miklos Spanyi playing the clavichord, a soft-sounding instrument but closer in mechanism to the fortepiano; and Marc-André Hamelin, whose light touch allows him to play the most difficult music at incredible speeds. Bezuidenhout's technique, along with the orchestra's sensitive accompaniment, created a completely different sound-world from more traditional performances of Mozart concerti: one that is warmer, less edgy or strident. The original instruments never overpowered the soloist. Fortes were loud but never LOUD.

The most moving music of the evening was the immaculately played Rondo in A minor that opened the second half of the program, a work both poignant and infinitely sad. This could also be said about the second movement Andantino of the Piano Concerto, K. 271, music that is mature well beyond Mozart's 21 years.

This was an exemplary concert in all respects. Congratulations to Mr. Bezuidenhout who, one hopes, will return on a regular basis as guest artist and mentor.

♫ *Alcina: Witch, Shrew and Termagant, But Most of All a Diva*
The English Concert, Harry Bicket (artistic director and conductor), Carnegie Hall, New York, 26.10.2014

Handel: *Alcina*
Concert Version

One could feel the excitement and sense the audience's anticipation well before this sold-out concert began. This was the final performance in a tour that took the cast and production staff from an opening in London on 10 October to venues in Spain, Austria, France and, finally, New York. I can only credit word-of-mouth for this awareness or, more accurately, "word of Web." Positive online reviews of concerts on tour quickly spread the news these days.

My thoughts were twofold. Either the singers would be exhausted (this was the last stop on their tour), or the opposite: at their best, having now performed the work many times. I would say that they came pretty close to perfection here, or as close as a concert version of an opera can be. It would appear that staged operas produced outside of the Met will continue to be semi-staged or concert versions with minimal space in which to sing and interact, at least until money for the arts from public and private sectors starts to flow again.

The performers here were not in costume, except for Joyce DiDonato who wore a Cruella de Vil-style gown. The vocalists did the smart thing, singing and acting as if they were in a fully staged production. Singers exiting a scene would move to a near or distant chair depending on the demands of the libretto. Eye contact between members of the cast gave the audience some sense of connection between characters. For example, near the beginning of the opera when Bradamante/Ricciardo expresses bafflement at Morgana's *coup de coeur,* she rolls his/her eyes as if to say, "Give me a break. You can't have fallen in love with me. We just met!"

It would serve little purpose to summarize the plot line. Here, as in many Baroque operas, the libretto is simply an excuse to for the composer to write music that is appropriate to the emotions expressed in the text. A large number of Handel's libretti are no more than templates: women dressed as men or vice versa (*Alcina, Admeto, Xerxes, Floridante*), done to test the fidelity of their affianced or as a means of discovering a truth that could not be revealed otherwise until the end. Other templates are framed on the false assumption that a character is dead but is later revealed to be alive (*Agrippina, Ariodante*). *Alcina* succeeds here not so much for the words or the drama, but for the inspired music of Handel and the consistently high quality of both the orchestral and vocal parts. While there were some weaknesses, the overall excellence of the ensemble overrode any small complaints.

When one of the vocalists stands out so clearly from the rest of the cast it becomes a somewhat difficult balancing act to give a fair reading of the other soloists. This was noticeable, for example, when DiDonato's pitch-perfect voice, fully at ease, traverses the difficult aria in Act III, "Ma quando tonerai." Each note was clear and sharp yet had enough volume to carry to the back of the hall. The wonderful "Sta nell'Ircana" (certainly a happy aria for the two horn players who were finally given their chance to join the orchestra in the only music they were to play that evening) was beautifully sung by Alice Coote. Under other circumstances, this aria would have knocked the socks off the audience members, given Coote's virtuosity. Yet this was tempered by the fact that it paled in comparison to DiDonato's previous aria.

The other sopranos and mezzos varied in vocal quality, with Anna Devin as Oberto the surprise of the evening. Her voice was better suited than the other vocalists in a performance where the orchestra played in an historically informed style. The combination of a sparing use of vibrato and a naturally beautiful voice produced a pure and youthful sound not heard elsewhere on stage. On the other end of the spectrum, Ben Johnson as Oronte had a more traditional operatic voice, one that did not seem quite right for this production.

In earlier reviews of Harry Bicket and his ensemble, I had cause to comment on a coolness that marred his orchestral playing. This came through less here because his orchestra was, as it should be, secondary to the vocalists. Although there seemed to be an improvement in the orchestra's enthusiasm in the second and third acts, Bicket tended to fall into a groove that flattened out the differences between arias, mostly due to his tendency to standardize the tempi. The waning variety made the final half of the performance a little tiresome. While with Handel you can never have enough of a good thing, too many arias taken at similar tempi can make them sound the same.

The audience was as pleased with the singing as any I can remember since the demise of the New York City Opera. There, too, in their many landmark revivals of Baroque operas, cheering was almost mandatory at the end of all but the most minor arias. The performance here, scheduled to run about 3 hours ran almost a half hour longer due to the shouting and cheering of the audience. It was well deserved.

♫ *Maurizio Pollini Wanes but Does it Matter?*
Maurizio Pollini (piano), Carnegie Hall, New York, 19.10.2014

Schumann: *Arabeske* in C major; *Kreisleriana*
Chopin: Prelude in C-sharp minor; Piano Sonata No. 2 in B-flat minor; Berceuse in D-flat Major; Polonaise in A-flat Major

Encores:
Chopin: Nocturne in D-flat major; Scherzo No. 3 in C-sharp minor; Etude in C minor, "Revolutionary"; Ballade No. 1 in G minor

The seasonal reappearances of some of our greatest pianists in the Stern/Perelman auditorium at Carnegie Hall are always an event. The audience knows that whoever is on stage has something special to offer. Many solo musicians say they've played at Carnegie Hall, but few really—or rarely—have. The cognoscenti know to ask, "Stern, Zankel or Weill?" There is a considerable difference in size between Weill's 270 seats, Zankel's 600 and Carnegie Hall's 2800. Pollini may have waited eight years after he won the Warsaw International Chopin Competition to feel confident enough to accept offers to play publicly; but when he did, he went straight to the top, performing in Carnegie's main hall.

The key phrases that pepper so many Pollini reviews can be found in Alan Hughes' 1968 *NY Times* review of that first concert at Carnegie Hall: "as swift and steely a set of fingers as any pianist today," "beautifully if somewhat coolly played," "clean articulation" and "long lined-melody…shaped aristocratically." Hughes significantly closes his review with what has now become for many critics an apologia for this giant of the piano: "Does he play Beethoven? Does he play Bach? Who cares when he plays Chopin…so splendidly."

Almost 50 years later, another critic refers briefly to an earlier performance of this same program as having missed notes, blurred passages and the absence of Pollini's former technical brilliance. And his conclusion? "It doesn't matter," since Pollini has "bestowed the music of Schumann and Chopin" upon an "audience of his loyal subjects."

What does matter then? Pollini may be a king and the audience his loyal subjects, but what if he's not wearing any clothes. It seems easy enough to reject young competitors who are hoping for a first prize but flub, or musicians who are applying for orchestral positions but don't quite have what it takes. Sure, it is hard to ignore effort, but the alternative is a dangerous one: the lowering of expectations and the rise of mediocrity.

The *Arabeske* that opened the program lacked a clarity of line, hindered either by the peculiarities of Pollini's custom piano or the overuse of the sustain pedal. The conversational nature of Schumann's music demands that the voices

79

talk clearly to each other. Here, as in some of the other pieces, there was a peculiar clumpishness in the left hand that buried the lower voices. For the same reasons, the "zum Schluss" section that closes the work never sounded, as it should, delicate and wispy.

Pollini, a student of the idiosyncratic Arturo Benedetti Michelangeli is known for his cool classicism. Perhaps he was attempting in the *Kreisleriana* to broaden his playing style, to be less cool and outward looking and, to paraphrase the second section's heading, to be *sehr innig*. At moments he seemed unsure, and he certainly didn't show the confidence and technical prowess we have come to expect from him.

He did seem more comfortable with the Chopin works. The Prelude in C-sharp minor sung out well but something was lost in the crescendos. The Piano Sonata No. 2 held up well too, but the Scherzo and particularly the Finale were rushed, as if the pianist wanted it to be over. The Berceuse lacked the silvery tones that were hidden beneath the sustained pedal marks that Chopin wrote for it. By this time, I was almost certain that this dull sound was due to the piano, which I noticed was rushed onto the stage and perhaps not completely adjusted. The concluding Polonaise in A-flat was workmanlike, without the bravura and jittery tension that informs the performance of a Horowitz. The speed was there but little else.

Happily, in the four encores Pollini gathered some kind of strength from the applause or was able to relax. There was no question here of waning technique. Two of the encores were played at Pollini's first recital, and he seemed at ease enough to tear through these bonbons with aplomb.

♪ *Zelenka's World*
Gonzalo Ruiz (oboe), Kathryn Montoya (oboe, recorder), Dominic Teresi (bassoon), Rob Nairn (violone), Avi Stein (harpsichord), Charles Weaver (theorbo, Baroque guitar), Paul Hall, Juilliard School of Music, Lincoln Center, New York, 23.9.2014

Zelenka: Sonata in F major for Two Oboes, Bassoon and Continuo
Bach: Chromatic Fantasy and Fugue
Handel: Sonata in G minor
Bach: Sonata in C major for Oboe and Continuo (arr. Ruiz)
Vivaldi: Sonata in A minor for Recorder, Bassoon and Continuo
Zelenka: Sonata in G minor

Bach, Handel and Vivaldi are such huge figures that they have hidden a number of nearly-great composers in their shadows. We've heard of Telemann and Domenico Scarlatti, but there were many more composers, often associated with particular courts or parishes. For example, Christophe Graupner at the Darmstadt court, through the pioneer recordings of Geneviève Soly, has been revealed as a composer of substance with a signature sound that is beguiling and even mildly addictive. Gottfried Heinrich Stölzel at the court in Gotha was a prolific composer of over 1300 cantatas (most lost or incomplete) whose vocal and sacred music has elements that certainly stand up to Bach's.

Maybe these other composers will find their heyday in the future, but as for Zelenka, he has been and continues to be a cause for the Historical Performance department at the Juilliard School. Zelenka's third sonata from the ZWV 181 collection was performed back in January 2014; and in November 2013, his most famous work, *Hipocondrie à 7 Concertanti*, was given an appropriately woozy reading. This October, Masaaki Suzuki will be performing Zelenka's *Missa Patris* with Juilliard415 and the Yale Schola Cantorum.

Born in Prague, Zelenka was most closely associated with the city of Dresden, first as a violone player at court and then as a church composer. The Czech music of his youth never really left him, and his use of rustic, folksy dance rhythms imbues his work with a spirited jauntiness. Part of the reason Zelenka's music hasn't been performed much was that for some reason it was locked away in a Catholic church (Zelenka was a Lutheran). The other part is that his music is very demanding for musicians. Take the opening of the 5th Sonata from ZWV 187 collection. Starting off à la Vivaldi with all instruments in unison, it suddenly spotlights the violone player with a run of several measures of 16th notes and 32nd notes, which are then given over note-by-note to the oboe. But what makes it sound uniquely Zelenkian is its out-of-balance themes. In addition, triplets are thrown in but not in any logical way. Rob Nairn deftly handled these difficult runs. The piece was a challenge to the players, who went beyond mere technical prowess into the core of the work.

The Chromatic Fantasy and Fugue, a staple in the Bach repertory, is frequently given a dramatic interpretation whether performed on piano or harpsichord. This understanding of the work as heavy and emotional is perhaps based on its title. Even though an organ has not been specified, it falls into the category of organ works with similar names, the toccatas and fugues or fantasias and fugues. Ari Stein played the harpsichord as if it were a clavichord, expressive and sensitive to the touch. The chromatic pages were never pounded out, the fugues were never exaggerated.

Handel's Op. 2 was not intentionally written for publication but had to be put out in the market to compete with plagiarized or stolen musical scores carrying Handel's unauthorized name on their covers. Given the fact that Handel compiled the set in a way that made it playable by the most common instruments might belie this fact. Why else would he specify that the obligatto instruments are interchangeable? They can be played by recorder, violin or oboe and continuo. Unannounced for this performance was the introduction of a Baroque guitar as a substitute for the theorbo, which did have a slight effect in lightening the work's colors. Some borrowed passages, such as the fourth movement's use of themes from *Rinaldo*, were recognizable.

Gonzalo Ruiz had to dig deep to come up with a transcription of Bach's Flute Sonata BWV 1035 for oboe and continuo. Transposing it to C made it possible. If it was his intention to make the oboe sound like a flute, the smooth legatos of a flute never came through. We do know that Bach admired the D minor Oboe Concerto by Benedetto Marcello enough to transcribe it for keyboard. Bach never wrote an oboe sonata or concerto, so it's nice to have one available for oboists. Mind you, this is a difficult and complex work in either format, and Ruiz is to be congratulated for bringing more Bach into the world even if it's a surrogate.

The Vivaldi Sonata for Recorder, Bassoon and Continuo waits for the second movement to put the bassoonist in the spotlight; although it was written for recorder and bassoon, it is the recorder that gets Vivaldi's attention. The only problem in this performance was with tempos. Both largos were played like adagios or even andantes. This was especially true of the largo cantabile which was too fast to produce a singing quality and reduced the impact of the allegro molto conclusion.

The final Zelenka Sonata is in his typical style: an obsessive repetition of a 6-note motif supported by an unstable continuo in the first movement, and a demanding second movement with a fugue that appears from nowhere. With a fugue as complex as this in the second movement, one wonders what Zelenka will do to prevent the final movement from seeming anti-climactic. Following a slow movement, the allegro ending comes in with a fugal theme that never quite follows the rules. Though close to being a canon, it never quite gets there either.

All in all an adventurous recital, as we've come to expect of the Juilliard faculty.

♫ Bach and Reger: They Might Be Giants
Paul Jacobs (organist), Paul Hall, Juilliard School of Music, Lincoln Center, New York, 8.9.2014

Reger: Fantasy and Fugue on BACH
Bach: Chorale-Prelude: *Von Gott will ich nicht lassen*; Prelude and Fugue in D minor ("Fiddle")
Reger: Intermezzo; Introduction, Variations and Fugue on an Original Theme

The works by Max Reger presented here date from the first five years of the 20th Century. During this period, Mahler's Third, Fourth and Fifth Symphonies, Busoni's towering piano concerto and Bruckner's Symphony No. 9 were premiered. While Reger's "Introduction, Variations and Fugue on an Original Theme," the centerpiece of this program, lasts only 35 minutes, it shares the grandeur and complexity of its musical contemporaries.

Clearly Paul Jacobs found this work worth the time it took to master, as he confirmed through his playing and his comments during an evening of music and explication. The sold-out concert's demographics were quickly surveyed by Jacobs who asked the audience to raise their hands if it was their first organ recital. There was only a scattering of hands which might explain the warm reception given to the soloist at the end of the recital: music of this density, dissonance and duration is not easily appreciated.

Although Jacobs stated that little in the score specifies which stops to use and when, and thus requires additional effort on the part of the performer to determine a fitting timbre, the score is quite unequivocal about how it should be played. Instructions for which manual(s) to use, which couplers not to use (*nur Coppel zum*), and when to pause and when not to (*Keine pause!*), as well as detailed tempi and dynamic marks make the work even more challenging. Jacobs accomplished the nearly impossible: quickly pulling stops, switching from keyboard to keyboard and applying virtuosic techniques on the pedalboard all at the same time. And it's impressive to see him do all this without a sheet of music in front of him!

As part of his opening remarks, Jacobs sampled the motifs of the variations and of the fugue. This was a smart thing to do as it clarified the work's structure. Knowing what to look for made it easier to follow the variations which often flowed one after another without pause. The main motif could be clearly discerned in each of the variations, some of which were surprisingly light-hearted. Dissonances abounded and chromaticisms were ever present; yet even though it edged close to atonality, it never really escaped tonality's pull, ending as Bach's works often did on a colossal dominant pedal point.

Reger's "Intermezzo" proved that he was capable of composing music that never raised its voice above *piano* except for a brief measure which starts as a *forte* but ends as a *piano*. This is about as delicate a piece as can be imagined for an organ: one soft voice being echoed by an even quieter upper voice. Jacobs used the choir and swell manuals to clarify and differentiate the musical lines.

The opening work, "Fantasy and Fugue on BACH," is Reger's take on Bach's own variations as most prominently used in *Art of the Fugue*. As Bach did with his variations, Reger also transposes, inverts and retrogrades the theme. If that isn't enough, the theme becomes the motif of not only a complex fugue, but a double fugue at that.

Who would ever state that any of Bach's organ works could serve as a respite, a quiet point in the middle of a storm? The two Bach pieces seemed tame in comparison to the works surrounding them. This Choral Prelude is one of many Bach wrote as improvisations on choral texts for religious services. The Prelude and Fugue in D minor has as its distinguishing feature the fact that the fugue is almost a note by note transcription of the second movement of the G-minor Sonata for solo violin.

For his encore Jacobs played the fugue from Bach's A-minor Prelude and Fugue, referring to it as "little." It might have been little to him but the audience certainly thought it was "great."

♪ *Zinman is Welcomed Back to the States After 19 Years as Conductor of Tonhalle in Zurich*

Mostly Mozart Festival 7: Joshua Bell (violin), Lawrence Power (viola), Mostly Mozart Festival Orchestra, David Zinman (conductor), Avery Fisher Hall, Lincoln Center, New York, 19.8.2014

Boyce: Symphony No. 1 in B-flat major

Mozart: Sinfonia Concertante for Violin and Viola in E-flat major
Beethoven: Symphony No. 3 in E-flat major ("Eroica")

English music had somewhat of a heyday starting in the mid to late 16th century with the music of Thomas Tallis, William Byrd and John Dowland. It continued with Henry Purcell in the late 17th century and Handel in the early 18th. Although some of my fellow English reviewers on this site may disagree, there wasn't another composer of substance in England until the late 19th and early 20th centuries with Edward Elgar and Frederick Delius. Thomas Arne, an almost exact contemporary of Boyce, is best known by crossword players as the four letter word for the composer of "Rule Britannia." There were few composers of note in the England in which Boyce flourished. The Continent fared a little better with the sons of Bach, W. F. and C. P. E., Gluck and Stamitz. Born in 1711, Boyce had few competitors when he was offered the job as Master of the King's Music in 1755, and he continued in that role for over 20 years.

Boyce was not a major player in the development of the incipient classical period as were his continental counterparts. C. P. E. Bach was writing Sturm und Drang music well before the "official" beginning date of that artistic period; Gluck was reforming opera; Stamitz was creating the modern symphony orchestra. Boyce and, later, the youngest son of Bach, Johann Christian, were writing music that was in reaction to the thick, heavy music of the Baroque. Although Mozart had met the youngest Bach and wrote musical transcriptions of some of Bach's music, this is music for the dilettante, fluffy background music that requires little effort to understand.

Zinman instilled life into this short Boyce symphony by sharpening the attacks and speeding up the tempi. Well played by the Mostly Mozart Orchestra, the tiny movements, even with the repeats, took barely 10 minutes.

What a difference in talent between Boyce and Mozart. The double concerto known as the Sinfonia Concertante for Violin and Viola is one of Mozart's greatest accomplishments. It is a work that gives considerably more pleasure live then recorded. Because the sound from the solo violin and solo viola mix and blend with each other, it's hard to know which instrument is playing what at any given time. I believe Bell was playing the infamous "Gibson ex Huberman" Stradivarius. It had a wonderful sound and Bell played as if it were made for him. Its depth and warmth would make it even more difficult to know what instrument is being played, the low notes of the Strad having such a rich "viola" timbre. I wasn't thrilled with Lawrence Power's performance: his cavalier approach never sounded convincing. He accompanied the orchestra when not soloing. It was not just this look-at-me performance of the orchestral viola part but it was the superficiality of his interpretation itself that disappointed me. Granted, he clearly had mastered and memorized the work's ritornello viola part, but the result was that he continued in the solo parts as if he were still a member of the orchestra. It also was a bit unkind to Joshua Bell, standing there while his fellow soloist was soaking up all the attention. I am sure many in the audience wondered why Bell wasn't playing along with the orchestra like Powell. Bell has nothing to worry about.

Zinman came through with a powerful and well-structured Beethoven "Eroica." He never settled for the automatic pilot that many conductors turn on when they play a work time and time again. From the opening chords and timpani drum beats, I experienced a kind of energy I hadn't felt from this symphony in quite a while. This was no rote performance. Zinman brought specific orchestral groups to the forefront so that they were heard above the usually dominant string section, which gave clarity to musical lines that are often buried beneath the strings. He took the huge crescendos of the first movement and made them huger. Starting at a very low *pianissimo* he cranked up the volume to the loudest *fortes*. This never seemed artificial but rather appeared to come organically from what preceded it. The second movement was less a funeral march than an heroic march not towards death but towards life. The dominance of the tympani as it was played in the middle of the second movement was chilling. The brass was brazen in both the second movement and the hunting horns of the trio section of the third movement Scherzo stood out clearly from the background. The finale was a bundle of energy, nonstop whirlwinds with cascading runs that I can't remember hearing as clearly and with such speed since Toscanini recordings with the NBC Symphony Orchestra. Filled as it is with false codas, the final movement often seems endless. I never felt that here. The music raced to the finish but it never felt rushed.

I'm sure Zinman will be missed by the Zurich Tonhalle orchestra and audience, but it's nice to know he will be back in the States as an itinerant conductor or, perhaps, conductor of an American orchestra. There are many orchestras that would benefit from his leadership, but I'd best leave that topic for another time.

♫ *The Fairy Queen: A Production Evoking the Spirit of Purcell*

The Sebastians, Jeff Grossman (musical director), Christopher Caine (director and choreographer), East 13th Street Theatre, New York, 18.8.2014

Purcell: *The Fairy Queen*

I had some difficulty starting this review. No, not the normal writer's block, but rather a struggle to find the adjectives that would do justice to this performance. Well-done, excellent, captivating, seductive, clever, charming: yes, it was all these. But there was something special that this performance had, and the only word I can think of to describe it is one that can be dull and emotionally neutral, but is also filled with all sorts of issues: "authentic." This word normally takes me somewhere that I don't want to go: historically informed productions, original instrumentation, vibrato-less playing, white voices, temperaments and correct pitches. There were parts of this production where one might question the authenticity of the performance. But it was authentic, not because it followed or didn't follow certain stylistic guidelines, but because it carried with it what I see as the spirit of Henry Purcell. We'll never know, of course, the specifics of the actual productions in his lifetime, but I can't imagine that they were very far from this performance. I was captivated from beginning to end, caught up in the group's unflagging energy and enthusiasm. We know New York is the home of many talented people hoping for a break, but to put together a troupe of such multi-talented performers is a credit to the dell'Arte Opera Ensemble team and Christopher Caines.

This particular production is similar in concept to William Christie and Jonathan Kent's 2009 performance from Glyndebourne, revived the following year at the Brooklyn Academy of Music. Both creatively incorporated text from Shakespeare's *A Midsummer Night's Dream*, in a sense using it to make the semi-opera whole. Christie/Kent's *Fairy Queen* was lavishly produced, with imaginative sets and costumes plus well-known singers. Both productions had their moments of anachronism with occasional topical subjects added to the text, be it "Brooks Brothers" used as a synecdoche (but uttered a little too frequently here), or Kent's copulating rabbits in the earlier production. (Don't ask!) Both incorporated actors, vocalists and dancers, but the key difference is that in the Christie/Kent version, there was only one person on stage capable of multiple skills: Robert Bolt, who acted, sung and played the flute. In the Caines version, many are multitalented.

One of the weaknesses of an otherwise fine recent production of Handel's *Acis and Galatea* was the clear discomfort of the vocalists who awkwardly stood around as dancers from Mark Morris's troupe flew by. A little acting skill was all that would have been required for the soloists to overcome their anxiety. Baroque opera is a mixed art form, each genre requiring different or multiple talents. The talents needed for a semi-opera are different from what's required for an *opéra-lyrique* or an *opéra-ballet*. The real success of this performance was the ability of most members of the troupes to break down the barriers between art forms. When all are involved and all work together as an entity, the parts are subsumed to make a greater whole.

Not every aria was pitch perfect, not every actor was a Hamlet, not every dancer had twinkle-toes or was expected to dance like Aynsley Inglis or Luke Tucker. Purcell writes that we should "sing while we trip it on the green." Tripping on the green requires no dancing lessons. There was some exceptional singing here, voices that should be heard and appreciated by a wider audience. There was an energy that is rarely present in other performances as a result of everyone being on stage most of the time. Vocalists came out from the crowd, sang and slipped back to the group.

The musical accompaniment may have been stripped down, but there was never a feeling of thinness. When needed, Baroque trumpets were added. The musicians performing the obbligato parts of some of the arias never drew attention to themselves, and at the quieter moments never "disturbed" the characters' "sleeping sense."

Purcell was that rare composer who seemed to have had an endless fount of melodies. These wonderful songs and arias, whose motifs would fill happily any other composers' notebooks, are for Purcell literally throwaways. It was entirely appropriate to draw the curtain covering the picture of Purcell in the last act.

However, it was clear that he had been with us through the entire production.

♪ *Handel's Teseo: Weak Plot, Great Music*
Mostly Mozart Festival 6: Philharmonia Baroque Orchestra, Nicholas McGegan (conductor), Alice Tully Hall, Lincoln Center, New York, 17.8.2014

Handel: *Teseo*
Semi-staged Concert Version

It seems every Handel opera is made up of two stories. The first story is, of course, from the libretto. The second story, whether apocryphal or not, is the one that often surrounds the opera's creation and production. Some examples: in preparation for his opera *Ottone*, Handel, so the story goes, was faced with a diva who refused to sing one of his arias. Handel is said to have grabbed her by the waist, threatening her with defenestration. Another involves the premier of *Theodora*, poorly attended due to an earthquake that shook London a few days before the opening. It drove a good number of likely audience members, those who could afford to, out of London. They returned but only after three performances. The opera was never again to be revived in Handel's lifetime. Other stories involve machinations with theater managers, impresarios and prima donna castrati such as Senesino and Farinelli.

The second "story" of Teseo involves stolen theater revenues. Handel had successfully sold out all the tickets for its opening two nights only to find that the theater manager had absconded to the continent with the box office receipts. The company decided to continue the run but never recouped income from those two performances. This may not seem a major financial loss for all involved; but when an opera was considered a success if it played a mere dozen times, as is the case of *Teseo*, it was a substantial loss of revenue.

As for the "real story," the libretto is not one of Handel's best. Not that anyone would ever compare any Handel libretto to Shakespeare, but in the great Handel operas such as *Giulio Cesare, Orlando* and *Hercules*, the composer and librettist found the right formula to create characters with some depth of personality. Here the characters are thinly drawn and the plot stretched beyond what is necessary, a plot that borders on bombast. For most Baroque operas, or any opera for that matter, suspending disbelief is necessary to attach our eyes to the stage and our ears to the music. But here there are plot lines that have so little logic that even suspending disbelief is difficult to do.

Teseo's libretto suffers more than most operas from multiple iterations of *deus ex machina*: instantly negating all that went before. First there is the sudden reversal of Medea's previously uncontrollable rage. From a fire-breathing termagant wreaking Hell on Agilea and Teseo one moment, to a bearer of good-tidings and reconciler the next: this is too broad not to find humorous. Even the peripatetic Charles Burney, Handel's friend, music scholar and admirer of his music, commented that the opera's dénouement merrily skips along, a happy ending regardless of what came before. One of the main sources for the libretto of *Teseo*, Lully's *Thésée*, makes it clear that Medea's quick reversal was a strategy to allow her to come up with some other form of revenge and not a change of heart.

The second impossible-to-believe incident is the magical appearance of Minerva who sends Medea away and wishes the couples a happy future. This conceit mirrored the conclusion of Lully's *Thésée*. The last half hour is a half hour too long to support the thin plot. If we weren't to lose the fifth act aria, "Morirò, mà vendicata," beautifully rendered by Dominique Labelle, the opera could have ended with the first improbable conclusion of Act IV. The fact that this is the only Handel opera with five acts and the fifth is the weakest in the production makes me think Handel was trying to make a connection to Lully's *Thésée*, written in five acts.

There was a questionable decision to go comic as a way of solving the weak plot problem. This is after all a "serious opera." The switch from seria to buffo occurs with the entrance of the loafish King Aegeo played by Drew Minter and continues on and off through the rest of the production. I'm not sure I minded. For one thing, it validated the over-the-top yet convincing performance by Ms. Labelle and smoothed the way to the happy ending.

Vocally and instrumentally there was barely a missed beat. *Teseo* has been a favorite of McGegan who first performed it in 1985. It's hard to believe that Drew Minter, the King, was a member of the original production. Other members of the group have kept the cast nearly intact over the years making it a paradigm for their dedication and respect to the leadership and accomplishments of Nicholas McGegan.

The instrumentalists were on-stage at this performance in the pit-less Alice Tully Hall, forming an offbeat semi-circle around the conductor. McGegan, as usual, danced his way through the music, occasionally playing the harpsichord. The singing and acting was almost uniformly good. Drew Minter had some difficulties in the middle and low ranges. Robin Blaze started off a little weak, but came into his own, doing a superb job in the duet with Céline Ricci, "Unito a un puro afetto," and the solo aria "Più non cercà liberta." The ever-reliable Amanda Forsythe was in top form as were both Amy Freston and Céline Ricci. In the aria, "M'adora l'idol mio" even the one or two slips on the part of the oboist Mark Schachman did not take away from this amazing display of voice and instrument. The great Baroque soprano, Dominique Labelle, acted and sang the role of the termagant Medea for all it was worth, not missing any chance the libretto offered to spew her venom.

The venerable Philharmonia Baroque Orchestra was well balanced and the solo obligatto instrumentalists breezed through *Teseo*'s difficulties while giving the audience a reason to focus on some of Handel's most appealing music.

♫*Noseda Conducts a Fiercely Individual Beethoven's Ninth*

Mostly Mozart Festival 5: Erika Grimaldi (soprano), Anna Maria Chiuri (mezzo-soprano), Russell Thomas (tenor), Ildar Abdrazakov (bass), Concert Chorale of New York, James Bagwell (director), Mostly Mozart Festival Orchestra, Gianandrea Noseda (conductor), Avery Fisher Hall, Lincoln Center, New York,

Beethoven: Overture to *The Consecration of the House*; Symphony No. 9

In June of 1977, Voyager 1 was launched. In its cargo was a set of recordings called *The Voyager Golden Records*. One of these contained an eclectic selection of music ranging from Peruvian panpipes and drums to Chuck Berry's "Johnnie B. Goode," and included two excerpts from Beethoven's works: the first movement from his Symphony No. 5 and the Cavatina from the String Quartet No. 13. It's a shame there were only 90 minutes of music on this analog gold-plated copper disk and no room for Beethoven's 9th. I'd like to see what an alien's reaction would be to this particular work. Perhaps it would understand what humans are truly capable of achieving.

In Noseda's nearly perfect performance of the 9th last night, every note played was right in place, tightly drawn and sharply in focus. From the opening *sotto voces* to the huge crescendos that follow, Noseda clearly had his own vision. This was no lush, velvety interpretation in the grand tradition of the large symphony orchestra. Pulling back from the detailed music to its overall sound, I was reminded of performances that are historically informed. Lean, taut and crisp are adjectives not often heard when referring to Beethoven's music, but for Noseda, clarity of the musical lines was paramount. With fewer instrumentalists than are usually used for this symphony, he worked every orchestral group to their max. In the opening movement, the upper hand was, unusually, given over to the winds, the strings almost acting as accompaniments. And why not? Normally, the sounds of the strings section would be drawn out over and above the other orchestral groups, in effect raising their dynamic level; the strings would be played a notch up, for example from *ppp* to *pp* (or the winds would be played a notch down from the strings).

In the past, I've often felt that sufficient time hasn't been given to rehearsals, particularly during a festival such as this one. Here I had no such problem. Seeing Noseda's rapport with the musicians and singers, no one would know that he was a guest conductor. The orchestra caught his enthusiasm and sent it right back out to the audience. Only in the third movement did I feel a lack of structure. This might have simply been disappointment that the third didn't reach the heights of the other movements. Certainly there was no problem with the technical aspects of the playing.

The final movement is ultimately the summation and litmus test for all that precedes it. Beethoven himself knew this when he embedded motifs from the three previous movements near the finale's beginning. The most difficult aspect here is to keep everything under control and in balance but not so tightly as to inhibit the orchestra and chorus. Noseda held that fine line, aided by the excellent soloists. The vibrant chorus under the leadership of James Bagwell belied the fact that they numbered only 50.

I'm not sure what Noseda thought of the audience's interruptions, but I could understand why they applauded after each movement. He may have planned on quickly segueing from the third movement to the fourth, which could be the reason he brought the soloists on stage at the pause between the second and third movements. Any chance this might have happened was prevented by the audience's enthusiasm.

The opening overture to *The Consecration of the House* acted both as a warm-up and a preview of the music to follow. Musically it borders on the bombastic, particularly in comparison to the earlier Leonora and Egmont overtures.

Needless to say, the audience's applause was tumultuous at the end of the 9th.

♪ *Mark Morris's Acis and Galatea Adds Mozart to the Mix*

Mostly Mozart Festival 4: Mark Morris Dance Group, Mark Morris (director and choreographer), Philharmonia Baroque Orchestra and Chorale, Nicholas McGegan (conductor), David H. Koch Theater, Lincoln Center, New York, 7.8.2014

Handel: *Acis and Galatea*

Acis and Galatea was written during Handel's stay as composer-in-residence at Cannons, the idyllic country estate of the Duke of Chandos. The original production was barebones: three sopranos, a tenor and a bass, who also served as the chorus. The orchestra consisted of two violins, two cellos and two musicians on oboe and recorder. This allowed the entire group to perform *Acis* in a large room such as those available in the spacious mansion. (Many years ago a traveling troupe was able to do a full production of *Acis* at my daughter's elementary school in a large classroom.)

For later productions, Handel augmented the orchestra, adding trumpets, horns and flutes. Mozart filled out the orchestra even more in his arrangement, most drastically by replacing the Baroque wind of choice, the oboe, with the recently invented keyed clarinet. So here at Lincoln Center we had a Baroque band on original instruments conducted by a Baroque specialist, Nicholas McGegan, performing an updated, non-Baroque version using Baroque instrumental and vocal techniques.

There are some gains made when using Mozart's orchestration, including his magical transformation of *secco* recitatives into seamless *accompagnatos*. His substantive changes in orchestration allow *Acis* to be performed in a space as large as the Koch Theater and, at times, Mozart successfully fills out the very thin orchestral lines. But what is largely missed is the purity, clarity and intimate timbral colors of the original version. When the chorus sings Mozart's arrangement of "Wretched lovers," we hear the Mozart of the Masses and the Requiem, not the haunting Monteverdi-like madrigal with its meandering counterpoint from the original score. Mozart's decision to use the keyed clarinet to replace the recorders or oboes as the obbligato instrument obviates the point of several arias.

90

Mark Morris choreographed a magnificent dance that clearly has been thought through and well-rehearsed. Even some of his attempts to add levity to the choreography were successful: the Pilobolus-like metamorphoses of the dancers in imitation of Polythemus's stride when "ample strides" is sung; or the clever grouping of the dancers into a flock of sheep at the mention of flocks. Yes, there were Morris's obvious "dancing out" lines of text: the waving of hands when a character leaves, or everyone on stage pointing in the same direction when Acis sings, "Where shall I seek the charming fair." But this production never reaches the sophomoric lows of Morris's version of Purcell's "King Arthur," where the famous aria, "Genius of the Cold," was sung from inside a refrigerator.

The staging left something to be desired: abstract backdrops that looked at times like a forest, a snow-covered street, a city skyline or a mobile home. The costumes were simple, sheer fabric that breezed along with the dancers, almost taking on a life of their own. There was nothing in the costumes that approached the brilliance of the Morris-Mizrahi production of Rameau's *Platee*, but nothing has come—and may never come—close to that collaboration.

In contrast to most operas with dancing, the music was subservient to the choreography. Perhaps the dominance of the dancing, which continues without stop from beginning to end, led to some degree of tepidness in the overall performance. The singers were generally stiff and inflexible, and only in the final few arias did they really seem to mesh with the dance troupe and generate a sympathetic warmth. These final moments leading to the requisite happy ending brought to mind the poignant and plaintive production of Purcell's *Dido and Aeneas* with Morris himself as Dido.

The singing never did soar but there is not much soaring in the score itself. Douglas Williams had the most interesting role as the lecherous and gluttonous Polpyphemus. Thomas Cooley started off a little weakly but gained strength as the work progressed. Yulia Van Dooley sang well but seemed overwhelmed by the action going on around her. The same could be said of the chorus-like role of Michael Chybowski as Damon, the shepherd friend, who like Belinda in Purcell's *Dido* tries to respond positively to the lovers' plaints.

Conductor McGegan and his Philharmonic Baroque Orchestra, now in its 34th year, were spot on. Everything was played to perfection, with special praise due to the clarinetists and to the valveless horn players, who are always to be complimented for successful performances on their devilish instruments.

♫ *Emerson String Quartet Plus Martin Fröst Equal a Recital to Remember*

Mostly Mozart Festival 3: Emerson String Quartet (Eugene Drucker and Philip Setzer, violins; Lawrence Dutton, viola; Paul Watkins, cello), Martin Fröst (clarinet), Alice Tully Hall, Lincoln Center, New York, 14.8.2014

Haydn: String Quartet in G minor
Mozart: String Quartet in E-flat major; Clarinet Quintet in A major

Both the Emerson and the Juilliard are great string quartets and popular with New York concertgoers. The Juilliard, of course, has the home-town advantage by carrying the Juilliard School's name. It also has considerable seniority with a history that goes back 30 years further than the Emerson's. But David Finckel, the former cellist for the Emerson, has been a New York fixture since he and his wife, pianist Wu Han, took over artistic responsibility for the Chamber Music Society of Lincoln Center in 2004. His involvement in the New York and New Jersey music scene during this period has been substantial.

Last year saw Finckel's departure from the Emerson and the arrival of Paul Watkins as the quartet's cellist. It has been almost a year since Watkins first appeared with the group at the 2013 Mostly Mozart Festival. At that time, I praised his quick assimilation into the Emerson, no easy task for a newcomer filling the chair of Finckel whose departure was the first change ever to the group's makeup since its inception in 1976. Watkins certainly appeared at ease here, relishing the few times his instrument was scored to carry the prominent musical line.

As shining an example of great chamber music as the Emerson's first half of the concert was, it didn't come close to the second half, dedicated to Mozart's meltingly beautiful Clarinet Quintet. Like much music from Mozart's last years, this is one of his great transcendent works. Very little music can stand next to it and not come out seeming smaller. I grew up on a Benny Goodman recording done live from the 1956 Berkshire Festival, and I felt for many years that there was no reason to listen to any other recording, so perfect did it seem. I was so enamored of this music that for years I took an unusually dissonant series of chords in the first Trio of the Minuet as having been written by Mozart. In point of fact, it was simply a defect in the recording. I realize now, of course, that although the music itself may be perfect, the performances (or recordings) may not be.

This particular interpretation by the Emerson and clarinetist Martin Fröst supersedes any other I can remember hearing over the years. I'm not sure how often Fröst has appeared with the Emerson, but they all seemed exceptionally at ease, playing with a fluid consonance and an empathic accord. Normally I'm fussy about the freedom performers take with a composer's tempo designation, but here their laid-back first movement tempo was nothing if not limpid, the musicians opting for clarity of line above all. There was no issue with contrasts between the playing of a noticeably slower first movement and a second movement which, unusually for Mozart, is designated Larghetto rather than Andante or Adagio. So poignant was the playing that I was little bothered by the continuous tête-à-tête going on in the row in front of me; I shut my eyes and focused intensely on the music, only snapping back at the end of the final movement to take in the most spontaneous and generous applause I have heard in quite some time. If it weren't for the fact that Fröst had to get to his next performance in the adjacent building, I'm sure that an encore would have been appreciated to quell the audience's fervor.

The two works that opened the recital were not in any way played less insightfully. The opus 20, No. 3 of Haydn was one of the composer's first quartets that could not easily take the label "Divertimento," a title given to some earlier quartets. This is music of substance meant to be listened to, not heard just as background music to a royal dinner. It may not have the seriousness and darkness that animate Mozart's works in G minor such as the 40th Symphony, the earlier 25th or the piano and string quintets; but it abounds in modulations, long rests, fermatas and soft endings, elements that would, in Haydn's later quartets and symphonies, add the idiosyncratic surprises that are his signature.

Mozart's E-Flat major is not an easy work to appreciate. As with the other string quartets in this group of six dedicated to Haydn, one hears a struggle going on, unusual for Mozart who, for the most part, had little difficulty composing. These works lack Mozart's easeful forward motion, their confident flow seemingly laden with additional weight. Although Haydn's appreciation of the quartets was effusive—he stated in a letter to Leopold Mozart that his son was the greatest composer he had ever met or had even heard of—Mozart, with his reworking of the pieces, may have felt he could do better. Whether this was simply a need Mozart had to be the best in whatever he did or some repressed paternal issues, I'd best leave to the experts.

The Emerson put all their prowess into every note, giving nothing that was not perfectly executed and much that will be remembered.

♫ Richard Goode Plays a Little Night Music, But Not Mozart
Mostly Mozart Festival 2: Richard Goode (piano), Stanley H. Kaplan Penthouse, Lincoln Center, New York, 31.7.2014

Bach: Preludes and Fugues Nos. 1 and 16 from *The Well-Tempered Clavier*, Book II
Schubert: Sonata in B-flat major

In my last review I bemoaned the lack of intimacy which Richard Goode could not quite effectuate in a hall the size of Avery Fisher. There was no similar problem with his solo performance on Thursday evening in the 230-seat Stanley H. Kaplan Penthouse on the campus of the Juilliard School. While not nearly as small as the venue in the famous Schubertiade painting by Julius Schmid, the Kaplan complemented the Schubert sonata that Goode performed as the main event of the evening. The program was part of the Mostly Mozart Festival's series of concerts at the Kaplan, appropriately entitled "A Little Night Music." The audience sits at tables of six and has a direct view of the performer against the backdrop of an illuminated New York skyline. A complementary glass of wine is offered before the hour-long concert begins at 10:00 PM.

Mr. Goode's recital opened with two preludes and fugues from Bach's *The Well-tempered Clavier*. While I have no quarrel with his decision to play pieces from this work, I could easily have chosen a half dozen more stimulating and exciting preludes and fugues which would have offered a sharper contrast to the massive sonata that followed. Goode, from a generation where every Bach keyboard player was judged by his or her ability to play in the fleet, *détaché* style of Glenn Gould, was surprisingly heavy-handed. In fact, the sole point of similarity between Gould and Goode was their habit of singing and humming as they played, in complete disregard of the audience.

Questionable too was Goode's use of the sustaining pedal. We know, for example, that Bach-specialist Angela Hewitt rarely uses the pedals and, when she does, uses them sparingly. Ironically, her favored instrument, made by Fazioli, has an additional fourth pedal, specially designed to dampen the sound without having an effect on the timbre. Andras Schiff, who in his earlier performances did use pedals, now avoids them completely. Clarity of line is critical for a successful interpretation of these pieces. They were written not only to prove their playability on an instrument that is equally tempered, but didactically as well, particularly in the fugues, to teach the separation of voices inherent in the counterpoint. Merging them through the use of sustaining pedals or lengthening the time for the notes to decay does just the opposite.

Ironically, many of the stylistic quirks that disappointed in Bach were a boon for Schubert as Goode gave a deeply personal reading of the last piano sonata. Employing moderate tempi and dynamics along with all the repeats, Goode forced the listener to either go with his flow or be left behind wondering when these endless reiterations of the primary motifs would end. Although written in the major key of B-flat, there is little of the lightness of a key signature that Schubert used for his String Trios and his upbeat Fifth Symphony. Even the sanguine fourth movement turns dark as it suddenly moves from *p* to *ff* with a series of F-minor chords that switch back just as suddenly to G-flat major. Goode dug into the music and brought out its soul. This was not a performance that Goode tried to make more accessible through technical finesse, crashing chords or dropping repeats. Those stylistic decisions can be left to the Richters, Pollinis and Kissins. Goode played this final sonata well aware that Schubert completed it in September of 1828 and died at the age of 31 in November of the same year.

♪*Mostly Mozart Festival: An Impressive Opening Concert*
Mostly Mozart Festival 1: Richard Goode (piano), Mostly Mozart Festival Orchestra, Louis Langrée (conductor), Avery Fisher Hall, Lincoln Center, New York, 29.7.2014

Mozart: Overture to *Don Giovanni*; Piano Concerto No. 23 in A major; Symphony No. 41 ("Jupiter")

As it inches its way towards the half-century mark, the Mostly Mozart Festival has had its share of ups and downs. Much of the credit for the ups must be given to music director and conductor Louis Langrée. Now in his twelfth season as head of the Festival, he has just signed a contract that extends his stay until at least 2017. He continues to imbue his concerts with an enthusiasm that charms his audience and, most surprisingly, in just the kind of works that confound one's expectations. You might exclaim, "Not another program made up of Mozart's

Greatest Hits," but no. "War horses" they may be, but the reins are tightly held and correctly used to get the most out of these old mares.

If a conductor and orchestra have been playing mostly Mozart together for the past dozen years, the audience should expect to get high-caliber performances. And they were not disappointed with this concert, the formal opening night of the Festival. Technically, this would be the third event in the series: the first, an outdoor performance of a commissioned work by John Luther Adams; and the second, a free concert in Avery Fisher Hall of music by Mozart, Gluck and Berlioz.

The overture to *Don Giovanni* set the tone for the works that followed. As in past seasons, Langrée used a smallish orchestra with modern instruments and never pushed the musicians to produce sounds that would not be considered "Mozartean." The strings played with limited vibrato, the winds and brass held back from overly resounding, and the hall itself was made more intimate by the yearly addition of acoustic pods above the musician's heads. The overture was taken at a moderate pace that vividly brought out the sudden sforzandos and fortes that alternate with the quieter measures. This was a performance made more effective by its restraint than by any emotional release. Langrée understands that the opera that follows has at its core the psychological issue of repression versus letting go.

Richard Goode is one of the few pianists these days who can be considered a specialist in Mozart. He comes to Mozart's music with an unhurried calmness that gives it room to breathe. In the concerto performed here, the piano was less like a solo instrument and more like a member of the orchestra. This resulted in music that was unusually well-balanced. Much of Goode's attention when not on the keyboard was directed to the conductor, as any good instrumentalist's would be. If only this performance had been in a smaller venue such as Alice Tully's Starr Theater or Carnegie's Zankel Hall, the intimacy that was potentially there would have been more clearly felt. Langrée and the winds in particular gave the first movement an almost bucolic ambience that was more than appropriate for a cool summer evening.

The concluding work, Mozart's Symphony 41, stylishly and lovingly performed, displayed the virtuosic talents of the instrumentalists. The orchestra seemed to grow in size as it progressed to its powerful conclusion.

The only decision I question was the choice of tempo. With the second movement Adagio taken more like an Andante, the contrast with a very different third-movement Minuet was lost. The same could not be said of the tempos in the third and fourth movements. The more rigid structure of the third movement gave way to a barely controlled whirlwind, complex in design and Baroque in its use of counterpoint.

It was a promising opening night that hopefully will be replicated as the Festival continues.

♪*Rameau among the Stars*

On Site Opera, New Vintage Baroque Orchestra, Jennifer Peterson (conductor),

Madame Tussauds, New York, 17.6.2014

Rameau: *Pygmalion*

The very existence of an opera company with the name "On Site" says much about the direction in which opera may be headed. With the recent revelation of the staggering amounts that the Metropolitan Opera must pay its orchestra, chorus and staff, it is no wonder opera companies are struggling to balance their budgets. Musical institutions that have survived a century and more despite the vagaries of the economy find themselves without needed government subsidies. What could seem more wasteful to our philistine politicians than money spent on opera attire and sets. Even the more enlightened and supportive European governments are tightening their belts around opera houses.

With a nod to both the financial requirements and opera of the future, On Site's vision seems to be one way of keeping this art form relevant and alive. This small group of singers, dancers and instrumentalists looks to match an opera's theme to its venue. In this case, what better place to "adorn" a performance of *Pygmalion* than a museum of wax figures? It's not the first time this had been done in New York: several years ago, a most successful performance of Haydn's *The Man in the Moon* was staged appropriately at the Hayden Planetarium.

Granted, this opera company wouldn't have a multi-million dollar machine built to stage the action of *The Ring*, or the expense of filling a pool with 1,600 gallons of blood-colored water to symbolize the impurity of Parsifal's temptations. But then again, how many times have the singers at the Met had the opportunity to be on stage with Julia Roberts, Kim Kardashian, Patrick Stewart and Robin Williams, albeit all made of wax?

Unfortunately, any performing troupe runs the risks inherent in being itinerant. You have little control of your venue: for instance, if you decide to stage the production outdoors, you run the risk of thunderstorms. Coincidentally, a contemporary of Rameau reported: "At the fortissimo of the reprise [to the overture to *Pygmalion*] there came a terrific flash of lightning, with thunderclaps. We were all struck simultaneously by the marvelous relation between the storm and the music. Assuredly this relation was not intended by the composer; he did not even suspect it."

During this particular production, it was not rain that interfered with the opera but a noisy air conditioning system, "tuned" very close to the sound level that noise-canceling headphones try to cover when one is on a plane. The resultant hum was a distraction to the soloists as well as a covering-up of the critical basso continuo accompaniment.

But this is glorious music, some of Rameau's best, beginning with the overture, a loosened version of the Lullian overture, played here vibrantly and at the right tempo by the New Vintage Baroque led by Jennifer Peterson. Although not an avid proponent of program music, Rameau uses imaginatively repeated notes in the upper strings to create a sound representing the sculptor Pygmalion's chiseling, and it was brightly reproduced by the orchestra.

I had a few reservations about Marc Molomot's voice. At the beginning, he showed some discomfort, perhaps due to the air conditioning problem, but this role is a tough one, reaching up as it does to the top of the *haute-contre* range. Most lovely are the pathos-filled falling sevenths, used here by Rameau almost as identifying leitmotifs in Pygmalion's arias.

Emalie Savoy handled the scorned Céphise convincingly: anger apparent in her eyes, and her voice properly expressing her rage and jealousy. She fares better in this staging than Rameau's original Céphise: here she wins Pygmalion's love and La Statue's return to her pedestal. I'm not sure why the decision was made to end the opera with the comeuppance of La Statue, but I rarely give credence to the irrational plot lines of French Baroque operas anyway.

The stellar performance of the evening was Camille Zamora's La Statue. To be clearly gifted as a singer is talent enough but to be a skilled mime as well is a rarity. Her gradual transformation from statue to human was riveting. As if she were singing a slow crescendo from pianissimo to fortissimo, her body broke out of her stone shell, not in a straight line but with a real sense of how it might be for a statue to become human, gaining two steps forward but losing one at the same time.

Pygmalion was the first of eight one-act opera-ballets that Rameau wrote late in life, and it's somewhat unbalanced. The plot is heavy with recitatives and arias in the opening scenes while the rest of the work consists of charming but irrelevant instrumental and ballet interludes. The dancers, often slightly out of synch and clearly constrained by the lack of space, had their Mark Morris moments but never seemed up to the instrumental playing. There was little attempt to bridge a connection to the wax figures, but if there had been, I suspect it would have been hard not to end up as sophomoric.

The remaining two performances of *Pygmalion* will move to a different venue but one that is also site-specific: the showroom of a company that manufactures display items including mannequins. In what would be a first attempt to use advanced technology, On Site Opera has partnered with Figaro Systems to allow owners of Google Glass to receive streaming virtual subtitles. This would certainly be a step up from the super-titles here which were weakly projected on the proscenium and which I, by happenstance, became aware of sometime in the third scene.

♫*Spark Missing from Haitink, Kavakos and the New York Phiharmonic*

Leonidas Kavakos (violin), New York Philharmonic Orchestra, Bernard Haitink (conductor), Avery Fisher Hall, Lincoln Center, New York, 8.5.2014

Webern: *Im Sommerwind*
Berg: Concerto for Violin and Orchestra
Beethoven: Symphony No 3, "Eroica"

It wasn't the end of the subscription season for the New York Philharmonic on

Thursday night, but it certainly felt that way. There were a number of empty seats, but part of the problem might have been the fear of having to sit through works by two members of the Second Viennese School of composition, Webern and Berg (the third member being Schoenberg). Could it be possible that serious concert-goers still quake at the mention of their names, composers who flourished 50 to 100 years ago?

Well, there was little to be frightened about. The Webern piece was far from the sparse, bare, overly studied music that made him infamous. Written in 1904 and without an opus number, this orchestral work has a student feel about it. One hears in it the influences of Strauss, whose major tone poems had been written; Mahler, who had already premiered his Symphony No. 5 and was in the process of writing his Sixth; Schoenberg, who had written his *Verklärte Nacht* five years earlier; and Wagner, who died the year that Webern was born.

Derivative as it may be, there is much to enjoy in this imaginative and well-orchestrated piece. Webern was very specific in both his annotation of the score and instrumentation but, sadly, the Philharmonic did not appear to get it. Only the brass section seemed prepared and in unison; otherwise, tempos were slack and the playing was lackadaisical. The opening passages, annotated with the exact same marking as Wagner's *Siegfried Idyll*, "sehr bewegt" (very agitated), was played softly but lacked the required nervousness. This is the kind of music that the NYP does well under Alan Gilbert (who performed it with the orchestra in 2010), but Haitink did not have whatever spark was needed to enliven the performance.

When successfully played, the Berg violin concerto is that rare work that triumphs on the technical level as serial music yet goes beyond any other work of its time in communicating the raw emotions felt by the composer. Expectations were high given the combination of violinist Leonid Lavakos and conductor Bernard Haitink. This was especially true for me, having been disappointed with the Philharmonic's last performance of the Berg with Frank Peter Zimmerman and Alan Gilbert in 2011. Unfortunately, the problem with balance in the 2011 performance became an issue here too. Both Zimmerman and Kavakos failed to dig into the score, and the Philharmonic may have played loudly but lacked the frenetic energy that the score demands. One need only listen to Isabelle Faust with conductor Claudio Abbado to understand what was missing in Kavakos's execution.

Beethoven's symphonies have undergone serious rethinking as to the correct tempo to be used and whether or not to take the repeats. The longer symphonies, such as the Third, could become turgid when played too slowly and moribund if repeats are added to the mix. Beethoven's metronome markings are of little help and, if anything, they complicate the issue. The first movement of the Eroica has a metronome marking of 60, putting it roughly in the category of adagio; yet Beethoven gives the textual tempo as allegro con brio. If we trust the metronome the tempo should be very slow. If we trust Beethoven's descriptive annotation, the conductor would need to double the orchestra's speed. Even more confusing is the fact that there is no consistency from work to work. For example, the allegro con brio first movement of the Fifth Symphony has a metronome speed of 108.

Those who grew up on Toscanini's Beethoven hear the Third as an energetic, rhythmic romp, with every movement, save the Marcia Funebre, allegro or faster. Haitink's disappointing Third took all the repeats in an endlessly slow first movement that never got off the ground. The second movement, seemingly played at a similar tempo as the first, never sounded dirge-like and its middle section *crescendo* never reached the expected emotional heights. Even the Presto final movement didn't catch on fire.

The numbed audience had to wait until the conductor turned around and gestured to them to applaud, and they did, but rather coolly.

♪*Too Tame and Too Well-Behaved: Juilliard415 Plays Corelli*

Juilliard415, Monica Huggett (director), Madison Avenue Presbyterian Church, New York, 25.4.2014

Corelli: Concerto Grosso in D major; Violin Sonata in G minor; Trio Sonata in D minor; Violin Sonata in B-flat major; Trio Sonata in A minor; Violin Sonata in C major; Violin Sonata in F major; Concerto Grosso in F major

There were many fine moments in this, the first of two concerts devoted to the seminal Baroque composer Arcangelo Corelli. The two concerti grossi from the composer's most famous set, the Opus 6, were warmly played. Monica Huggett ceded her role as soloist in the trios and violin sonatas to give her Juilliard students the chance to display their skills.

What was lacking had little to do with the performance itself and, to my mind, a lot to do with the composer. I don't question Corelli's important role in the development of the concerto or his influence on composers such as Geminiani, Locatelli and Tartini. He was revered in his time and his published sets of sonatas, trios and concerti grossi were extraordinarily popular. But contemporary renown is not the best basis on which to judge the quality of a composer's work: Salieri's operas were more highly regarded in their time than Mozart's, while Graupner and Telemann were considered better candidates for a position in Leipzig than Bach.

Great Baroque music is complex, often convoluted, rich in counterpoint, willing to go to the edge of dissonance and free to roam to foreign modulations. At its best it is music that is rhythmically complex, filled with color and written as if were being improvised at the moment. The French word "baroque" means "irregularly shaped," and composers of Corelli's generation and before wrote music that was irregular and misbehaved: Froberger, Schmeltzer, Legranzi, Muffat, Frescobaldi, Biber. Michael Taylor in *The New Grove Italian Baroque Masters* writes that Corelli's music is "predictable, over-simple or even commonplace." He then says that the contrapuntal movements are "admittedly too stiff when they are strict and too haphazard when they are free." Corelli himself is quoted as saying his compositions were written to "show off." For whatever reason, he limited his scores to a range of notes that didn't go above D on the highest string and, so the story goes, refused to play a higher A note as a member of an orchestra conducted by Handel.

Corelli's music is not only limited in range but in color and orchestration as well. Vivaldi might have written one concerto 500 times, but variety of instrumentation was never an issue. Corelli limited his compositions to strings only, but Vivaldi ran the gamut from solo violin concerti to the most imaginative combinations such as the Concerto *con molti stumenti*, RV 558, for two mandolins, two chalumeaux (a predecessor to the modern day clarinet), two theorbos, cello and strings. Corelli's mostly brief movements never seem to go very far from their initial statement. His music may lay well in the hands of the string player, but not well in the ears of this listener.

The playing of the students assigned the solo violin parts improved in technique and confidence from first sonata to last, making me think that the order of performers paralleled a progression in school training and curriculum. Francis Liu and Anne Lester comfortably handled the double stopping as well as cadenzas. Laura Rubenstein, joining in as second violinist to Monica Huggett on one of the trio sonatas, couldn't quite compete with Huggett. Often cellists are not given much attention, but the two here, Caroline Nicolas and Sarah Stone, really had their work to do and it didn't go unnoticed.

Corelli used various incomplete cadences to join movements without pause. If pauses between movements are taken as a chance to turn pages of a score, as was done here, it leaves the audience hanging, waiting for the next movement to resolve the suspension.

The final Concerto Grosso in F major brought the ensemble together again as the bookend to the opening Concerto Grosso, with Monica Huggett joining in as the leading voice of the *concertino*.

One last point. Why bother to include in the program that it is "strictly prohibited" to take photographs or make videos when nothing is done about audience members blatantly raising their cell phones to record the performance?

♫*William Christie Brightens New York's Baroque Music Scene*
Juilliard415, William Christie (musical direction), Benoît Hartoin (musical preparation), Vélez Blanco Patio, Metropolitan Museum, New York, 11.4.2013

Leclair: Ouverture in G major (from Overtures et sonates en trio)
Couperin: *La Sultane* (from MS 129.949, Lyons, Bibliothèque Municipale); *Concert instrumental sous le titre d'Apothéose du Lulli*

Juilliard415, William Christie (conductor/director), Corpus Christie Church, New York, 13.4.2014

Charpentier: Sonate à 8; *Actéon: Pastorale en musique*

The Juilliard415 concert in the Metropolitan Museum's Renaissance Vélez Bianco Patio opened with an *ouverture* by Jean Marie Leclair. This *"ouverture"* is not the overture as we now know it but rather a form of suite which—to make things more confusing—has as its first movement an *ouverture* or, more correctly, an *ouverture à la française*. Created by Lully, it has a rhythmic, stately pacing with double dotting and strongly accented chords. It then goes into a quick fugue, usually on a short theme, that creates a kinetic contrast to the slow repeat that follows. The musicians understood what was needed and played this and the other two movements with charm and grace: adjectives that epitomize Leclair's music.

Francois Couperin's *La Sultane* was probably his only work for a quartet, adding a viol da gamba to the group of three who usually made up his musical ensemble. The viol adds a darker and deeper color to the mix and gives more body to the slow movements. Even the titles of the tempos have a euphonious sound: *gravement, gayment, tendrement, légèrement*. This music was played with flourish and grandeur.

Couperin's *Concert instrumental sous le titre d'Apothéose du Lulli* is one of two Apothéoses that he wrote; the other was for Corelli. After Lully's death, there was an effort made to open France up to the musical styles of other countries, and Couperin's instrumental sets *Les Nations* and *Les Goûts Réunis*, as well as the two Apothéoses, are representative of the attempt at musical accord. Even in this piece for Lully he endeavored to reconcile the two composers, which never would have happened.

What is unusual about this work is the text that accompanies the music. The composer asked that the appropriate lines be read before each of the first nine sections. It really is necessary because this music was meant to be programmatic, music that describes or tells a story. Here there would be no way to determine what he meant to describe from the music alone (as opposed to music that imitates its subject, such as birds, storms, etc.). How would one know for example that the *très vite* of the third movement is meant to be the flight of Mercury to the Elysian Fields? William Christie was the reader, chiming in between movements with a description of the music that would follow: each miniature played with grace and élan.
*****

From William Christie's very first performances and recordings as conductor of his newly-formed Les Arts Florissants, he has made the revival of Charpentier's music his cause. Even the name he chose for his orchestra, Les Arts Florissants, was the title of a Charpentier chamber opera. Rebuilding Charpentier's reputation has been a long struggle for Christie but a successful one, and many early music enthusiasts are now cognizant of the depth and complexity of this composer.

Charpentier himself had a recognition problem during a good part of his life. When Louis XIV made Lully superintendent of music, composers were forbidden to stage musical events without his approval. Even after Lully's death, his followers (who during Rameau's time would be called Lullistes) were still committed to performing only music by Lully and his disciples. Much of Charpentier's music, including *Actéon*, was considered inappropriate, immoral and, the worse damnation of all, "in the Italian style."

Since 1989 Christie has been coming to New York with Les Arts Florissants to present major but little-known works from the Baroque period. His first BAM productions had a tremendous impact on the revitalization of Baroque opera. Here was this obscure music of tremendous depth and complexity, complemented by the use of original instruments and stylized singing and dancing. Although Christie revived many works by major Baroque composers, it is Charpentier to whom he always returns.

Although *Actéon* is labeled a Pastorale with its outdoor settings and hunting scenes, its center is really a tragedy. The high point of the opera occurs when Actéon is changed into a stag and tragedy arrives as he is ironically torn apart by the very hounds that had been searching for him in his human form.

This concert version of Charpentier's chamber opera was enlivened by the expressiveness of the soloists. Kyle Stegall's Actéon was intense and convincing, and he showed another, more dramatic voice than the one I admired in his role as the Evangelist in Bach's *St. John Passion*. Virginie Verrez dazzled in the role of Junon. Raquel González as Aréthuze/Diane had a strong voice, but her performance did not change my earlier opinion that her voice is too operatic for music from the Baroque period.

It is always a special event when Christie comes back to New York. We look forward to his return

♪*Right Music in the Right Place*

Cynthia Roberts (violin), Owen Dalby (violin), Katie Rietman (cello), Simon Martyn-Ellis (Baroque guitar), Clarion Orchestra, Steven Fox (conductor/director), Fabbri House, New York, 12.4.2014

Caldara: *San Elena al Calvario* in G minor
Vivaldi: Concerto Grosso in A minor; "La Primavera," *Le quattro stagioni*; Sinfonia in G major; "L'inverno," *Le quattro stagioni*; Lute Concerto in D; Sinfonia in G

What better venue for an almost-all Vivaldi program than the wood-paneled Italian Renaissance library at the Fabbri House. Unfamiliar music mixed with the familiar, from a rarely heard Antonio Caldara work to "Spring" and "Winter" from Vivaldi's *Le quattro stagioni*.

Caldara, eight years older than Vivaldi, was a prolific composer, more prolific in vocal music, at least, than Vivaldi. Caldara wrote around 100 operas alone (Vivaldi claimed he wrote 94, although we only know of about 50). His vocal music included more than 40 oratorios, 110 masses and hundreds of other forms, mostly sacred in style. Not much is made of a possible connection between Vivaldi and Caldara, but it would be unlikely that they never met. Both men were born in Venice: Caldara left in 1699 when Vivaldi was 22.

San Elena al Cavario is one in a set of twelve sinfonias that Caldara arranged from his own sacred canatas and oratorios, and it is reminiscent of Vivaldi's Concerto in B Minor, "Al Santo Sepolcro." Both works blur the line between concerto and sinfonia, a term often used to describe an overture to an opera. Slightly more complex than an overture, sinfonia are usually from two to four movements. Here, in *San Elena*, all the strings came into play as one by one they joined the fugue in a quiet opening that led to a vigorous second section. It was a perfect introduction to the music that followed.

There was no doubt about the provenance of the group's instruments: the Baroque strings are so much mellower than their modern-day counterparts. The warm acoustics helped: the music seemed to be reflected by the dark wood of the library. This came about as close as one could imagine to hearing the music as it might have originally been performed.

The Concerto Grosso in A minor, scored for two violins, strings and basso continuo, fell into the hands of Johann Sebastian Bach and re-materialized in the form of an organ concerto. Vivaldi might have thought he had written music for two soloists and bass, but Bach saw the soloists as two hands playing an organ with the basso continuo played on the pedalboard. In any case, this performance of Vivaldi's original score excelled, with Cynthia Roberts and Owen Dalby in top form.

If played well, with a small ensemble and a willingness on the part of a conductor to go beyond the hundreds of performances heard piped into elevators and telephones on hold, Vivaldi's *Le quattro stagioni* can still charm the listener. This was the case here. Aided by the library's ambiance, the music came to life: birds, thunderstorms, murmuring streams and cracking ice were all readily conveyed. Owen Dalby was a strong and confident soloist in "Spring," but Cynthia Roberts in "Winter" played close to the edge of what can possibly be done on a violin. It's how one might think the Red Priest would have played it, and would have expected it to be played.

After the intermission, Steven Fox stepped away, handing the leadership to concertmaster Cynthia Roberts. This was not an unusual practice in the Baroque era, and it worked fine with the Sinfonia in G. The same cannot be said of the performance of the Lute Concerto in D. Simon Martyn-Ellis gave a brief history of the lute and the Baroque guitar and opted to play Vivaldi's concerto on the soft-toned guitar. Martyn-Ellis played elegantly, but miscommunication between him and the basso continuo, cellist Katie Rietman, led to an unfortunate imbalance in the outer movements that rendered the guitar inaudible for some of the time.

The closing work on the program brought Steven Fox back to conduct the ensemble, and the concert ended in fine fiddle.

♫*A Diabelli to Join the Greats*
Mitsuko Uchida (pianist), Carnegie Hall, New York, 9.4.2014

Schubert: Piano Sonata in G major
Beethoven: 33 Variations on a Waltz by Diabelli

Over a four-year period in the 1980s, I waited impatiently for the release of another set of Mitsuko Uchida's landmark Mozart sonata recordings. Sure, there were plenty of sets of Mozart's piano music available, from Walter Klien's budget set for VoxBox to Christoph Eschenbach's expensive set from DGG. But Uchida had a way with Mozart that made me understand the appeal of these oft-times slight pieces, and she brought her talents to the Mozart piano concerti, her recording of them reaching the top of anyone's list. She is doing the same now with the Beethoven sonatas, combining a fabulous technique with sharp intellectual acumen.

At Carnegie Hall this week, she was like a sprite who had flown onto the stage, bowing once and seemingly unaware of the audience. In fact, after the intermission she started playing without waiting for a number of people to get to their seats.

Of all the major composers in the classical period, I've always found Schubert to be the one least capable of writing a decent development section in sonata form. Sometimes, when the music is catchy, as it is in the Symphony No. 9 or the C-major Quintet, it doesn't really matter: one is so enthralled with the music that one can suspend critical judgment. The G-major Sonata is not one of those pieces. In the first movement, the development section simply repeats the same theme with minimal variations; I counted some 30 iterations of the opening eleven chords (not as bad as the D-major with 60 iterations of the six-chord opening). Even the best pianists, and that includes Mitsuko Uchida with her ability to bring freshness to the work, cannot overcome the sonata's repetitiveness. Alfred Brendel, who considered this piece to be the very definition of the poetic, gave a quite different rendition, defined by a sensibly speedier performance time, particularly in the first movement which he completed in about twelve minutes, whereas Uchida took about twenty. As a point of reference, Sviatoslav Richter takes 26 minutes.

Ms. Uchida's *Diabelli Variations* was a different experience completely. Here she brought power and poetry to each variation with subtlety and a superb technique. One may have wanted a little more humor in Variation 13 with its out-of-place hiccups, or in Variation 22 with its play on Mozart's "Notte e giorno faticar" from *Don Giovanni*, but this was more than compensated for by her attention to detail. The presto movements flew by, not as a blur but as discrete notes. In Variation 19, marked Presto but really meaning "as fast as you can," Uchida had something going on, whether it was the pedals or her attack, that made me think I had never heard it before. In Variation 24 she turned the *Fughetta* into a devotional and mournful prayer. A variation such as the 28th verges on both dissonance and madness, and Uchida played it as if written not by Beethoven but by Ligeti. As in many of the performances of Bach's *Goldberg Variations*, the final few *Diabelli Variations* are often played without pauses between them. The last few epitomize all that went before. Here there was poignancy, resignation, intellectual fire and a final nod to the simplicity of the original waltz, ending as the work does with the simplest of minuets. At the conclusion there was no drama, none of the usual waiting for her to lift her hands from the keyboard as a signal that the audience could now applaud. For her the performance was over;

for us it will join the other great Diabellis, those of Stephen Kovacevich, Peter Serkin and Vladimir Ashkenazy, lingering in our memories as one fantastic recital.

♫Bach's Youngest Son Composes Works in the Style of his Elder Brothers

Xenia Löffler (oboe), Raphael Alpermann (harpsichord), Akademie für Alte Musik Berlin, Georg Kallweit (concertmaster), Zankel Hall, Carnegie Hall, New York, 8.4.2014

J. S. Bach: Orchestral Suite No. 1 in C major
J. C. Bach: Concerto for Harpsichord, Strings and Basso continuo in F minor
C. P. E. Bach: String Symphony No. 5 in B minor
Concerto for Oboe, Strings and Basso continuo in E-flat major
J. C. Bach: Symphony in G minor

The Akademie für Alte Musik Berlin has done some sharp thinking in the creation of programs for their American tour. They must have realized that concerts offering standard Baroque repertory can become boring for both musicians and audiences, and selected a number of works that are seldom heard. They also alternated programs from city to city: "Italy versus Germany" (music of Handel, Vivaldi, Telemann, etc.) in Denver; "Bach Family" in Washington; and "Italy versus Germany" in Boston. The enthusiasm and freshness expressed by the musicians may have been enhanced by a few days break from these works before the performance in New York. Whether we got the better program, I'm not sure, but I would hazard a guess that we did.

The one familiar work on this program was J. S. Bach's first orchestral suite. The smaller size of the instrumental group allowed for a particularly clear window on the two oboes and bassoon. Often the bassoon is treated simply as the supporter of the harmonic line and even when listed as a member of the *concertino* group it often takes a secondary role. Here, though, the bassoonist, Christian Beuse, stood his ground, giving a virtuosic performance with the two oboes the quieter partners of the trio of soloists.

The other works on the program are not often performed, although in 2014, C. P. E. Bach's tercentenary, much of his music has become available live or recorded. The style of the two Johann Christian Bach works is atypical of the considerable output of the youngest of Bach's sons. His music in general is colorful, *galante* and looks more toward Mozart and the future than backward to his elder brothers, Wilhelm Friedemann and C. P. E. So close is the F-minor Concerto to W. F. Bach's signature concerti, filled as they are with dramatic, tortured phrases and sudden changes in mood and dynamics, that there are still questions as to whether this concerto was in fact written by W. F. Bach and not Johann Christian.

Harpsichordist Rafael Alpermann was a wonder at the keyboard in the Concerto in F minor. The finale, a dizzying Prestissimo, was deftly handled. Only a more potent harpsichord might have added to the concerto's blazing spirit.

Both of the J. C. Bach compositions here are Sturm und Drang works, the kind of music that C. P. E. Bach wrote well before and after this brief period on the road from pre-classical angst to the music of Haydn and Mozart. Written in 1770, Op. 6, No. 6 is one of the rare works Johann Christian scored in the key of G minor. It would be easy to draw a line from J. C. Bach's symphony to Mozart's G-minor symphonies, particularly the earlier "Little G Minor" written only three years after J. C. Bach's. J. C. Bach's catalog shows a mere five pieces in G minor; Mozart wrote fewer than ten works in this key, one of them being the 40th Symphony.

C. P. E. Bach's Oboe Concerto reveals another side of the composer. It is more peaceful than the other works on this program and served as a nice respite before the fiery Symphony in G minor that closed the concert. Xenia Löffler is a real oboe virtuoso but she made no big show of it, adhering instead to the concerto's quiet nature.

The encore, the first movement of Haydn's Symphony No. 3, was brightly performed and provided a fitting end to a thoroughly enjoyable concert, both well-conceived and well-played.

♫Bach's St. John Passion Takes a Place Where It Belongs

Soloists with members of the Yale Schola Cantorum, Juilliard415 and members of the Yale Baroque Ensemble, Masaaki Suzuki (conductor), Alice Tully Hall, Lincoln Center, New York, 4.4.2014

Bach: *St. John Passion*

Appreciation for the Passions of Bach sometimes comes slowly. At first the recitatives seem endless, the chorales simplistic and numerous, the number of arias few and far between; and when the arias do appear they are slow in tempo and dire in mood. Those familiar with Bach's cantatas won't find here the glorious brass fanfares that open many of them, or the upbeat arias with obbligato accompaniment. In fact, neither Passion even requires brass instruments. One can slip a CD of Bach's cantatas in a car's player and drive merrily along, but it would not likely be the same if the Passions were played instead.

The two extant and essentially complete Passions are the *St. John Passion* and the *St. Matthew Passion*, and the music and text of the *St. John* have been considered weaker than the later *St. Matthew*. Although Mendelssohn revived both, the *St. John Passion* never got the attention it deserved until Schumann conducted it 1851, calling it "one of the profound and perfected works of Bach." It is only in the last 50 years or so that the *St. John* has been judged on its own merits, and it now even has proponents who consider it better than its younger sibling. John Eliot Gardiner in his exhaustive yet eminently readable *Bach: Music in the Castle of Heaven* devotes about 50 pages to the *St. John* but only 36 to the *St. Matthew*. Gardner states that the *St. John* "packs a more powerful dramatic punch than any Passion setting before or since."

There is in the *St. John Passion* a sense of soul-searching inwardness reminiscent of Bach's earliest cantatas, and one could convey the ambiance of the *St. John* by just reading their titles alone. These early cantatas express a deeply religious, tortured, almost morbid fervor felt so strongly in *St. John*: "Out of the Depths, I Call Lord to Thee"; "Christ Lay in the Bonds of Death"; "I Have Much Affliction"; and "Weeping, Wailing, Worrying and Fearing." The famous *St. John*'s opening chorus which comes out of nowhere, *de profundis* as it were, with shouts of "Herr, unser Herrscher," has a power that even for Bach is rare. Few other opening works (overtures if you will) convey so much of the drama to come. The overture to Mozart's *Don Giovanni* comes to mind but little else.

Masaaki Suzuki has always had a way with the *St. John Passion*, having recorded it for CD and DVD several times. Viewing a performance of this Passion done over fifteen years ago, I could barely discern any changes in his approach to the work here. Even the way the instrumentalists and chorus came and went onstage was similar. This might be considered unusual: many conductors are never satisfied, always striving for ways to get closer to the music. But Suzuki in fact has this work down cold and so close to perfection that any changes would likely harm it. The only major differences between the two performances was Suzuki's use of an alto instead of a countertenor and some changes in instruments used for the basso continuo.

In both Passions the key to a successful performance is the Evangelist. Kyle Stegall's reading of the Gospel came close to that of Ian Bostridge, under whom he, not surprisingly, studied. The sweetness of his voice was a pleasure to listen to and at times almost made the musical parts seem secondary to the text. He did a fine job of the word-coloring techniques that Bach used so frequently. For example, in the recitative "Da verleugnete Petrus" there is the text "wept most bitterly." Bach stretches the word *weinete* almost two measures to simulate the sounds of weeping.

The other major singers came out from the chorus when needed. Sara Couden gave appropriately mournful readings of the alto arias. Molly Netter's voice was crisp and clear, white yet warm. She gave an excellent rendition of the poignant aria "Zerfleisse, meine Herzen," the equivalent of the even more touching "Erbaume Nicht" from the *St. Matthew Passion*. On the other end of the vocal spectrum Edmund Milly gave an authoritative, confident voice to Jesus as did Andrew Padgett in the role of Pilate.

The chorus and orchestra were a little muddy at the start but quickly pulled themselves together as the words and music were carried along by the devoted conducting of one of the world's great Bach specialists, Masaaki Suzuki.

♫*Rameau's Platée: No Frogs in Throat Here*
Soloists, chorus and orchestra of Les Arts Florissants, Paul Agnew (conductor), Alice Tully Hall, Lincoln Center, New York, 2.4.2014

Rameau: *Platée*
Concert Version

I've been lucky enough to attend two major productions of *Platée*: the New York City Opera's revival in 2004 and the Opéra Garnier's revival in 2006. Whether due to lack of funding or other causes, this performance from Les Arts Florissants was a stripped-down concert version of Robert Carsen's well-reviewed revival at the Theater an der Wien and the Opéra Comique, and it suffered from that.

Carsen's staging in Europe placed the cast in the middle of a high-fashion show, with Jupiter dressed and made up to look like designer Karl Lagerfeld, Juno in Coco Chanel and La Folie costumed à la Lady Gaga. It's an interesting conceit, putting a character like Platée in a place where being out of fashion is sufficient reason for him to be made into a pariah. However, the fashion-show concept wasn't made clear in this concert version, and information on the setting would have helped place the opera in context and clarified some of the costuming and connections.

Losing the staging also meant losing the dancing, which left the audience without anything of visual interest for long stretches at a time. Mark Morris's choreography at the City Opera and Laura Scozzi's in the Paris production tightened and filled the opera's many non-vocal interludes which, as well played as they were here, were ultimately just too static.

To compare these three productions of *Platée* is to realize that Rameau provided for an extremely wide range of interpretations. The libretto is so silly that there could hardly be anything done to it that would make it sillier. The 2006 Paris production with Paul Agnew as Platée is set in a theater with rows of balcony seats facing the audience as if the actors on stage were watching us. With the cast running up and down the staircases and sitting expressionless, this could have effectively been choreographed by Pina Bausch. In contrast, the 2004 NYCO production opens in a gay bar with partly clad men soliciting each other, and it sets the characters in a cartoon-like swamp. Outrageous costuming by Isaac Mizrahi added to the success of this production.

So what were we left with? I was telling someone this morning about the performance and was asked who the group was. Upon being told "Les Arts Florissants," her response was, "Oh, then it had to be good." Of course she is right. Every production I've ever seen by this group rises far above those of any other historical performance ensemble. Season after season through "Le Jardin des Voix," William Christie has been able to consistently train many of the vocalists who so enthusiastically sing and act in his musical world. One may question some decisions as to tempo and dynamics, but there is no question about the musicians' capabilities. They make no attention-grabbing show of their skills, and at this performance many players smiled and laughed, charmed as much by the characters as was the audience. There are no questions about technique. Christie has so successfully mastered Baroque practice that it would be hard to find the harshest critic of early music performance who would feel the need to question him on issues such as vibrato (absolutely none), instruments (all original) and scores (nothing cut, all da capos taken).

The highlight of *Platée* has always been La Folie's "Formons les plus brilliants concert." While not quite as outrageous as Jennifer Smith's La Folie in the 2004 production where, dressed in sheets of music, she hands them out to the orchestra, Simone Kermes gave her own maniacal reading: improvising the melismas and adding a last note two octaves above the actual aria's final notes. If she has been called "Lady Gaga of classical music" by the press, she has found here in *Platée* the right vehicle and costume.

There was no attempt to present Platée her/himself as a frog as is done in the other productions. In truth, Marcel Beekman's Platée came closer to the historical portrait we have of the actor Jelyotte who played Platée in the premier in 1745. Beekman, who at times fell into the role of the Australian cross-dresser/comedian Dame Edna, acted and sang a little too broadly. He never conveyed the expressive sensitivity of Paul Agnew, whose anger at being hoodwinked was both repulsive and touching. Jean-Paul Fouchécourt, from the 2004 NYCO production, is the voice I hear when I think of Platée.

We should be happy for whatever Rameau and William Christie we are offered, but I hope that in the future Les Arts Florissants will be able to stage this work in New York in the way it deserves.

♫*Paul Lewis: Brains and Brawn Synthesized*
Paul Lewis (piano), Zankel Hall, Carnegie Hall, New York, 26.3.2014

Bach: Chorale Prelude on "Nun komm, der Heide Heiland" (arr. Busoni)
Beethoven: Piano Sonata No. 13 in E-flat major, "quasi una fantasia"
Bach: Chorale Prelude on "Ich ruf' zu dir, Herr Jesu Christ" (arr. Busoni)
Beethoven: Piano Sonata No. 14 in C-sharp minor, "Moonlight"
Liszt: *Schlaflos, Frage und Antwort*; *Unstern! Sinistre, disastro*; *R. W.—Venezia*
Mussorgsky: *Pictures at an Exhibition*

Encore:
Liszt: Piano Piece in F-sharp major No. 4, from *Fünf kleine Klavierstücke*

Paul Lewis has never conveyed in person or in photographs the impression of being one of the super-physical pianists of our day: a Kissin, a Hamelin or a Berezovsky. In fact, he has presented the opposite image, one of *weltschmerzian* seriousness, a Schubert maybe but not a Beethoven. This is true even though it was Lewis's highly praised recordings of Beethoven sonatas that brought him into the forefront of world-class pianists. His sensitivity, coolness and reserve distinguished him from the legions of Beethoven sonata exponents, the Schnabels, Gilels and Richters. Lewis himself wrote in 2008: "Much is made of the physical force of Beethoven's music. While it is true that there is often a strong physicality about it, it would be wrong to assume that his extremes are predominantly physically violent…. A *sforzando* shouldn't always hit you between the eyes, a fortissimo shouldn't always punch below the belt."

Maybe not below the belt, but there were some heavy punches thrown here. Take, for example, the Presto agitato from Beethoven's "Moonlight Sonata." In Lewis's CD from 2007, there are instances where the second chord that completes the opening phrase can barely be heard. Here there was no mistaking that Beethoven marked these *sforzando.*

Muscularity vying with sensitivity could be a heading for this program. The sensitive side was reflected (as he symbolically genuflected) in the introductory Bach pieces played without pause before each Beethoven sonata. The chorale preludes, "Nun Komm, der Heide Heiland" and "Ich ruf' zu dir, Herr Jesu Christ," in transcriptions for piano by Busoni, set the tone for what followed. Lewis made a strong musical connection in choosing the Chorale Prelude BWV659 with a phrase that repeats a few measures into Beethoven's Sonata No. 13.

All the works on the program were in dialectical opposition: loud and soft, sacred and profane, leading to a synthesis of both. That synthesis came at the end of Mussorgsky's *Pictures at an Exhibition:* its conclusion at "The Great Gate of Kiev" succeeded in an imaginative way to end this recital at the doors of heaven.

The second half of the program also opened with short pieces, this time by Liszt. Not much can be said about these three fragments which seemed no more than pages from a notebook. Coming in at about ten minutes, all three sketches were mercifully brief: the kind of piano music that Liszt churned out in volumes. Only in the final section of the *R.W.-Venezia* does there seem to be a reason for its inclusion, harkening back to Beethoven's da-da-da dum.

If there was any question as to Lewis's ability to confidently negotiate works requiring tremendous strength, it was put to rest in his performance of Mussourgsky's *Pictures at an Exhibition.* Although Lewis's interpretation of this manic-depressive masterpiece may not have had that in-the-blood closeness to Mussourgsky as it had in the hands of a Pletnev, Richter or Kissin, it did have Lewis's own stamp upon it. This uniqueness clearly came from a careful reading of the score: every section had its own personality. Even the rondo-like returns to the "Promenade" seemed less like iterations than the introduction of totally new themes. Lewis understood just what is gnomic about the "Gnomus" movement, filling it with gnarly, spidery turns and twists. At times Lewis nearly pushed away his piano bench as if he needed more room to come down on the keyboard. This changed the character of a sketch such as "Bydlo," often played as a plodding and lumbering walk, into an earth-shattering trek.

The manic sections of this work did not escape Lewis either. The flittering "Tuileries" and scampering "Marketplace of Limoges" and especially the "Ballet of the Unhatched Chicks" all caught the over-the-top comic spirit of the score.

The only cavil I had was with the "Catacombs," an awfully difficult piece to pull off successfully. The freedom given the performer by the many fermatas in the score allows for a range of interpretations that can run as fast as a minute or as slow as five. Played too slowly, as Lewis did here, it becomes just a series of chords; too fast and it loses its morbid character.

This was just a minor blip, if a blip at all, in an otherwise intelligently conceived and totally convincing recital.

♫Uncommon Handel: Surprisingly Rewarding

Handelfest 2014: Soloists and Chorus of the American Classical Orchestra, Thomas Crawford (director), Alice Tully Hall, Lincoln Center, New York, 19.3.2014

Handel: *Concerto a due cori* in B-flat major; *Concerto a due cori* in F major; *Jubilate*; *Alceste*

Several years ago I reviewed a concert by a Baroque orchestra whose conductor was due back the following day to his military post. He had had only a few days leave to prepare and rehearse for the concert, which included a challenging concerto by Johann Fasch for two horns. It was not a pleasant experience. This wasn't simply a problem with intonation but with the soloists not being able to get the right notes from their horns. Perhaps with more rehearsal time both soloists and orchestra would have had a better chance of succeeding.

And perhaps not. We've come to accept that if a horn player is to be authentic he must use a natural horn. The issue of what the "correct" choices are to achieve perfect intonation in Baroque brass is a complicated, convoluted and controversial one. Many factors are involved: venting, bore size, use of hand stopping and embouchure to name just a few. Ultimately the question becomes which is more important, correct intonation or authenticity. As a critical listener, I find myself focusing nervously on the brass players, fearing the next note will go off to another octave to the detriment of the musical experience. At this concert the four players used natural horns with B-flat crooks and a combination of embouchure and hand-stopping to produce the required notes. Given the fact that there were intonation problems from one or more horn players (not an unusual occurrence), I would have preferred the so called "Baroque" horn which is vented but not valved. The end result of more than fifty years of research into the issue of historical performance shouldn't be to leave us sitting on the edge of our seats.

These two appealing concerti each consist of identical but opposing choirs: HWV332 for two oboes and bassoons and HWV333 for two horns, two oboes and bassoons. Borrowing from one's own earlier works or from works by other composers was not at all unusual in the 18th century, and both concerti do borrow from other sources. The most obvious and familiar is a verbatim transcription in the B-flat piece of "And the glory of the Lord" from the *Messiah*; the third movement of the F-major concerto emulates the aria *"Orribile lo scempio"* from Vivaldi's *Tito Manlio.*

The *Jubilate*, a compilation of verses from the Psalms, was Handel's first foray into music with an English text. Even in this early work he was borrowing his own music, some of it from his time in Rome. The natural trumpets included here were played skillfully and without intonation difficulties by John Thiessen and Carl Albach. The soloists, who are members of the choir, sang with varying quality, with baritone Timothy McDevitt standing out from the others.

The main course for the evening came after the intermission with an unexpectedly fine semi-staged (costumes and dancing but no stage settings) production of Handel's *Alceste,* incidental music for a lost play by Tobias Smollett. There is much beautiful music here and much beautiful singing as well. In fact, everyone contributed to its success. The orchestra members lined up along the back stage were balanced and attuned to the singers and dancers upstage. The choreography, limited somewhat by the lack of space, was traditional ballet (as opposed to performance in the style of Baroque dancing). Lindsey Jones and Weaver Rhodes animated the incidental sections, with Ms. Jones a stunning and ethereal Alceste. Marguerite Krull was superb as the goddess Calliope, handling the long melismas with grace and ease. Baritone Robert Balonek's one aria, "Ye fleeting shades, I come," was persuasive, polished and robust. The only weakness here was the demanding role given to tenor Randall Bills who never seemed totally comfortable in the upper ranges and was unsteady in some of the long vocal lines.

Clearly, everyone put much time and effort into making this production something substantial, and it was acknowledged by an appreciative and enthusiastic audience.

♪A Varied Program of Baroque Music Handled Royally by Tafelmusik

Tafelmusik Baroque Orchestra, Zankel Hall, Carnegie Hall, New York, 17.3.2014

Veracini: Overture in G minor
Delalande: "La grande piece royale": "Suite de symphonies pour le souper du roi," No. 7
Bach: Concerto for Two Violins, Strings and Continuo in D minor
Handel: Concerto Grosso in B-flat major
Vivaldi: Concerto in G minor for Two Cellos, Strings and Continuo
Marais: Suite from *Alcyone*

A criticism leveled these days at some Baroque groups is their penchant for showing off: they seem to equate being historically informed with being histrionically informed. Aside from taking inordinately fast tempi, these groups often demonstrate to their disadvantage an ability to dance as they play, perhaps feeling that more than just playing the notes is required to keep the audience's attention. No one really knew until Beethoven's time and the invention of the metronome how fast an allegro was or how slow an adagio should be. But if the music is of interest, it doesn't need extra adrenaline to make it convincing.

Tafelmusik has been performing Baroque music for over 30 years, and has never felt the need for excess. They have concentrated on perfecting their broad repertory not by training musicians to be virtuosi but, more importantly, by playing as members of one body producing one sound. Refined, gracious and elegant are words that come to mind.

The works here were intelligently chosen from a cross section of Baroque music; none except the Bach double violin concerto is very well known. Each of the main styles of Baroque music was represented: Veracini and Vivaldi from Italy, Delalande and Marais from France, Bach from Germany and Handel from Germany through Italy to England.

Veracini's Overture had its first Carnegie Hall performance last year at Zankel by the Venice Baroque Orchestra. At the time that I reviewed the concert I was not familiar with Veracini's name, and I was pleasantly surprised by the quality of his work. If this piece weren't entitled "Overture," it could easily be taken as a concerto for two oboes with its traditional alternations between orchestral sections and solo oboe sections. This is even more prominent in the Largo. The final Allegro had tremendous energy as it rushed with a strong rhythmic drive to the conclusion. The oboists, John Abberger and Marco Cera, drew sweet and mellow sounds from their Baroque instruments, so different from the sharp metallic sound of the modern oboe. It makes it easy to understand why the oboe was a favorite of Louis XIV (and thus all the oboe music written for him).

The oboes, as well as the bassoon, are again prominent in the Delalande suite from "Music for the King's Supper." It's only recently that an interest in the French Baroque has reawakened. This music had been thought of as simply so much pomp: frilly and decadent, written to please the greatest dandy of them all, Louis XIV. Attitudes have changed, particularly in the reevaluation of the operas of Lully.

It is apt that Tafelmusik chose Delalande's piece which was written specifically to be played while royalty sat down at the table to eat. Telemann wrote a famous set of instrumental works which he could have named Tafelmusik, but he decided that "Musique de Tables" was more appropriate. Whatever the title, the performance here was lovely, enhanced by the excellent oboes and bassoon. The music would whet anyone's appetite for more…music.

Bach's double violin concerto is always interesting to see in a live performance. It is difficult when only hearing the work to discern which violin at any given moment has taken center stage. What was noticeable in this performance was the imbalance at times between Jeanne Lamon's softer manner responding to the phrases of the more aggressive playing by Aisslinn Nosky. Perhaps this was planned as a way to distinguish the two instruments, but in any case watching both violins toss themes back and forth is one of the great pleasures of this concerto.

There are many great concerti in Handel's two sets of six concerti, the Op. 3 and 6. The one performed here, Op. 3, No. 2, is noted for its lyrical Largo highlighted by its solo oboe. It also has a grand and complex third movement Allegro with fugal voices interrupted by unexpected fortes.

The Vivaldi concerto for two celli opens in an atypical fashion: the two solo celli play the concertino role first with the orchestral ripieno not appearing for ten measures, reversing the usual orchestra first, soloist(s) second template. Again, as mentioned above in regard to the Bach double violin concerto, there was an imbalance between the two instrumental soloists, with Christina Mahler considerably more aggressive than her counterpart Allen Whear. Nonetheless, this was exciting Vivaldi and amazing cello work from both.

The Suite from Marais's *Alcyone* opens with the classic Lullian *Ouverture*: a short beginning of double dotted notes, a middle section based on a brief fugal theme and a repetition of the opening section. The selection of dances omitted the famous tempest scene which requires tympani, but did include a chaconne with its imaginative variations on a repeated bass line, ending with a repeat of the opening theme. The closing *Tambourins* had to settle not unpleasantly for Allen Whear striking his cello as a substitute for a tambourine. A movement from Handel's Op. 6 Concerto Grossi was the encore of this thoroughly pleasing concert.

♫ A Fitting Celebration for C. P. E. Bach on his 300th Anniversary

Scholar and Lunatic or the Roots of Romanticism: The Four Nations Ensemble (Tatiana Chulochnikova, violin; Antonio Campillo, flute; Loretta O'Sullivan, cello; Joshua Lee, viola da gamba; Andrew Appel, harpsichord and clavichord), Salon/Sanctuary Concert Series, Abigail Adams Smith Auditorium, New York, 8.3.2014

J. S. Bach: Prelude in C major, WTC Book 1
Mozart: Fantasia in D minor
C. P. E. Bach: Rondo in A minor; Sonata for Flute & Continuo in E minor; Sonata for Viola da gamba & Continuo in C major
Telemann: *Deuxiéme Suite*
C. P. E. Bach: Sonata II for Flute, Violin and Continuo in B flat

What better day to program a concert around the life and works of C. P. E. Bach than on the 300th anniversary of his birth? He was the second surviving and most successful son of the seven children born to Bach's first wife and second cousin, Maria Barbara. If we believe that genius can be inherited then C. P. E. and his older brother, Wilhelm Friedemann, received their talents from both parents. The brothers started off with similar potential, excelling in school and at the universities they attended, but W. F. squandered his capabilities on gambling and alcohol. His sometimes wild music has flashes of brilliance as well as a poignant melancholy that at times borders on the bathetic.

This evening's Salon/Sanctuary concert was more of an event than a simple recital, opening as it did with a conversation between keyboardist Andrew Appel and musicologist James Johnson on a variety of topics centering on C. P. E. Bach and his times. C. P. E.'s life and works are filled with contradictions. For a time he was highly regarded as a composer of keyboard pieces, "Sonatas for Connoisseurs and Amateurs," and the Bach of renown, not his father. C. P. E. had a strong need to be recognized as an intellectual and moved in those circles in Berlin and Hamburg. His book on the art of playing the keyboard is still referred to as a major source of keyboard technique.

His instrument of choice was the clavichord, and he wrote volumes of very personal and introspective music for it. Appel demonstrated what a delicate sound it produces, so soft that even from the front rows it was barely audible. As intimate as the venue was, there was really no way to bring all the audience in close enough to appreciate its sound. The familiar first prelude from J. S. Bach's *The Well-Tempered Clavier* required the listener's memory to fill in unheard gaps. The more dynamic pieces that followed hopefully reached some of the audience. If not, we have at least learned to be sure to get a seat in the first rows at the few clavichord recitals we may attend.

The Rondo Wq56/5 from "Sonatas for Connoisseurs and Amateurs" is as good an example as any of C. P. E.'s style. This is not a piece to approach lightly, and not a piece that one might want to improve with one's own ornaments as is done with works by his father. It takes a certain sensibility to craft the right phrasing, timing and touch and to follow the detailed markings that make it very clear what C. P .E. wants. Andrew Appel had the right attitude and the technical finesse to tease the keys to produce the desired effect (or more precisely the correct *Affekt*).

The resources currently committed to promoting his music, such as *Carl Philipp Emanuel Bach: The Complete Works*, mean much has been made available to "connoisseurs and amateurs" alike. The more one hears this music the more one realizes that without C. P. E., Mozart would still have written brilliant scores but not the music that we know today. Every technique imaginable used by Mozart in his piano concerti can be found in one or more of 50+ concerti that C. P. E. wrote for keyboard. Not to diminish the genius of Mozart's Fantasia, K. 397, but its uniqueness doesn't seem as unique having heard similar improvisatory openings, long fermatas, rapid changes in tempo, unexpected key modulations and sudden dynamic outbursts in C. P. E.'s Rondos and Fantasias.

Considering that C. P. E. was flautist Frederick the Great's personal accompanist for thirty years, there are only a small number of authenticated flute concerti and sonatas. Although these works can be difficult and demanding, especially at fast tempi, they were certainly within the professional level of Frederick the Great (as we know by the works he himself composed and the 300 or so concerti written for him by his in-house composer, J. J. Quantz). Frederick found out soon after hiring C. P. E. that this young composer couldn't churn out—or wouldn't—the number of works asked of him. C. P. E.'s flute sonatas in general are written in a more conservative style, so much so that several thought of as having been written by J. S. Bach were probably works by C. P. E.

Antonio Camillio, backed by Loretta O'Sullivan and Andrew Appel on basso continuo, rolled with the rhythmic flow of the Sonata in E minor. This is music that paces itself, music that should not be rushed, and the ensemble quietly let the music carry them to its conclusion. The final Minuetto is a Minuet in name only: the traditional trio section is replaced by two variations on the first theme.

The three Sonatas for viola da gamba show C. P. E. at his finest. Dare I say that they are more interesting, emotionally potent and musically complex than his father's three (BWV1027-1029)? Obviously, he learned from his father what was needed to write music for this expressive instrument, and did that and more. J. S. Bach's sonatas have mostly been performed by cello and piano to good effect, but few versions of C. P. E.'s sonatas that I've heard on modern instruments have captured the expressive quality of original instruments. To be captivated and caught up in this music is to begin to understand the composer's appeal.

As a respite from the strange world of C. P. E. Bach, the ensemble chose the *Deuxième Suite* from Telemann's Paris Quartets. Telemann, a "Renaissance Man," was a chameleon capable of changing musical styles. His overtures, suites of dances and chamber music, whether in the French style as here or in the Italian or Polish style, are delightful and convincing imitations of popular dances of the day. They were played with charm and finesse by the ensemble.

The Sonata for flute, violin and continuo that concluded the concert begins with a typical C. P. E. theme, bouncy and slightly off-balance, and although the flute and fortepiano are able to "sing" these notes, they are not really singable. The composer plays with these motifs by breaking them up, changing the length of the phrases and moving them across measures into syncopations. Another signature technique of C. P. E. is the use of simple repeated notes in the bass line, so simple in fact that a first year piano student could play it with ease. This type of harmonic support is so prevalent in his music one could build an argument that, as the son of the greatest proponent of counterpoint, he overreacted in making sure there was as little counterpoint in his music as possible. The middle movement, sensitively played here, is full of melancholy and yearning and leads to a final movement even more playful than the first one.

A fine evening then that made no compromises in the discussion, demonstrations or program, and a birthday party that would certainly have pleased the composer of the day.

♫Handel's Samson: Larger than Life
Soloists and Chorus of the American Classical Orchestra, Nicholas McGegan (conductor), Alice Tully Hall, Lincoln Center, New York, 4.3.2014

Handel: *Samson*
Concert Version

Music used as a means of personal expression or to pour out one's heart and soul was rarely a reason for composing prior to Beethoven and Schubert. Now and then there was a composer so overcome by emotional turmoil that music was an act of catharsis. Gesualdo, the 16th-century Prince of Venosa who killed his wife and her lover, wrote madrigals of extreme dissonance and darkness that came from his repentant soul. However, before the 19th century most composers wrote music as a commodity for a paying audience (Handel), a praying audience (Bach) or at the request of royalty for whom they worked (Haydn). These composers got up every morning, went to work and then came home and told their wives that they had had a busy day. "What did you do today?" "Oh, I finally finished that B minor Mass." Vivaldi claimed that he could compose a piece of music faster than

116

it could be copied out.

Handel was a shrewd businessman who did what he had to do to earn a living. He struggled with impresarios, prima donnas and theater owners. Arias were added or subtracted to his vocal pieces based upon which singers were available. If he couldn't write operas when in Rome due to a papal ban, he wrote cantatas or oratorios, often with themes more secular than religious. Later on in London, where he started losing money due to competition from other opera companies, he began writing oratorios based mainly on Biblical themes. Oratorios didn't require staging, scenery and expensive Italian vocalists.

Special attention is given to Handel for his *Messiah* and there may be some truth in the stories of inspiration that allowed him to write the whole oratorio in less than a month. But within a week or so after completing *Messiah* he was already back at work writing *Samson*.

This is a big oratorio with over 70 numbers lasting almost 3 1/2 hours when performed in its entirety. Nicholas McGegan, who recorded a complete version of the work at a performance in Göttingen in 2009, here cut some aria da capos and parts or all of some recitatives to bring the performance down to the 3-hour range. The orchestra of over 30 instruments and a 24-member chorus were close to the number Handel used at *Samson*'s premier. Although McGegan's conducting is enthusiastic and committed, he often does not quite get the crisp, bright colors that we've come to expect from Baroque conductors such as William Christie and John Gardner.

It's not that Handel's oratorios are easy for the chorus and soloists, but in general they don't make the demands of his operas. That's not surprising since the availability of English-speaking singers was limited: Handel often used actors who were not capable of singing on the level of the top Italian singers, and certainly weren't comparable to the castrati in his Italian operas. If *Samson* were an opera, the role of Micah, for example, might have been given to the great Italian castrato Sensisino. Here, Virginia Warnken, whose voice I have admired over the years, needed more pep and energy to breathe life into Micah, a character who came across as somewhat dull and uninspired.

Tom Cooley, who is featured in McGegan's recorded performance, was convincing as the conflicted Samson. His voice was somewhat tight for his first few arias, but he loosened up and came into his own in the duet between Samson and Harapha, "Go, baffled coward, go." Andrew Padgett as Harapha gave a fine performance and excelled in the aria, "Honour and arms scorn such a foe."

The members of the chorus who came forward as minor characters in the oratorio often sounded better than the principals. Sarah Brailey as the Philistine Woman was certainly a match to the excellent Megan Chartland's Dalila in the lovely echoing duet, "My faith and truth, O Samson, prove."

Both the chorus and orchestra were well-balanced with little overpowering of the soloists. A more prominent sound from the brass, when called for, would have added bite to the overall orchestral coloring.

♪*Vienna State Opera's Salomé: Strauss is in Their Blood*
Soloists of the Vienna State Opera, Vienna Philharmonic Orchestra, Andris Nelsons (conductor), Carnegie Hall, New York, 1.3.2014

Richard Strauss: *Salomé*
Concert Version

Here's a little-known fact that can vie with the most obscure statistic given by any sports announcer: this staging of *Salomé* was the 3000th performance of a Strauss opera by the Vienna State Opera. Perhaps it comes as no surprise then that *Salomé* was far and away the best showing to date by the Vienna Philharmonic—the orchestra of the Vienna State Opera—at Carnegie Hall's "Vienna: City of Dreams" festival. After a somewhat lackluster series of concerts the VPO returned on Saturday night fired up and with a different conductor: Andris Nelsons, the new director of the Boston Symphony.

The reputation preceding the VPO's appearances here has been that of a great orchestra which sometimes is not so great. *Gramophone* rated it the third best orchestra in the world, right behind the Berlin Philharmonic and the Royal Concertgebouw, yet added this caveat: "It must be admitted that the Vienna Philharmonic, for all its deserved fame, does not always sound like the best orchestra in the world. It plays too many concerts, for one thing…they can even sound brutal, like a second-rate symphony band. Sometimes the playing sounds boring."

We forget that musicians are human, and that it's difficult to avoid the effects of the circadian clock. An orchestra from Europe in New York even a few days before a concert might not be at their best if the concert begins at 8PM and one's body clock says 2AM. I can't speak for the second of the four VPO concerts this week, but there was a definite improvement from the first evening's disappointing reading of Beethoven's Ninth to a satisfying if not superb concert version of *Wozzeck* to a brilliant performance of *Salomé*.

Andris Nelsons turned up the heat on what is already one of the hottest operas ever written. All involved seemed to gather energy from one another, an energy that strengthened as the opera progressed to its inevitable finale. There were some unbalanced moments when the orchestra should have been more careful about overpowering the singers, but that can be excused when a conductor is perhaps not totally familiar with a venue's acoustics or the strengths and weaknesses of the soloists. This happened with some of the male singers, in particular with an otherwise satisfying Tomasz Konieczny as Jochanaan. Less critical attention need be given to these imbalances when surtitles are available as they were here.

This concert performance was enhanced by placing the three main characters together on stage left, which allowed for some limited but meaningful interactions. The previous night's *Wozzeck* employed a similar setup, but there the interaction was minimal, even though several opportunities presented themselves for Matthias Goerne as Wozzeck and Evelyn Herlitzius to face off.

Gerald A. Siegel as Herod was appropriately apoplectic, and Jane Henschel as Herodias, repeating the role she played in a 2012 production, bristled with glee as Salomé got the best of Herod. Gun-Brit Barkim as Salomé was by far the star of the opera, and her amazing performance received a good 10-minute standing ovation (which might have run longer had there been enough space on stage for all the principals to comfortably accept the cheers and bravos). The soprano, who has roots in the Komische Oper Berlin, was anything but comical here. Having that rare voice which must cover a range from low G-flat to B_5, her obsessive cries for Jochanaan's head raised the rafters. Only at the very end did her voice show a ragged edge, but still it was a tremendous feat.

♪Kristian Bezuidenhout: A Convincing Performance Dazzles on Many Levels
Kristian Bezuidenhout (Fortepiano), Zankel Hall, Carnegie Hall, New York, 27.2.2014

C. P. E. Bach: Rondo in C minor
Mozart: Piano Suite in C major; Minuet in D major; Gigue
C. P. E. Bach: Sonata in E minor
Mozart: Rondo in A minor; Prelude and Fugue in C major; Piano Sonata in A major

Encore:
Mozart: Andante Cantabile from Piano Sonata in C major

This was a most engaging program on multiple levels, carefully planned and convincingly executed. It successfully showed the underestimated influence of Carl Philipp Emanuel Bach on the young Mozart and, in Mozart's Prelude and Fugue in C Major, the influence of C. P. E. Bach's father, Johann Sebastian.

C. P. E. Bach was a prolific composer and a highly regarded intellectual who at the time overshadowed his father: during his life, he was the famous Bach. It was not until the 19th century and the rediscovery of J. S. Bach's works that he replaced his son as the Bach of renown.

We are now seeing a re-awakening of interest in this second son of Johann Sebastian. In a project that was started in 1995, Miklós Spányi has accomplished his goal of recording all of C. P. E. Bach's keyboard concerti by 2014, the 300th anniversary of the composer's birth. Spányi still has many years left to complete the recording of all of C. P. E.'s solo keyboard music; he has produced 27 discs so far. Both the Brilliant and Hanssler labels have released large boxed sets of C. P. E. Bach's music as well.

Kristian Bezuidenhout's short speech during the concert mentioned the tercentenary as well as the dearth of interest in this most under-appreciated composer. The choice of instrument upon which to perform his works, an issue that is still problematic, was also addressed. Bezuidenhout's excellent-sounding fortepiano is in some ways a compromise since it is known that the delicate and low-volume clavichord was C. P. E.'s preferred instrument. Dynamically responsive to the touch, it would have been inaudible past the hall's first few rows.

The opening Rondo was a paradigm of C. P. E.'s wrought and mannered style which belied the incipient *galante* style of his contemporaries. Unexpected pauses, sudden dynamic changes, harmonic suspensions and modulations to unrelated keys conspire with long runs up and down the keyboard that end suddenly in silence or a barely audible pianissimo. As if all this weren't radical enough, C. P. E. ends the Rondo with a repetition of all but the final opening note, leaving the piece tonally unresolved. This is music that almost skips the "classical" period and goes right to the emotional heart of the romantic era.

Who knew that Mozart wrote a characteristic suite in imitation of the Baroque era's common set of dance movements: it was a surprise to me. Only a genius like Mozart could have composed such a convincing throwback to the previous century's popular French-influenced style. Unusually, Mozart ended this suite without the traditional gigue, but Bezuidenhout cleverly completed it by going straight into two orphaned Mozart dances, a minuet and a gigue.

Bezuidenhout continued the first half of the concert with a sonata by C. P. E. Bach followed by Mozart's Rondo in A minor, used here to "complete" the Bach sonata. The last movement of the Bach Sonata in E minor ends so quietly that the quick segue into Mozart's Rondo seemed to be a natural conclusion.

The final work on the program, Mozart's A major Sonata K.331, was preceded by a J. S. Bach-infused anachronism: the Prelude and Fugue K.394. Bezuidenhout's deep sensitivity, intelligence and technical skills were present here as in the earlier works.

Bezuidenhout came on stage with his shirt sleeves rolled up as if ready to tackle anything, and he did so with a rare understanding and an ability to reveal the connections between Mozart and C. P. E. Bach, the man whom Mozart himself said was the "father of all of us."

♫ *Vienna Philharmonic Orchestra Begins Extended Stay at Carnegie Hall*

Vienna Philharmonic Orchestra, Franz Welser-Möst (conductor), New York Choral Artists, Joseph Flummerfelt (chorus director), Carnegie Hall, New York, 25.2.2013

Schoenberg: *Friede auf Erden* for Chorus and Instruments ad lib
Beethoven: Symphony No 9 in D minor

This was the opening concert of the "Vienna: City of Dreams" festival at Carnegie Hall, and what better way to begin than with a performance of Beethoven's Ninth Symphony, played by an orchestra intimately connected with the composer. The festival, which focuses on the musical legacy of Vienna, includes seven programs by the Vienna Philharmonic, concert versions of Berg's *Wozzeck* and Strauss's *Salome*, the complete Beethoven violin sonatas performed by Leonidas

Kavakos, Schubert's *Die schöne Müllerin* with Mattias Goerne and Christopher Eschenbach and more. There will also be special events, lectures and films.

The program began with Schoenberg's brief *Freide auf Erden* which has some affinities—and some antipathies—vis-à-vis Beethoven's Ninth. The texts of both works proclaim a victory for peace and love, but Beethoven later in life believed that brotherhood and love for one another were possible, while Schoenberg ultimately rejected his earlier optimism. Twenty or so years after Schoenberg wrote this piece he stated, "When I composed it…this pure harmony among human beings was conceivable." Both of these works make impossible demands on the chorus, but Joseph Flummerfelt and the New York Choral Artists handled the challenges admirably. Their performance of *Friede auf Erden* was carefully balanced and avoided the possibility of going over the top into screeching. The work jumps between tonality and atonality but concludes with a tonal cadence; it was to be Schoenberg's last tonal work.

Perhaps it was my anticipation that led to a sense of disappointment in the performance of the Ninth. As one might expect from the Vienna Philharmonic, it was a traditional reading. Tempi and dynamics were conservative, but even if old-fashioned, a performance doesn't have to be wan and lacking in electricity. One thinks of Toscanini, who still had a foot in the 19th century but drew from the players in his orchestra a fire that at this concert was started too late.

The last movement brought an awakening of both conductor and orchestra. In fact, my complaint here is that the fire spread too quickly and the final chorus verged on being out of control. This over-intensity felt pushed rather than evolving naturally from the previous movements. Except for mezzo Zoryana Kuspler, who had a weaker voice, the soloists seemed to be singing for another conductor and orchestra and were overheated. This is not to say that powerful singing is inappropriate for the Ninth, but coming after the pale performance up to this point, it felt like the vocalists were singing Wagner rather than Beethoven.

♫ *Jordi Savall and Juilliard415 Bring Magic to Music for Shakespeare*

Stage Music in the Plays of William Shakespeare: Juilliard415, Juilliard Actors from Group 45, Jordi Savall (director), Manfredo Kraemar (concert master), Baryshnikov Arts Center, New York, 24.2.2014

Johnson: Music for *The Winter's Tale*; Music for *Macbeth*
Locke: Music for *The Tempest*
Purcell: Music from *The Fairy Queen* (based on *A Midsummer Night's Dream*)

Encore:
Rameau: Final Contredanse from *Les Boréades*

What a magical concert this was, so replete with sumptuous music that the only thing I missed were the words that accompany the gorgeous melody of "Love's sweet passion" from *The Fairie Queen*:

If Love's a Sweet Passion, why does it torment?
If a Bitter, oh tell me whence comes my content?
Since I suffer with pleasure, why should I complain,
Or grieve at my Fate, when I know 'tis in vain?
Yet so pleasing the Pain, so soft is the Dart,
That at once it both wounds me, and tickles my Heart.

The magician here was Jordi Savall, both Oberon and Prospero to the musicians and actors. From the opening orchestral salvo to the hand-clapping encore, everything meshed in a perfect harmony seldom experienced at other such events.

The program featured masques and incidental music from Shakespeare's two most phantasmic plays, *The Tempest* and *A Midsummer Night's Dream*. Before each musical segment, a short introduction was given and an excerpt was performed, which helped one put the music that followed into a more meaningful context. Starting with selections from Robert Johnson's music written to accompany Shakespeare's own productions, the program mesmerized.

Jordi Savall joined in as an instrumentalist only in the opening Johnson pieces, preferring instead to conduct from the podium. Bowing, without a smile, he struck a pose of severity that belied the bucolic, unaffected music he was leading. It wasn't until the encore that one saw the warmth and humanity which, in addition to his musical command, have earned him innumerable awards and carried him to the top of the early music profession.

I've always considered Henry Purcell the Shakespeare of music, only stopped by a premature death from achieving Shakespeare's renown. Early critics and students of Shakespeare argued a nature versus nurture source of his genius: did the playwright's preternatural talents spring full-blown from his head? Or was it the result of immense book reading or a photographic memory? The same question can be asked of Purcell, whose music is rife with melodies that appear and disappear so quickly that one wonders whence the source of this musical stream.

This question of Purcell's genius has been partially answered for me by hearing Matthew Locke's Music for *The Tempest*. The opening Introduction is so close harmonically to the Overture to *Dido and Aeneas* one might think it was the ground for the latter. The middle movement of *The Tempest*, a sarabande, is a haunting lyrical interlude whose shifting harmonies place it far beyond its time and had to have influenced Purcell. The "Curtain Tune" that comes towards the end of the suite must be one of the earliest uses of dynamics to depict a storm: crescendos that are marked "lowder by degrees" and decrescendos as "soft, softer, softest." This piece goes musically beyond even Purcell's winter storm scene from his *King Arthur* into the instrumental world of Rameau.

I would have to give the name of everyone on stage to fairly and adequately praise this production. Savall was lucky to have the eminent violin virtuoso Manfredo Kraemer as concert master. His clean intonation and well-judged articulation were a model for the rest of the players. Trumpeters Timothy Will and Caleb Hudson have to be singled out for their peerless playing, as close to perfection as anything I've heard on the Baroque trumpet, particularly in the "Echo" movement of *A Midsummer Night's Dream*. The recorder players, Lindsay McIntosh and Allen Hamrick, gave a plangent reading of the delightful "Birds' Prelude."

For an encore, Savall led the group in the final *contredanse* from Rameau's *Les Boréades*. For this he asked the audience to clap their hands when the opening theme was played. This would be the first time since elementary school that I was asked to clap out a rhythm. It's good to know that I can still do it.

♪*Fabio Biondi, with a Change of Clothes and Venue, Performs Bach*

Fabio Biondi (violin), Kenneth Weiss (harpsichord), Weill Recital Hall, Carnegie Hall, New York, 20.2.2014

Bach: Violin Sonata in G major; Violin Sonata No. 6 in G major; Violin Sonata No. 4 in C minor; Italian Concerto
Locatelli: Sonata in D minor

Encore:
Bach: Cantabile, ma non poco Adagio from Sonata for Violin and Harpsichord in G major

Weill Recital Hall has always been a most conducive venue for chamber music. (Its original name was just that: Chamber Music Hall). Its small number of seats, under 300, and classic design give it an air of formality not felt in its younger sibling, Zankel Hall. Although, pleasant to be in and home of most of the Baroque Unlimited series concerts, Zankel's modern broadcast studio design at time clashes with the music performed on stage.

Yet even at the more traditional Weill, I was slightly surprised to see the two musicians come out in tuxedos. I knew then that this concert would be a different experience than Fabio Biondi's all-Vivaldi program a week earlier at Zankel. At that concert, Biondi was the strolling violinist, playing music that did not require him to be glued to a score; and when playing movements from the *Four Seasons* made it evident that this was music for which no support was needed. Thankfully, Biondi and his group, Europa Galante, have not fallen into the shake-and-bake style of playing of certain Baroque ensembles whose soloists emphasize critical moments with pelvis grinds not seen since Elvis in his heyday.

It is easy to differentiate Vivaldi's *Gebrauchmusik* (Hindemith's term for music written to be used for mundane purposes) from Bach's religious-based music, where even some secular chamber music bore the SDG initials (For God Alone) next to Bach's signature. Bach knew and admired Vivaldi's works and transcribed a number of Vivaldi concerti into solo keyboard works. Maybe a little more of the spirit of Vivaldi would have added some warmth to the musicians execution.

Both musicians, but Weiss more so, relied on their scores, which gave some rigidity to the pieces played. It could be simply that the many soloists and some conductors who perform without scores have made us come to expect that level of performing acumen all the time.

Biondi certainly knows his stuff and was relaxed as ever: not surprising for someone who has been in front of audiences since he was twelve. He dug into the fast movements with the same dexterity that he has given to all music that he performs. The slow movements and especially the passionate, lyrical Siciliano from the Fourth Sonata were played with much pathos.

I would have loved if Biondi had programmed one of the solo violin sonatas or partitas, given that Weiss had the opportunity to play alone Bach's Italian Concerto: a performance that was particularly convincing in its intelligent use of the harpsichord's second manual to differentiate the "solo" instrument from the "orchestral" instruments. Weiss also had a chance to show his skills in the harpsichord-only third movement of the Sixth Sonata.

Biondi closed the recital with a work of the Italian contemporary of Bach, Pietro Locatelli. As would be expected Biondi was right at home here, bouncing back all the virtuoso techniques thrown at him by his countryman. The encore was an alternative version of the Adagio from the Sixth Sonata which was quite interesting and very different from the original movement played earlier.

♫*A Windy Season of Vivaldi*
Europa Galante, Fabio Biondi (director and violinist), Zankel Hall, Carnegie Hall, New York, 11.2.2014

Vivaldi: Overture to Concerto in G major for Oboe, Bassoon and Continuo; Allegro from Concerto in C major for Oboe and Continuo; Allegro from Concerto for Violin and Orchestra in E major, "La primavera"; Cantabile and Allegro from Concerto in D major for Flute, Strings and Continuo, "Il gardellino"; Allegro from Concerto in E major for Violin, Strings and Continuo, "L'amoroso"; Allegro from Concerto in G minor for Violin and Orchestra, "L'estate"; Largo and Allegro from Concerto in D major for Recorder, Oboe, Violin, Bassoon and Continuo, "La pastorella"; Presto from Concerto in G minor for Violin and Orchestra, "L'estate"; Allegro from Concerto in F major for Violin and Continuo, "L'autunno"; Largo and Allegro from Concerto in G minor for Flute, Strings and Continuo, "La notte"; Concerto in B-flat major for Violin and Continuo, "La caccia"; Allegro from Concerto in F minor for Violin and Orchestra, "L'inverno"; Largo and Allegro from Concerto in F major for Oboe, Recorder and Bassoon, "La tempesta di mare"

Encore:
Telemann: "Der stürmende Aeolus" from *Water Music* Suite in C major, "Hamburger Ebb und Fluth"

Fabio Biondi and Europa Galante are at the top of my list of European original-instrument groups, and the performance here only reconfirmed it for me. Biondi has been a tireless advocate for Vivaldi and other Italian composers of the

Baroque era. In addition to his role as violinist and director of the group, he has also reconstructed many Vivaldi operas. This has been no easy task, and in some cases, where parts of operas were lost, Biondi has substituted arias from other works by Vivaldi or a contemporary. Borrowing music was common in Vivaldi's day, and some of the operas revised by Biondi, such as the underperformed masterpiece *Bajazet*, should really be considered, as was most of this program, a *pasticcio*.

The concert could be described both as a group of pastiches (mix-and-match movements) and as a series of *sinfonias*. Baroque composers were very lax about titles. "Sonatas, suites, symphonies and overtures" were used indiscriminately as titles for different combinations of instruments and different arrangements of the music. Here Biondi put together a series of movements from various Vivaldi concerti. The pieces were grouped together in the standard Vivaldi concerto structure of fast, slow, fast. The opening concerto, for example began with an Allegro from the Concerto for Oboe and Bassoon; continued with its slow movement; and ended with the final Allegro movement from RV449 for oboe.

Adding to the surprises in this unusual program, Biondi included movements from the work that many of us most associate with Vivaldi, *The Four Seasons*. Incorporating movements from this overplayed music in a different context made for a fresh appreciation of this really quite masterful set of concerti. Considering how often this music is played and how frequently it is performed on auto-pilot, one had no sense here that Biondi and his group were playing a work that has become the stuff of elevator music.

The performers' handling of every nuance was clearly thought out and practiced, and the flexibility and sense of ease that each musician displayed made for an unusually satisfying evening. They were able to pinpoint the right moment to improvise or to build to a crescendo or to arpeggiate a chord; and when one needed to hold a fermata a tad longer than usual, or needed to emphasize rapid transitions from alternating high notes to triplets. Biondi's signature cadences, so prominent in his accompaniment of arias, are appealing because they run against the expected, traditional loud final notes. As if to show the audience that he was well aware of this flaunting of tradition, he ended the concert on an exaggerated *ppp*.

All the soloists excelled. Oboist Paolo Grazzi's piquant playing in the opening concerto set the standard for the rest of the concert. Marcello Gatti and his Baroque flute had the audience as well the musicians hypnotized, as if they had been listening to a snake-charmer. This was especially true in the lyrical Cantabile of the famous "Il gardellino" concerto. Subtle variations in the da capo's highly ornamented repeats were sublime. One normally doesn't pay much attention to the basso continuo in a Baroque group, but the double bass score called for rapid playing of this unwieldy and ungainly giant, and it was handled impeccably by Patxi Montero.

Biondi announced the encore with the amusing comment that the audience would not have to listen to another Vivaldi work, and the group

proceeded to give an energetic rendering of the storm movement from Telemann's *Water Music* (*Hamburger Ebb und Fluth*).

♪ *The Complete Brandenburgs on an Off Night*

Freiburg Baroque Orchestra, Gottfried von der Goltz (violin and director), Petra Müllejans (violin and director), Alice Tully Hall, Lincoln Center, New York, 5.2.2014

Bach: Brandenburg Concertos: No. 1 in F major; No. 6 in B-flat major; No. 2 in F major; No. 3 in G major; No. 5 in D major; No. 4 in G major

Recordings have often required a rearrangement of the parts of a complete set. For instance, the six Brandenburgs or the nine Beethoven symphonies are sometimes boxed out of sequence. To avoid splitting a movement midway because of a need to flip the disc, or to fill the recording in the most efficient way, an audio editor might place Beethoven's Third Symphony on one side and the Fifth on the other. But why rearrange a live performance of works that are clearly marked by the composer to be in a specified order.

I asked this question last year of Baroque violinist Elizabeth Wallfisch, who had just led an unordered performance of the Brandenburgs at the Montreal Festival (the concerti were played in a sequence of 2, 5, 4, 1, 6, 3). She answered that it wasn't her decision and she would have done it Bach's way, but she thought the producers might have wanted to open both the concert and its second half with larger works. I would hazard a guess that a similar rationale was used by the Freiburg musicians: wanting to open and close with as many orchestral members as possible on stage as possible. The First Brandenburg requires the most players, and the Fourth, which ended the program, is large enough to include doubled instruments without compromising the composer's intent. This cannot be said of the Sixth Brandenburg which calls for a smaller ensemble and less diverse instrumentation.

The First Brandenburg is the most complex of the set: it's the only Brandenburg with more than three movements and demands much from all the musicians. This is a work that can easily sound cacophonous, and even more so when played on original instruments, as it was here. The rapid changes between the ripieno and concertino sections and the extremely difficult scoring for two natural horns requires a well-seasoned orchestra with virtuosic soloists: exactly what one expects from the Freiburg Baroque. Unfortunately, this performance of the First never quite came together. Their 1990 DVD of the Brandenburgs focused on the soloists, and the horn players in the First never missed a beat, which cannot be said about the horn soloists here. Violinist Gottfried von der Goltz played the violino piccolo in a way that contradicted the description of the instrument in the program notes as a "sweet-toned mini-violin." Whether the problem was with the instrument or the player, the sounds produced were harsh and shrill.

For Bach, the Sixth Brandenburg deserved its place as the grand finale in

the set, and for many it's the greatest of them all, but this performance lacked both depth and dimension. The violas should have sounded rich and resonating, not weak and thin as they did here. The acoustics and the inherently small sound of original instruments were part of the problem.

The Second Brandenburg, scored for violin, recorder, oboe and trumpet solos, succeeds or fails on the playing of the trumpet. So difficult is the trumpet part that I always feel a sense of relief when the concerto ends. In many cases, when performed on the impossibly difficult clarino trumpet, I'm happy if only the highest notes are flubbed. The instrument was so hard to master that Bach's eldest son stopped writing for it: he couldn't find anyone willing to play it. Jaroslav Rouček made a valiant effort to keep within the trumpet's tessitura but wasn't able to rein in the instrument enough to allow the audience to stop focusing on him and give their attention to the music itself.

The second half of the concert was more relaxed: the remaining concerti are free from the technical challenges of the first three. The Third Brandenburg was well performed and lacked only the improvisatory-style second movement often used to replace the bare two chords that Bach provided.

The Fifth Concerto, along with the Fourth that concluded the concert, were played on the level one expects from a group with such a reputation. The famous virtuosic cadenza which concludes the first movement of the Fifth gives the harpsichord its only chance to shine, and the music worked here exactly as intended: the voice of the harpsichord rose as each instrument faded away, taking the stage as soloist for a grand conclusion. In the Fourth Brandenburg, second violinist Petra Müllejans dug into the music with an intensity missing from von der Goltz's vacant posturing. The Fourth ended the cycle with more verve than any of those that preceded it.

The encore, the last movement of Telemann's Concerto in F for two horns, was played with such intensity and energy (as well as perfectly pitched horns) that it made me wonder why the Freiburg Baroque had chosen to tour with the Brandenburgs when it is clear that the ensemble have lost their fire for these works.

♪Not as Simple as 1-2-3: Trios Performed by Juilliard Baroque

Juilliard Baroque, Gonzalo X. Ruiz (oboe), Robert Mealy (violin), Dominic Teresi (bassoon), Jeffrey Grossman (harpsichord), Paul Hall, Juilliard School of Music, Lincoln Center, New York, 23.1.2014

Handel: Trio Sonata in B-flat major
C. P. E. Bach: Sonata for Oboe and Basso continuo in G minor
Telemann: Fantasia for Harpsichord, No. 2 in D minor
Zelenka: Trio Sonata in B-flat major
Telemann: Trio Sonata in G minor from *Essercizi Musici*
J. S. Bach: Sonata for Violin and Basso continuo in G major; Trio Sonata in F major, arr. Ruiz
Juilliard Baroque consists of faculty from the Juilliard's renowned historical

performance department and is one of two ensembles that give public concerts during the school year. The second ensemble is Juilliard415, a student group that varies in size from a few chamber music players to a full-blown orchestra. For the last several semesters the teaching group has opened the public concert season.

Except for one of Telemann's rarely performed fantasias for harpsichord, the program consisted of various examples of the Baroque trio sonata. One would think that a trio is just that: Beethoven's "Archduke" Trio is for piano, violin and cello, and Schubert's string trios are for violin, viola and cello. Baroque trios are not that simple, and the first piece on the program exemplifies the complexity of what later became a standard musical form.

The title of Opus 2, printed in one of Handel's collected editions, is: Sonatas or Trios for Two Violins, Flutes or Hoboys (oboes) with a Thorough Bass for the Harpsichord or Violincello. In later publications Handel had a final say before his sheet music was printed, but in this case his publisher, John Walsh, saw an opportunity to broaden his customer base by transposing keys where needed so as to make the works playable by the broadest combinations of musicians. If a musician purchasing the scores wasn't part of a trio then he could still buy it for personal use: the cover stated that the score could be either for a soloist ("sonata") or for a trio. This is really no more than good public relations and clever advertising, and Handel himself was no slouch in regard to selling his products, whether scores or operas.

Tonight's performance added one other instrument not included on the cover page: the bassoon, used here along with the harpsichord as the "Through Bass" (basso continuo). Handel didn't skimp on the basso continuo's role, which is usually a simple accompaniment, and here included several virtuosic passages for the bassoon, all handled agilely by Dominic Teresi. The "trio" of four were exemplary, the only issue being Robert Mealy's lack of the aggressiveness needed to balance properly with Gonzalo Ruiz's forceful oboe.

C. P. E. Bach's output, although no match for his father's, was voluminous: 80 or so concerti, hundreds of sonatas, mostly for keyboard, and over 20 passions are just part of his legacy. This year is his tercentenary and hopefully a time to revive this underrated composer. When we talk about Sturm und Drang, we forget that all of C. P. E. Bach's music was of this kind. His works invariably are what Robert Mealy so appropriately characterized as "edgy" (on the cutting edge). Even this brief sonata, written in his late teens or early twenties, shows aspects of his *sui generis* musical output: syncopation, unbalanced phrases, a simple harmonic line of repeated notes (in clear contrast to his father's complex harmonic lines) and unusual cadences that are invariably a surprise. The third movement is in an odd form which would appear to be a theme and variations, but the variations have little to do with the opening theme. A final da capo repeat of the opening theme, typical of the theme and variation form, ends this unusual sonata. Ruiz played with conviction, negotiating the sharp curves with apparent ease.

Telemann's set of Fantasias for Keyboard is almost unique in his vast musical output. He was, like Vivaldi, a prolific producer of instrumental and vocal

music, but shied away from works for solo keyboard. One commends Jeffrey Grossman for his dexterous performance and for choosing one of these rarely-played pieces. Yet as a whole, these 36 Fantasias confirm for us, and probably did for Telemann too, that keyboard music was not his cup of tea.

Jan Dismas Zelenka is another off-beat composer most famous these days for his slightly crazy suite entitled *Hipocondrie à 7 Concertanti*. (It was performed last April by Juilliard415.) The trio sonata performed here has elements typical of this eccentric composer: it opens with a melting violin solo repeated by the oboe, then broken up and tossed back and forth between the two instrumentalists. Towards the end of a seemingly ordinary first movement Adagio comes a series of dissonances that throw the work into another realm altogether. The second movement Allegro is complex and technically challenging, handled by all with flair and fervor. The bassoon alone has long and intricate runs that would confound most but was played flawlessly by Dominic Teresi. The largo here is reminiscent of the *Hipochonrie*'s tango-like *Lentement*.

There are only two violin sonatas with basso continuo confirmed to have been written by Bach. The G major BWV1021 opens with another lyrical and effusive Adagio, similar in style to the earlier Adagio from Zelenka's trio. Robert Mealy was in his element here, producing a sound that makes one understand why advocates of historically informed practice feel so strongly about the use of original instruments.

The group of Trio Sonatas were written by Bach as organ exercises for his eldest son, Wilhelm Friedemann. They are demanding works and require the player to be dexterous enough to play an entire bass line using only the pedalboard. There have been many arrangements of these works, most commonly for string trio (violin, viola and cello) but also combinations that include recorders, flutes and even guitars. Gonzalo Ruiz played his own transcription which fell comfortably in his range. This showcase of virtuosity ended a delightful evening that warmed and rewarded an audience courageous enough to have braved the frigid cold outside.

♪*Radamisto: Not Your Ordinary Student Production*

Juilliard Opera and Juilliard415, Julian Wachner (conductor), Peter J. Sharp Theater, Juilliard School of Music, Lincoln Center, New York, 20.11.2013

Handel: *Radamisto*

Handel was a prolific composer of operas: *Radamisto, Riccardo Primo, Rinaldo, Rodelinda, Rodrigo, Roxana,* and that is just the Rs. There are even more As (11). All in all, Handel wrote around 40 operas - not as many as Vivaldi, who claimed to have written 94, but a respectable number to be sure.

According to Handel's early biographer, Charles Burney, *Radamisto* "was more solid, ingenious and full of fire than any drama that [he] had yet produced in this country." It was also the first opera in which Handel included horns which gave the music much more color and pomp. Until the final scene when everything that went before is reversed and those who, moments earlier, were at knifepoint now hold hands in happy reconciliation, there is an unrelenting oppressiveness in this opera that is unusual for Handel. There is no comic relief, no momentary bliss when lovers connect, just the continual death threats that never materialize.

The staging was simple but effective. Chairs were used to break up the space and acted as dividers at times. The lighting cleverly created shadows on a scrim as the singers would periodically "disappear" by facing the wall. No hints were given as to time and location, but the costumes would seem to indicate the action takes place during Roman times. There are few references to what country we are in. Anthony Hicks, in his notes to a recording of this opera, states that the country under siege should be Iberia, while others have situated the events in Armenia.

Tiridate, played here with convincing commitment by Aubrey Allicock, was a ruthless tyrant whose only desire was to conquer, be it a new country or the wife of the leader under siege. Allicock's baritone handled some quite low notes easily, and he had no problems in rising clearly above the orchestral accompaniment. Equally adept as actor and singer, his rock solid performance made him the backbone of this production.

All the other vocalists were strong and got stronger as the plot advanced. The first half of the opera was slow with little in the way of action, while the second half was entirely engrossing. Elizabeth Sutphen as Tigrane started off a little tepidly, but by the second half came into her own. I've commented positively elsewhere about Mary Feminear and Pureum Jo, and both were even stronger in this production. Virginie Verrez established herself early on as the strong-willed Zenobia, wife of Radamisto, in the powerful aria "Son contenta di morire."

Countertenor John Holiday as Radamisto was the surprise of the evening. His rich, natural, unforced voice never sounded false, and the ease with which he expressed all kinds of emotions was wonderful. His performance of the famous "Cara sposa, amato bene" was achingly beautiful as was the similarly paced "Qual nave smarrita." His voice was equally impressive in arias that required dramatic strength such as the show-stopping "Vile! Se mi dai vita" with its long and difficult melissmas.

Julian Wachner and James Darrah made some smart decisions. They were right to use the second edition of *Radamisto* but, more importantly, they were sensible about including or excluding middle sections and da capos. As beautiful as "Qual nave smarrita" is, it comes late in the opera and would have run a good seven or eight minutes if the repeats hadn't been skipped.

The Juilliard415 orchestra members did an exceptional job backing the singers, seldom overpowering them, and the soloists who accompanied some of the arias did so masterfully.

Now that we have lost the New York City Opera as our main source of Baroque opera revivals, we can look forward to the Juilliard Historical Performance and the Opera Studies departments continuing to bring back to life these wonderful but neglected works.

♪ *Carnegie Hall Baroque Series Opens with Arcangelo*

Alina Ibragimova (violin), Katherine Watson (soprano), Nicolay Borchev (baritone), Arcangelo, Jonathan Cohen (conductor and harpsichord), Zankel Hall, Carnegie Hall, New York, 18.11.2013

J. S. Bach: Concerto for Violin and Orchestra in A minor
J. C. Bach: "Mein Freund ist mein" from *Meine Freundin, du bist schön*
Handel: Concerto Grosso in D minor; *Apollo e Dafne*

Not that many years ago New York was considered way behind both in its scheduling of Baroque music concerts and in its ability to support upstart groups. While other major American cities such as Boston and San Francisco had thriving early music groups and concert series, New York's were few and far between. Some NY groups managed to hang on with encouragement and support from European conductors who specialized in early music; the presence of Andrew Parrott helped keep the New York Collegium in operation for almost a decade. This group's spirit has re-materialized under the name of the Clarion Music Society, a name that had been used by an early music group started in the mid-1950s by Newell Jenkens. Under the recent leadership of Stephen Fox it has given some under-appreciated concerts that stand with the best.

Interest here in early music gained momentum around the time that the Historical Music Department in the Juilliard School established. Now in its fifth year, that program has been a source not only of professional-level players and groups but also of concerts and operas. Over the years Juilliard has brought in some of the best HIP conductors in the world, including William Christie, Jordi Savall and Nicholas McGegan. There are at least six new early music groups based in New York that have appeared in the last year or two and consist of graduates from Juilliard.

The Baroque Unlimited Series at Carnegie Hall has scheduled a wide range of early music groups since it began in 2004-2005. This season opened with a new group formed in 2010 by English cellist and conductor Jonathan Cohen. Listening to the opening work on the program, Bach's A-minor Violin Concerto, a work that I've heard at least a dozen times in the past year, I felt a nagging ambivalence. Here was a group of young early music players giving their all but not adding anything new. Has the New York Baroque music scene changed so radically that I'm complaining that there are too many new groups? No, but now that there are so many groups performing here we may need to be a little more critical. We shouldn't just be thankful to have concerts of this music available every day of the week in some theatre or church, but we should raise the bar as we do with any other classical performer or group. Emmanuel Ax, Evgeny Kissin, Maurizio Pollini, Mitsuko Uchida and Andras Schiff all give solo recitals at Carnegie Hall, and one need only listen to them to see why they are special.

I don't yet see yet what Arcangelo has that earns them a visit to Carnegie Hall. Alina Ibragimova was an ardent, accomplished soloist and I have no complaints to make about her talent and abilities; but Rachel Pine's performance of the same work at the Montreal Chamber Music Festival this past spring excelled in every way. The same can be said for Nanae Iwata, a Juilliard Concerto Competition winner, and her performance of the A-minor Concerto in March of 2012. Ms. Iwata took a very personal approach to this concerto, avoiding any showiness, and the result was a cool yet surprisingly satisfying interpretation.

Johann Christoph Bach's "Mein Freund ist mein" (not to be confused with J. S. Bach's duet of the same name from his Cantata 148) is basically a chaconne with vocal accompaniment. Katherine Watson would have more successful had she varied her dynamics. After the first thirty or so iterations monotony set in. She did a much better job with Handel's *Apollo e Daphne* where she definitely had more interesting material in both recitatives and arias. Baritone Nikolay Borchev as Apollo gave a solid dramatic reading in the semi-staged production, only flagging a bit towards the end. The tenth of Handel's twelve Concerti Grossi was played energetically and brightened by the optional oboes that Handel added to some of his concerti in later editions of this opus. Although Handel did not specifically include oboes in this concerto, Cohen chose to do so, which added much color to the score.

The audience's enthusiasm and applause brought the group back to play an encore: the last movement from the Opus 6, No. 10 that they had performed earlier. Whether the group wasn't prepared or was miscued on the upbeat, the oboists (playing on difficult keyless original or recreations of original instruments) went badly out of tune: an unfortunate ending to a generally satisfying concert.

♪Met's Die Frau: Without a Shadow of a Doubt, a Great Production

Soloists, Metropolitan Opera Orchestra, Vladimir Jurowski (conductor), Metropolitan Opera, Lincoln Center, New York, 12.11.2013

Richard Strauss: *Die Frau ohne Schatten*

What are we to make of this opera and its strange albeit beautiful world? It opens *in medias res* with the Nurse and the Messenger discussing the fact that this is the twelfth time in the past year that he has come bearing a demand to the Empress from her father, the mysterious spirit who controls this world, that she return to him. The Messenger then tells the Nurse that this time the Empress, who is half-human and half-gazelle and has no shadow, must obtain a shadow from the human world within three days or she will have to return to her father; her husband, the Emperor, will be turned into stone. Does this make any sense? No. What it does do is provide the librettist, Hugo von Hofmannsthal, with material for a fairytale, and the composer, Richard Strauss, the inspiration for some of his most gorgeous music. Long sweeping musical lines roll in, and languorous moments such as the Third Act's "Vater, bist du," a precursor to the heart-rending "Beim Schlafengehen" from his *Four Last Songs,* make this one of Strauss's greatest operas.

Strauss had composed some strange operas before this including *Ariadne auf Naxos*, *Elektra* and *Salomé*, but nothing as phantasmagoric as *Die Frau ohne Schatten*. The opera and its story are not based on familiar myths or Biblical characters as in his previous operas, and the audience at its 1919 premiere found it incomprehensible. The staging required tremendous resources from singers, designers and orchestras, and it took another half century for *Die Frau* to enter the repertory of contemporary opera houses. Few could put on the kind of magic show that the Met produced here.

This production is a revival of one from 2001, and it has lost none of its opulence. The two sets are built on the theater's stage-raising elevator: the opera begins in the fantasy world which rises to reveal the all-too-human, slovenly Dyer's house where the refrigerator is filled with beer cans and the wife fries fish in a space near the dye vats. The husband, Barak (the only named character in the opera), spends his time playing rough-house games with his brothers. His wife is a self-centered termagant. Between the human and the spirit worlds is a staircase where the characters can climb back and forth.

The staging of the other-world space was stunning, with mirrored floor, walls and ceiling. There were several scenes that particularly impressed me. The Emperor's red falcon, who originally lead him to the Empress, returns a number of times and somersaults around the mirrored walls, at times seemingly a blur of red. Jennifer Check deserved the round of applause she received for her acrobatics. Another spectacular scene was in Act III when the spell on the Emperor is broken, freeing him from a stone encasement. For this he wore a cape made of mirrors that caught and reflected the light and was reminiscent of the Commandatore scenes in Mozart's *Don Giovanni*.

Within its own logic the opera stands up well, but ultimately it becomes moralistic, preaching "go and be fruitful" philosophies supported by voices of the unborn, and simplistic clichés such as it is better to be a human than a god.

There were a few miscues, a sour turn here and there, but mostly brilliant singing.

Anne Schwanewilms, who played the same part in the very different Christof Loy production, fit the role of the Empress well and was quite impressive in her final rejection of the shadow. Although the original libretto lists the Empress as the leading female vocalist and the Dyer's wife several singers below her, the applause for Christine Goerke's knock-out singing over shadowed that for all the other roles.

The orchestra under the direction of Vladimir Jurowski was so brilliant that I found myself focusing on the instruments. Strauss's use of the brass section rivals Mahler's, and the Metropolitan's brass are nonpareil.

This was a magical production with every one of its 220-or-so minutes riveting in every way.

♫*Speed Counts*

Miah Persson (soprano), Stephanie Blythe (mezzo-soprano), Frédéric Antoun (tenor), Andrew Foster-Williams (bass), New York Philharmonic Orchestra, Bernard Labadie (conductor), New York Choral Artists, Joseph Flummerfelt

Bach: Cantata No. 51, "Jauchzet Gott in allen Landen"
Handel: "Let the Bright Seraphim," from the oratorio *Samson*
Mozart: Requiem (Completed by Robert D. Levin, 1993)

No amount of research will ever be able to answer definitively the question of how fast or slowly a Baroque score should be played. Since there were no metronomes in Bach's day, even if a score is annotated we can't be sure about the speed. When the tempo is indicated (adagio, allegro) or a movement is designated a dance (sarabande, gigue), then the conductor should be more circumspect about the tempos that he takes. But how fast is an allegro? How slow is a sarabande? In the case of songs and arias, the words themselves determine the pacing. "Haste, haste to town" should be played fast; "When I am laid in earth" would, of course, be slow.

The most sensible approach is to take a tempo that allows every musical line to be heard as clearly as possible; respects the composer's phrasing; and isn't so fast that the instrumentalist is not confidant and comfortable with the score. The latter is very important in a small orchestra where mistakes, miscues or misinterpretations can't always be covered by another musician.

At previous concerts conducted by Labadie, an early music specialist, I admired his ability to draw from modern orchestras a sound closer in color to his own period instrument group, Les Violons du Roy. The orchestra here consisted of members of the New York Philharmonic playing modern instruments, and the simplest way to emulate an early music sound is to reduce vibrato. As far as I could tell, this method was used for the two Baroque pieces on the program, but it wasn't enough: the fast arias were too fast and the slower ones lacked warmth.

Bach's Cantata No. 51 is a showcase for all involved, but specifically for the soprano and trumpet soloist. The soprano needs to be comfortable in the wide range of middle C to high C. The trumpeter has to have complete control of his instrument and needs to match the soprano in long stretches of sixteenth notes. The first aria has a fiendishly difficult trill on the G above the staff, and Matthew Muckey performed brilliantly. He used a modern trumpet designed to ease the difficulty of playing these notes; the trumpet used in Bach's time was valveless and required the trumpeter to use only his lips and tongue to produce notes.

Miah Persson's voice, accurate enough in all ranges, was too thin to overcome the unforgiving acoustics of Avery Fisher Hall. The recitative in this cantata is one of Bach's most poignant, and I missed the emotional impact that I've felt in other performances. This held true for the Handel aria as well. I know Ms. Persson has appeared in many opera productions, and I wonder if she toned down her "opera voice" and turned up her "white voice."

There are enough substantive changes in Robert Levin's version of Mozart's Requiem that we should approach it the same way we approach Bruckner's symphonies. Brucknerites don't talk about his Second or Seventh symphonies but his Carregan Edition Second Symphony or his Haas Edition Seventh Symphony. The same should be done for Mozart's Requiem whose various editions began with Franz Xavier Süssmayr at the dying Mozart's bedside. The overall accomplishment of Levin's changes is to make the work seem more like Mozart's other great Masses through the addition of colors and contrasts not completely fleshed out in the traditional score. Like the many valid revisions of Bruckner's symphonies, this version seems equally acceptable and can stand on its own.

The soloists and chorus gave the Requiem a strong reading. Stephanie Blythe demonstrated what an "opera voice" should sound like in Avery Fisher Hall: she sang with enough strength to overcome the Hall's weak acoustics. Tenor Frédéric Antoun had a particularly distinguished voice.

♪Thunder and Agitation: Music Not Quite Ready to Be Sturm und Drang

Dresden and Berlin: A Celebration of Two Courts, 12th Annual Jerome L. Greene Concert, Juilliard415, Nicholas McGegan (conductor), Alice Tully Hall, Lincoln Center, New York, 4.11.2013

Zelenka: Symphonia to *Sub olea pacis*
Benda: Symphonia No. 7 in D major
Pisendel: Violin Concerto in D major; *Imitations des caractères de la danse*
Zelenka: Hipocondrie à 7 Concertanti
C. P. E. Bach: Symphony in E minor

The years covered by the works on this program (1720-1760) saw a seismic shift in music from the ornate, highly charged, convoluted, even raucous late Baroque to the genteel, formal and disciplined music of the Classical period. Bach's two eldest sons had careers that highlight the risks of being a composer during such a period of artistic upheaval. C. P. E. had few problems, carving a niche for himself in the Court of Frederick the Great who gave him a wide berth to write music that was both experimental and personal. J. S. Bach's eldest son, W. F., was also very talented but wasn't quite comfortable writing in the style demanded by the music arbiters of the day (being an alcoholic and a gambler didn't help either). His music is stylistically very much like Zelenka's *Hipocondrie*.

This bizarre piece starts with the typical dotted rhythms of a French *ouverture*. Something, though, is just slightly off, enough to create a sense of wooziness. If Zelenka gives any one instrument the symptoms of hypochondria it would be the bassoon which at one point sounds like it has a bad case of hiccups. McGegan and orchestra struck just the right balance (or off-balance) to convey a sense of illness-induced unsteadiness. Throughout this work the lower instruments literally toot their way to the conclusion as the music modulates into parallel minor keys, the work ending with a return to the opening tempo and a coda that comes close to, but is not quite as dissonant as, the one Mozart wrote for his *Musical Joke*.

Franz Benda's D-major Symphony is a pleasant enough gallantry but only interesting in its sharply rhythmic final movement. Without implying that this movement has any programmatic content (not that this would be uncommon for music of this period), there certainly is a lot of braying and hee-hawing. The syncopated measures give another rhythmic boost to the music's jauntiness. This piece and the works that followed were expertly played and, I should add, expertly danced by Maestro McGegan.

Pisendel's name is often associated with Vivaldi, who befriended him on the former's trips to Venice as a member of the Dresden Orchestra. Both men were exceptional violinists and exchanged concerti as tokens of friendship, including a set of concerti and sonatas specifically written for Pisendel by Vivaldi. Vivaldi could almost have written the D-major concerto performed here, but Pisendel's formatting differs from the template that Vivaldi used. It would be atypical of Vivaldi to wait so long after the opening for the violin to make its entrance and even more unusual to give the violinist an improvisational cadenza solo for his opening salvo. Edson Scheid was more than equipped to deal with the virtuosic challenges of the piece, and McGegan kept everything moving unrelentingly, conducting at the full tempo of presto, never abating even during its most demanding measures.

The second half of the concert opened with Pisendel's *Imitations des caractères de la danse*, which just might be one of the shortest of the popular dance suites written in that period: seven different dances ending with a "concertino" in less than seven minutes. Particularly of interest in this suite are the Musette and a Passepied that speeds up to a fevered pitch before the transition to an almost-as-fast Polonaise.

Written in 1763, C. P. E. Bach's Symphony in E minor is technically part of the so-called "Storm and Stress" period that covered the 1760s and 1770s. It is typical of the music of this brief period in its use of sharp shifts in mood and tempo. Bach, though, did not reserve his use of the minor key for his Storm and Stress symphonies as did Mozart (the two symphonies in G minor, No. 25 and No. 41). In fact, C.P.E Bach was writing keyboard sonatas in this style as early as the 1730s and completed his 40 or so concerti for keyboard by 1760. The late E-minor symphony explores some of his Storm and Stress techniques: sudden shifts in dynamics, unbalanced phrasing, unexpected transitions between movements and long poignant slow movements, often punctuated by loud outbursts and long silences. This music was meant to surprise, and McGegan drove the orchestra to a frenzy with hard punches into the air, only to drop his boxing gloves for kid gloves during the softer moments.

McGegan responded to the audience's warm applause with another symphony by Benda, briefly telling the audience that this symphony (No. 10 in G major) was only two and a half movements. In fact it was even less than that. The second movement barely ran past the thirty-second mark. It was a fitting conclusion to this entertaining program: an offbeat hurdy-gurdy-like first movement punctuated by quick staccatos from the bassoon, and a final movement centered on a comic interplay between the horns and the winds. It was only here that the winds couldn't quite come together, a small complaint for an otherwise professional performance.

All-in-all, a thoroughly enjoyable evening.

♫ *András Schiff's Monumental Performance of Two Great Piano Monuments*

András Schiff (piano), Carnegie Hall, New York, 5.11.2013

Bach: *Goldberg Variations*
Beethoven: *Diabelli Variations*

It has been nearly sixty years since Glenn Gould recorded Bach's *Goldberg Variations* and forever changed the way we listen to Bach. There have been many great musicians before Gould who tried to revive interest in Bach, and in particular the *Goldberg Variations*, but none were able to accomplish what Gould would with the release of his forty-five minute 1955 recording.
Beethoven's *Diabelli Variations* received their first performance at Carnegie Hall in 1912, yet Bach's *Goldberg Variations* had to wait another thirty years until Ralph Kirkpatrick played them on a harpsichord at what is now Weill Recital Hall. At that time, Olin Downes, the music critic for *The New York Times*, stated that this music seemed to provide pleasure to "musicians," "connoisseurs" and "the musical elite of the city."

It's not that there has been a dearth of pianists who've played and even specialized in Bach. In the 1930s, Edwin Fisher's performances of Bach were the models for his generation, and his style of playing Bach was passed on to some of his students such as Alfred Brendel and David Barenboim, neither one known as a great Bach interpreter. Wanda Landowska became the next Bach advocate, but she was stymied by her choice of an instrument (a Pleyel harpsichord) that overpowered Bach and had little flexibility in sound without resorting to its clunky manual stops. Rosalyn Tureck treated Bach with a zealot's insistence on total adherence to Bach's testament. Glenn Gould's arrival was for her the coming of the Anti-Bach. Gould's performances were idiosyncratic, iconoclastic and irreverent, just the opposite of Tureck's.

András Schiff's studio sessions for his first *Goldberg Variations* recording took place in December 1982, barely three months after Gould's death. Schiff was a natural to continue in the Gould tradition. His tempi were fleet without being excessive, his ability to adjust each hand to draw out musical lines was never exaggerated, and his choice of taking repeats was never arbitrary. He took over Gould's role as the Bach interpreter par excellence, and only Angela Hewitt has come close to taking the title from him.

The András Schiff who appeared last night for his final recital in his Bach Project cycle was a different pianist from both the one who made his earlier recordings (1982, 2001) and the person appearing a few nights ago on stage performing Bach's Six Partitas. At last night's concert, there was no tepidness, no lack of variety that would have dispersed at intermission a good part of the audience as it had done last week. In fact, from what I could see, few people left at intermission, considering that both the Bach and Beethoven works are considerably more demanding than the Partitas.

Whatever is it was that made the difference between these two appearances, Schiff was in top form for this mammoth undertaking. There was some magic that he had last night that resulted in one of those rare events that is the goal of every artist in any performing art; and the reason why we keep going to events such as this in the hope of experiencing exactly that same magic. Each variation was crafted and shaped in such a way that it stood on its own, yet was also a necessary part of the whole that made it more than the sum of its parts. This was the kind of playing that can only come from the complete merging of the performer and the work, and is complemented by the audience's willingness to let go. Schiff's conceptual grasp of the work's structure was tectonic in nature. Pauses between movements varied from brief to long depending upon how much space Schiff felt was needed between each variation.

There was surprisingly little ornamentation, and when there was it was usually during the da capo of the second section. Every repeat was taken and there was no attempt to go beyond the urtext. The youthful Schiff would have played a repeat an octave higher, arpeggiated chords and used the sustain pedal to get one effect or another. The mature Schiff needed only Bach whose music provided all the effects that a pianist of Schiff's skills would ever require.

The haunting simplicity of the reappearance of the opening aria that closes the *Goldberg Variations* is one of the sublime moments in music. Unfortunately, this moment was shattered by premature applause. Here's Schiff's take on this lack of respect: "I would prefer it ideally if there was no applause at the end, just a wonderful silence. Unfortunately there is almost always someone who wants to show how well he knows the piece by applauding at the instant the final note has been played."

Beethoven also created a set of unique miniatures open to myriad interpretations by a myriad of pianists, each wanting at one time or another to add their own interpretations to the long list of their predecessors; few have the slightest chance of rising anywhere near the top. (A search of Amazon's catalogue lists 878 titles for Bach's *Goldberg Variations* and 275 for the *Diabellli Variations*). Any doubts about Schiff's stamina were swept away with a muscular and full-throated reading. He showed no signs of fatigue, hammering chords with as much intensity at the end as at the beginning. If he rested at times between movements, it was done not to catch his breath, but to give space after the more expressive or lyrical movements.

This time the audience held back their applause until Schiff felt it was the right time to break the mood by lifting his hands from the keyboard.

At the Partitas recital, Schiff may have given the audience a subtle musical statement in the selection of his encore. He chose the brief first-year-piano-student's C-major Invention from Bach's pedagogical set of 2-Part Inventions.

The simplicity of the encore seemed to imply that if this was all he could play, he was ready to call it a night.

For last night's encore, he performed the second movement from Beethoven's Opus 111, not a work that one would ever think of using as an encore, especially after having played the two huge works. If he felt the need to tell the audience that he was barely winded, this eighteen-minute encore surely proved it.

♫*András Schiff: Winding Down as He Nears the End of His Bach Project*

András Schiff (piano), Carnegie Hall, New York, 30.10.2013

Bach: Partitas: No. 5 in G major; No. 3 in A minor; No. 1 in B-flat major; No. 2 in C minor; No. 4 in D major; Partita No. 6 in E minor

There are few pianists capable of filling the space left by the early demise of Glenn Gould. Angela Hewitt would be one such pianist. András Schiff would be another.

Schiff shares Gould's preference for fleet speeds. They both aim for a clear separation of contrapuntal lines aided by a minimal use of pedals or, in Schiff's case, no pedals at all. Schiff, like the others, avoids legatos that might cover up hidden voices. Both pianists in their later years felt there was enough difference between their earlier performances and their current ones to warrant a second run-through. Gould had the opportunity to rerecord the *Goldberg Variations* once before his premature death. Schiff is in the process of reevaluating and rethinking his relationship to Bach during his *Bach Project*.

The result of Schiff's go-round, based on his performance of the Partitas here, is somewhat mixed. Tempi were surprisingly consistent with those from his youthful cycle. In fact, his performance here was, if anything, faster, particularly in the virtuosic gavottes and gigues that end most of the Partitas. Given the sheer amount of music played and the fact that every repeat was taken called out for something that might add variety. One such technique would be the implementation of ornamentation. It should be said that Schiff did use some ornamentation, but perhaps it was used too discretely. Given this sparsity and his complete avoidance of the sustain pedal it was not surprising to see many members of the audience leave at the intermission. Bach himself wouldn't think of playing the whole set in one sitting. In fact, the opposite may have been true: Bach intended these dances to serve as pedagogical keyboard exercises and not music that stands on its own.

Schiff's playing came to life in each Partita's opening and closing movements. The *Praeludiums* are not restricted in terms of rhythms and tempi as are the other sections written in dance form. The strongly accented sinfonias from the second Partita and the ouverture to the fourth Partita were given powerful readings. The other *Praeludiums* and the Fantasia are invitations to the performer to improvise or, at least, play the written score as if it were being improvised. In these introductions, Schiff was at his most inspired.

Similarly, Schiff dug into the closing gigues, playing them with a sharp and well-defined rhythm, keeping each line separate and varying the emphasis by bringing out the dominant motifs as they moved from hand to hand. The final gigue from the sixth Partita was played with so much conviction and authority that I imagined Schiff getting his second wind and continuing to play in this vein.

Schiff is celebrating his 60th birthday with what he calls the Bach Project: a series of six recitals covering Bach's major keyboard works played at various concert halls. The series has its conclusion with a performance of the *Goldberg Variations* at Carnegie Hall on November 5th. Just so that we do not think of him as a slouch, he will also play Beethoven's monumental *Diabelli Variations*. For the marathoner he is, Schiff is probably thinking of the Beethoven as nothing more than a long encore.

♪*The Tetzlaff Quartet: Doing it Their Way and Getting it Right*
Tetzlaff Quartet (Christian Tetzlaff and Elisabeth Kufferath, violins; Hanna Weinmeister, viola; Tanja Tetzlaff, cello), Zankel Hall, Carnegie Hall, New York 24.10.2013

Haydn: String Quartet in C major
Bartok: String Quartet No. 4
Beethoven: String Quartet in A minor

Christian Tetzlaff's schedule for November takes him to 13 venues as far apart as Hamburg, Philadelphia and Helsinki to perform 15 concerts. How he has the time to be part of a quartet is as much a wonder as is the exceptional quality of the quartet itself. There is no shortcut to the kind of performance the Tetzlaff Quartet gave here; no way that any group could achieve the results it did without a considerable amount of rehearsal time and practice. The rapport, trust and confidence that they radiated was palpable, and it resulted in music that was refined, polished and precise without the slightest bit of flashiness or showiness. Their attention to detail never interfered with the overall conceptual lines that governed each movement. This was playing on the highest level where each note carried the weight of authority.

There are few musicians who can be convincing enough to challenge a great composer's urtext. Glen Gould was one such genius, ignoring the historical assumptions about both Bach's music and Bach's likely interpretive style. He drew some contrapuntal lines out and hid others in seemingly arbitrary ways. Tempi were exaggeratedly fast or exceedingly slow. Legato lines were often played *détaché*. Yet it worked. He certainly took the starch out of the Cantor's collar and maybe was playing Bach the way Bach himself might have played his music.

I say this because there was much interpretative freedom in the Tetzlaff Quartet's playing. The opening Haydn Moderato was anything but moderate. This completely changed the character of the piece, taking it out of the somewhat lethargic world of many Haydn middle-period works and giving it the feel of later masterpieces such as the "Prussian" Quartets and those from the Opus 70s. How fast was it? The reputable Kodály Quartet slogs through the first movement in about ten minutes, the Tetzlaff in under seven. A lovely Adagio followed with its haunting theme played by the cello and its momentarily dramatic bursts of recitatives. Without stop the group went straight into the minuet, a piece that mixes a droning imitation of his patron's favored instrument, the baryton, with sudden modulations into the minor key. The fugal last movement ends with a coda sped up yet so convincing it belies the fact that although Haydn did not mark the coda *accelerando*, one wishes that he had.

The Tetzlaff played Bartók's Quartet No. 4 with equal mastery. With no specific connection between this quartet and the Haydn, the group performed it as if it were a natural progression from Haydn to Bartók. The same adjectives of refinement, precision and polish could be applied to all three works on the program. The Tetzlaff group could be faulted for not bringing out the romantic Hungarian folk motifs that always vie with the more modern, analytical elements in the quartets, choosing instead to capture the work's anxiety, edginess and taut frenetic energy; but it's hard to criticize something that works. In contrast to Haydn's lack of instructions on how to end his quartet, Bartók specifically sets up his coda with quick tempo changes from *Piu vivo* to *Meno mosso*, hammering home the final two measures by marking them *Pesante*. The brief second movement is a buzzy Prestissimo played *con sordino*, mixing pizzicati with glissandos and *sul ponticelli* (played as close to the bridge as possible). The third movement is a study in contrast, both agitated (agitato) and tranquil (tranquillo). The final two movements are a guided tour of string techniques: pizzicato to be plucked so hard that it bounces off the finger-board; *glissandi* (sliding) and col legno (strings played with the wood part of the bow). The Tetzlaff Quartet managed all these difficulties with authority, aplomb and humor (at one point hitting the music stands with their bows).

Beethoven's monumental Quartet Op. 132 is a rollercoaster of emotions, its five movements held in place by the third movement, the longest one in all of his quartets. The Tetzlaff performance was hypnotic, with the third movement designated as *Heilige Dankgesang* ("Holy Song of Thanksgiving"). It was so sublimely and prayerfully played that it bordered on silence; so soft that the muffled sound of the subway, generally not noticeable, here seemed like a sacrilege. When the players finished this movement, they held their bows up for the longest time that I can remember. For both the Quartet and the audience, it was a needed moment to recover from this ethereal interlude, before continuing with the sharply contrasting final two movements.

Loud applause had the group returning to the stage to play the Minuet from the third movement of Haydn's Quartet No. 3 from the Op. 20 set.

♩Juilliard415 in World-Class Performance of Rebel and Rameau

Chaos and Order: Dance Suites from the French Baroque, Juilliard415, Robert

Mealy (conductor and violin), Alice Tully Hall, Lincoln Center, New York, 21.10.2013

Rebel: *Les élémens*
Rameau: Suite from *Hippolyte et Aricie*; Suite from *Naïs*; Suite from *Les Indes galantes*

This performance by Juilliard415 was simply astonishing. Granted, there were a handful of alumni, faculty and guest artists included in the group of 30 or so players, but some 25 were students, ten of whom are in their first year of study in the Historical Performance program. The new students would have had only a month or two at Juilliard, but there was not the slightest evidence that any of the players were less than professional. Rameau's music is complex both harmonically and rhythmically, yet they never faltered. All played on original Baroque instruments or replicas: most of the wind and brass are less refined mechanically than modern instruments and demand more from the artist to produce their unique sounds. Robert Mealy, with his own playing to do, conducted with a light hand, yet the players were always totally in sync.

Anyone who has listened to Prokofiev's *Classical Symphony*, or to any music written "in the style of," will understand that it not uncommon to hear music that is anachronistic: music that refers back and is out of sync with the times. Then there is another type of anachronism that can be comprehended only when future generations look back. Beethoven's "Grosse Fugue" may not seem anachronistic to us in 2013, but we know that Beethoven's audience heard this as music out of sync with its time. Beethoven, I suspect, knew that he was writing music for the future.

It is less likely that Jean-Féry Rebel suspected that 200 years down the road the opening chords of his suite *Les élémens* would be called "tone clusters" and would be incorporated into the music of Charles Ives and his disciples. It was clear that the audience at this concert was taken aback by the dissonance of the first movement: it comes as quite a shock, the last thing one would expect to hear at a concert of 18th-century music. Unfortunately, the movements that followed were a more mundane mixture of dances and programmatic pieces representing the elements of air and fire. The movement called "L'Air: Ramage" was delightfully rendered by flutists David Ross and Melanie Williams.

To many Frenchmen, still under the shadow of the long-dead Lully, Rameau's opera *"Hippolyte et Aricie"* was considered nothing but cacophony. It so divided the musical world that those who favored Lully were called "Lullistes" and those following Rameau were called "Ramistes." It is hard to think of Rameau as iconoclastic or radical, but compared to his contemporaries, his music was nothing if not idiosyncratic. The noble and regal themes of gods and kings were challenged by Rameau's rambunctious operas with plots as diverse as the tale of a frog longing to replace Juno as the wife of Jupiter (*Platée*), to a vaudevillian pageant of delegates from exotic countries backed by music that supposedly reflected the visitors' own musical style (*Les Indes Galantes*). This was music that brought opera down to earth, opening it up to a diversity of themes never used before Rameau's time.

Last year I said this about a similar Juilliard415 concert: "It is a joy to see how the students have grown in confidence and ability and how quickly the Historical Performance department, now in its fourth year, has gained a reputation as one of the finest early music schools in the world." I would say the same this year but add that Juilliard415 has gained the reputation of being one of the finest early music orchestras in the world as well.

♪Haydn, Mozart and Who?

Lauren Snouffer (soprano), Hai-Ting Chinn (mezzo-soprano), Craig Phillips (bass-baritone), Clarion Orchestra, Steven Fox (conductor), Park Avenue Christian Church, New York, 16.10.2013

Haydn: *Overtura Covent Garden*
Bortniansky: Excerpts from the operas *Alcide* and *Le fils rival*
Mozart: Symphony No. 41 in C, "Jupiter"

When we think about the Baroque period, names like Albinoni, Bach, Corelli, Couperin, Handel, Purcell, Rameau, Scarlatti, Telemann and Vivaldi come to mind. Every month, it seems, there is the discovery of a "new" Baroque score or a "new" composer such as Steffani, Hasse, Graupner, Heinchen and Graun. When we move to the Classical period, we think of Mozart, Haydn, Beethoven and Schubert. Who then would follow? Perhaps the Bach brothers, but after that? Divienne, Dussek, Kraus, Baguer, Bortniansky: composers whose names are as unfamiliar as their music.

There could be several reasons why there hasn't been as much exploration in the Classical period as there has in the Baroque. Mozart so over-shadows his contemporaries that it might seem like a waste of time to research other composers and their works. Similarly, if the extant music of the day is not uniformly interesting, why bother finding more dull music. Works from the Baroque are rarely dull: that style required the ability to write complex, intricate music that at its worst is at least listenable. The rules of counterpoint and harmonics created an environment that allowed even non-geniuses to produce tolerable music. The change in style from the multi-voiced vertical music of the Baroque to the single-voiced horizontal music of the Classical period simplified the task of composing and often resulted in, well, simple music.

What are the compositional techniques that make for the greatest music of the Classical period? One need only look at Mozart's "Jupiter" Symphony and see how it uses Baroque elements such as fugues, dissonance, suspensions, chord inversions and distant tonal modulations to produce its finest moments.
From the Bortniansky samples at this concert, it would be impossible to make any judgment as to the quality of his musical output. Bortniansky received his education from the prolific but stolid Galuppi. With ten years of study in Italy under his belt, he came back to the Russian court capable of writing music in both the French and Italian styles, but today he is known mostly for his liturgical

works.

Steven Fox presented the premier of instrumental and vocal music by Bortniansky that he edited from scores he discovered in the British Library. The opening instrumental music from *Alcide*, "Danza degli Spiriti," was bright and vibrant, rich with the warm sounds of the orchestra's early instruments. Lauren Snouffer's voice matched the orchestral timbre, and she sang the aria "Tu vedrai che virtù non paventa" with great conviction and expression. The acoustics in the Church may have affected the balance between singer and accompaniment, although there was no difficulty in hearing her voice.

The language changed from Italian to French for the remainder of the program. Snouffer stood out in the arias, backed by mezzo Hai Ting Chinn and joined by bass-baritone Craig Phillips. Phillips was fine in his solo aria, "En homme j'agirais sans doute," although his French enunciation could have been stronger.

Haydn must have liked his *Overtura Covent Garden*—he used it twice, as the first movement of Symphony No. 62 and as an alternate final movement of his 53rd symphony. Fox captured the pulsing energy of its exposition and contrasted this well with the more subdued minor-key middle section.

The performance of Mozart's last symphony was a brave undertaking and was, for the most part, well executed. The tonal color produced by the orchestra's early instruments was striking, highlighting instrumental lines not normally heard from modern instruments. The effect of this was to renew and refresh a work so often played by oversized orchestras. Moderate tempi were taken in all but the final movement which was played extremely fast. Some of the instrumentalists just couldn't keep up, and there were moments that seemed to confound the brass and wind sections.

♫*Sweeter Than Roses: Carolyn Sampson Sings Henry Purcell*

Carolyn Sampson (soprano), Beiliang Zhu (viola da gamba), Paul O'Dette (archlute), Kenneth Weiss (harpsichord), Weill Recital Hall, Carnegie Hall, New York, 10.10.2013

Henry Purcell: Songs
William Byrd: Third Pavan and Galliard in A minor, from *Lady Nevell's Book*
Christopher Simpson: "Division on a Ground" in E minor
John Banister: "Division on a Ground"

Henry Purcell's music has always held a special place for me. It's not at all difficult to see Purcell as the musical equivalent of Shakespeare. The genius of both men is unfathomable: neither had formal education that would account for their profundity; both had a purity and naturalness seemingly untainted by quotidian life. Historical influences and the sources of their works can be found but each, having created his own unique world, stands apart.

Purcell died at 37. He lived barely a year longer than Mozart did, and like Mozart he was astonishingly prolific. The Zimmerman catalog of Purcell works consists of nearly 700 anthems, sacred and secular songs, operas, odes and incidental music plus instrumental suites, fantasias and dances.

The first work on this program was "Thou wakeful shepherd." It's representative of a style of devotional songs whose libretto and score seem stark and bare but, when sung with the empathy and insight of Carolyn Sampson, the songs are found to be rich in content. The sudden changes that occur in the last four lines of "Shepherd" are particularly of interest. They go from confession and repentance to brief lilting melismas on the words "With joy I sing." This is then followed by the joyless repetition of the phrase "Yet who can die," and it concludes with the dispirited "so to receive his death."

Sampson's presentation of the songs was totally free of artifice. She seemed comfortable in all of Purcell's vocal ranges, and her attention to every word and ability to match the music to the text was totally convincing. So many early music sopranos look to Emma Kirkby as the ideal voice, crystal clear and "white" in its lack of vibrato. This kind of voice is best suited for sacred music such as the *Ténèbres* of Couperin or Charpentier, music whose long melismas would fill a cathedral with their purity. There is nothing cool about Sampson's voice: it is warm and natural with no loss of fervor or passion in being vibrato-less.

"Sweeter than roses" is a model of the subtle vocal tone coloring that Purcell was capable of using, and Sampson, in a text that runs only seven lines, captured all of it. The key words "cool," "breeze," "trembling" and "fire" received just the right intonation. The word "victorious," repeated twice as six-measure melismas, left no doubt as to what love has won.

Not all the songs on the program were as solemn or staid as the ones discussed above. "Man is for the woman made" is a tavern song with a harmonic line that is simple enough for anyone in any state of inebriation to play. "When first Amintas sued for love" is in a similar vein. The not-very-subtle double entendres are sung in the style of a sea-shanty or hornpipe with the concluding lines: "For soon he found the golden coast/Enjoy'd the ore, and touched the shore/Where never merchant went before."

In between Sampson's vocal sets there were interludes that highlighted the three accompanists. Paul O'Dette played the archlute, an instrument that is a somewhat smaller version of the more resonant and deeper-voiced theorbo. This was the first time that I've seen this instrument played solo, and it was fascinating to watch how the fretted strings were played like a lute at the same time as the fixed, un-fretted strings were plucked. This created a self-contained unit that sang and supported itself with its own harmonic bass line. Kenneth Weiss performed "Pavan and Galliard" by William Byrd with a delicacy that one might not expect from a harpsichord. Viola da gambist Beiliang Zhu played a spirited "Division on a Ground" by John Bannister.

As the harmonic support for the Sampson recital, these talented instrumentalists were never intrusive. They all formed a winning team in a concert that was truly outstanding.

♪*Beethoven's Ninth: Morning, Noon and Evening*

Julianna Di Giacomo (soprano), Kelley O'Conner (mezzo-soprano), Russell Thomas (tenor), Shenyang (bass), New York Philharmonic Orchestra, Allen Gilbert (conductor), Manhattan School of Music Symphonic Chorus, Kent Tritle (director), Avery Fisher Hall, Lincoln Center, New York, 3.10.2013

Mark-Anthony Turnage: *Frieze*
Beethoven: Symphony No. 9

Beethoven's Ninth Symphony: An App for the iPad, published by Touch Press
Beethoven's Ninth Symphony: Copyist's Manuscripts from The Royal Philharmonic Society and Juilliard School's Manuscript Collection.

Most music lovers would know the answer to "Where were you when you heard Beethoven's Ninth for the first time?" If they don't remember specifically where, I'm sure they would know when, and they would probably also know whose performance it was. It would not be uncommon for my generation to have first heard the symphony as performed by Toscanini and the NBC Symphony Orchestra on the RCA Victor label (1952); for those with access to a television set, it might have been its broadcast in 1948. For us there will always be a vinyl LP, scratches and all, playing somewhere in our minds.

Every performance of the Ninth is a gala event in and of itself, and the New York Philharmonic Orchestra's performance was no exception. For me it was the appropriate finish to a day devoted to this monumental work.

I began with Touch Press's *Beethoven's Ninth Symphony*, an application software product designed for the iPad. It's the latest attempt to integrate music, text and visuals and grew out of the Microsoft Home series of multimedia CDs from the mid-1990s. Earlier products like Microsoft Home's *Multimedia Strauss: Three Tone Poems* tried to merge different media but lacked the availability of computer power and storage capacity to accomplish what their designers could only imagine.

This new application allows the user to listen to the Ninth while any number of choices are available for viewing concurrently. There are four full recordings to select from and a choice of two scores that scroll across the screen in synch with the music. At any time during the playback, these variables can be changed. Karajan's performance can be switched immediately to Bernstein's, Fricsay's or Gardiner's; the score can be changed at any point from the copyist's manuscript to the most recently edited, near-urtext edition. The sometimes difficult notion of tuning becomes crystal clear when any of the other three performances are switched to Gardiner's. His tuning of A=430 sounds discordant and substantially lower in its register when compared to the higher-pitched traditional performances. A visual map of the orchestra viewed during the playback highlights the soloists or sections of the orchestra as they join in or drop out of the score, while a colored "BeatMap" sends vectors up and down the screen. Excellent commentary by   Beethoven aficionados and by orchestra

146

members and conductors while they listen to their own performances with headphones add to the cornucopia of material. If this isn't enough, a video of Bernstein's 1979 Ninth with the Vienna State Opera Orchestra is available: all this and more for the price of one of the four orchestral recordings.

In the afternoon I joined my colleagues to view two copyists' manuscripts of the Ninth, together for the first time at the Juilliard School's Manuscript Collection. Curator Jane Gottlieb explained that the Royal Philharmonic Society as a goodwill gesture for their 200th anniversary had funded and had made available to Juilliard and the Morgan Library the original commissioned copy of the score that Beethoven had prepared for the Society in 1825. It's the conductor's copy used by George Smart in the UK's first performance of the Ninth. It is also the edition used in the iPad application discussed above. The Juilliard copy was the score used to prepare the first printed edition. Viewing these scores reinforces the hackneyed but seemingly true image of Beethoven as mad genius. One can only stand in awe before these stained, yellowing pages and their scribbles: documentation of perhaps the greatest musical work ever.

Filled with the sensation of being as close to the great man as one can ever expect to be, I had the coincidental good luck to attend that evening's performance of the Ninth by the NYPO under the direction of Alan Gilbert.

The concert opened with a work commissioned to celebrate the 200th anniversary of the Royal Philharmonic Orchestra, Mark-Anthony Turnage's *Frieze*. Hopefully we've learned to be more accepting of new music so as not to be the target of future disdain for making the sort of derisive remarks about *Frieze* that Beethoven's early critics made upon hearing the Ninth: "a concert made up of Indian War whoops and angry wildcats," "the unspeakable cheapness of the chief tune, 'Freude, Freude!'", or "a morbid desire for novelty; by extravagance and by a disdain of rule."

Frieze was pleasant enough but, as often happens with commissioned scores, hardly identifiable as a commemorative to either Beethoven or the Royal Philharmonic Society. The first movement's opening notes and tempo and the second's long *fermatas*, albeit without drums, could superficially be inspired by Beethoven's first two movements. The third movement's opening with just strings could vaguely be compared to Beethoven's. As for the Ninth's massive finale, Turnage honestly and admiringly admits that he "didn't attempt to be in the shadow of the epic last movement." My real complaint would be that the work is not modern enough: with only a few degrees of separation, it might be considered a commemorative to the music of Leonard Bernstein.

The performance that evening of the Ninth was a not-wholly-successful synthesis of Gilbert and his orchestra. Here is a conductor sharp enough to realize that the Ninth is not a piece of music to be approached lightly: he waited four years into his tenure to add it to his repertory. The NYPO has played it almost 200 times over the years. Not that anyone on stage has been there since its first performance in 1846, but if we are to believe that orchestras like the Berlin Philharmonic and the Philadelphia have a particular "sound" carried down from retiring musicians to newcomers, the same can be said of the NYPO. Like the

Philadelphia Orchestra, the NYPO seems over the years to have developed suavity in sound from the string section, a less distinctive wind section and a brass section that at times reaches the outer circle of the Berlin Philharmonic's brass.

The first movement was workmanlike, not particularly bright or as dramatic as it should be. The second movement could have had more angularity, and more attention and discrimination should have been given to the rapid, almost disrthymic, use of *marcatos, fortes* and *sforzandos*. The third movement was less problematic, helped by the lush sounds of the strings, but it did not quite achieve the potency needed when the trumpet and horn calls break in toward the movement's end.

What can be said about the final movement, an all-out display of energy, some of which could have been used to fuel the previous movements. The four soloists and chorus, having waited 40 or so minutes to do their thing, did it with alacrity, vigor and dispatch. Was it moving? It can't help but be. Was it a great performance? Not really. Will Gilbert's next performance improve? You bet.

♪Kariné Poghosyan: Powerhouse Pianist Tackles Liszt (and Others)
Kariné Poghosyan (piano), St. Vartan Chamber Orchestra, St. Vartan Cathedral, New York, 25.9.2103

Schubert: *Ave Maria* (piano transcription by Liszt)
Bach: Keyboard Concerto in D minor
Liszt: From Book 2 of *Années de pèlerinage: Sposalizio; Après une lecture de Dante*

Watching Kariné Poghosyan at the piano, I was reminded of none other than Glenn Gould. As it happens, St. Vartan is located just a few blocks north of the old Columbia 30th Street Studio where he first recorded the *Goldberg Variations*. The kinetic energy, the singing and humming, even Gould's gesture of lifting his left hand as if conducting himself were all part of Ms. Poghosyan's performance. Gould, though, was a thorough anti-romantic. His forays into Mozart, Beethoven and Brahms were not successful; his notorious anti-everything performance of Brahms' First Piano Concerto with Bernstein conducting required Bernstein to explain to the audience that the tempi to be played were solely decided by Gould.

From the evidence of her performance here, Ms. Poghosyan is a Romantic. The opening Liszt work, a transcription of Schubert's *Ave Maria*, received the most effective reading of the evening: the dynamics were kept under control and she balanced the accompaniment in the right hand with the melody in the left.

Balance was more of a problem in Bach's Concerto in D minor. The members of the-newly formed St. Vartan Chamber Orchestra were overpowered by Ms. Poghosyan's fierce attacks on the keyboard. The entrance of the piano in the first movement had me wondering where she would go from there as she played with an intensity normally reserved for the coda. Bach did write music that could match Ms. Poghosyan's muscularity but that music was meant to be played on the organ. One needs to keep in mind that Bach's keyboard instruments (except for the delicate clavichord) responded with the same volume regardless of whether the touch was light or heavy.

Ms. Poghosyan was more in her element with Liszt's *Sposalizio*, his programmatic impressions of Raphael's painting of the marriage of Mary and Joseph. The opening pentatonic arabesques clearly foreshadow Debussy and his own arabesques for piano. The clarity of theses waves of notes is critical to the work's success but, unfortunately, they got muddied by a combination of over-pedaling and reverberation. Some of the reverberation can be blamed on the church's poor acoustics, but not much can be done about this short of placing dampers to prevent the blurring of the delicate arabesques and the crashing of chords that echoed back on themselves. Although one cannot expect pianists to adjust their performance techniques to satisfy the demands of a venue's acoustics, there are ways to ameliorate the problem. Considered use of the pedal and a better understanding of the results of the music's decay in this church might have helped.

The second Liszt tone poem, *Après une lecture de Dante*, demands a tremendous technique, which Ms. Poghosyan was more than up to. There were times, though, when a little more *leggierissimo* was called for. At other times, measures with the velocity markings of *stringendo* or *accelerando* were interpreted as if these were dynamic markings such as *crescendo*. *Crescendos* themselves often started at high volume so the dynamic rise couldn't increase enough for its effect to be felt.

Ms. Poghosyan has an impressive technique that when used with more consideration could reveal a great musical talent.

♫ Juilliard Historical Performance Program Opens Fifth Year With... Quintets

Monica Huggett (violin), Caroline Krause (violin), Daniel McCarthy (viola), Kyle Miller (viola), Michael Unterman (cello), Caroline Nicolas (cello), Paul Hall, Juilliard School of Music, Lincoln Center, New York, 24.9.2013

Mysliveček: String Quintet No. 1 in G major
Mozart: String Quintet in C major; String Quintet in G minor

This concert is the first of the Historical Music Department's fifth year. Last year's opening concert featured several faculty members in a varied program of Baroque chamber music; tonight's concert was less ambitious and technically not Baroque. There are, of course, no rigid boundaries, but traditionally the Baroque period runs from 1600 to 1750. This can be simplistically justified by putting Palestrina's death in 1594 as the end of the Renaissance, with Bach's death in 1750 marking the end of the Baroque and the beginning of the Classical period. Early music specialists like Roger Norrington and Nicholas Harnoncourt have moved the boundaries of historical performance way past Mozart to Beethoven, Schubert and even Bruckner. I could be wrong, but this may be the first program of Mozart that the Historical Music Department has presented.

The Mozart works were preceded by a brief string quintet, the first in a set of three, written by the Czech composer and friend of the Mozart family, Josef Mysliveček. The music of the period just before Mozart was odd, transitional, and referred to by the great scholar Robbins-Landon as the Barococo: fluffy compositions which rarely went beyond the music's surface. Quantz, Mysliveček, Boccherini and J. C. Bach all produced oodles of chamber music, sinfonia concertantes and, in the case of Quantz, hundreds of flute sonatas and concerti. The quintet performed here is pleasant music that Mozart imitated, and this can be heard in his earliest string quintet, K.174, where the monophonic simplicity and strict adherence to the classical agenda found in the music of Mysliveček were the norm. By the time Mozart wrote his last two string quintets, he was thirty years old and light-years beyond Mysliveček, writing quintets that are dense, complex and, particularly in the G minor, highly chromatic and heart-wrenchingly poignant.

Chamber music is the most difficult type to perform successfully. Soloists have only themselves to worry about if they fail during a recital, while members of an orchestra are generally covered by their fellow musicians playing the same musical lines. Chamber music demands not only complete accuracy but also total rapport with one's associates. There is no one on stage to cover mistakes: each note has to be exactly played and perfectly in-sync with the other players. Aside from the rare occasions when truly great musicians get together and play, most successful groups have members who fit together in style, temperament and level of skill. More than anything else, chamber music demands that each player knows what the other musician is doing. Chamber groups rarely rise to that level of accomplishment during their early years together and often fall apart if any member of the group decides to leave. Both the Juilliard and Emerson Quartets went through demanding searches for replacements this year, and the Emerson had considered disbanding if the right cellist could not be found.

The first violinist in a quartet is normally given the most prominent role, often playing as if a soloist in a concerto. Monica Huggett seemed to step down a notch here in both dynamics and tempi so as not to completely unbalance the group's equilibrium. The two Mozart quintets are demanding works that require not only advanced technical skills but a maturity that comes with experience. Tempi were generally on the slow side, and there were few instances when all the instruments coalesced. All the musicians were clearly talented and up to the complexities of the score, and their hard work does not go unnoticed.

An observation: There has been no final answer on whether Mozart intended the last two quintets to have the traditionally slow second movement replaced by the third movement minuet, and the traditional third movement minuet replaced by an andante. Some musicologists blame the original editor for this reversal when he set up the manuscript for publication. Monica Huggett and her group went both ways: the K.515 was played fast-slow-minuet (trio)-fast, while K.516 was played fast-minuet (trio)-slow-fast. The playbill did not make note of this change for K. 515 and had me trying to fit 3/4 time into 4/4 time to justify the error in the program guide.

♫Ian Hobson Begins a Series of 14 Recitals Devoted to Brahms' Works for Piano

Classical Inclinations in a Romantic Age: Works for Piano and Chamber Music with Piano, Ian Hobson (piano), Claude Hobson (piano), Edward A. Rath, Jr. (piano), Benzaquen Hall, DiMenna Center for Classical Music, New York

10.9.2013
Brahms: Scherzo in E flat minor; Variations on a Theme by Robert Schumann for four hands (I. Hobson, C. Hobson); Piano Sonata No. 1 in C major

12.9.20
Brahms: Piano Sonata No. 2 in F-sharp minor
Hungarian Dances, Book 1: nos. 1-5; Book 2: nos. 6-10; Books 3-4: nos. 11-21, for four hands (Hobson, Rath)

Musical completists come in various guises. There are the true marathoners who run non-stop to the finish, such as pianist Julian Jacobson who has performed all 32 Beethoven sonatas in about ten hours (with minimal breaks). The completist Leslie Howard has recorded all of Liszt's piano works on 99 CDs over a period of 14 years. Other notable completists include Nicholas Harnoncourt and Gustav Leonhardt with their complete Bach cantata series; and Scott Ross and his 555 Scarlatti sonatas. These last two accomplishments were the musical equivalents of running the 4-minute mile: once it was shown that it could be done, others were able to do the same. Then there are those completists who may not commit as much time and effort as the previously mentioned musicians but should get some credit for fulfilling their annual "Brucknerathon"–15 hours devoted to listening to all of Bruckner's symphonies.

Of course, when using the word "complete" one is putting oneself in the line of fire. According to one critic, the recording of Scarlatti sonatas by Richard Lester is "the first (and currently the only) truly complete recording of the Scarlatti's keyboard sonatas" with an additional 13 "authenticated" pieces. A complete set is only complete until the next set proves it otherwise.

Ian Hobson has been no slouch in the area of completeness with recitals or recordings of Beethoven's piano sonatas, Chopin's piano music, Rachmaninoff piano transcriptions and Schumann's entire opus for solo piano. His 14-concert Brahms series in New York this autumn, while not the first complete performance of Brahms' piano music, may be the first nearly-complete piano and chamber music cycle. An earlier Hobson series was, in fact, more "complete" with 16 concerts that included works for two pianos not scheduled to be performed in this series.

This said, how can one complain about incompleteness when offered the opportunity to hear this wonderful music, so much of it little known and unlikely to have been heard in recital. It gives the listener a rare chance to re-evaluate a composer whose music has been obscured by the image of a stodgy old man who composed dense, heady and convoluted music, music that pours like treacle. Chopin wrote elegant, haunting music, spun out like gossamer. Schumann's music, like Brahms', was fiery, explosive and impenetrable at times, but much of his output is miniature set pieces, brief excursions into childhood and nature. Then there is Liszt, whose music covers every possible form, with a large part consisting of transcriptions of other composers' works.

Most of us know Brahms' solo piano music from his later works such as the Rhapsodies or Intermezzos. Hobson played the first and second of Brahms' three sonatas from memory; all written in 1853 when Brahms was barely 20. While somewhat wild and unwieldy, in Hobson's hands they were engrossing works whose intensity and seriousness deserved the attention Hobson gave to them. The first sonata could be considered a piano puzzler with its phrases from Brahms' musical predecessor Beethoven. In addition to Beethoven's famous four notes from the Fifth Symphony, Brahms was clearly taken by the opening chords of Beethoven's "Hammerklavier" sonata, so much so that he uses a slightly varied form of it as his main theme. One also sees in these early works that his signature methods were stamped into the scores: for instance, the use of motivic kernels that grow into clusters of sound which are as unforgiving and demanding to play as the piano parts in his later piano concerti. Perhaps with age Brahms was able to create movements that could be seen, to paraphrase Ravel, as "nobles et sentimentales," but here even the slow movements are filled with fire and fury.

It is always difficult to make familiar music sound fresh, and this is even harder when the music has been associated with things pedagogical, trivial or just plain capricious. This was the case with the first ten dances from Books 1 and 2 of the Hungarian dances. So many of these delightful works have been stripped down for beginning piano students, commercials or as background music to movies or cartoons. Again, Hobson overcame much of the banality associated with these dances by focusing on them as serious works, applying a gravitas that lifted them from their usual campy environment.

The addition of the two hands needed for the 11 dances of Brahms' Books 3-4 required a different set of skills. Both Hobson, taking the role of the basso, and Edward A. Rath, Jr., as the soprano, avoided what seemed at times to come close to digital entanglement. Without the freedom for each to roam freely on the keyboard, these works were more docile and controlled. Several of the more dynamic dances seemed to foreshadow Ragtime music with its jumpy, syncopated rhythms.

Here and there Hobson made minor flubs of no consequence in a series where so much music is being played. He has yet to play in Cary Hall which hopefully will offer a warmer and more welcoming acoustic than Benzaquen Hall.

With so many opportunities to hear music that is unlikely to be performed again soon, New York music lovers should take advantage of this chance to attend what can only be called, to quote from Bach, a "musical offering."

♫A Tribute to Lorraine Hunt Lieberson

Mostly Mozart Festival 10: In Tribute to Lorraine Hunt Lieberson, Renata Pokupić (mezzo-soprano), Anna Stéphany (mezzo-soprano), Orchestra of the Age of Enlightenment, Laurence Cummings (conductor), Alice Tully Hall, Lincoln Center, New York, 22.8.2013

Handel: Overture and "Langue offeso mai riposa" from *Giulio Cesare in Egitto*; "Ah! Whither should we fly…" from *Theodora*; Concerto Grosso in B minor; "Where shall I fly?" from *Hercules*; Overture and "Lord to Thee each night and day" from *Theodora*; "Dopo notte" from *Ariodante*; Concerto Grosso in B-flat major; "Svegliatevi nel core" from *Giulio Cesare in Egitto*

Encore: Third movement (Musette) of Handel's Concerto Grosso in G minor

This tribute to Lorraine Hunt Lieberson is an acknowledgement of the mutual admiration between the late mezzo-soprano and New York City. In an interview shortly before her death in 2006, Lieberson said: "New York audiences are the most wonderful, albeit noisy and opinionated….They have taken me to their heart and I love them." She is remembered by New Yorkers who attended her performances at the Metropolitan Opera and the New York City Opera; anyone who heard her will never forget her. The emotional commitment that she put into her characters, her down-to-earth naturalness and the effortlessness of her vocal technique can only be described as angelic.

The program's vocal selections represented pieces for which Lieberson—who worked frequently with the Orchestra of the Age of Enlightenment—was known. Unfortunately, mezzo Renata Pokupić was under the weather, and she bowed out at the intermission. In the two arias she did perform, her voice was lackluster, and it wasn't helped by the muddiness of the orchestral accompaniment. Laurence Cummings' enthusiasm and energy did not initially carry over to the orchestra which struggled at times to keep up with his frenetic gestures.

There seems to be an established practice among some period instrument groups equating speed with a successful presentation of Baroque style. While opinions are divided as to what the "real" Baroque tempo should be (with one musicologist even calling for a halving of all tempi), there is little doubt that the pacing of the two parts of an *ouverture* need to be slow and fast. The opening to Handel's *Giulio Cesare* is a classic example of the *ouverture* as formalized by Lully. Its opening section should be played in a stately manner with emphasis on the dotted rhythms; the fugal second section should contrast sharply with the opening in tempo. Cummings started too quickly so that by the time the fugue arrived there was not enough room for the orchestra to accelerate. The string players struggled to keep up with his whirlwind style.

By the third work on the program, "Ah! Whither should we fly," Cummings' pacing was slower: a necessity for this mournful aria. Anna Stéphany has a plush mezzo voice, better in the upper range, and she gave a soulful reading of one of

Lieberson's signature arias.

The final work in a compositional set is often the high point of the opus. Handel's Concerto Grosso in B minor, the twelfth of Opus 6, is almost a gloss on a Brandenburg Concerto, with the concertino roles played here by solo violin, viola and cello. It has an affinity to the third Brandenburg whose brief transition to the last movement is mirrored in the fourth-movement Largo of Handel. Concertmaster Kati Debretzeni had the most challenging part, but she breezed through the toughest measures.

The aria "Where shall I fly" from *Hercules* requires a little bit of everything, from recitatives to long melismas and would be a true test of any singer's ability. Despite her indisposition, Renata Pokupić worked through the aria's complexities with admirable skill.

The second half of the program mirrored the first half in its selections of instrumental and vocal works. Cummings announced that Pokupić was unwell and that Anna Stéphany would sing all three scheduled arias. The audience was sympathetic, and the coolness of the orchestra and Cummings' somewhat zealous leadership seemed to ease. Although the overture to *Theodora* was still too fast, the orchestra's muddiness was gone.

Although Pokupić was originally scheduled to sing "Dope notte," it was clear from the fact that Stéphany at times sang long passages without looking at the score in front of her that it's an aria she knows well. It's another Handel vocal twister, and Stéphany came through winningly. The long applause was well deserved.

Cummings continued at his speedy state with the Concerto Grosso in B-flat major, but the orchestra and conductor were more in sync. The orchestral members were also more aggressive so one actually heard distinct instrumental lines that had been glossed over in the earlier concerto.

The powerful and moving "Svegliatevi nel core" from *Giulio Cesare* vividly concluded the program, with singer, orchestra and conductor giving the extra push that was missing in the first half. It was enough to bring back the singers and conductor several times and allowed an encore in tribute to Lorraine Hunter Lieberson. The pleasant, pastorale-like Musette from Handel's Op. 6, No.6 brought the performance to a fitting conclusion.

♫*Emerson Quartet Returns to Lincoln Center with New Member*
Mostly Mozart Festival 9: Emerson String Quartet (Eugene Drucker and Philip Setzer, violins; Lawrence Dutton, viola; Paul Watkins, cello), Alice Tully Hall, Lincoln Center, New York, 19.8.2013

Beethoven: The "Razumovsky" Quartets: String Quartet in F major, String Quartet in E minor, String Quartet in C major

The recent movie *A Late Quartet*, which appeared around the same time as the departure of the Emerson Quartet's longtime cellist, David Finckel, raised some interesting issues on the dynamics of a chamber music group. The movie's cellist is the senior member and the emotional center of the group, a role that might not be atypical in other chamber ensembles. The first violinist of the Endellion Quartet, Andrew Watkinson, in referring to the film, says: "The same could be said of our cellist, David Waterman. Oddly, I think the cellist quite frequently takes this role–perhaps because they are so often playing the bass line that holds the music together."

Both the fictional quartet and the Emerson faced similar alternatives: whether to disband or find a new cellist. Finckel has stated in interviews that the long-term plan had always been to agree to a date on which to end the quartet in toto. But, having found a new player, they now had to start thinking of themselves as a group that doesn't end but rather evolves. Since the Emerson has not had a change of members in 34 years, this was a critical moment in the group's history. Mr. Finckel, renowned as an advocate for chamber music, will continue performing with his wife, the pianist Wu Han, and plans on spending some time perfecting his role as soloist in works for cello and orchestra. He will also continue as director of Music@Menlo and the Chamber Music Society of Lincoln Center.

The Emerson took a middle-of-the-road approach to the Razumovsky Quartets, delighting in their complexity. Normally one would expect that any musical set would start with the easiest and progress to the more complicated. Oddly, the most modern-sounding and difficult quartet was the first and the "simplest" was the last, with the middle quartet in the minor key as the group's dynamic center.

How does cellist Paul Watkins with his obvious technical prowess fit into the group? A litmus test of the technical ability of a string player could be the finale to the last movement of the third Razumovsky. Marked Allegro moto, this final movement of the set is often played considerably faster than the final movement of the second quartet (which Beethoven actually marks as Presto). All the members of the group played just about as fast as humanly possible. One can imagine one virtuoso accomplishing this feat, but it is hard to believe that there are four players in the world with these skills all together on the same stage. There were no signs at all that Watkins had recently replaced a 30-year resident of the cellist's seat.

In general, the performance approached the music from a contemporary rather than a period perspective. Except for the aforementioned finale, these works were informed with a modern sensibility, and the classical themes of each movement were never overly emphasized. The group approached Beethoven's "melodies" as kernels of potential material to develop, rather than as complete forms.

I doubt this view would have been the same if the group had never heard, let alone performed, the music of Bartók. String quartets were written throughout the 19th and early 20th centuries, including those by Schubert, Schumann and Brahms, but it wasn't until Bartók in the second of his six quartets broke through the constraints of the diatonic scale into a new musical world that the quartet was free to go wherever the composer wanted.

♩*Grieving and Weeping, Rossini Style*

Mostly Mozart Festival 6: Maria Agresta (soprano), Daniela Barcellona (mezzo), Gregory Kunde (tenor), Kyle Ketelsen (bass-baritone), Mostly Mozart Festival Orchestra, Gianandrea Noseda (conductor), Concert Chorale of New York, James Bagwell (director), Avery Fisher Hall, Lincoln Center, New York, 13.8.2013

Beethoven: Symphony No. 2 in D major
Rossini: *Stabat mater*

Misconceptions persist about artists even when evidence is presented that clearly proves them inaccurate. One such fiction that naggingly refuses to die is that great works of art reflect the creator's state of mind at the time of composition. When Beethoven was writing the Symphony No. 2, he was in despair over losing his hearing. Sir George Grove quotes a close friend of Beethoven as saying, "You could not believe the indescribable, I might say horrible, effect which the loss of his hearing has produced on him." During the same period in which he wrote the Second he also wrote "Heiligenstadt Testament," declaring that he was hastening "to meet Death face to face." Many critics including Grove have expressed amazement that Beethoven in his Symphony No. 2 gave no evidence of his state of mind, that given his depression he wrote a happy work. The same inconsistencies have been found and questioned regarding Mozart who maintained his upbeat style even during periods of distress and upheaval.

Art offers a creator the opportunity to forge a new world where magical notes or strokes of a paintbrush take the artist out of the quotidian. Tragic music may come from a carefree artist as well as from a dejected one. We talk about the effect of the death of Mahler's daughter on the creation of his last three symphonies, but are the seven before any "happier," even the ones written during his joyful years with Alma?

In his Mostly Mozart Festival debut, Gianandrea Noseda made no attempt to find the tragic, if there is any, in Beethoven's Second. Tempos were brisk, and attention to detail was the hallmark of this performance. The orchestra played crisply and clearly, even highlighting a few phrases that I had never noted before. The MMFO seems to respond best to animated leaders, and Noseda's enthusiasm and energy were apparent throughout. The Second may be one of Beethoven's "undervalued masterpieces" as noted in the playbill, but no one told this to Noseda.

Noseda took on a bigger task in leading the orchestra in Rossini's *Stabat Mater*. While this is no masterpiece, it has delightful moments. Rossini had trouble with the piece (it has a convoluted compositional and performance history), and he wrote beautiful but often inappropriate music for the texts: music that could easily have come from a Rossini opera. The opening *Stabat Mater* is mournful enough, but the dramatic center does not support the words. "Cujus animam gementem," translated here as "Through her weeping soul," begins with an oompah-pah in the bass and continues its rollicking way through mourning, grieving, trembling and torment. (Cenerentola might have walked on stage without seeming out of place.) The duet "Quis est homo qui non fieret" is a catchy dance-like aria that gives the mezzo a chance to sing in her upper range and the soprano the opportunity to reach up to the high As. The contrast between the music and the words "Who is the man who would not weep" is almost comic. Finally, in the "Pro peccatis suae gentis" ("For the sins of His people"), we get music that somewhat reflects the text. Two of the arias are almost instrument-free, supported by just the low strings; perhaps Rossini felt that for these to be effective they would be better as plain chant than as operatic-style arias.

Both soprano Maria Agresta and mezzo Daniela Barcellona handled their arias with flair when needed and were sensitively subdued for the few laments in this lamentation. Gregory Kunde's voice was a little tight at first, but he warmed up as the work proceeded. Kyle Ketelson worked the wide range of bass-baritone with barely a weak spot.

The final "Amen, world without end," a most dramatic and tricky choral fugue, was a test for the chorus and orchestra. Noseda went all out to draw together the different groups of instruments and voices, and at the end barely a second passed before there were shouts of praise and a standing ovation.

♫Le nozze di Figaro All Dressed Up

Mostly Mozart Festival 4: Budapest Festival Orchestra, Ivan Fischer (conductor), Rose Theater, Lincoln Center, New York, 11.8.2013

Mozart: *Le nozze di Figaro*
Festival premiere

Given that the Mostly Mozart calendar consists largely of traditional performances of traditional works, expectations were high for Ivan Fischer's return to the Festival. His radical production two years ago of *Don Giovanni* was performed to great acclaim (including mine). That opera was starkly staged in a more intimate theater than the Rose, with scenery and props created from the contortions of a group of mimes, which emphasized the existential issues inherent in the opera. It was effective as both powerful theater and musical performance.

Sometimes the success of daring, anti-establishment events creates an environment that results in a roughing-out of the edginess of subsequent creations. This production of *Le nozze di Figaro* avoided the pitfalls that might have occurred had Fischer picked a Mozart opera fashioned as a dramma per musica (*Idomeneo*) or an opera seria (*La Clemeza di Tito*) rather than choosing an opera buffa. But as far as *Le nozze* goes, this staging could be considered conservative compared to Peter Sellar's 1988 version. The action in that production takes place in the Trump Tower on New York's posh Fifth Avenue. Cherubino is an awkward teenager; the Count, a business magnate; Susanna, a maid living in the building's laundry room; and Don Basilio, a sleazy, small-time crook.

Fischer's production is nowhere near Sellar's in its eccentricity. First, it is not a fully staged production. Fischer refers to it as a "staged concert," and the action occurs on platforms set between the left and right halves of the orchestra. Characters coming on or off stage negotiate a path between orchestra members. At the back of the stage is a rack of dresses that could be found in a dressing room, and the opera's opening scene has the characters putting on and taking off costumes to emphasize the role these clothes will play in the action. In a sense, though, there is little need to emphasize the importance of costume: Mozart himself is doing that. Operas and plays of this time and earlier abounded in "pants roles," and ploys involving changed costumes and changed identities were common. Cherubino is the paradigm of gender switching: a woman dressed as a man who dresses up as a woman. A masked ball hides the characters' identities in *Don Giovanni*, and in *Cosi Fan Tutti*, Ferrando and Guglielmo disguise themselves to test their fiancees' fidelity.

Fischer's *Don Giovanni* existed outside of time. *Le nozze* exists in an anachronistic world where most of the actors don outfits of the period but some don't (Bartolo, for example, wears a modern business suit). Fischer himself conducts standing or sitting in a chair to the right of the stage to avoid being part of the action, but at times he couldn't avoid it: most amusingly, he is included in the repartee during the duet, "Crudel! Perché finora."

The only stage props that are particularly striking are the mannequins dressed in 18th-century garb which hang above the stage, dropping down or rising back up as needed. For a moment when they first descended, I thought that they were really actors. Now, that would have been a theatrical coup.

The vocal performances were close enough to perfect to seem almost natural: the normal communication between characters as opposed to the more heightened artifice of many operas arias. Laura Tatulescu was a convincing Susanna. After an initially weak opening aria, "Porgi Amor," Miah Persson settled in as a strong and stunning Countess, receiving a deserved round of applause for the aria "Dove Sono." Hanno Müller-Brachmann, both as actor and singer, was somewhat weak as Figaro. On the other hand, Rachel Frenkel had a strong and secure voice, almost too strong for the ingenue role of Cherubino. The laureled baritone Andrew Shore was a bit wobbly initially but shortly steadied himself as Barolo. Ann Murray as Marcellina wouldn't even have had to sing—which, of course, she thankfully did—to receive warm applause from the audience.

The Budapest Festival Orchestra, often listed in the top ten orchestras of the world, continued holding their place with a peerless accompaniment. Fischer claims that he is "going through a personal metamorphosis, changing from a conductor into the dual role of conductor/stage director." As interesting as he is as a stage director, Fischer has a long history as a well-respected and honored conductor, and one hopes his role as Maestro will not be put aside.

♪*Louis Langrée Breathes Life into Festival Concert*

Mostly Mozart Festival 3: Isabelle Faust(violin), Mostly Mozart Festival Orchestra, Louis Langrée (conductor), Avery Fisher Hall, Lincoln Center, New York, 9.8.2013

Beethoven: Overture to *Die Ruinen von Athen*
Mozart: Violin Concerto No. 5 in A major, "Turkish"
Beethoven: Symphony No. 5 in C minor

Louis Langrée returned Friday evening to conduct what certainly has become his Mostly Mozart Festival Orchestra, having relinquished his leadership to conductor Jérémie Rhorer for several days this past week. Rhorer's program had a similarly constructed lineup: a Beethoven overture, a Mozart concerto and a Beethoven symphony. Aside from sharing this complementary formula, the performances had little in common. It's hard to believe that the superb playing last night was from the same orchestra that a few days earlier, under Rhorer's direction, had given a listless recital of works that are nearly equivalent in quality.

From the opening stacatti of the Beethoven overture I knew this concert would more than redeem its languid predecessor. The following brief march, meltingly taken up by the oboe and supported by the bassoon and horn, leads into the brief central subject. Echoes of earlier music and shadows of music to come abound in this barely five-minute gem. From the past came reverberations of both the final movement of Beethoven's Triple Concerto and the trial and initiation music from Mozart's *The Magic Flute*. From the future came adumbrations of the overtures of Rossini and in particular his overture to *William Tell*.

If Mozart's 5th Violin Concerto with Isabelle Faust as soloist was not entirely successful, it did come close to the mark. We had two strong personalities: Faust, cool and intellectual, and Langrée, fervid and rambunctious. Her performance of Berg's Violin Concerto is about as good as any out there, whereas Langrée is in his element with music that he can fire up, as he does with Beethoven. Although this was Mozart's final violin concerto, it still is an early enough work that the entire first movement could be played appropriately in the *stil galante*. This was Faust's approach to the concerto. Langrée went for a more dramatic, even tragicomic approach. The tremolos, for instance, that appear in the first movement created a kind of jittery, almost electrical quality at odds with Faust's coolness. Faust's quiet entry and jump into the *allegro aperto* seemed somewhat disjointed; her playing was majestic while the orchestra's was rougher and less refined. Faust could have dug in a bit. Mozart's music isn't breakable.

Faust and Langrée were better matched in the mellifluous second movement, coming together to sing an elegant and eloquent song which then leads into the surprising final movement. Here Mozart, aged 19, makes his final statement in the violin concerto genre. Choosing the most conservative musical form, the rondo, and the simplest tempo, that of a minuet, Mozart sets up the standard staging for a typical finale. Even the slightly foreboding modulation in the second iteration of the rondo doesn't seem extraordinary, but the third iteration, the so-called Turkish march, is something else. Here Mozart switches to 2/4 time and into the far-away key of A minor. With the inevitable return from these musical whirlings to the opening theme, Mozart plays one final trick in ending the concerto with a quiet run of the same grace notes used in all the cadences of the rondo's main theme.

159

After the intermission Langrée accomplished the difficult task of giving Beethoven's Fifth a new lease on life in a performance that abounded in energy and enthusiasm. Langrée pulled out all the stops: the orchestra snapped to attention, the string players sawed (and soared) through the four movements. I can't remember a more rousing segue into the final movement. It's good to have the orchestra back in the magical hands of Maestro Langrée.

♪Rhorer Returns to Lead Works by Mozart and Beethoven
Mostly Mozart Festival 2: Paul Lewis (piano), Mostly Mozart Festival Orchestra, Jérémie Rhorer (conductor), Avery Fisher Hall, Lincoln Center, New York, 6.8.2013

Mozart: Overture to *Le nozze di Figaro*; Piano Concerto No. 25 in C major
Beethoven: Symphony No. 1 in C major

When the choices for a concert program consist of works that are tried and true, it requires the performers to rise to the occasion: to recreate, not simply to repeat the works at hand. Sometimes the confluence of musical connections will simply light right up. At other times a performer will possess a charismatic charm that captures and captivates the orchestra, the conductor and the audience. Sometimes, as occurred here, nothing exceptional takes place. During the 2011 Mostly Mozart Festival, I wrote this about conductor Jérémie Rhorer and the Mostly Mozart Festival Orchestra: "Rhorer was more than enthusiastic, but the orchestra responded lethargically. This could have been a result of weeks of rehearsing unfamiliar or not commonly played pieces with different conductors, lack of sufficient rehearsal time, poor rapport between the conductor and the orchestra or a combination of any or all of these reasons."

I include the entire quotation as a ditto to the concert reviewed here. It is easy to go into auto-pilot mode if there is no attempt by the conductor to take control.

One might have hoped that Paul Lewis, the well regarded pupil of Alfred Brendel, would have been able to bring something special to the proceedings, but he too seemed uninspired, even as he attempted to give the Mozart concerto an air of grandeur and majesty. Strangely, Lewis, whose performances of the music of Beethoven and Schubert have been lauded all around, has barely touched anything by Mozart. His discography shows no Mozart and in concert, as best as I can determine, he has only the Mozart piano concerto played here (and recently performed at the Proms) in his repertory.

To be fair, I must say that there was hardly anything specifically wrong with the performances. The opening Overture to *Le nozzi di Figaro* was perfectly acceptable and went by so quickly that I thought that there might be something missing. (I hadn't realized that it is the briefest overture in all of Mozart's major operas.) The Piano Concerto No. 25 had few instances to praise or criticize. The cadenza to the first movement written by Brendel did not have the complexity and dramatic bite that can be found in those by Busoni, Robert Casadesus or

Friedrich Gulda. In the third movement, the modulations into minor keys during the development section lacked the darkness that should have been in sharp contrast to the rest of the movement's cheerfulness. I did like the different emphases Rhorer gave to the opening notes of the recurring main theme.

The performance of Beethoven's Symphony No. 1 was the sole work after the intermission, making for a less varied program and a concert that without intermission barely clocked in as an hour's worth of music. Although the symphony used conservative tempi, it seemed rushed and there were few "Bravos" from the audience, an unusual occurrence at a New York classical music performance.

I am curious about the next program in the series, another tried and true group of works. This time the orchestra will be led by the resident conductor, Louis Langrée, who is known to have a good rapport with his instrumentalists.

♩*Mostly Mozart Opening Concert: Flourishing Again*

Mostly Mozart Festival 1: Alice Coote (mezzo-soprano), Jean-Efflam Bavouzet (piano), Mostly Mozart Festival Orchestra, Louis Langrée (conductor), Avery Fisher Hall, Lincoln Center, New York, 30.7.2013

Beethoven: Overture to *Coriolan*
Mozart: "Ch'io mi scordi di te…Non temer, amato bene"
Beethoven: Piano Concerto No. 4 in G major
Mozart: "Parto, Parto, ma tu ben mio" from *La clemenza di Tito*
Beethoven: Symphony No. 7 in A major

In its 47 years the Mostly Mozart Festival has had periods when it flourished and periods when it languished. Luckily, we seem to be in an upswing. The original excitement in 1966 of having summer weeks filled with Mozart, whose music was thought to be illimitable, gradually died out and gave way to the necessary inclusion of Haydn, then Haydn and Schubert, and then composers as diverse as Monteverdi, Dvořák, Satie and Stravinsky. The conductors over the years have included Neville Marriner, Edo de Waart, Christopher Hogwood and, since 2002, Louis Langrée as both conductor and music director. Having one conductor for most of the Festival has improved the orchestra's performances considerably: they do not have to deal with a succession of differing maestros, each with a particular way of doing things.

This year's Mostly Mozart Festival focuses on Beethoven, a decidedly more fruitful subject than last year's exploration of the influence of bird songs on musical creation. The formatting of the opening night's program closely followed last year's with an overture, two Mozart arias, a piano concerto and a symphony. This eclectic array of differing forms provided a good introduction to the works of the two composers who will dominate the Festival. However, the opening concert made no attempt to select works that might reflect Mozart's influence on Beethoven. The latter's early piano concerti or symphonies would be more reflective of Mozart's style than the Piano Concerto No. 4 or Symphony No. 7.

161

Beethoven's dramatic overture to *Coriolanus* (a work by his contemporary, the playwright Heinrich Collin, not Shakespeare's version) was given a tightly controlled reading, closer in spirit to performances by Harnoncourt or Goodman than Reiner or Karajan. One may miss the latter two's massive chords that come from a full symphony orchestra with the tympani's booms echoing and reverberating through the hall, completely filling its sound space. But what we did get in this performance was clarity of both the inner and outer lines and the difficult-to-achieve balancing between the strings and the winds. The work's coda was particularly effective with its delicate *sempre più piano* followed by the three pizzicato notes that end the work.

Mozart's "Ch'io mi scordi di te" is perhaps the biggest gem in the collection of his under-appreciated concert arias. Written for soprano, piano and orchestra, it has one of those magical musical moments where we are surprised to have our expectations broken. Here, the vocalist, who would normally follow the recitative with an aria, comes in only after the piano plays the lilting opening theme. Alice Coote effortlessly delivered her warm mezzo voice to the back of the theater. In the second half of the program Ms. Coote came back to sing "Parto, parto, ma tu ben mio" from Mozart's *Clemenza di Tito*. In his final years Mozart was enamored of the recently introduced clarinet, and he used it here to accompany the mezzo's vocal line. Again, Ms. Coote gave a fine rendition of one of Mozart's last works.

Beethoven's fourth piano concerto was played here with a light and lyrical hand by the French pianist Jean-Efflam Bavouzet, a relaxed and delightfully summery performance. One need only look at the great French interpreters of Beethoven such as Robert Casadesus, Yves Nat or Alfred Cortot to appreciate Bavouzet's particular manner of performance: he played without overly dramatic gestures and was elegant without being fussy. Langrée understood fully what was required of him and the orchestra. To my surprise, I applauded spontaneously along with the most of the audience after the final notes of the concerto's compelling first movement. The brief, recitative-style second movement with its loud orchestral retorts to the piano's soft questions segues to the final movement.

The Mostly Mozart Festival Orchestra gave a vibrant, kinetic performance of Beethoven's Symphony No. 7. It was clear that the orchestra knew the work well enough for them to focus on Langrée and his interpretation rather than concentrating on the scores in front of them. Langrée kept a tight grip on the instrumentalists and, as a result, they gave a clear, forceful reading: a spectacular finish to an all-round superb evening.

♫*Concerti Galore: Bach Week Ends on an Up Note at Montreal Music Festival*

Rachel Barton Pine (violin), Elizabeth Wallfisch (director/violinist), Montreal Festival Ensemble, St. George's Church, Montreal, 25.5.2013

Bach: Concertos for Violin in A minor, Violin in E major, Three Violins in C major, Oboe and Violin in C minor, Violin in G minor, Two Violins in D minor

One should always be cautious when using the word "Complete" to qualify a historical composer's opus. Inevitably, a new work will be discovered or an old work reconstructed to invalidate the premise of completion. This new work will be added to the next "Complete" edition, which will remain complete until it isn't.

In the concert presented here, six violin concerti were performed, three of which are generally accepted as originally written by Bach for violin(s). The three others are reconstructions of harpsichord concerti, which may themselves have been reconstructions of now-lost violin concerti. The Concerto for 3 Violins, BWV1064R is a reconstruction of the Concerto for 3 Harpsichords, BWV1064. The same is true for both the Concerto for Oboe and Violin, BWV1060R, reconstructed from BWV1060; and BWV1056R, reconstructed from BWV1056.

Aside from stray fragments and the movement BWV1045 which, although scored for a solo violin, sounds more like a sinfonia that Bach might have written to open a cantata, the only violin concerto not included in this program is the reconstruction (BWV1052R) of the Concerto for Harpsichord No. 1 in D minor, BWV1052. There may be reasons why this one was omitted, but ultimately it is a scholarly decision based on whatever evidence is found convincing. Perhaps a better title for this concert might have been a vaguer "Bach Violin Concerti."

Rachel Barton Pine was soloist in all of the evening's concerti and gave characteristically sensitive interpretations. Hearing her pure notes effortlessly played in an unhurried, vibrato-less manner, I was reminded of just how bewitching historically informed interpretations can be. The simplest drawing of the bow across the string, free of fidgety wobbling, produces a tone that alone should convince anyone of the validity of these techniques. Even in the most demanding passages, one did not sense anything but complete oneness with her instrument: her violin radiated warmth with every touch of her bow.

The double and triple violin concerti gave the audience a quick lesson in "timbre." If there was ever a question of what a composer's reasoning is when he doubles, triples or quadruples the solo instrument, one need only listen carefully to the three lines in the Concerto for 3 Violins. Each instrument had a unique voice: Ms. Pine's, resonant and tempered; Elizabeth Wallfisch's, clear, sharp and bright; and Timothy Chooi's, smooth and mellow.

Only in the performance of the reconstructed Concerto for Oboe and Violin was the playing not of the highest quality. Theodore Baskin struggled in the solo part for oboe with a constricted and tight performance that seemed to put a damper on the rest of the players.

The Concerto in D minor for two violins had both master violinists in musical conversation in the first movement, with phrases tossed playfully between the two. The poignant Largo had the opposite effect of turning the two violins into one pure instrument. The final Allegro had both violinists coming together then moving apart, dancing in a joyous summation of this program and of the magical "Bach Week" at the Montreal Chamber Music Festival.

♪Bach's Brandenburgs in Montreal: Complete in Every Way

Soloists and Winners of the 2012 Canada Musical Instrument Bank Awards, Elizabeth Wallfisch (violinist/director), St. George's Church, Montreal, 23.5.2013

Bach: Brandenburg Concertos: No. 2 in F major, No. 5 in D major, No. 4 in G major, No. 1 in F major, No. 6 in B-flat major, No. 3 in G major

Why does one live concert succeed while another fails? The obvious answer is that a concert must be well performed, emotionally resonant and reflective of the musicians' intentions. Yet there are instances where everything comes together and goes beyond these qualities to a higher level of eloquence. For the audience in such a situation, nothing that occurs outside the music really matters. Technical and interpretative issues are subsumed by the nearly palpable sense of camaraderie between the artists and the audience.

This was the situation here. Did it matter that every seat in the church was taken and some members of the audience could only find places with a partial view, or that at times the musicians filled the stage so tightly that they might have feared accidentally bowing their colleagues. What mattered was the music: music played on an array of instruments of all shapes and sizes. Many of these were one-of-a-kind historical rarities whose resulting sound, aided by the unique acoustics of the church, were full yet at the same time unexpectedly intimate.

The ordering of the Brandenburgs was unusual in that it started with No. 2 and ended with No. 3. I'm not sure of the reasoning behind this, except for the fact that closing the concert with No. 3 gave all the string players an opportunity to be on stage for the final work of the night.

The Brandenburg No. 2 opened the concert with a flourish of fanfares. Trumpeter Jens Lindemann faultlessly shot rapid-fire notes that Bach wrote for an earlier instrument even more difficult to master than our modern-day one. Despite the unusually fast tempi that were taken for this concerto, Lindemann breezed through it with seeming ease.

Both flutist Jocelyne Roy and harpsichordist Hank Knox were outstanding in the Brandenburg No. 5. The harpsichord is the instrument in the spotlight here, acting as a major player rather than just a supporting member of the basso continuo group. In no other Brandenburg, and perhaps in no other work by Bach, does an obbligato harpsichord play non-stop from beginning to end. The improvisatory-like cadenza of the first movement only gradually gains focus as instrumentalists drop out one by one as if they were precursors of Haydn's vacationing musicians in his "Farewell Symphony." Now completely alone, the harpsichordist is faced with 65 bars of daunting runs and arpeggios of 16th and 32nd notes, some even written as triplets. Getting to the end measure is an accomplishment in itself, and Knox is to be congratulated for getting there error-free.

Not that Elizabeth Wallfisch was in any way inactive in the previous concerti, but No. 4 really gave her an opportunity to show her stuff. Along with the caressing playing of recorders by Vincent Lauzer and Alexa Raine-Wright, Ms.

Wallfisch tackled the fiendishly difficult violin role in the *concertino* sections with thorough mastery. In fact throughout the evening she never for an instant wavered in control of all three of her roles: leader, soloist and member of the orchestra's string section.

One can understand why Bach's Brandenburg No. 1 is the first in the set: it makes use of more instruments than any of the others and is the prototype for all that follow. Each concerto is uniquely colored, but the first is *sui generis*. It is the only one with four movements, and its final movement is comprised of the names of dances; technically, it's more of a suite than a concerto. All the instrumentalists had a chance to step out from the crowd as if they were introducing themselves to the audience. Special mention should be given to the horn players Jocelyn Veilleux and Louis-Phillipe Marsolais, who succeeded in a challenging score.

After the brashness of the No. 1, No. 6 came as a needed respite. Bach perhaps felt that the last work in a set should be one of an unusual nature: both the Cello Suite No. 6 and the Brandenburg No. 6 are markedly different from their predecessors, the former written for its highest register, the Brandenburg for its lower. The unhurried warmth that came from the normal string section's violins, violas, celli and double bass was enhanced by the viola da gambas played by Betsy MacMillian and Elin Söderström. What can be said about this Brandenburg's second movement other than that it is ethereal?

The concluding No. 3 had all the string members tightly fitted across the stage. The energy radiated by the previous concerti seemed to have been harnessed and applied to this one: a fitting finale that upon completion had the audience jumping out of their seats, giving the players well-deserved applause and bravi.

This was an exceptional concert, one sure to be on my list of best concerts of the year.

♪Suite Fifteen: *Winners of the 2012 Competition Open "Bach Week" at the Montreal Festival*

Montreal Chamber Music Festival, St. George's Church, Montreal, 22.5.2013

Bach: Selections from Sonatas and Partitas for Solo Violin; Suites for Solo Cello

Fifteen finalists from the 2012 Canada Council Musical Instrument Bank Competition demonstrated exactly what made them winners, with each musician on an historic violin or cello playing movements from Bach's solo cello suites and solo sonatas and partitas. A brilliant showcase for these young virtuosi, it should help put to rest any doubts about the future of chamber music, any mistaken thought that it's the music of a dying generation.

As part of the winners' prizes, each has been given an historic instrument to use for a period of three years. The instruments themselves are from the $36 million collection of strings curated by the Canada Council Musical Instrument Bank.

What a treat it was to both hear a well-chosen selection of some of Bach's finest solo music for strings, and to have the pieces played on unique instruments by individuals who had their own strong views as to how they wanted their brief solos to sound. Running the gamut from the clean, intellectual, yet elegant violin playing of Matilda Kaul to the romantic, lush performance by Arnold Choi on the cello, every soloist had something to say and nearly all said it with genial panache.

It would be ungracious for any critic to take a position on what was "correct" playing and what was not. The use of vibrato ranged from heavy—Emmanuel Vukovich's take on Bach's famous D-minor Ciaccona—to non-existent in the hands of Jonathan Chan (Fugue and Allegro from the Sonata No. 1 in G-minor). Similarly, each instrumentalist had his or her own notions as to both tempi and dynamics: some stayed near the urtext while others went far afield in personalizing their own interpretations.

As each soloist had his or her own musical personality, each instrument had its own timbre, small but resonant in Chan's hands but large and full in Véronique Mathieu's Presto from the Sonata No. 1. The variety of sounds was astonishing and made this a dream program for both string and Bach enthusiasts.

Individual performances were at the least serviceable and breathtaking at their best. The difficult Prelude to the infamous Suite No. 6, debatably written for a five-stringed violincello piccolo, was formidably handled by Rachel Desoer. Her clear, easeful control of the strings near the very top of the cello's tessitura hypnotized the audience. Carissa Klopoushak's velocity in the Presto of the Partita No.1 was plainly in the no-speed-limit zone. Ariel Barnes did right by the Prelude to the 4th cello suite; he brought out the various colors from the opening motif which is modulated every which way, creating at times a sonic illusion that the same phrases can be heard in two ways at the same time. Andréa Tyniec's polished reading of the *Tempo di Borea* from the Partita No. 1 was full of grace.

There were a few minor disappointments. Se-Doo Park didn't quite succeed in mastering the technical difficulties of the gavottes and gigue from the sixth cello suite. Emmanuel Vukovich tried to squeeze a little too much meaning out of the Ciaccona, extending its length beyond one's attention span. I'm sure that there was some logic as to why certain pieces were played da capo while others weren't, but I couldn't see it.

Impressive as well was the audience who clearly understood that applause wasn't expected until after the performers had completely finished their sets.

♫Mozart and Bruckner: Lightness and Heaviness
Emanuel Ax (piano), New York Philharmonic Orchestra, Alan Gilbert (conductor), Avery Fisher Hall, Lincoln Center, New York, 24.4.2013

Mozart: Piano Concerto No. 25 in C major
Bruckner: Symphony No. 3 in D minor

Alan Gilbert in his notes on this program uses three adjectives that precisely describe Emanuel Ax's playing: lightness, elegance and warmth. Whether he is doing Mozart, Chopin or Barber, he never pounds, never throws himself about, never overly gesticulates. His playing could be seen as emotionally detached and his touch on the keys verging on *détaché*, but this is not the case. A great pianist can coax *fortes* from a keyboard without hammering the keys. Here Ax's light touch brought out the element of silence in Mozart's music: the music or non-music that exists between notes. Not that Ax ignored the legato markings in the score, but this was legato played on its edge.

Ax's lyrical playing matches the concerto itself, a work rife with melodies. The opening fanfare gives way to a long exposition before the piano enters about three minutes into the work; when it does, a new theme opens. The piano eventually picks up and repeats the main theme and the secondary theme, often called the "Marseilles" motif. This eight-note motif becomes the elemental structure that weaves in and out of the concerto in every way possible. The rhythmic first five notes are repeated at every turn: played outright, chopped off, repeated over and over in the forefront and background. The cadenza by Alfred Brendel (no Mozart cadenza exists) has become the common one, and Ax played it with gracious dignity.

In contrast to the middle movements of many other concerti piano concerti, the second movement is relatively upbeat, without the frequent changes in modulation that are the central elements of more heartfelt ones. Much of the writing is for woodwinds and horns which places it in the realm of Mozart's more rustic works like his divertimenti. The slightly faster than usual tempo was not at all inappropriate. Although the third movement is listed as an Allegretto, it has the feeling of a rondo. The main theme is repeated after a new theme is played and, in rondo style, this is done twice.

This performance was about as good as it gets.

With Bruckner's Symphony No. 3 we are in an entirely different world. It's hard to get a handle on most Bruckner symphonies, difficult to compare performances when there are so many versions. Even if we were to compare Leopold Nowak's editions of No. 3, we would have to ask which Bruckner version we are we listening to: the 1873 or the 1889? Gilbert chose the 1889 version "convinced that [this is] the one that finally satisfied him." Is there a big difference between these two? If one looks at the timings, for example, Gilbert finished the piece in just under an hour. George Tintner in his recording of the 1873 version runs 77 minutes. It would take a dedicated Brucknerian to be able to compare the 17 or so versions of his nine-plus symphonies, let alone discern one from another. Bruckner was so insecure that he felt anyone who was willing to "correct" his symphonies could do so better than the composer himself. In terms of manuscripts, scholars have found at least nine versions of No. 3 in various draft stages.

Gilbert did a superb job of controlling this monster, and only a few times did it seem that he went too far with the massive crescendos. The symphony has some upbeat, less tortured music that is lacking in the later symphonies, and Gilbert presented the quieter moments of lyrical sweetness quite effectively. The brass players, so important to all of Bruckner's symphonies, pierced through the massive musical clusters with a spiking élan. The whole orchestra is to be congratulated on a dynamic performance.

♪Voices in a Garden
Les Arts Florissants, William Christie (director/conductor), Brooklyn Academy of Music, Brooklyn, 19.4.2013

Rameau, Monteclair, Dauvergne, Grandval, Gluck, Campra: "Le Jardin de Monsieur Rameau"

Le Jardin des Voix: Daniela Skorka, soprano; Emilie Renard, mezzo-soprano; Benedetta Mazzucato, mezzo-soprano; Zachary Wilder, tenor; Victor Sicard, baritone; Cyril Costanzo, bass

Since 2002, on a biennial basis, William Christie has held auditions to select a small group of promising vocalists for Le Jardin des Voix. Ultimately, they will either join Les Arts Florissants or move on with impressive credentials. Those who are accepted into the program receive intensive singing lessons and training by Christie and others in preparation for joining Les Arts Florissants on a worldwide tour. This changing group of young singers made its fifth appearance in New York to perform a program fittingly entitled "Le Jardin de Monsieur Rameau."

As a clear sign of the growing interest in this project, BAM changed venues this year from the smaller Harvey Theater to the main building, the Harvey Gilman Opera House. This was a tradeoff: some intimacy was lost but it enabled a larger audience to hear the single performance. However, due to the fact that there were still two performances to run at the Gilman of Charpentier's *David and Jonathas*, the vocalists had to cope with the wooden room that serves as the opera's set.

The soloists, all well-versed in Baroque vocal style, gave alternately serious and comic readings from Rameau and the other composers. The first selection, from the prologue of Monteclair's *Jephté*, featured a sampling of various musical elements, starting with an overture in the style of Lully: slow dotted and double dotted rhythms, followed by a return to the beginning theme. It is not usual but Christie took the repeats on the overture. A dance movement follows leading in to the first aria, which is sung to the tune of the rigaudon. The catchy rigaudon theme, unusually, continues through the next aria as well, closing with a sweet flute-driven chorus.

The most charming and droll aria of the evening had to be Grandval's cantata "Rien du tout." Nicolas Racot de Grandval was a contemporary of Rameau, known more for his dozens of plays than his musical works. The cantata, winsomely sung by mezzo Emilie Renard, parodies his contemporaries, including Monteclair. The singer tells the audience that she has grown weary of music, unable to satisfy everyone's differing taste. Asking the audience to request an aria that is serious, comic, languorous or chromatic, she sings each word and is accompanied by the orchestra in that particular style. She then sings an aria is each style but becomes more and more frustrated because no one will tell her what they want. Renard did a great job singing and acting and caught the exact spirit of every phrase.

Arias from Gluck take us solidly into the 18th century. One normally thinks of Gluck as the stark, dramatic and somewhat emotionally cool composer of such operas as *Orfeo ed Euridice, Armide* and *Iphigénie en Aulide*. It comes then as a surprise that he wrote this Vaudevillian opera, *L'Ivrogne corrigé*. The theme of a recovering alcoholic is not something you might expect from this composer, the champion of reformist opera. Gluck complained about the silliness of Baroque opera and wanted to strip it of over-decoration and exaggerated actions: to, in fact, go back to the purity of the ancient Greeks. The group nonetheless did their best with this too-broad comedy, hamming it up a bit and doing so with palpable enjoyment.

Excerpts from another opera, whose name was taken by an early music group, *Europa Galante*, followed after the intermission. This opera by Campra is considered to be the first of a genre called "opéra-ballets." As Gluck later rebelled against the overly ornate and fantastical operas of his time, Campra's *Europa Galante* avoids exotic tales of love and war. Instead it presents a series of portraits of courtship in various countries. The entire cast plays a role here, and again the singers' voices and acting were professional in a way that seems more solid and well-balanced than most other performances of Baroque theater and music.

Of all the Rameau arias that followed one stands out, and that is the vocal quartet "Tendre Amour." This aria gains its power from falling somewhere between a canon and a chaconne. Each voice comes in as in a round. It was meltingly sung with an unearthly harmony and just the right intonation.

We have to thank William Christie for his foresight and dedication, for looking towards the future and the continuation of this premier company.

♫*Unusual Mozart, Colorful Janáček, Dramatic Schumann*

Jonathan Biss (piano), Elias String Quartet (Sara Bitlloch and Donald Grant, violins; Martin Saving, viola; Marie Bitlloch, cello), Carol McGonnell (clarinet), Eric Reed (horn), Brad Balliett (bassoon), Zankel Hall, Carnegie Hall, New York, 10.4.2013

Mozart: Piano Concerto No. 13 in C major
Janáček: Concertino for Piano and Chamber Ensemble
Schumann: Piano Quintet in E-flat major

The Piano Concerto No. 13, K.415 is part of a set of concerti (with K.413, 414 and 449) written by Mozart in the specific hope of earning a substantial recompense. He was successful in selling subscriptions to a series highlighting these concerti, but his later attempt to sell manuscript copies on a subscription basis failed. His advertisement for the scores was meant to appeal to both professionals and amateurs: professional musicians would perform them with an orchestra and purchase all the parts, while amateurs or less wealthy musicians would only need to buy the scores for piano and strings. Mozart may have underestimated the skill required for an amateur to perform the works and, as a result, this business venture did not succeed.

Even if there was not historical evidence from contemporary accounts, advertisements and Mozart's letters that he had specifically intended these works to be playable by both amateur and professional, one only needs to look at the scores. The first movement of K.415 runs about 325 measures of which nearly 200 are for piano and strings without orchestral accompaniment. By comparison, Mozart's final piano concerto, K.595, which is not intended for amateurs, has about 300 measures of which just 64 are for piano and strings.

This was the first time I had heard a performance of a Mozart piano concerto performed with a string quartet instead of an orchestra, and it took a little while to adjust to this stripped-down version. The opening sounded thin and scratchy. I certainly missed the horns and tympani that explode at the first *forte* of the orchestral version, but the lyrical second movement didn't seem to want for lack of other instruments. Jonathan Biss might have lingered less on each note as if each one were packed with equal potency. The final movement has its best moments in the transitions back to the rondo's refrain, but not having the orchestral accompaniment lessened the power of these expressive moments.

Janáček's Concertino for Piano and Chamber Ensemble is imbued with the spirit of Czech folk music. It's hard not to feel that this work had some influence on Bartók: in effect it is a "Concerto for Orchestra" without orchestra. While none of the movements here have the brazenness of Bartók, they each have their own quaint folksy quirkiness. Janáček's subtitles for each piece connect them intentionally or not to the music of his opera *The Cunning Little Vixen*. The opening combination of piano and French horn plods in an off-balance manner that does seem appropriately named "grumpy hedgehog." The frenetic piano and clarinet flit about in the second movement like the "fidgety squirrel" they are meant to represent. All the instruments join in to create the sounds of night creatures in the third and a "scene from a fairy tale" ends this delightful work.

The performance of Schumann's Piano Quintet continues Biss's probing exploration of this composer. While I questioned some of his musicological comments and programming decisions in an earlier review, overall his performance of Schumann's works is well thought out and convincingly played. Although one hears Beethoven's influence in the Piano Quintet, it really is Schubert whose music is behind it. This is most clearly heard in the lieder-like second movement's haunting funereal themes and the lyrical trio section of the Scherzo. If there is any Beethoven to be heard in this piece, it is the final movement's dynamic lead-up to the ending fugue.

The Elias String Quartet played with agility and vigor, and the three additional musicians enthusiastically added their technical expertise to the colorful Janáček Concertino.

♪You Don't (Des) Say

Metropolitan Opera Orchestra, Harry Bicket (conductor), Metropolitan Opera,

Handel: *Giulio Cesare*:

Should I have been disappointed by the sudden absence of the indisposed Natalie Dessay for this second night's performance of Handel's *Giulio Cesare*; or should I have been pleased that her replacement was Danielle de Niese, the soprano who took the part of Cleopatra in the original 2005 Glynde*bour*ne production? Peter Gelb's appearance on stage before the performance brought expectant moans from the cognoscenti, who knew that he would be announcing a change in the cast. If my internal applause meter was correct there were considerable more "ahs" at the mention of Danielle de Niese's name than at the mention of Natalie Dessay's. De Niese seems to have captured the demanding hearts of New Yorkers. Her appearance last October at New York's hot, all-music-is-welcome-here nightclub, Le Poisson Rouge, revealed a down-to-earth charmer. Her performance in the Met's pastiche *Enchanted Island* was widely hailed.

The Met intelligently reproduced the staging of the Glyndebourne production almost to a T: all the original major designers were involved in the remake. The most critical change from the original was the casting of a countertenor in the role of Caesar as opposed to a mezzo in a pants role. Sarah Connolly was astonishing and absolutely riveting in the Glyndebourne production. David Daniels hit the right notes, but otherwise he paled in comparison.

Other members from the original cast included the ever-reliable Patricia Bardon whose complex character of Cornelia ran the gamut of emotions from desolation at the loss of her husband to anger and rage toward his killers. The opening "Ombra mai fu"-like "Priva son d'ogni conforto" was poignant. The duet with Sesto, "Son nata la lagrimar," was well sung by Bardon but unfortunately marred by Alice Coote's inability to match Bardon's over-powering voice. Cornelia's sudden change in character as expressed in her final aria, "Non ha più che temere," convincingly reflected the trauma of the preceding events as well as her awareness that her once dependent son can now stand on his own.

Two secondary characters from the original production, Christopher Dumaux and Rachid Ben Abdeslam, excelled in singing, acting and dancing. Dumaux as Tolomeo added a physicality to the role not generally present in the rest of the cast (outside of de Niese). As the classic villain, his voice carried venom and cruelty in every note, and his gratuitous violence towards Cornelia and Cleopatra was palpable. The counter-tenor Rachid Ben Abdeslam was outrageous as Cleopatra's confidant, Nireno. Both his "Bollywood" dancing and his stylized singing of "Qui perde un momento" did not seem, surprisingly, inappropriate either to the opera or to the words of the text. This was true with all the dance numbers which supplied Shakespearean moments of comic relief from the tragic tale unfolding.

Alice Coote in the pants role of Sesto, Cornelia's son, was convincingly sullen throughout the entire opera. If her voice didn't quite thrill as did Angelika

Kirschschlager's in the original cast, this is not meant to be a disparagement. Guido Loconsolo, as the evil advisor to Tolomeo whom he ultimately abandons, sang with a forceful tenor voice. His evil ways and his lust for Cornelia mirror those of his malevolent master, Tolomeo.

There was, of course, much beautiful music. If there was one showstopper it would have to be "Se pieta" which closes Act II. Discussing this aria in an interview, de Niese stated how physically draining and exhausting the piece is to sing. There are few ten-minute arias of this emotional depth that can hypnotize an audience, but this one did. A similar statement applies to "V'adoro, pupille" from Act II. The aria "Va tacito" is a rarity in Baroque opera with an obbligato horn accompanying the singer. Daniels, while lacking the vocal projection he's had in the past in this aria, nonetheless proved convincing. "Se in fiorito ameno prato" from Act II is a joyful and bubbly aria with solo violin accompaniment. Delightful as it is, it seems out of place in this opera, more reminiscent of the rustic "Sweet bird" of *l'Allegro ed il Penseroso* or the pastoral songs in *Acis and Galatea*.

Harry Bicket led a stripped-down Metropolitan Opera orchestra in a supportive and stylish fashion. There was no attempt to "go authentic," which was the case with Glyndebourne's original production under the direction of William Christie. If that had been tried here it might have resulted in a volume too low to fill a hall as big as the Met.

Now that both *Enchanted Island* and *Giulio Cesare* have been such successes, how about a selection from the dozens of Baroque operas that have been successfully produced in Europe in recent years? Any opera from Lully, Vivaldi or Rameau would be welcomed.

♫*András Schiff: Better at Keyboard Than Podium*

András Schiff (piano and conductor), New York Philharmonic Orchestra, Avery Fisher Hall, Lincoln Center, New York, 3.4.2013

Bach: Keyboard Concerto No.5 in F minor, Keyboard Concerto No.3 in D major
Mendelssohn: Sinfonia No. 9 in C major, "Swiss"
Schumann: Symphony No. 4 in D minor

The list of prominent soloists who, successfully or not, have tried a hand at conducting is nearly endless. These changes midway or late in a soloist's career have historical precedents in Berlioz, Liszt, Wagner, Toscanini, Szell and Bernstein. Today the list would include Ashkenazy, Eschenbach, Barenboim and Pletnev. There are obvious reasons for this shift in musical occupation including loss of flexibility or illness, and less obvious ones such as wanting control over an orchestra or the desire to broaden one's musical landscape.

Soloists who test the waters may find that directing a large group of musicians requires a strong personality, one able to gain respect from an orchestra's sometimes intractable members. During an interview with the keyboardist Miklós Spányi, I asked him about his attempts at conducting and he replied: "For a certain time I preferred conducting to performing, but I realized that it might be better to leave that job to the professional conductor. Conducting from the harpsichord is one thing, but standing in front of all those people is not my...cup of tea."

To expand on Spanyi's comment, conducting from the keyboard is barely conducting at all. Depending upon the demands of the piano score, the pianist/conductor may have little time to lead the orchestra. In the two concertos by Bach here, the piano basically is played non-stop and, in the dual role of soloist and frequent basso continuo, there is little time for the pianist to lift a hand from the keys. This style of conducting relies on the orchestra to play successfully on its own. The F-minor Concerto's two outer movements were a little rough around the edges, but this was redeemed with a poignant middle Largo. The Concerto No. 3 fared better, with Schiff clearly distinguishing between the left and right hand voices: this was the kind of technique that made Schiff the Bach pianist of his time. His trademark *détaché* playing, clearly influenced by Glen Gould, is more measured, less eccentric and warmer than the earlier Gould. It was difficult to spot but towards the end of the middle movement Schiff uses the pedal ever so slightly to sustain the bridge between several measures. This was a solid performance with the orchestra improving considerably from the opening work.

It wasn't until the Mendelssohn sinfonia that one could see the conductor's full style, and perhaps this is not the best choice of pieces on which to judge Schiff's skill. *Playbill* states this is the first performance ever of the piece at Carnegie Hall, which leads to the question: why hasn't it been played before? Well, the answer is simple: it's pleasant but insubstantial. Some of the other string sinfonias are less ambitious and can be accepted on their own terms, but the 9th attempts too much and Schiff didn't quite reach the level of intensity that is needed.

The Schumann Symphony No. 4 was performed in its later version of 1851. Schiff conducted the movements without break, as specified on the original 1841 version, which was closer to a symphonic fantasy than a traditional symphony. The piece was convincingly played, but there were moments when it seemed that Schiff was not really controlling the orchestra, that they knew this piece well and were playing on autopilot.

This was Schiff's first conducting gig with the Philharmonic, and I was inclined to be more lenient with him. In point of fact, he has been conducting (though not full time) since 1999. Overall it was a moderately successful performance from a first-rate pianist and a well-intentioned conductor.

♫*The St. Matthew Passion: Glorious Bach, Confusing Production*
Orchestra of St. Luke's, Iván Fischer (conductor), Carnegie Hall, New York, 28.3.2013

Bach: *St. Matthew Passion*

Bach is in the air and in the ears of New Yorkers with the kind of attention usually reserved for a composer's commemorative year such as 1985 (Bach's 300th birthday) or 2000 (the 250th anniversary of his death). New York's classical music station WQXR is nearing the end of a ten-day marathon of all of Bach's music. It began on March 21st, the 328th anniversary of Bach's birth, and it ends on Easter Sunday. Their "Bach 360°" festival includes free concerts, "How Bach Changed My Life" contests and, for donations, a gift of a funereal black Bach tote bag that was announced along with witty puns on the word "todt." At the same time, the NY Philharmonic is nearing the end of a month-long festival entitled "The Bach Variations."

Carnegie Hall presented the *St. Matthew Passion* in 1992 and again in 2007 with a performance by Helmuth Rilling and the Orchestra of St. Luke's. Why such a long hiatus between productions of what is generally considered one of Western music's greatest achievements: a fear perhaps of being labeled old-fashioned, inauthentic or historically uninformed? As I wrote in a review of Bach's Mass in B minor, "What we are really talking about is nothing more than the continual changing of musical taste: each generation develops its own sensibility as to what is musically correct." A generation that will fill an auditorium to hear contemporary pieces is an audience that will also accept Bach's music whether presented on original instruments or not.

On Thursday night those who had looked online or read *Playbill* may well have been confused. The Carnegie Hall online information page indicated the performance would last two hours and thirty minutes including intermission, while *Playbill* gave the performance time as two hours and ten minutes. It would have been the quickest performance ever if the timings were true: no recording of the 1727 version has ever been done in less than two hours and thirty minutes. One result of this error was a slow departure of audience members who possibly had transportation deadlines or other obligations. With a work this sacred, complex and demanding of one's attention, the exodus made it difficult to concentrate on Part II.

Equally confusing was the stage setup. Bach's score requires two identical choruses and two almost identical orchestras. But what reasoning was there behind the second group having oboes and flutes in the front rows instead of strings as in the first group? I thought it was a brilliant idea to have the ripieno group leave the chorus to sing downstage the *cantus firmus* of the opening chorus, "Kommt, ihr Töchter, helft mir klagen." But why wasn't it done for the other chorus, "O Mensch, bewein dein Sunde gross," which also uses a *cantus firmus*?

Overall, however, the performance was excellent: well-constructed, moderate in timing, sensitive to the subtle changes in phrasing and pacing and emotionally potent. Most to be praised was mezzo Barbara Kozelj whose expressive rounded voice filled the hall, particularly so in "Buss und Reu." Dominique Labelle's voice moved a little too much into the operatic realm, and she flagged somewhat in "Aus Liebe will mein Heiland sterben." Both John Tessier as the Evangelist and Hanno Müller-Brachmann as Jesus carried the drama forward, attentive to the tone-painting Bach applies to so much of the text.

The members of Musica Sacra responded admirably to Fischer's well-judged conducting style. Although there was no problem in hearing the obligatto accompaniment for the single instrument arias, such as the violin in "Erbarme Dicht, mein Gott" or oboe in "Ich will dir mein Herze schenken," it might have been more powerful if they performed downstage with the solo vocalists.

For me, I doubt that any performance of the SMP will ever come close to the Jonathan Miller staged adaptations at BAM in 2001 and 2009, but this production was laudable. Hopefully, we will not have to wait years to see this monumental work again at Carnegie Hall.

♪Bach: A Break from the Rush Hour

Isabelle Faust (violin), New York Philharmonic Orchestra, Bernard Labadie (Conductor), Avery Fisher Hall, Lincoln Center, New York, 20.3.2013

Bach: Sinfonia from Cantata No. 42, "Am Abend aber desselbigen Sabbats"; Violin Concerto in A minor; Violin Concerto in E major; Orchestral Suite No. 3 in D major

I've been to several concerts with Bernard Labadie as conductor, but this was the first time I'd seen him conduct an orchestra other than his own period instrument group, Les Violons du Roy. I've also attended New York Philharmonic Orchestra concerts conducted by early-music specialists, but none have succeeded as well as Mr. Labadie in getting a period-instrument sound out of this orchestra. While both Alan Gilbert in his performance of Bach's Mass in B Minor and Labadie used smaller string sections, Gilbert's players were all over the place with vibrato (except cellist Carter Brey who used little, if any, perhaps in preparation for his Bach cello suite cycle). Labadie must have been stricter in his rehearsals in asking for minimal vibrato, and the string players took his instructions to heart. Their sound was fresh and clean.

The concert opened with Bach's sinfonia from his Cantata 42. "Sinfonia" had and has many meanings, but Bach used it to refer to an opening to a cantata that is purely instrumental and not vocal. Many of his sinfonias were taken from earlier works: the sinfonia for Cantata No. 52, for example, comes from Bach's Brandenburg Concerto No. 1. Sometimes Bach reprised the movement in its entirety, but at other times, as in the opening to Cantata No. 29, he transcribed a work that had been written for another instrument, in this case the Prelude to his second violin partita. The project probably took him as long to do as it would to write a sinfonia from scratch. The sinfonia performed here is of unknown provenance but it certainly sounds like a movement from a concerto with two sound groups that play against each other. The soloists are a bassoon and two oboes, and the second group is the orchestra. Unfortunately, Labadie didn't isolate the groups as well as he should have, and much of the solo playing was drowned out by the orchestra.

Isabelle Faust performed the two violin concerti with such ease and comfort that you forgot how demanding the scores are. The second movement of the A-minor concerto was played with a naturalness and sensitivity that seemed completely egoless. No grand statements were made here, just the music as if it were being played for the first time. Her Stradivarius, the so-called "Sleeping Beauty," did anything but sleep. Its timbre is otherworldly, and the purity of her sound was helped by her minimal use of vibrato and her subtlety in phrasing. I barely heard the orchestra when she was soloing: Labadie rightly chose to be no more than a support for her all-encompassing playing.

For the third orchestral suite, Labadie brought in other members of the NYPO. Before the downbeat, I questioned the need for him to double or triple the instrumentalists, but again his decision was the right one: the density of the score was well able to support a larger orchestra. This is music of a near grandiloquent nature, based on the French music of Lully and his successors; the overture follows Lully's style even to the use of a short motif in the middle section. The justly famous and poignant Air never sounded as sweet as it did here. Perhaps the final movements were faster than would normally be the case for the specified dances, but in the end everything seemed just right, including the promised one-hour length of this charming Rush Hour Concert.

♪Messiaen: Most Definitely to the Stars

Juho Pohjonen (piano), Laura Weiner (French horn), Ian Sullivan (xylorimba), Jared Soldiviero (glockenspiel), Ensemble ACJW, Robert Spano (Conductor), Zankel Hall, Carnegie Hall, New York, 19.3.2013

Messiaen: *Des canyons aux étoiles…*

Andras Shiff recently talked about his synesthetic experience of associating colors with certain keys: C major is white, G major is green and B minor is black. Messiaen goes a step further, claiming that he "paints colors for those who see none." What he is really saying is that he translates the colors of the world into music which can be "heard" as colors. Messiaen's mystical world mixes and matches senses, and his music reflects this process. "Music," Messiaen states "is a perpetual dialogue between space and time, sound and color…a dialogue which ends in a unification." Listeners must suspend their normal way of listening to allow his unique sound-world to take over their own senses.

What better place to inspire a composer like Messiaen than Bryce Canyon and its natural marvels. As Messiaen states: "I had to raise myself from the depths of the canyons to the beauty of the stars…I had only to keep going in the same direction to raise myself up to God." One is so taken by the sheer beauty of *Des canyons* that when the composer scores a traditional grand swelling crescendo in the coda to "Bryce Canyon et les rochers rouge-orange," we forget how far outside the tonal world we have been.

An ornithologist, Messiaen was particularly interested in incorporating bird calls into his music, and four of the twelve movements of *Des canyons* feature bird songs. Here and in other works such as the *Catalogue d'oiseaux* and *Petites esquisses d'oiseaux*, he often reserves the solo piano as the imitative instrument. But these are not simply imitations of bird songs. There is always something else going on, whether it's a clash of orchestral sections or chords that as Messiaen states are needed after each note "to reproduce the timbre."

Messiaen employed a variety of methods to convey the visual world, and he was not above using clichéd techniques to convincingly legitimize the movements' titles. In the opening movement, "Le désert," a wind machine produces the whooshing sounds associated with desert winds, along with his own invention, the geophone, whose pebbles shaken across a drum-like surface sound like shifting sands. Yet, if this were all, his composition would be nothing but a demonstration of what bad program music is. Beyond his imitation of natural sounds are the mystical connections that serve as the work's integumentary system: bells lightly touched, riffs from the glockenspiel, tremolos from the strings, arpeggios from the piano. Everything glitters and shimmers. This primal "music of the spheres" slithers and squelches. It provides what a philosopher would call the ontological being of beings.

There is some spectacularly difficult music in this score, but the Ensemble ACJW overcame all of the technical issues. It was clear that every member of the orchestra, under the able hands of Robert Spano, was committed to the performance. Laura Weiner not only played her French horn exquisitely, she did so without a score in front of her. Elsewhere, I have spoken of my admiration for the pianist Juho Pohjonen and his performance here only adds to my list of encomiums. The percussionists take a major role, and Ian Sullivan and Jared Soldiviero, on the xylorimba (an extended xylophone) and the glockenspiel respectively, played with awesome virtuosity.

♫ New York Philharmonic's 17-Year Wait for Bach's Mass in B minor
New York Philharmonic Orchestra, Alan Gilbert (conductor), Avery Fisher Hall, Lincoln Center, New York, 13.3.2013

Bach: Mass in B minor

As Alan Gilbert states in his program notes, "We are at the tail end of a period in which Bach and other Baroque composers have become the almost exclusive domain of musicians who adhere to what is known as 'historical performance practice.'" Indeed, for a masterwork such as the B-minor Mass to go through a 17-year hiatus before being performed again by the NYPO may speak volumes about the influence of the historically-informed movement. But what we are really talking about is nothing more than the continual changing of musical taste: each generation develops its own sensibility as to what is musically correct.

The first (albeit incomplete) New York performance of the Mass in B minor in 1828 used 98 singers and 68 musicians. Tastes change: by the late 19th century, performances with 200 or more vocalists were considered not big enough. The first complete performance in New York City, by the Oratorio Society in 1900, consisted of 72 instrumentalists and a chorus of 500 and was praised by *The New York Times* for being "in accordance with the tonal balance usual in Bach's day." Ten years later, Albert Schweitzer complained that, "Even with a choir of 150 voices, there is a danger of the lines of the vocal polyphony coming out too thickly and heavily in a way directly opposed to the nature of Bach's music."

A similar debate existed over the issue of OVPP (one voice per part), an idea proposed and defended by Joshua Rifkin in the early 1980s. The praise heaped on a recent recording by the Dunedin Consort using Rifkin's revised OVPP edition confirms that this approach is still alive and kicking. Gilbert and the NYPO were somewhere in the middle ground with a string section of 30 or so and a chorus of 60. When the chorus was singing forte they sometimes overpowered the orchestra, but otherwise the two were well balanced. Considering the glowing reputation (and rightly so) of Anne Sofie von Otter, she seemed off her mark: her voice lacked her usual angelic heft. In the first duet with Dorthea Röschmann, "Christe eleison," both singers were vocally on the same level. In the second duet, "Et in unum Dominum," Ms. Röschmann soared while Ms. Otter stayed on the ground.

As it has done in the past with music of the Baroque, the orchestra took a mixed approach to the issue of vibrato. While there are debates as to its use, limited vibrato seems the right way for string players to perform the music of this period. Some NYPO musicians, such as cellist Carter Bray, clearly stayed away from vibrato. Violinist Glen Dicterow, on the other hand, moderated his use of vibrato when playing the *obligatto* violin arias but slipped back into the vibrato groove when not soloing.

Although the first half of the concert lacked instrumental timbre and vocal color, this changed in the second half with the resounding "Patrem omnipotentem," "Et resurrexit" and "Osanna in excelsis." No one wrote more joyous, spine-tingling music than Bach, and Gilbert drew the best from both singers and instrumentalists. The members of the brass section, whose playing is so important for the success of these movements, ably handled their difficult scores.

Alan Gilbert continues to surprise with his fearless ability to successfully perform works normally reserved for specialists. From Bach to Beethoven to Bruckner, from Janáček to Ligeti and Lindberg, Gilbert successfully interprets them all, breathing new life into this very traditional institution.

♫ Jonathan Biss: Music and Didactics

Jonathan Biss (piano), Zankel Hall, Carnegie Hall, New York, 12.3.2013

Schumann: *Fantasiestücke*, interspersed with
Janáček: Selections from *On an Overgrown Path*, Book 1
Mozart: Minuet in D major, Adagio in B minor
Schumann: *Davidsbündlertänze*

The program list above has been slightly modified from the Carnegie Hall *Playbill* to match the information for this concert on Jonathan Biss's site.

"Interspersed with" was included in the site's concert listing but not in *Playbill*. It came as a surprise to me: I am not against didactic concerts but I like to know what is in store.

What if I specifically chose to attend this recital to hear Schumann or Janáček? I might be disappointed to discover that I would be listening to a hacked-up version of Schumann's *Fantasiestücke*, interspersed with selections from Janáček's first book of *On an Overgrown Path*. Part of the experience of listening to a collection of works is appreciating and understanding its entire structure, and that was not possible here. When I hear a collection of small pieces the anticipation of what's to come is part of the pleasure.

It is beyond me why Jonathan Biss states in his *Playbill* introduction that "the *Fantasiestücke* are not so much a cycle as a collection of character pieces" but the movements of *Davidsbündlertänze* "lose much of their meaning–if not their beauty–when heard in isolation." All of Schumann's collections of piano pieces are thought out. Simply hearing the consistent use of a fast tempo alternating with a slow tempo implies intentionality on the part of the composer. Nothing prevents a pianist from playing these pieces individually, but if the whole is played the pieces should be done one after the other as the composer intended.

Even if we accept Biss's premise with regard to piece-to-piece relationships, his pedagogical argument is sophomoric. Which composer has not been influenced, sometimes strongly, by the works of an earlier composer? Soler by Scarlatti, Mozart by Haydn (and vice versa), Schumann by Chopin or Liszt by Schumann: any composer who chooses a format used by earlier composers is going to reveal their influences. Chopin's *Preludes* might not have been written if Bach had not created his two books of preludes and fugues. Bartók may still have written his sonata for solo violin, but a movement marked tempo di ciaccona without Bach's *Chaconne*? Unlikely.

There was no doubt that Biss was committed to his thesis. He played both the Schumann and the Janáček with ardor and conviction although ultimately each composer suffered from the disconnect of interspersion. Would Biss's interpretations of these pieces be different if he were not trying to prove a point? Certainly adding Mozart to the formula makes clear the untenability of his approach. A simple if slightly eccentric Minuet by Mozart is given the heavy weight of being, according to Biss, "Mozart at his most unapologetically ridiculous." Really? The trio portion of this minuet with its slight dissonance was played by Biss as if it were Stravinsky in his neoclassic phase. The more substantial Adagio in B minor is, Biss claims, "an unrelieved human catastrophe in musical form." I have no idea what this means, but how does either Mozart work reveal a connection between him, Schumann and Janáček? Biss again states the obvious: "Mozart, too, had an extraordinary feeling for drama and psychology in music."

By the time Biss sat down to play with true drama, devoid of any ideology, the *Davidsbündlertänze*, my exasperation had nearly taken the best of me. Hearing Schumann performed without any overhead in a well-judged, if slightly too romantic manner redeemed somewhat the first part of the concert.

♫A Run Through the Barococo

Veronica Cangemi (soprano), Jérôme Pernoo (cello), Ensemble Matheus, Jean-Christophe Spinosi (director and violin), Zankel Hall, Carnegie Hall, New York, 6.3.2013

Handel: Overture and "Frondi tenere ... Ombra mai fù" from *Serse*
Vivaldi: "Gelosia, tu già rendi l'alma mia" from *Ottone in Villa*; Concerto in D minor for Two Violins and Cello from *L'estro armonico*; "Zeffiretti che sussurate" from *Ercole su'l Termodonte*; Concerto in G minor for Two Cellos; "Se mai senti spirarti sul volto" from *Catone in Utica*
Popora: Concerto in G major for Cello
Vivaldi: "Siam navi all'onde algenti" from *L'Olimpiade*

In the mid-20th century, Barococo became associated with DeKoven, a New York radio announcer who used the term in a positive context. His ideal Barococo composer was Vivaldi or Albinoni: the outer movements of their concerti met DeKoven's criteria of being fast, strongly rhythmic and short. He was the equivalent of a pop-music deejay who plays only "oldies but goodies." There were few recordings in the Barococo style when DeKoven started broadcasting, but a brief surge of interest in Baroque music arrived with the Beatles and their use of Baroque-style backgrounds in "A Day in the Life" and "Penny Lane." The Swingle Singers' a capella group, Wendy Carlos's "Switched-On Bach" and Joshua Rifkin's "The Baroque Beatles Book" all gave impetuous to the popularization of Baroque music.

DeKoven would have loved the works on this program. He would have skipped the slower pieces and played the outer movements of the Vivaldi concerti and the Popora's Cello Concerto over and over. The faster the tempo, the louder the fortes, the longer the crescendos, the more laudatory his praise would have been. No one is certain how fast these movements were played originally, but we do know that there is no marking in Baroque scores for crescendos: crescendos and decrescendos were first used in the mid-18th century. Unwarranted and sudden changes from *pp* to *ff* are common Barococo trademarks, and both the instrumentalists and the singer Veronica Cangemi were guilty of these exaggerated gestures.

Vivaldi's vocal output was mammoth and, with the revival of interest in his operas, we are seeing a more mature style than in his instrumental music. The quality of his approximately 45 operas, 80 pasticcios and 100 stray arias vary: *Il Giustino* and *Arsilda* contain little more than instrumental music with the voice as a solo instrument, often simply doubling the instrumental accompaniment. But there are dozens (hundreds?) of arias that are as exciting and powerful as any written by Handel. *Bajazet*, *Motezuma* and *Ercole su'l Termodonte* are filled with glorious music from start to finish.

Jean-Christophe Spinosi and his group have been recording the complete collection of Vivaldi manuscripts found in the Library of Turin. While these have been highly praised, comparisons with recent recordings by Fabio Biondi and

Alan Curtis show Spinosi oblivious to the subtleties of the music. This was also true with the Zankel Hall performance. For the sake of Ms. Cangemi, whose voice barely kept up with the instruments, Spinosi might have slowed down. Although her singing was technically accurate, it sounded strained. Overly dramatic gestures distracted from the performance rather than enhancing it, high notes were screamed and melismas were stretched out to a ludicrous length. Just a quick listen to Vivica Genaux, Roberta Invernizzi or Patricia Ciofi makes this clear.

There were some successful moments, mainly from the virtuoso cellist Jérôme Pernoo who demonstrated his remarkable ability. The almost unknown cello concerto by Porpora was the highlight of the evening. Pernoo played at a nearly impossible speed, at times reaching down almost to the bridge to bring out the instrument's highest notes. Popora has only recently been revived and is mostly known for his arias, many of which were "borrowed" by Vivaldi for his own operas or used to fill his many pastiches. If Porpora's talents, as evinced in this cello concerto, are also present in his other instrumental works, they are certainly worth exploring.

The one encore, Vivaldi's "Agitata da due venti" from *Griselda*—spine-tingling when sung by Cecilia Bartoli—fell flat for this reviewer.

♪*Stephen Hough: No Amateurs Need Apply*
Stephen Hough (piano), Carnegie Hall, New York, 4.3.2013

Chopin: Nocturne in C-sharp minor, Nocturne in D-flat major
Brahms: Piano Sonata No. 3 in F minor
Hough: Piano Sonata No. 2, "Notturno Luminoso"
Schumann: *Carnaval*

In this month's *BBC Music Magazine*, Stephen Hough has contributed an article entitled "A Masterpiece or Not? That So Often Depends on How it is Performed." From the title, one would think it a clichéd subject: of course a great performer has the power to make or break any work. He or she can make any piece a masterpiece or, if poorly played, a "not-masterpiece." But what Hough discusses is a different issue: "Why is it that some works performed by anyone, if minimally played correctly retain their masterpiece status, while other pieces require an exceptional artist to make them seem great?"

Hough mentions Brahms' First Piano Concerto as an example of making "sense in any decent performance," whereas his "'Second Concerto' requires a much more subtle interplay between instruments and tempos to have a full impact." The piano in the Second is on from the second measure and plays almost continually until the end; the First can almost be played without the piano, so dominating is the orchestra.

How would Mr. Hough analyze his own concert? Do the two Nocturnes of Chopin require a masterful performance or just a playing of notes to be acceptable? I can't imagine someone doing these pieces with technical accuracy but without a point of view or an infusion of emotion. In the first Nocturne,

Hough took a darker look at the score, using more pedal than usual and putting emphasis on the left hand. This made it contrast more sharply with the second Nocturne in D-flat major. But even the D-flat major, often played dreamily, in Hough's hands was toughened up. The melody was there but less in the forefront.

By any standard, Brahms' Piano Sonata No. 3 would fall into the group of masterpieces requiring a high level of attention for the performance to succeed. Hough played the work by the 20-year-old Brahms as if the composer needed to express his adolescent rage and exorcise his devils. The colossal structure held together even if there were moments when the playing seemed overwrought.

It was a whole other world when Hough played his own piano sonata, an interesting and relatively accessible piece as far as contemporary music for piano goes. Much of this accessibility came from the indirect references to other composers and the use of a repetitive motif to hold the piece together. The beginning run of dissonant chords brought to mind Charles Ives; the more mellow parts could have been from one of Messiaen's *Vingt regards sur l'enfant-Jésus*. The use of disparate chords followed by a virtuosic burst of runs and arpeggios, varied and repeated many times, is a signature of Messiaen's keyboard works. It was interesting to note that the other works on the program were performed without score, but his own composition required both score and page turner.

Hough really came into his own in a multicolored performance of Schumann's *Carnaval*. Every piece had its individuality and character. Hough seemed to settle into his comfort zone, more relaxed than in the first half of the concert, delighting in the variety of these miniatures. A few pieces were played a bit too hard: the *"valse noble"* was a waltz but it was not very noble, and the *"papillons"* were a little too heavy to float. Any possible thoughts that Hough may have made some wrong interpretative decisions were simply blown away by the thoroughly convincing final character piece. If this was a march by David against the Philistines, my suggestion to the Philistines would be to retreat quickly.

The resounding coda was met with equally resounding applause.

♫ *A Goldberg to Dream About*
Juilliard415, Monica Huggett (leader), Peter Jay Sharp Theater, The Juilliard School of Music, Lincoln Center, New York City, 27.2.2013

Bach: *Goldberg Variations* (transcribed by Dmitry Sitkovetsky

I can't think of another work that contains so much potential, such unlimited possibilities to shape itself, as the *Goldberg Variations*. Every interpretation that meets its demanding technical requirements has something to offer. There are no performances that can be considered definitive, no one standard way to play it. Depending upon musicians' decisions on tempo and velocity, it has been played in as few as 38 minutes (Glenn Gould, 1955) and as long as 94 minutes (Roslyn Tureck, 1959). Even if one were to add back the 38 minutes of da capos to Gould's recording, Ms. Tureck's performance would still be 18 minutes longer.

What other work in the history of music has been as transcribed, transposed, rearranged and "corrected." Versions exist for two pianos, harp, organ, guitar, digital synthesizer and accordion (a thoroughly convincing performance by Teodoro Anzellotti). There is even a "re-performance" of Glenn Gould's 1955 recording on a Yamaha digital piano that is an exact replication of Gould's. And then we have Uri Caine's jazzed-up version with viola da gamba, drums, electric bass and turntables.

As far as transcriptions go, that of Dmitry Sitkovetsky stays very close to home. Bach wrote the *Goldberg Variations* for a *Claviercembal mit 2 Manualen* and never goes beyond three voices at a time, usually two upper and one bass. This makes it a natural for string trio: violin, viola and cello. In its orchestrated version here, the other string players back or double the voices, giving it a depth and warmth more strongly conveyed than with a simple string trio.

This is the first time I've heard Sitkovetsky's version played on period instruments, and what a performance it was. With Monica Huggett playing first violin along with three star virtuosi students—Samuel Park, violin; Daniel McCarthy, viola; and Michael Unterman, cello—the Juilliard Historical Performance's student orchestra created a colorful and vibrant reading. Ms. Huggett's phrasing was immaculate. Her sensitivity to all the subtle changes in tempo and rhythm conveyed much more information from the score than the keyboard version. The variable gradations available to a string player made the music sing.

Although there are many brilliant performances on the keyboard, instruments like the harpsichord are inherently limited in their sonic range. Control over volume and decay are limited on these instruments (less so on the piano), but limitless on strings. Particularly with a work like the *Goldberg Variations* each voice needs to be attended to and expressed individually. Playing the work with strings allows each instrument to have total control over every line.

So it was with the canons. These musical "rounds" can be difficult to follow, but here, where a different instrument picked up and repeated the theme, the structure of the movement became perfectly apparent. The pathos of the slow thirteenth variation touched me as if I were hearing it for the first time. Ms. Huggett made sensible choices about taking or not taking the da capos. The 25th variation, if played slowly and with all the da capos, tends to throw the construction of the entire work out of balance. Wisely, Ms. Huggett did not repeat the "B" section of this variation so as not to extend its somber mood. The final variations, often taken together with minimum pauses, never seemed rushed.

The orchestra of 14 musicians was one less than in Sitkovetsky's original recording for Nonesuch in 1993. That was a spirited performance, but the use of modern instruments made it colorless. Here, the maturity and professionalism of the student group was astonishing. The soloists played their parts as if they had lived with this music for their entire lives. Michael Untermann's playing in the 26th variation was breathtaking, repeating the difficult scoring in each of the sections without once seeming to strain.

This was a concert to be remembered and one against which other performances of this masterpiece should be judged.

♪*The Heirs of Tantalus: A Pasticcio of Blood and Song*
Members of The Sebastians Chamber Orchestra, The Broad Street Ballroom, New York, 22.2.2013

Handel, Monteverdi, Scarlatti: *The Heirs of Tantalus*

The *pasticcio* is the musical equivalent of a culinary goulash: add some of your old arias, steal a few more from your contemporaries, compose an overture (or just take an old *sinfonia* and call it an overture), package it and you have a new opera ready for a world premiere. From Monteverdi's time until copyright laws came into effect, this process was often a way for a composer to complete a work and beat a deadline. Many of Handel's *pasticcios* can be sourced to his own earlier works. Vivaldi's underrated *Bajazet* contains arias from Hasse, Giacomelli and Broschi. Anyone who saw the Metropolitan Opera's brilliant *pasticcio*, *The Enchanted Island*, which consisted of arias from multiple Baroque composers, knows that a well-chosen potpourri of arias makes for a fine night at the opera.

The scope of this *pasticcio* was sensibly judged, with no attempt to match the scale of the Met's production. The two soloists and the instrumentalists were on a small stage, while the three actors moved about the aisles and often leaned against a spotlighted column. This required some audience swiveling, but the cast enunciated clearly most of the time so that it was not always necessary to face them. With the actors serving as narrators and Roman personages–the equivalent of an operatic recitative–a tale was told of bloody and perverse characters and events from the House of Atreus to Nero's Palace.

From the opening overture to the final duet with its typical Baroque turnaround in mood from torment and loss to the words "Alas, in this mortal life/the greatest happiness a heart can expect/is to be free from care," the audience was treated to an operatic episode of *I, Claudius*–gruesome yet amusing at the same time.

Handel's *Agrippina* and Monteverdi's *L'incoronazione di Poppea* are, appropriately, the main sources for the arias. Ottone's opening aria, "E pur io torno," was rendered by countertenor José Lemos in a shaded and expressive interpretation that went from hope and comfort to despair and emptiness within minutes. Jessica Gould's canorous voice comfortably negotiated the jaunty runs of the aria "Non ho cor che per amarti." Monteverdi's "Pur ti miro" was sung meltingly by the duet. While not strictly a chaconne, which carries the bass line from beginning to end, this aria derives its pathos from the chaconne's tempo and rhythm. "Come nube" was the evening's highlight, with a text in which Handel beautifully tone paints the significant words flies, wind, fire and cold.

Mention should be given to the instrumentalists and in particular to oboist Meg Owens who deservedly took the seat normally reserved for the concert mistress.

The venue was a real find both in terms of acoustics and style. Folding chairs were set up in the center of what used to be a bank's public space, a circular area in the style of the Pantheon's interior. Tiled Roman columns added to the illusion that we were in a building from the Roman era.

A great deal of time and thought must have been spent on this production. Hopefully it will be staged again and for a longer period than one night.

♩Radamisto: In Need of Some Dolce Vita
The English Concert, Harry Bickett (director, harpsichord), Carnegie Hall, New York, 24.2.2013

Handel: *Radamisto*
Concert Version

Henry Bickett brought his early-instrument group, The English Concert, and Handel's *Radamisto* to the United States after well-reviewed performances in England. In fact, this review is the third for S&H. The casts on both sides of the Atlantic differed only in the replacements of Tigrane and Farasmane: the minor role of Farasmane was ably handled here by David Kravitz, and the pants role of Tigrane was sung superbly by Joélle Harvey. Her sonorous voice showed no strain in the difficult "La Sorte, Il Ciel, Amor."

The revival of Handel's operas was a long time coming. There were no performances of any of them from the last five years of his life up to 1920 and a production of *Rodelinda* in Germany. Performances of other operas such as *Giulio Cesare* and *Serse* followed, but arias were stripped of their da capos and most *recitatives secci* were removed. The role of Giulio Cesare was "corrected" by transposing his arias down an octave; women singing men's roles were apparently deemed as offensive to audiences as men singing within the tessitura of a soprano or alto. Every opera ultimately ended up as a pastiche of itself, often glued together with arias from other composers.

One can still find in print a recording of *Radamisto* (originally released in 1961 and re-released in 1998) done in German with a standard symphony orchestra and a basso in the role of Radamisto. This recording claimed to be the first one based on the 1720 original version (HMV 12A) but how this can be the case with a basso in the lead role and the libretto in a "non-original" language?

The version used by The English Concert here is a mix of the original two productions from 1720, the latter one modified to accommodate the vocal range of the Italian castrato Senesino. David Daniels sung the title role and, dare I say, this is the first time that he did not seem to stand out in a lead role. But given that this is a concert version with a particularly complex plot and a plethora of arias, it would be difficult to find any singer who could refine each aria to its exact emotion.

The issue of performance practice is really the key to *Radamisto's* success or failure. Elsewhere I've distinguished between schools of historical performance which are often associated with the culture in which the groups evolve.

Representing the English school throughout its long history, The English Concert has been stylish, authentic and even adventuresome in its programming, but in comparison to current Italian Baroque groups, such as Alan Curtis's Il Complesso Barocco, Fabio Biondi's Europa Galante and Andrea Marcon's Venice Baroque Orchestra, the English group seemed lifeless here. Over the years, The English Concert has changed little as other performance groups have advanced their own styles. Of the 70 or so recordings the English Concert has made, only two of them feature complete operas.

This concert version of *Radamisto* was well sung, but the lethargy of the orchestral accompaniment made for a dull affair. Tempi were deadeningly slow. Arias that are particularly stunning, such as Tigrane's "Deh, fuggi un traditore" where the urgency of fleeing from the tyrant is a showpiece of virtuosic singing, were not included. The same could be said for Tridate's "Stragi, morti, sangue ed armi" whose "the trumpet calls out with martial sound" would have had the audience out of their seats.

With so many groups worldwide committed to replicating the glorious performances that made operas by Handel and Vivaldi compelling for their contemporaries, it's a shame not more have reached American shores.

♩Hearing Familiar Music Anew
Christian Zacharias (piano), Orchestra of St. Luke's, Pablo Heras Casado (conductor), Carnegie Hall, New York, 7.2.2013

Beethoven: Overture to Goethe's *Egmont*
Chopin: Piano Concerto No. 2 in F minor
Debussy: Five Préludes (orch. Hans Zender, 1991; US Premiere)
Schumann: Symphony No. 4 in D minor (original version, 1841)

Pablo Heras Casado knows what he wants to get from his players, and he does so with authority, confidence and self-effacement. The opening work, Beethoven's overture to the incidental music of Goethe's *Egmont*, is one of a number of compositions that he wrote for a specific function. Unlike Mozart, who rarely differentiated between "personal" music and *gebrauchsmusik*, Beethoven could only be inspired if he felt the subject reflected his high standards or political beliefs. Hence, he left us with probably the largest collection of bombast by any major composer. *Wellington's Victory* (the so-called "Battle Symphony"), the overture and incidental music to *King Stephen* and music for mechanical clock do not show Beethoven in his best light.

Goethe's *Egmont* is different. The story of a hero who gives his life for his country, it espouses themes of brotherhood and liberation from tyranny. Casado gave a vital and intense reading of the work, but it never sounded overplayed. A good orchestra and conductor have no need for super fortes to convey the composer's intent: excitement and pleasure can be had through a more relaxed playing, and that was the case here. When the coda arrived with a crescendo that starts with a half measure rest followed by a fermata and a nearly audible passage marked *ppp*, we realized what magic Beethoven and Casado had spun.

In an earlier review I questioned Casado's condoning of the decision to use a reproduction of an 1829 fortepiano for a performance by Kristian Bezuidenhout of Schumann's 1849 *Introduction and Allegro Appassionato* ("Concertstück"). In fact, it would have made for an interesting performance if that instrument had been used here for Chopin's second piano concerto. It's far more likely that fortepianos were still in use in 1829 when Chopin wrote his concerto than in 1849 when Schumann wrote his work for piano and orchestra.

Christian Zacharias used the standard Carnegie Hall instrument of choice, the Steinway Model D. The Steinway is not the best piano for all types of music, but it served as an ideal instrument for Zacharias's fleeting and lithe interpretation of Chopin. Here the soloist and conductor were perfectly matched. Chopin had a knowledge of every sound that a piano could produce, but this did not extend to instruments for the orchestra; Carado recognized this and deferred to Zacharias. Honestly, I don't remember focusing visually or auditorily on Carado and the orchestra: the piano dominated and the orchestra served more as accompanist than as equal partner.

One never knows what to expect when one sees "orchestrated by" after a work's title, and there is always Ravel's orchestration of Mussorgsky's *Pictures at an Exhibition* as the standard against which other orchestrations are judged. Zender's orchestration of five preludes from Debussy's two books of preludes for piano, while not quite as imaginative as Ravel's, holds its own kind of charm. As an orchestration goes, it is pretty much a note-by-note rewriting of the piano score. A chord or note marked sforzando is played by a percussive instrument, and glissandos are meted out to the harp. All five pieces were brightly and colorfully performed, aided by the bizarre sounds of several unusual instruments like the musical saw.

Listening to a different version of a work that one knows well is often an odd experience. For one thing, it makes you question whether you really know the music as well as you think you do. Sometimes an earlier version sounds superior to the standard version only because it adds interest to a work that has been heard too many times, and Schumann's 1841 "original" version of his fourth symphony is a good example. The earlier version has a looser structure that seems closer to the heart than the later, more tightly constructed score. Both conductor and orchestra played ravishingly and succeeded in reinvigorating this old warhorse.

♫ *Juilliard Baroque Serves a Repast of Nations*
Juilliard Baroque, Corpus Christi Church, New York, 10.2.2013

Couperin: Selections from *Les Nations*

History did not make it easy for future generations to understand Couperin's life or music. Correspondence has not survived, and very few contemporary accounts exist of the man who was the French king's harpsichordist.

Couperin lived during an era when old forms were being replaced with new ones whose coinage was up for grabs. Simphonie did not refer to our four-movement works but was a generic term for any music played with more than one instrument. Overtures were overtures to operas, but also dance suites such as the four *ouvertures* of Bach. Passacailles and chaconnes were totally interchangeable names for pieces based on a repeated ground; Couperin himself named one of his pieces *Chaconne ou Passacaille*. *Les Nations: Sonades et suites de simphonies en trio* is the full title, and it obfuscates more than it informs. Like Couperin's *Pièces de clavecin*, *Les Nations* is divided into *ordres*. Couperin insisted on calling the opening abstract movements *Sonades* and the following dance movements Suites.

What do these appellations mean? Except for the tempo designations they give no information to the performers or the audience. Couperin must have found some pleasure in labelling his music with mysterious titles. While many of his keyboard works are simply named for their tempo, others are either character pieces (*pièces de caractère*) or outlandish jokes: *Les Baricades Mistérieuses*, *Le Tic-Toc-Choc*, *Les Culbutes Ixcxbxnxs* and *Les Notables & Jurés Mxnxstrxndxurs*.

The very form of *Les Nations* is sui generis. The opening *Sonades* are clear representatives of the Italian style *sonata de chiesa*, prominent in the music of Corelli. Usually there are four movements, alternately slow and fast, but here there are between six and eight. The dance movements that follow are French in style. Juilliard Baroque performed the entire first *ordre* and parts of the second and third, but only the opening *sonade* of the fourth.

The Juilliard Baroque consists of world-class authorities on period instruments. Monica Huggett's 1984 recording of *Les Nations* under the direction of Jordi Savall is the standard against which other recordings are compared, and the quality of their performance here certainly was on that level. If one's interest in these pieces flagged, only Couperin can be blamed. *Les Nations* includes both early and late work, and the earlier pieces lack the confidence of the more mature ones. The dance suites were much livelier, particularly in the third suite, where the music could have been written by Rameau in his *Pièces de Clavecin* (another misnomer for a work that can be played solely on the keyboard or with violin and keyboard).

The most interesting movements, and the ones given the most enthusiastic performances, were the Chaconnes and Passacailles. Rhythmically catchy, their recurring motives are in fact variations on a theme. Always unpredictable, Couperin ends only one suite with a Passacaille; the others are embedded in the suite or, as in *L'impériale*, followed by a short anti-climactic *menuet*.

The relatively small church held in the sound which would have died out in a larger venue. Thanks to the Juilliard Historical Music Program for another challenging and rewarding production.

♪*Kristian Bezuidenhout: A Revelatory Recital at Carnegie Hall*
Kristian Bezuidenhout (harpsichord), Weill Recital Hall, Carnegie Hall, New York, 12.2.2013

Kerll: Toccata in G minor, Passacaglia in D minor
Couperin: Allemande, Courante and Sarabande for Harpsichord in E minor
Froberger: Toccata No.16 in C major, Partita No. 12 in C major
Handel: Allemande from Suite No. 3 in D minor, Courante from Suite No. 4 in D minor, Aria and Variations from Suite No. 3 in D minor
Bach: Toccata in D minor, Partita in A minor (after Solo Violin Partita No. 2 in D minor, transcription for harpsichord by Lars Ulrik Mortensen)

Although I could satisfy my thirst for music by listening solely to the harpsichord, I see why others cannot. At times pulling back from the music itself and just hearing the instrument's grating, piercing sound makes me question my obsession with it. Wanda Landowska, the first modern musician to bring the harpsichord out of storage, played a Pleyel that was so immense sounding that when all registers and both manuals were used at the same time (which her instrument could do) a chord could be sustained for 25 seconds. The Pleyel certainly did correct some of the instrument's legendary weaknesses, sustaining notes and allowing changes in volume (although not gradually). Even though this type of harpsichord, custom-made for her, disappeared, many musicians after her continued playing in an earth-shattering style. Fernando Valenti, a student of Ralph Kirkpatrick, the major advocate of a softer approach to the harpsichord, rebelled against him and used a Challis harpsichord that was a model of discord. Today Pierre Hantai plays the harpsichord as if Scarlatti had written Beethoven's *Hammerklavier*.

Bezuidenhout's instrument here was a double manual 1994 French harpsichord by D. Jacques Way and Marc Ducornot that had a remarkable tone. Every note glowed. Bezuidenhout used the second manual and hand stops sparingly, but effectively enough to vary phrasing and articulation as needed. This was not the case in an earlier concert in Alice Tully Hall. Bezuidenhout's instrument of choice then was a fortepiano whose sound barely reached past the first rows of the orchestra. His harpsichord here made one feel as if the acoustics for this auditorium were specifically designed to give the instrument ideal support.

A charming speaker, Bezuidenhout at one point addressed the audience and explained what connected the works he had chosen: all were related in one way or another to Froberger. He is credited with creating the Baroque suite as a series of dance movements, and his works were the progenitors of the suites of Handel and the suites and partitas for keyboard by Bach. At times, the music on the program reminded me of the recently rediscovered Christophe Graupner who composed over 40 partitas, or Silvius Weiss's voluminous output of suites for the lute. I am not aware of any connection between Froberger and these composers, but it would seem impossible that they were unaware of him.

The program included three toccatas, a form that gave a composer the opportunity to write down his own improvisations, music that would otherwise have been lost. Virtuoso passages, fughetti or fugues, and arpeggios are all the stuff of toccatas. Bezuidenhout dove into these toccatas and into all the pieces with verve and confidence, but the transcription of the chaconne from Bach's Second Partita for solo violin lost its grandeur and its inner line in the flood of rushing notes with a tempo that was too far from the norm for any chaconne. But Bezuidenhout excelled in the other works on the program. There was no showmanship here, but rather a clear desire to please the audience and make for an enjoyable evening. The selection of pieces from the underappreciated suites of Handel were pitch-perfect, receiving, as did all the da capo pieces, well-judged ornamentations. The encore was the Allemande from Bach's Fourth Partita and could not have been more poignantly played.

This recital would turn even the most adamant skeptic of the harpsichord into an admirer. It would amaze me if anyone hearing the performance could complain about this sweet-sounding harpsichord or the exquisite playing by Bezuidenhout.

♪Venice Baroque Orchestra: When Wild Works
Venice Baroque Orchestra, Andrea Marcon, (director), Zankel Hall, Carnegie Hall, New York, 6.02.2013

Vivaldi: Sinfonia from *La Senna Festeggiante*; Concerto in G minor for Flute and Strings, "La notte"; Concerto in F major for Bassoon and Strings; Concerto in C major for Flautino and Strings
Veracini: Overture in G minor for Two Oboes, Bassoon and Strings
Porpora: Concerto in G major for Cello and Strings
Geminiani: Concerto Grosso in D minor (after Corelli's Violin Sonata, "Folia")

Encores:
Vivaldi: Allegro from Concerto in D major for Violin
Telemann: Presto from Concerto in E minor for Flute and Recorder

From Mozart's adaptation of Handel's *Messiah* to the rediscovery of J. S. Bach by Mendelssohn in the 1820s through the 19th and most of the 20th centuries, performances of Baroque music were based on the assumption that this was music that somehow needed to be "corrected." Sir Thomas Beecham's notorious re-orchestrations of Baroque composers such as Handel and Leopold Stokowski's overblown transcriptions of Bach were done to make this music palatable to their audiences.

It wasn't until the 1970s with the performances of Bach's cantatas by Nicholas Harnoncourt and the symphonies of Mozart by Christopher Hogwood that a reaction to this approach began to take hold. The cries of the proponents of the school of historically informed performance (HIP) were "To the Text!" Concerts and recordings of Baroque music had to be historically correct. The instruments needed to be either original or accurate replicas, tuned to a pitch a half step lower than today's. Every aspect, from the number of instrumentalists and chorus members to positions on stage to the absence of vibrato and use of *notes inégales*, were to be authentic.

The only problem with following these rules is that there was and is much disagreement as to what was really "authentic." How many chorus members were there in Bach's performances of the Mass in B minor (if in fact he did perform it in his lifetime)? Was it one voice per part as argued by Joshua Rifkin and his supporters? Did the string players at that time bow completely vibrato-less as Roger Norrington insisted? What was the correct tuning, considering historical confirmations of ranges running from below A=400hz to A=480hz? (Today's traditional instruments are standardized as A=440hz and Baroque instruments generally at A=415hz.) As for the question of *notes inégales,* Wikipedia will give you that answer in 7000 words!

So where in the dialectic process are we now? Have we reached a kind of synthesis where we all agree on some common performance rules? No, but we're probably close. We may never again accept a performance on the order of Leonard Bernstein's recording of Vivaldi's Concerto for Diverse Instruments in which most of the Baroque instruments are replaced by modern-day descendants. But it is now more acceptable for non-period orchestras to play Baroque music if they at least attempt to follow some of the rules regarding reduced vibrato, fewer instruments per part and basso continuo on the harpsichord instead of piano. The current freedom from the strict style requirements expected from HIP groups has given way to a range of performance practice from conservative groups like The Academy of Ancient Music (less conservative now under the baton of Richard Egarr than with his predecessor, Andrew Manze) to the insanity of Red Priest. Yet a true synthesis that agrees on standards for all has yet to occur.

This leads us to the performance by Andrea Marcon and the Venice Baroque Orchestra. Yes, they have original instruments pitched at A=415hz and use *notes inégales,* one instrument per part (except for the strings) and little vibrato. They have all the prerequisites needed for a HIP, right? Wrong! The one detail not followed, a major one, is that the players pretty much ignore the text, adding sforzandos, crescendos and accelerandos that are nowhere to be found in the composers' scores. The opening sinfonia from Vivaldi's serenata *La Senna Festeggante* has notations by Vivaldi himself, some of which were not followed.

Marcon is a Baroque scholar and was involved with reconstructing and performing the recently discovered serenata, *Andromeda Liberato.* So what is his justification for these broad interpretations? In an interview, he states: "In Italian music, especially Vivaldi, because the music is not so rich harmonically and so on, it has to be treated differently. We know from documents of the time that Vivaldi played with a lot of colors and dynamics, and that is what we try to do, too. Interpreting Italian music means almost that you are manipulating what is written. We play what is written, of course—we don't change a single note. But we add so much that the piece almost sounds new."

The qualities that made this concert succeed in spite of its wildness were the sparkling freshness and the enthusiasm of all the members, and these traits make the Venice Baroque Orchestra stand out from other equally skilled groups. While the renowned Il Giardino Armonico under the direction of Giovanni Antonnini has played here as well, their wildness was, well, wild. Anna Fusek

performed the same C-major concerto for flautino as Antonnini did in his appearance, but her playing was spirited and invigorating while Antonnini's was shallow and stale.

The rarely performed opening sinfonia from the wonderful serenata *La Senna Festeggiante* brought out parts of the score I've never heard, in particular the flautino in the first movement. In the second movement Marcon changed emphasis from the string instrumental line to the cello which imaginatively refreshed the brief but tender Andante.

Although the famous flute concerto, "La notte," was played immaculately by Michele Favaro, the bassoon concerto with its dark coloring overshadowed the former. The keyless bassoon was played by one of several multi-talented musicians, Giulia Genini, who also plays the alto recorder.

After the intermission the group performed a work by a contemporary of Vivaldi, Francesco Maria Veracini's Overture in G minor–a work and a composer unknown to me–which was well constructed and beautifully performed. Might some group revive this composer, as Reinhold Goebel and the Musica Antiqua Köln did with Johann David Heinichen in the mid-1990s?

Nicola Popora's concerto for cello was another new one for me. He has been part of the recent revival of interest in Baroque opera, and his arias are often found "borrowed" by his fellow Venetian Vivaldi in the latter's operas and pastiches. Much of Porpora's music was written for the renowned castrato, Farinelli. The cellist in this performance, Daniele Bovo, succeeded in a virtuosic rendition that demanded as much dexterity on the cello as Popora demanded of Farenelli's voice.

Geminiani's *Variations on "La Folia" after Corelli* are in fact variations on variations and one of many versions written by composers going as far back as the 16th century. Corelli's were written for violin and basso continuo, C. P. E. Bach's for keyboard and there is even one written by Gregorio Paniagua in 1980 that has, among other instruments, tablas, sitars and drums. The Venice Baroque Orchestra tossed off these variations with confidence and aplomb.

The first encore, the Allegro from Vivaldi's Concerto in D major for Violin, is rarely played and Marcon explained to the audience that they would realize why. Gianpiero Zanocco, listed as the sixth violinist of the seven on stage, breathtakingly performed the almost impossibly difficult violin part which requires a technique few violinists possess.

♪Barenboim's Beethoven: Ending on the Right Note

West-Eastern Divan Orchestra, Daniel Barenboim (conductor), Carnegie Hall, New York, 30.1.2013

Beethoven: Symphony No. 1 in C major, Symphony No. 8 in F major, Symphony No. 5 in C minor

No conductor alive today has been quite as controversial as Daniel Barenboim. His political positions vis-à-vis the Israeli-Palestinian question have made him a

pariah in most of the countries from which members of the West-Eastern Divan Orchestra come: Israel, Palestine, Turkey, Lebanon, Jordan, Egypt, Syria and others. To what degree these political and philosophical issues affect his musical world might be opaque, but its ambience was part of this performance.

The extra-musical metadata came not in the form of some type of program music–the opening of the Fifth Symphony never has and never will be the "Hand of Fate"–but in an attitude of sober-mindedness and staidness that really only worked to the conductor's advantage in the Fifth Symphony. Certainly the first movement of Symphony No. 1 deserved some of the descriptions used in the concert's Playbill: it "begins with a musical joke," its "ostensible grandeur is a charade," the winds are "decorated by jaunty accents." The conductor himself when asked, in a recent interview with *The Economist*, "Why Beethoven?" responded that Beethoven is never superficial, cute or frilly. Perhaps not, but both the First and the Eighth have a level of humor that was missing in this performance. From the First's opening "wrong chords" to the flute and bassoon's comic "Ahh" response to the cello's "A-umph" in the third movement, we should be hearing a more light-hearted Beethoven. The Allegro molto e vivace should surprise, as each measure hesitantly gains a note in the first four measures, but it didn't.

Barenboim did somewhat better in the Eighth Symphony with a snappy opening. This revved up the first movement as the strings established an underlying motion and momentum that carried it forward. The orchestra may have put more drama than humor in the measure-long rests and interludes when only the winds played, but overall the first movement came off fine. The so-called "metronome parody" of the second movement could have been crisper, the *sempre staccato* more sharply delineated. The third movement, probably the most "classical" of Beethoven's minuets and trios, came across with its rustic quality intact. The finale bore too heavy a weight for a movement of such lightness.

Both Barenboim and his orchestra came into their own with the Fifth Symphony, a work that seemed designed to match music and these players. The violas and celli were appropriately lush sounding in the second subject of the second movement. The tympani and horns of the final movement were excitedly brash, as they need to be. Barenboim ably arched the construction of the last movement, avoiding reaching overly loud fortes during its many crescendos. He was aided by the wonderful acoustics of Carnegie Hall.

♫New York Philharmonic's Messiah Done Just Right

Layla Claire (soprano), Tim Mead (countertenor), Kenneth Tarver, (tenor), Alastair Miles (bass), The New York Choral Artists, Joseph Flummerfelt (director), The New York Philharmonic Orchestra, Gary Thor Wedow (conductor), Avery Fisher Hall, Lincoln Center, New York, 18.12.2012

Handel: *Messiah*

With so many *Messiahs* performed this week, there was little chance of avoiding

one, short of staying home and watching "A Chipmunk Christmas" on TV. The one that interested me the most was the performance to be conducted by the early music specialist, Emmanuelle Haim. I've never seen her conduct, and I was curious how she, a specialist in Baroque performance, would lead the New York Philharmonic. A few days before the concert, I checked the event on the NYP site and there was no mention of her at all. It was a disappointment, but her replacement was Gary Thor Wedow, another Baroque specialist.

There really is something about the *Messiah* that captivates the listener no matter how many times it has been heard. Every note moves and every aria satisfies. A frequent complaint about Handel's arias is that the standard A-B-A form can drag. The arias in the *Messiah* are all to the point, so much so that one is amazed at their inventiveness. Like his countryman Henry Purcell, Handel wrote so felicitously that many melodies, heard briefly, seem like throwaways.

Wedow's configuration of a select group of members of the Philharmonic was well-balanced with orchestra, soloists and chorus never drowning each other out. Reduction in the amount of vibrato varied from musician to musician, resulting in an accompaniment which was neither overly Romantic nor strictly Baroque. There were a few miscues, but nothing critical to the performance. The basso continuo was the standard harpsichord and bass supplemented by a virginal for the *recitativi secco*. This unusual choice of instrument was played by Wedow from a standing position at the podium. I didn't quite understand the reason why this instrument was used, particularly in such a large venue, and I was surprised I could even hear it. It turns out that it was amplified.

The performers were all top notch and the inclusion of a countertenor, Tim Mead, added a colorful element to the vocal tapestry. The number of young and exceptionally talented countertenors performing today has grown from a time when you could count their numbers on your fingers. Not only did Mead cover the difficult vocal range, but he did so without any sign of strain or discomfort. Layla Claire's ethereal soprano was meltingly touching. Tenor Kenneth Tarver started off a little weakly, but soon came into his own. Basso Alastair Miles was competent if at times a little unsteady. The pitch-perfect playing of the trumpet by Matthew Muckey deservedly received audience acclamation.

The chorus, vibrant and enthusiastic, gave their all to every number. From the Hallelujah Chorus to the final Amen, all the forces played as one, immersed in the intensity of Handel's fevered scoring. The premature applause midway during the Amen was, in the spirit of the season, smilingly forgiven by the conductor.

♪*Rameau Turns French Opera Topsy-Turvy*

"Demons and Monsters: The Theatrical Orchestra of Jean-Phillipe Rameau," Robert Mealy (violin and director), Mary Feminear, Pureum Jo (sopranos), John Brancy (baritone), Davone Tines (Bass-baritone), Juilliard415, Alice Tully Hall, Lincoln Center, New York, 14.12.2012

Rameau: Suite from *Castor et Pollux*; Suite from *Dardanus*

194

It's hard to believe now how radical, dissonant and cacophonous Rameau's first operas sounded to the Parisian public. When Marc Minkowski's recording of Rameau's first opera, *Hippolyte et Aricie*, came out, a sticker on the cover stated that this opera shocked and outraged its original audience, that it was so revolutionary it changed the course of music history. Few who hear the opera today, without knowing what came before, will be shocked by the music, but it did indeed turn conventional French opera on its head.

Here was music whose strange harmonies, unusual instrumentation, long set pieces and provocative prologues made the current French operas, mostly unsuccessful imitations of Lully, just seem plain dull. Even the themes of Rameau's libretti went far beyond the narrow range of Lully's subjects. Pollux's struggle with the fraternal love that prevents him from accepting the love of Télaire and Phébé was a topic never dealt with in French opera before Rameau. *Les Indes Galantes* is a series of entrees of exotic foreign dignitaries and their fantastic entourages. The much later *Platée* involves a frog-like being, living in a swamp, who believes that Jupiter will abandon Juno sand marry her.

The two suites of this program are taken from the early *tragédies en musique: Castor and Pollux* and *Dardanus*. While revivals of Rameau's operas had a recent, short-lived period when there was enough funding to support expensively staged productions or recordings for major record labels, we now get concert versions or collections of orchestral suites and arias. From Marc Minkowski we even get *Une Symphonie Imaginaire*, a compilation of "17 of Rameau's best orchestral moments" as stated in one review.

This performance featured four excellent singers, all well-versed in Baroque style and a nearly-professional orchestra of students led by the Baroque specialist Robert Mealy. The full color of Rameau's music was emphasized by the oboists and bassoonists standing up when their contribution was prominent. It was nice to see and hear details too subtle to be picked up on a recording, such as the several notes played on the triangle in the minuets of the first suites. A few liberties were taken in dynamics, particularly in the repeats of some of the dance movements. The first set of gavottes were taken at an unusually slow tempo compared to the more traditional gavotte tempo in Act IV of the same suite.

Mary Feminear gave a moving reading of "Tristes apprêts," an aria reminiscent of Handel's much earlier "Lascia la spina." Pureum Jo's voice was unalloyed and supple. She breezed through several arias from *Dardanus* with ease and aplomb. The pure, rich bass-baritone of Davone Tines was one of the highlights of the evening, and John Brancy sang even better than he did in last year's Rossini one-act operas at Juilliard.

It is a joy to see how the students have grown in confidence and ability and how quickly the Historical Performance department, now in its fourth year, has gained the reputation as one of the finest early music schools in the world.

♫*Prequel to Così Fan Tutte: So, Do They All?*

Orchestra of the Second Instrumental Unit, Ryan McAdams (conductor),

Company XIV, Austin McCormick (Choreography), The Italian Academy for Advanced Studies in America, Columbia University, New York, 13.12.2012

Dawe: *Così Faran Tutti*

Jonathan Dawe is one of our most talented and distinctive—yet little-known—contemporary composers. He will be looked back upon as one of the few librettists and composers of contemporary opera whose originality captivates and endears, whose music is both "modern" and deeply rooted in the past. Like Charles Ives's scores, which at first seem gratuitously dissonant but ultimately resolve and reveal their grounding in traditional American music, so does Dawe's music hearken back to Baroque and Classical opera. We've neither heard nor seen his operas—or have we?

Dawe's genius lies in his ability to deconstruct an earlier composer's music, to fractalize it, breaking it down and then piecing it back together. This is no mere automatic process like randomizing notes. The result is music that, if not recognizable, seems familiar. In *Così Faran Tutti*, the overture's fanfares, for example, echo Mozart. The continuo accompaniments to the recitatives (off-key in this case) mark the work as Mozart as well.

Calling itself a prequel to Mozart's *Così Fan Tutte, Così Faran Tutti* plays on Mozart's ambiguous title (translated variously as "So do they all," or "All women are like that"). The small change in gender ("Tuttc" to the masculine form "Tutti") sums up the difference between these works. In Mozart's opera the women are blamed for falling prey to their suitors' deceptions: all women are like that. In Dawe's version everyone is to blame. Everyone "does it."

Opera frequently teeters on the edge of inanity. In Mozart's *Così*, the two couples meet their disguised lovers and within seconds fall in love, minutes later fall out of love, get betrothed and get un-betrothed, and all within a single day. Alfonso exaggerates how the news of Ferrando and Guglielmo leaving for the army is the worst thing in existence, worse even than their deaths would be. At the end, the opera's myriad complications seem to resolve themselves in an instant.

By comparison, Dawe's characters almost always go completely over the brink. They sing long arias about the most minuscule and minor events. And it's not just the two couples who fall in love with each other instantly: everyone falls in love with everyone else, men with women, women with women, men with men. This is what Norman O. Brown referred to as "polymorphous perversity," not in the way Freud used this term to describe infants, but rather as the human ability to engage in any and all kinds of sexual activity.

Similarly, Dawe expands upon the clichéd ruse of having a masquerade party where the simple addition of a bandit's mask over the eyes appears to completely disguise everyone. Taking this to a ridiculous level, Dawe has the women, whose body types could not be more different, come dressed as each other, clearly identifiable to anyone who's not blind. The final, hysterically funny scene ends with all the characters in Despina's bedroom (and with as many as can

fit in her bed) impersonating each other. Despina, fearful of the return of Alfonso, tries to empty the room. Alfonso, previously depicted as a philosopher/scientist completely obsessed with his own ideas, barges in, singing in falsetto and wearing a wig to make him appear as Fiordiligi.

All the singers, dancers and instrumentalists were exceptional. Ryan Adams's conducting was enthusiastic, spirited and committed to a score that is very complex. The dancers were lithe and suggestive, and the choreography by Austin McCormick was on a par with his delightful Baroque-style production earlier this year of *Judge Me Paris*.

The venue was the elegant theater of the Italian Academy with the seats arranged more sensibly than for the production of Dawe's *Cracked Orlando* in 2010. The presence of a panel LCD screen, not always visible to all, gave subtitles to the Italian text.

What I said in my review of *Cracked Orlando* holds true here: "Mr. Dawe is to be congratulated for composing a rare, uncompromising work that needs no defense for its dissonance and atonality, is genuinely appealing in its own right, and puts to rest the complaints of those who still think the term 'modern music' is an oxymoron."

♪*Anderszewski's Bach Steps Back*
Piotr Anderszewski (piano), Carnegie Hall, New York 6.12.2012

Bach: French Suite No. 5 in G major, English Suite No. 3 in G minor, Italian Concerto, English Suite No. 6 in D minor

Encore: Sarabande from Partita No. 1 in B-flat major

I first heard Piotr Anderszewski on his recording of Beethoven's *Diabelli Variations*. I found it special, and it remained so for me until Ashkenazy's recent CD of the same work. The common critical praise of Anderszewski's performance is his ability to let Beethoven speak for himself. There is so much vibrancy, complexity and variation in the work that it doesn't need to bear the weight of a pianist's personality. But there was one point when Anderszewski disregarded Beethoven, and it was at a crucial moment. The penultimate chord in the score is followed by an eighth-note rest immediately followed by the final chord marked *f*. Anderszewski takes the eighth-note rest as if it were a five second fermata before striking the final chord as a *p* not an *f*. Looking back at it now, it seems as if he were making a statement that he may have followed Beethoven's score to the tee, but he didn't have to.

There was some magical Bach at Carnegie Hall. Anderszewski's well-judged use of ornamentation, flourishes and arpeggiation on the repeats was exemplary. In the *Loure* of the French Suite No. 5, he brought out clearly the melodic line for the left hand buried in the B section. In the gigues, he matched Glenn Gould in velocity. He executed the repeat of the second gavotte of the English Suite No. 6 an octave higher than Bach wrote it, reproducing what it

might have sounded like when played with an open lute stop on the harpsichord. The dark D minor prelude to the suite hearkened back to the improvisatory style of Frescobaldi preludes, toccatas and canzones. In the Italian Concerto the lines of the "soloist" against the "orchestra's" accompaniment sounded so authentic that it seemed the pianist might be coming in slightly ahead or behind the "orchestra."

But the moderately paced dances such as the allemandes, bourées and gavottes lacked, at times, a rhythmic pulse. The faster dances had speed to spare, but when played too fast, as he did, the essential contrapuntal lines blurred: the voices dropped out in a whirlwind of virtuosity. The sarabandes, particularly the one from the English Suite No. 6, were as slow as any I've heard. It's hard not to compare this lumbering interpretation to the notorious 25th variation of the *Goldberg Variations* played by Glen Gould in his 1955 performance that consumed 6:30 minutes out a total of 39 minutes: the time it took him to finish the 30 variations. Let us hope that Anderszewski comes to his senses as Glen Gould did in his second recording of the *Goldberg Variations* in which he played the 25th in a more sensible 4:16 minutes.

Few purists these days still defend the notion that Bach has to be played on a harpsichord for the listener to experience the real thing. To do this would be to miss out on some of the best piano performers of recent times: Glenn Gould, Andras Schiff and Angela Hewitt, to name a few. Gould was certainly eccentric, but rarely failed in the qualities one might think Bach himself would have admired: clarity of line, control of phrasing and technical finesse. Since Bach's rediscovery in the mid-19th century, we've had to listen to overly personal, soulful Bach that steals the heart of this joyful music. Although we may have gone overboard in the other direction in an attempt to recreate the true Bach, we are now willing to enjoy the possibilities inherent in the piano: that is, when the piano is used to expose the music of Bach rather than as here cover it with overly virtuosic speed-fests or Romantic histrionics that put our understanding of Bach back a century.

♫Juilliard415 Morphs Again

Juilliard415, Bohemian Club at the Kosciuszko Foundation, New York, 3.12.2012

Castello: Sonata decimasesta from *Sonate Concertate in Stil Moderno, Libro II*
Farina: Pavana Seconda from *Ander Theil newer Paduanen*
Rosenmüller: Sonata no.10 in F major from *Sonate*
Corelli: Trio Sonata no. 6 in B minor from *Sonate a tre*; Sonata no. 12 in G major: Ciaconna from *Sonate da camera a tre*
Vivaldi: Concerto in G minor

As with any student orchestra, the makeup of the early music group Juilliard415 changes from one year to the next as students graduate and new ones come in. Fortunately, there is continuity with experienced seniors sharing their knowledge with younger players. But unique to any early music group is the demand made

upon it to morph into the myriad combinations of instrumentalists needed to cover the staves of a composer's score. No 19th century or later chamber work would be written—as Bach did for most movements of his *Musical Offering*—without specifying an instrument. If the instrument could cover a line's range, whether keyboard, oboe, violin or flute, that was okay for Bach. Play Schubert's Quintet in C major with a contrabassoon instead of a double bass and watch the audience walk out. In this concert, Corelli's Trio, written for 2 violins, replaced the first violin with a flute and sounded as "correct" as the original.

The historical precedent in the Baroque period allows for changes in instrumentalists depending upon which musicians are available to perform and what their level of expertise may be. This can be seen in the music of Vivaldi who, as a music teacher in a girl's orphanage, almost always composed with a specific student or student group in mind. Hence there are the odd combinations of *concertino* groups ranging from simple two-violin concerti to the concerti for diverse instruments such the RV 555 concerto for 3 violins, oboe, *viola all'inglese*, *chalmeleau*, 2 cellos, harpsichord, strings and continuo. Bach too continually transformed works to other formats: a harpsichord concerto to one for violin, or another composer's oboe concerto into a keyboard work.

The concert presented here by the current Juilliard historical performance group consisted of two ensembles. It was the first time I've heard the students without a staff or guest conductor and, without meaning to disparage this performance or any of the performers (many of whom I have praised in previous reviews), the program wanted for the presence of a conductor/leader. Monica Huggett, Gonzalo Ruiz or a guest instructor like William Christie, Jordi Savall, Steven Fox or Richard Egarr would have added a level of panache and enthusiasm.

The program was designed to track the development of the Baroque chamber sonata from the extravagant style of Dario Castello (played admirably here), with its sudden changes in tempo and dynamics; to the German Johann Rosenmüller with his take on the techniques of the Italian violin school; through Corelli, the most influential composer of the group, whose early Trio sonata mix of both "church" and "chamber" form leads to Vivaldi. The latter's Concerto in G minor, like most of his concerti, follows the more modern of Corelli's forms, the chamber (*da camera*) style of fast-slow-fast.

The interesting history of the G minor concerto revolves around the fact that it was not written for Vivaldi's girl students at the orphanage, but for performers and composers from Dresden who were so enamored of Vivaldi that they came to Venice to learn from him. The concerto was written and sent back to Dresden with one of the visiting musicians. Although it starts off like a violin concerto, the other musicians, who are normally relegated to the background ripieno, come up front as part of the soloist *concertino* group. This allowed Vivaldi to provide the virtuosi of the Dresden orchestra with music to show off their skills. Nanae Iwata stood out in this concerto, as she has in other performances, for her vibrant Baroque technical finesse in the manner of her mentor, Monica Huggett.

Both ensembles were technically adept and particularly skilled at following the lead violinist whose use of rubato required the players to keep a sharp eye on his every move. Like a conductor waiting for the soloist in a concerto to finish his cadenza, failure to look at the first violinist could have resulted in coming in too soon or too late.

♪Aimard Approaches Debussy from Another Side

Pierre-Laurent Aimard (piano), Carnegie Hall, New York, 15.11.2012

Debussy: Préludes, Book II
Holliger: *Elis (Three Night Pieces)*
Schumann: Symphonic Etudes

The core education and training of most musicians is based on a repertory that starts in the 17th or 18th centuries and continues through the years, trailing off to a considerably smaller body of works from the 20th and 21st centuries. Most soloists' suitcases are filled with music from Bach through Ravel, but over the years they may pick up "modern" pieces, often works that have been written for them or which they feel obliged to tackle. Evgeny Kissin rarely goes beyond the standard repertory except for Prokofiev and Scriabin and, more recently, Samuel Barber. The same could be said of Martha Argerich who occasionally will play something by Lutoslawski.

A contemporary pianist would come naturally to a composer such as Debussy from his emersion in music of the 19th century: Chopin, Schumann, Liszt and Brahms. The expectation is that the pianist's interpretation would be a continuation of the grand tradition. If the pianist had a choice of playing the first book or the second book of Préludes, the first would be considered more accessible.

But what would this music sound like if the pianist approached it from the opposite side of music history? What if he were a student of Yvonne Loriot and Pierre Boulez? What if his repertory up until recently consisted of works by György Ligeti, George Benjamin and Elliott Carter (whose final work was written for the pianist)? What if at the age of sixteen he won first prize in the Messiaen Competition?

It should be said before anything else that Pierre-Laurent Aimard's performance on Thursday evening was exquisite, both immaculate and flawless. He played without a score (except in the short work by Holliger), and seemed to think through and analyze every note. There was nothing dreamy, lulling or insubstantial about the Debussy, no hazy poem filled with accolades to the moonlight. This was radical music in its day, and Aimard played it seriously. It would seem he sees something almost sacred in Debussy. This was particularly true in his performance of the seventh prelude, "La terrasse des audiences du clair de lune." With the amount of time given to the gaps before and after this prelude and the attention to every note, Aimard gave it the color and feel of one of the "régards" from Messiaen's "Vingt régards sur l'enfant-Jésus."

Sitting down to play the Debussy, Aimard waited for what seemed like several minutes before raising his hands to the keyboard. For an encore, which it took the audience several minutes to convince him to play, he performed a short work by Elliott Carter, "Fratribute," from his *Tri-Tribute*. Aimard referred to it as an "Homage à Carter": quite a lovely work. After the final note he lifted his hands and froze for what seemed forever before letting the confounded audience applaud. After the final note of the Debussy, some members of the audience shouted and applauded inappropriately, before he even had a chance to lift his hands from the keyboard.

His serious approach to the preludes unfortunately left the humor out of some of the pieces whose titles or score markings clearly indicate Debussy intended them to be playful. I'm not sure how Debussy expected a passage marked "ironique" to sound but Aimard passed this by. Debussy's sixth prelude, "General Lavine-eccentric," is to be played in the style of a cakewalk but it needed a little more eccentricity, as did the parody, "God Save the King/Queen," in the ninth, "Hommage à S. Pickwick, Esq. PPM. PC."

Aimard, intentionally or not, gave the audience no chance to applaud before beginning Schumann's Symphonic Etudes. Considering that the last note of Holliger's *Elis (Three Night Pieces)* requires the pianist to reach into the piano to pluck a string, it would have been inappropriate to applaud his derrière. By the time he got back to his chair, it was too late to acknowledge his interpretation of this delightful Webernian miniature.

It was only after Aimard finished playing Schumann's Symphonic Etudes (including the five posthumous etudes) and stood up to accept the audience's applause that one realized how much energy, both physical and mental, it took to perform these difficult variations. Aimard looked pale and drained, although this did not show during his execution. Some of Schumann's later etudes require tremendous stamina. One movement is marked "Presto possibile" and Aimard took this to heart. The final "Allegro brillante" could have stood alone in its Lisztian virtuosity.

"Brilliant" would be the apt word to describe this entire recital.

♪ *Triumph of Handel, Christie, Juilliard415 and Soloists*

Raquel Gonzáles (soprano), Ying Fang (soprano), Rachel Wilson (mezzo-soprano), Spencer Lang (tenor), Juilliard415, William Christie (conductor), Alice Tully Hall, Lincoln Center, New York, 27.10.2012

Handel: *Il Trionfo del Tempo e del Disinganno*

The first decade of the 18th century was one of the most unusual and prolific periods in the history of vocal music. Opera had been banned by Pope Innocent XII, and that policy continued until the death of his successor, Pope Clement XI, in 1710. But similar to American Prohibition when alcoholic beverages were often produced with the tacit approval of the very people who established the ban, vocal music was commissioned by men close to the Pope. Two cardinals

(Ottoboni and Pamphili) and one Marchese (Ruspoli) sponsored soirees where composers like Handel and Alessandro Scarlatti presented cantatas and oratorios.

These works were basically operas without staging, traditionally in two sections and modeled after medieval morality plays. The libretti consisted of debates among personified Platonic ideals as to who was smarter, more powerful or more beautiful. Some were based on mythological stories so as to avoid any association with the sacred, but Handel in his many interpolations of old arias into new works made little distinction between the sacred and the profane. Often the text was meant to be edifying and frequently, as in the case of *Trionfo*, it was just plain dull. The big exception to the rule was Handel's brilliant *L'Allegro, il Penseroso ed il Moderato*. That libretto works better than most because it is based on a poem by John Milton. It was under this ban that Handel at the age of 22 wrote his first oratorio, *Il Trionfo del Tempo e del Disinganno*. Based on a libretto by Cardinal Pamphili, the oratorio must have pleased Handel: he revised it in 1737 and again in 1757, and borrowed many arias from it for use in later productions, the most famous transformation being that of Piacere's "Lascia la spina" into Almirena's "Lascia ch'io pianga" in *Rinaldo*.

The oratorio's opening is not the French-style overture favored by Handel (a slow, stately, heavily dotted entrance, followed by a short-themed fugue and ending with a repetition of the opening), but rather a classic fast-slow-fast Italian sonata. The story goes that Handel had written his usual French overture for this work, but Corelli, who was a member of the orchestra, stated that he did not understand the French form. Handel, out of deference to the great violinist/composer, wrote a new Italian-style sonata to replace it.

Not that this new opening was any simpler for the orchestra to play. The violins and the oboes have much to do and there was some struggling from both instruments in the performance here. William Christie held nothing back, and as the work progressed both groups settled into a more comfortable playing of Handel's demanding score.

Ying Fang and Rachel Wilson, who both appeared earlier this year as soloists in a cantata by Handel, have improved considerably. There were moments when Ms. Fang's vocal coloring reminded me of a young Magdalena Kožená. Ms. Wilson sang a heart-rending "Lascia la spina," softening her vocal coloring to a hue closer to Baroque vocal style. The same could be said of Raquel González, whose voice also seems to have lightened since her appearance with Christie during his previous visit to Juilliard. Tenor Spencer Lang excelled in every aria, intensely involved with the text and expressing emotion with every word.

Highlights of the performance included Ms. Gonzalez's rendering of "Fosco genio," with its odd jumping chromaticisms and strange, tricky cadences; Ms. Fang's vocal gymnastics in "Una schiera di piaceri"; and the duet by Fang and González, "Il voler nel fior degl'anni," with its virtuosic oboes and recorders. The most exceptional piece in the oratorio, perhaps, is the quartet "Voglio tempo per risolvere" with its complicated vocal combinations revealing a level of artistic maturity not seen in Handel's other early arias. "Tu del Ciel," sung tenderly by Ms. Fang, ends the work on a peaceful note rather than with the usual upbeat finale.

♪Tharaud's Varied Program from Scarlatti to Ravel

Alexandre Tharaud (piano), Weill Concert Hall, Carnegie Hall, New York, 24.10.2012

Scarlatti: Sonatas in E major, A minor, C major, F minor, D minor
Ravel: *Miroirs*
Chopin: Sonata No. 2 in B-flat minor
Liszt: "Funérailles" from *Harmornies poétiques et religieuses*

His fingers seem to extend across the entire keyboard, and they snap back after a run of chords as if they were made of rubber. Alexandre Tharaud reminds one of Vladimir Horowitz, and the comparison is not far-fetched: in addition to their long fingers and similar way of attacking the keyboard is their love for Scarlatti. No major composer since the 18th-century has left behind so much music, but so little background on that music and even less about himself. We know that Scarlatti was music teacher to Princess Maria Barbara of Portugal–later Queen of Spain–for over 30 years. Copies of two 15-volume editions of sonatas written out by the Queen's copier were found in Parma and Venice, but not one piece of paper from Scarlatti's own hand. There have been conspiracy theories that, aside from the musical scores, everything of and about Scarlatti was made to disappear. Apart from some anecdotal stories, such as the contest in Scarlatti's youth with Handel as to who was the better harpsichordist and who the better organist (Scarlatti won the former and Handel the latter), virtually nothing is known about him. Perhaps the inability of history to make a personality out of Scarlatti has limited the public's interest and has resulted in his music being underappreciated and underplayed.

There are 550-plus sonatas and, aside from a few simple, childlike pieces, not one can be considered a dud. Specific ornamentations and trills are bountiful in Scarlatti's scores, but rules as to whether they should fall on a note or before it are still open to debate. Although most of the sonatas are marked with a tempo description of the most general kind, few of them have any dynamic marking This is not unusual, given the fact that aside from instruments with double manuals and those capable of changes in register, dynamic changes were not possible on the harpsichord of Scarlatti's time. Even though Queen Maria Barbara of Spain was one of the first purchasers of a pianoforte, Scarlatti continued to write for her in a style suitable for the earlier instrument.

The sparseness of playing indicators can be seen by the performer either as a demand that the works be played exactly as written, or as an invitation to fill in what is not there. In fact, this dichotomy generally falls in line with which instrument is played. The more restricted interpretations use the harpsichord (Kirkpatrick, Ross, Leonhardt); the more improvisatory use the piano (Horowitz, Pletnev, Sudbin and Tharaud). However, there are exceptions with freer interpretations on the harpsichord (Landowsa, Hantai, Valenti), and stricter interpretations on the piano (Schiff, Meyers, Grante).

There is no question to which school Tharaud belongs. Scarlatti's E major sonata was just a warm-up. A minor opened crisply with a flourish but failed to reveal and emphasize the audacious syncopated chromatic scales that run up and down individually and jointly. A speedy run through of C major was imaginatively phrased and smoothly played, but this piece's quirky theme works best when played on a harpsichord and even better when played using the lute stop. The lyrical F minor was performed with just the right touch and sensitivity, and the wildly virtuosic D minor, with its repeated notes and dissonant chords, was a good example of how well Scarlatti can be played by a pianist of Tharaud's ability.

Ravel's *Miroirs* takes us into the first years of the 20th century and represents one of the varied paths that music was to take throughout the 1900s. Scriabin, Vaughan Williams, Schoenberg, Ives, Rachmaninoff and De Falla were all born within three years of Ravel, and each composer followed or created his own style, be it late Romantic, mystical, nationalistic or avant-garde. Ravel's *Miroirs*, in addition to being in the forefront of the impressionist movement, also looks back to programmatic music of the 19th century: "Noctuelles" (Night Moths), "Oiseaux tristes" (Sad Birds) and the rest of the movements imitate the sounds of nature.

Tharaud's performance was captivating from the start. The ability to fine tune his velocity and to control the timing of phrases was there from the opening "Noctuelles." His "Oiseaux tristes" had an almost eerie edge to it. "Une Barque sur l'océan" uses techniques and phrasing that seem somewhat clichéd, but Tharaud successfully steered the boat to shore. Only "Alboradodel gracioso" lacked clarity of line and color, but I may be prejudiced by my familiarity with Ravel's richly-hued orchestral transcription.

Whether coincidentally or deliberately, Tharaud chose two funereal works, Chopin's "Funeral March" Sonata No. 2 and Lizst's "Funérailles" from *Harmornies poétiques et religieuses*. The first movement of the Chopin was played with tremendous energy and intensity, the massive runs of chords attacked with hands that seemed to bounce off the keyboard. The opening of the third movement, "Funeral March," is so overplayed that it is easy to forget there is some astoundingly beautiful music within it, and Tharaud was sensitive to the slightest variations. The final movement, normally taken at lightning speed, in Tharaud's hands sped by so quickly that it sounded like a coda to the third movement.

"What else is our life but a series of preludes to that unknown Hymn, the first and solemn note of which is intoned by Death?" Liszt's famous explanation of his orchestral work, "Les Préludes," can be applied to his work in general with some slight changes: "What else is our life but a series of preludes leading to nowhere." Tharaud did a fine performance of this work in spite of its bloviation.

The first encore was the poignant transcription Bach wrote for a Benedetto Marcello oboe concerto. The second encore came as an amusing contrast to the all the music before it: variations on Gershwin's "The Man I Love."

♫ *For Connoisseurs and Lovers of Music*

The Flute King: Emmanuel Pahud (flute), Les Violons du Roy, Bernard Labadie (conductor), Zankel Hall, Carnegie Hall, New York, 22.10.2012

Benda: Sinfonia No. 1 in C major
Frederick I, King of Prussia: Flute Concerto No. 3 in C major
Quantz: Concerto for Flute in G major
J. S. Bach: Ricercar a 6 from *Musical Offering*
C. P. E. Bach: String Symphony No. 5 in B minor, Concerto for Flute in A major

The title of this review refers to a published set of keyboard sonatas by C. P. E. Bach entitled *Für Kennen und Liebhaber*. Translations for "*Kennen*" range from "connoisseur" to "expert." "*Liebhaber*" could mean "amateur" or "enthusiast." The distinctions were clear to Bach and his contemporaries: the sonatas in this set are equally playable by both groups. The first group would be challenged by the complexities of the difficult pieces, while the second would find delight in those with simpler melodies. No denigration was implied; if it were, no "Liebhabers" would have bought his scores.

I say this as a prelude to a concert whose first half was pleasant enough in its late Rococo elegance to please the "Liebhabers" in the audience. Although, from their spontaneous recognition in the encore of J. S. Bach's *Badinerie* from his second suite and their laughter when Pahud played it half-seriously, I would say that most of the audience were *Kenners*.

It was the second half of the concert that made this performance special. The highlight of the evening was the Ricercar a 6 from Bach's *Musical Offering*. The instrumentalists stood in a semi-circle around the conductor, and slowly each of the six voices spoke, only to be covered by the entrance of another voice, until the double bass's notes stormed in. At this point all 16 instruments weaved in and out, carrying their individual lines to the final notes. The theme, a simple motif written by Fredrick the Great, lent itself to this kind of development, but it took a composer like Bach to see the theme's potential and set it free. It's interesting that the great variations of Bach, *A Musical Offering*, *Art of the Fugue* and the *Goldberg Variations*, and similarly Beethoven's *The Diabelli Variations*, are based on insipid themes. It is almost as if the composers thrived on the melodies' shallowness and the fact that any variations could only be improvements!

Bernard Labadie could not have done a better job controlling this wild ride: every line was clear and every entrance of that line was distinct and audible against the musical background. The strings were rich and lush without ever going over the top, and this version of the *Musical Offering* produced a sound much like a Bach organ work. By having fewer players on stage, Labadie avoided making the piece sound as if it were a transcription by Stokowski. The same performance with double or triple the string players would have given the work a heftier and inappropriate styling.

It was Bach's eldest son, Wilhelm Friedemann Bach, who suffered most from not being able to find a way out from under his father's shadow and musical style. The works that he wrote have an imbalance that is woozy and schizoid. Brilliant as W. F. was, the brother closest to him in age, Carl Philip Emmanuel, was successful in freeing himself from his father. Like his older brother, C. P. E. wrote eccentric music, but he had the capacity to lead a normal life: financially solvent and admired and respected as composer and keyboardist to the royal courts of Berlin and Hamburg.

We get glimpses of these eccentricities in the symphony performed here. In the first movement there are sudden jumps, modulations, pregnant pauses and changes in tempo: all trademarks of C.P.E. Bach. You get glimpses of this period style in the music from the first part of the program, but the spark of genius is not there.

Labadie gave an intense and passionate reading of the C. P. E. Bach symphony and was well onboard for Emmanuel Pahud's rendition of the A minor flute concerto. As strongly as Pahud had held our attention in the first half of the program, he was unquestionably more committed to this masterful piece of music. The wild outer movements were in sharp contrast to the poignant, heartbreakingly slow second movement. Both Labadie and Pahud took a moment of silence before playing this movement, perhaps needing some time to prepare themselves for the intensity of the work's *innigkeit*.

What better praise can I give to Pahud then to compare him favorably to another great flautist, who had a similar interest in music of this era and played it both mellifluously and fluidly many times upstairs at Carnegie Hall: Jean-Pierre Rampal.

♪*Baroque in Pieces, But Nothing Broken Here*
Krista Bennion Feeney (violin), Melanie Feld (oboe), Stephen Taylor (oboe), St. Luke's Chamber Ensemble, The Morgan Library & Museum, New York, 12.10.2012

Biber: Sonata No. 3 in F major for Violin and Continuo
Albinoni: Concerto for Two Oboes in C major, Op. 7, No. 11
Bach: Violin Concerto in A minor, Orchestral Suite No. 1 in C major

When the best of the best get together to perform music they clearly love, a good time is guaranteed for all. The St. Luke's Chamber Ensemble are members of the Orchestra of St. Luke's which was founded in 1979. Since then they've recorded over 70 albums, won four Grammy Awards, commissioned over 50 new works and premiered 150+ new works. Both Ensemble and Orchestra have succeeded where so many others fail.

The Morgan Library concert consisted of two familiar works by Bach, one work by the under-appreciated Tomasso Albinoni and one by the recently revived master of the violin, Heinrich Biber. Sonata No. 3, like much of his violin music, was written to show off his own virtuosic skills. Double-stopping, *bariolage*, emulation of bass ostinatos and pedal points are all techniques used here and in the other seven sonatas in this set of eight. No. 3 starts out with a *praeludium*, which could as well be called fantasia or toccata, an opening piece meant to sound as if it were improvised. The mixture of fast and slow runs leads without pause to a lovely group of variations. The final movement may sound familiar as it has a repeating ground similar to Pachelbel's Canon. Although marked as *Variatio*, it is really a poignant chaconne, one of the common rhythmic forms popular in Europe at the time. Best of all was the surprise ending: the piece stops in the middle of a violin riff.

Krista Bennion Feeney's performance was a showcase of violin technique. Her approach to the Biber sonata achieved the right mix between Romantic vibrato and cool Baroque style, and technical difficulties, of which there were many, didn't seem to faze her. It was both captivating and convincing, and on a par with performances of the work by violinists such as Andrew Manze and John Holloway.

Vivaldi or Albinoni? It's really difficult to tell, not only in the Albinoni piece performed here, but in any of his concerti. An older contemporary of Vivaldi, born 17 years before him and living ten years longer, Albinoni clearly influenced the younger composer. The concerto played here is part of the earlier of two sets of 12 concerti, most for oboe. This demanding work was deftly played by Melanie Feld and Stephen Taylor. As in the previous piece, modern instruments were played in a persuasive Baroque style, but I did miss the warm and mellow coloring of period oboes.

Ms. Feeney returned for another solo role in Bach's A-minor violin concerto. A challenge for performers of works that have been overplayed through the years is the need to take the audience back to the time when these compositions still sounded fresh. With their vivacity and élan, the St. Luke's Chamber Ensemble was able to revivify both this work and the Bach Orchestral Suite No. 1 that followed.

The group covered the orchestral requirements of this suite in a one-instrument-per-part format. This could have produced a thin sound, but through a combination of performance volume and the fine acoustics of the Morgan's theater, the musical voices were full and distinct. There was a slightly humorous moment when the final notes of the concluding *Passepied*, a generally slow dance, ended. The audience wasn't quite sure if the suite had indeed finished: our usual expectation with Bach is that his works end with a gigue or a similar quick tempo.

♪ *Webern, Brahms and Half a Bach*
Minsoo Sohn (piano), Zankel Hall, Carnegie Hall, New York, 6.10.2012

Webern: Variations for Piano
Brahms: Variations and Fugue on a Theme by Handel
Bach: *Goldberg Variations*

If Minsoo Sohn had heeded the words of the grande dame of Bach pianists, Roslyn Tureck, he would have reconsidered his decision to skip the repeats in his performance of Bach's *Goldberg Variations:* 'In Bach's music the repeats are essential... This is inescapably true in the *Goldberg Variations*, which are so alive with contrapuntal variation. Without repeats the *Goldberg Variations* are a tour de force. With them the music is fulfilled, becoming the Odyssey of variation form that it truly is." Roslyn Tureck is referring to Glen Gould's 38-minute recording made three years before her comments, but she could have just as well been talking about Sohn's 31-minute performance here. Of course, there is no law requiring him to play repeats but by not doing so–particularly those that have different first section end bars–the pianist is in fact not playing notes written by Bach to be performed.

The other major issue is that some part of the audience was drawn to this recital based on hearing Sohn's recent recording of the *Goldberg Variations* on the Honens label. On this CD Sohn not only plays every repeat, but also applies to them the subtlest and most sensitive ornamentation I can ever remember hearing. It is a shame we were not given the opportunity to hear them performed live. Adding these repetitions would have made this one of the great *Goldbergs* of the twenty-first century. This accolade is no small claim given the competition he's up against. A search on "Goldberg Variations" on Amazon comes up with 871.

Sohn has an uncanny ability to control his touch in such a way as to make one think each line of music is being played on a different piano or by a second pianist. This was apparent from the opening aria where the upper and lower lines seemed to roll like waves. The same could be said for the three-voiced canons which were both luminous and pellucid. The clarity of the marching bass of the sixth variation, the subtle shading of the phrases of the eighth, the "variations" in touch as each voice enters in the fughetto of the tenth variation, the almost comical fluttering of the 11th and the 17th, the ravishing poignancy drawn from the 13th, the frenetic quavers racing around the keyboard of the 20th, the rubato creating a sense of hesitancy and uncertainty in the 25th, and the effortless playing of the difficult 28th and 29th with their combinations of trilling and hand-crossing, are just the highlights of his masterly interpretation.

The virtuosity here was no simple showmanship. Each variation seemed carefully thought through, decisively stated and played with the muscularity to prove it.

Webern's brief three-movement set that at one time seemed so impossibly radical, in Sohn's hands came off as being of its time (it was written in 1936). The short sub-segments of the tone rows played variously in inversion and retrograde tied the phases together within the movement; the three movements then tied together as a whole. Wisps of sound connected it in ways that made it seem both similar to and the opposite of the tonal world of the dying romantic tradition.

Sohn's interpretation of Brahms' Variations and Fugue on a theme by Handel was more than technically adept, but lacked the imagination and conviction of his Bach. The variety of both musical forms and composers represented in Brahms' Variations from Bach to Beethoven to Schumann, while not requiring the pianist to have a degree in musicology to perform successfully, does require a deep understanding of the music that Brahms himself had inherited. It is to be hoped that in the future Sohn will reappraise this set of variations as well as his decision to drop the repeats in the *Goldberg Variations*.

♫*Chaconne: Gotham Early Music Scene Does the Devil's Dance*
The Art and Ecstasy of the Chaconne: The Sinfonia Players, Christine Gummere (artistic director), Society for Ethical Culture, New York, 4.10.2012

Biber: Passacaglia for solo violin
Mazzocchi: "Sdegno campion"
Bertali: Chiacona for violin and continuo
Monteverdi: "Quel sguardo sdegnosetto"
Purcell: Chacony in G minor; Dido's Lament from *Dido and Aeneas*; 3 Parts on a Ground in D major
Couperin: "Le Rossignol-en-amour"
Lully: Passacaille d'Armide from *Armide*; Chaconne de Galatée from *Acis et Galatée*
Leclair: Chaconne from *Le Deuxième Récréation de Musique*
Stölzel: "Bist du bei mir"
Bach: Chaconne from the Partita in D minor for unaccompanied violin
After Arañés: Gran Chacona

Chacona, chaconne, ciacona, chacony, ciaccona and chiacona all refer to a dance form so captivating that it was banned at one time for being music of the devil. It usually begins with an accented second beat, but not always. The ground that the music dances above and around repeats continually the same notes, but not always. It is mostly in triple time, but also in common time. It is claimed to have its roots in places as disparate as Mexico, the Caribbean, Africa and Spain. There is something inherent in its beat that makes improvisation and variation a natural. Regardless of what is played above the bass ground, the repeating motifs will drive the piece forward to an appealing musical end. As Alex Ross states in an essay on the chaconne, it is "perfectly engineered to bewitch the senses," resulting in its most intense form as "a little sonic tornado that spins in circles while hurtling forward." If one wants to understand the appeal of Philip Glass's music, they need look no further than to the history of the chaconne.

The chaconne has an opposite effect when played slowly: it can be soothing and limpid. The prime example here was the performance of Couperin's "Rossignol-en-Amour." Originally written as one of several hundred miniatures for solo keyboard, Couperin himself suggested the upper line could be taken by a flute and the ground played on the keyboard. Susan Miller took to heart his tempo request to play this piece "slowly and very tenderly." She successfully kept a fluid and cohesive hold on the music even when it was approaching silence.

Heinrich Biber's Passacaglia for solo violin is the final piece in his set of violin sonatas entitled *The Rosary Sonatas*. (It is also the only sonata in the set with normal tuning.) Because of the allure of the chaconne form (indistinguishable from the passacaglia) it was not uncommon to end a major musical set or work with a chaconne. Both Rameau and Purcell end operas with this dance and hearing it almost charms the audience into wanting to get up and dance. Unlike Bach's *Chaconne*, Biber's strictly enforces the playing of the repeating ground throughout the entire piece, even opening with it before the upper voice comes in. Judson Griffin gave the work a glowing reading, clearly articulating the four bass notes while doing dancing variations above them.

A playful badinage was acted out between Grant Herreid, with his long threatening theorbo fretboard and the mezzo-soprano Maria Todaro before and after she sings Virgilio Mazzocchi's 'Sdegno campion." I would question though the disparity between the words and her vocal interpretation. The text is a call to arms in praise of the anger required to summon up the fury needed to destroy the enemy. Ms. Todaro's sweet voice gave rich expression to Mazzocchi's song: admirably done yet seemingly at odds with the words.

The Bertali chiacona for violin and continuo starts with a five-note ground repeated continually, changing tempi and dynamics but never the notes themselves. The violin score is a true test of one's virtuosity which, when passed, results in the piece sounding as if it were improvised. Theresa Soloman's playing was exemplary. The only disappointment was that it ended so quickly, breaking the hypnotic spell it cast upon the audience.

Monteverdi's "Quel sguardo sdegnosetto" from his *Scherzi musicali* is another work requiring virtuosic skills and a wide ranging voice. This performance revealed the less serious side of Monteverdi (*Scherzi musicali* are musical jokes) with Ms. Todaro leaping through the higher ranges of her tessitura with ease. A "whiter" voice might have better complemented this song but Ms. Todaro gave a spirited and energetic rendition.

By the time the chaconne reached Henry Purcell, the rules governing it were beginning to break down. In the Chacony in G minor Purcell allows the bass ground to be picked up by other instruments and bounced back and forth between the string players. In the 3 Parts on a ground, Purcell starts off in 6/8 time but midway goes to the "normal" 3/4 time. In both pieces there are variations demanding awesome technical skills which the instrumentalists clearly possessed. The penultimate aria from Purcell's *Dido and Aeneas* with the most pathetic lines ever sung, "Remember me, but ah! forget my Fate," received an earnest and fervid reading by Ms. Todaro.

The dancers in the second part of the program worked their charm in two chaconnes by Lully. It was good to see again Baroque dancing choreographed in the manner of Catherine Turocy and the relocated New York Baroque Dance Company; and to know it is still represented in New York in the persons of Patricia Beaman and Carlos Fittante. The dancers, in traditional period garb and masks danced with their outstretched arms in sensitive synchronization to the music.

The under-appreciated Jean Marie Leclair is represented here by a chaconne from his *Deuxième Récréation de Musique*. We are in a new world with the bass line starting off as in a traditional *ostinato* style but then joining in with the other instruments, following the spirit of the form but hardly any of its rules. The movement ends quietly with the original bass line back where it belongs. The instrumentation here was the flute and violin, but could have been played by two violins as well.

"Bist du bei mir," originally ascribed to Bach but now attributed to G.H. Stölzel, was lovingly sung by Ms. Beaman. Claire Jolivet started out a little hesitantly but quickly took control of the monumental chaconne from Bach's D minor partita for unaccompanied violin. Her flawless technique rendered a reading that was both majestic and deeply personal. It should come as no surprise that although composers of the 18th century, such as Leclair, Rameau and Boismortier, continued to write chaconnes, it wasn't until the 20th century with Bartók's sonata for solo violin (which includes a chaconne) that any composer felt he had anything additional to say that had not already been said before by Bach.

The entire group, led by the dancers in Spanish attire, joined in Grant Herreid's arrangement of Juan Arañés's Gran Chacona. This vivid recreation of music and dancing on a Spanish street brought out the wild nature of the form. The clacking of castanets ended the evening, while delightfully opening the Gotham Early Music Scene's sixth year.

♫ *18th-Century Concert in 19th-Century Salon*

Anthony Roth Costanzo (countertenor), Bradley Brookshire (harpsichord), Jared Angle (dancer), Troy Schumacher (choreography), Salon/Sanctuary Concerts, The Player's Club, New York, 28.9.2012

Handel: "Rompo i lacci" from *Flavio*; "Aure deh per pietà" from *Giulio Cesare*
Purcell: "Secrecy's song" from *The Fairy Queen*; "Music for a while" from *Oedipus*; "The Evening Hymn" from *Harmonia Sacra*
Bach: Chromatic Fantasy and Fugue
Vivaldi: *Qual per ignoto calle*
Scarlatti: Sonatas in B-flat Major, G Major, D Minor
Handel: "Pena tiranna" from *Amadigi di Gaula*; "Vivi tiranno" from *Rodelinda*

In an earlier review of the wild fractal opera *Cracked Orlando* I wrote: "Anthony Roth Costanzo seems to improve each time I see him, from his performance in Handel's *Ariodante* at Juilliard to his role as Armindo in the New York City Opera's production of Handel's *Partenope*. I look forward to seeing him at the Met some time in the near future." Indeed, Mr. Costanzo did appear this past season in the Met productions of *Rodelinda* and the Baroque pastiche *The Enchanted Island*. In the latter he stood out in a small role as Fernando, but also had the opportunity to replace David Daniels, who was ill, as the lead singer.

In a gala concert to mark the opening of the new season, Salon/Sanctuary presented a recital by Mr. Costanzo, backed at the harpsichord by Bradley Brookshire. In addition, Jared Angle joined Mr. Costanzo in a ballet of Vivaldi's cantata *Quel per ignoto calle*. The concert was held in the period salon of the Player's Club (purchased by the actor Edwin Booth and modeled after the Garrick Club in London).

Emoting and gesticulating on stage is tremendously difficult for a soloist.

It requires the performer to concentrate on the words and their meaning without getting distracted. This is particularly true of Baroque arias where the level of artifice is very high: men singing women's roles, women singing men's parts, the frequent occurrence of *dei ex machina,* improbable coincidences and illogical endings. There's often a fine line between being emotionally convincing and tragic and just plain looking foolish. This was not the case with Mr. Costanzo, who from his first note exuded confidence and an assurance that nothing that he didn't mean to be silly would be sung here.

Mr. Costanzo began with Handel's "Rompe i lacci" from Act II of *Flavio.* Guido, who is in love with Emelia, has just found out that her father has forbidden them to marry, and he sings of wanting to put asunder his love for her. In the original production this aria was sung by the great Italian castrato, Senesino. As with many of the arias that Handel wrote for his star singer, this is a showpiece for the performer with long 16th-note melismas on the word *lacci.* Mr. Costanzo sang this, like every aria which followed, flawlessly. The aria "Aure deh per pietà" from *Giulio Cesare,* again originally sung by Senesino, received an earnest and heartfelt reading.

I've always found Henry Purcell's music some of the purest and most unspoiled works by any British composer. There is an innate ability to grasp the very nature of the music and express it in a unique way that makes me think of Shakespeare. The genius of both men went far beyond what they could have possibly learned. In "Secrecy's song," there is a Shakespearean-like sexual suggestiveness in the stretching of the word "pleasure." "Music for a while" was lovingly sung over a repeating ground and "The Evening Hymn" appropriately ended the Purcell songs.

Mr. Brookshire then performed an instrumental interlude, Bach's Chromatic Fantasy and Fugue, a showpiece that demonstrates both what the performer can do and what the particular harpsichord has to say. I was initially surprised at the overly bright and snappy sound of the instrument, but I warmed to it. Modeled after a 1738 German harpsichord, but with a second manual, Mr. Brookshire's keyboard produced a varying timbre. This instrument came pretty close to the sound of Bach's and his contemporaries' keyboards.

Mr. Costanzo returned with Jared Angle to sing and dance to Vivaldi's secular cantata, *Qual per ignoto calle.* Mr. Angle is to be congratulated not only for his sensitive dancing, to apt choreography by Troy Schumacher, but also for his ability to do so in a limited space. While I wouldn't add dancing to Costanzo's CV, he did a fine job as the rejected lover, singing and acting the role with conviction.

The only disappointing part of the evening's performance was Mr. Brookshire's Scarlatti. There are many sonatas to choose from Scarlatti's vast output, and Mr. Brookshire picked some of the more difficult ones. Beginning with K.545 and what seemed like a continuation of his tuning, he hesitated after the first measures but continued playing even after this false start. There are some wildly rhythmic and syncopated measures here with an outrageous series of quavers played against a bass line in octaves. Mr. Brookshire had the *Prestissimo* tempo right, but wasn't able to do justice to the sonata's surprises.

K.146 and K.141 fared better. 141 is noted for its rapidly repeated notes with a strongly accented often dissonant bass line. It also features hand-crossing which, before Kirkpatrick refuted the theory, was used as a criteria for determining a sonata's chronology. It was previously thought that as Scarlatti aged he developed such a belly that he couldn't reached over it to cross hands and thus a crossed-handed maneuver would date the sonata as being written before his weight gain.

The evening concluded with two more Handel arias. "Pena tiranna," though not as famous as "Ombra mai fu," has the same emotional weight. Mr. Costanzo's attention to each word gave it a clarity and warmth that are the hallmark of his singing. "Vivi tiranno" ended the program on an upbeat note. Terrific performances in an atmospheric venue, small enough to feel you are part of a salon concert at a private home: what more can you ask of an evening's entertainment?

♫ *Juilliard Faculty Passes Their Senior Performance Test*

Juilliard Baroque, Monica Huggett (violin), Sandra Miller (flute), Sarah Cunningham (viola da gamba), Kenneth Weiss (harpsichord), Paul Hall, Juilliard School of Music, Lincoln Center, New York, 24.9.2012

Telemann: Concerto No. 2 in D major
Forqueray: "La Régente" from Suite 3, *Pièces de viole*; "Le Carillon de Passy" from Suite 4, *Pièces de clavecin*
Blavet: "Les Caquets" from Sonata No. 2 in D minor; Presto from Sonata No. 1 in G major from *Sonates mêlées de pièces*
Telemann: Sonata No. 1 in A major from *Quadri/Six quatuors*; Sonata No. 1 in A minor from *Nouveaux Quatours en six suites*
Rameau: Concert No. 5 from *Pièces de clavecin en concert*
Encore:
Rameau: *Tambourins* from Concert No. 3, *Pièces de clavecin en concert*

The Historical Performance department at Juilliard, now in its fourth year, held its first major recital of the new school year with members of the faculty demonstrating their skills. As with most of the performances in previous years, the house was packed. The members of the Juilliard Baroque group vary from concert to concert, with Monica Huggett usually serving as leader-director. This year Sarah Cunningham has joined the faculty and group as viola da gambist.

The selection of works on the program was broad enough to give every instrumentalist a time to shine. Ms. Huggett had several passages from the Telemann pieces to show her virtuosity. Sandra Miller played mellifluously the Blavet Presto movement of the Sonata No 1 from *Sonates mêlées de pièces*. Sarah Cunningham excelled in a piece from Forqueray's Suite 3 from his *Pièces de viole*, and Kenneth Weiss played the "Le Carillon de Passy" from the Suite 4 of Forqueray's *Pièces de clavecin* with great delicacy.

It is easy to see why three full pieces by Telemann were on the program. There is no "complete" edition of Telemann's works, and estimates of his total output range from 3000 to 4000 pieces. Many of these have been lost, but nonetheless his body of work is a candy store where groups of musicians can find scores that match their instruments. Want something for oboe, recorder, violin and basso continuo? Got that. Just two oboists without basso continuo? That too. Two horns and two violins with basso continuo. Of course.

As in previous faculty performances, much of the audience's attention focused on Huggett whose skills are nonpareil. No technical difficulty seemed to phase her, and her violin produced a warm, rich and slightly dark intonation. Although the viola da gamba is not as showy as the violin, Cunningham's expertise was apparent.

The two works by Forqueray have a bizarre history. Antoine Forqueray was viola da gambist and composer at the court of Louis XIV. With little time for his children and under constant pressure from his wife, he sent his son Jean-Baptiste to live with his grandfather. When the grandfather died, Jean-Baptiste, already a proficient viola da gambist, moved back with his father. Forqueray *père*, jealous of his son's musical abilities, had him falsely imprisoned for debauchery and stealing. Ten years later, the son, having achieved fame as a musician and composer, was exiled from France by his father for the same "crimes." A few months later the exile was rescinded, Jean-Baptiste returned, and his father moved to an estate outside Paris. Two years after Forqueray *père* died, Forqueray *fils* came out with two honorific publications: a series of suites for viola da gamba and a transcription for keyboard, advertised as written by Forqueray *père*. Although it is still debated, the consensus is that it is the work of Forqueray *fils*.

Interestingly, the solo pieces done by Cunningham and Weiss were written and published by Forqueray in additional versions: "La Regente" and "Le Carillion de Passy" are available for both viola da gamba and keyboard.

The concert ended with one of the wonderful "concerts" from Rameau's *Pièces de clavecin en concert*. The fifth of the set, stylishly performed here, may well have been chosen for its opening *pièce caractéristique* entitled "La Forqueray." To top off this beguiling evening, the group performed as an encore the *tambourins* from the third concert. Its humorous and rustic rhythms were captivating, with Weiss in particular playing in a manner that set the audience laughing.

♫*Einstein on the Beach: Fresh and Clean after 20 Years*
Robert Wilson, Philip Glass, Lucinda Childs, Philip Glass Ensemble, Brooklyn Academy of Music, Brooklyn, 19.9.2012

Philip Glass: *Einstein on the Beach*

There is a great disparity between the opinion of Philip Glass's music that is held by many listeners and the music itself. Mention his name and someone will sing something in *solfège*, or mouth a repetitious phrase over an implied pedal point.

Mention that you are going to a production of a Glass opera that runs over four hours without intermission, and you are told that you are crazy. I myself can be accused of this mindset, at least towards Glass's music since the trilogy of *Einstein on the Beach*, *Satyagraha* and *Akhenaten*. There are some exceptions, works that have grown on me over the years–the chamber opera *The Photographer* (1988); the soundtrack to the movie *The Thin Blue Line* (1988); and the first "qatsi" documentary, *Koyaanisqatsi* (1982)–but neither *Powaqqatsi* (1988) nor *Naqoyqatsi* (2002) work for me.

It is 20 years since *Einstein on the Beach* was last performed, a long enough time for all concerned to eschew any remembrance of having been overwhelmed or overloaded by the music. As the text says many, many times, "It could be fresh and clean," and it was. *Einstein* is successful both as an artifact reflecting the Zeitgeist of the period in which it was written, and as a work of art that stands outside of time. Although first performed in 1976, it is very much a product of the 1960s. The hypnotic music harkens back to cult groups whose never-ending repetitions of "magic" words transported them into an altered state of mind. Cartoonish grimaces, over-exaggerated gestures, comic book trains and buses realized in the pop style of Peter Max, a mock trial out of the Marx Brothers' *Duck Soup*, a toy rocket ship on a clearly seen wire straight from the cheap sci-fi films of schlock director Ed Wood: all examples of what could be classified as camp. The penultimate scene of the opera, which takes place in a space machine, is modeled after similar images of workers operating machines in the camp classic *Metropolis*.

The production itself was a masterpiece of synchronization. As if to confirm this systematization, the actors all wore wristwatches. However, sometimes the symbolism, even though very much of the period it is reflecting, is sophomoric. Gyroscopes, clocks going backwards in time, a building backdrop in the style of De Chirico, halo-like objects floating across the stage: all would be a gold mine for a college student's assignment to interpret what these symbols "mean."

Glass's music succeeds here partly because it's still fresh, and as the play progresses it falls naturally into the background, which overcomes the problem one can have when listening to the music in private. It only becomes the center of attention when the acting and dancing stop. The high point musically was the wildly virtuosic violin solos by Antoine Silverman. Very much like the early Baroque violin works of Legrenzi, Navara and Valentini, Glass demands both intense concentration and nearly impossible technique. At times it resembled the prelude from Bach's Partita No. 3 for solo violin played at *prestissimo*. Another high point was mezzo-soprano Hai-Ting Chinn's solo near the end of the opera, which sounded like Emma Kirkby singing Couperin on amphetamines.

There were two major dance intermezzos, but only the second one was attention-grabbing. The first featured traditional pirouettes, arabesques and pliés, but the second one, driven by the organ all stops out, was energetic, exhausting and exhilarating.

Of course in an opera this long, with the demands it places on both the audience (who handled their private intermissions considerately) and the players, there are bound to be weak moments: Scene 1B at the back of the train went on too long, as did the Space Machine of Scene 3B.

Overall, I doubt that anything this season will come close to *Einstein* as a theater, music and dancing event. Two days later, and I'm still haunted by it.

♪Rhyming and Miming in 17th-Century Venice

Venezia from the Streets to the Palaces: Le Poème Harmonique, Miller Theater, Columbia University, New York, 12.9.2012

Monteverdi: "Dormo Ancora"
Castello: Sonata Concertate in Stil Moderno
Monteverdi: "Lamento della Ninfa"
Manelli: Bergamasca: "La Barchetta passaggiera"
Ferrari: "Chi non sà come Amor"; "Son ruinato"
Anonymous: "Villanella ch'all'acqua vai"
Manelli: Canzonetta; "Sguardo lusinghiero"
Jacarà: "Aria alia napolitana"

Taking advantage of the paucity of major musical events between the end of the festivals and the opening of the autumn concert and opera season, Columbia University's Miller Theater presented a semi-staged program of the music of Venice from the middle and late 17th century. It was a wise decision: New Yorkers and visitors filled the Miller Theater the first night, and the second and final performance was completely sold out. Music from this period is not often played in venues of this size, and it is not always easily appreciated. Although considered part of the Baroque era (1600-1750), the music creates a completely different sound-world than that of even a decade or two later. The opening aria from Monteverdi's *Il ritourno d'Ulisse in patria*, for example, written in 1640, is miles apart from the arias of Cavalli's later operas of the 1650s and 1660s and light-years away from the operas of Purcell in the 1680s and 1690s.

Le Poème Harmonique set out to recreate the atmosphere and dynamics of a concert in 17th-century Venice. Certainly, a great effort was made to determine which instruments would accurately reproduce the sounds of that period. All were original or replicas of original instruments, some rarely seen: a lirone, a viola da gamba-like instrument; a colascione, a long-necked lute; a violone, an early version of the double-bass. When pizzicato was required the bowed instruments were moved horizontally and plucked like guitars. All the musicians appeared relaxed and played as if they were part of a private consort. Johannes Frisch in particular was exceptional, handling the difficult violin passages with ease.

The stage was lit by candles and dim lights on the music stands; midway through, a few more lights appeared at the front of the stage. The long wait for the first piece to begin may have been planned to give the audience time to get in the mood. When tenor Jan Van Elsaker slowly came on stage, he did so with small steps and hand gestures, and the opening aria could not have been more appropriate: "I do not know if I am awake, or if I dream still." Unfortunately, this would not have been recognized by many in the audience–even if everyone had been given the texts and translations–as we were all literally in the dark. To experience something close to an original performance, you need to understand what the vocalist is singing. For the most part, the soloists neither acted nor mimed clearly enough to give more than a general sense of the texts.

And what a shame! The one masterpiece here, Monteverdi's "Lamento della Ninfa," as poignant as it is without words, is so much more so if they are understood. Monteverdi was a tone-painter. For example, the effect of the dissonant double suspension on the opening chorus's "her grief was visible" is lessened without the context. Similarly, it would have been more compelling had we known that "her lost love she thus lamented" was the reason the trio ends their choral commentary on a dying fall. Although the three male voices sang with appropriate expressiveness, Claire Lefillâtre pushed her voice a little too operatically. This madrigal succeeds best when sung by a cooler and whiter voice then Lefillâtre used here. (Having heard her earlier this year performing Couperin's *Leçons de ténèbres*, I know her voice has that capability.)

Making it even more difficult to follow, one piece ran into the other without a gap. Of course, it would not be in the spirit of 17th-century Italy to have translated super-titles, but then again we were all sitting in an "inauthentic" air-conditioned theater.

In spite of these qualms, I thought the performance had tremendous energy and enough variety to hold the audience and, responding to sustained applause, two encores followed. Whether totally successful or not, the show did reflect the Miller Theater's willingness to explore less visited corners of music history, and I look forward to an adventuresome season ahead.

♫Andrew Manze's Magical Conducting

Mostly Mozart Festival 8: Stephen Hough(piano), Mostly Mozart Festival Orchestra, Andrew Manze (conductor), Avery Fisher Hall, Lincoln Center, New York City, 22.8.2012

Bach: Orchestral Suite No. 3 in D major (arr. Mendelssohn, ed. David)
Mendelssohn: Piano Concerto No. 1 in G minor
Mozart: Symphony No. 41 in C major, "Jupiter"

The overall success or failure of any music festival depends on the usual set of variables: choice of composer and compositions, orchestra, conductor, soloist, program selection and the performance itself. This year's Mostly Mozart Festival was particularly noteworthy in its attempt, consciously or not, to freshen up some of the tried and true musical masterpieces. This was accomplished in two ways: first, through the unusual matching of conductors and orchestras, the second, by the choice of unconventional editions of familiar works. Both elements were present in Tuesday night's performance.

Andrew Manze has been conducting for close to ten years, but it is hard not to think of him as the great Baroque violinist whose large discography revived interest in many unknown composers of the 17th and 18th centuries. As a conductor, he has risen quickly in the ranks, and one can see why. In addition to his energetic and totally committed style, he brought with him some magic fairy dust that turned a traditional orchestra into an early-music group.

So here we have a Baroque violinist turned historically informed conductor leading a traditional non-early-music orchestra in a version of a Baroque masterpiece edited to make it playable by a "modern" 19th-century orchestra! Yet so convincing was this performance it would be hard to differentiate the standard edition from Mendelssohn's altered one. The first major modification was the addition of clarinets to the orchestra to substitute for the difficult trumpet parts that Bach wrote for higher-ranged valveless trumpets.

The other major change was in the second movement. Concertmaster Ruggero Allifranchini performed the famous "Air on a G String." Mendelssohn's version calls for a violin soloist; the other first violinists put down their bows. Again, without listening carefully you'd think this version was the original one. Clearly Allifranchini knows how to emulate 18th-century bowing as it was clean of any vibrato, although in other parts of the concert many string players weren't controlling their vibrato. Manze was still able to get the effect he wanted: a stylized rendition, brimming with charming dance rhythms, biting and incisive string playing and vividly colored wind and brass.

In his performance of the first Mendelssohn piano concerto, Stephen Hogue seemed to thrive on the energy of the conductor and orchestra. Hough and Manze took a pleasant enough piano concerto by the 22-year-old Mendelssohn and turned it into a work far beyond its seeming simplicity. Both Hough and Manze's involvement with the work was tactile. Playing from memory, Hough moved quickly along through the final catchy third movement themes and received the audience's rousing applause. Unable to quell the audience, he performed an encore that needed no introduction: the "Träumerei" from Schumann's *Kinderszenen*.

Mozart's "Jupiter" Symphony received a vibrant, nearly electrifying interpretation. Manze conducted with his whole body. He brought out some wonderful effects by revealing buried motives normally not heard, such as the whispering strings in the transitions of the first movement or the bright and breezy wind playing in the third movement *Minuetto*. The finale was a non-stop whirlwind of sounds redoubling with intensity at the coda's conclusion.

♫One Step Back to Brahms

Mostly Mozart Festival 7: Joshua Bell (violin), Mostly Mozart Festival Orchestra, Louis Langrée (conductor), Avery Fisher Hall, Lincoln Center, New York, 18.8.2012

Mozart: Symphony No. 1 in E-flat major
Schubert: Symphony No. 4 in C minor, "Tragic"

Brahms: Violin Concerto in D major

How many degrees of separation are there between Brahms and Joshua Bell? Surprisingly, there is only one. Bell plays the "Gibson ex-Huberman," the same 1713 Stradivarius given to the 13-year-old virtuoso, Bronislaw Huberman, in 1895. The following year the child protégé performed the Brahms Violin Concerto at a concert attended by Brahms himself.

His biographer, Max Kalbeck writes: "As soon as Brahms heard the sound of the violin, he pricked up his ears, during the Andante he wiped his eyes, and after the Finale he went into the green room, embraced the young fellow, and stroked his cheeks. When Huberman complained that the public applauded after the cadenza, breaking into the lovely Cantilena, Brahms replied, 'You should not have played the cadenza so beautifully.'"

How Joshua Bell ended up owning this instrument is a story in its own right (see my interview with Josh Aronson, the director of "Orchestra of Exiles"). I can't speak for Brahms, but Bell's performance must certainly have been on Huberman's level. Few renowned soloists play with such élan or put so much energy and enthusiasm into a work likely to have been performed hundreds of times. Not for a moment was there any sense of the violinist's flirting with auto-pilot—an easy switch often turned on for warhorses. As offhand praise of the orchestra: from Bell's first entrance, the musicians remained in the background, seeming as captivated as was the audience by his charismatic presence.

It would be particularly difficult to hazard a guess as to how much credit for the success of the Brahms can be attributed to the instrument itself. Given the violin's infamous history and the nine months spent in restoration, one has to give it more than simply second billing. To my ear, the sweetness and evenness of every note regardless of its dynamic would support its claim as being second fiddle to no one.

The first symphony of Mozart, written at the age of nine, while no more than fluff is pleasant fluff. Mozart shows himself as a talent capable of taking any kind of music given to him and incorporating it into his own composing style. Here, under the influence of Bach's youngest son, Johann Christian, Mozart creates a symphony imitative of but not quite up to the charm of Bach's early Opus 3 symphonies. Although the piece was well played by Langrée and the Mostly Mozart Orchestra, I only question the inconsistent use of vibrato: its absence was clearly intended by the concertmaster, but inconsistently applied by the other string players.

The Schubert 4th Symphony deserves more exposure than it has been given. Its introductory Adagio with its uncertain modulations into distant keys looks backwards to Haydn's overture to *The Creation* and forward to Mahler's mysterious symphonic openings. The Andante in the unusual key of A-flat major starts out in true Schubertian lyrical style but two minutes into the movement surprises us with a loud F minor chord. This eerie modulation leads to what we would think of today as silent movie music: an accompaniment to a scene of the villain tying the heroine to the rails. The third movement goes way beyond the traditional Minuet and Trio. Its use of syncopation and uneven accents makes it seem like an inebriated parody of itself. The fourth movement is based on a seven-note phrase that is tossed back and forth between the first violins and the flute and oboes. Later abbreviated versions of this motif carry the movement to its foreboding three-*sforzando* conclusion.

All these works were exactingly detailed by Langrée and the Mostly Mozart Festival Orchestra—an accomplishment that seems to be the norm as the festival moves into its final week.

♪*Mostly Wrong Yet Mostly Right*

Mostly Mozart Festival 5: Kristian Bezuidenhout (fortepiano), Freiburg Baroque Orchestra, Pablo Heras-Casado (conductor), Alice Tully Hall, Lincoln Center, New York, 9.8.2012

Schubert: Symphony No. 3 in D major
Schumann: Introduction and Allegro appassionato, "Concertstück"
Mendelssohn: Symphony No. 4 in A major, "Italian"

What is one to make of musicians who have staked their careers on the tenets of the "Historically Informed Performance" (HIP) movement but have recently been performing music in a style that is unquestionably historically incorrect? Kristian Bezuidenhout plays a reproduction of a late-date fortepiano (*ca.*1820) which must be one of the last ever made commercially, and was most certainly by Schumann's time as quaint as a Pleyel harpsichord (instrument of choice for Wanda Landowska) would be to a modern day pianist. It is as inconceivable to believe that Schumann's or Mendelssohn's orchestras played with instruments in the style of the 18th century as it is to believe that Stokowski's approach to Bach reflected an historically correct style.

The Freiburg Baroque Orchestra has been around for 25 years as a model HIP group. At the time of its founding, the HIP movement was accepted as a valid approach to music before the 1830s. Music by Monteverdi, Purcell, Bach, Mozart, Beethoven and Schubert may have used the bowing, phrasing and pitch of instruments of their generation and before, but by the second quarter of the 19th century this style would have been considered antiquated. Scarlatti had access to the early Christofori fortepianos in the 1720s. It would be a short view of the history of the piano to think 100 years later fortepianos were still a dominant force in keyboards.

Yet if there is no historical justification for this kind of interpretation, there are valid artistic ones. Both the Schubert and Mendelssohn symphonies were played with a freshness that gave new life to the works. In some ways it was like turning the treble up on an amplifier: music once covered by the heavier patina of modern day instruments came to the forefront. This could be heard in the first movement of the Schubert symphony where the wind instruments shimmer and shine. As different as the strings in a Baroque orchestra sound from today's strings, the winds and brass had a more unique timbre. Valveless brass, wooden flutes, oboes with a choice of coloring (*oboe d'amore*, *da caccia*) create a wholly different sound-world.

As much as the instruments made a difference, so did the players. Like their predecessors at this Festival, the Chamber Orchestra of Europe, they are virtuosi in their own right and have no official conductor. Not to disparage Maestro Heras-Casado, but I suspect they were capable of doing a fine job without him.

The Schumann piece is unusual and infrequently performed. Attempting it on the fortepiano was a greater challenge than even Kristian Bezuidenhout was capable of overcoming. This was a favorite of Sviatoslav Richter, and his many performances succeeded through his use of powerhouse techniques that left no room for competition on a piano let alone on a fortepiano. As would be expected, even the gentlest orchestral moments drowned out the soloist, and during the many dramatic moments all one heard were tinklings. Balance is critical at all times, particularly between a soloist and an orchestra. When the soloist's very instrument cannot produce a dynamic loud enough to be heard over the orchestra then the composer's intent has been betrayed.

Note: In my review of the Mostly Mozart concert on 5 August, I wrote about the annoying ubiquity of the piped-in bird calls. I am happy to say that the bird songs are now played only as the audience initially enters the concert hall. (22 August) Note to above: I chirped too soon. The birds were back but at least they were caged. None got into the men's room, and they seem to have been chased away from the Rose Theater. (23 August)

♫Schubert's "Real" Unfinished Symphony

Mostly Mozart Festival 4: Garrick Ohlsson (piano), Mostly Mozart Festival Orchestra, Susanna Mälkki (conductor), Avery Fisher Hall, Lincoln Center, New York, 7.8.2012

Schubert/Berio: Rendering
Beethoven: Piano Concerto No. 5 in E-flat major, "Emperor"

Luciano Berio's exploration of new forms of music was unrelenting. One of the first composers to work with electronics to transform the human voice, he was a major influence on many modern composers. Yet, unlike many of his ilk, he had no ax to grind with music before his time. Boulez might have shouted, "All art of the past must be destroyed," but Berio, born the same year as the French composer/conductor, would never have supported that type of radical call to arms. His famous arrangements of folk songs run the gamut of styles from the Renaissance through and beyond Cantoloupe.

Berio's tying together and filling out of the musical fragments that were left behind at Schubert's death is a wholly different achievement than that of Cooke completing Mahler's Tenth or the recent "completion" of the Bruckner Ninth by a group of musicians. Cooke had close to a hundred pages of Mahler's orchestrated score, and Bruckner had already completed a good part of the last movement of the Ninth Symphony. Schubert left no completed orchestrations, just pages of first thoughts written out on the two piano staves. Berio knew that there wasn't enough material to complete a whole symphony, but unlike the other "completists" he did not fill in the missing parts with what he thought the composer, if still alive, might do; rather he added his own music. In some ways it's reminiscent of the Baroque practice of improvising connections between movements, such as the transition between the first and third movements of the Bach Third Brandenburg Concerto, written with only two notes: a musician was expected to improvise the rest.

Susanna Mälkki conducted a vibrant rendition of this work, smoothly integrating Berio's music into Schubert's. The transitions shimmered and glistened, aided by the delicate sounds of the celeste. The true Schubert sections looked forward to what the Tenth Symphony might have been: a clear line to Bruckner. Where some of Berio's music could seem like static, Mälkki grounded it so that it didn't sound like a radio tuned a megahertz or two from its true station ID.

One expects that someone as imposing as Garrick Ohlsson would sit down at the keyboard and produce a sound equal to or greater than a Richter, Gilels or Agerrich. But quite the opposite occurred here. Ohlsson gave a refined, almost elegant interpretation of Beethoven's Piano Concerto No. 5, with effortless attention to detail. Few pianists perform like this today, and Artur Rubenstein comes to mind as Ohlsson's stylistic predecessor. Subtle tonal expressions showed the lyrical side of this work. Ohlsson worked with a palette of colors as much as he did with a range of dynamics. The second movement Adagio was poetic in the extreme, and the only disappointment for me was the lack of surprise when the second movement suddenly goes without pause into the delightful third movement.

♫And No Birds Sing
Orchestra of Europe, Yannick Nézet-Séguin (conductor), Alice Tully Hall, Lincoln Center, New York, 5.8.2012

Mozart: Overture to *Don Giovanni*
Bach: Concerto for Violin and Oboe in C minor
Mendelssohn: Symphony No 3. in A minor, "Scottish"

The theme for this year's Mostly Mozart Festival is bird songs and their influence on composers. There will be (or were) discussions as well as a bird walk through Central Park. I have no problem with this and have refrained from commenting earlier in fairness to the Festival and its promoters. But having attended five concerts so far, I must say that the bird songs that are being piped through the lobbies of Avery Fisher Hall and Alice Tully Hall have quickly become tiresome and inescapable (owl hoots in the Alice Tully men's room!). Leaving the concert hall still enveloped in the music's sound-world, I was rudely brought to earth by the chatter of mockingbirds, catbirds and wood thrushes (from what I can remember of ornithology). We all live with enough ambient noise and would expect, no matter how well intentioned, that the city's premier music center would be the last place to be adding aural intrusions to our already overly noisy environment.

Yannick Nézet-Séguin and Lisa Batiashvili returned to Alice Tully Hall after their admirable performance the other night of the Beethoven Violin Concerto. For this concert, Ms. Batiashvili was joined by oboist Francois Leleux of the Chamber Orchestra of Europe. Both soloists and orchestra played the first movement with sharp accentuations and a strong forward rhythmic propulsion. The musicians were generally well-balanced with the oboe occasionally overpowering the violin. This was partially due to Ms. Batiashvili not pushing hard enough but also to the oboist filling the musical space with what seemed to be twice as many notes as the violinist. The second movement, marked Adagio, is in all respects a *Siciliano* similar in style to the second movement of the keyboard concerto BWV 1053; both pieces are in 12/8 time and start out with pizzicati played by the violins and violas, lulled along by a mellifluous rocking motion. Echoing each other, the two soloists other gave a sensitive and expressive turn to this movement and the piece concluded with a lively Allegro.

Although this was not a "mostly Mozart" program, the concert did begin with a charmingly expressive interpretation of the Overture to *Don Giovanni*. Yannick Nézet-Séguin brought out less of the Overture's tragic overtones than its melodic material. Perhaps, if this were actually the lead-in to an opera performance, one would expect to feel a little more *frisson* than was given here, but this was a concert aria.

Nézet-Séguin seems to thrive on fast tempi, and in the concluding Mendelssohn "Scottish Symphony" he was in his realm. Take out un poco, non and assai from the movement headings, and you are left with a bright and energetic symphony whose movements would be marked Andante con moto, Allegro agitato, Vivace troppo and a final Allegro vivacissimo-Allegro Maestoso. The third movement Adagio, a heartfelt paean interrupted by seismic changes, leads into the final movement's dramatic representation of the Scottish barrens.

It is fortunate for Philadelphia and its orchestra to have acquired Maestro Nézet-Séguin as principal conductor—and for New York as well, to know he is only a short distance away.

♩ *What a Difference an Orchestra Makes*

Mostly Mozart Festival 2 & 3: Lisa Batiashvili (violin), Chamber Orchestra of Europe, Yannick Nézet-Séguin (conductor), Alice Tully Hall, Lincoln Center, New York, 2.8.2012

Beethoven: Violin Concerto in D major; Symphony No. 3 in E-flat major, "Eroica"

Christiane Karg (soprano), Julie Boulianne (soprano),Toby Spence (tenor),

Andrew Foster-Williams (bass-baritone), Concert Chorale of New York, James Bagwell (director), Mostly Mozart Festival Orchestra, Yannick Nézet-Séguin (conductor), Avery Fisher Hall, Lincoln Center, New York, 3.8.2012

Beethoven: Symphony No. 2 in D major
Haydn: Missa ("Nelson Mass")

These two back-to-back concerts had so much in common, the first one segueing so felicitously into the second, that it is irresistible not to review them together. The first concert ended with Beethoven's Third Symphony and the second began with Beethoven's Second. Both performances were conducted by the energetic Yannick Nézet-Séguin. Both orchestras received similar instructions from Mr. Nézet-Séguin: his body speedily changing positions, leaving no doubt as to what at any given moment each section of the orchestra should be doing. *Sforzandi* had the conductor punching the air or beating an imaginary kettle drum with both hands. Although neither orchestra was playing or attempting to emulate original instruments, Mr. Nézet-Séguin was clearly following the lead of Sir Roger Norrington whose tempi in his recordings of the Beethoven symphonies were based on the composer's hyperkinetic metronome markings.

What was apparent though was the difference in quality between these two performances.

Granted, the Mostly Mozart Festival Orchestra picked the short end of the stick, getting the Second Symphony instead of the Third: a general consensus would place the Second at the bottom and the Third somewhere near the top of the "Top Nine" list. The Chamber Orchestra of Europe also had the edge in being in a more intimate venue, but the problems with the second night went way beyond external issues to the heart of each orchestra. I can't speak directly to the issue of rehearsal time, since I have no idea how much time each group committed to preparation; but it was more than apparent that the COE played, paradoxically, as if it they knew the piece by heart, yet were playing it for the first time. Like the Orpheus Chamber Orchestra, they perform without a conductor, requiring that each member handle those duties on his or her own. Like Abbados' Lucerne Festival Orchestra, they are handpicked virtuosi in their own right.

The Mostly Mozart Festival Orchestra, on the other hand, was lusterless. The opening Adagio of the Second was a dull affair. The transitional material between sections of the symphony were murky. The super-express tempi of the COE's musicians that made for so much excitement, in the hands of the MMFO instrumentalists became no more than a race to get to the end as quickly as possible. Beethoven's signature sforzandos–spiky thunderbolts that felt like electrical shocks–were mere thumps in the second concert. Even Nézet-Séguin's reading of the Second Symphony Larghetto, here more like an Andante, couldn't hide the orchestra's lethargy.

The addition of a chorus for Haydn's "Nelson Mass" did add an element of excitement to the second program, but balancing problems nagged many of the masses' segments. Again, the question of rehearsal time comes to the forefront, since those hours are key to correcting unbalanced behavior. Only the tenor Toby Spence and the bass-baritone Andrew Foster Williams were able to push their voices past the middle of the theater. The quick tempi again caused some instrumentalists to come in too late or too early.

The first concert's All-Beethoven program began with the Violin Concerto in D. This was a rock solid performance with no attempt to place the concerto in any non-traditional context: no original instruments (e.g., Zehetmair, Brüggen), no radical cadenzas (Schnittke, Kremer), no overdubbing of the piano version (Kopatchinskaja, Herreweghe). Lisa Batiashvili's cadenza, though, was not the traditional (Joachim's) but the rather more difficult one by Fritz Kreisler. Here as in every other part of the concerto Batiashvili exuded confidence and an easygoing manner that contrasted successfully with Nézet-Seguin's more frenetic conducting.

The COE has recorded the complete Beethoven Symphonies under the direction of Nikolaus Harnoncourt. At that time it was released in 1991, it was a revelation: Harnoncourt conducting a non-"historically-correct" performance applying his period theories to a more traditional orchestra. The result was so successful that most modern orchestras these days follow Harnoncourt's guidelines for pre-20th century compositions: lessening vibrato and rubato, reducing orchestra size and even dropping the standard pitch down as much as a semitone. It might have been interesting to compare the live and recorded versions of the two symphonies, but this recording came out in 1991 and I doubt that few, if any, of the instrumentalists performing here would have been old enough to have participated in these earlier performances.

"Fun" might be too simple and overused a word to use in relation to these "heavy" masterpieces of music; but to call the first concert "fun" and the second "not fun" would not be unjust descriptors.

♫Mostly Mozart Festival Opens with…Mozart

Mostly Mozart Festival Opening Night. Nelson Freire (piano), Lawrence Brownlee, (tenor), Mostly Mozart Festival Orchestra, Louis Langrée (conductor), Avery Fisher Hall, Lincoln Center, New York, 31.7.2012

Mozart: Overture to *La clemenza di Tito*; Piano Concerto No. 20 in D minor; "Misero! o sogno…Aura che intorni spiri"; "Un' aura amorosa" from *Così fan tutte*; Symphony No. 38 in D major, "Prague"

The Mostly Mozart Festival opened its 46th season with an all-Mozart program directed by conductor Louis Langrée. This Festival, like any other long-lived series, has had its individual as well as overall ups and downs. During the middle years, as its popularity waned, the Festival tried to attract a new audience by expanding its composer list, so that by 1997 the Mostly (Not) Mozart schedule consisted of no less than 32 composers. A strike cancelled most of the 2002 season. Mr. Langrée made his debut as conductor in 2003, and he is due congratulations for keeping Mozart in the forefront.

If this opening concert is any indication of what lies ahead in both selection and performance, we are in for a pleasant month. I was familiar with Nelson Freire in the 1970s, but seem to have lost sight of him until his magical recordings of the Brahms piano concerti in 2006 made me realize what a great pianist he was and is. I think of him along with Radu Lapu, another pianist who seemed to drop out of view only to return to the concert hall more of a master of the instrument than when he was young virtuoso.

What approach can one take to Mozart's D-minor concerto that hasn't been used before? For one thing, one can address it without the preconception that because it is in D minor, the key of Mozart's Requiem and much of Don Giovanni, it must be tragic. Langrée's opening measures were certainly dramatic enough, with heavily accentuated syncopations and sudden dynamic changes from *p to f*. But once the soloist came in with new motifs not played before, he put his stamp on the music, declaring it more *dramma giocoso* than *seria*. He was amazingly consistent in style and conception, even choosing the briefest of cadenzas in the first and last movements, as if to say "This poetic work need not be unhinged by crescendos, banging chords and liberal use of rubati. Its poetry will speak for itself." As gently as this piano concerto was played, there was no doubting that Freire had a strong overall concept of how he wanted it to be heard by the audience. Indeed this was as crisp, confident and summery an interpretation as I've ever heard. Perhaps he has a different concept of the work when he plays it in winter….

The enthusiasm of the orchestra and conductor that accompanied the pianist was a continuation of the spirited reading of the concert's opening work: the overture to Mozart's opera *La clemenza di Tito*. The completion of *La clemenza di Tito* was definitely after *Die Zauberflöte,* but it is more than likely that specific parts of each score were written at the same time. (See Christoph Wolff's recently published iconoclastic book about Mozart's final years, *Mozart at the Gateway to his Fortune.)* One can hear a number of exact phrases straight out of the earlier work.

To give the audience a taste of the vocal aspect of Mozart's genius, Langrée programmed two arias for tenor, one a concert aria, the second an aria from Mozart's *Cosi fan tutte.* Lawrence Brownlee started off a little weakly in the opening aria, "Misero! o sogno…Aura che intorni spiri." I question why this specific aria was chosen out of dozens of other opera and concert arias: it is mostly a recitativo accompagnato which gives the tenor little to work with until the very end. Brownlee handled the more well-known "Un' aura amorosa" from *Cosi fan tutte* with a deep, warm, almost baritone coloring that showed no element of strain and reached clearly to the back of the theater.

The final work on the program, Mozart's Prague Symphony, received a sparkling interpretation that sounded much larger than one would expect from the number of musicians on stage. The bleachers placed in back and to the sides of the orchestra and the acoustic pods hanging from the top of the theater are the traditional changes to the venue when this festival occurs; and, as in the past, they take away some of the hollow overtones that often fill the theater during its regular season.

♫Exemplary Mozart Ends New York Philharmonic Subscription Season

Emanuel Ax (pianist), Jennifer Zetlan (soprano), Jennifer Johnson Cano, (mezzo-soprano), Paul Appleby (tenor), Joshua Hopkins (baritone), New York Choral Artists, Joseph Flummerfelt (director), New York Philharmonic Orchestra, Alan Gilbert (conductor), Avery Fisher Hall, Lincoln Center, New York, 20.6.2012

Mozart: Piano Concerto No. 22 in E-flat major; Mass in C minor, "Great"

It may have been that everyone was simply grateful to get indoors to escape the heat from this summer's first record-breaking day, or that it was the last program of the year in the NYPO's subscription season, but whatever the reason the musicians gave a nearly faultless performance of two of Mozart's masterpieces, the E-flat piano concerto K.482 and the Mass in C minor K.427. The music felt refreshing, and even the "Great" Mass, while not completely without serious moments, was unusually (and successfully) light-spirited.

What I wrote about Emanuel Ax's recent recital holds true with this performance of the E-flat piano concerto: "His playing was not the type to draw attention to itself: the piano was never pounded, and he never made manifest the fact that there were passages that required substantial prowess." The concerto opens with emphasis on the winds, as if it were a wind divertimento or one of Haydn's or Mozart's Sinfonia Concertantes. The clarinet in this concerto (which debuts here as a member of the Mozart orchestra) joins the flute and bassoon in a subdued but colorful first movement, punctuated by fanfares from the brass. With the gentlest touch Ax made his solo entrance almost as if he were interrupting the orchestra with his playing. Even the cadenza to the first movement was taken by Ax at a leisurely pace and in the least showy manner. Gilbert and company backed up Ax without ever crowding him, and the wind soloists too were given the room they needed to fully paint the pastel-like colors of this lovely concerto.

The second half of the evening was given over to Mozart's Mass in C minor. It is a somewhat odd work, not written for any specific occasion or sacred event but meant to fulfill a vow Mozart made when marrying Constanze. Mozart may have realized in mid-creation that giving his wife a Mass was probably not the best way to celebrate a marriage and left it incomplete. At one point he refers to it as a "cantata Mass" which is probably a more apt description of the work. Its "greatness" seems to be in Mozart's ability to select and manipulate parts of the liturgy and go beyond the structure of the Mass.

The solemn and bleak opening of the Kyrie could substitute for the first movement of the Requiem. The chorus holds back nothing, but after that first Kyrie eleison is sung Mozart has a solo soprano sing a most poignant Christe eleison as the music suddenly changes in color and tone. Jennifer Zetlan pitched every note exactly right, and they came across as clearly as if she were right in front of you. The difficult passage in the first movement that drops to B and then to A below middle C and the jumps back to a high A was done exceptionally well. Mezzo-soprano Jennifer Johnson Cano also had a wonderful voice and rendered an ardent version of the solo Laudamus te. Only in the soprano duet, Domine Deus, did both singers sound shrill. Tenor Paul Appleby couldn't quite sing on the exceptional level of the sopranos. The baritone, Joshua Hopkins, in his small part, helped make this performance stand out.

This all-Mozart program made me reflect on the upcoming Mostly Mozart Festival. With every passing year the Festival, understandably, features less and less Mozart: after 46 years, any audience might tire of hearing the same composer over and over. But if this concert was an indication of what can be done to make Mozart fresh again, maybe it's time to re-title the festival "Mostly Mozart Redux."

♫New York Philharmonic: Expansive with Nielsen, Limited with Beethoven and Korngold

Leonidas Kavakos (violin), NY Philharmonic Orchestra, Alan Gilbert (conductor), Avery Fisher Hall, Lincoln Center, New York, 14.6.2012

Beethoven: Overture to *Coriolan*
Korngold: Concerto in D major for Violin and Orchestra
Nielsen: Symphony No. 3, *Sinfonia espansiva*

For the New York Philharmonic's penultimate subscription concert of the season, Alan Gilbert selected a grab bag of works to perform. Gilbert has always tried to find some connectivity between the works on a program, and the Korngold Violin Concerto in D major hearkens back to Beethoven's concerto in the same key. In the playbill, Gilbert states that Beethoven and Nielsen "work well together…both (share) a terseness of expression and dispassion." With a little creative editing, one can perhaps see an even greater similarity between Beethoven's opening of the *Coriolan* Overture and the Nielsen Third Symphony:

The concert began with Beethoven's dramatic overture, but Gilbert gave this work a somewhat desultory reading. We have come to expect a certain richness and color from the Philharmonic, but did not get that here. It struck me that perhaps the piece did not get the rehearsal time required. It really wasn't until the Nielsen symphony that the orchestra snapped into place, and they gave that piece a crisp and coherent performance. Unfortunately, this was not the case with either the Beethoven or the Korngold.

I have admired Leonidas Kavakos since his landmark recording of the original 1904 version of Sibelius's Violin Concerto, and looked forward to his interpretation of Korngold's concerto. One need only listen to the recordings of Jascha Heifetz, who premiered the work, or Itzhak Perlman's 1981 disk to hear the unabashedly Romantic nature of the concerto–exactly what was missing from Kavakos's performance. Sure, the vibrato used in the recordings is over the top, but it is passion and not technique that define the music. Korngold himself is quoted as saying that his work "is more Caruso than Paganini." Kavakos was underwhelming, often drowned out by the orchestra. The tepid pace of the first

228

movement, marked Moderato nobile, obliterated any contrast with the similarly paced second movement, marked Romance.

By contrast, Gilbert's reading of Nielsen's Symphony No. 3 was brilliantly rendered. From the opening unison chords to the explosive finale, Gilbert held the orchestra under tight rein. Nielsen was a master of orchestral color, knowing exactly what timbre was needed to match which musical line. I've always been impressed with composers who are so sure of what they want us to hear that they will call for an instrument or voice for only seconds or minutes. A case in point is Ives requesting a viola and/or a flute for a brief accompaniment to his monumental Concord Sonata. Nielsen brings in two vocalists here to sing wordlessly for several minutes in the second movement. Why? Because it is right.

Gilbert's project to record the complete symphonies of Nielsen is certainly well-considered. While this recording cycle might not be anywhere near the magnitude of Bernstein's resurrection of Mahler, it is certainly a good start for such a young conductor. Now, if he is looking for a new cycle to perform once the Nielsen is complete, how about a complete set of Martinu's symphonies?

♪Mozart String Quintets at Montreal Music Festival
Afiara Quartet, Cecilia Quartet, Barry Shiffman (viola), Michael Tree (viola), Montreal Chamber Music Festival, St. George's Church, Montreal, 29.5.2012 and 31.5.2012

Mozart Quintets: No. 1 in B-flat major, No. 2 in C minor, No. 6 in E-flat major, No. 5 in D major, No. 4 in G minor, No. 3 in C major

The six string quintets by Mozart span his lifetime, from the first, composed when he was 17, to the last, written in the year he died. By the age of 17, he had already written 170 works, but the First Quintet was his most inspired chamber work to date, competing only with the 3 Divertimenti, K. 136-138, in quality. It is possible that he was moved to write this work after hearing Haydn's Opus 20 set of quartets. Mozart was a keen observer and apparently could play back from memory anything he heard. One can see Haydn's influence here in Mozart's use of rests, syncopation and counterpoint. The false reprise that concludes the piece is a classic Haydn trick: leading us to expect a repeat of the main theme, but instead stopping short of it, as if to say, "Finished! On to the next masterpiece." The Afiara Quartet, aided by the eminent violist and founding member of the Guarneri Quartet, Michael Tree, gave an earnest if somewhat tepid reading of the work. Michael Tree has always been the most circumspect of players and was so in this piece, but I wonder if his presence may have been intimidating to the group. This was certainly not the case with their recital in New York in January 2012 when the additional member of the group was Denis Brott.

The Second Quintet is usually given short shrift. Desperate for money, Mozart needed a piece to add to what would become known as the Third and Fourth Quintets for a subscription concert. He quickly transcribed his Serenade K. 388, written five years earlier. Charles Rosen does not even mention this work in his chapter on string quintets in *The Classical Style*; Einstein in his *Mozart, His Character, His Work* goes as far as to say that Mozart "should never have arranged this work as a quintet for strings." The Serenade is awash with colors of woodwinds that can't be replicated by stringed instruments, yet the Cecilia String Quartet succeeded in giving the Second Quintet an appropriately somber reading. Mozart's minor-key works make up only a small part of his output. It is almost an oxymoron to refer to the original piece as a "dark" serenade, but here there is none of the levity commonly found in Mozart's serenades and divertimenti. Who but Mozart would write a minuet, the least serious of any movements, in the contrapuntal style of Bach with a canon for the first part and a trio which repeats the opening canon except in retrograde? Min-Jeong Koh always seemed to be in control as leader of the group, and Barry Shiffman as second violist added richness and depth to this enigmatic transcription.

The Quintet No. 6 in E-flat major is a Mozartean mixture of gusto and gloom with motifs starting out with promise and then modulating to different and distant keys. Here the Afiara Quintet caught on early, with the cellist Adrian Fung energetically taking an unusually prominent role, particularly in the buzzy first movement. The trio section of the minuet shows Haydn's prominent influence in the hurdy-gurdy sound. The Afiara Quartet, with Barry Shiffman as the second violist, played without the stiffness shown in the first work on the program and impressively dug in for the contrapuntally complex final movement.

The second concert of this complete Mozart quintet cycle began with the Fifth Quintet in D major. Starting with a slow introductory exchange of questions asked by the cello, the Fifth quickly moves into a lively Allegro. To give balance to this movement, Mozart unusually brings back the opening theme in its Larghetto tempo only to start up and immediately end with the same opening Allegro theme. The Adagio starts off sweetly in G major but quickly modulates to D minor for a few minutes of drama before returning to and finally ending on a peaceful note. A rocking, slightly off-balance minuet with a trio of rising arpeggios leads to a busy contrapuntal finale. The Cecilia Quartet tossed off these difficult and complex perambulations with ease again, helped by the temporary odd man in, Barry Shiffman.

What seems to be everyone's favorite, and understandably so, the Fourth Quintet was the penultimate piece on the program. The heart-rending opening movement with its quick chromatic bitter-sweet turns and yearning cries from the violas affects us like little else in Mozart's music. Aside from a few pieces of juvenilia, G minor was used as the key signature for only five works, all special in their expression of pathos: the best known are the 40th Symphony and its earlier cousin, the 25th, both works special in their bare expressiveness. Atypical in many ways, this quintet has a logic of its own: the usual tempi (fast, slow, minuet and finale) are shifted here. Given the tragic quality of the opening movement, a second slow movement would create an imbalance which does not occur when a quicker paced minuet is used. The Adagio third movement leads into an even slower opening fourth movement of longing not heard again until Schubert. The concluding Allegro is another contradictory "sad gigue" in 6/8th time.

Expectations at St. George's were high for this particular work, and there are many great performances over the years with which to compete. Expressive but not really practiced in coming together as one, the Afiara made a valiant effort but couldn't quite reach the heights this work demands.

The concluding work, Mozart's No. 3 in C major, suffered in comparison to the G minor and should probably have been scheduled in the middle of the program. Beginning with a simple rising run of the cello with the other strings playing single repeated notes, the first theme should really be called a motif, as it consists of only four notes played in response to the cello. Barely has the first movement started when Mozart moves into the minor key on the opening's second iteration. Another unusually placed second movement minuet with an unusually poignant trio leads into a touching third movement Andante consisting of a most prominent conversation between first violin and first viola. A bouncy, upbeat Rondo concludes this calmest of all the quintets, and this adventurous cycle of concerts as well.

♫Bravo Bartók: James Ehnes and Friends in Montreal

James Ehnes (violin), Andrew Armstrong (piano), James Ehnes String Quartet, Montreal Chamber Music Festival, St. George's Church, Montreal, 28.5.2012

Bartók: Bravo Bartók!

Every spring for the last 17 years Montreal has hosted their Chamber Music Festival. The event has grown from a few concerts to 18 this year over a three-week period. The venues have also changed, and the Festival is now held at St. George's Church, with a stage covered by baffles that improve the acoustics. The schedule for this year included several jazz bands, all 15 quartets by Shostakovich over four nights, Bach's cello suites on two nights and the Mozart string quintets on two nights as well.

The Festival's founding director is cellist Denis Brott, whose energy and enthusiasm are unlimited. Looking to expand the program's reach beyond Montreal, Brott came to New York this past January with the Canadian Afiara Quartet to introduce the Festival to New Yorkers. The performance at the intimate WMP Concert Hall was exemplary, and it encouraged me to attend this year's Festival.

For Bravo Bartók!, violinist James Ehnes created a program that started with one of Bartók's early works and ended with one of his last. Written while Bartók was still a student, the Violin Sonata in C Major is pleasant enough, although youthfully derivative of Brahms, particularly in the first movement where Bartók copies Brahms' signature use of parallel thirds. The second movement starts off as if it were a funeral march, but speeds up in the style of Brahms' Hungarian Rhapsodies; Andrew Armstrong took in stride the movement's demanding arpeggios. Although Hungarian folk elements are present here and there in the first two movements, it's not until the final movement that we clearly hear anything of the later Bartók and his modal folk-dance themes and harmonies.

The performers had the choice of emphasizing the sonata's backward-looking style with its elements of Brahms' and Franck's sonatas, or looking ahead to Bartók's later works and even some early Schoenberg. Given the work's fairly obvious tonality and late romantic glow, Ehnes might have made a stronger case for this sonata by looking back.

By the time we get to the third and fourth quartets, 24 years have passed. The fourth, which sounds so modern on first hearing, hovers tonally around C major, and this key signature is often given with the title. The first movement could be considered to be in sonata form, although hidden behind the movement's glissandi, trills and marcatos. The second movement continues with Bartók's bag of tricks, using *sul ponticelli* to create the buzzing insect sound that appears in so many of his orchestral works as well. The middle third movement acts as a bridge to the fourth and fifth movements which are mirror images structurally of the first two movements: the fourth's snap pizzicato mirroring the second's use of pizzicato, and the fifth with its strong thematic relationship to the first movement. The newly formed James Ehnes Quartet may not have the magical sound that emanates from groups with years of experience playing these works together, but they gave a vibrant reading, with Ehnes smoothly handling the work's technical requirements.

The Solo Violin Sonata, commissioned and first performed by Yehudi Menuhin, is one of Bartók's last works. There is no way to write a solo violin sonata without knowing that it will be judged against the unequaled sonatas and partitas for solo violin by Bach. Bartók was fearless in composing this work, and wrote two movements whose names reference Bach's set of pieces. The first movement, Tempo di Ciaccona, takes its title from the last movement of Bach's second solo violin sonata. The Ciaccona is a chaconne mostly in the grandeur of its spirit and tempo, but occasionally one does hear Bach in Bartók's use of multiple stops, and in his attempts to emulate a bass line.

The designation *Fuga* is used by Bach for several movements, and Bartók's fugue has both a Baroque-style theme and elements of a true fugal execution. This can be said of the Bach-like Adagio and the gigue-like Presto as well. Ehnes gave an authoritative performance. Handling a piece this difficult is no mean accomplishment and Ehnes was unfaltering in negotiating its vertiginous heights.

The final work on the program was the brief Quartet No 3, which is really one movement and a coda. The opening moderato with its various string techniques segues into a frenetic second movement that could be the second theme and development of a sonata form, with the third movement a recapitulation of the exposition. The coda compresses into its few minutes the spirit of the preceding movements, ending with a boisterous and upbeat finale to this challenging and rewarding concert.

♪*Salome in Concert: Unstaged But Not Unbowed*

The Cleveland Orchestra, Franz Welser-Möst (conductor), Carnegie Hall, New York, 24.5.2012

Strauss: *Salome*
Concert Version

Carnegie Hall waited 69 years after *Salome*'s first performance in Dresden in 1905 to stage it (with a dream cast including Birgit Nilsson, George Shirley, Norman Bailey and the Chicago Symphony led by Georg Solti), which speaks to the work's controversial libretto. Harold C. Schonberg's 1974 adulatory review of this first Carnegie Hall *Salome* could, with a change in names, be copied and pasted here.

The crux of any performance of *Salome* has always been the presentation of Jochanaan's head to Salome and her necrophiliac response. Directors have tried everything to make this scene seem believable, from Salome singing to a head in a closed silver serving dish, to kissing or fondling an all-too-realistic-looking severed head, to singing to it while drenched in blood. In a worst-case scenario, it can come off as comically over the top, and even some successful interpretations can't avoid making this scene bathetic.

What can be done with it to avoid even a hint of falseness? Don't act it, just sing it. When the singing is as rich, emotionally rife and note-perfect as it was in this production, your mind stages its own performance of a lifetime. In an unusual change from traditional concert performances of opera where the singers stand stage front, here the main characters were placed like members of a chorus in bleacher seats above and to the left and right of the orchestra. This integration of the soloists with the instrumentalists could have been a problem with less powerful singers drowned out by the instrumental swellings in front of them. Aided by the renowned acoustics of the hall, only Garrett Sorenson's voice was occasionally buried by several orchestral explosions. While Nina Stemme in her Carnegie Hall debut may not have had the vocal reach of Birgit Nilsson (who, according to Schonberg, could "had the doors been open...been heard in Albany"), she did come close to bringing down the rafters.

Certainly there was no question, even without costumes and staging, that this Salome was one psychotic, obsessive, nymphomaniacal bundle of id. Her series of "I-want-his-heads" were like no other tantrums ever heard (even from two-year-olds in cabin class on an intercontinental flight). Herod, played and sung with persuasive authority by Rudolf Schasching, was just a fly in Salome's spider web. Jane Henschel in the role of Herodias egged her daughter on with a comic levity that gave everyone, cast and audience, a moment to catch their breath. Eric Owens' otherworldly voice, both out of the depths off stage and apocalyptically prophetic on stage, conveyed an obsessive strength matched only by Salome.

Gramophone might have upped its ranking of the Cleveland Orchestra's not inconsiderable position of seven (out of a listing of 20 top orchestras of the world) if this performance had been heard by those involved with the assessment. It is difficult to believe that the score has been in the orchestra's hands for just a few weeks, so tightly together did they play. Welser-Möst brought out some of the most lush and sensuous sounds from the strings that I've heard outside of the Berlin Philharmonic. This was true not only for the surging crescendos but for the shimmering tremolos, so soft that it seemed like the sounds could only be coming from a harp or celesta.

Without the constraints of having to synchronize the orchestra with the singers and staging, as would be required in its operatic version, Welser-Möst took advantage of this freedom to speed the music along. This helped color and intensify the driving frenzy of the singers moving towards the inevitable "Kill that woman." It was barely a second after these final words were sung that the audience was on their feet shouting bravos to that same woman.

♪*Judge Me Paris: A Baroque Burlesque Opera*
Directed, choreographed and conceived by Austin McCormick in association with Morningside Opera and SIREN Baroque, Company XIV, 303 Bond St. Theatre, Brooklyn, 20.5.2012

Judge Me Paris: A Baroque Burlesque Opera
Excerpts from *The Judgment of Paris* by John Eccles, with additional music by Vivaldi, Marais and Eccles (from *The Mad Lover*). Libretto by William Congreve with additional text by Jeff Takacs

What should one expect when the press release for an event specifically states, "No one under 16 will be admitted"? And the event in question is not an explicit play or movie but an opera of the Baroque period? To be honest, *Judge Me Paris* would hold little shock for any 16-year-old who is willing to ignore peer pressure and attend an opera, let alone one from the early 18th century.

The bawdiness in this turned-around version of John Eccles's *The Judgment of Paris* was not only effective but, in fact, may have been closer to how the opera was originally produced. Contemporary playwrights Thomas Shadwell and William Congreve and earlier playwrights William Wycherley and George Etherege filled their plays with double entendre, sexual innuendo, adultery and cuckolding. Shadwell complains in a preface to his first play, *Sullen Lovers,* that the main characters in the works of his contemporaries are "most commonly a Swearing, Drinking, Whoring Ruffian for a Lover and an impudent ill-bred tomrig [harlot] for a Mistress."

Although costumed in "whoring" attire, the dancers and singers refrained from overly explicit gestures and put more emphasis on suggestive actions and movements. Upon entering the theater and seeing that the cast, in various stages of *déshabillé*, were already "on stage" (the stage being a large dressing room) did make one feel like a voyeur. During the performance, the actors/actresses' use of a handheld video camera focused closely on each other enhanced this sense of being an outsider peeking in. When the video was played back on the wall and floor, the second or two time delay created an effective sensation of disjuncture.

Given the number of early operas over the past few years that have been put through the grinder only to come out a different but wholly valid theatrical experience, it speaks to the malleability of this art form. The inevitable comparison of *Judge Me Paris* with the Met's recent Baroque opera pastiche, *The*

Enchanted Island, show that both are valid and successful recreations of Baroque style and practice regardless of the difference in scope and size. Both operas borrow freely from several composers, a practice not uncommon in the Baroque period itself, although *Judge Me Paris* does take more liberties with both the music and the staging. The addition of an anachronistically obnoxious Zeus, broadly played by Jeff Takacs, shifted the emphasis away from Paris to the tawdry machinations of an all-too-human con artist. Modern-day songs, including one with Zeus on a guitar, moved the opera out of the 18th century. SIREN Baroque's four instrumentalists were supportive as well as attentive to the singers and dancers. The two recognizable Marais pieces, "Sonnerie de Ste-Geneviève" and "Variations on La Folia," were played with an unusual freshness. The arias from the Eccles opera were delightfully rendered with just the right period vocal touch. At its best moments the music could have been written by Purcell.

The choreography may have suffered a bit from the weight and awkwardness of the dancers' attire, but it was a nice change from the ultra-formality of Catherine Turocy and the overly programmatic choreography of Mark Morris. Sean Gannon as Paris, on stage and dancing through most of the production, is to be admired for both his grace and his stamina.

If you can, go see *Judge Me Paris*–and take your 17-year-old with you.

♪*Emanuel Ax Presents a Diversity of Variations*
Emanuel Ax (piano), Carnegie Hall, New York, 17.5.2012

Copland: Piano Variations
Haydn: Variations in F minor
Beethoven: 15 Variations and a Fugue on an Original Theme in E-flat major, "Eroica Variations"
Schumann: *Études en forme de variations*

Variations upon a theme informed Emanuel Ax's choice of works for this recital at Carnegie Hall. A variation itself is really no more than a formal numbered structure that is the basis of music. From early music on, the idea of playing a theme and then varying it runs through forms like chaconnes, fandangos, dance movements, fugues, the sonata with its development section and cadenzas with their improvised riffs. In fact, the most basic of any musical form would be A-B or, in da capo form, A-A-B-B, "B" being a variation on "A."

Composers have written variations from the most simplistic (e.g. Mozart's keyboard variations on "*Ah, vous dirai-je, maman*" or "Twinkle, Twinkle") to those great monuments of keyboard music, Bach's *Goldberg Variations* and Beethoven's *Diabelli Variations.* In most variations the theme is apparent in every movement; in rare instances they are not audibly recognizable (as in Bach's *Goldberg Variations* where only the formal pattern A-A-B-B and harmonic infrastructure of the theme connect the individual variations).

In Copland's *Variations for Piano*, the five-note opening, while varied in numerous ways, would be difficult to break down formally into numbered movements. The notes that form the motif are handled as if they were a shortened Schoenbergian 12-tone scale. It was clear that Ax was attempting to perform this work as a lyrical, tonal composition, making even the parallel seconds and ninths seem normal. He respected Copland's sometimes odd expressive requests, such as "threatening" in reference to a run of arpeggios or "simply, naively" to a group of chords. The poetic approach Ax took here with Copland was applied to all the other pieces which followed in the program. If the audience expected a flashy, virtuosic recital like many others in this series, they didn't get it from Ax. His playing was not the type to draw attention to itself: the piano was never pounded, and he never made manifest the fact that there were passages that required substantial prowess.

Haydn's Variations in F minor were played with a very gentle touch, the volume barely rising except in a few passages marked *forte*. Even the excellent acoustics of Carnegie Hall could not help this performance which would have been better suited to a much smaller venue. If I were asked to give brief description of the interpretation, it would be "small sounding."

Ax's take on Beethoven's "Eroica" variations was also small-voiced, and not until the fugal variation did it sing out loudly. These variations lack the wildly imaginative quality of Beethoven's *Diabelli Variations*, and in no way do they approach their later orchestral counterpart, the last movement of Beethoven's Third "Eroica" Symphony. Although some of the variations are nearly the same in both works, the piano version wants for the instrumental color inherent in an orchestra. Ax's performance perhaps tried too hard to find the soul of this work. He would have been more successful emphasizing differences in dynamics and tempo between variations rather than searching for a musical depth that isn't there.

Schumann's Symphonic Variations were given a more sensitive and lyrical reading than the muscular versions one hears in recordings by Pollini, Richter and Horowitz. When a work as demanding as this is chosen as part of a recital, you can be sure that it will be used to showcase a performer's ability to handle the work's massive chords and challenges. The Agitato, Presto possible and Allegro brillante all require formidable technique. Ax has this ability but, as in the other works on the program, he chose to let the music speak for itself. The result was a fluid, romantic interpretation more suited to Chopin's works.

Ax's first encore was Liszt's "Valse Oubliée," No.1, which he played with panache. The Chopin that followed, the "Grand Valse Brillante," took me back to the first time I heard him perform. Ax had just won the Artur Rubenstein International Piano Competition, and recorded an all-Chopin program for RCA. It was one of those LPs that I played so often it was eventually scratched beyond playability. Elements of Ax's performance on that record were still apparent in this recital.

♪Kissin's Hair-Raising Performance of Barber's Sonata
Evgeny Kissin (piano), Carnegie Hall, New York, 3.5.2012

Beethoven: Sonata No. 14 in C-sharp minor, "Moonlight"
Barber: Piano Sonata
Chopin: Nocturne in A-flat major; Sonata No. 3 in B minor

In a review of Kissin's performance last year at Carnegie Hall, I mentioned how only by suspending my disbelief in both Kissin's Dorian Gray-like immutability and his automaton-like presence could I relax and enjoy the recital. He sailed through an all-Liszt program, seemingly unaware of Scylla and Charybdis following his every note.

Was he less of an automaton than last year? Yes and no. For one thing, he managed to smile at the audience in response to their applause, and he seemed to be a bit less rigid in his playing style. The big change was to reveal itself later in the program.

Some warhorses in the right hands are capable of recovering their freshness—not necessarily the first thrill of hearing the music, but at least the understanding of what made the work so appealing in the first place. Kissin, unfortunately, was not able to reawaken any interest in the "Moonlight" sonata. The first movement was overly coddled. Instead of letting the music flow, it felt like Kissin was holding back, expecting the rubato to be all he needed to give an edge to the Adagio. The second movement's phrasing was choppy, and the last movement was nearly pummeled to death with over-pedaling and pounded *sforzandos*.

But the memory of this experience was pretty much wiped away by Kissin's powerhouse performance of Samuel Barber's Piano Sonata, Op. 26. What must the audience have thought if they know Barber only as the composer of the tepid "Adagio for Strings?" Perhaps the members of the Russian community at the recital were not surprised as the Barber work does bear similarity to Prokofiev's piano sonatas. Common to both are their off-center asymmetrical rhythms, syncopated and jazzy.

His muscular approach made the classic recording of Barber's Sonata by John Browning sound like Debussy. Kissin managed to make the first movement both modern and traditional at the same time. The second movement's light-fingered *leggero* had just the right impish quality, fleeting away in minutes. The more traditional Largo was played with sensitivity to its lilting and hesitating rhythms. The final movement was a showcase of virtuosity: a *moto perpetuo*, opening with a fugue and continuing with a combination of Gershwin-like rhythms and Bach-like counterpoint.

Even with the intermission smartly programmed after the Barber, it was more than anticlimactic to come back to the old Kissin. Not that the Nocturne in A-flat and the Sonata No. 3 of Chopin were poorly performed, but it felt as if Kissin had flipped his auto-pilot switch back on. The sonata's first movement was slowed to the point of losing its cohesiveness. The second movement had a little more sparkle and Kissin revealed the classic Minuet and Trio basis of the Scherzo form. Kissin does best with works of bravura, and his final minutes lifted the audience (figuratively and literally) out of their seats.

Perhaps the still-young Kissin will have realized his abilities to go beyond what he has been doing and the repertoire that he has been given or has chosen. It is clear that he has an affinity for works of the 20th century–his recordings of Scriabin and Prokofiev confirm this. Let us hope next year he will still look like an 18-year-old child prodigy, but choose repertory more deserving of a 40-year-old master of the piano.

♪Student Groups Join to Create "The Creation"
Yale Schola Cantorum, Yale Baroque Ensemble, Juilliard415, Masaaki Suzuki (conductor), St. Bartholomew's Church, New York, 30.4.2012

Haydn: *Die Schöpfung*

Where better to hear Haydn's late oratorio, *The Creation*, than in the resplendent St. Bartholomew's Church. The Byzantine façade hides a huge but much simpler space, with cushioned chairs instead of pews. On this occasion, most of the chairs were filled. The performance was a joint effort between Yale and Juilliard featuring their three exemplary student performing groups: the Yale Schola Cantorum, the Yale Baroque Ensemble and Juilliard415, all led by guest conductor and Bach specialist, Masaaki Suzuki.

What does the chaos of creation sound like? Haydn wrote his version of the creation at the tail end of the Age of Enlightenment. The music has its dissonant moments and more surprises than his Surprise Symphony, but still clearly speaks in the voice of Haydn: not his earlier Sturm und Drang voice but that of the late London symphonies. Comparing Haydn's "Representation of Chaos" with the opening "La Cahos" from *Les élemens* by the 18th-century Baroque composer Jean-Féry Rebel makes Haydn seem tame. Haydn's opening overture has several sudden explosions, the most prominent one occurring a little past the midpoint after an appealing flurry of off-key natural horns. The orchestra twice pounds out a 7-note phrase (seven days of the week?). Later we get an even more emphatic explosion on the last word of "and there was light." This musical surprise should have the audience jumping out of their seats, but unfortunately Suzuki didn't turn the volume up quite high enough to shock the audience, and this was one of his few interpretative mistakes.

In an example of early program music, Haydn has the orchestra mimic birds, water and insects. This too had been done before, in Handel's *Israel in Egypt*, a work that Haydn likely heard in London. Handel presents a series of orchestral representations of the plagues, more specifically the raining down of frogs and the destruction of crops by locusts.

The four soloists (normally five, but John Taylor Ward sang two parts) are all current graduate students in the Yale Schola Cantorum. All four, perhaps intentionally, sang their parts with softer, gentler and more upbeat voices then those heard in other performances of this work. One critic has called this Haydn's most cheerful work at the happiest point in his life. This may have been the happiest period of his life, but I'm not sure if I would go so far as to call this oratorio cheerful, although there were cheerful moments, particularly in the Adam and Eve sections. John Taylor Ward was faultless in the roles of Raphael and Adam; he stood in for bass Dan Moore and deserves extra praise for it. Referred to elsewhere as a baritone, he was able to successfully reach down to hit some very low notes, notes that would be hard even for a bass to sing. This was true in both "Roaming in Foaming Billows" and later in "Now heaven in fullest glory shone."

Jessica Petrus as Gabriel truly had an angelic voice, especially when she reached up to the high E at the end of the aria, "The Marvelous Work Beholds Amazed." Steven Soph had perhaps the strongest voice and Megan Chartrand, who had a small role as Eve, sang formidably. I was lucky enough to be seated near the orchestra, but I wondered if their voices and the church's acoustics allowed for them to be heard clearly in the back.

There was no doubt as to the chorus's ability to project to the last row. They sang and the instrumental ensemble played with professional prowess under the leadership of Maestro Suzuki. Having almost completed the recordings of all the Bach cantatas, Suzuki would find this particular blend of chorus, orchestra and soloists a familiar combination for him, and he led them enthusiastically throughout this exceptional performance.

♪The Storm Within the Calm: Richard Goode Plays Schumann and Chopin

Richard Goode (piano), Carnegie Hall, New York, 25.4.2012

Schumann: *Kinderszenen, Kreisleriana*
Chopin: Nocturne in E-flat major, Scherzo No. 3 in C-sharp minor, Waltz in A-flat major, Waltz in C-sharp minor, Waltz in F major, Ballade No. 3 in A-flat major

Encores:
Chopin: Mazurka in C major
Beethoven: Scherzo from Sonata No. 18 in E-flat major
Janácek: From *On the Overgrown Path*, Book I

It is always a surprise when you hear a musician perform works outside of what, rightly or wrongly, you consider his standard repertory. Richard Goode playing Schumann and Chopin is not as radically unexpected as early music specialist Nikolaus Harnoncourt performing *Porgy and Bess*, but he is most often thought to be a specialist in Bach, Beethoven and Mozart.

Goode's recital of works by two geniuses of early Romantic piano music was top-notch in almost every regard, though perhaps not quite on the level of Claudio Arrau playing Schumann or Artur Rubinstein performing Chopin. The recital was musical poetry from start to finish, and the audience was captivated. Since the urtext of the first work played, the 13 *Kinderszenen*, has no tempo markings (except for "Ritter vom Steckenpferd"), performances of these miniatures are all over the place in length. The famous "Träumerei," for example, takes Lang Lang 4:11 to complete while Horowitz in one version does it in 2:24. Most of Goode's tempo choices were well considered, and only in "Fürchtenmachen" would I have wanted a little more speed and "fright." I liked the way that in "Am Kamin" he was able to emulate two lines of voices talking in front of a fire.

Although Schumann's masterpiece for piano, the *Fantasie* in C major, was not played here, it is interesting to see this work as the missing third of a series of increasingly more complicated compositions. Even if the *Fantasie* was started before the two works on this program, it was not revised until after Opus 15 and 16 were completed. This leads to a clear progression in terms of complexity, maturity and probably psychological disturbance. The opening "Ausserst bewegt" of *Kreisleriana* starts with a theme similar to the central section of the *Fantasie* and continues in an almost schizophrenic manner with all except the final movement played in extremes: "*Sehr*" is the adjective used to describe all the movement's tempi. Goode could have taken the virtuoso's way of playing the fast sections as loudly and speedily as possible, but he opted for a more controlled, crafted and ultimately a more satisfying reading of the score.

The same poetic emphasis was used to shape the Chopin pieces. The Nocturne in E-Flat received an almost classical reading, never raising its voice even in the crescendo from *p* to *ff* near the end of the score. Virtuosity can't be avoided in Chopin's Scherzos, and Goode provided proof that he could play runs of octaves as well as anyone. The Scherzo in C-sharp minor goes back and forth from frenetic to gentle arpeggios, and Goode performed this difficult work without unduly disturbing the calm that imbued the entire recital.

The three waltzes caught the strong rhythms of dance, but here a lighter touch may have been needed. Having grown up listening to Dino Lipatti's 1950 recording of the waltzes has jaded me and, I'm sure, many others into being unable to hear this music without comparing it to Lipatti's version, to the detriment of any other.

The final work, the Ballade No. 3 in A-flat major, seemed almost like a recap of all the preceding Chopin. It begins with lilting delicate harmonies of a conversation-like melody, but soon massive chords mutate the original melody into a fiery and demanding emotional statement.

Of the three encores, the Beethoven Scherzo from his Sonata No. 18 in E-flat major was the most moving: a reminder of how great a Beethoven interpreter Goode is.

What can't be analyzed and dissected here is the charisma that Goode brings with him. Walking onstage as if he were taking a leisurely stroll, he sits down and plays with an almost eerie calm, immediately capturing the audience's attention for the duration of the concert—as only a few master pianists can.

♪*Reviving Vivaldi: Juilliard Plays All Vivaldi Program*

The Glories of Venice: Juilliard Historical Performance Faculty, Juilliard415, Monica Huggett (director), Corpus Christi Church, New York, 22.4.2012

Vivaldi: Concerto in F major, Concerto for Violin, Flute, Oboe, Bassoon and Continuo in G minor, Bassoon Concerto in D minor, Concerto for Two Horns in F major, Flute Concerto in D major "ll gardellino," Concerto for Oboe and Bassoon in G major, Concerto per solennita di S. Lorenzo in D major

On a rainy Sunday afternoon we were treated to an all-Vivaldi concert by the Juilliard Baroque (faculty) and Juilliard415 (students). It would be hard to say who was or was not a student, so professionally did everyone perform.

Vivaldi has suffered over the years from jokes centered on the notion that all his music sounds the same: the old saw is that he didn't write 500 concertos, but rather wrote one concerto 500 times. And if one mainly hears myriad recordings and performances of "The Four Seasons," his music can sound trivial.

The truth is that Vivaldi wrote most of his instrumental music on demand as material for students, but he is due more respect now with the revival of both his sacred music and a large body of operas. The recovery of over 450 works found in the Library of Turin which the CD label Naïve is in the process of recording (currently at 56 volumes on its way to 100 by 2015) gives reason to believe Vivaldi looked at opera as his true art. While some Vivaldi arias and sacred pieces are simply voices being doubled by the orchestra, there are many others that are of exceptional merit and compete with Handel in musical quality.

The first two concerti performed here were part of 25 *concerti da camera* recovered from the Turin Library cache. These works are ideal for presenting Vivaldi concerti with a limited number of musicians, and the Juilliard groups made these chamber concerti showcases for their technical skills.

The opening Concerto in F major is unusual in several respects. Instead of his usual three movements, Vivaldi uses a four-movement form, the *sonata da chiesa,* found most prominently in the works of Corelli. This concerto, like the one that followed, uses the same instruments that play the ripieno (orchestral forces) to play the concertinos (one instrumental solo). The usual basso continuo of keyboard and bass stringed instrument was replaced entirely by bassoon, and the excellent bassoonist Domenic Terasi added bounce and color to the music. The impossibly-difficult-to-play natural horns improved their intonation considerably in the third movement.

The other found work, the Concerto for Violin, Oboe and Bassoon, includes a continuo that frees the bassoon for other business. Unfortunately, although named as a soloist, the bassoon never gets a chance to solo. The second movement dialogue between the oboe and flute melds in a way that blurs the line between the instruments, and it was tenderly played by Gonzolo Ruiz and Sandra Miller. A chaconne, a common form used by most of Vivaldi's contemporaries but rarely by Vivaldi, provided a spirited end to the concerto.

A favorite instrument of Vivaldi, the bassoon finally got a chance to solo in the D minor Concerto. Teresi took the long runs with ease, producing a warm and earthy tone.

At a concert last year, a Baroque performance group presented a double horn concerto by a Bach contemporary, Johann Friedrich Fasch. Although the group considered itself Baroque, the solo horns were modern-day French horns. It was clear from their first notes that they had not practiced adequately, and wrong notes on a horn are not easy to disguise. Here, fortunately, two brave natural horn players, R. J. Kelley and Nathanael Udell, took on Vivaldi's Concerto for Two Horns. Using only embrochure and a hand in the instrument's bell, they were able to make this formal hunting horn sing. Some slightly off moments are not unexpected, given how difficult it is to reshape one's mouth or open and close the bell as needed.

All the concerti on this program were unfamiliar—not difficult to accomplish when there is so much unplayed Vivaldi music to discover—except the Flute Concerto in D major, known as "The Goldfinch." But with Sandra Miller as soloist, it was good to hear it again. Her discreet use of improvised ornaments on the da capos in the languorous second-movement Largo was particularly appreciated.

Every once in a while, Vivaldi hits the mark on rhythmically interesting instrumental material, and the Concerto for Oboe and Bassoon is one of those concerti. There is much of interest in the back and forth of the oboe and bassoon, and the sound mix of these two double-reed instruments make it difficult to see where one instrumental line ends and the other one begins. The last movement brings back themes that are closely related to the first movement.

The closing Concerto in D major was the star of the show. The opening Andante creates a sense of dramatic foreboding and leads into a French baroque fanfare with horns used as trumpets. In the Naïve series of Vivaldi's works, the conductor Alessandro de Marchi uses the last two movements of this concerto to replace the lost overture to the military oratorio, "Juditha triumphans." Although there are solos for other instruments in the last movement, the amazing violin cadenza by Monica Huggett was the highlight.

And who said Vivaldi's music is clichéd?

♪Rarely Played Busoni Quartet Makes Its Carnegie Hall Premiere
Brentano String Quartet (Mark Steinberg and Serena Canin, violins; Misha Amory, viola; Nina Maria Lee, cello), Weill Recital Hall, Carnegie Hall, New York, 19.4.2012

Busoni: String Quartet No. 2
Beethoven: String Quartet in B-flat major with *Grosse Fuge*

Busoni's Quartet No. 2 was written in 1887, somewhere between Brahms' and Dvořák's early quartets and Schoenberg's and Dvořák's late quartets. I had never heard the work before, and my initial impression was that it was derivative: part Bach, part Beethoven and part Brahms. The fact that it had never been performed at Carnegie Hall in its 120-year existence seemed to be an implicit judgment of its worth. However, there was no question about the Brentano Quartet's commitment to the piece, and they played with prestigious technique and boundless energy.

But I had a nagging feeling that I was rushing my opinion of the work. With the score in hand I listened to the handful of available recordings, and not only did I begin to see the work's attractiveness but also how stellar the Brentano's interpretation was. Sensitive to the score's shifting phrasing and its off-beat, occasionally syncopated progressions, the Brentano deftly handled the complex manner in which the themes (motifs, really) are developed. The *fughettos* come and go naturally without seeming artificial or contrived. The second movement uses as its main theme a drone-like cello line with the first violin soaring that is quite charming. The third movement is a Scherzo with a brief middle trio and a return to the opening theme, and the final movement, filled with quick changes in tempo, uses counterpoint in several fugal segments. Although the work is no undiscovered masterpiece, it holds its own as a not easily classifiable composition by a composer who himself might be considered unclassifiable.

Beethoven's String Quartet in B-flat major presents a choice of two final movements: the *Grosse Fuge* or a more traditional Rondo. Conservatives hear in the *Grosse Fuge* the music of the past, dismissing the dissonant modern parts; lovers of modern music hear it as if it were written in the 20th century. The piece is just as likely to be performed by the Arditti Quartet as the Juilliard Quartet, and each ensemble claims the work as their own.

I reviewed elsewhere a performance of the Op.130 and *Grosse Fuge* which was played traditionally and which left me awestruck. The Brentano's approach was to push the work into the 21st century, avoiding the emotional impact that makes the music come alive. The movement marked *Alla danza tedesca* did not have the pulse that should have made it seem danceable. The Cavatina lacked warmth until the coda, when the attempt to be poignant seemed overindulgent.

Nowhere in the score is there a marking for playing the strings with *spicatto*, yet this was how most of the fortes were played. The *Grosse Fuge* sounds modern enough without the sawing and slashing of the strings to prove its raw modernity. The performance of the work should carry you away with its intensity and fire rather than leaving you cold. I am certainly not looking for the overly romantic interpretations by quartets of the early 20th century such as the Budapest or Bush quartets, but we have been through a period of researching performances as they were practiced in the composer's lifetime. The resultant knowledge should lead us to interpretations more in the spirit of what the composer was hoping to accomplish.

Nevertheless, this particular reading of the score was well appreciated by the audience. The Brentano's vision is certainly a valid one, and their playing was immaculate on every level.

♫ The Splendors of Dresden and of the Oboe

The Splendors of Dresden: Juilliard415, Gonzalo Ruiz (conductor and oboist), Rosemary and Meredith Willson Theater, Juilliard Music School, Lincoln Center, New York, 12.4.2012

Fasch: Suite in G major
Telemann: Suite for Two Flutes, Strings and Continuo in E minor
Bach: Oboe Concerto in D minor
Telemann: Septet (Concerto) for Three Oboes, Three Violins and Continuo in B-flat major
Heinchen: Concerto and Suite con Violino, Oboe e Traverso in G major
Telemann: Suite for Two Flutes, Strings and Continuo in E minor

This delightful and spirited performance by the students of Juilliard's Historical Performance Department was led by Gonzalo Ruiz, the eminent oboist and faculty member. This year alone the students have performed under the leadership of some of the foremost conductors in early music: William Christie, Monica Huggett (Faculty), Richard Egarr, Ton Koopman, Jordi Savall, Steven Fox and Masaaki Suzuki. Each conductor brought a personal style of conducting, but also ideas on the technique of playing Baroque instruments. Monica Huggett has a wealth of knowledge of stringed instruments; Jordi Savall, the viola da gamba; and Gonzalo Ruiz, the oboe.

Lully was one of the first composers to use oboes, probably transitioning from the older pre-oboe instrument, the shawm, and his unique sound is always recognizable by the oboe's prominence. Any composer who was influenced by him carried this particular timbre back to his own country. In addition, Lully's opera overtures became the standard form for most Baroque operas that followed, and the popularity of the form soon allowed composers to expand the use from an opera introduction to a suite of dances taking the name overture (and beginning with a traditional overture as well). The first two works on this program began with Lullian overtures: a slow opening section heavily accented with dotted rhythms, followed by a fast fugal middle, closing with a return to the opening tempo. This and the dances that followed were conducted with an emphasis on each movement's unique rhythmic pulse. The Fasch suite, a rarely played work, exemplifies the kind of music that has unfortunately been neglected.

How different really is Baroque music from popular dance music when it is performed with the energy of Mr. Ruiz and his students? For propriety's sake the listener holds back the urge to shake one's head, tap one's shoes or conduct with one's finger. This vital rhythmic drive was felt here in even the slower dances.

The centerpiece of the program was the amazing performance of Bach's BWV 1059, most often heard as a solo keyboard concerto but perhaps originally written for oboe. If this were the case, Bach would have needed a top virtuoso to play the note-filled score, and the Juilliard is lucky to have someone of the caliber of Mr. Ruiz on staff.

He came on stage with a stocking covering his scalp, which was explained in the program notes as a way of preventing sweat from dripping down his face and reaching his mouth. His performance revealed the possibilities of the oboe. At a recent concert of Il Gardino Armonico, the piccolo player and leader of the group, Giovanni Antonini, played a signature solo from a Vivaldi piccolo concerto. This solo part was played as fast as possible and although no notes were missed the music was rather superficial: a series of empty notes. By contrast, Ruiz's solo was no auto-pilot performance; if anything his success in playing the difficult score was a result of the tension inherent in the work's risks. The students played along conductor-less, but they clearly were able to hold their own.

John David Heinchen is even less known than Fasch, having officially been "rediscovered" by Reinhard Goebel and the Musica Antiqua Köln. Deutsche Grammophon's advertisements for this recording in 1992 called Heinichen "The Vivaldi of the North," just as Dresden has been called the "Florence of the North." The concerto performed here has a wonderful middle section Allegro with brilliant writing for oboe and transverse flute.

The choice of venue—one of Juilliard's more intimate performance rooms—only enhanced the whole musical experience.

♫*Mozart Opts for Constanza Years Before Meeting Her*

Gotham Chamber Orchestra and Chorus, Neal Goren (conductor), Gerald W. Lynch Theater, John Jay College, New York, 11.4.2012

Mozart: *Il sogno di Scipione*

This free-spirited and imaginative production of Mozart's early opera *Il sogno di Scipione* succeeds in a way that other anachronistic stagings of opera do not. The conceit of a dream (*sogno*) provides the license for the director to create a staging that goes beyond the restraints of reality. Since the opera was never performed in its entirety in Mozart's lifetime (and not revived until 1979), there really is no precedent as to how it would have been or should be staged. The Gotham's interpretation conceptually mirrors the one performance on DVD, recorded at the 2006 Salzburg Festival.

It is hard to believe that this opera was written by a boy of 16, and even harder to believe that it is Mozart's seventh opera. The libretto tells of a dream had by the young Scipione, the future defeater of Hannibal. Waking in a bedroom, Scipione finds himself if not in a *ménage à trois,* definitely *à trois.* Michele Angelini as Scipione is asked to choose between two women, personifications of Fortune (Susannah Biller as Fortuna) and Constancy (Marie-Ève Munger as Constanza). Tempted by Fortuna, who dresses and undresses and appears in various states of dishabille, Scipione resists her wiles and chooses, as Mozart himself did, Constanza.

Il sogno di Scipione suffers from a plot based on a simple kind of personification that was typical of operas, oratorios and masques written at the turn of the 18th century. Handel's *Il Trionfo del tempo e del Disinganno,* with characters named Beauty, Time and Pleasure, and his more famous *L'Allegro, Il Penseroso ed Moderato* are examples of libretti based on personifications. The music has an older-generation feel to it with its da capo arias, more Baroque than *galant.* Much of the singing consists of highly embellished arias typical of Handel, Hasse and A. Scarlatti.

This is early Mozart, but it is not easy Mozart. The cadenza-like melismas at the completion of the arias were sometimes hard work for the young singers. But whatever was lacking in reaching the high C's was made up for in enthusiasm and spirit. The strongest vocal performance came from Arthur Espiritu's Publio who sang majestically while hopping around on one leg. The non-sequitur ending with its appeal to patrons by the soprano Rachel Willis Sørenson was expertly sung, but her attempts to be flirtatious were not greatly convincing.

Goren led the orchestra in a bright and brisk rendition of the overture and settled in to a comfortably paced regimen that was well-balanced and supportive of the singers. This was an adventuresome and imaginative introduction to the young Mozart's accomplishments.

♪Fox Leads Juilliard415 and Clarion Society in Exceptional Baroque Concert

Nanae Iwata (violin), Julia Bullock, Heather Engebretson, Ying Fang (sopranos), Rachel Wilson (mezzo-soprano), Spencer Lang (tenor), Davone Tines (bass-baritone), Juilliard415, The Clarion Choir, Steven Fox (conductor), Alice Tully Hall, Lincoln Center, New York, 23.3.2012

Corelli: Concerto Grosso in D major
Handel: *Silete venti*: Motet for Soprano and Orchestra
Bach: Violin Concerto in A minor, *Magnificat* in D major

Conductor Riccardo Muti has over the last ten years performed and recorded concerts that have been universally praised. Credit is always given to the conductor, but equal or greater accolades are given to his two orchestras. What is so exceptional about these orchestras is that all the members are handpicked by Maestro Muti. Every conductor is involved in the hiring of new orchestral members, but few are able to hire more than replacements for the usual turnover of staff.

Likewise, the students in the Juilliard School's Historical Performance Department, while not selected by a particular conductor for an orchestra, have been admitted only if they excel. There are just a handful of equivalent early music departments in universities, and getting accepted by Juilliard defines you as a soloist placed among an orchestra of soloists. The Department is only in its third year, but Juilliard415 can truly be considered among the top professional Baroque orchestras of the day.

These students also have been exposed to master classes and conductors who are the most prestigious in the world. They have had to deal with each teacher's individual personality, had to unlearn and learn again what each conductor demands of his or her own orchestra. As Monica Huggett, Artistic Director of the program has stated, "How many musicians in history have under their belts French, Italian and German styles. These students might be asked to play any one or all of these styles on any given school day."

Steven Fox had his turn with this orchestra and the group responded with sparkle. Choosing one of the bedrocks of Baroque music from Corelli's Opus 6, Fox was pulled in by the work's rhythmic pulse. This concerto gave the violinist Samuel Park, in the concertino sections of the piece, the material for a short but spirited demonstration of virtuosity, on par with any that I've heard in this work

In Rome at the turn of the 18th century, Handel had connected with Corelli, whose concerto grossi were a major influence on his own cycles of concerti grossi (Opus 3 and 6). One might think that the unusual motet chosen as the next piece on the program, *Silete venti*, was from this period. In style it is reminiscent of the series of cantatas Handel wrote for the religious leaders of Rome in 1706-1707, but current scholarship puts it much later, in the mid-1720s. While the cantatas are decidedly secular, this motet is considered to be a piece that could be performed in a church; but even a quick reading of the text reveals that taking out one word (Jesus) would convert it into a secular motet.

Ying Fang had a lovely voice, warmer than many sopranos who sing Baroque arias, but for a work of this nature the song and the singer were a good match. Steven Fox and the orchestra kept back when she was up front. Kristin Olson, whose oboe seemed to be ever-present, added much color to the orchestral palette.

Nanae Iwata is to be commended for her determination to give a decidedly personal vision of Bach's A minor violin concerto. At no point did she cede her soft sound for the sake of virtuosity. At times a tad behind the orchestra, she maintained a steady, confident and self-effacing technique. The lush second movement, usually a showcase of vibrato, here sounded even more poignant without it. At one point, towards the end of the final movement, I had a momentary sense of transcendence when everyone was perfectly in accord.

There was no question of holding back for Bach's *Magnificat*. Fox conducted most of the more rhythmic movements off the ground. The "Et exultavit spiritus meus" sung by Julia Bullock was strong and vibrant. Heather Engebretson's "Quia respexit humiltatem" smoothly segued into the always surprising "Omnes generationes" from the Chorus. Both Spencer Lang and Davone Tines gave resonant readings of their respective arias. "Esurientes implevit bonis" might have benefited from a slightly lighter voice than Rachel Wilson's, particularly against the two lilting flutes. The chorus was sharp, clear and responsive to Fox's every gesture.

Of the three performances of the *Magnificat* that I've seen this season, this was the most compelling. It would be hard to resist any concert that showed such enthusiasm, energy and freshness by all involved.

♫Ian Bostridge Is the Star in Bach's St. John Passion

Ian Bostridge (tenor), Neal Davies (bass-baritone), Karina Gauvin (soprano), Damien Guillon (countertenor), Nicholas Phan (tenor), Hanno Müller-Brachmann (bass-baritone), Les Violons du Roy and La Chapelle de Québec,

Bernard Labadie (conductor and music director), Carnegie Hall, New York, 25.3.2012

Bach: *St. John Passion*

When MP3 players were in their infancy, with five gigabytes of free space, compressing the music data down to a low-quality 125kb allowed storage of about 100 CDs. My solution for storing opera CDs was to not record the recitatives. In so many Handel and Vivaldi operas, the long texts, nearly spoken, with only a basso continuo to support the singer, were a waste of precious disk space. If I wanted to follow the opera's story, I would do that listening to the CD at home with a libretto in hand.

But what about the Bach cantatas? I tried stripping out recitatives in a few, but when I listened to them I felt like I was listening to the Best of Bach or Bach for the Unborn. Bach somehow was different. If the text was long but more meaningful or poetic than the usual prose, he would call in extra instruments to enhance the libretto. What a shame it would have been to miss out on the miraculous *recitativo accompagnato* from BWV 61.

Why am I bringing this up? Because the particular success of this performance of Bach's *St. John Passion* came from the moving, pure and precise voice of the Evangelist, sung by the eminent Ian Bostridge. His captivating voice in the recitatives was a pleasure to listen to and almost made the musical parts seem secondary to the text. He did what Bach himself did by emphasizing key words and giving them extra color. For example, in the recitative "Da verleugnete Petrus," there is the text, "wept most bitterly." Bach stretches these words to simulate the sounds of weeping, and Ian Bostridge rendered them so pathetically that it indeed brought tears to one's eyes.

The other soloists were competent and often more. Countertenor Damien Guillon didn't quite project his voice far enough in the aria "Von den Stricken meiner Sünden," but did give a solid reading of "Es ist Vollbracht." This aria is one of the few, if any, by Bach that actually has the soloist join in at the coda after the instrumental recapitulation. Karina Gauvin gave a strong account of "Ich folge dir gleichfalls," one of the few upbeat pieces in a work that is, even for Bach, unusually dark. Neal Davies as Jesus had little to sing, but gave a needed authority to the role. Hanno Müller-Brachmann in "Mein teurer Heiland lass dich fragen" was able to maintain a nice balance when the chorus joined in to interweave their voices with his in a Chorale. Nicholas Phan sang well, but inevitably suffered in comparison to Bostridge.

The chorus and orchestra sang and played with a comfortable fluidity. Only in the opening chorus were they out of synch, which made me think that I was listening to the beginning rumbles of Haydn's oratorio, *The Creation*. This disconnect may have occurred due to Labadie starting the performance before the orchestra was quite ready. But from this point on, the singers and instrumentalists provided a firm ground to support this admirable production of what has always been considered, perhaps unfairly, as the *St. Matthew Passion*'s weaker sibling.

♪*Ton Koopman and Amsterdam Baroque Perform Bach the Old-Fashioned Way*

Teresa Wakim (soprano), Bogna Batosz (alto), Tilman Lichdi (tenor), Klaus Mertens (bass-baritone), Amsterdam Baroque Orchestra and Choir, Ton Koopman (conductor), Carnegie Hall, New York, 15.3.2012

Bach: Cantata BWV 104, "Du Hirte Israel, höre"; *Magnificat* in D major; Cantata BWV 147, "Herz und Mund und Tat und Leben"

At the time the Amsterdam Baroque Orchestra was founded, there were only a handful of early music performance groups and they were considered radical in all respects. One of the complaints about the early music groups' playing was that it was too cold. This would naturally be the case since the instruments used to perform are originals or copies of originals that lack in richness what they gain in timbre. All the instruments are played without vibrato, a practice that reduces, particularly in the strings, the warmth we have come to expect from contemporary instruments. At the same time what is gained by the absence of vibrato is a clarity of line.

As often happens when there is a reaction against the reigning style in art, it initially triggers an overreaction. These early groups were fairly brash about what they felt was the "true" way of playing early music, and armed with little more than an ideal of a purer music, they made mistakes on every level. Issues over vibrato, debates as to what the correct tuning should be (somewhere between A-400hz and A-430hz), equal temperament, *notes inégales*, valveless, vented or ventless brass, Baroque bowing methods and types of bows: it took decades of scholarly research to come up with some consensus on how this music should be performed. Much of the unified front of the early historically informed performance groups splintered as newer discoveries were made.

The one-voice-per-part (OVPP) movement of Joshua Rifkin became the basic structure of groups directed by Andrew Parrott, John Butt, Paul McCreesh and others. Nicholas Harnoncourt's set of the complete Bach cantatas used only boy singers in its chorus and as high soprano soloists. Tempos and styles often varied by country: Italian Baroque groups were speed demons, French groups heavily into ornamentation and Northern Europeans tended toward more moderate tempos.

Joshua Rifkin defended the OVPP rule by ignoring the first-hand evidence of Bach's own statements, preferring to use the evidence of Bach's contemporaries such as Telemann whose manuscript performance scores clearly indicated OVPP. Ton Koopman has held to a moderate approach through all this in-fighting from the beginning. Sticking closely to the few extant Bach documents such as the *Entwurf* of 1730 where Bach requested that the Thomaskirche provide him with 36 members for the chorus (I counted 25 for this performance) and 24 instrumentalists, Koopman seems closest to getting it right.

When tempos are indicated there is less room for misconstruing the pace, but none are indicated here in this score. At the opening of this concert, the chorus performance of "Du Hirte Israel, höre" struck me as a bit slow. Digging up an old recording of the 104th cantata done by Fritz Werner in the 1950's, I was in for a surprise: Werner takes twice as long as Koopman with the opening chorus.

Throughout this performance the soloists concentrated on making sure every word was clearly enunciated. This complemented the conductor whose focus also seemed to be on making sure every note was heard. The balancing of the various groups so that one group wouldn't drown out another was exemplary. Tenor Tilman Lichdi and soprano Teresa Wakim gave the most intense performances. Wakim's pure white voice informed her arias with a silvery brilliance lacking in Bogna Batosz's arias. The ubiquitous Klaus Martens disappointed by declaiming the wonderful aria "Beglückte Herde, Jesu Schafe" with its poignant double oboe d'amore accompaniment.

The *Magnificat* is one of Bach's masterpieces. It sounds fresh on every hearing, and this performance was no exception. The musicians and chorus soared in both the opening and closing choruses, and the intervening arias showed the range of color the orchestra was capable of producing. Not to denigrate in any way the trumpet players who performed with bravura, but they lacked the éclat that can only come from ventless instruments.

The concert concluded with Cantata BWV 147, known mostly for its great chorale, "Bleibet Meine Freude", sung twice in different stanzas. But the real gem is the aria with solo violin and continuo, "Bereite dir, Jesu, noch itzo die Bahn," touchingly sung by Teresa Wakim and elegantly played by concertmaster Catherine Manson. It is an aria reminiscent of the centerpiece of Bach's *St. Matthew Passion*, "Erbarme Dich."

As a most appropriate response to the applause, Koopman performed again the Gloria from the *Magnificat* as an encore.

♫Beethoven's Missa Solemnis: Difficult Work, More Difficult Circumstances

Christine Brewer (soprano), Michelle de Young (mezzo-soprano), Simon O'Neill (tenor), Eric Owens (bass-baritone), Malcolm Lowe (violin), Boston Symphony Orchestra, Tanglewood Festival Chorus, John Oliver (conductor), Carnegie Hall, New York, 6.3.2012

Beethoven: *Missa solemnis*

The *Missa solemnis* is one of the most challenging scores for a conductor, whose worst nightmare might be having to perform it on less than 24 hours' notice. John Oliver, a last-minute replacement for Kurt Masur who was the replacement for James Levine, received mixed reviews at his Boston premiere in late February. This Carnegie Hall concert was his fourth live performance with the Boston Symphony Orchestra and the Tanglewood Festival Chorus, and the interim week must certainly have helped him pull some of the looser elements together. While this was far from a seamless presentation, all the parties involved were self-assured and enthusiastic. If at times they weren't a tightly knit group, how many other performances of the work are totally cohesive, outside of those by Toscanini, Klemperer or Beecham?

The opening Kyrie epitomized the pluses and minuses of the entire reading. It started off with a muddy sound, the orchestra overpowering the soloists at their entry, and as a result one missed the impact of the solo quartet's voices, which should pierce through the massive sound layer in their cry for mercy. But once the soloists established themselves as a presence, they had the fortitude necessary to move the piece forward. Similarly, the chorus—without scores—sang with confidence, their eyes fixed on the conductor's spare gestures.

The unusual ending of the Kyrie (the final note is a *pizzicato* from the strings marked *pp* with a fermata) and the chorus's sudden declamation of "Gloria" always comes as a surprise, and it did so here even if the groups were slightly out of balance. The chorus again excelled in some very difficult music even though it was at the expense of vocal clarity. Distinct enunciation in a work like this that demands so much vocally is difficult, but it should be lucid enough for the audience to at least be certain the chorus is singing "Credo" and not "Crucifixus."

The Credo is another challenge for any chorus, and the Tanglewood Festival Chorus met it head on. At one point, on the word *omnipotentem* at the beginning of the Credo, the sopranos in the chorus are asked to hold a B5 note for almost four measures. Is this Beethoven's way, as he states at the beginning of the score, of permanently instilling religious feelings in the singers? If so, I should think that every chorus member might have been converted. The high point of the evening was the magical violin solo that precedes and continues through the Benedictus. Malcolm Lowe played radiantly, in spite of some brief instances where the soloists and chorus overpowered him. One of those special musical moments, this violin solo seems to appear out of nowhere and disappears just as quickly. This approach was also used Richard Strauss in the ecstatic solo entry of the violin in "Beim Schlafengehen" from *Vier letzte Lieder*.

The coda of the *Missa Solemnis* is unusual for Beethoven in that it is surprisingly brief. The final notes came so suddenly that Oliver seemed shocked himself, dropping his hands (the traditional symbol that it is okay to applaud) midway through the last note.

♪ *Simon Trpčeski Debuts at Carnegie's Zankel Hall*
Simon Trpčeski (piano), Zankel Hall, Carnegie Hall, New York, 27.2.2012

Liszt: Prelude and Fugue in A Minor (after Bach), Petrarch Sonnet No. 104 from *Années de pèlerinage*, *Les jeux d'eaux á la Villa d'Este*, Hungarian Rhapsody No. 2 in C-sharp minor
Schubert: 16 German Dances; Fantasy in C major, "Wanderer Fantasy"

A musician's choice of what to play at a debut concert is a calling card for the audience. One might not expect an aspiring pianist at his Zankel Hall debut to play, as Jeremy Denk did, thirteen of Ligeti's impossibly difficult Études and follow with Bach's *Goldberg Variations*, but one does look forward to more than virtuosic show pieces.

Simon Trpčeski's performance revealed little about either the pianist or the composers. At times it seemed that he was on auto-pilot, his hands doing one thing, his body and mind somewhere else. During the pauses between pieces, he seemed annoyed at the few coughs from the audience and exhibited twitchy eccentricities. His manner of lifting his hands after a difficult passage or at the end of the piece was a gesture that seemed to say, "Look at me." Was he expecting a standing ovation when he stated at one point that he is a popular star in his home country of Macedonia, but not in New York?

He is certainly a powerful pianist, reminiscent of others such as Boris Berezovsky, Lazar Berman or Boris Berman, capable of drawing massive sounds from the keyboard. This was evident in the opening Liszt transcription of Bach's organ version of the Prelude and Fugue in A minor. Here Trpčeski was able to impressively produce an organ-like sound from the Steinway, and gave listeners the impression that the pedal points were coming from the pedalboard and not the keyboard.

Tremendous energy was also shown in the Hungarian Rhapsody No. 2, but it was a poor choice out of the nineteen possible rhapsodies. He must be aware that the piece has been taken apart for comedic purposes by everyone from Mickey Mouse to the Marx Brothers to Mel Blanc's version in "Daffy Duck's Rhapsody."

His performance of the minor 16 German Dances of Schubert was heavy-handed and lacked the required lightness of touch that would make these throwaways listenable. Pounding the keyboard through Schubert's "Wanderer Fantasy" does not produce a particularly interesting interpretation even though Trpčeski had more than the necessary dexterity to play this challenging piece. You only need to listen to Alfred Brendel's delicate yet rhythmic performances of the Dances and sensitive and poetic playing of the "Wanderer Fantasy" to see what the proper approach to these works should be.

The potential is there for Trpčeski's interpretative abilities to grow to equal his technical skills. At that point we might have an artist as popular in New York as he is now at home.

♪ Well, He Certainly Got Around: St Luke's Chamber Ensemble Circling Bach

Circling Bach: Myron Lutzke (cello), Elizabeth Mann (flute), St. Luke's Chamber Ensemble, Brooklyn Museum, 25.2.2012

Rossi: Sinfonia Grave, Sonata Settima Sopra L'Aria d'un Balletto, Sonata duodecima Sopra la Bergamasca
Vivaldi: Concerto for Cello in A minor
Handel: Concerto Grosso in F major

C. P. E. Bach: Flute Concerto in D minor
Geminiani: Variations in D minor, "La Folia" after Corelli

Having just attended a concert in a series called "Refracted Bach" where the "Gilded Goldberg Variations" were played, it did not seem strange to be at a concert entitled "Circling Bach." Bach has, since his resurrection by Mendelssohn in the 1820s, been transcribed, transposed and varied upon by everyone from his own sons to Leopold Stokowski, and his scores have been rewritten for instruments as diverse as the harp, harmonica, accordion and Theremin. The circle of composers who influenced him are numerous: Vivaldi, Corelli, Buxtehude, Böhm, Telemann, d'Anglebert. His own circle of influence has extended into the 20th century as seen in the music of Ives, Berg, Hindemith and Stravinsky; and to our current day in Phillip Glass, John Adams, Terry Riley and Steve Reich.

Salamone Rossi is best known today, if known at all, for his madrigals and for the fact that he was Jewish. While there was no direct connection between Rossi and Vivaldi or Bach (Rossi died 50 years before either was born), Bach might have known both Rossi's use of the *stile antico* and his forays into the new *stile moderno* with its prominent use of counterpoint. The performance of these slight pieces would have benefited here from the timbre of original or original-style instruments. The addition of the cittern, resembling a mandolin although not of the mandolin family, added a lute-like sound that was very appealing.

The next work in the program, Vivaldi's Cello Concerto in A minor, must have been written for a particularly talented cellist: it requires considerable virtuosity, particularly in the final movement. Its unusual opening solo, supported only by the basso continuo, continues for nearly a minute before the orchestral ripieno comes in with a completely different theme. In fact the orchestra never plays the cello's theme and the cello never plays the orchestra's theme. The Andante second movement was poignantly rendered by Myron Lutzke, who also handled the difficult third movement Allegro with finesse. It would be hard to consider this unusually constructed concerto as one of the 500 concerti that Stravinsky joked were really one concerto written 500 times.

One connection between Bach and Handel's Concerto Grosso Opus 6, No. 9, can be found in their common practice of appropriating previously written material for use in "new" compositions. For the second and third movements Handel simply took two movements from his Organ Concerto HWV 295, the so-called "Cuckoo and the Nightingale," and rewrote the organ solo for strings. Bach had done the same many times. Although, surprisingly, there are no extant organ concerti by Bach, we do have a transcription for organ of the first movement of the Concerto for Keyboard in D minor, BWV 1052; Bach used this as the opening of a "new" cantata, BWV 146. Part of Handel's twelve brilliant Concerti Grossi, No. 9 is in some ways a synthesis of the whole set. Playing with a sensitivity to the different emotive elements of each movement, the SLCE was particularly fine in the intense and unusual central fugue.

253

The most neglected composer of the 18th century has to be C. P. E. Bach, yet the second son of J. S. Bach was more popular in his day than his father ever was. According to C. P. E. scholar Jane R. Stevens, this flute concerto may not have been a transcription of the Concerto in D minor for Harpsichord H.425/W.22, but in fact the reverse: the flute concerto might be the original version of the score. Regardless of origin, this concerto in either form is wonderfully imaginative and inventive. Elizabeth Mann deserved a standing ovation for mastering the incredibly difficult solo part, and the orchestra gave supple support, neither disappearing into the background nor being so forward as to drown out Ms. Mann.

Geminiani's Variations on "La Folia" after Corelli are in fact variations on variations and one of many, many similar compositions. Corelli's were written for violin and basso continuo, C. P .E. Bach's for keyboard and there is even one written by Gregorio Paniagua in 1980 that has, among other instruments, tablas, sitars and drums. The SLCE enthusiastically tossed off these 24 variations with confidence and aplomb.

♪And Then the Earth Shook and Trembled: Rattle, the BPO and Bruckner's Ninth

Berlin Philharmonic Orchestra, Sir Simon Rattle (conductor), Carnegie Hall, New York 24.2.2012

Bruckner: Symphony No. 9 in D minor with the US premiere of the final movement. Performance version by Samale-Phillips-Cohrs-Mazzuca (1983–2011)

Carnegie Hall has been both blessed and cursed. The main concert hall, officially the Isaac Stern Auditorium/Ronald O. Perelman Stage, is considered to be ideal acoustically. Unfortunately, it sometimes suffers from being right next to a subway station. There were moments in this concert when one thought a train had made a wrong turn and ended up in the hall: the floor shook as far back as our seats in row W, but the vibrations came from the stage, not the subway.

The performance revealed an image of Bruckner far from that of the country bumpkin who had childish ambitions of being the next "B" in the pantheon of Bach, Beethoven and Brahms. He is still seen by some as the idiot savant who built pointless crescendo after crescendo only to have nothing at the crescendi peaks: a musical Sisyphus never quite reaching his goal. As to the caveats about his old-fashioned style of composing, which looked backward and not forward, one only had to hear Sir Simon Rattle and the Berlin Philharmonic to ask if there has ever been a Scherzo more tragic and less Scherzo-like, or an Adagio more poignant and at the same time more apocalyptic. If Bruckner's life-long quest was be the next Beethoven and to write a ninth symphony on the level of Beethoven's Ninth, in this monumental work he was not far from his mentor's own masterpiece.

Only rarely is there an interpretation that makes us want to reexamine a composer's works in a particular genre or even his entire output. In our time one thinks of Glenn Gould and his iconoclastic reinterpretation of J. S. Bach's keyboard music, Leonard Bernstein's revival of Mahler or Sir Thomas Beecham's "rediscovery" of Delius. Here, from the *ab initio* (or should we say *de profundis*?) tremolos played pianissimo to the final three pizzicati of the third movement Adagio, the audience was held spellbound. Any orchestra under any conductor can play loudly, but few can inject such raw terror into each sonic burst that it becomes almost too painful to hear.

Working with one of the great orchestras of the world, Herbert von Karajan built the BPO into a successful but tightly controlled group prepared to succeed in any environment. Rattle has deconstructed this model and rebuilt it in a different fashion. Every member played as if in a chamber music group. The violins swayed with abandonment that couldn't be imagined in von Karajan's day. Conducting the entire work without a score, including the recently completed fourth movement, Rattle made gestures here and there but never imposed himself on the instrumentalists.

It seems only fair to suspend critical judgment on the US premiere of the reconstructed fourth movement. Started in 1983, first performed in 1991 but still considered a work in progress until 2010, this finale deserves to be heard several more times before it's reviewed. Unquestionably, it has the Bruckner signature sound, the grand crescendos, the prominence of the brass. Whether it matches Bruckner's other final movements and creates a conclusion that feels right remains a question. This premiere has generated much excitement and expectation, so mentioning the opinion of a detractor might add some balance. This is particularly important as it comes from one of the great Bruckner conductors, George Tintner: "It is not meant cruelly when I say that I for one am glad that Fate did not grant him his wish [to complete the symphony before he died]…for the *Finale* is unworthy of what is perhaps Bruckner's greatest music… The various efforts of brilliant scholars who have recently made performing version of Bruckner's *Finale* will be of entirely historical interest."

Frequently today, part of a music critic's comments focus on how rude the audiences are. The sold-out audience for this concert was exemplary: barely a rustle, cough or "ahem." It was 90 minutes of Bruckner, and the reception bodes well: the time may have finally arrived to place him on a pedestal next to Mahler.

♫*Norrington's Classical Equation: 2 x 39 + 1 =*

Jeremy Denk (piano), Orchestra of St. Luke's, Sir Roger Norrington (conductor), Carnegie Hall, New York, 16.2.2012

Haydn: Symphony No. 39 in G minor
Beethoven: Piano Concerto No. 1 in C major
Mozart: Symphony No. 39 in E-flat major

The series of Sturm und Drang symphonies Haydn wrote from the mid-1760s through the early 1770s are arguably his best symphonic works. One can't overestimate the influence C. P. E. Bach had not only on Haydn but on most composers of the time. Mozart is quoted by the music critic J. F. Rochlitz as having said of C. P. E., "He is the father. We are the children." The elements that distinguish Bach's instrumental music—sudden changes in dynamics and tempi, unexpected modulations to distant keys, silence used as a dramatic effect and dissonances where least expected—are all hallmarks of these Haydn symphonies.

Written in 1770, Haydn's 39th symphony falls right in the middle of this phase of his symphonic development. It's in the same key that Mozart would later use for his two symphonic forays into this dramatic style: the G minor symphonies, 25 and 40. Having recently heard Haydn's 26th symphony (the first of his *Sturm and Drang* series) performed on original instruments or replicas by students in the early music department at the Juilliard School, I still had the rough, complex, almost raucous timbres of these instruments in my mind. The Sturm und Drang symphonies look back to the Baroque and benefit more than Haydn's other symphonies from a historically informed approach. Although the OSL used instruments that were neither original Baroque instruments nor replicas, their playing technique gave a fine sense of the rich coloring that these symphonies offer.

Sir Roger Norrington made reference to the early music style in a number of ways. The most prominent feature was the immaculately clean, vibrato-less playing of the strings, and his unusual arrangement of the orchestral seating added to the period flavor. While the instrumental layout changed for each piece based on the scoring, generally the orchestra partially surrounded the conductor with the wind and brass players on the outside wings, first and second violins across from each other and the violas and celli in the middle. Having the wind instrumentalists stand up when needed allowed the sounds of the oboists, flautist and clarinetists to be heard clearly over the other instruments. Both the brass and the tympani accentuated the score with a freshness and crispness not heard in more traditional performances.

Norrington was one of the early proponents of historically informed performance, and one of the first conductors to apply period playing techniques to composers as late as Bruckner. His insistence on playing by the metronome markings, even in the metronome's earliest use by Beethoven, was controversial, but now it is common practice to play at these accelerated tempi. Surprisingly then, I found the third movement minuet slower than it should have been, dulling the contrast between it and the previous movement. This held true for the trio section of the minuet as well, which was missing its usually sharp distinction from the surrounding outer sections.

The change in the orchestra's layout was even more radical for the Beethoven piano concerto. This time the circle required the string players to position themselves with their backs to the audience. The piano and pianist faced the conductor who was standing in the center of the circle, which created the appearance that the audience was the recipient of the conductor's gestures. This also required the fallboard to be removed from the piano in order for the instrumentalists to see the conductor. These mutations generated a refreshingly well-tempered, even *galant* reading of the score, and Jeremy Denk played effortlessly through the entire work. It was not until the cadenza that one realized the effort required from the pianist. (Having seen Denk perform *The Goldberg Variations* and the Ligeti *Preludes* in the same evening, I had no doubts about his stamina.) Never raising the piano's voice or engaging in virtuosity by hammering the keyboard, his rendition of this cadenza made me wonder if it was even written by Beethoven, so unBeethoven-like it was in its self-effacement. The audience spontaneously broke into applause at the end of the first movement: clearly, this wasn't a breach of protocol but a heartfelt appreciation of Denk's rejuvenating approach to this well-known piece.

The concluding work, Mozart's 39th symphony, has little in common with Haydn's symphony of the same number. Here, with a much larger orchestra than for the earlier works on the program, there were some balancing problems, and one missed the richness of the strings when they competed with the winds and brass. My first impression of the orchestra was that they were so tightly knit that Norrington's mild gesturing was barely needed, but the Mozart would have benefited from a less laid-back conducting style.

All the members of the orchestra played flawlessly, but special mention should be given to the clarinetist, Jon Manasse, who was outstanding in both the Beethoven, played from the right side of the orchestra, and the Mozart, played from the left. The brief but poignant duo in the second movement of the Beethoven concerto had Denk turning his head in deference to the clarinet, as if the two were members of an intimate chamber group.

♫ *Goldberg Variations: Refracted and Re-Gilded*
Refracted Bach: Dessoff Choirs' 2012 Midwinter Festival: Steven Ryan and Catherine Venable (piano), Weill Recital Hall, Carnegie Hall, New York, 7.02.2012

Bach/Holloway: "Gilded Goldbergs"
New York Premiere

This performance is part of the Midwinter Festival organized by the Dessoff Choirs to explore the ramifications and "refractions" of Bach's music through the centuries. Tonight's concert probably came closest to the Festival's descriptive ideal: Bach's music refracted through the sensibility of other composers—in this case, Robin Holloway. There have been many modifications made over the centuries to the *Goldberg Variations*, most of which fall into two categories. The most common is the transcription or transposition of the work for other instruments: harp, accordion, guitar, string trio, two pianos or orchestra. The second features an artist's modifications, improvisations or variations; within this group there are versions that more or less retain the identity of the original music.

Uri Caine's 2000 reworking of the *Goldberg Variations* is probably the most ambitious ever undertaken. It starts with the main theme played on a fortepiano as written, but then crosses over to everything from rag to jazz, chorus to string quartet, waltzes to tangos. Running well over two hours and comprising 70 variations, it takes to heart Bach's tacit license to allow his music to be played on whatever instrument a musician desired. At this point in Bach's life he was more concerned about perfecting his art and ensuring his legacy than the practical concern of who played what. One of Bach's last pieces, *The Musical Offering*, has only a few movements that specify any instrumentation at all.

The Rheinberger/Reger transcription (1883, 1903) for two pianos comes closest to what Robin Holloway stated was his initial desire to "clarify the close-weave canons or manage the fiendish hand-crossing numbers." Josef Rheinberger allocated the more difficult contrapuntal lines to four hands over two pianos to make the original more playable. Max Reger then took Rheinberger's *Variations* and, as he did with many of Bach's works, filled in harmonic layers which he felt was necessary for the music to be appreciated by modern ears. The end result stays reasonably close to the original work.

Although there was one variation, the Messiaen-like 18th, which I couldn't connect with its source, I was able to keep up with Robin Holloway's version by running through Bach's variations in my head. (Having the score of the original work might have helped one understand Holloway's changes.) What is so unusual about Bach's *Goldberg Variations* is that he never actually develops the upper melody. He writes variations on the inner harmonic flow of the aria rather than the opening aria or theme itself. This differs from themes and variations by other composers like Beethoven: as far as he goes tonally and thematically from Diabelli's original waltz, it is always recognizable in every variation.

Holloway does the same as Bach, changing harmonies, modulating through keys, keeping most variations intact but also deconstructing others. In the famous 25th variation (which has been controversial since Glen Gould took six and a half minutes to play it in his 38-minute 1955 recording), Holloway makes sure our interest is held by breaking it apart and then splicing the pieces back together again. The heavy dissonant chords in many of the variations as well as the tone clusters in the 29th are reminiscent of Charles Ives's Concord Sonata where two or more things are going on at the same time. Ives's explanation is that as a child he remembered hearing two bands heading into town from different directions and playing different tunes. Some of this polytonal writing is done here as well.

The 19th variation (entitled "Ländler and Trio. 'Brief history of Austro-German music in triple time'") was the most fun to listen to and seemed so natural it could almost pass as the original. Beethoven integrated only one external reference in his 22nd variation of the *Diabelli Variations*, "Notte e giorno faticar" from Mozart's *Don Giovanni*. Holloway gives us at least nine here, all from three-quarter minuets, ländler and waltzes, including minuets from a Haydn symphony, Mozart's 40th Symphony, and Beethoven's 8th, and references from Brahms and Richard Strauss (*Der Rosenkavalier*).

One does not need to know any of the above to enjoy these playful variations on variations. The polished technique of Steven Ryan and Catherine Venable was formidable, and I can only imagine how tremendously demanding rehearsal time must have been. I couldn't say if there were any wrong notes played, particularly in a variation such as the 10th which is entitled "Robust and a bit gormless. Wrong-note music." But there's no question that the pianists vividly conveyed the spirit of both the composer and his transcriber in an elegant and majestic way.

♪If Only Nightingales Could Sing as Well: Vivica Genaux at Carnegie Hall

Vivica Genaux (mezzo-soprano), Europa Galante, Fabio Biondi (conductor and violin), Zankel Hall, Carnegie Hall, New York, 2.2.2012

Vivaldi, Nardini, Locatelli

Encores:
Giacomelli, Broschi

If the orchestra had not left the stage and the lights had not come up, the audience would have happily stayed for more. The already lengthy recital started at 7:30pm and continued till close to 10:00, but people showed little inclination to leave their seats except to stand and applaud Vivica Genaux's final encore, "Qual guerriero in campo armato." This signature piece, written by Riccardo Broschi for his brother Carlo (aka Farinelli) and included in Vivaldi's *Bajazet,* demonstrates what one might think the human voice could not achieve. Excluding perhaps Bel Canto it was not until Giacinto Scelsi's *Canti del Capricorno,* written in the 1960's, that anyone tried to push the human voice to its limit. At one point in the aria, a *melisma* written on the first vowel of "*battaglia*" continued with 16th-notes for 13 measures. If Ms. Genaux found a way to breathe during this aria it was not evident. There were no tricks here or in any of arias. She avoids using the aspirates sometimes employed by singers who can't quite get out all the written notes, and the result is uninterrupted long legatos that are crucial for the arias' success.

The evening's program consisted of short instrumental works of the Italian Baroque interspersed with arias from Vivaldi's operas. The opening Sinfonia revealed a considerably more laid-back Fabio Biondi than I've seen and heard in the past. Biondi and Europa Galante have certainly held their own in the unspoken internecine contest of Italian Baroque groups (Concerto Italiano, Venice Baroque Orchestra and Il Giardino Armonico) as to who can play the fastest. The two dominating Italian groups of the 1970's and 1980's, I Musici and Il Solisti Veneti, were well intentioned advocates for the Italian Baroque but made little attempt to distinguish their performance style from that of other periods. The result was music that was played too slowly and sounded thick and stodgy.

Most of the recent Italian groups have often gone overboard in the opposite direction. What I Musici performed in 12 minutes, Il Gardino Armonico completed in eight. Here the Vivaldi concerto for two violins did not seem rushed and was played immaculately by Biondi and group member Andrea Ragnoni. Sounding at times like Bach's own double concerto written 20 years later, this concerto's difficulties were sloughed off with an elegant panache. The Locatelli concerto grosso, a throwback to the multi-movement concerti of Legrenzi,

259

Stradella and Uccellini, received a brisk but not overly so reading of the fast movements and delicate, sensitive interpretations of the slow ones. Written a generation after Vivaldi, the violin concerto by Nardini is a delightful little gem, composed in the 1760s and played with a judicious use of vibrato by Biondi (but not by the strings): another example, perhaps, of a more mellowed Biondi.

In Vivaldi's time, it was not unusual to borrow from one's own works or steal works from other composers. Without having access to the urtext, one can never be certain who wrote what. The first aria of the evening, "Quell'usignolo," from *Farnace*, is particularly confusing with regard to its provenance. It was either written by Vivaldi as stated in the program notes, or by Giacomelli as presented in Ms. Genaux's CD "Arias for Farenelli." Regardless of who wrote it, no nightingale could sing like Ms. Genaux or cover her wide vocal range.

The high point of the evening was the aria "Come in vano" from Vivaldi's *Cantone in Utica*. This amazing piece of vocal magic is a virtual non-stop display of leaps, trills, runs and arpeggios. Ms. Genaux's voice stayed consistently steady through her amazing tessitura, reaching deep down in her chest for the low notes and smoothly running up to the higher ranges without a bit of strain.

Along with her superb voice, what remains in my head is Ms. Genaux's sparkling presentation. Not restrained by the conventions of performing in an opera, Ms. Genaux put her entire soul into each aria, swaying and shimmying as if she were given license to do whatever she felt. This joy spread contagiously through the audience, evincing Ms. Genaux's miraculous voice, Biondi's and his orchestra's top-notch skills and the remarkable creativity of Vivaldi and his contemporaries.

♪The Three Sopranos: William Christie Conducts Students from Juilliard's Historical Performance Program
Katherine Whyte, Raquel Gonzalez, Lilla Heinrich Szász (sopranos), Juilliard415, William Christie (conductor), Alice Tully Hall, Lincoln Center New York, 26.1.2012

Purcell: Excerpts from *The Fairy Queen*
Rameau: Excerpts from *Les Fêtes d'Hébé*

It is no surprise that William Christie chose excerpts from Purcell's *The Fairy Queen* to showcase students from the Juilliard School's Historical Performance program. *The Fairy Queen* is a work close to his heart. Christie's classic recording of this semi-opera in 1989 was wonderfully spirited, and last year he directed it at the Brooklyn Academy of Music to rave reviews.

To do the entire opera, Christie would have needed a chorus, a cast of about 25 characters, additional instruments and four hours of performance time. The selections performed here were based on the musicians on hand, and only in the song "Now the night is chas'd away" did they perform music that requires the additional resources of a chorus. In its place, the instruments picked up what would have been the choral *ritournelle*. Prominently absent from *The Fairy*

Queen excerpts was the ardent aria, "If love's a sweet passion."

The instrumental selections were played with an enthusiasm and professionalism that is truly delightful to hear from a group so young. These students are coming into the historically informed performance world at the right time: the instruments that were so difficult to play in the earlier days of historically informed performance are now more easily mastered. Although the trumpets used here are vented (true Baroque trumpets are without valves and vents), it is still admirable to see these students play them with such ease.

Katherine Whyte, had the right tessitura and vocal style for the Purcell arias but, I wish her voice had been strong enough for the audience to clearly hear the words. This was particularly true with the Act V plainte, "O let me ever, ever weep," one of the most moving of all of Purcell's music and similar in style to Dido's Lament, "When I am laid in earth," from *Dido and Aeneas*. After hearing Lilla Heinrich Szász in the second part of the concert, I thought that she would have had just the right "whiteness" for this aria.

Rameau is another composer high on Christie's list, and his music was represented in last year's program with Juilliard415, as well. That performance featured only instrumental music, but here vocal music was included. The chosen excerpts came from Rameau's little known opéra-ballet, *Les Fêtes D'Hébé*; Christie was involved with resurrecting the work and recorded the first complete performance in 1997.

Two very different sopranos shared the arias from this opera, Raquel González and Lilla Heinrich Szász. Ms. González certainly had a voice that could be clearly heard in the last row, but not really a voice for Rameau. Christie's recording features Sophie Daneman, Sarah Connolly and countertenor Jean-Paul Fouchécourt all of whom have voices free from more modern vocal styling. Lilla Heinrich Szász straddled the middle ground between the other two sopranos and was just right: a stronger voice than Ms. Whyte, yet correctly Baroque; a cleaner voice than Ms. González yet free of her more modern mannerisms. I will say though that Ms. Gonzales's final aria "Eclatante trompette" did match in spirit the concluding instrumental fireworks.

Christie led the students as a sympathetic and positive teacher. Many of his gestures, aside from those highlighting sections of the orchestra when needed, were instructions to play softly. It was fascinating to see how intensely he listened to the arias that did not require him to conduct (they were accompanied by the basso continuo): he sat in a chair at one end of the stage as if a member of the audience, enthusiastically congratulating the musicians upon completion. This stepping back and letting go is the sign of a teacher who truly cares for and nourishes his students. He displayed a similar attitude with his elite student group, *Le Jardin des Voix*, during their performance at BAM last year.

This yearly recital by Juilliard415 and William Christie is eagerly anticipated, and rightly so.

♪Epiphanies at a Musical Hideaway: Beethoven and Schubert at WMP Concert Hall

Montreal Chamber Music Festival, Denis Brott (cellist), Kevin Louks (piano), Afiara Quartet, WMP Concert Hall, New York, 20.1.2012

Beethoven: Sonata for Cello and Piano in A major
Schubert: Quintet in C major

The venue for last night's concert, the WMP Concert Hall, is adjacent to a repair shop for rare violins. The old-world look of their shared storefront seems out of place on a block that has over the years held hardware stores, bodegas and illegal phone stores that would unlock a cell phone for a price. Passing the storefront on my way to the subway, I was drawn to the concert schedule taped to a window above an array of instruments. Inside, what was once a commercial lobby is now a salon with chandeliers, gilded mirrors, 70 chairs and a wooden shell that holds a concert grand Bösendorfer. (It's nice to hear a piano in concert these days other than a Steinway.) In addition to raising the performers and instruments to a more visible level, the shell was also designed to improve acoustics. If there was anything less than perfect in this performance it was that the players did not compensate for the smaller acoustical space. Particularly in the Schubert, the five musicians almost sounded like an orchestra.

But what an orchestra! Every note was played to perfection, brimming with emotion, plus a performance of Schubert's Adagio that made me feel this has to be the saddest, most doleful music ever written, almost too painful to hear. I had forgotten how ravishing a work this is. Having terminally scratched my old Columbia Masterworks LP performance with Isaac Stern and Pablo Casals and torn to shreds the green cover with use, I knew every single note but also realized last night how I was familiar with just this one particular performance, recorded at the Prades Festival in 1954. I've heard the Quintet played over the years, but this was the first time I truly listened to it since I was a teenager.

The moments of sheer transcendent beauty abounded from both the music and the musicians. The brief and soft introductory motif, played once by the violinist and repeated by the cello, leads with only a measure or two of notice into an agitated first theme with the cello continuing obliviously to play the opening motif. The second theme takes advantage of the second cello to play along with the first in a haunting duet.
The development section of this first movement shows Schubert using dissonance that would rarely be heard again until the end of the century. Chords shriek as if in pain. After several hesitant repetitions of the opening theme convinced the listener that each iteration is the beginning of the recapitulation, it does finally come back, leading to the movement's two ominous final chords, one *ff* and the other marked *p*.

The Adagio consists of the simplest group, two dotted figures and a slur with a grace note. Schubert knew how to squeeze from this phrase every possible melodic and harmonic element. First violinist Yuri Cho played as if the music was playing her, so possessed did she seem with Schubert's spirit. A performance like this adds credence to the view that Schubert knew his life was nearing its end, that this last great masterpiece, written the year he died, would be one to define his legacy.

The bouncy third movement leads the listener to think that here at least is music that is not crying *de profundis*. Strongly accented double-stops and long runs of quavers in the light-colored key of C major fool us into believing all is well until the trio brings us back into the world of the Adagio. The scherzo form, based on the older minuet, always has as its contrasting central section a trio. Traditionally it is a light-hearted, often rustic dance, but not here where it vies with the Andante con poco mosso from the B-flat Trio as to which is the most heart-rending.

Whether the final movement is upbeat or a wild Totentanz is debatable. Both the Casals recording and the performance by the Afiara Quartet treat it successfully as high drama. The intensity of the Afiara's playing was palpable, and I found the lead-in to the coda and the coda itself enthralling.

None of the above should take away from the exceptional opening performance by cellist Denis Brott and pianist Kevin Louks of Beethoven's Sonata for Cello and Piano. With the exception of one brief moment where the naturally big-sounding Bösendorfer overpowered the cellist, the players were in perfect accord.

Mr. Brott prefaced the work with a reading of Beethoven's "Immortal Beloved" letter. Half the letter was recited before the first movement and the other half before the third. Sensitive to every nuance, both players demonstrated the emotional connection of the Sonata to Beethoven's state of mind at the time.

It wasn't just the technical prowess that made the evening so special. Virtuosity is simply a given—commitment of one's entire being to the music is not.

♫*Mehta and Bruckner: A Triumphal Reunion with the New York Philharmonic*

New York Philharmonic Orchestra, Zubin Mehta (conductor), Avery Fisher Hall, Lincoln Center, New York, 12.1.2012

Bruckner: Symphony No. 8 in C minor

Poor Bruckner: unappreciated until his final years, and even then facing constant barbs from critics and bewilderment from conductors. The intended conductor of the premiere of the Eighth Symphony bowed out, admitting that he found the work incomprehensible. The influential reviewer and Bruckner's (as well as Wagner's) perennial nemesis, Eduard Hanslick, called the Eighth "interesting in detail but strange as a whole and even repugnant." He went on to say that "the listener is simply crushed under the sheer weight and monotony of this interminable lamentation." More than 100 years later, comments like those still abound: friends and colleagues find it incomprehensible that anyone would voluntarily sit through well over an hour of "dismal long-windedness" (Hanslick again).

No one finds it strange if a gathering of Mahlerians make a pilgrimage to Mahler's birthplace, yet Brucknerians who do the same are looked on as eccentric bumpkins: words used to describe the composer himself. In addition to complaints about the insufferable length of Bruckner's symphonies are the cavils about his endless repetitions, yet Schubert's D major piano sonata which has over 60 iterations of the opening six chords is considered a masterpiece. Philip Glass's compositions are nearly synonymous with the word repetition, yet his music is continually in demand. Perhaps Bruckner would not have been as poorly received today if he had died at 31 or driven a taxi before becoming a great composer. Many composers are odd in some way: Gesualdo, murdering his wife and her lover; Beethoven living with chamber pots all about; or Scriabin writing music that would hasten and serve as the accompaniment to the end of the world. By comparison, Bruckner was merely a rustic rube or an idiot savant.

We're lucky that so many conductors have gone beyond these prejudices and been captured by the beauty of Bruckner's symphonies. Eugen Jochum, Gunter Wand, Herbert von Karajan, Wilhelm Furtwangler and Sergiu Celibidache, just to name some conductors from the recent past, were all great Brucknerians. Zubin Mehta has talked about breaking down in tears upon his first hearing of the Adagio of the Eighth Symphony.

At this performance, Mehta's usual conducting style was somewhat constricted. There was hesitancy in his gesturing to the sections of the orchestra which dampened and dulled some of the moments when sharp accents were needed. The monumental crescendos at their highest peaks were at times a bit too jagged and raw. Some brief woodwind solos were buried by the strings, but the strings did a fine job sustaining the symphony's underlying pulse, mainly through long stretches of tremolos. There was no lack of technical confidence on the part of the instrumentalists (aside from a few rough spots from the horns), and the orchestra seemed both passionate about the music and committed to their one-time leader. It was clear that Mehta too felt a strong affinity with the musicians. Conducting without a score, he literally had nothing between himself, the music and the players. In contrast with Alan Gilbert's performance of the Second Symphony, there was no question that Mehta understood how the correct shaping of each element is like fitting a piece in a huge puzzle. The completed puzzle revealed the monumental spirituality of Bruckner's last completed symphony.

♫Haydn, Schubert and Ravel Open New York Philharmonic Spring Season

Anne Sofie von Otter (mezzo-soprano), New York Philharmonic Orchestra, Alan Gilbert (Conductor), Avery Fisher Hall, Lincoln Center, New York, 28.12.2011

Haydn: Symphony No. 88 in G major
Schubert: Six Orchestrated Songs
Ravel: *Ma Mère l'Oye, La Valse*

Haydn's Symphony No. 88 falls into that nether space between the Paris

Symphonies (82-87) and the London Symphonies (92-104). Somewhat of a hybrid work, it reveals elements of Haydn's early- and middle-period styles while looking forward to the symphonies that follow. In some respects, it's an early run-through of the popular "Surprise Symphony" No. 94: both are written in the same key, have the same instrumentation (except for doublings of the flute and oboes in the 88th) and surprise us with a totally unexpected dynamic jump from *pp* to *ff* with *sforzando* marked on the three beats. What is also unusual about this symphony is that both the first and second movements are each driven by only one theme. Haydn was such a master at this point in his career that he could take any motif and vary it enough to sustain interest in the entire movement.

However, there was a stodginess in the Philharmonic's playing of this work that was resistant to Gilbert's attempts to liven it up. Almost dancing at times, Gilbert was clearly looking for a spikiness in the heavily accented first movement. This was true as well in the musette-like trio of the third movement with its asymmetrical accents that lacked the punch of Haydn's notated *fortzandos*. If I were more of a mystic I would almost think that the spirit of Leonard Bernstein (who recorded this symphony with the NYPO in 1963) conducted the final movement. Both conductors repressed the bouncing rhythms of the movement, opting instead for an old-fashioned smoothness in the strings.

The unusual orchestral transcriptions of several of Schubert's popular songs brought to mind the vocal music of Mahler. Most were by Max Reger, a prolific composer, who published dozens of his own waltzes, songs and fantasies as well as transcriptions of works by Bach, Beethoven and Schubert. These scores were meant for home use or, in this case, small orchestras. He specifically avoided a heavy hand in the transcriptions of these songs, aiming for pieces "so simple that any orchestra can play them at sight." He did accomplish his goal: the orchestration shimmers and glitters, coloring the singing but never drowning it. That these Schubert works are familiar was confirmed by the gentleman in back of me who, several notes into "The Trout" stated loudly "I know this song and I like it." Anne Sofie von Otter has an obvious affinity for these pieces and sang them all regally, with authority and confidence. Only in "To Sylvia" could one question her dramatic gestures: she seemed to be expressing irony while singing words that do not appear to be ironic at all.

I'm not the best critic to write about the performance of Ravel's *Ma Mère l'Oye* ballet suite: I've never found him of much interest except for his String Quartet. Perhaps this music is pleasant enough when used to accompany a ballet, but not having dancers to distract me, I found the 30 minutes insufferable. Certainly, it made his *Boléro* seem tolerable by comparison. *La Valse* was thematically catchy and rich in color, if somewhat clichéd in its deconstruction of the waltz. One only has to listen to Mahler's many symphonic waltzes to understand the decadence inherent in this dance form.

♪*Bach and Messiaen: Varieties of Religious Experience*
Atlanta Symphony Orchestra Chamber Chorus, Norman Mackenzie (director), Orchestra of St. Luke's, Robert Spano (conductor), Carnegie Hall,

New York, 15.12.2011

Bach: Brandenburg Concerto No. 3 in G major
Messiaen: *Trois petites liturgies de la Présence Divine*
Bach: Magnificat in D major

Bach and Messiaen represent two opposite types of composers of religious music. Both shared the belief that they were writing their music for the glory of God alone. In fact, Bach himself ended his compositions with the abbreviation SDG, *Soli Deo Gloria.*

Bach's religious music, though, is external, public and communal. It proselytizes and threatens damnation to the unbeliever. It demands that we go through the trials of life "weeping, wailing, worrying and fearing" (Cantata No. 12). It also asks us to "ring out songs, resound strings for the blessed time when God will prepare our souls to be his temple" (Cantata No .190). His work follows Luther's call for music to be a way of bringing people together to participate in the liturgy.

On the other hand, Messiaen's music expresses the composer's personal religious beliefs and inner struggles. It too resounds with the glory of God, but this God is a private one. Messiaen sings praises not only to God but also to his manifestations: his fascination with bird songs resulted in the seven books of *Catalogue d'oiseaux* for piano. Messiaen picks up on the tradition of the French sacred music of Charpentier and Couperin. The solitary voices of their *Leçons de Ténèbres* have a strong emotional connection to Messiaien's masterpieces for piano, *Les Visions de l'Amen* written just before and *Vingt regards sur l'enfant-Jésus* written just after the work performed here.

The Brandenberg Concerto No. 3 served as a prelude to the religious music. It was played by members of the Orchestra of St. Luke's without a conductor and they might have fared better with one. There were both articulation and balancing problems. The basso continuo line lacked clarity, and it was difficult to distinguish the orchestra (ripieno) from the soloists. The two half-note movement, often stretched out with a leading improvisation by the continuo, provided no sense of transition to the last movement. Only in the final movement was there any feeling of coherence.

Messiaen's *Trois petites liturgies de la Présence Divine* is a work that one would hardly think could stir up controversy. Yet the work's uncertain religiosity and Messiaen's own explanation that was handed out to the audience led to what was called "Le Cas Messiaen." One critic wrote about this most harmless work as being "of tinsel, false magnificence and pseudo-mysticism…with dirty nails and clammy hands with bloated complexion and unhealthy flab, replete with noxious matter, looking about anxiously like an angel wearing lipstick." The libretto itself is an odd mixture of Biblical quotations, the writings of St. Thomas Aquinas and Thomas à Kempis and Messiaen's own religious musings. The instruments added to the orchestra, particularly the ondes martenot, also became a controversial issue for more conservative music critics who questioned whether it was an appropriate instrument for a religious work. Other unusual instruments included celesta and vibraphone.

Robert Spano handled this diverse group with commanding authority. Not quite as musically complex as other orchestral works of Messiaen and still mostly tonal, the music and singing go from almost near-silence to *Carmina Burana*-like vocal raucousness. The piano part written for his future wife, Yvonne Loriod, dominated the other highlighted instruments. The celesta mostly doubled the piano part, and the ondes martenot's role was, thankfully, minor. The sounds generated by this instrument's electronic innards must have sounded other-worldly at the time, but now it seems almost comical, as if played as background music for a Captain Video TV episode or a grade-B 1950's sci-fi movie.

The concluding work in this concert was Bach's *Magnificat*. Spano made no pretensions of performing it in early music style. But it was a fine performance by any standard. Only the mezzo-soprano, Sasha Cooke, strained as soloist in "Et Exultavit," but she improved considerably in "Esurientes." The final movement, the Gloria Patri, was as all-out rousing and vibrant as any performance I can remember.

♪*Metropolitan Opera Presents World Premiere of a Baroque Pastiche*

Metropolitan Opera Orchestra and Chorus, William Christie (conductor), Metropolitan Opera, New York, 31.12.2011

The Enchanted Island

[These comments are based on a viewing of the final dress rehearsal.]

The Metropolitan Opera, rarely at the forefront with productions of new operas, has chosen to present an opera that is both new and old. Following the precedent of composers of the 18th century, who recycled their own music as well as music of their contemporaries, the production team has taken music from the Baroque composers Handel, Vivaldi, Rameau, Purcell, Campra, Rebel, Ferrandini and Leclair. Although some of the names listed here are familiar, none of their music is. It might have been easier to include more familiar music, but not doing so speaks to the integrity of the production. The libretto, written in English by Jeremy Sams, closely reflects the sensibility of the composers of the original music: the common weaknesses found in both gods and men, the persistence of love (and lust), the role of chance and change, the demands made on those at the top and the bottom of the social hierarchy, the mutability of sexual attraction and the need for forgiveness. The libretto is sometimes successful in its attempts to be funny in a topical way and clever in the use of contemporary jargon, but not so successful at other times when even the cast seems to know that their lines are falling flat.

What makes this production so special and worthy of attending live or in

HD is the participation of some of the best performers of Baroque music today. William Christie's involvement alone is an imprimatur of authenticity and high quality. The cast is a Baroque opera lover's dream: the soloists are all familiar with Baroque performance style and sing the difficult music with ease. Only Placido Domingo's voice lacks early music styling, but this is made up for by his acting: his appearance as the god Neptune adds a sense of camp in a scene reminiscent of Busby Berkeley spectacles. The staging is wildly creative in its use of both traditional operatic elements and modern computerized visual effects.

Perhaps in the future the Met will look back more often to the past and revive other forgotten masterpieces such as Leclair's sole opera, *Scylla and Glaucus*, or Vivaldi's *Bajazet*. Lully, whose music is not included in this pastiche, is eminently eligible for revival following the successful performance this year of *Atys* at the Brooklyn Academy of Music. Several operas by Lully have been produced elsewhere but have not made their appearance in New York: *Thésée* and *Psyché* at the Boston Early Music Festival; *Bellérophon*, *Roland* and *Proserpine* among others in French productions by Christophe Rousset and Hervé Niquet.

♪Mahler's 10th: Not Perfect Enough for Mahler Himself

New York Philharmonic Orchestra, Daniel Harding (conductor), Avery Fischer Hall, Lincoln Center, New York City, 1.12.2011

Mahler: Symphony No. 10 ("Cooke III" version)

So much has been said and written about Mahler's unfinished symphony and its completion by various parties that I won't add to the catalogue. A history of both the symphony and its recordings can be found on our parent site, MusicWeb International. If the size of that discography seems excessively long (almost 10,000 words), think what its length would be if it included every recording made since the article's publication in 2000.

The decision to complete a work left unfinished at a composer's death should be based on knowledge of the composer's intentions and relationship to the score. Undoubtedly, had Mahler lived longer he would have completed this symphony. We don't know exactly why Schubert did not complete his "unfinished" symphony, but we do know he lived for another seven years. No one has completed that score in a way convincing enough to serve as the standard performing edition (as opposed to, say, Franz Xaver Süssmayr whose completion of Mozart's Requiem is generally considered definitive). Some works are left unfinished because the composers felt there was no chance of them ever being performed. And then there is Scriabin's *Mysterium*, which has its own set of problems: the composer's instructions require the symphony to be played for seven days when, upon completion, the world will end and start up again with a race of supermen.

Daniel Harding has made Mahler's Symphony No. 10 his signature work, and recorded it to rave reviews on the Deutsche Grammophon label. His performance here, while not quite on the level of his recording with the Vienna Philharmonic, revealed a vision of the work that would seem to be beyond the ken of someone so young. Like all Mahler, the 10th requires a conductor with enough self-assurance to harness the massive resources needed to successfully tame the beast. This job is made even more difficult since so much of the music is ersatz Mahler. It's a major accomplishment to present a coherent performance of the two movements assumed to be nearly finished before his death, the first and the third. The second and fourth movements, which are relatively short by Mahler's standards, are less problematic because of their simpler structure. But the fifth movement, which is about as long as the previous three movements combined, is a real challenge.

Did Harding convince us in this final movement that we were listening to anything reasonably close to what Mahler had intended, or for that matter to music that could be considered a great work of art? Would this movement, if it were not associated with Mahler, stand on its own? I think not. Was this at least listenable? Yes, it was colorfully orchestrated, with a few brief turns where you could hear the distant echoes of the composer and even of other composers such as Bruckner.

Mr. Harding and the New York Philharmonic made a valiant attempt to stamp Mahler's name on every note played, but the final judgment was made by Mahler himself when he wrote, "All that is not perfect down to the smallest detail is doomed to perish."

♫The Long Road to Carnegie Hall: Christian Zacharias' Debut Recital

Christian Zacharias (piano), Carnegie Hall, New York, 13.12.2011

C. P. E. Bach: Sonata in A minor, Rondo in C minor
Brahms: *Klavierstücke*
Beethoven: Sonata No. 31 in A-flat major
Schubert: Sonata in D major

What piqued my interest most about this program was Christian Zacharias' decision to include C. P. E. Bach in his debut recital at Carnegie Hall. His four recordings of Scarlatti speak for his talent and passion for Baroque keyboard music. Would his sensitivity carry over to a composer who in many ways is the opposite of Scarlatti? Where Scarlatti's music is truly "baroque" in its boldness, wild virtuosity and theatrical flair, C. P. E. Bach, the second eldest son of Johann Sebastian Bach, was looking for a way to be emotionally expressive in a controlled way. The pianoforte and clavichord were his instruments of choice. Most of Scarlatti's music was for the harpsichord (or very early pianoforte) where, unless he was playing a double manual instrument, the music could be fast and slow but not loud and soft (*piano* and *forte*). For the most part, C. P. E. avoided writing contrapuntally, often replacing the bass with a simple harmonic line: a few of the same notes played repeatedly. Even if he had wanted to follow in his father's footsteps he knew that to survive as a musician he had to be shrewd. He would have to adhere to the style of the day (or create the style of the day) or suffer the fate of his older brother, Wilhelm Friedemann, stigmatized for life as old-fashioned.

How does one successfully perform on a piano works that were written for an instrument which produces sounds on the level of a lute or non-amplified guitar? This goes way beyond the debate as to whether music written for harpsichord should be played on a piano: Glenn Gould put that question to bed 50 years ago. Very few pianists have succeeded on the piano with C. P. E. Bach. Mikail Pletnev's show-off style and overemphasis of the composer's manic moments is not very appealing. Danny Driver's CD is warmer than Pletnev's but lacks the C. P. E. spark. Glenn Gould has it right in one of his two recordings of C. P. E.'s sonatas.

Zacharias was as close to being on the mark as anyone I've heard playing C. P. E. Bach on piano. Applying a light and subtle touch to the keyboard and a limited but effective use of the foot pedals, he made the concert hall feel as if it had shrunk to the right size. In a style both dispassionate yet committed, he escaped the temptation to exaggerate the sudden changes in dynamics and bizarre key modulations. What often seems crazy in C. P. E.'s scores sounded perfectly reasonable here. The Rondo's surprise ending with that "missing" note had a stronger effect than in performances where the entire work is played wildly.

Zacharias succeeded where others have failed due to his good sense of the balance between playing to be heard and playing too loud; somehow this pianist knew how to work with the magical acoustics of Carnegie Hall. That is quite an accomplishment for someone performing here in his first recital.

However, his performance of Brahms seemed too controlled and not passionate enough. An intermezzo is one of those musical appellations like prelude, impromptu or interlude that could mean pretty much anything, from slow to fast, loud to soft, tender to dramatic. The three intermezzi and one rhapsody (another generic musical phrase) did not come to life in this performance, never quite reaching Brahms' complex and idiosyncratic music world.

His Beethoven fared somewhat better. Zacharias played in a cooler style than one is used to hearing these days, and his sensible phrasing and tempered use of rubato clearly delineated the complex lines of this penultimate sonata. He was at the top of his form in the final movement's ending fugue, reveling in the counterpoint.

Of all the major composers in the classical period, I've always found Schubert to be the one least capable of writing a decent development section in sonata form. Sometimes, when the music is catchy, as it is in the Symphony No. 9 or the C major Quintet, it doesn't really matter: one is so enthralled with the music that one can suspend critical acumen. The D major sonata is not one of them. In the first movement of the sonata, the development section simply repeats the same theme with minimal variations; I counted nearly 60 iterations of the opening six chords. If one listens to the openings of the first three movements, they are nearly indistinguishable from one another. As for the rondo, the main theme is cute in the way Carl Czerny's superficial exercises or Clementi's piano music can be. This sonata, written while Schubert enjoyed a rare happy vacation outside Vienna, makes us appreciate that he didn't vacation more often: he was most profound when he was the least content.

[Note: The two encores, the rarely heard Scarlatti K.55 and the delightful Mozart Rondo K.485, were exceptionally well-played.]

♪Not Your Usual School Recital: Juilliard Students Show What They've Learned

Juilliard 415, Monica Huggett (leader and violin), Peter Jay Sharp Theater, Juilliard School of Music, Lincoln Center, New York City, 2.12.2011

Handel: Concerto No. 1 in B-flat major, Concerto No. 2 in B-flat major, Concerto No. 6 in D major, Concerto No. 3 in G major, Concerto No. 4 in F major, Concerto No. 5 in D minor
Telemann: Quartet in D minor for Two Flutes, Bassoon, and Basso continuo

Admirers of Baroque music know that the name Monica Huggett on a concert's program notes is a guarantee that what they will be hearing will be of the highest quality. This is true whether she performs in a recital, conducts a student orchestra or is part of a chamber music group like the faculty-staffed Juilliard Baroque. The concert presented here was, as expected, a great success: Ms. Huggett led students of the Historical Performance Department in a charming program of Baroque music including the lesser- known of Handel's two concerto grosso sets, the Opus No. 3.

It's hard not to be impressed with the musical achievement of this group (and the exceptional training they must be receiving from the faculty). Several students perform on a level that would qualify them to join a professional Baroque orchestra. This accomplishment is made even more astonishing by the fact that they are playing on original, or copies of original, instruments with none of the modern keys added to make instruments like the flute and oboe easier to play. The stringed instruments and their bows are different enough from the ones on which they were trained to play to require students to forget what has been drummed into them since their first music lessons: the bows are held differently, the strings tuned differently and vibrato is to be avoided. As for the brass instruments, well, just forget everything you've been taught, such as using your fingers to play the instrument.

Like most of the instrumental music published by Handel, the Opus 3 set of six concerti grossi was written to be played by amateur musicians. Amateurs were much closer then to what in our day would be considered professionals. In Handel's time any player(s) who excelled would take the more virtuosic obbligato part of the score, while the "amateurs" would be part of the orchestral section (ripieno). Each concerto in the set highlighted one or more instruments. The

271

Concerto No. 1's solo instruments are the violin and oboe with the most difficult playing reserved for Ms. Huggett's violin. Kristin Olsin's oboe playing in this concerto was fluid in the slow movements, pointed and rhythmic in the faster ones. Outstanding string playing dominated the first movement of the Concerto No. 2, while the oboe and bassoon carried most of the other movements. The fourth movement, strongly resembling Handel's opening movement of his Opus 1, No. 11 flute sonata, leads into an oboe dominated gavotte, reminiscent of Lully's dance pieces.

Other highlights of this performance included the flute playing of Antonio Campillo Santos and the sharp-shooting 16th-note runs by violinist Nanae Iwata in the Concerto No. 3. In the Concerto No. 6 only two movements are printed in the original edition, but it is possible that the orphan overture HWV 327 might have served as the brief segue to the final Allegro and as a way to restore the concerto to its Fast-Short-Fast state. Performed here by Ms. Huggett and flutist Christopher Matthews, the back and forth dialog between these two instruments was short but ravishing. The masterful playing of the Concerto No. 4 with its wonderful Lullian overture was for me the epitome of the evening. Only in the difficult Concerto No. 5 did the group seem somewhat under-rehearsed and unable to catch their breath in Ms. Huggett's exceedingly fast race to the end.

It is a major accomplishment that the Historical Performance division of the Juilliard has succeeded so well with a student program that is, after all, only in its third year.

♫An Italian in Egypt: Rossini's Rarely Heard Moïse et Pharaon

The Collegiate Chorale, American Symphony Orchestra, James Bagwell (conductor), Carnegie Hall, New York, 30.11.2011

Rossini: *Moïse et Pharaon*
Concert Version

The Collegiate Chorale's eclectic programs, ranging from a revival of a Kurt Weill musical to Handel's *Israel in Egypt*, have always been presented with enthusiasm and gusto. These events require massive resources: a symphony orchestra, soloists and a chorus of two-hundred and fifty singers. As in the past, *Moïse et Pharaon* was a one-time performance, but in the best of all possible worlds, a successful production like this one should be offered again to those who hear about it later through the press and the internet.

The score of this opera has been handed down in an 1827 version, the result of Rossini bowing to the exigencies of evolving tastes, political and financial realities, and the language of the country in which he was residing. The source for *Moïse et Pharaon* was his earlier opera *Mosè in Egitto*. The new libretto, now in French, was redesigned by eliding, reshuffling and augmenting that work to make it more in keeping with changing French taste.

There is a considerable disconnect, most noticeably in the first and second acts, between the music and the text. The overture is classic Rossini with his signature coda consisting of rapidly accelerating crescendos, which seems an inappropriate lead-in to a story whose central theme is religious persecution. The first two acts were particularly static with much proselytizing and goings back and forth on whose god(s) are the true gods. As the synopsis in *Playbill* ironically states, "It takes another three acts to let the people go." The librettists must have known that without the addition of some character development, the work would end up being knocked down a step from an opera to an oratorio.

What was only partially developed in the first half of the opera becomes the main theme of the second half, a story that persists to the end of the opera: the love between Moses' niece Anaï and the Pharaoh's son becomes the central subject of the final two acts. Other singers come on stage to augment the cast and the added story line puts a face on the characters who were previously only sketched out. The music changes at the beginning of Act III with an overture of a more serious and complex nature than the earlier two, and orchestra and chorus seemed connected now that drama and serious music had taken central stage. Given Rossini's ability at orchestral coloring, it is surprising that he didn't take advantage of musically voicing the plagues, instead of simply mentioning that they were wreaked upon the Egyptians. It has always been the highlight of Handel's telling of the same story (minus the lover's tale) in his oratorio, *Israel in Egypt*.

There were several miscues and flubs by the orchestra, mainly in Acts I and II. The musicians were not fully in rapport with one another until after the intermission. If there was a halftime pep talk by the conductor, it would explain the better playing in the second half. The singers ranged from adequate to superb. James Morris was an ideal choice in the role of Moïse, his voice convincing in its authority. Kyle Ketelsen couldn't reasonably compete with Morris, but sang the role of Pharaon confidently. Marina Rebeka as the emotionally torn Anaï fared well with most of the more difficult bel canto arias, but was unquestionably one-upped by the glorious voice of Angela Meade. The most disappointing part of the evening was the very minor role Miss Meade had in the production; it was not surprising that her profile in *Playbill* states she has won 53 competitions. Special mention should also be given to Eric Cutler whose role as Aménophis was bold and undaunted.

For Rossini-ites, the big surprise of the evening was the opera's *pianissimo* ending. It would be tricky to try and outdo musically the parting of the sea and the drowning of the Egyptians, but all the same there was a slight letdown in not getting the big Rossini coda.

♫ *An All-Around Musician: Jeffrey Kahane Conducts and Performs*
Sheryl Staples (violin), Liang Wang (oboe), New York Philharmonic Orchestra, Jeffrey Kahane (conductor, harpsichord, piano), Avery Fisher Hall, Lincoln Center, New York, 22.11.2011

Bach: Concerto in D minor for Oboe, Violin and Strings
Mozart: Symphony No. 33 in B-flat major
Beethoven: Piano Concerto No.1 in C major

Jeffrey Kahane has succeeded where others have failed in leading members of the New York Philharmonic in a spirited concert of music that spans the 18th century from Bach to Mozart to Beethoven. In a previous concert, Alan Gilbert led and soloed with Frank Peter Zimmerman in Bach's Concerto in D minor, a work similar in style and substance to the D minor Concerto for Oboe and Violin performed here. Gilbert actually used a smaller ensemble of 16 players to Kahane's 20, but made little attempt to moderate the vibrato or temper the more Romantic tendencies of the orchestra. The result was a performance that was muddy at times and seemed to be working against the acoustics of the hall. (The New York Philharmonic, aware of the problem with performing early music, hangs large pods from the ceiling during its Mostly Mozart Festivals.)

Kahane, conducting from the harpsichord as part of the basso continuo section of the orchestra, clearly had an understanding of what was required to brighten and enliven the concerto, and the orchestra played crisply, with a minimum of vibrato. The soloists, Sheryl Staples and Liang Wang, were generally well-balanced with the violin occasionally overpowering the oboe. The second movement marked Adagio is in all respects a *Siciliano* similar in style to the second movement *Siciliano* of the keyboard concerto BWV 1053; both pieces are in 12/8 time and start out with pizzicati played by the violins and violas, lulled along by a mellifluous rocking motion. Echoing each other, the two soloists other gave a sensitive and expressive turn to this movement and the piece concluded with a lively Allegro.

The next work, Mozart's Symphony No. 33, brought a few more instruments on the stage but kept the harpsichord. This wasn't because Mozart included the instrument in the score, but based on historic information, he often improvised on one when a keyboard concerto preceded a work without a keyboard. I'm not sure if Kahane was following the bass line, as he would for earlier works where the keyboard is part of the basso continuo section, because whatever he was playing was totally drowned out by the orchestra. The famous Jupiter theme, as mentioned in the program notes, suddenly appears out of nowhere in the development section. This four-note theme, the basis of the last movement of Symphony No. 41, is also the theme of Symphony No. 25.

Kahane might have had difficulty conducting while playing the harpsichord if he didn't have the score on an iPad. I've seen the device used by a pianist who turned pages with two wireless buttons next to his piano pedals, but this was the first time I'd seen it used by a conductor. For the pianist at the earlier concert, the iPad was positioned horizontally, but for Kahane the score was positioned vertically. (I can see this device being used for a Bach or Mozart score, but I'm not sure if a Mahler symphony could be rendered legibly on the screen.)

No iPad was needed for the Beethoven. Applying a light and slightly *détaché* touch to the keyboard, Kahane interpreted this early work as looking backwards to Mozart rather than forward to Beethoven's own later works. The cadenzas were stunning examples of virtuosity with substance. The first-movement cadenza was written by Beethoven, but the one in the last movement was Kahane's transcription of Beethoven's own cadenza. This was a masterly rendition that took some techniques from the early music stylebook but never sounded too small or thin. It would be hard to say in which capacity Kahane excelled more: a conductor and as a pianist he is altogether one great musician.

♪Gardiner and Toscanini: Beethoven Comes First
Orchestre Révolutionnaire et Romantique, Sir John Eliot Gardiner (conductor), Carnegie Hall, New York, 16.11.2011

Beethoven: Overture to *Egmont*, Symphony No. 7 in A major, Symphony No. 5 in C minor

Midway through Sir John Eliot Gardiner's elemental performance of Beethoven, I had a sense of déja vu. I was experiencing again the extraordinary emotions that I had felt listening to these Beethoven symphonies for the first time. Those recordings by Toscanini and the NBC Symphony Orchestra from the 1950s and the symphonies played here are surprisingly similar in style: raw, taut, driven and, at times, even frenzied. The timpani were rifle shots, the violins strained to the point of near dissonance, the brass sounded calls for help, and the bass strings rumbled like an imminent earthquake. Yet how different the conductors and orchestras are: Toscanini, with one foot still in the 19th century, was a stern, temperamental and demanding Maestro, bred in the Italian operatic school where the conductor was the unquestioned authority. Gardiner is a product of the early music movement, a scholar and even-tempered conductor who is known mostly for his energetic Bach cantata cycle and revivals of French and English Baroque composers.

Toscanini's orchestra used modern instruments, revised scores and techniques out of the late 19th and early 20th centuries (not greatly different from the symphony orchestras of today). Gardiner's orchestras use original (or copies of original) instruments of the period, valveless brass, Baroque tympani and wooden winds. The strings produce minimum vibrato, as do singers and choruses.

What brings these two opposite musicians together is their demand that the composer's music is what should be performed, his intentions followed to the best of one's ability. For Toscanini, conducting wasn't an excuse to impose one's own interpretation on the score. If Beethoven gave metronome markings considerably faster than what would seem plausible, one could assume Beethoven knew better than a conductor how the piece should be played. If, as in early music, the original source has no annotation at all, then a conductor such as Gardiner needs to make his decision based on historical support. Both Toscanini and Gardiner aimed for clarity above all else, a return to a conducting style that allows the audience to clearly distinguish an oboe from a flute, a trumpet from a trombone.

Even more so than Toscanini, Gardiner is able to lead his orchestra from the softest pianissimos to the most chilling fortes. From the redoubtable oboist who was as close to a soloist as any other member of the orchestra to the fearless trumpeter dependent on his ability to use mouth and lips instead of fingers to produce the required notes, every instrumentalist is a virtuoso in his or her own right.

The dominating feature of each piece in this performance was its unrelenting pulse. In some ways, Beethoven's bass line acted as it would in earlier music, serving as the unremitting ground upon which the main symphonic line is based. There was always a sense of an inexorable moving forward as if slowing down would cause the whole work to collapse. This is not an easy thing to do, and Gardiner accomplished it with great finesse. In doing so he was dancing on the edge of cacophony. One misfired trumpet call or horn volley and these great symphonies would have gone over the edge into bombast. To everyone's delight this never happened: the audience's response was as loud as the final notes of the Fifth Symphony.

♪ *Daniel Taylor and Deborah York Perform Handel to Perfection*
Arias and Love Duets: The Theatre of Early Music, Deborah York (soprano), Daniel Taylor (conductor, countertenor), Weill Recital Hall, Carnegie Hall, New York, 15.11.2011

Handel: Passacaglia for Violin and Viola, from Suite No. 7 in G minor
Excerpts from *Rinaldo, Tolomeo, Giulio Cesare, Rodelinda*

While doing some research on the arias performed here, I thought that the roles and voice ranges did not seem to coincide. My problem was that I was confusing Handel's *Rodelinda* with *Rinaldo*. This mistake is not difficult to make since there are also operas written by Handel named *Radamisto, Rodrigo* and *Riccardo Primo*. (I won't go into the As.) Depending on whether the 1711 or 1731 version of *Rinaldo* is performed, various arias are included or not. It is not uncommon to see the role of Rinaldo played by a soprano, or a contralto playing Bertario in *Rodelinda*. To add to the confusion, at this performance the arias were not sung in strict program order.

These problems might bother a reviewer, but all the listener heard was glorious singing, supported by a committed group of instrumentalists. Cynthia Roberts was superb in the role of first violinist, playing with flare and with an awesome technique. The other instrumentalists were also right on with every note, including David Jacques who played the Baroque guitar and not the lute as stated in the program.

Although the program notes indicated that the opening work, a "Passacaglia" from Handel's seventh suite for keyboard, was a late 19th-century transcription for violin and viola by John Halvorsen, this was not the piece played here. Halvorsen's score is filled with notations on how to play each note; aside from a metronome marking and tempis described as molto energico, allegro con fuoco and più mosso, for example, there are spicattis,
ponticelli and flautati. The urtext of Handel's score has no markings at all. I'm not sure what the group was playing, but it was far closer to what Handel wrote than to Halverson's transcription.

The duet that followed, "Scherzano sul tuo volto" from *Rinaldo,* had the two singers' voices intertwining and crisscrossing each other in a vocal range that made one question who was the fiancée and who the fiancé. Later in the concert we heard Daniel Taylor in full voice, but here he clearly held back, letting Deborah York's voice dominate the duet.

Similarly, "Cara Sposa," the best known piece on this program, was touchingly sung by Mr. Taylor. He has an angelic demeanor which well suits songs of lamentation, and he performed this one effortlessly. "Bel Piacere," sung by Ms. York, uses a technique common to Vivaldi: after a brief opening ritornello, the first violin doubles the soloist note for note, stopping only for the instrumental ritornellos. The effect is quite moving, with the violin creating a birdsong-like accompaniment to the singer's voice. "Se il cor ti perde," a duet from Handel's *Tolemeo,* is very similar in style to "Schezano sul tuo volo." Written in the key of F-sharp minor, both duets weave the voices in, out and around each other: the harmonizing is ethereal and almost other-worldly.

The second half of the program opened with the overture to *Giulio Cesare,* which is an almost perfect example of a true Lullian overture. The only clue that it's by Handel is the length of the fugal middle theme: Lully motifs are always just a few notes, while Handel's run over several measures. Ms. Roberts and her group put so much spirit into their performance that it seemed as if a full orchestra was on stage. "Tu la mia stella sei" followed, a difficult aria that York tossed off with ease, reaching up to the highest vocal register without undue strain or thinning out.

The group returned to *Rodelinda* and a more familiar aria performed by Daniel Taylor: "Dove sei," a lament made poignantly touching by Taylor's attention to each word and meaningful but not overly-emotional gestures. This led into a wonderful and difficult aria, "Se pieta di me non senti" from *Giulio Cesare.* Built on a chromatically descending triplet played repeatedly through the entire piece, with Ms. York's impassioned voice doubled or echoed by the strings, this was certainly the most moving aria in the concert, and the applause that followed was appropriately long.

Taylor then took the stage and graciously thanked the New York audience for giving him the opportunity to play in Carnegie Hall. It was thrilling to him, but even more so to his mother, who was in the audience. He stated that his natural voice was that of a baritone and that he was able to use this range in this next aria, "Domero la tua fierezza." Loosening his ponytail as he took on the role of the mad Tolomeo, he tackled this wild aria with all its jumping notes and wide intervals. If there was any question whether this angelic countertenor could belt out dramatic arias, it was answered here. His exaggerated gestures and emphatic holding of the low notes was tremendous fun after so many rueful songs.

Taylor dedicated the final duet from *Rodelinda,* "Io t'abbraccio," to a deceased friend. Appreciative applause continued until the ensemble returned to do an encore of their first duet, "Scherzano sul tuo volto."

♪ Bernard Haitink Returns After 33 Years to Lead the Philharmonic

Cynthia Phelps (viola), Carter Brey (cello), New York Philharmonic Orchestra, Bernard Haitink (conductor) Avery Fisher Hall, Lincoln Center, New York, 10.11.2011

Strauss: *Don Quixote*
Beethoven: Symphony No. 6 in F major, "Pastoral"

It's always interesting to hear conductors explain their choice of programming. Earlier this season, Alan Gilbert gave "sadness" as the common connection of an unusually disparate choice of works, which is as vague as saying that "music" is what links the works on a concert program. Bernard Haitink in an interview in *Playbill* states that his program choices will succeed because the Pastoral following *Don Quixote* "brings you back to a more intimate music making." Not to dispute the Maestro, but intimate is not a word I would use to describe a Beethoven symphony played by a moderately-sized orchestra inside a hall that seats an audience of over 2500. But aside from the difference in orchestral size, these two works are indeed closer than they might appear at first glance. Both are on the quieter end of each composer's compositions. There is certainly drama in each, but as Strauss tone poems go, *Don Juan, Death and Transfiguration, Thus Spake Zarathustra* and *A Hero's Life* are considerably more dramatically intense than *Don Quixote*. As for Beethoven, the Pastoral is by far his most peaceful symphony. Both works start and end quietly and, of course, both works are representative of program music: common for Strauss, but much rarer for Beethoven.

For a conductor of such renown, Haitink appears to be the opposite of what we think of as a "Maestro." His style of conducting while not quite as restrained as his most famous predecessor at the Chicago Symphony Orchestra, Fritz Reiner, is one of reserved and concise gestures. Even in the sections marked *fff*, the orchestra never seemed to reach the loudness or even blaring that at times occurs when Alan Gilbert is leading. In *Don Quixote* the second variation with its wild and dissonant tremolos sounded not so much like Mahler as Webern. This clarity allowed one to pick out voices that are not normally heard but sacrificed, for example, the intense storminess of the seventh variation and the fierceness of the opening of the ninth. The third variation, the longest in the work, is also the one most difficult to make interesting. This variation suffers from the inherent silliness of program music: attempting to imitate what music never can. Aside from mimicking the sounds of nature, it is impossible to tell a story with music. In this variation we are supposed to hear a conversation between the cello (Don Quixote) and the viola (Sancho Panza). The best one can do here to give the section interest is to increase the tempo, which, unfortunately Haitink, didn't do. (Although the program notes state that Strauss never wrote an official program guide, one was included in the *Playbill*, furthering the illusion that you can appreciate music by following a tone poem's story line. The result is that the listener, instead of focusing attention on the music, concentrates on the program, trying to "hear" a story that's not there.)

The performance of Beethoven's Pastoral symphony succeeded and suffered from the same stylistic considerations as the Strauss opener. The opening movement starts out briskly and continues at a moderate pace. At times there are moments of great lucidity such as at the end of the development section of the first movement where the brass stands out distinctly from the rest of the orchestra. The woodwind imitations of bird calls at the end of the second movement were lovingly performed. While the fourth movement's thunderstorm was furious, it wasn't furious enough. The final movement's gentle iteration of the main theme was repetitious.

Over the past few decades, many conductors have successfully breathed new life into Beethoven's symphonies: Roger Norrington, Nicholas Harnoncourt and John Gardiner among them. Those conductors and orchestras that do not have access to original instruments can always cut down on their use of vibrato and work with Beethoven's own metronome markings (as controversially fast as they are).

Yet even with all of these issues, one cannot ignore the New York audiences' expectations, and I understand why: it has been 33 years since Haitink conducted the NYPO. This was a rare opportunity to attend a performance by a member of the fading generation of conductors old enough to have heard Strauss's music while the composer was still alive.

♫A Poet Returns: Juho Pohjonen at Zankel
Juho Pohjonen (piano), Zankel Hall, Carnegie Hall, New York. 3.11.2011

Beethoven: Sonata No. 15 in D major
Debussy: *Estampes*
Chopin: 24 Preludes

In a review of Juho Pohjonen's performance of Mozart's Piano Concerto No. 23, I referred to him as a poet whose playing is "delicate, graceful and effortless." I can add more adjectives for his recital here: intense, committed and thoughtful would be a start. If his choice of works was meant to show all sides of his talent, he made wise decisions, and opened his recital with a limpid and affable performance of Beethoven's Sonata No.15. The gentle first movement with its softly played staccato bass line leads into a poignant theme that sets the pattern for the rest of the sonata. Even the Scherzo, usually in Beethoven's hands the most frenetic form, is tempered here. This sonata is one of Beethoven's least showy works, and it confirmed that Pohjonen is one of the least showy pianists around. One need only compare his style to that of a contemporary, Lang Lang, to make the point clear.

One of the most impressive of Pohjonen's skills is his ability to create subtle gradations of color through a masterly control of the keyboard. With his demand for complete dynamic control of the piano, Debussy would seem to be an ideal composer for this young man, and he is. Pohjonen's fingers seemed to barely touch the keyboard, yet he was able to draw out sounds awash with shadings. The concluding measures of the first movement of Debussy's *Estampes* entitled "Pagodes," with its cascading 32nd notes, were played with ethereal lightness. He forcefully carried forward the strong Spanish dance pulse of the second movement, "Soirée dans Grenade," and was adept at imitating the sound of rain in the concluding "Jardin sous la Pluie."

The concert concluded with the demanding 24 Preludes of Chopin. Not since Pollini's classic recording of this work in 1990 have I heard such a strong and convincing performance. From the fleet *Agitato* opening to the concluding "Storm" prelude, nothing seemed difficult or demanding. Some might question the tempi of many of these miniatures: the entire 24 pieces clocked in at around 25 minutes, an exceptionally fast pace compared to Pollini's 36 and Ashkenazy's 39. But I never sensed any Prelude was rushed, and if anything he may have lingered on some of the slower pieces. The warhorses like numbers four and seven never sounded clichéd, an accomplishment in itself.

Much has been made of Pohjonen's cool manner. But why should he or any artist betray his nature just to please the audience? One could instead be thankful that a musician is willing to share his or her amazing abilities in a concert hall and leave the smiling to chorus lines.

♪ *The Art of András Schiff: A Performance of His Own Three Bs*
András Schiff (piano), Carnegie Hall, New York, 31.10.2011

Bach: Three-Part Inventions
Bartók: Piano Sonata
Beethoven: 33 Variations on a Waltz by Diabelli

For several years during the 1980s András Schiff was mainly known as a Bach specialist. His recordings of all of Bach's major works, while not quite given the hallowed status of Glenn Gould's Bach, were deservedly treasured. Like Gould, Schiff rerecorded the *Goldberg Variations* 20 or so years after his first take on it, and this second performance, done live in concert (meaning no weeks of editing and cutting as in Gould's recordings) was even more universally praised than his first.

I wondered how his performance of Bach's Three-Part Inventions would compare to his 1985 recording. Written as exercises for Bach's many children, the Two- and Three-Part Inventions were meant to be played in progressive groups, from the easier two-part study pieces to more complex works with three lines of counterpoint. In addition to keyboard technique, they were also meant to teach clarity of musical line, so that all voices were distinct. The 15 little three-part pieces are not particularly interesting musically so it takes an imaginative player on the level of Gould in the past and Andrea Bacchietti today to overcome their pedagogical torpor. Unfortunately Schiff's execution here cannot be placed next to the performances of those two artists. The works don't easily accommodate a piano, and certainly not a grand piano, unless they are played with lightness and delicacy. There were no crescendos possible on the harpsichord, so building to large climaxes as Schiff did totally distorts the music. I'm not suggesting that the piano be played as if it were a harpsichord, or that the Inventions should only be played on a harpsichord, but to ignore these exercises' raison d'être is ultimately to dismiss the composer's score as irrelevant. It's the performer's choice as to tempo since Bach doesn't specify any, but some of the Inventions were played here at an unconscionably slow pace; this was particularly true of the fifth, sixth and eleventh.

Schiff is devoting his time in New York to his "In the steps of Bartók" theme for Carnegie Hall's Perspective series, and chose this Bach work as a pedagogical forerunner of Bartók's six-volume *Mikrokosmos*. However, he could just as well have played some of the more interesting Preludes and Fugues from Bach's *The Well-Tempered Clavier*. An ardent aficionado of the Bösendorfer piano, Schiff has been known to ship his personal piano to performance sites, and perhaps a Bösendorfer might have been made available for him at Carnegie Hall (even with the hegemony that Steinway holds here). The Bösendorfer has a silvery tone, not thin like a harpsichord but more appropriate for playing 18th-century keyboard music than the Steinway with its bigger sound. It was only in the final invention, number 15, that Schiff produced the kind of fire that was needed in the previous 14.

After brief applause, Schiff literally jumped into the Bartók sonata as if he had been offered water at an oasis. There was no compromising here. The Steinway responded to his fleet fingers and the scale-stretching chords, awaking members of the audience who had nodded off during the Bach. With its jazzy rushes of sound and distant echoes of Hungarian folk tunes, this sonata was full of flare and fire. The middle movement with its pulsing ground leads into the concluding Allegro molto with a repeating staccato requiring even more strength than the sonata's first movement.

The two great variation sets for keyboard, Bach's *Goldberg Variations* and Beethoven's *Diabelli Variations*, have become de rigueur for skilled pianists to perform and record at some point in their careers. Anderszewski, Ashkenazy, Kovacevich (twice) and Richter among others have masterfully interpreted the variations on the silly little theme that obsessed Beethoven to the extent that he wrote 33 variations when asked to contribute just one to Diabelli's compendium. Beethoven's mad genius inspired him to create a set of compelling short masterpieces. Every emotion imaginable can be found here, from the comical number 13 with its misplaced near-silent echo of preceding chords, to the 22's parody of Leporello's "Notte e giorno faticar" from *Don Giovanni,* to the profound and poignant number 31.

Schiff's uncompromising vision squeezed out meaning from every note. He carried through until the end with the most intense concentration: when the final massive chords were played, it was only premature applause from the audience that awakened him from his rapt state.

And there certainly was no stinting, compromising or perfunctoriness in Schiff's choice of an encore. There was no bowing and rushing off to a late dinner for this artist. He played the entire Op.109 sonata by Beethoven in a performance that was even more intense than his *Diabelli Variations*. The encore went on for over 20 minutes, and I was so dazzled at this point that I found myself wishing that he would respond to the next round of applause with Beethoven's *Hammerklavier* sonata.

♫*A Taste of French and Italian Baroque: Jean-Paul Fouchécourt and Gaële Le Roi*

Duetto/Duo, Jean-Paul Fouchécourt (tenor), Gaële Le Roi (soprano), Ryan Brown and Elizabeth Field (violins), Loretta O'Sullivan (violoncello), Andrew Appel (harpsichord), Scott Pauley (theorbo), Weill Recital Hall, Carnegie Hall, New York, 30.10.2011

Lully, Charpentier, Lambert, Vittori, Cavalli, Melani, Monteverdi

In a gracious gesture, Ryan Brown, conductor and founder of the Washington-based Opera Lafayette, dedicated the opening excerpts from Lully's *Atys* to William Christie. It was a fitting compliment since Mr. Brown's group, at the forefront in reviving Baroque operas for the past 16 years, would have to have been inspired by works discovered and performed by William Christie and Les Arts Florissants. Brown has specialized too in unknown works by little known composers such as Sacchini, Francoeur and Monsigny (whose delightful *Le Déserteur* was performed here last year). Those who are in Washington or in Versailles in February will have the opportunity to attend Opera Lafayette's world premiere of Monsigny's *Le Roi at le fermier*.

Starting with Christie's revival of *Atys* at BAM, New York audiences have been exposed to more French Baroque music this season than in the past, and in particular to Lully. A generation ago this music was dismissed as frilly, simplistic and overly ornate: good as background to events with pomp and circumstance, but not to be taken seriously. The operas of this period can seem filled with over-the-top libretti, gods coming down to vie with humans, deus ex machina events and exaggerated expressiveness. This is true but then so are most operas from *The Magic Flute* through *The Ring* cycle. It is the music that ultimately matters, and French Baroque's dancing dotted rhythms, syncopations and the continual *ostinati* are instantly captivating.

One of the most ubiquitous signatures of French Baroque music is the chaconne. There is something inherent in its beat that makes improvisation and variation a natural. Regardless of what is played above the bass ground, the repeating motifs will drive the piece forward to an appealing musical end. As Alex Ross states in an essay on the chaconne, it is "perfectly engineered to bewitch the senses," resulting in its most intense form as "a little sonic tornado that spins in circles while hurtling forward." One need only understand the appeal of Philip Glass's music to appreciate the chaconne's power.

The chaconne has an opposite effect when played slowly: it can be soothing and limpid. Fouchécourt's choice of *air de cours* by Michel Lambert included two chaconnes which are distinctly calm: "Vos mépris chaque jour me causent mille alarmes" and "Ma bergère." Fouchécourt sang these and other arias with great artistry and expressiveness. His voice still retains its idiosyncrasy and the distinctiveness that was so critical to the success of his well-known performance in Rameau's *Platée*.

Here as in the Rameau opera he used gesture and exaggeration to highlight the words, emphasizing text that clearly was meant to be comic. The humorous "My bergère" ends with the lines "She loves her flock, her crook and her dog/And I can love no one else but her." Fouchécourt literally barked the penultimate line. The other Lambert songs were enchanting if not as interesting verbally. They express the ubiquitous theme that love is pleasurable pain: "I do not sing to beguile my sadness/but rather to prolong it," or "Alas, if in my unhappiness I find so much delight I would die of pleasure if I were happier."

The program opened with some selections of scenes from *Atys*. The brief opening *ritournelle* led into Fouchécourt's first aria, "Allons, allons." Fouchécourt's voice was well-centered and natural sounding. His voice falls into the category of high-tenor (*haut-contre*), and only once or twice did the music require him to go beyond his range into falsetto. Joining him in *Atys* was Gaële Le Roi who matched or even went beyond Fouchécourt in theatrical expressiveness. Compared to Fouchécourt her voice at times lacked clarity and sweetness, and in her aria from Melani's *Empio Punito* she had difficulty reaching down to her lower range.

I am not sure why large stretches of *recitativos secce* were chosen when so much more is available in the way of accompanied recitatives or just traditional arias. This was particularly true of the excerpts from Vittori's *La Galatea*. In addition, closing the recital with a scene from Monteverdi's *L'incoronazione di Poppea* was not out of keeping with the rest of the program, but this scene is not representative of the opera which is as dark as a Shakespearean tragedy.

Despite my few cavils, this was an extremely pleasant evening. The instrumentalists were right on the mark and gave sound coloring and exceptional attention to detail. Ryan Brown's easy virtuosity adds to his already commendable reputation as a conductor. The audience was remarkably in tune with the performance, perhaps erring on the side of coolness but completely coughless and silent during the frequent retuning moments common to Baroque stringed instruments. The ambiance and sharp acoustics of Weill Recital Hall only added to the pleasure of the evening.

♫ Scholl, Bicket and *The English Concert* Perform Purcell to Perfection

Andreas Scholl (countertenor), The English Concert, Harry Bicket (conductor), Zankel Hall, Carnegie Hall, New York, 20.10.2011

Biber, Purcell, Muffat

Harry Bicket and his generically named The English Concert joined countertenor Andreas Scholl in a delectable program of vocal and instrumental works by Henry Purcell with brief introductory appetizers by Heinrich Biber as the first piece performed and by Georg Muffat for the opening after the intermission. Biber's "Sonata a 6" is in a modified fast-slow style with the valveless solo trumpet alternating with the strings, except at the end where the trumpet joins the strings for a fugue-like coda and final fanfare. The trumpeter Mark Bennett, fearless and undaunted, played the difficult trumpet part, creating the sounds by only the shaping of his lips (embouchure).

Henry Purcell is the greatest native-born English composer, which excludes Handel, born in Halle, and includes Elgar. Although only 36 when he died, the Zimmerman catalog of his works goes up to number 850. No one really knows from where his skill in writing music came. He never left England, yet his knowledge of the French style of music was completely internalized. At 18 he replaced the deceased Matthew Locke as Master of the Music for the King.

Why his music is not better known is a mystery. Yes, there have been productions of his main semi-operas *The Fairy Queen*, *King Arthur* and *Dido and Aeneas*, but there are hundreds of works never performed. Both William Christie for his productions of Purcell's works and Robert King for his recordings of the complete odes, anthems and songs should be commended.

Bicket and Scholl made their contribution to boost Purcell's reputation in this performance at Zankel Hall. Scholl, his voice slightly weak at the beginning, warmed up and gained body as the concert progressed. The opening "Sweeter than roses," because of its difficult harmonic shifts going from the languorous "First trembling made me freeze" to the explosive roulades of the next line, "That shot like fire o'er," should have been performed later when Scholl's voice had found its groove.

"Music for a while" opens with the basso continuo playing a ground that is continually repeated through the entire work. This harmonic technique is common in Purcell and his contemporaries as a way to weave a melody without having to write the bass line. The cello and harpsichord sensitively served as the accompaniment in this song. The song "An Evening Hymn" is a prayer before bedtime which ends oddly with a "Hallelujah." Scholl handled this oxymoron by taking a middle position of being neither too pious nor too joyous. Then came the delightful chaconne which ends *King Arthur*, followed by the opening overture. Perhaps, one of Purcell's most touching pieces of music is the mesmerizing "O, Solitude, my sweetest choice." Another song based on a repetitive ground, the bass replays the motif 28 times, resulting in not quite a Philip Glass moment but somewhere near there. Scholl's sensitive reading of this poem brought out its haunting emotions.

At this point in the concert, there were some last-minute changes. "Shepherd, shepherd, leave decoying" from *King Arthur* was played by the orchestra but not sung by Scholl. The reason is simple: it is written to be sung by two singers in the soprano range. Andrea Scholl is a wonderful singer, but may not be good enough to sing two voices (even if they are only doubled). Having confused the audience with not singing what he was programmed to sing, he sang the aria from the Winter Scene: "What power art thou." Without knowing the context, one might not understand the gasps of breath taken by the Cold Genius woken by Cupid in the libretto. (Mark Morris in his version of *King Arthur* for the New York City Opera, has this song performed by the singer inside a refrigerator!) Scholl sang very well but the piece works better when done, as it usually is, by a bass.

The symphony from Act V is very much a throwback to an earlier musical era with the violins bouncing back and forth motifs in the style of the pre-Vivaldi schools of violin playing. The magical and soulful song "Fairest isle," followed by the overture to Act I, led to the intermission.

The "Passacaglia from the Sonata No. 5" by Georg Muffat is a good example of a confusion in musical categorization. The observant listener might ask what the difference is between a passacaglia and a chaconne and the answer is none. Perhaps in the composer's mind, passacaglia seems to express a freer form than the strict chaconne, but over the years they have merged into the same form. This work requires tremendous technical skills, particularly from the first violinist, and Matthew Truscott admirably played some of the more difficult variations.

Purcell's "One charming night," a catchy tune with a sensuous instrumental combination of woodwinds, was another highlight of the evening. The instrumental "Dance for the Followers of night" is so close in spirit to the classic dances written by Lully (and even includes the tambourine, a common instrument in Lully's orchestra) that it seems amazing Purcell never received musical training in France.

Next came one of the pieces added at the last minute to the program: "If music be the food of love," with lovely melismas sung by Scholl. A little later he performed the second added song, "Strike the viol," from one of Purcell's many odes. Without tempo markings and dynamic indicators it's the choice of the performer, but I would have preferred a more lively interpretation than Scholl gave: the words themselves say "in cheerful and harmonious lays." These two songs replaced the poignant "If love's a sweet passion," which ends, as is common in Purcell's odes, with a choral ritornello. It is not unusual, where choral resources are not available, to simply have the instrumental accompaniment replace the chorus, which could have been done here.

Dido's Lament from *Dido and Aeneas* gave Scholl the opportunity to use his abilities to express the most heartfelt feelings imaginable in this most pitiable song. How can anyone not resist the final line of the song: "Remember me, but ah! Forget my fate"? The program appropriately ended with the chaconne that ends *The Fairy Queen*. This practice of ending a Baroque opera with a chaconne is common in many operas of this period from Lully to Rameau.

Although not revealed by the conductor or the singer, the encore was another Purcell gem, "Here the deities approve" from the ode "Welcome to All the Pleasures." Another song based on a repeating ground, this work really hits its mark after the words are sung and the instrumental ritornello builds to a glorious finale. An encore of "Music for a while" provided an irresistible finish to an irresistible concert.

♪Lorin Maazel Returns to His Favorite Orchestra, the New York Philharmonic

Nancy Allen (harp), Robert Langevin (flute), New York Philharmonic Orchestra, Lorin Maazel (conductor), Avery Fisher Hall, Lincoln Center, New York, 13.10.2011

Mozart: Symphony No. 38 in D major, "Prague"; Concerto in C major for Flute and Harp
Debussy: *Jeux, poème dansé*; "Ibéria" from *Images pour Orchestre*

Has any conductor in history had as long a relationship with an orchestra as Lorin Maazel with the New York Philharmonic? His first appearance as their conductor was in 1942 at the age of 12, in Lewisohn Stadium in front of 8500 people. While the seven years (2002-2009) that he contractually directed the NYPO is nowhere near Eugene Ormandy's record 43 years with the Philadelphia Orchestra, one can see why there is a special bond between this conductor and orchestra. The rapport was evident with every note played.

Mozart's Symphony No. 38 is unusual in several respects. Haydn had begun using slow introductions to his first movements in symphonies as early as his sixth and in every one of his last 15, generally to great effect, but the 38th was Mozart's first attempt to use this stylistic method. He certainly must have had opera overtures in mind while writing: the opening sounds like a cross between the overtures to the just-completed *Marriage of Figaro* and soon-to-be-completed *Don Giovanni*. As for a similarity to *The Magic Flute* overture, we have that in the opening string measures:

Although Mozart wrote many three-movement symphonies, most of them were early compositions. I suspect he felt that the 38th really had four movements, with the first being the long, slow introduction. If Mozart's requested repeats are taken, this Adagio can take upwards of 15 minutes to perform, more than the length of any of the movements that follow.

From the opening notes it was evident that Maazel's interpretation of the work would be a serious one. He conducted without a score and drew an intense, dramatic reading from the orchestra. A master of detail, Maazel educed lines and phrases so clearly delineated that they revealed unheard music. So much of this symphony consists of fragmented motifs that connecting them requires a conductor of Maazel's stature and an orchestra that knows exactly what the conductor is looking for. This is particularly true for the development section of the final movement which puts the orchestra through instrumental exercises in counterpoint. My only qualm, and this is a conductor's choice, was that the da capos were not taken.

The Concerto for Flute and Harp is an oddity by any standard, but there are other strange combinations in Mozart's catalog: the violin and viola *Sinfonia concertante* or the lesser known one for oboe, horn, clarinet and bassoon. Even Köchel himself, not knowing how to categorize it, put it not unwisely under "wind concerti," and it does share the *galant*, courtly, aristocratic demeanor of the two earlier flute concerti. I've been spoiled by recordings that normalize the volume of the two solo instruments, and was struck by how much more music the flute actually carries than the harp. Certainly it was not the fault of Nancy Allen if at times she was inaudible when playing the quiet (*piano*) measures in the score. The accompaniment was kept appropriately in the background, without any attempt to draw attention to itself. The flautist Robert Langevin was clearly aware of the problem of potentially drowning out the harpist and pulled back when it was Ms. Allen's turn to play, but short of amplification, there seems to be no method to compensate for the hall's poor acoustics. Yet all in all, this was a fine performance of a delightful work.

The second half of the concert was devoted to Debussy. If these works were meant to show off what the orchestra could do or did do under Maazel's reign, they certainly excelled. *Jeux* is a difficult and complex work with little of the tonality required to make it immediately accessible. This is not *La Mer* or *L'Après-midi d'un faune*. Rather, it's looking in the direction of the orchestral music of his disciple, Ravel, or Stravinsky, whose *Le Sacre du printemps* had just been premiered.

The excerpt "Ibéria" from *Images pour Orchestre* is closer to the Debussy that most of us know. While not programmatic in the way that the works of Debussy's elder contemporary, Paul Dukas, were (e.g. *Sorcerer's Apprentice*), this tone poem still attempts to musically mirror the work's titles. The final section, "Morning of a Festival Day," starts off quietly but quickly evolves into a musical festival, giving Maestro Maazel the opportunity of showing the world what a first-class ensemble he helped to create.

♪He Called For His Fiddlers Three, and Did They Fiddle

Juilliard Baroque's "The Three Fiddlers": Monica Huggett, Cynthia Roberts, Robert Mealy (violins), Phoebe Carrai (cello), Avi Stein (harpsichord), Paul Hall, Juilliard School of Music, Lincoln Center, New York, 27.9.2011

Buonamente: Sonata a tre violini from *Sonate e canzoni...libro sesto*
G. Gabrieli: Sonata XXI a tre violini from *Canzoni e sonate*
D. Gabrielli: Ricercare #7 in D minor
Baltzar: Consort for Three Violins
Matteis: Divisions in D minor
Purcell: "Three Parts upon a Ground"
Marini: Sonata "in Ecco" from Sonate and Passacaglio from *Per ogni sorte di strumento*
Uccellini: Sonata duodecima from *Sonate, sinfonie et correnti, libro II*
Blow: Prelude, Morlake Ground
Fontana: Sonata Sestadecima a tre violini from *Sonate*
Vierdanck: Capriccio for Three Violins from *Ander Theil Capricci*
Pachelbel: Canon and Gigue in D major

What makes the difference between a routine performance and one that sparkles is ineffable. When the performance is by a chamber group the rapport between

287

members is critical, and there was no question about rapport being there in this first event of the Juilliard School's Historical Performance season. Monica Huggett led the other three string players in a performance of mainly unknown works of the 17th century, and the enthusiasm of the group was contagious.

In other Baroque groups, the players sometimes go on autopilot. Think of the poor musicians playing "The Four Seasons" to tourists three or four times a week at the Sainte-Chapelle in Paris. What would they give to have a chance to perform first-rate music from virtually unknown predecessors of Vivaldi, as was the case here.

One wonders what Ms. Huggett's source is for this wonderful musical cache. At a concert by her students at Juilliard last year, there were works by some of the composers listed above but also pieces by Castello, Rossi, Legrenzi, Bertali and Jarzębski. Some names may be recognized by those interested in Baroque music, but outside of specialists their names and music are scarcely known.

The Buonamente sonata which opened the concert begins with a slow almost improvised fantasia, progressing to a faster more imitative section where each instrument repeats the first violinist's passages. It then returns to the tempo of the first section, but ends with the fast imitative runs of the second section. This piece was played with both poignancy in the slow sections and spirited élan in the faster ones.

One normally thinks of Giovanni Gabrieli as a composer of fanfare music for brass. It came as a surprise to hear a sonata from his *Canzoni e sonate* performed for strings, yet one could almost hear the trumpets and trombones as played by the Juilliard Baroque.

Phoebe Carrai performed one of the evening's highlights, the Ricercare No. 7 by Domenico Gabrielli. Ms. Carrai gave an accomplished presentation of this precursor of the Bach cello suites, which starts off with what sounds very much like the theme of Bach's *Art of the Fugue*. This short motif with variations, although not a dance movement as are those of Bach's suites, had nearly the emotional impact of one of his great cello sarabandes.

Thomas Baltzar's Consort for Three Violins consists of 10 dances, several of which were played here. These delightful excerpts look forward to the Baroque suite of dances of Bach, Handel and Telemann. There was less use of imitative techniques by the strings in these movements which gave them a more modern sound. Nicola Matteis, who flourished just a little later than the previous composers on the program, gives more independence to the cello in his spirited Divisions in D minor. The term "division" refers to a form that breaks down or "divides" the theme as a method of creating variations.

A chaconne by Purcell ended the first half of the concert. The chaconne, like its less ubiquitous cousin, the fandango, has an elemental, almost hypnotic quality created by the continuous variations played upon the repetitive bass. Most Baroque composers wrote chaconnes, all different yet in some ways all the same.

It took a couple of repetitions of Marini's Sonata "in Ecco" to realize that the echoed strings initiated by Ms. Huggett were coming from offstage. The echo effect was another popular conceit of the Baroque period and the performance here was particularly amusing. The Uccellini piece that followed is a slight work with an interesting tempo and a rhythmic change midway before it closes with the original tempo. Next came John Blow's lovely prelude and ground; another chaconne, it could have been written by one of his predecessors, William Byrd or even Louis Couperin. Giving the string players a brief rest, Ari Stein played this harpsichord solo with loving sensitivity.

The sonata for three violins by G.B. Fontana reverts back to a more traditional musical style. Here the third violin is left out of the opening back and forth repartee between first and second violinists. Robert Mealy waited for his chance later on to outdo both of the violinists with improvisatory virtuosic playing and excelled as soloist.

After another slight work by Johann Vierdanck in the traditional imitative style with the second and third violinists repeating the first violinist's passages, we finally come to a work that is not only well-known but "over-known", the Pachelbel Canon in D, performed here with the less frequently played Gigue. Like the Adagio attributed to Albinoni the Canon in D has become such a commonly played theme for TV and movies that something special has to be done to refresh its original appeal. Recorded transcriptions abound, from serious instrumentations for piano, for guitar and for lute and harp to the outrageous inclusions in Star Trek and Techno Rock mixes. There are even Hip Hop interpretations and something entitled "Sotthing [sic] Music to Calm Your Mind." Happily there is also the Juilliard Baroque to strip away the patina and expose the Canon in D in its original state.

Appreciative thanks go to the group for giving life back to the Canon and new life to all the works performed.

♪Berg Replaces Beethoven in a Concert Of the "Three Bs"
Frank Peter Zimmermann (violin), Alan Gilbert (violin and conductor), New York Philharmonic Orchestra, Avery Fisher Hall, Lincoln Center, New York, 5.10.2011

Bach: Concerto for Two Violins in D minor
Berg: Violin Concerto
Brahms: Symphony No. 3 in F major

One has to admire Alan Gilbert for his provocative programming, tying together works by three very different composers on the basis of the common mood of sadness. There is more than just sadness that connects Bach to Berg. In the final movement, Berg clearly quotes from a Bach chorale, going so far as to incorporate Bach's own harmonization. The connection with Brahms' third symphony stretches Gilbert's thesis. Symphony No. 3, as tonally vague as it is, ultimately ends in F major, the same key of Beethoven's sixth and eighth symphonic works that certainly could not be considered sad. Except for the decidedly upbeat (as upbeat as Brahms ever is) symphony in D major, the first and fourth are in the traditionally "sad" keys of D and E minor. Gilbert ends an interview about the line-up stating, "Somehow these works work really well together, I think, on a program."

Regardless of whether the three works performed last night had a common theme–musical programs, after all, are not Sunday crossword puzzles–it was nonetheless another adventuresome programming effort by Mr. Gilbert.

A quick look at the fascinating NY Philharmonic digital archives reveals that not much Bach has been performed at Avery Fisher Hall by the New York Philharmonic in recent years. In fact, this was the first performance of the Bach double violin concerto since April of 1985. Donal Henahan in *The New York Times* complained that the concert was old-fashioned and ponderous; and that the two soloists, associate and assistant concertmasters, showed "sturdy competence but no special flair or rhythmic variety." And 26 years later, his issues with that performance are the same ones most critics would have with last night's concert.

Gilbert nodded his head only once to Baroque historically informed performance practice by resizing the orchestra to the acceptable 16 players: four first violins, four second violins, four violas, four celli (although I could only see three), two double basses and a harpsichord continuo. Was there much else that Gilbert could do to inform the work with some standard early music techniques? Short of giving his orchestra Baroque instruments and bows and sending them across the street to the Juilliard School's Historical Performance division for a crash course in playing without vibrato and with dotted rhythms, not much. He would also have had to request that the acoustic pods that were installed during the summer's Mostly Mozart Festival to reduce reverberation, brighten the higher registers and repair the flat radio sonority that came from onstage, be reinstalled. Nevertheless, both instrumentalists played with flair and vitality and Gilbert's skill as a violinist (he started playing at five and appeared as orchestral soloist at ten) is another feather to put in his hat.

The Berg Violin Concerto that followed was also somewhat disappointing. Zimmerman contributed his major role with appropriate emotional conviction, evidently well-versed in the subtleties of this difficult but moving work. The problem had much to do with balance. There is a wonderful point in the first movement where the flute plays a lovely little refrain that the soloist echoes. The brass came in at that moment so forcefully that the soloist was drowned out, but part of a conductor's job is to be a virtual recording engineer, preparing the orchestra so that the balance between soloist and orchestra allows independent audibility of all instruments.

The Berg concerto is that rare piece of "modern" music that is on some level accessible to most listeners. It's dramatic, touching, angry but ultimately accepting of one's place in life, with the final movement's chorale echoing the resignation of Bach's unsung words, "Es ist genug." Certainly this is not an easy piece, nor a particularly happy one, but the unsmiling faces of the orchestra members bowing for the applause made this audience member feel funereal.

The third symphony of Brahms concluded the concert. This work is another difficult creation by a difficult composer. The third looks forward to Bruckner and Mahler, whereas Brahms' other symphonies look back to

Beethoven. For these symphonists, the conductor needs to keep in mind that there is a conceptual line connecting the movements which needs to be understood in its whole as well as in its parts. Bruckner, for example, needs a tremendously broad perspective that holds the ambiguous sections together; otherwise all we hear are scraps of music that come and go with no connection to one another. Brahms' third symphony has a similar nature, at least in the first and last movements where fragment phrases predominate. The third movement is the most familiar, composed in the form of the traditional minuet and trio, the main theme repeated so many times that we walk out humming it. But the other movements need the conductor's help to make them appealing.

Perhaps Gilbert was worn down by the weight of the melancholic nature of the program: an adventuresome effort, but not a particularly satisfying one for me.

♪In Lully's Garden: Other Flowers Flourish Alongside Atys
Les Arts Florissants (orchestra), Le Jardin des Voix (vocalists), William Christie (conductor), Brooklyn Academy of Music, Brooklyn, 25.09.2011

Le Jardin de Monsieur Lully
Semi-staged

Lully's *Atys*, performed last week at the BAM Opera House, is the epitome of the great French composer's later stage style, the *tragédie en musique*. Operas of this type, written in the last 13 years of his life, emphasized drama over music and ballet. Last night's performance gave us the opportunity to see and hear works in Lully's other major styles, where music is the center of attention.

The performance was meant to be a showcase for William Christie's Le Jardin des Voix, an ongoing master class of young singers trained in early music repertory. Eventually some will go on to join Les Arts Florissants or other early music groups, and it was clear from this performance that these vocalists are already near the top of their profession.

The program opened with excerpts from a very early comédie-ballet: *Ballet de la revente des Habits*. The *symphonie* that begins this work is not the symphony as we know it today, but "symphony" in the sense of "being in harmony with." Musically, it just means instruments playing together. This was followed by a delightful *recitativo accompagnato* sung by Anna Reinhold, who also played Cybèle in the acclaimed production of *Atys*.

The program continued with a group of more substantial musical excerpts, this time from *La Grotte de Versailles*, a transitional work referred to variously as a comédie-ballet, petit opéra, pastorale or eclogue. The libretto was by Philippe Quinault (the librettist of *Atys*), and was the first text he wrote for a Lully production. It fails to go beyond the standard themes of love's torments, the joys of country life versus city life and the plaints of a shepherd mooning for the unattainable; the shepherds and shepherdesses find happiness in escaping to the fountains and *grottes* of Versailles. Despite the uninspiring words, all the singers took on their roles enthusiastically, singing the excerpts with a silvery intonation both alone or in unison. The section ended with a popular musical conceit, that of the echo: one voice singing a phrase and the other(s) repeating part or all of it in a softer voice.

Taking a break from Lully, Christie chose several pieces by Michel Lambert. Lambert, 20 years Lully's senior, is best known for his plaintive *air de cours*, songs written with simple accompaniment for one to four voices. Here again, the themes revolve around love and death. Of the four airs performed the most interesting is the round-like "Il faut mourir," with the recurring quizzical line, "We must not change but die." Once again, the singers performed with appropriate poignancy, bringing back to life a form of music that has been nearly forgotten.

Music by Marc-Antoine Charpentier, whose most vocal advocate is William Christie, came next. This *pastorale*, "Il faut rire et chanter," was sung spiritedly by the cast and confirms the notion that where great music is played, text is secondary. Based on the typically clichéd themes mentioned above, most of the text doesn't rise much above a ditty, yet the music is lovely, rich with both vocal and instrumental complexity that succeeds in spite of the clichéd words.

After the intermission, the group returned to perform more Lully. The opening ritournelle from the *Ballet de la Raillerie* with its repeated phrases could be a chaconne if it weren't in triple-time. A duet followed, sung by Rachel Redmond and Anna Reinhold and mocking a very real subject of the day: French vs. Italian music. At the time this music was composed there had been an ongoing debate as to which country's music was "better" at expressing the most emotion. Italy mocked the music of France for its pathos, tenderness, ornate ornamentation and over-the-top extravagance; France mocked Italian music's empty virtuosity, unpleasantly high-range vocalism and lack of refinement. Since Lully literally controlled what music could be staged in France and where, this debate would raise its head to become a real issue only after his death.

The excerpts that followed on the program are from the comédie-ballet *Le Bourgeois Gentilhomme* with a text by Molière, and a selection chosen from the entree "Ballet des Nations." The music is exceptional, with typical Lully instrumental accompaniment: prominence given to wind instruments with doublings on flutes and oboes (Louis XIV's favorite instrument). Here castanets were used, rather than Lully's scored maracas, and the instruments gave a clear Spanish flavor to the music.

Next was the aria "Dormez beaux yeux adorables" from the comédie-ballet *Les Amants Magnifiques*, a ritournelle sung by the sopranos and almost sounding like a lullaby. Two airs followed from another comédie-ballet, *Les Plasirs de L'Ile Enchantée*, Lully's first stage production to be done at Versailles. The final work on the program: excerpts from Act III of Lully's last full production the pastorale-héroique *Acis and Galatea*. Opening with a captivating instrumental passacaille and continuing with charming vocal warmth, the singers completed this magical pastiche with exceptional finesse. My only caveat is that I wish the cast of singers had not been directed to dance in Baroque style, even if it was generic movements and gestures. But this was a slight bit of amateurish staging in an otherwise totally professional and exhilarating production.

♪Lully's Atys: A Brilliant Production of an Opera Where Drama Outshines Music

Soloists, Les Arts Florissants, William Christie (conductor). Brooklyn Academy of Music, Brooklyn, 20.9.2011

Lully: *Atys*

Much has been said and written about the performers and the staging of William Christie's production of Lully's masterful opera *Atys*. And rightly so: last evening's performance at BAM was as close to perfect as can be imagined.

What struck me most was how well this production's disparate patches were sewn together into a seamless whole. Although the text was written by the renowned dramatist Philippe Quinault, it is likely that it was Lully in collaboration with King Louis XIV who chose the topic and made the dramatic decisions. If this was not quite a Wagnerian one-man show, it came very close to being one.

Most operas are dominated by the music. Even in operas with tightly integrated music, drama and dancing–Wagner's, for example–it's the music that is at the forefront. In *Atys* the musical demands are less important than the dramatic ones. None of the singers are required to go beyond their given tessitura. Countertenors are not needed: none of the music requires that voice range. Most of the recitatives are sung as *ordinaire*, accompanied not by the orchestra but by a keyboardist and plucked string bass instrument. Long recitatives without orchestral accompaniment can make for very dry stretches, and this was the case in the first two acts where much time was spent vocalizing the play's exposition. Appropriately perhaps, recitativo secco is another expression used for this kind of oration.

This focus on drama as opposed to music helps explain the opera's popularity with viewers who might find Lully's music in his other works for stage impenetrable or tedious. Thinking back to 1994 when I saw Christie's production of Charpentier's *Médée* at BAM, it was the music that dominated. Perhaps that is why *Médée* has not had the popularity of *Atys*, although it is regarded as musically superior even by Christie himself. He states in the book accompanying his second recording of *Médée* that of all his fully staged productions, including *Atys, Médée* is the one that's most important, the one whose effect on the staging of music is "immeasurable."

As for the choreography, it would be interesting to see how the brilliant dancing that was done in this production compares to Christie's 1986 premiere. The discoveries made in the area of Baroque choreography over the last two decades have been substantial. For one thing, we've learned that Baroque choreography was as concerned with the matter and manner of gesture, arm positions and pantomime as it was with ballet movements themselves, and this production successfully incorporated these advances.

Here then is true drama—love, jealousy, revenge, murder, trickery and remorse—which is what keeps our attention for four hours. From the traditional opening prologue which, like those of other Baroque operas, has little to do with what follows, to the frozen character left on stage as the final curtain descended, it was the drama on which we were most focused. This becomes even clearer to the viewer when the company takes its bows and curtsies, with the prominent members of the cast doing so individually. Could you recognize every performer and the role each played? Would you remember which singer sang which aria in what act? This is not a criticism of the production, but is the result of following Lully's wishes to the letter.

Baroque opera, like any musical genre, takes time to appreciate. Christie has done us a service by discovering this old-new musical source, and the influence of his original production of *Atys* on the classical music scene cannot be underestimated. Christophe Rousset, Mark Minkowski, Hugo Reyne and Hervé Niquet, all former members of *Les Arts Florissants,* have made successful careers as conductors of Baroque groups and have all done productions and recordings of French Baroque music. Inspired by Christie, these conductors have clearly wiped away the notion that French Baroque music is nothing more than music for the dilettante, pompous music used mainly to open BBC television programs.

♪Mozart's "A Little Night Music" at Lincoln Center

Mostly Mozart Festival 7: Jennifer Koh (violin), Shai Wosner (piano), Stanley H. Kaplan Penthouse, Lincoln Center, New York, 24.08.2011

Mozart: Sonata in E-flat major, Sonata in C major, Sonata in B-flat major

The last time I was in the Stanley H. Kaplan Penthouse at Lincoln Center, a small space that holds about 180 people, it was to hear Sir Roger Norrington talk about the concert he would be performing that evening devoted to C. P. E. Bach. The chairs were arranged in rows facing a lectern. To the audience's surprise, Sir Roger walked in wearing sweatpants and a C. P. E. t-shirt which set the casual tone.

This was not how the venue was arranged for last night's recital. As you arrived, you were offered a glass of wine and ushered to a table in a room set up as if it were a cocktail lounge. This "Little Night Music" was "little" because it lasted about an hour, and "night music" because it started at10:30 PM. The audience was a mix of old and young, and it seemed just the right place to impress a date with how sophisticated and sensitive you are.

Mozart's violin sonatas are some of his earliest works. His Op. 2 and 3 of 1764 were written when he was eight. They and many of their successors were really sonatas for keyboard with violin obbligato (an odd word that can mean its opposite, as in this case: "not required"). But by the time the two later sonatas played here were written, each part shared the stage equally. It wasn't until Beethoven wrote his middle period violin sonatas that the form truly became the violin sonata we know today.

Those lucky enough to sit at a table near the raised platform where this chamber music recital was performed were given the rare opportunity to experience the kind of closeness Mozart's audience had in his day. Jennifer Koh played to perfection and her accompanist on the piano, Shai Wosner, played immaculately. Both were sensitive to the dynamics of their instruments so that when the pianist brought out an important line, Ms. Koh would stand back and turn down her volume. Her 1727 Stradivarius, warm and rich in tone, seemed to play itself. Koh is known for her strength and fire, but she really only exhibited that once, in the coda to the Sonata in B-flat major.

At the beginning of the development section of the first sonata played and at the coda at the end of the first movement, Mozart introduces the four-note theme that he would use in the finale of his last symphony, the "Jupiter." The second movement was played with an achingly beautiful tenderness. The jaunty third movement ended cheerily after six variations.

The Sonata in C major opens unusually with an Adagio of great expressiveness, leading right into an Allegro molto. The opening Adagio is repeated and the movement ends with a return to the Allegro molto. The sonata's second movement is *Tempo di Menuetto,* not a true Minuet which would have a middle trio section, but paced as if it were one. Although the violin is far from just an accompaniment here, the real work is given to the pianist, who handled the difficult passages with ease.

Another poignant theme opens the last work on the program, the Sonata in B-flat major. This Largo lasts barely two minutes before it races into a lively Allegro, again with long runs on the piano. The Andante, lovely as it is, may have been slowed down a little too much resulting in an Adagio played with just too much expressiveness. The final movement ends with a quick showpiece for the violinist that made the listener want to stay and hear more even as midnight approached.

♫New York's Mostly Mozart Festival Winds Down

Mostly Mozart 6: Bertrand Chamayou (piano), Mostly Mozart Festival Orchestra, Jérémie Rhorer (conductor), Avery Fisher Hall, Lincoln Center, New York, 23.8.2011

Haydn: Symphony No. 22 in E-flat major, "The Philosopher"
Mozart: Piano Concerto No. 12 in A major, Symphony No. 29 in A major

As creative and talented as he was, Haydn was still expected to report to work daily and do his job, which was to write and perform music. We recognize Haydn as a genius, but to the Esterhazies, for whom he worked most of his life, he was a servant, a mere artisan. (Bach too thought of himself as an artisan, teaching his children how to play and compose music as another father of the time might teach his sons to be blacksmiths.) Haydn's 100-plus symphonies certainly equal a mere mortal's lifetime effort. But there are also over 400 songs, 130 trios for baryton (a cello-shaped instrument favored and played by the Prince), 25 operas, 70 string quartets, and more. His level of consistency is astonishing: the difference between his weakest music–probably what he wrote for the *Lire Organizzate* (an instrument related to the hurdy-gurdy)–and his greatest, works on the level of "The Creation," is very small. By comparison, Beethoven's compositions went from the bombastic Wellington's Symphony to the Ninth, a significant difference in quality.

All this is said in preparation for reviewing last night's performance of Haydn's Symphony No. 22. There have certainly been more spirited performances of this and other symphonies from the early to middle period of Haydn's life. Conductor Jérémie Rhorer was more than enthusiastic, but the orchestra responded lethargically. This could have been a result of weeks of rehearsing unfamiliar or not commonly played pieces with different conductors, lack of sufficient rehearsal time, poor rapport between the conductor and the orchestra or a combination of any or all of these reasons. The difficult, spirited and well-played opening hunting calls from the doubled French and English horns gave a false promise that the rest of the symphony would be equally energetic. For me, this is not top Haydn, like the middle-period Sturm und Drang symphonies, but the quality of all the symphonies is so consistent that it would be hard not to enjoy any played reasonably well.

Looking at the dates of the two Mozart compositions, it might seem surprising that his 12 piano concerto was written eight years after his 29th symphony, but he had written just eight concerti for piano before he hit his stride with the ninth. Mozart took the piano concerto seriously, and felt uncomfortable at a young age with tackling its demands. It wasn't until he befriended the so-called "London Bach," Johann Christian Bach, that Mozart wrote his piano concerti numbers three through five (one and two were juvenilia), which were based on transcriptions of J. C. Bach's piano sonatas.

Bertrand Chamayou has been widely recognized for his achievement in having performed Liszt's *Transcendental Études* more than 40 times between 2003 and 2005. Of course, playing Mozart requires a very different sensibility and I can't be sure that Chamayou has it, but it was a satisfying performance nonetheless. I do question the solidarity of soloist and orchestra, which was once or twice off their mark but mostly on and provided a sensitive accompaniment overall.

Although the first movement was fine, I thought the second movement, played more adagio than the marked tempo of Andante, sagged. The final movement, a Rondo, is filled with brilliant themes, each with material enough for a movement in itself. Unusually, Mozart wrote cadenzas for all three movements of this concerto, and Chamayou handled them admirably without unnecessary flash or bravura.

Many of Mozart's early symphonies are really *divertimenti*, music to be diverted by and not listened to, and they are nowhere near the level of Haydn's early works. Only in No. 25 in G minor did Mozart really start exploring the possibilities of the genre. From then on most of his symphonies are models of the form as it began its long development through the 19th century.

The opening Allegro moderato of No. 29 has a fire not found in earlier symphonies. Reflecting a depth of feeling and poignancy beyond Mozart's years, the Andante second movement is emblematic of the Mozart we can't resist. A Minuet follows with the kind of intensity associated with the Scherzo, a form soon to join the Minuet as an alternative for the third movement of a symphony. (Beethoven's Scherzi in his later symphonies were anything but one-two-three dances.) The final movement has a complexity and richness that carries us through to a coda that always catches the listener by surprise. The recurring cadence leads back to the main theme so many times that when the symphony does conclude, it takes a few seconds to realize that it's over. Rhorer did a fine job with this work, justly pacing each movement and bringing out voices that you wouldn't normally hear unless it were played by a smaller group on original instruments.

The concert was pleasant enough overall but often lackluster, a quality not uncommon towards the end of a long festival, particularly one as intense, demanding and high-quality as this year's Mostly Mozart.

♫Poetic Inspiration: A Poet Tackles Mozart
Mostly Mozart Festival 5: Juho Pohjonen (piano), Mostly Mozart Festival Orchestra, Jonathan Nott (conductor), Avery Fisher Hall, Lincoln Center, New York, 17.8.2011

Stravinsky: *Symphonies of Wind Instruments* (1920, rev. 1947)
Mozart: Piano Concerto No. 23 in A major
Beethoven: Symphony No. 4 in B-flat major

This Mostly Mozart Festival program, though not mostly Mozart, was nevertheless the composer's night in terms of both the high quality of the music and the exceptional playing by the soloist. Just as I was remembering a Mozart piano concerto performed last year by Stephen Hough at the series' closing concert (which I did not like), Jonathan Nott and pianist Juho Pohjonen came on stage.

What could this conductor, soloist and orchestra possibly offer to rekindle my feelings about a piece of music that I've lived with all my life? The answer is simple: have a poet play the piano. I am not using "poet" or "poetic" as a substitute for romantic: there was nothing romantic about this performance. In point of fact, it was quite the opposite. It started out with a moderately paced Allegro, played crisply under Nott's direction. It seemed forever before Pohjonen lifted his hands to play the Steinway, but when he did, from the very first run of 16th notes, I knew this performance was going to be special. He played the keys as if they were simply an extension of his body. This was the most, delicate, graceful and effortless performance of the work I have ever heard. It would seem that his ability to get to the core of this music could only be achieved after years of mastering the work's technical and musical aspects, yet as far as I can determine it was his first performance–an amazing achievement considering that Pohjonen has only been concertizing since 2005. In both his slightly hunched-

297

over-the-piano style and in his ability to so sensitively bring out each line of music, he reminded me of the great Glenn Gould. It would be interesting to hear him perform Bach.

The pianist was called on stage to standing ovations and played an encore by Edvard Grieg, "The Bridal Procession Passes" from *Scenes of Country Life*. This delightful little throwaway may be familiar to some as it was used again in his *Peer Gynt*. Pohjonen played the piece nimbly. He could, I am sure, have chosen from some dozens of dazzling scores that would impress his audience with his technical prowess but in keeping with the poetic nature of his performance chose a bit of poetry, instead. Bravo!

The program opened with Stravinsky's *Symphonies of Wind Instruments*. Surprisingly, there is no mention in the program notes that the real source of these works is not the late 18th-century masters, but the late 16th-century Giovanni Gabrieli. His *Sacrae Symphoniae* of 1597 and others contain instrumentalists who played together in sympathy with each other, hence one definition of symphony.

I found the performance somewhat lifeless. It should have been spiky and jazzy but was very thin and flat. It may not have been a piece that either the instrumentalists and/or the conductor felt strongly about. A performance as poor as this makes the music sound like what one thinks "modern music" is: disconnected, disjointed, and without memorable phrases or tunes, but this would not have been the case had it been played with more commitment.

The performance of Beethoven's Fourth Symphony had tremendous verve and vitality with the brass and percussion at times overpowering the strings. I probably was not the only one whose eyes kept focusing on the tympanist. There were no long breaks for him in this performance and his playing was impeccable. This symphony could have been given a subtitle like the "Eroica" or "Pastorale" if the appellation weren't such a mouthful: Beethoven's Fourth Symphony, "The Tympani." The concert ended on a festive note with all stops out from the instrumentalists. Chalk up one more event to a series that has been in all respects inspired.

♪*Solid Fare from Mozart and Mendelssohn, Goulash from Dvořák*

Mostly Mozart Festival 4: Takács Quartet, Andreas Haefliger (piano), Avery Fisher Hall, Lincoln Center, New York, 7.8.2011

Mozart: String Quartet in D major, "Prussian"
Mendelssohn: String Quartet No.2 in A minor
Dvořák: Piano Quintet in A major

Although known mostly for their long list of award-winning recordings of Beethoven and Bartók, the Takács Quartet certainly holds their own with other composers as evinced by this varied program at the Mostly Mozart Festival. As in most chamber groups that have had long life spans, the Takács has intelligently chosen the right replacements over the years. The two remaining members of the original quartet founded in 1975 are Károly Schranz, second violinist, and András Fejér, cellist. The addition of Edward Dusinberre, an Englishman, as cellist and Geraldine Walther, an American, as violist has turned this Hungarian quartet into an international chamber group.

The Takács began the program with the first of Mozart's three "Prussian" quartets written for the amateur cellist King Frederick William II of Prussia. The fact that the King's playing skills were limited clearly shows in the cello part. It is rare in Mozart to have, as he has here in this quartet–or in any of his other works for that matter–three of the four movements marked with the same tempo. Even the second movement, marked Andante, is only a few bars-per-minute away from the other three movements marked Allegretto. Rarely does the note length go beyond a 16th note (semiquaver) and only at the end is there a brief foray into 32nd notes (demisemiquavers). One doesn't need to read music to understand the simplicity of the cello's part in these measures from the first movement:

To be honest, I'm not a great fan of Mozart's string quartets. The first 13–all written before 1773–are little more than divertimenti. It wasn't until 1782, after meeting Haydn and hearing his quartets, that Mozart approached the genre as a serious form. Even the six pieces dedicated to Haydn are problematic. Charles Rosen in *The Classical Style* writes that these works "struggled to assimilate Haydn's language" resulting "in a constant alteration of awkwardness with his more natural grace." (Rosen devotes a chapter to the string quintets but not one to the quartets.)

However, the first "Prussian" quartet in the hands of the Takács may make me rethink my dislike–at least for this particular work. By not trying to find drama or complexity in the score as other chamber groups do, the Takács concentrates on the work's inner spirit which is all sweetness and light, warmth and mellifluousness. Mozart was just entering his last musical phase where complexity became less important, past the point where he had to prove himself to anyone–particularly his father, who died two years before these works were composed.

As precocious as Mozart was, it is hard not to be impressed by the early works of Mendelssohn. His 12 early symphonies, written between the ages of 12 and 14 are certainly more substantial than the symphonies Mozart wrote at this age. It really wasn't until Mozart was 17 that he wrote his first mature symphony, the 25th, known as the "Little G." Similarly, this Mendelssohn quartet, written at the age of 18, is more complex and mature than most of Mozart's at the same age and only comparable to one other quartet of this period, Mozart's D minor, written when he was 17.

In the first movement a short opening adagio is followed by the main theme–a skipping motive so full of potential that it dominates the entire movement and is a major element in a varied form in the other movements as well. The poor secondary themes of this Allegro vivace are left to fend for themselves. This skipping theme seems at times as if it were about to turn into a fugue but never does. The meltingly tender reiteration of the main theme by the viola right before the coda was all I needed to hear to understand why Geraldine

Walther was chosen as their violist. The second movement presents a theme quite similar to the first, particularly where the tempo changes from Andante to Poco piu animato. The third movement is again the main theme–re-measured, re-noted, but clearly there. The Presto is Mendelssohn's hat-tipping to the opening instrumental recitative-like introduction to the last movement of Beethoven's Ninth and the quartet's inner fugue a reference to, perhaps, the *Große Fuge*. Near the closing of this movement, the opening theme of the first is reiterated, as it is in Beethoven's Ninth where earlier themes are replayed in a different context. The Takács performed this fiery work with a total commitment and complete solidarity that define a top-notch chamber group.

It is surprising how much music Dvořák wrote: over 200 works in his lifetime. He is, of course, known mostly for his warhorses, the "New World" Symphony, the Cello Concerto, the "American" Quartet and the *Slavonic Dances*. (As a musical side-note: "If you don't know whose romantic work is being played on your radio, your best odds are to guess it's Dvořák.") Like much of Dvořák's music this quintet is full of bravura, both saccharine and cloying at the same time. The opening measures with the cello playing a melody as the piano plays arpeggios is a very odd beginning. The movement does go on and on with not a tremendous amount to say. The second movement is a "Dumka," a characteristic folk music form most famously found in the "Dumky" Trio, where all six movements are in this style, and in the *Slavonic Dances*. This movement of the quintet, neither interestingly structured nor memorable, comes close to the 15-minute mark, about 14 minutes too long. The third movement Scherzo is thankfully brief and the Finale races, but not fast enough, to a quick wrap-up with a clichéd four note (dum da da dum) ending.

The Takács Quartet and Andreas Haefliger gave this piece their all, and the audience was able to bring them back on stage only two or three times before the lights abruptly came on. Could the theater lighting technician have felt the same as I did?

♫ *Mozart's Unsolemn Solemn Vespers*

Mostly Mozart Festival 3: Lucy Crowe (Soprano), Soloists of the Concert Chorale of New York, James Bagwell (director), Mostly Mozart Festival Orchestra, Iván Fischer (conductor), Avery Fisher Hall, Lincoln Center, New York, 9.8.2011

Mozart: *Ave verum corpus*; Symphony No.41 in C major, "Jupiter"; *Vesperae solennes de confessore*

In a brief conversation with Maestro Iván Fischer, he talked about how he had been aiming for a "unified," seamless production the other night of *Don Giovanni*. I facetiously suggested he could cut the intermission, which to me was more like an interruption. In the *Playbill* for last night's performance he states, "I am interested in an organic unity of performance especially in the case of operas." This philosophy was certainly carried over to the program he conducted last night. Where normally there would be a silent break (except for the ubiquitous coughers) between pieces or audience applause, Fischer had the organist play an improvisatory or improvisatory-style interlude. This made the brief sacred choral work, *Ave verum corpus*, seem like an other-worldly overture to the profane last symphony of Mozart. The work itself is a small gem, under five minutes, and in its simplicity could be mistaken for a Christmas carol. A very late work, it has that shimmering, ethereal aura also heard in the three adjacent Köchel numbers: the works for glass armonica. The transcendent Clarinet Concerto was also composed in the same month. In Mr. Fischer's hands, the motet glowed.

In *Vesperae solennes de confessore*, plainchant antiphons sung by a tenor in the chorus were interpolated between most of the movements. The effect of this was to both unify and to separate the parts of the whole. The musical question as to whether to fill the gaps between sections of the Vespers, as is done in the full liturgical service, goes back at least as far as Monteverdi. When Andrew Parrott recorded Monteverdi's "Vespers of 1610" with both plainchant and instrumental interludes, it came as a surprise to some and as a revelation to others. In fact, this radical version (also with only voice per part) probably did come closer to how it sounded when it was actually performed as part of the Vespers liturgical service. On one side we have the liturgical tradition saying that the composers, de facto, expected it to be performed with fillers; and on the other hand, there were those who felt these interludes had the effect of breaking up the work by adding music that, as far as we know, neither composer intended to be added.

For a work that is supposed to be solemn, there is little solemn about this Vespers. Most of the movements are marked Allegro or Allegro vivace. Scored for strings, trombone, tympani and bassoon (*ad libium*), this sacred work was performed brightly and with much élan by both orchestra and chorus. The *Laudate pueri* (no tempo) demonstrated how easy it was for Mozart to switch musical styles, from strictly Classical to High Baroque. This contrapuntal movement became the Kyrie of Mozart's final work, his Requiem. The high point of the Vespers, as well as the program, was the sublime "Laudate Dominum." Along with "Et incarnatus est" from the Mass in C minor, this aria, although not requiring a coloratura range, reveals its inner luminosity with a voice a little less white than Lucy Crowe's. Nonetheless, it would take a heart of stone not to be moved to tears listening to this lustrous nonpareil.

Fischer conducted a crisp, festive performance of the Jupiter Symphony, emphasizing the brass and tympani. Tempos were moderate. His ability to bring out thematic material, particularly from the lower strings, was exemplary. It would have been interesting to have heard this work played by his own Budapest Festival Orchestra which played so brilliantly in *Don Giovanni*, but certainly the Mostly Mozart Festival Orchestra could hold its own, and did so in last night's performance.

♪ *Bodies that Sing: An Imaginative Re-creation of Don Giovanni*

Mostly Mozart Festival 2: Budapest Festival Orchestra, Iván Fischer (conductor and director), Rose Theater, Lincoln Center, New York, 4.8.2011

There are not many three-and-a-half hour performances so intense that one feels freed from the usual gravity of time, so tightly wound that the intermission seems more like an interruption, and with an audience so totally in tune with the performers that applause for individual numbers actually seems necessary to clear the charged air and ready it for the next jolt. The conductor, standing on the podium, his back to the audience as they enter, patiently waits for the right time to lift his baton and dives straight into the overture, taking us with him, not coming up for air until the end of Act I.

All this was part of the experience of attending last night's Mostly Mozart Festival performance of his masterpiece, *Don Giovanni*. Referring to the production as a "staged concert version" does not do justice to the large-scale concept here. The staging was minimal with no props at all, although thinking back on the performance, I could swear there were rapiers and pistols! Fischer would have used the same stage elements even if this work were to be performed at the Met. The focus of the production is on the base physicality of Don Giovanni's *Weltanschauung*. Don Giovanni, always the existential anti-hero, here conflates sexuality with a perverse rejection of the sentient human body. He kicks, beats, throws down, steps on and murders with no sense of the body's threshold of pain. Windows, tables, walls, furniture, a wedding carriage: all are made from human flesh. Don Giovanni's Christ-like assumption not to Heaven but to Hell appropriately ends with his body being torn to shreds.

How was all this accomplished? How was all this perfected with only two previous performances in Budapest? Credit has to be given to Mr. Fischer as both musical and theatrical director with his intuitive sense of who would best sing and act each part. I don't remember seeing or hearing a finer cast, both as singers and actor/actresses. Laura Aiken's dress must have been fireproof. As Donna Anna, she was molten fury, eschewing her fiancé's selfish platitudes. Her voice effortlessly covered all ranges with no sense of the difficulty inherent in an aria such as "Crudele?…Non mi dir, bell'idol mio." Tassis Christoyannis's smarmy Don Giovanni acted and sang every line with a sneering sense of grandiosity. His descent into Hell was horrific. José Fardilha outdid himself as Leporello, his bass voice capable of switching timbre as quickly as he switched his loyalties. Myrtò Papatanasiu as Donna Elvira sang touchingly of her abandonment, sensitively revealing her all-too-human capacity to be enthralled by Leporello disguised as Don Giovanni. Sunhae Im's meltingly sweet voice was the very essence of the ingénue, and her Zerlina convincingly ran the gamut from coy to seductive. The Commendatore, Kristinn Sigmundsson, epitomized the role: robust, statuesque, with an ideal *basso profundo* that at its deepest, darkest range could set the theater floor vibrating.

The most imaginative staging decision, one that added a whole other level of visual pleasure to this performance, was the addition of 15 actors from the University of Theatre and Film in Budapest. Each student is required to be competent in singing, dancing, acrobatics and acting. Mr. Fischer saw them perform in Budapest, and on a whim he hired them for this production. Their role here can best be described as a cross between the dance/acrobatics of Pilobolus and the miming street actors who periodically pop up in urban areas. Their creative ability to form themselves into objects strikingly enhanced the psychological and philosophical framework that Mr. Fischer sought to present.

Aside from one minor anachronistic moment when Don Giovanni plies the posse with marijuana as a way to spur them on to hunt for Leporello, the production was flawless. Where equivalent attempts have been made to modernize Mozart's operas or make them relevant, none that I am aware of have done so without failed gimmicks and tricks or sophomoric incidents. This production will stand as a hallmark against which all others will be judged.

♩Only Mozart Opens Mostly Mozart Festival

Mostly Mozart Festival 1: Christian Tetzlaff (violin), Antoine Tamestit (viola), Susanna Phillips (soprano), Mostly Mozart Festival Orchestra, Louis Langrée (conductor), Avery Fisher Hall, Lincoln Center, New York, 3.8.2011

Mozart: Overture to *Le nozze di Figaro*, Sinfonia concertante in E-flat major for Violin and Viola, "Crudele?...Non mi dir, bell'idol mio" from *Don Giovanni*, "Bella mia fiamma...Resta, o cara," Symphony No. 36 in C major, "Linz"

In my first review of a Mostly Mozart concert last year, I expressed gratitude that that particular concert was "Mostly Not Mozart." Having attended numerous performances under the 18-year leadership of Gerard Schwarz, I grew weary of quickly rehearsed, spiritless concerts. Anthony Tommasini of *The New York Times* refers to this period as "the dreary days."

Those days are certainly over. Louis Langrée took over from Schwarz in 2002 and has made it his own festival. Last night's opening performance seemed like a return to the golden days. Even Avery Fisher Hall felt less humongous and, while not quite intimate, certainly warmer. Acoustical pods hanging from the ceiling dampened the theater's usual screechy resonance; filled grandstands on the stage may have also aided in this aural improvement.

The program was an ideal first-night summary of the major Mozart forms: opera, concerto and symphony. The Overture to *Le nozze di Figaro* was cleanly articulated and moderate in tempo. I'm not sure what the turnaround in instrumentalists is from year to year, but this certainly didn't sound like a pick-up group. The players showed no first-night jitters and performed as if they had been playing together for years (and maybe they have).

The Sinfonia concertante in E-flat major is one of the dozen or so pieces by Mozart that ensure, should most of his other scores disappear, he would still be considered one of the great composers in history. The back and forth between the violinist, Christian Tetzlaff, and the violist, Antoine Tamestit, was so smoothly delivered that it would be difficult in some passages to discern where the violin ends and the viola begins. Mozart enhanced this bonding by retuning the viola to

303

fill any register gaps between the two instruments. I felt the third movement might have been played a tad slower, but that is a minor issue. I was curious about the note at the bottom of the *Playbill* listing for this piece that states they "will perform Mozart's own cadenzas." We have, unusually, Mozart's own cadenzas for the first and second movements. (In a concerto for solo instrument, the performer was expected to improvise his own cadenzas. This is the case with Mozart's piano concerti.) But in a double concerto it would be nearly impossible to improvise a cadenza; Mozart had to provide them for the performers. In the case of the piano concerti, many alternative cadenzas have appeared but few stand up in quality to the ones written by Beethoven. As for alternative cadenzas for the Sinfonia concertante, I'm sure that someone has written one, but it would be a fool who would think he could improve upon the original. I certainly would be interested in hearing any, but I've failed so far in even finding a reference to such a work.

After the intermission, Susanna Phillips performed two arias, one from *Don Giovanni* and the other a concert aria written a few days after the premiere of that opera. Both are lovely and were sung warmly by Ms. Phillips. One certainly understands the desire to have an aria from this opera on the program, given the fact that it will be performed this week as part of the festival, but why choose two arias so close in style and both in C major?

The final piece was the Mozart Symphony No. 36, played spiritedly by Mr. Langrée and orchestra. It was a finely honed performance though not quite as clearly delineated as the Sinfonia concertante. In the other works presented this evening all the repeats were taken; here, in the Poco adagio second movement (played closer to an Andante), the repeats were omitted. As a result, the contrast between the 6/8 meter of the second movement and the 3/4 time of the Minuet was slightly dulled. I would be curious if the second performance of this work were more relaxed, not being under the constraints of the radio and video schedule to finish in exactly two hours.

These are minor complaints about an opening-night concert that promises well for the series. As Raymond Ericson stated in his review of the very first Mozart Festival Concert in August of 1966: "You can't go wrong on Mozart."

♫ Peter Brook's Flute-less *Magic Flute*
Lincoln Center Festival: Peter Brook (director), Soloists, Franck Krawczyk (piano), Lynch Theater, New York, 8.7.2011

Mozart/Peter Brook: *A Magic Flute*
American Premiere

What would a performance of *The Magic Flute* sound like if there were no flute, without an overture, without the three boys and the three ladies, no orchestra, shortened or elided arias, juxtaposed scenes, a singer singing a ditty not in the original opera–plus music from other works of Mozart's? It would not be *The*

304

Magic Flute, but *A Magic Flute.* Peter Brook's production makes no pretensions of being just another elaborate, grandiose, modern, relevant, even magical version of Mozart's masterpiece. In some ways, it might be better defined as an "anti-opera." Brook attempts to get to the core of this work, stripping away all the irrelevant parts so that even when it comes to scenery all we are left with is a stage filled with bamboo poles.

This version would certainly be a disappointment to purists. Sung to a libretto "freely adapted" by Brook, the pianist Franck Krawczyk and Brook's one-time assistant, Marie-Hélène Estienne, the production is more theatrical than operatic. To be precise, if you break the production down into three elements, staging, acting and singing, no one part is given undue emphasis. All are of equal value. The way the cast responded to the closing applause epitomized this equality. No cast member stepped out of rank to receive his or her individual ovations. In some ways, the production has the sensibility of the "radical" theater of the 1960's: works done at La Mama, the experimental theater of Jerzy Grotowski and Brook's work informed by the Theater of Cruelty and Theater of the Absurd.

"Absurdly," the production was done as a multi-lingual singspiel, the "sing" being done in German and the "spiel" in French (and a couple of words in English). The suicide attempt by the hapless Papageno was staged with a symbolic tree that seemed straight out of the opening scene of *Waiting for Godot.* The tree, created from crossed bamboo poles, looked like the beginning of a game of Hangman. Two actors, William Nadylam and Abdou Ouologuem, fill in for characters absent in this production and act as a Greek chorus as well. Both were also adept at handling the bamboo props—shaping them into a temple, a wall or a prison.

Masonic elements that Mozart emphasized were secondary to the philosophical principles of Sarastro. Brook also weakens the vengeful evil power of the Queen of the Night, making her eventual submission to Sarastro's beliefs seem inevitable. Every scene was compressed: the arias shortened and the da capos not taken.

The singers in this cast change from performance to performance. I saw the second cast and found the singers adequate to the demands of their roles; only Pamino, played by Agnieszka Slawinska, excelled in her arias. Leila Benhamza, in the demanding role of Queen of the Night, hit the impossible high notes in her two major arias, but only did so by shouting them.

The most interesting performer was on stage but neither sang nor acted: pianist Franck Krawczyk. Aside from his technical prowess, Krawczyk's adaptation was right on the mark, vibrant during the lighter scenes and foreboding during the darker ones. The moments when music was needed to provide an interlude that isn't in the original score were filled with music from other Mozart works. They blended in so well that in an interlude following the three trials Krawczyk's interpolation of the improvisatory opening of Mozart's Fantasia K. 397 seemed totally appropriate.

It was interesting to note how some of the arias in this performance foreshadow the style of Schubert's songs. In Sarastro's final aria, "In diesen heil'gen Hallen," the piano accompanies the singer with Schubert-like runs, ripples and quick modulations. Emotionally, one feels the commonality between these two doomed composers: Mozart with his dark undertones and Schubert's morbidly fixated songs.

While this might not be a version of *The Magic Flute* that I would want to see regularly, it is good sometimes to see a performance of a work that clears away the cobwebs, refreshing parts that have begun to sound hackneyed. It allows you to rethink works that have become war horses. Here Peter Brook, at his late age, successfully sees and connects with Mozart's autumnal vision of what man must do to be allowed to enter the temple of the next world.

♪ *Festival Review: Boston Early Music Festival*
Boston Early Music Festival, Boston, 12.6.2011–19.6.2011

The Boston Early Musical Festival that ended this past week occurs biennially and has done so for the last 30 years. This year the event attracted an estimated 15,000 people with hundreds of concerts, operas, master classes, lectures and exhibitions. I'm not sure how the attendance compared to previous years, but at a lecture-recital given by fortepianist Kristian Bezuidenhout, he was told that he would need 50 handouts. He was short by about 100 leaflets.

I was only able to join the Festival for the last three days, but that was enough to share in the excitement and anticipation of events with some of the great specialists in early music. In addition to Bezuidenhout, there was the young countertenor Philippe Jaroussky (more about him later); the vocal groups The King's Singers and the Canadian Les Voix Baroques; members of the Freiburg Baroque Orchestra; Peter Phillips and the Tallis Scholars; Jordi Savall; and the list goes on.

The BEMF Festival and Exhibition Guide runs over 300 pages. Fortunately, it reproduces most of the concerts' programs, adding details to the somewhat skimpy playbills handed out at each performance. It was an absolutely necessary informational source for all the events.

Keyboard Mini-Festivals
As part of the BEMF, there were two "mini-festivals," the first one an exploration of the organ. The second, which I attended, was devoted to the keyboard. Following the year's main theme, "Metamorphosis: Change and Transformation," it was titled "The Keyboard as a Catalyst for Change and Transformation." The offerings ranged from a musician whose lecture basically consisted of announcing the title of the work to be played, to a performer who spent much of his time talking, which just left a short period to play music.

The recital hall was the First Church of Boston, a modern space that is not quite intimate but has surprisingly good acoustics, particularly given the small dynamic range of the keyboards played. Peter Sykes introduced all three sessions, one devoted to the harpsichord, one to the fortepiano and one to the clavichord.

Each instrument had two keyboardists presenting their specialty.

Harpsichord

Sykes first played a work by the North German Georg Böhm, whose transformation was to write a suite in the French style with a classic Lully *ouverture* to open and a series of dances in the French style to follow. The next piece, a work by Dietrich Buxtehude, transformed a traditional Lutheran chorale into a four-movement suite. Sykes then performed a transcription by Bach of a trio sonata of Johann Reichen, who was one of many contemporaries whose work Bach adapted. Like most everything he touched, Bach improved Reichen's sonata, never expanding the source, but always reducing the voices to contrapuntal lines playable on a keyboard. In transcriptions of some concerti by Vivaldi, only a master such as Bach could have accurately transformed a fully orchestrated concerto into a work for two hands. As for Sykes' performance, he didn't particularly impress me with his playing. It was technically accomplished, but was both stiff and lacking in expressiveness.

More exciting and vibrant playing came from Luca Guglielmi who played two of Bach's concerto transcriptions, by Vivaldi and Marcello. If it weren't for this piece, Marcello's name would not be known today at all. Handel's transcription of his own Concerto Grosso Op. 6, No. 6 was a delight, as was Bach's arrangement of his Suite for Lute in G minor—which itself is a transcription of his fifth Solo Cello Suite.

Fortepiano

Christoph Hammer's topic was "*Ciarlattani*-Mozart in Competition." *Ciarlattani* or "charlatans" is a strange word to use for Mozart's competitors whether apocryphal or true. The performers Mozart competed with were composers in their own right; one can't feign virtuosity or improvisational skills. Changing the order from the program listing, Hammer gave a charming performance of a sonata by the unknown composer Ignaz von Beecke. Mozart is thought to have competed with Beecke in 1771 playing a fortepiano—and actually lost that one, admitting in a letter of having become rusty on the fortepiano. In a subtle and powerful performance of Mozart's Fantasia in D minor, Hammer used the work to demonstrate what kind of improvisational skills Mozart might have presented during these contests.

The most famous competition was that between Mozart and Muzio Clementi in 1781. However, of the two Clementi pieces that Hammer played neither in fact was the one that Clementi used in his contest, his Sonata in B-flat, Op. 47, No. 2; Hammer began with another sonata in the same key, the Op. 24, No. 2. The opening movement starts with a theme that Mozart stole for his overture to *The Magic Flute*, 10 years after Clementi wrote this piece. The second Clementi work, meant to be a parody of Mozart's keyboard writing, was thankfully brief. Hammer's recital ended with Mozart's Variations on a Theme by Paisiello. The second performer/lecturer for the fortepiano segment was Kristian Bezuidenhout, who scheduled only a single work, the Mozart Sonata in G major.

This performance was meant to exemplify Bezuidenhout's theories as to how one should approach Mozart's less-annotated scores—those written for his personal use, as opposed to his public commissions necessarily annotated for publication. I must say that whatever theoretical framework Bezuidenhout applied to his performance resulted in one of the most beautiful interpretations I have ever heard of a Mozart sonata, subtle and alert to every nuance.

Clavichord

For this segment the audience, initially spread about the room, was told to move as close to the stage as possible if they wanted to hear every note. We were also advised not to applaud to break the mood, but to wave our performance leaflets, all in respect to the soft-spoken clavichord. Michael Tsalka began with a variety of works from relatively unknown composers: starting with the Renaissance composer Antonio de Cabezón, he continued with the better known Froberger, a set of Bach variations entitled *Aria Variata* in A minor, and then a short piece from the Mexican Baroque composer Joseph de Torres. All were well-played and showed the keyboard's wide range of tonal depth and its sensitivity to the lightest touch. Tsalka played with his fingers curved over the keyboard, almost like they were cramped, but it didn't seem to hinder his ability to play, which he did with much sprightliness. Since I was to interview Miklós Spányi the next day and had never seen him play, I felt it was important to be as close as possible to the stage, both to observe his technique and to hear clearly the music emanating from this softest of instruments. In fact I was able to get a seat in the front row, the clavichord keyboard facing the audience. Unfortunately the page turner (Peter Skypes) stood next to Spányi right in my line of vision, completely blocking my view. The nice lady beside me saw how upset I was and kindly switched seats with me. Seeing him play was important, since his technique was quite different from Tsalka's, his long fingers stretched out almost effortlessly across the keyboard, reaching each note with ease.

Spányi began with a transcription by C. P. E. Bach of his own Sinfonia in F major. Just as his father was able to transcribe for two hands fully orchestrated works, so too could the son. Spányi's fingers sped across the keyboard, the original first movement difficult enough to play in its original manifestation, let alone in a transcription for two hands. The second movement, an Andante, was an exercise in key pressure control. Using precise fingering, Spányi was able to apply just enough pressure to give stress to the keys that require them. Two pieces from C. P. E.'s published collection followed and were played immaculately. Four movements from *The Art of Fugue* brought this late Bach work down to a human level. A virtuosic set of variations by Beethoven ended the cycle. And so the long day's mini-festival (9:00AM to 4:00PM) ended.

Steffani: *Niobe, Regina di Tebe*

The festival centerpiece was the American premiere of Agostino Steffani's *Niobe, Regina di Tebe*, one of hundreds—if not thousands—of operas from the 17th and 18th centuries by composers such as Hasse, Graun, Jommelli, Popora,

Destouches and Campra. Some of these (by Lully, Conradi and Blow) have seen the light of day due to the arduous efforts of the BEMF.

French Baroque opera has been luckier than its German or Italian counterparts. France's operatic revival has its roots in the early discoveries by William Christie, whose performances of Charpentier sacred and secular music led to productions not only of Charpentier but of Lully as well. Christie's disciples, Reyne, Rousset and Minkowski, have added to this revival, and Sir John Gardiner also contributed with his early productions and recordings of Rameau and Leclair operas. It's odd that aside from the revival of Monteverdi and Vivaldi, few Italian Baroque opera composers have generated any interest. Much, of course, has to do with the money needed to produce most of these elaborately costumed and staged works–and with large groups of singers talented enough to sing with the high tessituras that these operas required. France's government-funded arts councils have been tremendously generous to organizations such as the Centre de Musique Baroque de Versailles that are attempting to restore their musical heritage. With over 1,000 editions printed and nearly 50 CDs published in the last 20 years, the French are well on their way to uncovering their musical history.

Steffani's opera, *Niobe, Regina di Tebe*, is very much in the French style. This is not unexpected, Steffani having met Lully and attended his operas five years before he himself wrote his first opera. *Niobe* is filled with the elements of French opera beginning with a typical Lully-style overture. The stylized dancing, with its exaggerated hand and arm gestures and mime-like overly-emoted facial expressions, was wonderfully choreographed by Caroline Copeland and Carlos Fittane. The music, filled with dotted rhythms, had an instrumental timbre that seemed at times like only oboes and bassoons were being played. Costumes and stage settings, accurately designed from records and drawings of the period, were brilliantly rendered. The plot, too convoluted to discuss here, is both tragic and comic. Humorous episodes include the trapping and taming of a bear, and the comic presence of a philosophizing feminist, played and sung farcically by the countertenor José Lemos who brought an element of modernity and relevance to the text.

As for the singing: what a treat! The entire cast sang like the music was in their blood. There was no drifting into classical or romantic vocal mode. Purely sung with little difficulty in the upper ranges, this was a model of Baroque technique. To be singled out for their exceptional brilliance are Amanda Forsythe as Niobe and the nonpareil countertenor Philippe Jaroussky. Mention should be made about the venue: the Cutler Majestic Theater, an ornate masterpiece of the American Beaux-Arts period with its Rococo influence just an era away from the Baroque period music being played onstage. Acoustics were excellent as well.

This was such a captivating opera. The fact that it ran over four hours was of no consequence: it totally beguiled from beginning to end.

Mozart String Quartets
Kristian Bezuidenhout was back to play the two Mozart Piano Quartets, K. 478 and K. 491, with members of the Freiburg Baroque Orchestra: Petra Müllejans

(violin), Gottfried von der Goltz (viola), and Kristin von der Goltz (cello). These works come from two different worlds. Only a small percentage of Mozart's oeuvre are written in a minor key and those in the key of G minor are tragically intense. Out of 40-plus symphonies that Mozart composed, only the 25th (the "Little" G minor) and the 40th are in a minor key. Mozart, who was fairly strict in following classical period music forms, particularly in the opening movement of his instrumental works, surprises us here not by any deviation from the rules, but in our expectation. Just as we hear the lead-in to what should be the exposition's second theme, Mozart gives us the same theme as the opening – only this time in the major key of B flat. Then, as if we are not getting our money's worth with only one theme, Mozart opens the development section with a brand new one. The poignant second movement follows a traditional "A-B-A" formula, with each section rife with heartfelt melodies. As if to correct the seriousness of the previous movements, the concluding Rondo opens with a bouncy theme and ends brightly, although the mood of the first movement returns briefly in the middle.

The second Piano Quartet in E-flat major is all cheer and luster, but without the interesting complexity of the G minor Quartet. As in the previous quartet, the instrumentalists performed impeccably. Bezuidenhout made the fleeting runs up and down the fortepiano with ease and helped put the performances near the top of my experiences of listening to chamber music.

Handel: *Acis and Galatea*

This chamber opera was performed at the New England Conservatory's Jordan Hall to what appeared to be a full house. The staging was unusual in that instead of characters playing their roles as Arcadian shepherds, nymphs or rustic country folk, the director framed the work as a play-within-a-play: 18th-century characters rehearsing *Acis and Galatea* in their 18th-century costumes. It's an interesting conceit that probably added more confusion to an already confused plot. With most Baroque operas, it's always better to sit back, suspend your disbelief and enjoy the singing and the music. This relatively youthful work of Handel, age 33, is filled with so many catchy tunes, that one wonders whether a 1718 Hit Parade would have its top ten songs straight from this opera. Even the overture, a whirlwind of sound with the strings alternating with the woodwinds, is memorable. The diction was so clear that I couldn't mistake what I thought I had heard in earlier stagings. In the first line of the opening aria, instead of "Oh, the pleasure of the plains," I heard "Oh, the pleasure of the pain." Every aria was sung to perfection. The surprise character who stole the show was the bass Douglas Williams, wearing an eye patch to denote his role as Polythemus, a Cyclops. Galatea, played by Teresa Wakim, sang on the level of Amanda Forsythe in *Niobe* and that is no small accomplishment.

What more can be said about a nearly perfect production except to thank everyone involved for their tireless devotion to making every aspect of this opera succeed. In addition to the brilliant contribution both musically and operationally by Paul O'Dette and Stephen Stubbs, I would thank many of the teaching staff at Juilliard Historical Performance: Robert Mealy, Cynthia Roberts, Phoebe Carrai,

Robert Nairn and Gonzalo Ruiz.

♪*Cunningly Good: Janáček's "Little Vixen" Performed in New York*

The New York Philharmonic, Alan Gilbert (conductor), Doug Fitch (director), Karole Armitage (choreographer), New York Choral Artists, Joseph Flummerfelt (director), Metropolitan Opera Children's Chorus, Anthony Piccolo (director), Avery Fisher Hall, Lincoln Center, New York, 22.6.2011

Janáček: *The Cunning Little Vixen*

Magical is the word that comes to mind when describing last night's opening of Janáček's *The Cunning Little Vixen*, in the final concerts of Alan Gilbert's second season with the New York Philharmonic. This simple story needs no videos, no fractal light shows, no robotic scenery. In fact it just might be a rarity these days, a total–or at least nearly total–analog production. It's hard to imagine what fancy digital devices would add to a work of art so completely self-contained. The libretto and the music (Janáček did the texts as well) are so seamlessly intertwined that at any given moment it would be impossible to determine the source of the work's *affekt*. From the shimmering opening, convincingly conducted by Gilbert, to the insistent and percussive final bars, everything seemed so rightly in place that to change one note might be to change the whole.

The magic began with children imaginatively costumed as insects and animals of the swamp. Directed by Doug Fitch, they accurately captured each being's idiosyncrasies–the rubbing together of a fly's legs, the winged movements of the dragonfly, the stinging action of the mosquito. The scenery and costuming avoided anything overly outlandish.

The Avery Fisher Hall stage itself was extended out several rows into the orchestra with a zig-zagged runway allowing access to the aisle. At one point a fanciful insect ran up the aisle towards the exit, only to be blocked by a man with a cane slowly wending his way. It took a couple of seconds to realize that he wasn't part of the production.

The children performed their dancing so professionally that it was a joy to see. At one point, after a long dance interlude, they exited the stage with timing so perfect that the last to leave did so exactly on the music's final note, no mean feat. The costumes and machinations of the hens in the first act add levity to a work that quickly moves from a poetic opening to a prosaic ending. Up until this point it would seem entirely reasonable to ask why the opera would not be appropriate for children, adding it to the likes of *Hansel and Gretel* or *The Magic Flute*, perfect vehicles for parents to use as a tool to expose children to music. But this opera is no *Peter and the Wolf*. Squeezing life cycles into minutes, Janáček expresses another side of humanity. Here we have seduction disguised as love, marriage as a doomed enterprise, and old age as a time of emptiness.

The same cycle occurs in the animal world. The vixen "Sharp Ears," acted and sung with a smooth naturalness by Isabel Bayrakdarian, begins life as a spunky kid and, as a member of the Forester's family, is given the education of being exposed to humans. As she gets older and wiser, she sheds some of her naïveté, tricking the hens into coming near enough for her to kill them. Ultimately, she falls victim to her pride and the life cycle continues with a new vixen, not very different from the old one.

In addition to Gilbert's conducting and the orchestra's vibrant playing, all the singers' voices fell naturally into the musical whole. While there were no grand arias to help judge their vocal capabilities, none of them pushed their voices unnecessarily. Super-titles were beamed unobtrusively on a curtain above the stage, but the singers' diction made it almost unneeded. The English translation was modernized but not excessively so.

As to whether the *The Cunning Little Vixen* will rank with last year's hit production of *Le Grand Macabre*–also directed by Fitch–I can't imagine it being considered as anything other than a cunningly grand success.

♫*The Fairy Queen Hits the Big Apple*

Big Apple Baroque and Dušan Týnek Dance and Theatre, The Kaye Playhouse, Hunter College, New York, 14.6.2011

Henry Purcell: *The Fairy Queen*

This Purcell work is often classified as semi-opera. Some of the libretto is spoken, some sung: a cross between opera and set stage pieces (masques). Much of the text is taken straight from Shakespeare's *A Midsummer Night's Dream,* and *The Fairy Queen* is (even without going into its musical components) a hybrid of theatrical forms. Add to this mix the composer Henry Purcell, writing in a number of musical styles–the French style of Lully, the Italian style of Giovanni Draghi and the English style of John Blow–and you end up at best with a patchwork quilt and, at worst, a mishmash.

The theatrical demands of *The Fairy Queen* are onerous: a cast of 25 (in addition to the main singers), a production crew of 32, a dance troupe of nine, and an orchestra of 25 members. To say this production, the first of this magnitude for the Big Apple Baroque and the Dušan Týnek Dance Theatre, didn't stand up to the one produced **at** the Brooklyn Academy of Music under the direction of William Christie is only to repeat the admission made in the playbill that this was a "production…mounted without the customary props of space, time or money that normally underpin an entertainment of this scale and scope."

The music that Purcell wrote for this opera is glorious, one memorable aria after another. Purcell had, like Mozart and Schubert, the ability to create wonderful melodies that sound as natural as human speech, that appear and disappear never to be heard again. The music spans a range of emotions from the drunken "Fill up the bowl" to the heartbreaking "Let me weep" (the sister aria to "When I am laid to earth" from Purcell's *Dido and Aeneas).* Purcell's method, one that he used so often in his odes and welcome songs, is to begin with a ritornello leading into the vocal line, and then towards the end have the chorus and/or orchestra pick up and end the aria. The orchestral pickup not only reiterates the theme but develops it as well.

The opening night performance suffered from first-night jitters, at least in the first three acts. In the masque scenes of the final two acts, the acting and singing improved considerably. Interspersed with the arias are interludes often filled with short dances. The dancing was quite professional, if a little derivative of the choreography in Mark Morris's takes on Purcell's "Dido and Aeneas" and "King Arthur."

Although the staging lacked props, the same cannot be said of the costumes, which were abundant, eloquent and colorful. However, some of the production decisions were the oddest I've ever seen. In Act III, at the king's birthday party, the king is equipped with a pair of sunglasses and a cell phone. Anachronism can be amusing, but it has to be meaningfully placed. One can't have ambulances arrive to take Hamlet and Horatio to the hospital unless this anachronistic conceit was established early in the play. A video played on the backdrop and meant to enhance "Let me weep" might have been interesting in another context. This short film done in the silent movie style of Carl Dreyer or the more recent manner of Robert Bresson was quite impressive, but proved to distract one from concentrating on the Fairy Queen's most poignant aria.

Confusing as well was the playbill, the synopsis being a hodge-podge of details of the fictional libretto mixed inextricably with sources from Purcell's time. It also includes references to scenes that have been elided from the actual performance. Confusingly, no bios are given for any cast or production member, but pictures of the dancers and their bios are fully detailed.

The one outstanding singer, Lynn Norris, with a truly gorgeous voice able to clearly reach all of the audience, demonstrated her understanding that Baroque vocal style is not the same as 19th-century vocal style.

♪NYPO Offer a Beethoven Bonbon, Some Currier Caffeine and a Dollop of Brucknerian Schlag

Anne-Sophie Mutter (violin), Alan Gilbert (conductor), New York Philharmonic, Avery Fisher Hall, Lincoln Center, New York, 2.6.2011

Beethoven: Romance in F major for Violin and Orchestra
Currier: *Time Machines* (*World Premiere*)
Bruckner: Symphony No. 2 in C minor

Alan Gilbert continues to create adventuresome programs that mix familiar works with brand new or rarely performed ones. Tonight's relatively familiar piece was Beethoven's Romance for Violin and Orchestra in F major. The new work was Sebastian Currier's *Time Machines*, a concerto written for Anne-Sophie Mutter. The rarely performed Bruckner Symphony No. 2 ended the evening.

Anne-Sophie Mutter gave an easeful, elegant performance of the Beethoven Romance. If overplayed, the lyrical first theme can easily sound treacly, but Ms. Mutter didn't allow this to happen. The work is in rondo-sonata form with each new theme modulating into a minor key and the central section acting as a brief development in sonata form. Although little is known of this work's pedigree, the quiet and inconclusive coda leads one to suspect that it could be the second movement of some lost or unwritten violin concerto. There is such a sense of expectation at this moment that one can almost hear the beginning of the imagined concerto's finale. This was the world premiere of Ms. Mutter performing under Mr. Gilbert's leadership, and she surely should have been pleased by his responsive accompaniment.

The other world premiere, Sebastian Currier's *Time Machines,* a seven-movement concerto commissioned by Ms. Mutter, followed the Beethoven. Mr. Currier certainly had no doubts as to Ms. Mutter's technical abilities, and she played the demanding piece with little evidence as to how difficult it must have been to master. The concerto was mature and accomplished, complex yet accessible. Mr. Currier's deconstruction of his composition in the printed program, though helpful in understanding its underlying musical structures, was not needed to enjoy its unique sound world (just as one does not need to understand the intricacies of the harmonic and canonic world of Bach's *Goldberg Variations* to enjoy its musical realization).

Each movement has its own distinct voice. The first is a buzzy whirlwind of instrumental colors, the violin mostly used as emphasis, and ends with impossibly fast violin runs at the lowest dynamic level. The second movement is made up of clever and amusing "delayed" responses or echoes of the violin's short phrases. The third movement is all snapping, virtuosic percussive sounds and pizzicati, the cacophony seeming to last only seconds. The fourth movement, a virtuosic showpiece that Ms. Mutter played with rapid-fire bravura, is highlighted by what sounded like a piano but was probably the vibraphone. The fifth is the most highly inventive movement, complex, frenzied and heavily orchestrated. I found this movement humorous, as if it contained conversations between wood thrushes, while the final notes sounded not unlike ducks quacking. The sixth movement was the only one that seemed derivative, a brief work that could have been part of any set of Webern's pieces for orchestra. The final variation, entitled "harmonic time," was almost lyrical, opening with Ms. Mutter sounding as if she were about to play a late romantic concerto *à la* Sibelius. The similarity ends quickly yet the movement remains lush and lyrical, a heart ready to burst.

Mr. Gilbert concluded the concert with one of the least known of Bruckner's output, the Symphony No. 2. This was a daring move on Mr. Gilbert's part: he could have chosen the more accessible Fourth or the monumental Ninth, but the Second would never be close to the top in anyone's Bruckner's Top 10. Yet the Second is as representative of Bruckner's works as any other, and to get caught up in its magic gives one the key to opening the door to his other mystical chapels. Not since Bach has a major composer written music so entirely in *Soli Deo Gloria* as Bruckner, nor has any composer's entire opus seemed as if it were part of one integrated whole. On one level, Bruckner's symphonies appear to be a variation on Liszt's *Les Préludes:* "What is life but a series of preludes to that unknown song, of which the first solemn note is sounded by death."

Every crescendo that Bruckner wrote walks a tight line between being emotionally convincing and bombastic, but unless poorly conducted never becomes the latter. Like few other composers he demands that listeners suspend their disbelief and give the music room to make itself believable.

In the *Playbill*, Mr. Gilbert writes, "I could conduct [Bruckner] every day for the rest of my life and be satisfied as a musician." His exquisite recreation of Bruckner's musical spires might just accomplish with this composer what Bernstein was able to do with the next generation's great symphonist, Gustav Mahler.

♫Hallelujah: Handel and Beethoven Choral Works in New York

Paul Appelby (tenor), Rachel Rosales (soprano), Charles Perry Sprawls (bass), Nancianne Parrella (organ), Jorge Ávila (violin), Arthur Fiacco (cello), Choir and Orchestra of St. Ignatius Loyola, Kent Tritle (conductor), Church of St. Ignatius Loyola, New York, 25.5.2011

Handel: Concerto in G minor for Organ and Orchestra
Handel: "Foundling Hospital Anthem"
Beethoven: *Christum am Ölberge*

In a city as large as New York that offers music of all kinds every evening of the year, it is easy to forget how active churches are in adding to its musical life. Last night's concert followed another substantial one performed at a church just one block north the week before. Some churches present their own choruses and orchestras, while others serve as venues for outside groups. For audience members who are not church goers, it is often a visual as well as auditory treat. The secular façade of the Church of St. Ignatius Loyola hides a late-19th-century mix of Baroque and Roman basilica elements with a long nave and an interior paved partly with pinkish marble. It also houses the largest track organ in New York City, with over five thousand pipes.

The organ, rising above the back choral loft, has a magnificent sound. Handel played these organ concerti, though, on a small positive organ with registrations probably limited only to open and stopped flute ranks. If Handel had played the Concerto in G minor on an organ such as this one, the sounds of other instruments would have been drowned out. This brief opening piece was played on the organ with solo violin and cello, and without amplification this reduction of Handel's score to a trio would have been totally covered by the organ. Here the result of amplification, plus not being able to see the players in the chorus loft, made it feel like listening to a recording of the work rather than a live performance.

The following composition, "The Foundling Hospital Anthem," was performed in its original version. There also exists a revised version, and I wish the choice here had been to do that one. Handel added one aria and modified some of the choruses so that they were sung by soloists instead. These changes redefined the whole emotional tenor (ahem!) of the work. The revised score opens with a solo aria by the tenor introduced by violins played in unison. The soloists take over some of the chorus's parts, such as in the line beginning "O God, who from the suckling mouth," sung in the revised version by an alto. Handel also added the delightful and winsome aria "The people will tell of their wisdom," an angelic give-and-take between two sopranos. The first two choruses were not written specifically for this anthem, but were borrowed instead from his earlier work, the "Funeral Anthem for Queen Caroline." By making these revisions, Handel was looking to change the elegiac mood into something more upbeat.

That being said, the performance of this original version was a solid one. The conductor Kent Tritle knew exactly what he wanted from his musicians and singers. The surprise was the "Hallelujah Chorus" from *The Messiah* in its original placement as the final chorus of the anthem. I wondered if it would have been appropriate for the audience to have stood up during its performance!

The major work on the program was Beethoven's *Christum am Ölberge*. While this is Beethoven's only oratorio, he wrote many other pieces for chorus and/or soloist and orchestra. Often these works, including the one performed tonight, were quickly written to meet a specific event; the accession or death of an Emperor, or a political event such as the Congress of Vienna, and are bombastic with cloying texts. Tonight's oratorio compares in quality with better written works for chorus and orchestra such as the Fantasia for Piano, Chorus and Orchestra and the larger *Missa Solemnis*. Despite the sacred tradition, the recitatives, arias and choruses are operatic in scope.

Paul Appleby, the tenor, had just the right voice for the role of Jesus, presenting a powerful, yet emotionally fragile figure. I might have wished he were a little more in sync with the other members in regard to when he was required to be seated, but this didn't impact his fine singing. Rachel Rosales didn't have the sweetest voice and strained a bit in some of Beethoven's difficult arias, but still was able to give a strong performance. The bass Charles Perry Sprawls had too short a role to comment on his voice. Both the orchestra and chorus, under the direction of Mr. Tritle, played flawlessly and knew how to deal with the Church's acoustics so as not to have one group overpower the other.

♪Handel Done Right by the Clarion Music Society

Chorus and Orchestra of the Clarion Music Society, Steven Fox (conductor), Park Avenue Christian Church, New York, 17.5.2010

Handel: *Judas Maccabeus*

George Frideric Handel was known to be a shrewd, if occasionally misguided, businessman. In his biography of the composer, Christopher Hogwood states that at the time of writing *Judas Maccabeus*, Handel showed signs of "healthy opportunism slipping into a slightly weary pragmatism." The libretto was written by Reverend Thomas Morrell (a new librettist for Handel), and much of it is just plain old doggerel. But when Handel received it, he began composing almost immediately.

In this case his judgment was good. *Judas Maccabeus* may not be anywhere close to the top in popularity of Handel's works, but it was second only to the *Messiah* in the number of performances done during his lifetime. As a pragmatist Handel knew just what to do to stack the deck in favor of a theatrical success. He holds back much of the military and war pieces until the last third. The trumpet doesn't appear in the work until "Sound an alarm," the 36th out of 54 numbers, in Steven Fox's abbreviated production. And even in this aria it's not until the da capo that the trumpets actually come in.

From this point on, no one sleeps: the music is so wonderfully intense that I wished Mr. Fox would have done the entire oratorio (about 68 numbers), but I could understand why he didn't. First, it would have added half an hour to the performance which already ran a good two hours. Second, for whatever story this oratorio is meant to tell, the items removed had no impact on the "plot." Finally, the rejected pieces were in most cases slower tempi and Mr. Fox excels in fast-paced music. I only regret his not having included the spirited "So rapid thy course is" and the plaintive "Wise men, flatt'ring, may deceive us," both from Act II.

The singers were particularly impressive. Steven Caldicott Wilson had a slow start, but was formidable in "Sound an alarm." Both Lauren Snouffer and Silvie Jensen sang with great poise and élan. Daniel Taylor's Priest reached a whole other level of beauty in "Father of Heav'n." Indeed, his ability to produce such a wonderful rounded bell-like sound so effortlessly is something *from* "Heav'n." Jesse Blumberg sang warmly and sensitively. Commendations are always owed to any and all players of the torturous valveless instruments. It is said that Bach's eldest son, W. F. Bach, who was somewhat behind the times, went fruitlessly in search of musicians to play valveless horns and trumpets for his old-fashioned cantatas. They were too difficult for most to play.

What can I say about Steven Fox that I haven't said before? Adding to my last rave review, I can attest that having experienced his recent conducting with two different orchestras, where he achieved similar impressive results, there is no questioning his ability to draw out from musicians their best possible playing. Clearly, he has a tremendous rapport with musicians, and this ability makes him a conductor to follow.

♩Schoenberg Does a Strauss Waltz, Strauss Writes an Adagio for Strings, Brahms Joins in a Gypsy Dance

Jupiter Symphony Chamber Players: Adam Neiman (piano), Paul Neubauer (viola), Maurycy Banaszek (viola), Barry Crawford (flute), Vadim Lando (clarinet), Anton Barakhovsky (violin), Lisa Shihoten (violin), Suren Bagratuni (cello), Good Shepherd Church, New York, 16.05.2010

Johann Strauss II: "Emperor Waltz"
Richard Strauss: *Metamorphosen*

This concert was another fine performance of unusual repertory, brilliantly played by little-known musicians. The last of a series of 20 inventive programs that started in September 2010, the concert was planned to end on a high note and it didn't disappoint.

The program opened with a Schoenberg transcription of a work by a composer who could be considered his exact opposite, Johann Strauss II. Schoenberg himself said: "I don't see why when other people are entertained I too should not sometimes be entertained…. It would be hypocritical of me to conceal the fact that I occasionally step down from my pedestal and enjoy light music."

Schoenberg also implied that only light music that had some depth was worth bothering about. He seemed to have found something of interest in the "Emperor Waltz," enough to make the effort to shrink a whole orchestral score into a work for six players. The end result is much more serious, and more amusing, than the original. The differences between the original and the transcription are subtle and mostly done "behind the scene": changes in harmony, added counterpoint and instrumental color. This transcription emphasizes the bass instruments and transcribes some of the instrumentation to the flute, clarinet and piano. The result is a work that sounds as if it were written for an accordion or street band with its inebriated oom-pah-pah beat. The choice of solo instruments to replace a full orchestra section gives the work a fresh touch.

The instrumentalists played the piece to the hilt, putting it through all of Strauss-Schoenberg's musical peregrinations. They highlighted all the facets of the score that made the original such a popular work.

We are in a whole new world with Strauss's *Metamorphosen* in a transcription by Rudolph Leopold. It is less a transcription than a reduction of players from 23 strings to six, and it results in a more intimate reading of a monumental work. Strauss originally referred to it as an "Adagio for about 11 strings," and indeed it has much in common with Samuel Barber's *Adagio for Strings* which came 10 years earlier. They both are funereal in nature, bent on creating a somber musical environment. The *Metamorphosen* though reaches back towards Wagner and the Schoenberg of *Verklärte Nacht* and is considerably more difficult than Barber's work. It's easy to catch on to Barber's poignant piece with an opening main theme that hits you in the face and doesn't do much else after that. Strauss's goes on for twice as long, through varied key modulations, producing a deeper harmonic depth. It leads one through a dark landscape with only a few hopeful moments. I was mesmerized from start to finish, caught up in its passionate despair. This is not the Strauss who slowly leads you to the rapturous climaxes of his popular tone poems; to understand it the audience has to go with its sorrowful flow. The players maintained the work's expressive and mournful mood to its bitter end.

A much more upbeat work concluded the program and the season: Brahms' Piano Quartet No. 1. This is perhaps Brahms' most successful work, at least of his middle period, filled with delightful themes. (Interestingly, Schoenberg transcribed this piece for full orchestra.) The first movement alone has four astoundingly beautiful themes: the opening piano motif taken up immediately by the cello, the lyrical second played by the cello, the soaring third by the violin and viola and the rollicking fourth by the players in unison. This last theme, in the recapitulation, changes surprisingly from a jaunty to a melancholy one, modulating to the minor key as the movement ends on a quiet note. The second movement is a speedy Intermezzo with even an even speedier Trio section marked Animato. After a return to the original tempo, the movement ends with a flourish in the piano, again ending softly in a *pp*.

The Andante Brio opens with a classic Brahms-style theme, similar in spirit to the *Academic Festival Overture*. As the work's slow movement, it doesn't provide much peace, with stormy chords from the piano filling its central section. It seems that Brahms here, as in his first piano concerto, is writing the symphony he didn't feel that he was yet capable of writing.

The final movement is the famous Rondo alla Zingarese with its rustic country dance rhythms and poignant middle section. The piano has a workout that requires tremendous dexterity. As would be typical of this country-band music, the piece builds up to a frenzy with Brahms concluding this masterpiece with the designation Molto presto. The work, rife with challenges on all levels, as well as the two preceding pieces, was handled admirably by all involved. The entire series presented exceptional performances of unusual repertory that deserves to be better known.

Note: Even though I could not see the pianist Adam Neiman play, I was aware of the fact that there wasn't a page turner present, and he didn't seem to be turning pages himself. An announcement was made that he was using an iPad 2. After the concert we spoke briefly, and he said that he was reading the score from the iPad using an app that costs $5. The iPad connected wirelessly to two remote pedals near the piano's pedals (which cost an additional $110).

♪Dramatic Performances in an Ideal Setting: Mozart and Dohnányi Quintets

Lily Francis (violin), Ida Kavafian (violin/viola), Jessica Lee (violin), Mark Holloway (viola), Nicholas Canellakis (cello), André-Michel Schub (piano), Rose Studio, Lincoln Center, New York, 12.4.2011

Mozart: String Quintet in C minor
Dohnányi: Piano Quintet No. 1 in C minor

In an earlier review I mentioned that chamber music played in an intimate setting can magically enhance the listener's experience. With an audience of about 100 clearly devoted music-goers, the Rose Studio was just right for last night's excellent performance of two very different quintets.

The first work on the program was Mozart's String Quintet, K.406/516b. I've added "516b" to avoid a seeming anachronism. This quintet, a transcription by Mozart of his Serenade for Winds K.388, was meant to serve as the third member of a set of quintets, the other two being K.515 and 516. The Köchel number 406 was corrected by Alfred Einstein to K.516b in the third edition of the Mozart catalog since the transcription was done around the same time as 515 and 516.

The opening motif, played forte by all five, set the tone not only for the Mozart but for the fiery Dohnányi that followed. Neither piece was written with the dilettante in mind. Mozart composed just a handful of works in C minor (including the Mass in C minor, the Piano Sonata No. 14 and the Fantasia for Piano), and he didn't choose the key randomly. He transcribed the passionate intensity and rawness of the C-minor Serenade to complement the other two string quintets; all three were completed in the same year as *Don Giovanni* and share its hot-blooded spirit. The string quintet at the Rose Studio felt the work's temperament and temperature and played it with appropriate gusto.

The second movement, a poignant Andante in the relative major, brings a moment of peacefulness. But even this quiet interlude has some stretching of its harmonics, just to make sure we are aware that this is not an upbeat work, regardless of its starting and ending in the major key of E flat. As if there wasn't enough weight in the work to make it interesting, Mozart takes the classic minuet, the lightest movement in the traditional four-movement form, and, with a nod of the head to Bach, writes the "A" section as a canon. Still not satisfied he takes this same canon in the "B" section Trio and writes it in reverse. What Mozart has done is to create the musical equivalent of a palindrome. The final movement is a theme and variations. Actually it is a theme and variations with variations. The first three are typical for Mozart—adding triplets, modifying the theme by syncopation, changing emphasis on different notes—but by the fourth the da capo structure ends and the strict variation on a theme reverts to sonata form for a moment as it undergoes a development. This mixed form occurs quite frequently in Mozart's closing rondos where a development section is added to the middle, making the movement a cross between rondo and sonata.

As well-played as the Mozart was with Lily Francis as first violinist and Ida Kavafian as first violist, a certain authority was given to the performance of the Dohnányi Piano Quintet with Kavafian as first violinist. From the opening crescendo to the Finale's last chord, Kavafian exuded confidence and displayed a deep understanding of this work's inner structure.

It is amazing enough that this work was written by Dohnányi at the age of 18, but before publishing it as his Opus 1, he had already written some 70 earlier pieces. This quintet is a late 19th-century masterpiece. It is slightly derivative, but the music is so well conceived that even if, in the first movement alone, you hear Brahms in the opening passages and Dvořák as the inspiration for the movement's second theme, you are still dumbstruck by the beauty of its melodies. At times one feels that the music is almost too big for a quintet: as Brahms' First Piano Concerto was jokingly referred to as his real first symphony, so this work seems to be stretching the bounds of its form.

The second movement continues at the zealous pace of the opening movement, pausing only briefly for the peaceful Trio section. Yet even here the quietude is broken, flaring for a minute and returning to the first section's dynamics to continue its fervent passage to a softer ending. An Adagio with a lovely melody played by the viola opens the third movement. It too has moments of fervid intensity before subsiding with a peaceful sigh. The Finale, a rondo-like movement, starts strikingly with a catchy, jaunting theme that fixes itself in your mind. Filled with big crescendos that are orchestral in their dynamics and a lyrical song first played by the cello then given to the others to comment on, this movement contains a bit of everything. This "everything" includes a perfectly constructed fugue based on the opening melody as well as Dvořákian moments. The movement ends as it began with tremendous bravura.

My kudos to all six members of the group for performing chamber music as it should be performed. They left the stage after this powerful recital looking tired, but the audience left the building invigorated.

♫Not Yet a True Mahlerian: Alan Gilbert Conducts Mahler's 5th
New York Philharmonic Orchestra, Alan Gilbert (conductor), Avery Fisher Hall, Lincoln Center, New York, 27.04.2011

Mahler: Symphony No. 5

In years past, every major symphony orchestra and conductor would have been obligated to follow the unspoken rule that they would never achieve the greatest heights in music until they performed and/or recorded all the Beethoven symphonies. Nowadays the same seems to hold true for those of Mahler. Even though it is an anniversary year (Mahler died in 1911), the number of performances as well as complete cycles is staggering. Every conductor, it seems, would like to be known as a "true Mahlerian."

Alan Gilbert has a long way to go in this regard, having conducted only three Mahler symphonies with the NYPO: the First on tour and outdoors, the Sixth last season, and now the Fifth. His performance of the Sixth Symphony back in September was moderately successful; as with this performance of the Fifth, I found some things to complain about but very little to praise.

The problems with last night's performance were more conceptual in nature than orchestral or technical, and had to do with Gilbert's difficulty in shaping the musical lines of Mahler's phrasing. To take examples from the first movement: right before the Funeral March begins there is a descending phrase played forte by the French horns. Without the right shaping, accenting and slight angularity, this can sound dull and flat rather than supremely tragic. Similarly, the Funeral March here is like most marches or waltzes in Mahler: never straightforward but always a bit sarcastic, bombastic or simply inebriated. Gilbert didn't quite get this. Mahler's irony was missing.

In the second movement, the tempo and dynamics were there, but the wildness that Mahler clearly specifies was diminished. He calls for the music to be played like "an intensely rushing storm" and with "the greatest vehemence." With such a description how can it be played other than fiercely and savagely? The opening attacks by the horns should sound like spikes going through metal. The return to the Funeral March tempo at the "Bedeutend langsamer" marking should be striking with the added upper voices, but wasn't. The transition from this movement into the Scherzo is marked "long pause follows." This pause separates the First Part from the quite different Second. I guess it's not really Gilbert's fault that what filled the long pause was a coughing epidemic, although I don't remember any such problem with Gergiev's Mahler. (I don't think anyone would have dared to cough in the latter Maestro's presence).

The third movement, marked Scherzo, is a mix of different moods, starting with rollicking horns played "powerfully, but not too fast," moving on to a slower ("ruhiger") section, back to the first tempo, on to a "Molto moderato," then to a smoother less raucous section ("Fliessender"), etc. More than the others this movement requires the conductor to create a musical arch that clarifies the beginning, the rich plaintive central section and the fiery "Piu mosso" and "Nach rascher" that conclude the movement. But here, the sudden changes in style and tempo seemed arbitrary.

What can be said about the Adagietto that hasn't been said before? As long as the movement avoids being histrionic on one side and overly limpid on the other, its pathos will come through. Gilbert may have erred slightly towards a conservative coolness, but it still was clear why this is Mahler's most appealing and popular piece, often performed by itself.

The final movement starts quietly but suddenly speeds up. Gilbert played this with tremendous vigor and intensity but pressed forward a bit too uniformly, so that by the time the coda was reached there was little room left for dynamic change. Gilbert's one and only feet-off-the-ground leap added a visual representation of the closing Allegro molto and final Presto, but was too late to produce its aural equivalent.

Perhaps, I've been a little too harsh since it was not in any way a terrible performance. For me, it just wasn't a satisfying one.

♫Leif Ove Andsnes at Carnegie Hall

Leif Ove Andsnes (piano), Carnegie Hall, New York, 7.4.2011

Beethoven: Sonata No. 21 in C major, "Waldstein"
Brahms: Four Ballades
Schoenberg: Six Little Piano Pieces
Beethoven: Sonata No. 32 in C minor

Leif Ove Andsnes may have scaled the Norwegian cliffs to breathe the pure air and be inspired to play Edvard Grieg's music on a concert grand perched on a precipice. Maybe he needs to do the same atop the Siebengebirge Mountains of Bonn to receive the spirit of Beethoven, born not far from there.

There was certainly thought put into the choice of works on this program, but Andsnes's attempt to find commonality among the pieces ended up sacrificing each work's uniqueness. The two compositions before the intermission do have moments where the composers hover near atonality, but by any standard these are exceptions not rules. There is not a tremendous amount of leeway for the performer to change tempo when the composer entitles a movement, such as the first movement of the "Waldstein," Allegro brio. Aside from a few accelerandos and ritardandos (even the brief eight-measure molto tranquillo near the end of the first movement is marked ma in tempo) there is no excuse for playing as slowly as Andsnes did; nor is there much room to play with dynamic changes. Although starting out softly at *pp*, the first crescendo to *f* occurs at measure 11 and to *ff* at measure 30. One could as readily rewrite Beethoven's music as to ignore his dynamic marking as Andsnes did here.

I always think of the opening theme of the "Waldstein" as sounding like a train with nearly identical repeating chords in the bass (16 in fact.) Andsnes played the movement rigidly, without any forward momentum. The same kind of playing occurred in the next two movements with no shaping of phrases, no regard for Beethoven's notational comments. It seemed like Andsnes was trying to draw out meaning from the score that was already there had he played it the way Beethoven meant it to be played. The end result was a dull fireless affair.

Brahms' Four Ballades fared better only because, in general, ballades are meant to be taken slowly, which the pianist did. But again, in the center of the first one, with a clear reference to Beethoven's most famous phrase from the Fifth Symphony played here 10 times over, Andsnes failed to capture Brahms' intensity. The lovely second one was not played with enough contrast between the opening Espressivo e dolce, the middle Allegro non troppo and the return to the first tempo. The short third ballade started off energetically then wilted. The fourth was funereal.

The highlight of the evening was Andsnes's playing of the key work around which the other pieces on the program were supposed to orbit. These six short pieces by Schoenberg, barely tonal, sparkled like diamonds. Here Schoenberg showed what potentially could be done by writing music on the edge of tonality. Not surprisingly, the audience, waiting for the moment when they could properly and sincerely applaud Andsnes for his accomplishments, gave their loudest approval.

The concert ended with Beethoven's last piano sonata, the Opus 111 in C-minor. What I would call the crux of this work occurs in the final movement when the meter suddenly changes to 12/32 but the tempo stays the same (*L'istesso tempo*). Beethoven here goes into a catchy, heavily syncopated segment that when played properly has a jazzy feel that makes it hard to keep your fingers from tapping out the beat. I found myself speeding up the music in my mind as if to encourage Andsnes to keep up with me, instead of slowly and "meaningfully" following behind me.

What did the audience feel about this performance, applauding enough to bring Andsnes out for three encores? I'm not sure, but the gentleman in the seat in front of me who was continually being poked awake by his wife during the concert, jumped up at the end to shout "*Bravo.*"

♪Jupiter Symphony Chamber Players in New York

Jupiter Symphony Chamber Players: Roman Rabinovich (piano), Vadim Lando (clarinet), Karl Kramer (horn), Dmitri Berlinsky (violin), Inbal Segev (cello), Good Shepherd Church, New York, 28.03.2011

Weber: Variations on a theme from "Silvana"
Kahn: Serenade in F minor
Mozart: Piano Trio in C major
Haydn: Divertimento a tré
Schoenberg: *Verklärte Nacht*

This concert was one of 20 performances in a series at Good Shepherd Church that runs from September to May. In earlier reviews, I praised both the selection of repertory, always programmed to mix familiar names and works with the unfamiliar, as well as the musicians' high level of technical and interpretive skills. Today's concert was no exception.

The first work on the program was a set of variations for clarinet and piano by Carl Maria van Weber. Known today mainly for his opera *Der Freischütz,* Weber was prolific in all musical forms: choral music, songs, concerti, piano sonatas and orchestral suites. He is also considered one of the great composers for the clarinet, writing mostly for the virtuoso Heinrich Bärmann. Because of the prominence of the instrument in works such as the overture to *Der Freischütz,* it might give the impression that Weber wrote much more music for clarinet than he actually did. Surprisingly, he wrote just six works for solo clarinet.

The work performed here was a set of variations on a theme from Weber's opera *Silvana.* The main theme begins with a clarinet playing a phrase that reminded me of the opening notes where it is joined by a bassoon in Mozart's "Voi Che Sapete" from *The Marriage of Figaro.* In fact, both works start with the same two notes and both are in the key of B-flat. Vadim Lando played the variations with élan where needed and a quiet sensuousness elsewhere. Roman Rabinovich's accompaniment was always sensitive to his colleague and vigorous in the piano's two solo variations.

The next piece was a serenade for piano, clarinet and horn by the composer Robert Kahn (1865-1951). In his youth, Kahn met and befriended Brahms, and it is clear from this serenade that Brahms' influence on him was substantial. In fact, Kahn outdid Brahms in writing trios for different configurations in an attempt to sell his scores to a broader range of players. For example, this serenade's score was published in nine different combinations for piano, horn, viola, violin, clarinet and oboe. The work, full of late-19th-century angst, was played with passion by the musicians.

The first half of the concert concluded with a delightful performance of Mozart's Piano Trio in C Major. Written in Mozart's prime between the 39th symphony and the three great last symphonies, it is in some ways a throwback to the earlier trio style of Haydn. Both Haydn and Mozart wrote piano trios, but Haydn wrote "Piano trios" and Mozart normally wrote "piano Trios." In the work performed here, however, Mozart's emphasis is clearly on the piano, with the other two instruments nearly relegated to obbligato roles. Rabinovich took the lead in this trio, performing with zest and always keeping an eye on the violinist to assure they were in synch.

After the intermission, Karl Kramer gave a brief introduction to the next work on the program, Haydn's Divertimento a tré for horn, violin and cello. He stated that the horn part, running through four octaves, was extremely difficult. He then asked the audience to wish him luck and proceeded to flawlessly play this technically challenging piece. At the high end of the instrument's range it takes embouchure and tight control of air supply to produce the notes, and Kramer handled both aspects with confidence and ease. Since Haydn wrote this work at a relatively early age and never specified which type of horn to play, one could assume he wrote the work for a virtuoso. In his later symphonies he made more realistic demands on the horn players.

The major work on the program was left for last: Schoenberg's *Verklärte Nacht,* a programmatic work based on a poem by Richard Dehmel in a transcription by the pianist Edward Steuermann. Schoenberg wrote the piece for a sextet and later transcribed it for string orchestra, so it was quite an accomplishment for Steuermann to convert a work originally scored for six strings down to three. (But then again, Liszt transcribed Beethoven's Ninth for solo piano!) Although this transcription doesn't come near the dark, rich, murky quality of the original, it does have the advantage of allowing one to pick up inner voices not normally heard. The violinist, Dmitri Berlinsky, ravishingly imitated the doleful voices of the two programmatic characters. The final dialogue, played in the violin's upper range, was piercingly beautiful. Although less music was given to the pianist and cellist, they handled their parts with discernment and empathy.

Given the quality of the playing, it is not surprising that the concert hall should have been filled on a Monday afternoon. The audience returns week after week, confident that successive concerts will equal or excel their predecessors.

Note: The following reviews from 2010-2011 do not have headlines.

♪Bach Collegium Japan, Masaaki Suzuki (conductor), Carnegie Hall, New York, 22.3.2011

Bach: Mass in B minor

This performance of Bach's Mass in B minor, as well as the previous evening's concert by the NHK Orchestra of Japan, is part of the JapanNYC festival. A more appropriate program could not be found to commemorate the disaster in Japan, and Clive Gillinson, Carnegie Hall's Artistic Director, requested a moment of silence before the concert started.

The historic debate as to what is the correct size for the Mass's orchestra and chorus is as complicated as it is for Handel's *Messiah*. Indeed, the Mass is like the *Messiah* in reflecting the sensibilities of the time. A large chorus had always been used, but by the late nineteenth century, performances with 200 or more vocalists were considered not big enough. The first complete performance in New York City in 1900 by the Oratorio Society of New York, consisting of 72 instrumentalists and a chorus of 500, was praised by *The New York Times* for being "in accordance with the tonal balance usual in Bach's day." In a very early nod to historical authenticity, Walter Damrosch, the conductor of the 1900 concert, had two oboe d'amores made in Germany for the performance, instruments unlikely to have been heard with a chorus of this size overpowering their fragile voices.

As early as 1911 Albert Schweitzer complained that, "Even with a choir of 150 voices, there is a danger of the lines of the vocal polyphony coming out too thickly and heavily in a way directly opposed to the nature of Bach's music." Today, no one will claim that a chorus of more than 50 or a large imbalance of vocal and instrumental resources would be true to the spirit of Bach's music. A similar debate continues over the issue of OVPP (one voice per part), an idea proposed and defended by Joshua Rifkin in the early 1980s.

Masaaki Suzuki's performance was somewhere in the middle ground of this controversy with an orchestra of about 25 instrumentalists and a chorus of four or five for each vocal line (Sopranos I and II, Altos, Tenors and Bass). Except for the bass and countertenor, the soloists returned in a graceful, rehearsed manner to their respective places in the chorus. Suzuki was so sensitive to the issue of balance that for "Et in Terra Pax" he moved the entire chorus from a left to right grouping of Soprano I, Alto, Bass, Tenor and Soprano II to a simpler grouping of highest to lowest vocal range. The chorus returned to their original configuration afterwards. The end result was a well-balanced performance with neither voices nor instruments overpowering each other.

Maestro Suzuki has nearly completed recording all of Bach's sacred cantatas (he is currently at volume 47) as well as all of his keyboard music, and he, the orchestra and the chorus are clearly well-experienced in Bach's choral style. A master harpsichordist, Suzuki carries over his knowledge of keyboard practice to Bach's orchestral and vocal music so that there is clarity to each polyphonic strand in the score, as would be required in a keyboard work.

There is no doubt that the Mass in B minor is a monumental piece of music, from its tragic opening "Kyrie" to its high point in the "Sanctus" (the vocal equivalent of vaulting a cathedral) to the ending "Dona nobis pacem," a paradigm of the entire work from its simple opening chorus to its massive full-blown finale. Yet ultimately, compared to Bach's 200 or so extant, tight and personal cantatas, the Mass seems overblown. This is partially due to its derivative nature: half or more of the sections are recycled from earlier material. Composed in a manner that, even with modifications, restricted Bach from the total freedom he had in creating a work such as the *St. Matthew Passion*, the Mass lacks the *Passion*'s solid structure and continuity. While not as derivative as the *Christmas Oratorio*, it does retain a feeling of being ever so slightly secondhand.

As for this performance, none of the soloists had particularly strong voices: all shared a common dynamic projection more suited for performances in smaller halls. My main complaint was with the bass, Peter Kooij, whose voice was weak and raw in his first aria, "Quoniam tu solus Sanctus." He improved somewhat (as did the performance as a whole) in the second half of the concert when he sang "Et in Spiritum Sanctum." Mr. Kooij has been an exemplary bass soloist in all but a handful of the Collegium Japan's recordings of the Bach cantata cycle, so his singing here was particularly disappointing.

The orchestra produced rich and multicolored sounds, even with the expected slight intonation errors of the tremendously difficult valveless horns and trumpets. The timpanist, Robert Howes, is to be particularly commended for his precise playing of his instrument. Ryo Terakado, the concertmaster, sensitively accompanied the soprano Rachel Nicholls in the aria "Laudamus Dei." The orchestra and chorus had only one real synchronization problem which threw them off for several minutes. This occurred right after the intermission at the beginning of the "Credo" when Maestro Suzuki began conducting before the musicians and chorus were ready. Tempos were also moderate.

I imagine how difficult it must be for the performers to find the inner strength necessary to perform music of such intensity and pathos given the tragedy that is being faced by their families and friends back in Japan. Congratulations to all the musicians for persevering through this difficult time to produce glorious music that consoles us all.

♫Dame Kiri Te Kanawa (soprano), NHK Symphony Orchestra, André Previn (conductor), Carnegie Hall, New York, 21.3.2011

Takemitsu: *Green*
R. Strauss: "Vier letzte Lieder"
Prokofiev: Symphony No. 5 in B-flat major

Death and its precursor, old age, were both the explicit and implicit themes in Monday night's performance by the NHK Orchestra of Japan at Carnegie Hall. Add to this program Tuesday night's performance of Bach's Mass in B

Minor performed by Bach Collegium Japan, and one wonders who had the prescience to program two nights of such funereal aptness. In a speech before the concert, Clive Gillinson, Carnegie Hall's Artistic Director, offered condolences to the victims of both the Japanese and New Zealand devastations. André Previn conducted an unprogrammed performance of Bach's Air from the Orchestral Suite No. 3. Upon its conclusion, the audience was respectfully sensitive enough not to applaud.

We can understand the correlation between old age and Strauss's last songs, written a year before his death and not played until a year later, but this concert presented other, more sensitive issues related to old age. The 81-year-old Previn was in terrible shape, hunched over with a cane to help him walk, seated while conducting, and giving only the barest of gestures (reminiscent of Fritz Reiner's non-gesturing normal style of conducting with the Chicago Symphony Orchestra). One might think that his ability to impart his vision of the works performed here would be impaired by his frailties, and this was indeed the case with Strauss's wonderful "Vier letzte Lieder." There was barely, if any, eye contact between Previn and the soloist, the visually, if no longer vocally, stunning and elegant Kiri Te Kanawa. It was a major accomplishment that both the conductor and the soloist were able to start and end at the same time.

I have to admit that I may not be an unbiased reviewer of Strauss's "Last Songs." I consider myself fairly calm and rational, but I become effusive every time I hear them. The famous violin solo in "Beim Schlafengehen" followed by the soprano's entrance with "Und die Seelen unbewacht" is one of the most moving moments in Western music. It was sad to hear little more than a semblance of Ms. Te Kanawa's voice. Her inability to project so that she could be heard past the middle rows of the hall was not helped by Mr. Previn's dynamic insensitivity to her vocal weakness. One can still hear glints of her glorious instrument, and her emotional connection to the music was clear, but listening to her 1979 recording with Andrew Davis and the London Symphony Orchestra of these songs only serves to demonstrate what has been lost in the intervening 30-plus years.

Previn fared better with Prokofiev's Fifth Symphony. With an orchestra as colorful as the NHK, it would be hard not to draw a vivid performance from the instrumentalists. At times, particularly in the first movement, the strings were almost too lush, not giving the other instrumental groups enough room to toot their horns, so to speak. The tempo of this movement was also a little too close to an adagio than to the andante it is. The spirited, inebriated second movement, a percussionist's dream (or nightmare), went better. Previn was able here to keep the restless pulse continually beating throughout while the strings played some of Prokofiev's catchiest tunes. The opening theme is one of the few melodies from this composer that after a few hearings get stuck in a groove of your brain. The lyric third movement does not stay lyrical very long, moving back and forth between intense crescendos and quiet, offbeat waltz-like phrases. The final movement starts as if it was going to be a repeat of the first, but quickly moves to the tempo's descriptor, giacoso: an accurate adjective for a movement chock full

328

of satiric circus ditties. The main theme itself ends with what clearly is a hee-hawing donkey bray. The symphony moves towards its end like a whirlwind, the braying still going on in the background, slowing down for only a second before concluding with a bang. This work's final few minutes provide an ideal showcase for an orchestra like the NKH to demonstrate its capabilities, and it admirably did so here.

A quick mention should be given to the opening work by Tōru Takemitsu: a brief, pleasant, if uninspired few minutes of ersatz late Impressionism, sounding as if it were stolen from the early borderline tonal works of Schoenberg.

Louis Armstrong once said that "musicians don't retire; they stop when there is no more music in them." This was a well-intentioned program hampered by two musicians who clearly have more music in them but no longer are at their best in a large concert hall.

♪Evgeny Kissin (piano), Carnegie Hall, New York, 9.3.2011

Liszt: various works

It is an interesting and very different experience attending a recital by a charismatic virtuoso. A critic needs to pay special attention when judging the success or failure of a performance by a legendary soloist. One must be particularly careful not to get caught up in the audience's mass mentality, yet still retain the ability to separate who the artist is from what the artist does. Those who dart up from their seats to clap, shout and cheer would do the same whether the artist played heavenly or atrociously.

I could not tell the exact demographics of the audience, but a quick glance showed considerably fewer white haired or balding men than at most performances in Carnegie Hall. While I was waiting at the entrance, a bus dropped off a class of teenagers. This was not your usual classical music audience, but then again this was not your usual concert.

Before Kissin entered, the feeling of expectation was palpable. When he walked on stage, affectlessly bowed and began playing, three thoughts came to me. My first was, "Here is living proof that Dorian Grey exists." How can someone look exactly the same at 40 as he did at 12, particularly someone who has borne the stresses of concert touring for the past 25 years? My second thought was, "Is he an automaton perfectly fine-tuned to play perfect music perfectly?" My third was, "Who cares?" The end result is that while not the most Romantic, soul-searching performance of these works, it certainly was close to the most accomplished, impeccable and peerless performance I have ever seen. Sit back and enjoy the ride.

And a ride it was. From the opening of the Ricordanza from the *Etudes d'exécution transcendante* to the final *fff* of the Tarantella from *Venezia e Napoli*, Kissin played impossibly difficult music as if it were all as transparent as Liszt's relatively simple Consolations. Pianissimos were delicately played, yet clearly audible. Fiery chords at higher volumes were never muddled and always crystal clear. For such an amazing virtuoso, Kissin never postured, exaggerated or felt the need to display any kind of unnecessary showmanship. If there was one phrase to describe his playing it would be the oxymoron Classically Romantic: emphasizing form over emotion, in a way similar to how Arthur Rubinstein approached Chopin. Kissin was peerless in his ability to give shape to every part of the music, from the smallest phrase to the entire work.

His performance of the massive Sonata in B minor shared all these qualities. Compared to the emotionally raw and almost terrorizing performance by Martha Argerich when she was 19, Kissin's interpretation was indeed tame. But what Kissin did do was make sense out of a work that still baffles audiences today. When he came to repetitions of the major themes, they sounded natural, whereas in other performances, they often sound clichéd and bathetic, forerunners of the overblown and schmaltzy themes of Tchaikovsky. From the technical side Kissin was flawless, showing no signs at all of stress, stringing impossibly difficult chords through chromatic runs as if he were practicing scales.

Kissin couldn't quite overcome the inherent dreariness of the "Funérailles" from *Harmonies poétiques et religieuses,* though he made a valiant attempt. Liszt's most attractive music are those works where he attempts to write melodic lines in the style of Chopin, but except for a lovely theme that enters midway and the delicate, almost inaudible coda, the rest of "Funérailles" suffered from lack of imagination.

The "Vallée d'Obermann" from *Années de pèlerinage* began as if it were a Chopin Nocturne, and Kissin was just as masterful in bringing out the musical lines in slow pieces as in the more dramatic ones. After a short outburst, Kissin ended the piece as quietly as it began.

The final work on the program, *Venezia e Napoli,* contains three movements. The first a gentle, swaying song evoking the gondoliers of Venice was warmly played with Kissin creating wonderful tinkling sounds from the high end of the keyboard. The second movement, simply called Canzone, is a slight piece with a rather uninteresting melody supported by continuous tremolandos and ending with rolling sextuplets in the bass. It seemed to exist merely as a transition. The concluding movement is the same piece that Jean-Yves Thibaudet played to end his recital a month earlier. Whereas Thibaudet used this dance simply as a vehicle to dramatically conclude his concert with a bang, Kissin found substance as well, emphasizing the movement's song-like qualities, without skimping on the piece's showy virtuosity.

Those who came to this recital with the idea that Liszt must be played with romantic Weltschmerz may certainly have been disappointed, but for those without any preconceived ideas, it was an evening to remember.

♪Akademie für Alte Musik Berlin, Zankel Hall, Carnegie Hall, New York, 7.3.11

Telemann: Overture in F minor
Bach: Brandenburg Concerto No. 5; Concerto for Violin and Orchestra in E

major
Handel: Concerto Grosso in F major
Telemann: Concerto for Flute and Recorder in E minor

One of the prominent themes in music of the Baroque period is, for lack of a better phrase, "Les Nations." Couperin's chamber music set entitled *Les Nations*, Rameau's opera *Les Indes Galantes*, Lully's Ballet des Nations from *Le Bourgeois Gentilhomme* and even Telemann's own *Les Nations Anciennes et Modernes* all speak to the Baroque period's acceptance of national styles and idiosyncrasies. Telemann and Handel were cosmopolitans, living in probably the last period before each country felt it had to have its own distinctive music.

Although the three composers in last night's concert were all German, much of their music was modeled after the French and Italian forms of the day. Telemann's music was strongly influenced by French contemporary dances. The concerti grossi, represented here by a Handel work, are based on a form invented by the Italian composer Corelli. Bach, somewhat more isolated, wrote keyboard works in the French style and transcribed music by the Italian composers Vivaldi and Marcello.

The program opened with Telemann's Overture in F minor, which has an Ouverture (Overture or Ouverture being the name of the form as well as the title of the opening movement) that could very well have been written by Lully. Here Telemann mirrors Lully's stately and slow-paced style, heavy on dotted rhythms, and his brief, fugal-like center section based on a theme of only a few notes. (By the time Bach wrote his four Ouvertures, these center sections were full-blown fugues.) The following movements are all dances with French descriptions. The heart of this work is the Plainte, performed almost romantically, each cadence stretched to squeeze out every poignant note. The AAMB played the final three dances without pause, a nice idea but a problem in practice. Since the tempi of the Allemande and Chaconne are similar, it takes a couple of seconds to realize that, in fact, the Chaconne has already begun.

The second work on the program, Bach's Fifth Brandenberg, received a conservative, well-articulated performance. Harpsichordist Raphael Alpermann sensitively ran through the difficult cadenza, to which he applied accents and lines of phrasing that gave freshness to a part of the work often played just as a showpiece for the performer. Except for the slightly over-enthusiastic cellist, Jan Freheit, who continued playing *forte* as the rest of the group lowered their volume and silenced their instruments in preparation for the cadenza solo, the whole concerto was exceptionally well-balanced.

Bach's E major Violin Concerto was performed by lead violinist Georg Kallweit, whose initial entrance as soloist was somewhat raw and thin. Thinking at first that this was the result of his Baroque violin, I soon realized that he must have made some adjustment to his technique to accommodate the acoustics of the hall, because moments later his violin came fully back to life. The central Adagio, one of Bach's most deeply felt instrumental movements, was beautifully played, exceptionally dark and rich in Kallweit's vibrato-less interpretation.

Handel's great instrumental cycle, the set of 12 Concerti Grossi, represents the high point of this Italian form (excluding the somewhat looser and less traditional Brandenburgs by Bach). The second concerto played here was particularly effective in bringing out inner voices lost in performances by larger groups.

The final concerto by Telemann is written for the unusual combination of flute and recorder. Here Telemann has in effect written a work that marks the transition from the older recorder to the newer, less nuanced, but more practical flute. (C.P.E. Bach in the same way denoted the end of the harpsichord with his concerto for harpsichord and piano.) The last movement, a raucous, rustic, Polish-style dance, was enhanced by the improvisatory appearance of a tambourine and spinning clacker played by various members of the group.

Throughout the concert the performers created an ambience of ease and comfort and a sense of intimacy that made the naturally warm Zankel Hall feel as if it were one's living room with a fire roaring in the fireplace. In contrast to an earlier concert in this series performed by their Italian counterparts, Il Giardino Armonico, no unnecessary showmanship or technique for technique's sake was needed to produce a delightful evening of music.

♪A Venezia! Il Giardino Armonico, Giovanni Antonini (director, flute, flautino), Zankel Hall, Carnegie Hall, New York, 24.2.2011

Castello, Merula, Castello, Legrenzi, Vivaldi, Galuppi: various works

In a program where the only familiar composer was Vivaldi, I assumed that his wind concerti would be the highlight of the evening. There was an air of anticipation as we waited for Giovanni Antonini, the director of the group and flautist, to appear. Even the players seemed expectant. He eventually strutted on stage and began playing the Vivaldi Concerto for Flautino, RV 444. Yes, he has amazing technique and breath control and is able to get incredibly rapid chirps out of the tiny little flute, but this was just virtuoso showmanship for its own sake. It was impossible for the listener to extricate the melodies from his rush of notes. Antonini cared little for tempo marks, playing the Largo as if it were an Allegretto, exaggerating cadences and creating codas with unmarked diminuendos and ritardandos.

I certainly am not a traditionalist in regard to Baroque performance. I love Anzellotti on accordion doing Bach's *Goldberg Variations*, the Dunedin Consort's one-person-per-role *Messiah*, and performances by Il Giardino Armonico in their Handel Opus 6 set (Handel's Concerti Grossi benefited from the speed and warmth of the group). But here Antonini sacrificed clear articulation, melody and rhythms for speed. Granted, Vivaldi's concerti are in no way monumental in comparison to Bach and Handel, but their melodies are catchy, the rhythms bouncy and second movements often soulful. In the second movement of the Concerto for Flautino, RV 443, Giovanni did slow down but not enough to bring out its heartfelt pathos. Equally annoying was his performing stance which the person next to me called the "pelvic school" style of playing: bending, lurching and swaying, adding unneeded body emphasis whenever he wanted to make a point.

The first part of the concert consisted of music from the Italian Baroque by little-known composers. The first two pieces were for four strings, but a string quartet far different from any written 100 years later. Very free in form, the works consist of short passages thrown back and forth among the musicians. These phrases are then developed in a way that makes them appear almost improvised; other characteristics are sudden changes in dynamics and tempo. The third piece on the concert was a Ciaccona for two violins and basso continuo. The chaconne is a form in triple time that uses a continuous repetition of a motif, usually only a measure or two in length, played in the bass upon which the upper voices seemingly improvise. The particular way the chaconne is accented on the second beat can have a mesmerizing effect. Almost all the composers of the Baroque period wrote one or more of them, ending in the nonpareil Ciaconna in D minor by Bach for solo violin. The chaconne played here, composed by Tarquinio Merula in the mid-17th century, is for two violins. In addition to the usual variations over the repeating bass, the second violin serves as a bouncing board for the motifs played by the first violin. This was delightfully handled by the two violinists, Enrico Onofri and Marco Bianchi.

Giovanni Legrenzi is often included in programs on the Venetian school in the period just before Vivaldi. Legrenzi died when Vivaldi was twelve, yet his influence on the younger composer was enormous, both in forms used and string technique. The sonata on this program is both representative of the modern side of Legrenzi with its more developed themes, and old-fashioned in its sudden dynamic and tempo changes. As in all the works in the first part of the program, the strings played with warmth and enthusiasm.

Although most of the pieces, including the improvisations that joined some of the disparate work, have been in IGA's repertory at least since 2000 when they were recorded on the album *Viaggio Musicale*, the work by Galuppi is new to the mix. A generation younger (1706-1785) than the other composers on this program, he is represented here by a composition once thought to be by Corelli. It was later determined that Galuppi wrote it but in the style of Corelli, and it certainly reminds one of the latter with its slow opening, fugal second movement and closing allegro.

One last caveat. The playbill states that these works are "three of Vivaldi's lesser-known wind concerti," but I stopped counting at 25 the number of recordings of all three. In fact, one of the early recordings of two of them (Vivaldi's RV 441 and 443) was performed by Leonard Bernstein and the New York Philharmonic Orchestra in 1958. Flautists such as Jean-Pierre Rampal and James Galway, among others, made the RV 441 concerto a standard repertory work.

♫London Symphony Orchestra, Valery Gergiev (conductor), Avery Fisher Hall, Lincoln Center, New York, 23.2.2011

Much of the criticism written about Mahler is based on the assumption that his music is deeply connected to his personal state of mind and events in his daily life. This is true of all composers, but more so for the neurasthenic Mahler. Completed in 1905 but not performed until 1908, his Symphony No. 7 apparently received only minor modifications during a three-year period that saw Mahler's relative happiness turn tragic with the death of his first daughter and the diagnosis of a serious heart condition. In addition to the traumas associated with his personal life, his long and fruitful relationship with the Vienna State Opera Orchestra turned sour, forcing him to resign.

Anyone who attended this concert and expected to be swept away by the melancholy one can feel when listening to Mahler did not find it here. Anyone hoping to find in Mahler's Nachtmusik 1 an eerie world of off-key marches, nerve-shivering Alphorn calls and the sounds of creepy frogs, insects and night birds, or to be transported in Nachtmusik 2 to a romantic forest where mysterious creatures live and fairies dance through the night would be greatly disappointed. This performance of Mahler's Seventh was not for the traditionalist.

Valery Gergiev's conception of this work is clearly revisionist. All the movements were taken at a clip, most noticeably No. 2 and No. 4, the two Nachtmusik movements. The first of these is usually performed as a Walpurgisnacht, opening with plaintive and suspicious Alphorn-like calls followed by a chromatic downward slide at the end of the first crescendo, a scary descent to the devil; a dance that sounds slightly off; and whimpering, shaky final notes. Gergiev avoids the ominous: the horn calls are conversations, not mysterious communications. The first chromatic slide lands on the ground with a thud and continues no further. The score's instruction for playing the march/dance that appears at the tempo change to "Sempre l'istresso" is "Nicht eilen, Sehr gemächlich." Mahler wants the conductor not only to slow down, but to lead the orchestra in a leisurely fashion, which Gergiev did, but he conducted it in a way more reminiscent of Elgar's formal marches written for royal occasions than of Berlioz's tragic "March to the Scaffold" from the *Symphonie Fantastique*.

The second Nachtmusik, marked andante amoroso, opens with a romantic violin solo. Again Gergiev's tempi edged toward the extreme and led to my one complaint: the orchestra overpowered the guitar and mandolin, two instruments that would make the movement into a real serenade. In Gergiev's performance we don't clearly hear the guitar until the coda, when most of the other instruments in the orchestra are silent and the guitar helps close the movement with a quiet ping.

The fact that these two pieces were completed at least a year before the rest of the symphony was written doesn't preclude the possibility of revisions having been made. But what Gergiev clearly sees is the elemental fact that Mahler wrote the original movements at a happier time in his life and left one Nachtmusik movement marked allegro moderato, which was played here just that way; and one Nachtmusik marked andante amoroso, played here as a romantic serenade.

The opening of the symphony sounded somewhat thin, and I wondered where Gergiev was going. It didn't take long to find out. Shortly into the first movement Mahler gives us a yearning motif marked "Mit grossem Schwung" that is often played with a strong accent on the first beat. Gergiev evened out the accents, making it less plaintive and more songful. Mahler specified that the conductor should take this passage with great élan, and that is exactly what Gergiev did. In other performances it can seem that midway through the movement Mahler lost his way, with every cadence appearing to be the final one. Gergiev kept a steady momentum going from beginning to end, smoothing over any choppiness and giving structure to the piece.

The Scherzo marked "Schattenhaft" is perhaps meant to be a less joyous movement, but Gergiev deemphasized the decadence of this waltz and put it more in line with earlier symphonic composers such as Schumann and Brahms. The trio has a looser structure than classical trio sections: several subsections of varying tempi return to the primary section not as an exact repeat of the opening but as if Mahler were writing a development section of classical sonata form. The movement ends with the winds imitating bird songs, but Gergiev sees them as songbirds while most other conductors see mourning doves.

Like the earlier movements, the Finale, which sounds as if it's going to segue into the overture to *Der Meistersinger,* is an orchestral showpiece. Gergiev has every section of the orchestra well trained and in the final movement let out all the stops: the brass flawlessly produced bright silver tones and the winds outdid themselves in rapidly running passages. The colors that Gergiev draws from the orchestra are synesthetic: one can literally hear the colors or see the music. The ability to make an orchestra play with such solidarity is rare these days and reminds me of the performances of the Chicago Symphony under Fritz Reiner (albeit with a very different conducting style). If this Mahler is representative of all of Gergiev-LSO performances, we have one great partnership here.

Alex Ross in his blog speaks of a friend recovering from heart surgery, listening to Mahler's Seventh and feeling a "quasi return to life, the symphony's convulsions and mysteries giving away to 'visions of transcendent joy and vitality'." What he relates is an apt description of Gergiev's life-enhancing performance here.

♫Jeremy Denk (piano), Zankel Hall, Carnegie Hall, New York, 16.2.2011

Ligeti: Études
Bach: *Goldberg Variations*

Jeremy Denk's piano recital at Zankel Hall would have been memorable had he performed only half of the program. It is one thing to take on the task of playing 45 minutes of some of the most difficult piano music ever written, György Ligeti's Études, which a generation ago would have been called unplayable. It brings to mind John Kirkpatrick's landmark premier recording of Charles Ives'

"Concord Sonata" (not to be repeated again for fourteen years), Geoffrey Douglas Madge's first complete performances of Sorbaji's *Opus Clavicembalisticum* or Marc-André Hamelin's recording of Alkan' s Grande Sonata Op. 33. Then think of the less virtuosic, but still technically, intellectually and emotionally demanding *Goldberg Variations* of Bach. Put these two together in one program and perform them brilliantly, as Mr. Denk did, and you end up with one appreciative audience and one very tired pianist.

Ligeti wrote his Études with the hope that one day they would allow him to join the Pantheon of other great étude composers such as Chopin, Liszt, Debussy and Scriabin. Does he accomplish this? I would say so. Like those of his predecessors, these have a pedagogical purpose, to present the pianist with exercises: chromatic runs up and down the keyboard, tremolos, crisscrossed hands, hand-over-hand and finger stretching chords. The pieces are tremendously demanding both harmonically and rhythmically; several of them require phenomenal technique and strength. There are no beginner's exercises here. It's as if Chopin had written all his Études at a level of difficulty comparable to that of his Op. 10, No. 12, "Revolutionary."

The more emotionally powerful études are those that rely on mammoth crescendi which start at *subito ppp* and end up, in the 13th étude for example, at *crescendo estremo fffffff*. As Mr. Denk queries in his blog, "How would 8 be different from 7?" One way he suggests is to "hurl my whole body at the piano as violently as possible and hope for the best." He doesn't quite do this, but he succeeds in producing some amazing sounds from his Steinway. The framing etudes, No. 1, "Désordre," and what is becoming a standard repertory virtuoso encore piece, No. 13, "L'escalier du Diable,"are the most dramatic, the ones that demand the most technical strength. No. 1 requires the right hand to play the white piano keys while the left plays the black keys. No. 3, a piece aptly titled "Touches Bloquées,"is a lesson in how not to play cross-hand. Here one hand literally blocks another hand, creating an unusual sense of hesitancy and frustration. The impressionistic No. 5, "Arc-en-ciel,"goes through several crescendi before ending in a whimper. No. 8, "Fém," sounds like a speeded up version of Debussy's "Golliwog's Cakewalk." No. 9, "Vertigo," is the downward opposite of the rising chromatic scales of No. 13. No. 11, "En suspens," is another Debussy-influenced étude. No. 12, "Entrelacs," is played here fast enough for one to notice an opening motif with a strong resemblance to the opening of another work of extraordinary technical complexity, Beethoven's quartet movement known as the Grosse Fugue.

This was a monumental performance. Mr. Denk clearly set a benchmark for the Ligeti and added another step on the escalier to this being considered one of the great étude sets of Western music.

After performing Ligeti's massive work, Mr. Denk played an imaginative, individual and very personal *Goldberg Variations*. I think that when next attending a performance I will bring a baseball scorecard to keep track of which sections of which variations are repeated and which are not. My slightly rough scoring shows the following totals for how each variation was treated in respect to repeats: AB

(14), AAB (7), ABB (1), AABB (8). Toward the end there were one or two instances where it was clear that Mr. Denk himself had lost track of whether he would or would not play the repeat. Of course, there is no law requiring him to play every repeat and sometimes dropping the repeats of some variations makes sense. The 25th Variation, which can be thought of as the work's crux, after which the remaining variations are performed with minimal pausing between them, can throw the entire work off-balance if dragged on too long. Glenn Gould's 1955 recording becomes lopsided with the 25th variation taking over 15% of the entire performance time. Mr. Denk made the right decision here by avoiding the repeats for this variation. But by not playing repeats, particularly those that have different end bars for the first and second time, the pianist is in fact not playing notes actually written by Bach to be performed.

It may be an off-handed compliment to note that Mr. Denk flubbed a few notes towards the end of the *Goldberg Variations*. For a performance this extraordinary, requiring such a tremendous effort, a random error or two just adds to this performer's exceptional humanity.

♪Manifest Legacy: Jeffery Kahane (piano), Cho-Liang Lin (violin), David Finckel (cello), Alice Tully Hall, Lincoln Center, New York, 9.2.2011

Beethoven: Piano Trio in D major for Piano, Violin and Cello, "Ghost"; Piano Trio in E-flat major for Piano, Violin and Cello
Brahms: Piano Trio in B major for Piano, Violin and Cello

It's unfortunate that this concert started off on a bad (non-musical) note: as the musicians were about to sound the first upbeat of the evening, a woman in the row behind me yelled loud enough for the entire audience to hear, "Will the car be there for us?" Her husband then continued the conversation, stating that they were sitting in the wrong seats. This was shouted, mind you, after it had been announced that the performance was being broadcast and that special attention should be given to ensure all electronic devices were turned off. The audience was asked to remain as silent as possible during the performance.

Whether this indiscretion actually rattled the players who clearly heard this aural intrusion or it was just a bad omen for the ensuing performance I cannot say, but they did not really recover until nearly the intermission. Every note was played correctly, but lacked the nervous energy one expects from the playing of Beethoven. The rapport that would normally bind the musicians to each other and to the music was missing. The delicate dynamic balance between the players that shifts as the composer requests specific members of the group to rise above the others was off. The slow movements, including the "Ghost" movement, were certainly heartfelt and warmly played. But great chamber music, more so than any other musical genre, requires not just playing the notes accurately, even if it's done with a superb technique. It also demands that each member of the group know exactly what every other member is thinking and playing. This is why, with some exceptions, the great chamber groups are those that have played together for decades, and have played the works on this program and other works from the standard chamber repertory countless times. To assume that a winning performance will be the result of simply putting great musicians together is as unlikely as it is to have exciting All-Star Baseball or Football Pro-Bowl games, where each player knows his role but has no idea how to play with his temporary teammates.

For whatever reason, in the final movement of the second Beethoven work, the musicians dug in and realized an explosive wrap-up of the Beethoven part of the program. I came back from the intermission with hope for a better-played Brahms and was not disappointed. The Brahms Trio was considerably more lively and energetic; the players complemented each other and fitted in as equal parts of the whole. This rich and exciting performance made the previously played Beethoven trios seem as if they were written by a minor composer. If an audience member had never heard of Beethoven or Brahms and was asked after the concert who was the greater genius, I doubt from this performance that anyone would have chosen Beethoven.

Why did the Brahms succeed where the Beethoven failed? This question goes to the ontological heart of each composer. Beethoven's chamber music demands that the players fill in the invisible spaces between the notes. In Brahms every space is taken. There is so much more information in Brahms; his themes have a complexity and denseness not found in those of his predecessor. The music, of course, demands that each soloist be an integral part of the group, in touch with and responsive to each other. But each musical voice in Brahms is more independent and the music itself provides the connections between members, whereas in Beethoven the instrumentalists need to make the connections themselves.

If the intent of this series is to demonstrate the clear passing of Beethoven's mantle to Brahms, then in this aspect it succeeded. The awkward title of the series, "Manifest Legacy" (ringing in my ears as "Manifest Destiny"), implies that Beethoven's works were manifestly (clearly, obviously) inherited by Brahms. Brahms was doing everything he could to avoid writing Beethoven's Tenth Symphony, but he couldn't prevent the symphonist in him from appearing in his chamber, vocal and orchestral works as well.

♪Music from the Time of Monteverdi: Soloists, Juilliard415, Monica Huggett (leader), Willson Theater, Juilliard School of Music, New York, 3.2.2011

It might seem like a strange way to start a review, but I am refraining from listing all the music played last night. This is simply because I'm not sure what actually was played. A note in the playbill stated that the ensemble would present selections from among the pieces listed within. Monica Huggett said to the audience at the beginning of the concert that several pieces listed would not be played due to time constraints, and she named them. After the intermission, Nathan Helgeson announced that he would be playing an additional work for dulcian (an early Baroque bassoon) accompanied by cellist Beiliang Zhu, written by a composer whose name I couldn't catch.

Even though there was no attempt to play these early-to-mid-Baroque pieces in any chronological order, it was interesting to note how the music changes from the earlier works of Castello, Buonamente, Jarzębski and Rossi to the later compositions by Legrenzi, Cavalli and Bertali. The earlier music is often more adventurous harmonically, more likely to stray to far-off keys, more likely to jump to another meter or suddenly change tempo. The later works, in contrast, are more refined, more melodic, less likely to be formulated by a simple canonic structure, but also less likely to take risks. With Legrenzi, in addition to hearing echoes of Vivaldi you can also hear the music moving ever so slightly towards the classical era and away from the elemental freedom of form of the earlier Baroque period.

Of the composers whose works were performed, I'm familiar only with the music of Salamone Rossi (madrigals), Giovanni Legrenzi (Northern Italian School, the most important mentor to Vivaldi) and Francesco Cavalli (composer of the seminal operas, *La Didone* and *La Calisto*). I felt better about my lack of knowledge when Ms. Huggett asked the audience if anyone had heard of the Polish composer Adam Jarzębski, and no one that I could see raised a hand. Anyone wanting additional information about the composers and their works could do no better than to read the detailed and well-researched program notes by Robert Mealy. As I have said in earlier reviews, Mr. Mealy's comments are exemplary.

In discussing Jarzębski, Ms. Huggett joked that the work that they would be playing should be an iTunes hit. She was not far from the truth. This work, as well as most of the others on the program, had an elemental jauntiness so rhythmic that it was hard to keep one's foot from tapping the beat. Many of the selections were canonic, giving each musician the chance to share the theme. Usually the canonic theme is started by the first violinist and is followed down the line of string players, varied and repeated again. The opening work by Dario Costello was almost fugal and very modern in its modulations which took it strikingly far from home. In this and in later works, Liv Heym, second violin to Ms. Huggett, was able to keep pace with Ms. Huggett. It almost seemed as if they were playing the memory game, Simon, where a series of notes are played that each player has to play back. If you played the theme correctly one note was added, and the one who succeeded in playing back the longest run of notes won the game. In this match, both players came in first. If at times Ms. Heym didn't quite have the intonation that Ms. Huggett had, it could partially be the difference in instruments. Ms. Huggett's violin was unusually deep and rich.

The other instrumentalists were equally accomplished. In one work, the gambist, Andrew Arceci, turned his instrument on its side, sat down and played his viola da gamba as if were a guitar. In the additional work presented by Mr. Helgeson, he made a great effort playing his dulcian in a canonic round against the cellist, Ms. Zhu. He got stuck once or twice trying to duplicate the musical phrases that Ms. Zhu sent him. Tatiana Daubek and Adriane Post were as proficient playing Baroque violas as they were with their violins. The excellent basso continuo, often hardly noticed, consisted of Jeffrey Grossman on organ and Daniel Swenberg on theorbo; they provided the support without which the music played would sound thin and lifeless.

I again commend Ms. Huggett for her adventurous choice of composers and the students for their upbeat, spirited and enthusiastic playing of this uncommon and unusual music.

♫ Jean-Yves Thibaudet (piano), Carnegie Hall, New York, 2.2.2011

Liszt: various pieces

Encores:
Liszt, Cherkasky, Brahms

It is not unusual to feel ambivalent about certain composers. One of my first classical LPs was the soundtrack to the romantic film biography of Franz Liszt, *Song Without End*. My parents refused to let me go to a movie that would now be rated G, and I accepted this album as a weak substitute. The LP was my introduction to Liszt: a 51-second excerpt from *Les Préludes*, a four-minute medley of themes from the First Piano Concerto and Hungarian Fantasies and one movement in common with Jean-Yves Thibaudet's recital, the third Consolation. Once I discovered Bach I decided I had no further use for this frivolous music.

Much of Liszt's music is bombastic and frivolous, but certainly not all. He wrote a mammoth number of piano pieces; Leslie Howard's *Complete Piano Works* comprises about 100 CDs. Much of this music consists of imaginative and virtuosic paraphrases of popular operas and concert music of the day. Liszt's transcriptions include all nine Beethoven symphonies and all the major Schubert song cycles, plus hundreds of other medleys, referred to as "paraphrases," "illustrations" or "reminiscences" on music from Bach to Wagner and beyond. The transcriptions avoid virtuosity for its own sake, but tremendous demands are still made on the pianist.

For this recital, Thibaudet chose to play Liszt's transcription of Isolde's Liebestod from Wagner's *Tristan und Isolde*. This work with its numerous crescendos and decrescendos can never quite replicate the growing tension created by a large orchestra, but Thibaudet might have been more effective in creating an orchestral sound had he been able to produce a greater dynamic contrast from soft to loud, particularly in the final crescendos.

The program eschewed Liszt's most popular compositions, except for the third Consolation, and instead presented rarely heard works. All were performed with tremendous élan and a blazing technique. Thibaudet made the most out of the opening Consolations, drawing out the work's Chopinesque melodies and dreamy harmonies. The impressionistic "Les jeux d'eaux à la Villa d'Este" from *Années de pèlerinage* with its continuous trills and tremolos sounds simpler to play than it really is. Thibaudet was able to get the right balance between the rumbling left-hand bass figures and the right hand which plays at the piano's highest range, emulating the sounds of a fountain.

Imitation of nature's sounds continued in the first of the *Deux Légendes* ("St. Francis: Sermon to the Birds"). Working within a restrictive tonal structure, Liszt didn't have the musical license that Messiaen had a century later when he composed his *Catalogue d'oiseux*; and 30 years later still, his *Petites esquisses d'oiseaux*. Liszt's score uses a G clef for the left hand as well as for the right. Only in the final measures does any note go below middle C.

Chopin is again the creative source for Liszt's Ballade No. 2 in B minor. This is a work on the level of any one of Chopin's four Ballades. With a potpourri of moods from near silent hymns to fiery chromatic runs, it is a textbook example of the Romantic piano form. Thibaudet captured every nuance and made its virtuosic runs seem like beginner's exercises.

The concert concluded with a tarantella, a classic example of amazing piano playing that was marvelous to watch but lacked any musical substance. Those in the audience lucky enough to sit piano-left were treated to a view of the pianist's hand disappearing in a rush of speed. Those on the right heard nothing more than empty notes.

Responding to the enthusiastic applause, Thibaudet returned to play three encores. The first two were simple, song-like throwaways, but the third was Brahms' substantial Second Intermezzo, played flawlessly by this masterful performer.

With so much of Liszt's music now available in this anniversary year, it might be the right time to weed through his hundreds of piano works for gems like some of the pieces performed by Thibaudet, and perhaps begin to raise Liszt's stature from the frivolous to the divine.

♫Kenneth Weiss (harpsichord), Paul Hall, Juilliard School of Music, New York, 31.1.2011

Bach: *Goldberg Variations*

The senior music critic for *The New York Times*, Anthony Tommasini, recently completed a fascinating series of columns and videocasts in response to a teenager's question, "Who are the ten greatest classical composers?" Bach was rightly chosen to head the list. With this precedent in mind, I hereby declare that within Bach's canon (no, not the variations marked *Canone* in the score!) the *Goldberg Variations* is his greatest instrumental work. I say instrumental rather than keyboard because there are so many transcriptions for various instruments that to call it simply a keyboard work would be to limit its infinite manifestations. There are versions for organ, two pianos (a little known but wonderful performance based on a Max Reger transcription), harp, accordion, guitar and even a synthesizer. What is truly amazing is that some of these instrumental performances (on the accordion, for example) are really top notch. In contrast to his two other mature masterpieces, the *Musical Offering* and *Art of The Fugue*, Bach at least specified on the cover of the *Goldberg*'s first edition a default instrument: a

"Clavecimbal mit 2 Manuelen." This all speaks to the greatness of the music, which is in fact as close to universal music as we have in the West.

Is there any other music strong enough to survive a range of tempi that runs the gamut of performance time from Glenn Gould's 38-minute 1959 Salzburg concert to Rosalyn Tureck's 94-minute 1957 performance? The time difference would still be substantial–almost 20 minutes–even if both had played all the repeats. Modern editions of the score show tempi designations as specific as poco andante, ma con moto and istesso movimento, which have no basis in history. In the urtext edition, Bach only gives two variations a traditional Italian-named tempo: Number 15, marked andante, and Number 22, marked alla breve.

I would classify Kenneth Weiss's performance as close to the middle in terms of conservative to liberal interpretive decisions. Up until the famous "Black Pearl" variation, number 25, he took all the repeats. His omission of the repeats here was the right decision, I think, given the stately pacing of the work up to this point. After that he was a little helter-skelter, taking some repeats and dropping others, but all within the window of what is often done after the "intermission" of the 25th to bring the work to a dramatic conclusion.

Mr. Weiss seemed able at times to overcome the inherent limitations of the harpsichord by bringing out inner voices in variations such as the 3rd and 6th. At times I would have wanted a little more fire, in the wonderful conversation that goes on in the 11th variation, for example. There was some slight muddling in the 12th and 17th, but this might have been the fault of the harpsichord, an otherwise bright-sounding copy of a Flemish Ruckers. Mr. Weiss worked the stops for almost every movement, which may have led to longer than desired pauses between the final variations. He also handled deftly the tricky 14th which, when played at a fast tempo, often ends up sounding as if the right and left hands didn't quite reach the finish line together.

There is a well-known but apocryphal story written by Bach's first biographer, Johann Forkel, 50 years after Bach's death, as to the genesis of the *Goldberg Variations*. Forkel states that Bach was asked to compose it by a nobleman so that it could be played nightly by his harpsichordist-in-residence, Johann Gottlieb Goldberg. The music was meant to act as a soporific to cure the Count's insomnia. It would be hard to imagine anyone falling asleep to this majestic music.

♫Soloists, Collegiate Chorale, American Symphony Orchestra, James Bagwell (conductor), Ted Sperling (director), Alice Tully Hall, Lincoln Center, New York, 25.1.2011

Kurt Weill: *Knickerbocker Holiday*

There was some question in my mind as to whether there was any precedent in submitting a review of a Kurt Weill musical to Seen and Heard. In a site search, Weill's name appears only about half a dozen times. One is a review of his *One Touch of Venus* (a rave review, by the way). Another is a piece on a three-day festival of Weill's music held at the Barbican Centre in January 2000, the centennial of his birth and 50th anniversary of his death.

Yes, this is unquestionably musical theater, but certainly not on the order of *The Addams Family*, *The Lion King* or *Mary Poppins*. There is much silliness in both the plot line and the acting, but Maxwell Anderson's introduction to his libretto makes it clear that this is not a lighthearted musical. Anderson writes of the play as a polemical vehicle meant to convey his nearly anarchic beliefs. He calls government a business that has a tendency to turn its members into gangsters, terrorists and plunderers who then hide their evil qualities behind a facade of patriotism. One line from the play spoken by Stuyvesant and quoted in Anderson's introduction is emblematic of his politics: the belief that government is nothing but a protection racket perpetrated upon its citizens by the assessing of exorbitant taxes.

Anderson's intentions are certainly not those of a benign lyricist. Even the most innocuous melodies that Kurt Weill could produce contain elements of Anderson's political agenda. In the song "What is an American," Anderson writes that a true American hates police and the legal system for one simple reason: a true American never does anything he is ordered to do.

This collaboration between Weill and Anderson mirrors Weill's more famous collaboration with Bertolt Brecht. In both Brecht's and Anderson's writing, politics peeks out from behind the curtain of their most famous operas and musicals. Radical statements are made but in contexts and situations that hide much of their radical rhetoric. For a new immigrant like Weill, who wanted desperately to rid himself of his German heritage and be accepted as true-blue American, Anderson was certainly a strange bedfellow.

The musical tells the story of Peter Stuyvesant's arrival from Holland to take the position of Governor of Dutch New Amsterdam. Everyone in the play is corrupt except the two young lovers, Brom, the Nelson Eddy to Tina's Jeanette MacDonald. (Eddy did play the role of Brom in the 1944 film version of the musical.) Peter Stuyvesant's governorship is simply a transfer of power from a corrupt council to a tyrant. The subplot contains elements of *The Marriage of Figaro*, but certainly not the genius of either Mozart or the librettist, Da Ponte. Both Anderson's Tina and Da Ponte's Susanna are being pushed into conjugal relationships with their superiors; both plays end with true love conquering all, while the superiors learn the wickedness of their ways. The envelope that wraps this play's plot and makes for some ironic and amusing theater is that everything going on here is taking place in the mind of Washington Irving. Irving, played convincingly by Bryce Pinkham, speaks and sings directly to the audience and, near the finale, to the actors as well.

Weill's score is a charming one, and it was sung and acted with enthusiasm and spirit. The cast contained no weak links. For a show that had only two performances, it certainly seemed well rehearsed: the cast handled all the lines and lyrics with ease and confidence. The most famous tune, "September Song," could easily have become maudlin, but was convincingly and movingly sung by

Victor Garber. Kelli O'Hara's operatic voice seemed a bit out of place; none of the male cast members sang operatically. Her songs might have sounded better without the amplification that did no justice to her upper range. In fact, the entire production would have gained in musical clarity without the amplification, even if the audience missed a few words. The orchestra and chorus clearly enjoyed what they were doing, and the conductor led both groups with a firm understanding of that era's musical style.

♪Radu Lupu (pianist), New York Philharmonic Orchestra, Christoph von Dohnányi (conductor), Avery Fisher Hall, Lincoln Center, New York, 19.1.2011

Brahms: Piano Concerto No. 1 in D minor

This performance is part of the New York Philharmonic's "Rush Hour Concert Series," which features one or two works lasting about an hour and starting at 6:45pm. The format has proved to be a pleasurable one: the audience need not chomp at the bit towards the end, racing up the aisles to catch a late train or competing with the exiting audiences from other Lincoln Center venues for available taxis.

Not that it was necessary to extend the applause time for Radu Lupu. Unsmiling, reserved and uncomfortable in front of an audience, he quickly left the stage after one acknowledgement to the house which gave all the players a well-deserved ovation. Looking in profile like Brahms himself, Lupu sat bolt upright on a standard chair and seemed to be absorbing the energy around him. The more difficult the music became, the more he gained in strength.

Brahms refrained from writing a symphony until he was 43, 18 years after writing this concerto, hesitant to assert himself as the heir to Beethoven's symphonies. Listening to the extended opening, which lasted a good four minutes (the 20-minute movement itself more than symphonic in length), one feels that this could be the opening to Brahms Symphony No. 0. Dohnányi conducted this introduction fiercely, drawing sharp, galvanized phrasing from the orchestra. Lupu matched the conductor with a muscular technique that seemed somewhat at odds with his motionless body. Yet when playing quiet sections such as the peaceful, flowing second-movement Adagio, Lupu softened his playing so that the balance in the interludes between the piano and winds were just right.

Lupu's athletic playing returned with the final Rondo, a broad and symphonic movement with an unusual central fugue that seems to nod its head at the fugal sections of Beethoven's Ninth. Brahms also surprises us with a cadenza which normally is the piano's last appearance before the coda but continues here for several minutes to its triumphal conclusion.

Dohnányi has chosen his pianists wisely, Radu Lupu for the First and Yefim Bronfman for an earlier performance of the Second. Both pianists and conductor complement each other in every aspect. All are mature interpreters who need not worry about technique but can concentrate on the details of the music itself.

♪Yefim Bronfman (piano), New York Philharmonic Orchestra, Christoph von Dohnányi (conductor), Avery Fisher Hall, Lincoln Center, New York, 13.1.2011

Widmann: *Con Brio,* Concert Overture for Orchestra
Schumann: Symphony No. 4 in D minor
Brahms: Piano Concerto No. 2 in B-flat major

An apt title for this sparkling program might be "All Is Not What It Seems." Young German composer Jörg Widmann's engaging "*Con Brio,* Concert Overture for Orchestra" could well have been entitled "*Con Brio,* Paraphrases on Themes of Beethoven." Schumann's Fourth Symphony might have been listed under its original name, *Symphonische Phantasie,* and Brahms' Second Piano Concerto, as it was expertly played here, could have been called "Symphony with Piano Obbligato."

Musical paraphrase brings to mind the dozens of piano pieces written by Liszt in which the source of the music is made clear by its title, or by the music itself, as in his *Rigoletto Paraphrase de Concert.* Widmann's paraphrasing is different. Without the program notes would one know that this work, commissioned by the Bavarian Radio Symphony Orchestra, was written specifically to precede and be shaped by Beethoven's Seventh and Eighth Symphonies? Of course, now that we do know, can't you hear the opening of the last movement of Beethoven's Seventh, the famous opening of the Fifth, the *Leonore* Overture, the finale to *The Creatures of Prometheus* and the opening of the second movement of the Ninth?

This was a delightful and wonderfully orchestrated piece. With only a slight adjustment in instrumentation, Widmann used the orchestra Beethoven would have used for his symphonies. But save for its cryptic allusions to Beethoven's musical themes and its moments of tonality hovering appropriately around the Seventh Symphony's A major and the Eighth's F major, this composition never for a moment sounded "Beethovian." Parts of the work were composed in a vertical style reminiscent of Charles Ives's *Concord Sonata* and Fourth Symphony. In both of them, Ives uses a technique similar to Widmann where multiple distinct musical phrases are played simultaneously rather than sequentially.

Widmann was able to bring out sounds seldom if ever heard from the timpani, crackling and scratchy notes that would normally have you covering your ears but that seemed entirely appropriate in the context of the piece. Christoph von Dohnányi held tight control over the orchestra, which is playing contemporary music these days with as much élan as they have always brought to the standard repertoire.

Just as Widmann's *Con Brio* was more a paraphrase than an overture, so it seems questionable to call the Brahms Second Piano Concerto a concerto, particularly in the way it was done by Yefim Bronfman. He made it clear both in his style of playing and his self-effacing mien that this was not a Piano Concerto but rather a Symphony with Piano Obbligato. For a good part of the work he sat patiently, hands in lap, listening and watching the performance as if he were a member of the orchestra, or of the audience for that matter. This was particularly true of the third movement with its poignant arioso for cello (later transcribed by Brahms into a song) but to some extent for all the movements.

Bronfman intentionally emphasized the "non-concerto" nature of the work. Playing without a score, he was in eye contact with the conductor whenever possible. This was no battle of egos à la Glenn Gould and Leonard Bernstein (albeit that was over Brahms' First, not Second, Piano Concerto). In fact, Bronfman clearly recognized that this piece required him to follow the conductor, that to perform in a different manner would be to gain control of the piano but to lose Brahms' concept of the entire composition.

If you were to take away the orchestra, the pianist would be left with a score void of any completed themes. We hear flourishes, but never the whole of any melody. If the piano concertos of Schumann, Chopin, Liszt or Tchaikovsky were played without an orchestra, they might sound stark but they would still reveal the true soul of the composition. If the same were done with Brahms' Second, we would hardly be able to pick out the skeleton of a coherent melody.

This was an exemplary performance, somewhat coolly played. Bronfman did not appear for a second to be perturbed by the difficult piano maneuvers required by the score. What was important was not technique (that would be a concern of mere virtuosos) but the transparency of detail revealed by transcending the piano's mechanical demands.

So we step back chronologically to a "non-symphony," Schumann's Fourth, which he originally entitled *Symphonische Phantasie*. Although this work is symphonic in its traditional four-movement construction, each movement having the standard symphonic tempo and meter, its internal structure is tampered with enough to be considered "fantasized." The first movement's most prominent theme occurs not in the exposition section but right where the development section begins. The recapitulation of the opening themes never occurs at the movement's end. Instead Schumann segues without pause into the second movement, a brief interlude of calm that proceeds without a break into the third movement's Scherzo. The Scherzo moves along traditional lines until the second trio is completed, and a repeat of the Scherzo's opening section is expected. Instead what we hear is a slow interlude leading up to the final movement which opens with none other than the first movement's most prominent theme.

Dohnányi's performance of the symphony was in the tradition of the great conductors of the twentieth century, men like Toscanini, Furtwängler, Klemperer or von Karajan, who conducted it in a manner confidently self-assured, solidly taut and always well detailed. As he did with the Brahms concerto, Dohnányi led the orchestra without a score: it was obvious that he was performing a work whose every note has been deliberated upon over his long career.

One walked out of the theater feeling lucky to have been present for this unusually satisfying program, enhanced by the collaboration of a major conductor and master pianist.

♪Thomas Hampson (baritone), Thomas Adès (piano), Tad Rosner (video artist), New York Philharmonic Orchestra, Alan Gilbert (conductor), Avery Fisher Hall, Lincoln Center, New York, 6.1.2011

Mozart: Symphony No. 40 in G minor
Mahler: *Kindertotenlieder*
Adès: *In Seven Days* (Concerto for Piano with Moving Image)

It has been noted by many in the press that Alan Gilbert has found a formula for presenting contemporary music to his New York audience and NYPO subscriber base that seems to staunch the flow of audience members exiting the concert hall at the sound of the first atonal phrase. From my vantage point, only a handful of the audience walked out during the New York premiere of Thomas Adès' *In Seven Days*. Mr. Gilbert's enthusiasm for and admirable commitment to the new music he is presenting has convinced his audience to give an ear (and in this concert an eye) to these compositions.

If this particular program was unified in any way, it was in its seriousness and melancholic temperament. It began with Mozart's Symphony in G minor, the second of only two minor-key symphonies he wrote and only one of a handful of Mozart pieces written in G minor. (The first movement of the String Quintet in G minor probably tops the list of Mozart's most sorrowful music.) The second piece was Mahler's *Kindertotenlieder (Songs on the Death of Children)*. Can there be a title for a song cycle and its accompanying music more melancholic than this? Although it might be over-generalizing to assign this mood to Adès' piece, certainly the opening movement "Chaos–Light–Darkness" is no Rossini overture.

Mr. Gilbert's Mozart was pleasant in an old-fashioned way and reminded me of nothing so much as the performance I grew up with: Felix Prohaska conducting the Vienna State Opera Orchestra. At the time that performance was considered to be on the more adventuresome side. As with Mr. Prohaska, Mr. Gilbert's conducting drew from the orchestra energetic, sharply accented rhythms using tempos more liberal than those usually played by major orchestras. I liked his attention to detail, for instance in the yearning two-note phrase at the end of the second theme, bounced back and forth between the strings and winds and the cellos and double basses. The tempo in the second movement was right on the mark, and the brass excelled in the last movement's exposition.

Thomas Hampson's history with Mahler goes back over twenty years with more than twenty recordings to date. His performance and recording of Mahler's *Kindertotenlieder* with Leonard Bernstein and the Vienna Philharmonic is considered a classic. Older and a bit lacking in the ability to project his voice to the last row, he still was able to move listeners to tears. Mr. Gilbert, as usual, conducted with tremendous finesse and seems to be headed in the direction of Leonard Bernstein as the NYPO's next great Mahlerian.

The final piece was the New York premiere of Thomas Adès' *In Seven Days*. This work, as Mr. Adès stated in a brief pre-performance conversation with Mr. Gilbert, was written in collaboration with his civil partner, Tad Rosner. The subject of the work, nothing less than the seven days of Genesis, has been tackled by many composers over the centuries, too many to enumerate, and the Adès-Rosner team have given themselves a tall order. Their method of composition was for a short segment of music to be written by the composer and then interpreted by the visual artist, who edited video clips and photographs of the buildings which house the two institutions that commissioned the work: Southbank Centre's Royal Festival Hall in London and the Walt Disney Concert Hall in Los Angeles. I'm not sure what the Southbank Centre's relationship is to the work at hand, but I could see Walt Disney's influence on the video representation of the music. Disney's attempt to visualize the music of various classical composers in *Fantasia* was considerably less amateurish than the visualizations of Mr. Rosner, even though *Fantasia* was created 70 years ago without computer editing equipment.

The music was pleasant enough, though difficult to pay attention to with the distracting video. So much of the music was derivative that I found it hard to stop my mind from coming up with names of composers whose music Adès was recycling: Britten, Stravinsky, Hindemith, Bernard Herrmann, Walton, Bax, Tippett, George Lloyd and so forth. From the visual side, the recycling was of old graphical clichés: Pac-Man characters, exploding fractals, space journeys done better on science fiction television, portals opening to the other world, amoeba represented by dots going through binary fission and less interesting graphics than found in the early video game, *Snake*s. If the goal was to match visual images to the music, it could have been done by simply clicking the "Random Alchemy" visualization option in Windows Media Player. There, at least, you would see true synchronization of music and image.

Credit should be given to the conductor, orchestra and pianist (Mr. Adès himself) for making the 30-minute work seem more pleasingly substantial than it actually was. Unfortunately, 30 minutes later it had been completely forgotten.

♪Hye Jung Lee (soprano). Julia Szabo (mezzo-soprano), Andrew Bidlack (tenor), Paul Houghtaling (bass-baritone), The St. Cecilia Chorus and Orchestra, Patrick Gardner (conductor), Carnegie Hall, New York, 23.12.2010

Bach: *Christmas Oratorio*

Of all the major choral works of Bach, the *Christmas Oratorio* is perhaps the least well-known. It lacks the architecture and the solidly constructed story line of the *St. Matthew Passion*, as well as that work's unified sensibility, the encompassing pathos that envelops the listener from beginning to end. It could not be compared to the Mass in B minor, another monumental piece that builds on itself, starting as a church but ending up as a cathedral. Even in performances with a small orchestra and one voice per part, the Mass in B minor sounds big. Not that there are no big choruses in the *Christmas Oratorio*. All six sections begin with one, rousing and joyous in all but the second and fourth.

Although the Oratorio contains beautiful music, Bach took much of it from earlier works, and it has the feeling of being patched together. In fact, it was not performed in its entirety in Bach's lifetime and the named sections are really individual cantatas performed on the holy days before and after Christmas. Each retains the classic Bach cantata format, beginning with a sinfonia and/or chorus, continuing with alternating recitatives and arias and ending with a traditional Lutheran Chorale. The cantata form used in this oratorio is less rigid than most— it intersperses choral numbers with vocal solos—but the overall structure is still that of a Bach cantata.

Bach made some attempt to unify the sections within the cantatas by reprising the opening chorus at the cantata's end or including references to the opening chorus in the ending chorale. He also created a common timbre between sections: one and three use a similar instrumentation, adding trumpets and tympani to the oboes and flutes. At first hearing, the opening of the third section sounds like a repeat of the opening of the first. The same appears true of the pastoral-like openings of the second and fourth sections.

This performance by the St. Cecilia Chorus, an amateur group that has existed since 1906, was led by guest conductor Patrick Gardner. David Randolph, the group's director and conductor for the past 45 years, died this year, and Mr. Gardner, as guest conductor, confidently handled both the chorus and the orchestra. Like his predecessor, Mr. Gardner made no attempt to follow Baroque performing practice. String players used full vibrato, and although there were some attempts to speed up tempi (for example in the first section's "Bereite dich, Zion, mit zärtlichen Trieben"), most arias were on the slow side. A few were even lethargic, like the closing chorale of the first section, "Ach mein herzliebes Jesulein!"

To be fair, one has to judge the success of a performance on its ability to accomplish what it does within the context of the specific style the conductor has tried to follow. Mr. Gardner was not attempting to emulate the early music techniques of his homophonic fellow conductor, John Gardiner. He performed the work with a chorus more than twice the size of the orchestra, and tended to stretch out final notes. At times the chorus overpowered the orchestra, and other times it sounded muffled. I found myself filling in the instrumental accompaniments, which were drowned out by the chorus, in my mind. As often happens in performances, particularly those that are only done once, it takes some time for the musicians and singers to warm up, and the second half of a concert clicks in a way that makes the listener feel they finally got it right. I am not sure why this happens, but you know when it does: the instrumentalists and the soloists/chorus sound as one. I felt this point was reached at the wonderfully jaunty, bouncing, infectious opening chorus of the fifth cantata: "Ehre sei dir, Gott, gesungen." From here on I was captivated with the performers' enthusiasm and the music's snappy rhythms.

The soloists were uniformly good. Hye Jung Lee, indeed, was superb. Her bell-like voice matched the sound of the flute in its ability to be heard clearly over the orchestral accompaniment. She also was the only soloist to sing in a Baroque style with minimum vibrato.

After the intermission, it was surprising that all the members of the group returned on stage except the mezzo Julia Szabo. Of course one wondered what had happened to her since several numbers required her voice. Near the beginning of "Flößt, mein Heiland, flößt dein Namen" in the fourth section, someone began shouting back at the soprano, Ms. Lee. It took a moment to realize that Ms. Szabo was echoing the answers "Ja" and "Nein" to questions chanted by Ms. Lee. Cleverly, Bach took this aria from his secular cantata "Herkules auf dem Scheidewege," which has as part of its libretto a conversation between Hercules and the nymph Echo. This was done quite effectively, and congratulations to the audience for restraint in not turning their heads around.

With its long history under the leadership of David Randolph and its democratic method of making decisions (including who would best serve as conductor), I hope this group chooses a new conductor as charismatic, dynamic and long-lived as Mr. Randolph, whose last appearance with the group was at the age of 95.

♫Soloists, Chorus and Orchestra of the Clarion Music Society, Steven Fox (conductor), Park Avenue Christian Church, New York, 15.12.2010

Bach: Cantata "Ich freue mich in dir"; Cantatas II and V from the *Christmas Oratorio*

When Bach is performed well, as it was tonight, one could almost think, "Why bother with any other music?" If played non-stop from beginning to end, the 200 or so extant cantatas would require three solid days to perform, not including intermissions and tuning of instruments. Add to this the Passions, Oratorios and Motets, plus several hundred instrumental works, altogether over a thousand cataloged numbers in the BWV listing, and Bach could keep most "Historically Informed Performance" groups busy for some time. Who would mind if after a few months the cycle started over again? I'm being facetious, of course, but a performance as perfect as the one tonight had my mind racing with similar thoughts.

I've listened to the Bach cantata cycle many times and am quite familiar with these works, or so I thought. But from the opening joyous and jaunty "Ich freue mich dir" of the Cantata BWV 133 to the soul-stirring choral reprise at the end of the fifth cantata of the *Christmas Oratorio*, I was aware how little I really know of these works. I had never noticed the beautiful interpolations of the wind solo refrains from the first movement into the final Chorale of the Cantata II. The repartee between the strings and the oboe d'amores, played by Gonzalo Ruiz and Luke Conklin, each group in respectful conversation, was new to me. I was mesmerized by the energy, enthusiasm, passion and attention to detail. Special commendation should be given to Sandra Miller who played the flauto traverso with great sensitivity and was particularly poignant in "Frohe Hirten" from the second cantata. Here she was clearly aware of the importance of playing softly, when not playing obbligato, so as not to usurp the tenor's role.

All of the singing was top-notch. So many altos and sopranos who perform as early music vocalists strive for a pure "white" sound at the expense of revealing their individual voices. This style may be more appropriate for works by composers of the generations before Bach such as Monteverdi, Lully and Purcell. Some HIP vocalists have moved away from what was once considered the ideal upper tessitura for Bach cantatas, the voice of the boy soprano, though this vocal ideal still persists at many early music performances. But not tonight: all the women soloists, to varying degrees, sang with their "true" voices, voices that I suspect you would recognize if you were asked to match vocal voice to speaking voice. There were fewer arias for the men, but each sang his part with confidence and authority.

Many members of the orchestra would be recognized by New York concertgoers as performers in various early music groups including the now defunct New York Collegium, and as teachers associated with the Historical Performance department at the Juilliard School of Music. After so many groups over the years have struggled and failed to put New York on the map as a center for early music performance, the Historical Performance department has done more in its brief two-year existence to attract top people than all the attempts to do so over the last 30 or so years of HIP. Monica Huggett and William Christie, both prominent forces in early music, are joined by Juilliard instructors like Cynthia Roberts (violin), Robert Mealy (violin), Sandra Miller (flute) and Geraldo Ruiz (oboe d'amore), just to mention some of the instrumentalists in tonight's concert.

I have seen Steven Fox several times, and I must say he outdid himself in this performance. I missed the premiere of this program at another venue two years ago, but can't imagine it being any better. His choice of tempo, his understanding of Bach and Baroque style, and his selection of seldom-heard repertory are unexcelled. Church acoustics can be a hit-or-miss component and a maker or breaker of a concert. Whatever magic was going on at this concert, it included the unusually warm and vibrant resonance that came from the hall. With a performance this special, it seems a shame that it will not be repeated, offering more concertgoers the opportunity of sharing in a wonderful and rare experience.

♪Karina Gauvin (soprano), Marie-Nicole Lemieux (contralto), Tilman Lichdi (tenor), Andrew-Foster Williams (bass), New York Philharmonic Orchestra, Bernard Labadie (conductor), New York Choral Artists, Joseph Flummerfelt (director), Avery Fisher Hall, Lincoln Center, New York, 14.12.2010

Handel: *Messiah*

There was a time when each generation of concertgoers knew exactly what to expect from a performance of Handel's *Messiah*. It's claimed that the first performance consisted of a chorus of 12 to 16 singers and an orchestra of strings (4.3.2.2.1), two trumpets, timpani, harpsichord and/or organ. Later generations expected the performances to be the aural counterpart of a fireworks display: the bigger the better. This reached its height of absurdity at the Handel commemoration ceremony in London in 1859, the 100th anniversary of his death, where a chorus of 2,765 and an orchestra of 460 performed the work. This practice irked George Bernard Shaw enough to rave that Handel's music "is murdered by the tradition of the big chorus! People think that 4000 singers must be 4000 times as impressive as one." New York was no slouch either when it came to huge choirs and orchestras. Its celebration of the 50th anniversary of the Handel and Haydn Society included a performance of *Messiah* with over 600 trained chorus members. As ersatz audiophiles feel that the louder they can turn up their amplifiers, the better is their equipment and musical experience, so did those generations of concertgoers assume that the more musicians playing, the better the performance would be.

Before the arrival in the 1970s of early music revisionists, one was likely to see, if not quite these grand numbers of musicians, certainly full choruses and orchestras. Tonight's performance was somewhere in the middle in terms of size with a chorus and orchestra of roughly forty each. Today, though, one can't even assume that a particular conductor will perform in his specialized style. Mr. Labadie has led his early music group, Les Violins du Roi, for the past 25 years. Although his performance tonight was by no means weak, I wonder how different a performance it might have been if he had conducted his usual band instead of the members of the New York Philharmonic. Although all the parts in this performance do constitute a whole, I wonder if they may constitute more than the sum of the parts in later performances.

As would be expected from a Baroque conductor, Mr. Labadie favored brisk tempi, which reminded me in "Why do the nations" of the current Italian fast-as-you-can style of playing Baroque music. At other times, I would have wished for a more polished sound from the vibrato-less strings. Mr. Labadie used to good effect the dynamics that Handel never notated in his scores, but not to an extent that made the music sound Romantic. Mr. Labadie's fellow countrywomen, Marie-Nicole Lemieux and Karina Gauvin, both of whose voices I admire from their recordings of Baroque operas, suffered from problems that, again, might have dissipated at later concerts. Ms. Lemieux, for example, in "He was despised" seemed to be disclaiming instead of singing her aria. Ms. Gauvin, her voice pure and crystalline at times, was slightly constricted and screechy at others. The bass, Andrew-Foster Williams, recovered quickly from a wobbly start in his opening recitative, "Thus saith the lord of hosts," to sing a riveting rendition of "Why do the nations." Tilman Lichdi did justice to the few arias he performed.

The chorus produced the best music of the evening. Attentive to every gesture from Mr. Labadie, these vocalists clearly articulated their lines without letting the words lead the music. Mr. Labadie, conducting without a score, enthusiastically and with much physicality was able to leap up in the air at peak moments without having to worry about coming down on a music stand. Some of the transitions between movements could have been played *attaca* and the "Hallelujah Chorus" seemed to catch the audience by surprise.

Being a completist, I question why, other than for reasons of time, movements are excised from whole works. Certainly, if the music were poorly written, dramatically illogical or of questionable authenticity, it could be cut. But this is not the case here. I missed particularly the lovely brief duet, "O Death where is thy sting," and the contralto aria, "If God be for us." There are few works other than the *Messiah* that are so consistently inspiring from beginning to end, each movement being a masterpiece in its own right and each excision a stolen work of art.

♩Music of the French Baroque: Juilliard415, William Christie (conductor), Peter Jay Sharp Theater, Juilliard School of Music, New York, 3.12.2010

Lully, Charpentier, Muffat, Rameau, Cassanéa de Mondonville: various works

Encores:
Charpentier, Rameau

Although tonight's program can't really be entitled "Christie's Greatest French Baroque Hits," this concert epitomized the music on which William Christie has built his career. Mr. Christie may not have been the first conductor to promulgate the work of the French Baroque (Jean-Claude Malgoire founded his Grande Ecurie et la Chambre du Roy in 1966); but amazingly the American (now French) citizen from Buffalo somehow broke through the closed French musical hierarchy to become the leader for the past 30 or so years of the Baroque revival in France. The Juilliard School should be honored to have him back again as a guest artist and teacher. His association with the Brooklyn Academy of Music, starting with his cutting-edge (if such a term can be used with music written in 1676) full-dress production in 1989 of Lully's *Atys*, led the way for later revivals of Baroque opera. The performers and conductors who have passed through Christie's Les Arts Florissants is a list of prominent names in early music performance: Marc Minkowski, Christophe Rousset, Hugo Reyne, Hervé Niquet and Juilliard faculty member Kenneth Weiss. One would expect several more names to be added to this list from the students performing here.

Mr. Christie presented the results of his training of the first- and second-year instrumentalists in Juilliard's Historical Performance program. With about the same number of instrumentalists as in his own Les Arts Florissants, the orchestra was large enough to perform a variety of works by composers from the 17th and 18th centuries. The group began with the brief overture to Lully's *Atys* and then continued with music by one of the mainstays of Mr. Christie's repertory, Marc-Antoine Charpentier. Charpentier has been doubly lucky. First he found a patroness for whom he acted as personal composer, and thus managed to escape Lully's tyrannical domination of the contemporary music scene. But he was forgotten until Christie's large discography of Charpentier's music brought him back to life. In a search engine look-up of "Charpentier" his name would never, before Christie's recordings, have appeared as it does now as "Marc-Antoine Charpentier" ahead of his namesake, "Gustav Charpentier," the composer of the opera *Louise*.

The Charpentier selection consisted of one of the very few purely instrumental pieces he wrote, the *Concert pour quatre parties de violes*. This short collection of dances is clearly a favorite of Christie's: he has recorded it several times. It is in fact a paradigm of the standard Baroque dance suite best known today in the collection of Bach's keyboard suites. It begins with a canon-like prelude and continues with an Allemande that could have been written by Charpentier's contemporary, the famous master of the viol and recluse St. Colombe, on one of his better days. The Sarabande with its echoes of the popular *La Folie* theme was followed by two lively gigues, one English and one French, a distinction that perhaps was better understood by composers of the time. A *Passacaille*, a common musical form that often ends Baroque compositions, completed the suite.

Georg Muffat, a curious figure in the history of music, was officially French, but thought of himself as German, even though his parents were Scottish and he grew up in Alsace. Based on the suite performed tonight, one must consider him "French by music," the same phrase that can be applied to his mentor, the Italian-born Lully. This suite is pure Lully, from the opening dotted rhythmic overture through the programmatically-named pieces whose titles in fact rarely have anything to do with the music being played. There is nothing of the poet in the beginning overture or of the "Jeunes espagnols" in the second movement, and they could be substituted for any other movement in the dance suite. This disconnect between the title of the piece and the music it was meant to describe reached its ultimate absurdity several years later in Couperin's *Pièces de Clavecin* with titles like "Les culbutes Ixcxbxnxs" or, even better, "Les fastes de la grande et ancienne Mxnxstrxndxsx."

After some brief Charpentier Noëls and an intermission, Mr. Christie moved his orchestra into the 18th century with music by Rameau and Mondonville. Rameau has required less resuscitation in recent years than Charpentier; Rameau's keyboard music was performed back in the 1930s and 1940s by Wanda Landowska and in the 1950s by Marcelle Meyers. Mr. Christie's contribution to the Rameau revival came in the form of full-blown productions of Rameau's operas in Europe and here in NYC at BAM.

The music played in the first half of the concert is unquestionably an acquired taste. It may have been a relief for the audience to grab on to Rameau's infectious rhythms and more modern orchestral colors in the second half, but many were unfamiliar with the music and unsure of the protocol of applauding. The program notes should really have indicated that traditionally the so-called *double* of a French suite is played without pause as was the case here with the "Deuxième Tambourin" of the *Pièce de clavecin en concert*. The same was true of the performance of the last piece, the suite from Rameau's opera *Les Paladins*. The two minuet movements were combined and most of the audience was waiting for the final contredanse before applauding, but it had in fact just been played. Even more confusing to the audience was Mr. Christie's switch from the small chamber group that performed the first two movements of the *Pièce de clavecin en concert* to a full orchestra playing Rameau's own transcription of the tambourin taken from his opera *Dardanus*. Mr. Christie had to notify the audience by a nod of his head that the piece had indeed ended.

I leave the best for last: a foot-stomping, head-bobbing (not from the well-mannered audience, but from Mr. Christie sitting on the side) performance of the little-known composer Mondonville's *Sonata Secunda*. The work, part of a set of six, was played in one of its many versions, this one for two violins, viola da gamba, bassoon and oboe. The star here was the oboist Priscilla Smith, who played the highly virtuosic score with tremendous skill and confidence.

It should be noted that the instruments played are original or contemporary reconstructions of period instruments. The horn and trumpet players in particular are to be commended for the successful mastery of their extremely difficult valveless instruments. The sounds that these instruments produce come from "lipping": varying the pressure and tension on the mouthpiece. Think of playing the piano without keys and you get an idea of the difficulties involved!

The enthusiastic audience called the players back with ovations that were forceful enough to warrant two encores. The final piece, a brief chaconne, was a fitting ending in true French Baroque fashion to a delightful concert.

♫Michael Hey (organ), The Juilliard Orchestra, Nicholas McGegan (conductor), Alice Tully Hall, Lincoln Center, New York, 22.11.2010

Handel: Organ Concerto in G minor
Haydn: Symphony No. 100 in G major, "Military"
Elgar: *The Wand of Youth*, Suite No. 2
Britten: "4 Sea Interludes" from *Peter Grimes*

It is not immediately apparent from the program notes but all the music performed here is of English origin. Handel had been living in England for 24 years before writing the Opus 4 set of organ concerti, and Haydn was in his second residency when he wrote his Symphony No. 100. As the English conductor Nicholas McGegan noted, 22 November celebrates the patron saint of music, St. Cecilia, and is the birthday of Benjamin Britten as well.

It's certainly reason enough for choosing these works, but there were others. As this was a student performance, the works selected were meant to highlight the skills of the orchestra members and, in the first piece, to give the soloist, Michael Hey, the opportunity to show his talents. Mr. Hey performed admirably, playing without a score in front of him and making the music seem improvisatory in the way that Handel might have played it. Mr. McGegan, a front-runner in the Baroque early music revival, needed to sacrifice Baroque historicity, given the fact that he was leading a group of students who neither specialized in Baroque playing practices nor played on original instruments. It was clear that the string players were told to tone down their use of vibrato, but even so they produced too large a sound and at times overpowered an organ set to play with most stops off.

There was no problem with the size of the orchestra in the next work, Haydn's Symphony No. 100. Egged on by the vivacious conductor, the orchestra used this late Haydn work as a showpiece for its skills. Mr. McGegan took a faster pace in both the opening and closing movements as if to demonstrate what the orchestra could do. A few notes not hit exactly by the horns and a cymbal player who didn't dampen his instrument and set off squeaky overtones were minor glitches in what was an otherwise vibrant performance.

After the intermission the musicians came back to form an orchestra that must have contained everyone in the school. I couldn't do a full count, but with no fewer than seven double bassists one gets an idea of the size. The Second Suite from Elgar's *Wand of Youth* consists of six movements, each based on themes that Elgar wrote when he was a teenager. Mr. McGegan drew a sharply chiseled performance from the orchestra. The first movement's march was particularly exhilarating, the violinists clearly giving added emphasis to the catchy main theme, a theme that might have been written by Elgar's contemporary in the US, John Philip Sousa. The third and fourth movements show the clear influence of Tchaikovsky, particularly *The Nutcracker Suite,* and the final movement ends the work in a whirlwind of sounds.

Although I've yet to acquire a taste for Benjamin Britten's music, the Interludes from *Peter Grimes* were certainly played well. The third movement, "Moonlight," which is often done by itself, demonstrated the orchestra's ability to do sensitive slow pieces as well as showpieces. The concert's final piece, the fourth movement's "Storm," prominently displayed the percussion section's talent.

Well-deserved applause was given to the orchestra and its conductor for presenting a carefully constructed program, performed enthusiastically by conductor and instrumentalists alike.

♪ Jupiter Symphony Chamber Players Series: Roman Rabinovich (piano), Nicholas Canellakis (cello), Vadim Lando (clarinet), Anton Barakhovsky (violin), Lisa Shihoten (violin), Dov Scheindlin (viola), Good Shepherd Church, New York, 8.11.2010

Reicha: Clarinet Quintet in B-flat major
Beethoven: String Trio in C minor
Franck: Piano Trio in F-sharp minor

In my review of the opening concert in this 20-concert series, I wondered if future recitals by the Jupiter Symphony Chamber Players would hold up to this level of playing? Unfortunately, I wasn't able to attend the intervening four concerts, but based on the one reviewed here, the answer is an unequivocal "yes." The same two attributes that made the first concert so successful also informed this one: virtuosic performers and unhackneyed, innovative programming of undeservedly neglected repertory.

Virtuosi they are: the list of awards won and venues played by the members of the group are extensive enough to validate their skills. Both Mr. Rabinovich and Mr. Barakhovsky started as child prodigies, and Mr. Scheindlin has earned his stripes as a member for five years of the Arditti Quartet.

This concert was subtitled "Radicals," but could have been more aptly entitled "Descendants" or "Inheritors." The line of influence runs from Beethoven through Reicha, a contemporary and friend, to Franck, Reicha's student. As for being radical, certainly there was nothing of that nature in the Reicha Clarinet Quintet, as delightful as it was. The Beethoven Trio was instilled here with a kind of fire that is not entirely appropriate to this early work. Sometimes playing a composer's early compositions, with the foreknowledge of later works, makes the music appear more radical than it actually is. Beethoven had written a similar trio three years earlier (the third trio of the Opus 3 set) that, if played in this manner, could equally have been called "radical." Only the Franck composition might fall under the designation not so much in concept as in practice. The Piano Trio, Franck's first published piece, certainly sounds ahead of its time with its cyclical theme structure: a method of unifying segments of a work by carrying the opening themes over to later movements, transforming them into other themes, only to return ab initio at the coda. This cyclical structure had been used, however, fifteen years earlier by Beethoven in his last group of quartets. If there was any part of the Franck which was future-looking, it was the pianist's score.

Mr. Rabinovich mentioned at the beginning of the Franck piece that it was "very difficult and complex." A glance at the score makes one think not of so much of Beethoven's influence but that of Charles-Valentin Alkan. Alkan, nine years older than Franck, of whom he was both a friend and a colleague, wrote monumental works for piano. What makes the Franck piece even more difficult than some of Alkan's compositions is that it allows the pianist no pause. Blocks of chords and arpeggios run continuously through every movement. There is some controversy as to the correct tempo of the first movement described as Andante con moto but given a metronome marking of 69. The usual verbal description of this number would be at the high end of adagio and andante con moto would normally be near the metronome marking of 100. The rare performances of this work have often followed the metronome marking, so a special award for bravery should be given to this group for playing the music as described by name and not by Franck's probably incorrect metronome reading. This increase in tempo adds to the technical demands of the pianist in particular. Normally there would be a slow middle movement that would allow the pianist to relax a bit, but not here. Franck has written the middle movement as an Allegro molto and the final movement, started without pause, as Allegro maestro. At the conclusion of the piece, Franck, as if making up for the absence of a pause between the second and third movements, places a two measure pause after a false finish. This allowed enough time for the enthusiastic audience to mistakenly get to its feet with bravos before the real final two measures were played.

All the works on this program were confidently performed, and gave the appearance of a simplicity which was not, in fact, the case. Mr. Rabinovich at 24 looks to be following the path of another virtuoso, the Alkan specialist, Marc-Andre Hamelin. At the conclusion of the concert the musicians walked off the stage as fresh as they had looked when they came on. It was as if they had finished a marathon without even needing to catch their breaths.

This was an all-around exceptional performance of unusual repertory by fearless virtuosi who, although able to attract a devoted audience that filled every seat (even for an afternoon performance), are owed and deserve more publicity and attention than they are currently receiving.

♪Christian Tetzlaff (violin and leader), Orchestra of St. Luke's, Carnegie Hall, New York, 28.10.2010

Mozart: Violin Concerto No. 3 in G major
Schoenberg: *Verklärte Nacht*
Sibelius: Suite for Violin and Strings
Haydn: Symphony No. 80 in D minor

The word "conductor" normally describes the person who directs, shapes and imprints his unique vision on the music played by the orchestra. "Leader," as stated in the program notes, is really a more accurate appellation for the person who directed tonight's performance. Whether playing as soloist or taking his seat as concertmaster, Christian Tetzlaff could only nod his head to signify the opening upbeat or the conclusion of a cadenza. The Orchestra of St. Luke's is New York's version of that other headless band, the Orpheus Chamber Orchestra, and both play exceptionally well without a conductor. It was quite interesting, though, to see St. Luke's play conductor-less a piece like *Verklärte Nacht*. The score is heavily marked with expressive notations such as *steigernd* (swelling), *leidenschaftlich* (passionately) or *hervortretend* (prominently or boldly). Each musician must not only play the right notes but must also be aware of all the changes in meter, tempo and key, *and* understand how the composer's playing directives should be converted into sound. For the most part, this conversion was done. There were some moments when, with just the leadership of Mr. Tetzlaff as first violinist, the orchestra could have used a conductor to help bring out the composition's special haunting ambiance. *Verklärte Nacht* is quite unique harmonically, and if played with great understanding creates an atmosphere that chills the listener with its shimmering angst. Under a conductor who had a conception of the piece as a whole and could draw the exact expressiveness needed from each musician as required, it would have been a more successful rendering of this early Schoenberg.

The concert opened with a performance of Mozart's Violin Concerto No. 3 which Mr. Tetzlaff started within seconds of appearing on stage. The words that best describe the sound coming from both him and the Orchestra of St. Luke's are two that I hate to use, but here seem particularly apt: "creamy" and "silky". I say this in a positive sense because the performance was quite moving. Mr.

Tetzlaff played with great panache and ease, as did the orchestra, and it seemed at times unbelievable that he was applying enough pressure on the strings for the notes to be heard at the back of the Parquet. Even more impressive was the fact that Mr. Tetzlaff wrote his own very imaginative and Mozartean cadenzas for the first and second movements.

Mozart's ending to the second movement is unusual. First, it is uncommon in a concerto for the instrumentalist to play as soloist after he completes the cadenza. And second, Mozart ends the movement exactly as if he were beginning it again, the only difference being that this time the violin rather than the orchestra plays the opening theme. After a few measures, though, Mozart simply ends the music in a whimper.

Sibelius's Suite for Violin and Strings is an odd composition. It is sad to think that this piece, written by the same composer who wrote one of the 20th century's greatest violin concertos, was the last music he completed; sad he remained so musically blocked until his death 30 years later that this was all he could produce. The suite, intended by the composer to be destroyed, did not suffer the same fate as his notoriously incomplete Eighth Symphony. To call it slight would be an understatement: three movements barely ten minutes in total. The first consists of off-beat rustic music in the style of "Ach! du lieber Augustin." The second movement starts off tenderly, stirs a bit in the middle and ends in its original mood. Only the third has some character: an amazingly virtuosic Moto perpetuo, accompanied by the strings playing pizzicato. Mr. Tetzlaff tossed off this difficult violin exercise as if it were a bonbon. Watching him play made me think of a film being shown at two or three times its normal speed.

The concert ended with one of Haydn's later symphonies, which is unusual in having D minor as its key signature. It had been 15 years since Haydn had written a symphony in that key: No. 26, named "Lamentione," for a melody from a Gregorian chant used as the basis of the second movement. However, in No. 80 Haydn does not use D minor as a means of expressing Sturm und Drang as he did earlier. Instead he takes the opportunity to play some jokes by using the seriousness of the key as a foil to poke fun at the rigid demands of the Sonata form. In the first movement where the development section would usually start, Haydn instead places an inebriated minuet. When the real development section starts there is a pregnant pause as if Haydn were thinking which direction he should go: the tragic opening direction or the wacky waltz direction. The movement ends with the waltz as if it were a confirmation from the composer that the days of Sturm und Drang are long over. The second movement is lyrical and deeply felt, sounding as though it were written in a minor key, but in fact it is in B-flat major. The minuet and trio return to the original D-minor key. The final movement plays with syncopation, at first between the members of the string section and then, in the development section, between the winds players. The orchestra performed this final movement, full of rapid passages and sharp soft-to-loud dynamics, quite proficiently.

As a whole, all the pieces on tonight's varied program were played exceptionally well. Perhaps, with a little more direction from a strong conductor, it could have been more than just exceptional.

♫Monica Huggett (director and violin), Phoebe Carrai (cello), Robert Mealy (viola), Sandra Miller (flute), Robert Nairn (double bass), Cynthia Roberts (violin), Gonzalo Ruiz (oboe), Kenneth Weiss (harpsichord). Juilliard Baroque, Paul Hall, Juilliard School of Music, New York, 20.10.2010

Mozart: Flute Quartet in D major
Hoffmeister: Double Bass Quartet No. 2 in D major
Giordani: String Quartet in A major
Mozart: Quartet for Oboe and Strings in F major
J. C. Bach: Quintet for Flute, Oboe, Violin and Harpsichord in D major

Congratulations! But to whom and why so soon? Because first prize goes not to the music and musicians but to the "Notes on the Program" written by Robert Mealy. They are an example of what all program notes should be: clear, concise and to the point. Mr. Mealy focuses briefly on the history of the composer, then the history of the piece and ends with a short discussion of the music itself.

In fact, some of these attributes can be applied to the pieces in tonight's program: "clear, concise and to the point." The opening quartet by Mozart revealed no great secrets. Tempi were moderate, compared to those of other period instrument groups, and traditional was the word that came to mind. It seems strange that a word that is usually applied to non-early-instrument performances should be apt for the playing of this quartet, but historically informed performances (HIP) go back so many decades now that one can certainly break out the adjectives traditional, modern and even radical as valid descriptions of any given performance, group or conductor. To put this in perspective, let's just say Nicholas Harnoncourt, Roger Norrington and Christopher Hogwood are traditional; Fabio Biondi, Andrea Marcon and Jean-Christophe Spinosi are modern (or are of the Italian school if you will); and Piers Adams (Red Priest) is an exemplar of the radical side of HIP. Liberties are taken with the composers' scores by the modern and radical groups, not only in their use of extreme tempi but also of non-indicated or exaggerated ornaments and cadences, violins attacked sul ponticello or sul tasto and instrumental codas ending with unmarked diminuendos and ritardandos. These performances are as distant from the composer's original intentions as was Leonard Bernstein's recording with the NY Philharmonic of concerti by Vivaldi.

I have no complaints about the Juilliard Baroque's traditional performance of the Mozart. There is enough loveliness in the piece to overcome any style of performance (well, maybe not by the Red Priest). The soulful second movement in B minor (a key rarely used by Mozart) is played pizzicato by the strings and is one of those great melancholy slow movements like the second-movement Adagio of the Piano Concerto No. 21. The wonderful transition, marked by a full measure's rest and designated attacca, that ends the second movement continues to delight and was handled by the group with great aplomb. The repeated five-note bird-like twitter, playable by the flute but given by Mozart to the violin, is one those little touches that no one but Mozart could do to make this phrase stand out; and stand out it did with the richness of Ms. Huggett's Baroque violin.

The second piece on the program was written by F.A. Hoffmeister, a contemporary of Mozart. This quartet is really a showpiece for the double bass, with Robert Nairn frequently reaching down to the bridge to reach the highest notes attainable. Playing this human-sized instrument with a large German bow, Mr. Nairn moved the double bass center stage from its usual place as part of the background support group known in early music as the basso continuo. It was impossible to focus on any of the other performers as they were most of the time mere accompanists. The violin occasionally raised its voice, but aside from the opening measures of the Menuetto, it and its fellow strings realized their voices would not be heard.

Tommaso Giordani (basically unknown to all of us except the writers of Grove's who found 1500 words to say about him) is often listed as the composer of "Caro Mio Ben." It is uncertain whether in fact it was this Giordani or a totally unrelated Giuseppe Giordani or Tommaso's father whose name was also Giuseppe. A composer mostly of comic operas, Tommaso also wrote some instrumental music. There is a lyric quality about the work played here which, as Mr. Mealy points out in his program notes, reveals "a new spirit of Romanticism in the midst of the balanced elegance of galant style." There are some quite touching forays into minor keyed themes, particularly in the first movement. Some difficult violin passages were, as expected, performed with ease by Ms. Huggett. In the second movement Mr. Mealy finally got a couple of minutes in the sun, with a few virtuosic measures. Giordani is certainly ripe for rediscovery, with just a handful of recordings devoted to his music available.

Mozart's Oboe Quartet, written a few years after the first Flute Quartet, was played lovingly by Gonzalo Ruiz. The Baroque oboe does not produce as piercing a sound as its modern-day keyed descendant. Both the recorder and the oboe were loud enough to be heard in this small venue but might have problems reaching parts of the audience in a larger theater. Mr. Ruiz clearly articulated the string of 16th notes in the first movement right before the tricky change in meter, with the oboe playing in 6/8 time while the others are simultaneously playing in 3/4 time. This is perhaps one of the first uses of polyrhythm. Mozart does something similar at the end of the first act of *Don Giovanni* when three different bands play in three different meters. In music history this probably doesn't occur again until Charles Ives writes his polyrhythmic version of multiple marching bands in several of his works.

The final piece, a quintet by J. C. Bach, included everyone who previously performed except for the double bassist and added the services of harpsichordist Kenneth Weiss. I rued the moment I saw that this was the only role Mr. Weiss was to play in this program: I consider him one of the lost treasures of American Baroque keyboard players who emigrated to Europe. This includes the late Scott

Ross, William Christie and Alan Curtis, among others. Although Mr. Weiss's part was small, he did contribute to the vibrant performance of a piece that shows again J. C. Bach's influence on Mozart: listen to the second movement, for example, and its use of pizzicato. Bach's forte was the concertante style of the Mannheim school, and he excelled at that school's use of colorful instrumental combinations. The piece played here was very much in the style of the many sinfonia concertantes he wrote. These were typically concerti for more than one instrumental soloist, giving each musician time to play with or against each other. This final work in the program was an excellent choice for each talented musician to display his or her considerable abilities.

♫The Collegiate Chorale, American Symphony Orchestra, James Bagwell (Conductor), Carnegie Hall, New York, 13.10.2010

Brahms: *Alto Rhapsody*; *A German Requiem*

It was quite a publicity coup for the Collegiate Chorale to have obtained the services of two soloists whose names have been in the news for several weeks now: Stephanie Blythe and Eric Owens. Both received positive reviews for their respective roles as Fricka and Alberich in the current Metropolitan Opera production of Das *Rheingold*. One assumes that tonight's switch to Brahms must have felt to them like a vacation from the arduous singing and acting in the Wagner opera. Here they were due to be soloists for only a relatively brief time. Ms. Blythe took center stage for under fifteen minutes and Mr. Owens for half of the Requiem's 10-minute third movement (with an additional minute or two in the sixth movement). The third soloist, Erin Morley, should be commended for her sensitive and heartfelt coloratura singing but also for her patience: she waited on stage for 40 minutes during the Requiem for her seven-minute performance of "Ihr habt nun Traurigkeit."

The program opened with Brahms' *Alto Rhapsody*, a piece not often played because it requires an orchestra, a chorus and a soloist for its brief 10 to 15 minutes. Brahms wrote this as a birthday gift, not for Clara Schumann but for her daughter, Julie: Brahms was known to be enamored not only of Clara but of her daughter as well. The music opens with the words "Who is that apart?" and continues with "The wasteland engulfs him," and then "Who drank hatred of man out of the fullness of love?" If the text of this work was indeed meant to seduce, we may now better understand why Brahms never married.

The introduction is a somber adagio in C minor played by the cellos and double basses with tremolos from the muted violins and violas, and it sounds more tragic than the Requiem which was written several years earlier. The music gets slightly more upbeat when it changes to a 6/4 poco andante, but then continues in a miry mix of aria, arioso and recitatives. At the heart of this work is the entrance of the chorus, as the music modulates to C major and returns to its original tempo. The last section never fails to surprise and stir, and Ms. Blythe, who has brilliantly recorded this music, obviously has it close to her heart. One knew from the first notes of her opening recitative, sung softly yet surely heard by those sitting in the rear balcony, that this was going to be a top-notch performance. There is often a tendency here for the soloist to be overly dramatic, trying to pour out emotion rather than letting the music do that. In some performances one senses the singer is in competition with the accompanying male chorus, but this was not the case here. Ms. Blythe didn't need to be center stage. She had already captivated the audience.

Without an intermission, the concert continued with *A German Requiem*. From a programming point of view the combination of this and the *Alto Rhapsody* may not offer the most variety, as the two works are seemingly cut from the same cloth. Within the Requiem itself, Mr. Bagwell might have attempted to stick more closely to the marked tempi: there were moments, particularly in the middle movements, when the momentum flagged. The sixth and seventh movements were more successful, starting with the change from andante to vivace in the heavily punctuated middle of the sixth movement. At one point the music resolves with what sounds like the final note, a joyous C major chord, but after a brief pause one realizes it leads into a short fugue. This last part of the sixth movement is so upbeat that it seems miles away from a dirge. The final movement is somewhat anticlimactic, concluding the Requiem on a gentle *pp*. Brahms had written and performed sections of this work as he finished composing them; the sense of finality we hear in some of the movements' codas may have in point of fact been, in earlier performances, actual endings of the work.

At its 1868 premiere, this work confounded the musicians and ultimately failed in its earliest version. Its complex and dense orchestration and use of counterpoint made it difficult for the instrumentalists to play it successfully. There were no such problems for Mr. Bagwell, his chorus and his orchestra on this night.

♪Soloists of Juilliard415, Monica Huggett (conductor), Peter Jay Sharp Theater, New York, 8.10.2010

Bach: Orchestral Suite No. 1 in C major
Cantata: "Süßer, Trost, mein Jesus kömmt"
Cantata: "Ich habe genug"
Orchestral Suite No. 4 in C major

Let me begin with what would normally be the final line of this review. Regardless of the small complaints I have, the concert was great fun, as much from the performance as from the thrill of seeing young and talented people taking up, with obvious pleasure, the playing of Baroque music. It was also encouraging to see so many prominent names associated with Juilliard's Historical Performance Faculty: Monica Huggett, Kenneth Weiss, Arthur Haas, William Christie, Jordi Savall and others. Over the years New York has buried almost all its Baroque orchestras, the latest being The New York Collegium, founded by Andrew Parrott in 1999.

Perhaps one or more graduates of this school might find the right formula for an Arts Florissants based here.

There was nothing easy about the pieces, nor was there any attempt to slow down, even when tackling technically difficult ones. From the slightly hesitant and constricted start of the first movement of the First Suite to the leave-no-man-alive Réjouissance of the Fourth Suite, the players seemed to grow in confidence. Aside from the Second Suite, which highlights the flute, I had never noticed how much the Orchestral Suites resemble concerti grossi. This similarity was made even clearer by having the instrumental soloists stand in front of the orchestra as would be done for any concerto. In the First Suite the soloists were two oboists and a bassoonist. This trio played well but couldn't quite get the propulsion to lift the suite off the ground. Specifically, the Forlane, a rhythmic dance in double time, suffered from a lack of pulse. In the trio sections of the first movement one could not help noticing the often ignored bassoonist who in a quiet way was playing amazing runs with virtuosic ease.

The next piece on the program was a short cantata. Soprano Ying Fang has a lovely whitish voice appropriate for the opening aria. Mezzo-soprano Lacey Jo Benter has a wonderfully dark, rich voice that added substance to the lilting rhythms of her aria: Bach here is picture-painting the words "His wonderworking hand will weave a wreath of blessings for me." Tenor Spencer Lang, who looks and sounds like Ian Bostridge, also has a beautiful voice, but unfortunately sang just one recitative.

The second cantata on the program was the justly popular "Ich habe genug." I was slightly disconcerted when two sopranos rather than the usual male singer(s) walked onto the stage. But in fact, Bach thought so highly of this piece of music that he wrote several versions which can be (and have been) performed by baritones, basses, sopranos, counter-tenors and tenors like Ian Bostridge. The heart-wrenching opening aria stands with "Erbarme Dich" from the *St. Matthew Passion* near the apex of vocal music. Deanna Breiwick's rendering was lovely. Also to be commended is the flutist, Emi Ferguson, who played the accompaniment without reading from the score. The orchestra at times drowned her out which was a shame because her playing was charged with considerable emotion.

The concert ended with a rousing rendition of the Fourth Suite. It takes a master conductor to achieve what Ms. Huggett did here: she and the orchestra performed the work successfully without four of the 12 instruments required by the score (three trumpets and tympani). Ms. Huggett conducted the piece as if these instruments were never part of Bach's manuscript: at times the music that you would expect to hear was simply not there. For example, the score calls for the opening upbeat to be performed by the three trumpets and tympani. Instead Ms. Huggett began on the second measure rather than the first. Each movement was taken at the fast end of the acceptable slow-to-fast scale, so much so that you felt pity for the oboists who played almost non-stop. The final Réjouissance was played faster than I ever heard it performed, and it was a fitting conclusion to an adventurous concert.

Bach, Duphly, Rameau, Scarlatti: various works

In a review of a harpsichord recital by Anthony Newman, I wrote: "There aren't a whole lot of globally prominent American harpsichordists these days, and many of those that are (were) went off to perform and conduct in Europe, such as Alan Curtis, Scott Ross and William Christie." One could add Lucille Gruber to this list. She too has lived abroad, splitting her time between performing in Europe and teaching, but not performing, in the States. According to the program notes, this recital was her first in America since 1979.

      The instrument on which she performed, noted in the guide as being a David Way 1999, should more accurately have been described as a Zuckerman harpsichord, probably made from a kit. David Way was the owner of Zuckerman's Harpsichords until his death in 1994. The fact that it is a kit is not meant as denigration, but might explain some of the harpsichord's tuning and action problems. It also might have contributed to the mistakes Ms. Gruber made in many of the pieces. (She herself admitted that she was not very familiar with this particular instrument.) Even though this harpsichord is modeled after a two-manual French-Flemish instrument of the late Baroque, Ms. Gruber was unable to coax from it whatever capabilities it might have for shaping or adding variety to the musical timbre. The lute stop, for example, could have been used more frequently, in particular with the da capos of the Bach pieces. The dynamic range barely changed even when the manuals were coupled. This wasn't helped by the acoustics of the church, which are more conducive to an organ than a harpsichord designed for a French chamber room.

      Ms. Gruber has her own views on Baroque keyboard performance, and it is a mixed bag of traditional and more liberal schools. At times her use of rubato stretched out the slower movements so broadly that it seemed like she would have been happier if the instrument had a sostenuto pedal. Her use of ornamentation was subtle but scattered, sometimes done in the beginning dance section and sometimes in the repeat. Her decisions on when and if to play repeats in the six Scarlatti sonatas were totally incomprehensible, and at various times arbitrary forms were chosen: A-A'-B-B', A-A'-B, A-B. It is common practice these days to play all the repeats, often with slight ornamenting of the da capo. Even the eccentric Glenn Gould was consistent in either not playing the repeats at all, such as in the first recording of the *Goldberg Variations*; when he did take the repeats they were done only when the score was so marked.

      Perhaps Ms. Gruber has taught and dissected some of these pieces too many times. Her didactic side showed in her choices of Scarlatti sonatas: K.367 is clearly written to teach how to play scales, the right hand going up while the left goes down the scale; K.455 is a practice piece for learning to play the same note repeatedly; K.119 has chords that stretch beyond an octave. Scarlatti wrote these as exercises for his patroness Maria Barbara, but the majority of the sonatas require tremendous agility and a full use of whatever resources the most modern and advanced harpsichords and pianofortes of the time could provide.

Rameau's "Les Cyclopes" was one of the few pieces for which Ms. Gruber did not need a score in front of her. Indeed, she seemed more comfortable with the highly ornamented scores of the two French composers. Aside from the thinness of this particular harpsichord, movements such as the Toccata of Bach's Sixth Partita and the Scarlatti sonatas require a strong, forward-moving, rhythmic pulse to reveal their power: a power that Ms. Gruber did not provide.

♩ Dancers of the New York Baroque Dance Company, Catherine Turocy (choreographer), Concert Royal Orchestra and Chorus, James Richman (conductor). Symphony Space, New York, 20.9.2010

Rameau: *Zéphyre* and other ballets

In the continuing debate as to how one should perform opera, music or ballet of the 18th century, it is a strange and ironic reversal when a traditional and conservative production seems more radical than current avant-garde stagings. The norm today, perhaps in a desire to attract a larger audience to French Baroque opera, is a tendency to mount these productions with as great a disparity between the music and the stage production as possible. The conductors William Christie, Christophe Rousset and Marc Minkowski have all directed Rameau operas with original instruments in an historically informed manner, but with staging, costumes and dancing as if Rameau lived in the 21st century. William Christie and Jose Montalvo's production of *Les Paladins* has the singers interacting with a backdrop video screen showing animated cartoon animals that also interact with humans dressed and undressed. Christie and Andrei Serban's production (choreography by Bianca Li) of *Les Indes Galantes* ends with William Christie going on stage to join Patrice Petibon, dressed as an American Indian chief, and the rest of the troupe in a chicken dance to the famous rondeau interlude from Act 3. Christophe Rousset-Pierre Audi's production of *Zoroastre* has the villains dressed in Nazi style trench coats, while the good guys and gals are clad in what look like white undergarments. Only the Marc Minkowski-Laurent Pelly (choreography by Laura Scozzi) Paris staging of Rameau's wildly inventive *Platée* and the Harry Bickett-Laurence Pelly (choreography by Mark Morris) Edinburgh Festival production avoid this disparity: it's the story of a frog who fancies herself Jupiter's wife only to find out in the finale that she has been the butt of the gods' joke.

What a refreshing experience then to see the NY Baroque Dance Company perform Rameau in the style of the time when the music was written.

I am not particularly knowledgeable about ballet, and can only say that the stylized dancing here was informed with an expressiveness that I've rarely seen elsewhere. With arms always gracefully raised and faces fixed, as if this were a silent movie, more meaning was conveyed than in a traditional ballet. Even the masquerade-party-style masks that were occasionally worn were capable of suggesting emotional states. Soprano Rebecca Choate Beasley as Cloris was the most expressive of all, her face at times showing fear, curiosity or happiness, with only the slightest change in countenance. The other two singers, Ann Monoyios as Zéphyre and Lianne Coble as Diane, sang with tremendous enthusiasm and a clear understanding of the vocal mannerisms of Rameau's time. The orchestra under the direction of James Richman never attempted to cover the singers or distract the audience from the dancers.

In addition to the full-length *Zéphyre*, the performance opened with a brief ballet made up of movements from two other Rameau Opéra Ballets: *Le Temple de la Gloire* and *Les Fêtes d'Hébé*. This newly choreographed suite was created by Ms. Turocy in celebration of the veteran dancer Rachel List's 20th anniversary as a member of the group. Ms. List performed her dedicatory dance with great aplomb as did the three other members of the troupe who joined her.

As a final note, it must be said that the presentation, although in period costumes, suffered from being in too small a space with barely enough room for the dancers to be at ease. I had to catch my breath for a moment when dancer Joy Havens put her foot down inches from the front stage only to catch herself, with an evident look of shock. Speeches by both Catherine Turocy and James Richman, although interesting, added an element of being in a school auditorium. My friend called it "The *Glee* of the 18th century." I do appreciate the fact that the theater lights were turned up high enough to allow one to follow the libretto, something not considered in most venues.

♫Mostly Mozart Festival 7: Stephen Hough (piano), Concert Chorale of New York, Mostly Mozart Festival Orchestra, Louis Langrée (conductor), Avery Fisher Hall, Lincoln Center, New York, 20.8.2010

Mozart: Piano Concerto No. 21 in C major; *Davidde penitente*

This was the closing concert for the festival, and I thought it might be appropriate to briefly look back at the history of Mostly Mozart Festival programming. In naming it "Mostly Mozart," the founders may have sensed that if the festival were successful, they might need a loophole to get out of such a confining title. Maybe 44 years ago it would have been inappropriate to have a "Mozart Festival" with music from other composers, but not now: major festivals for Bach, Handel and Haydn highlight other composer's pieces on their Web site.

Mozart was the one-man star of the show for only two years. Haydn shared the stage with him in 1968, Schubert in 1970 and 1971, Bach in 1972 (when you bring in Rosalyn Tureck and Anthony Newman to perform you'd better allow Bach to be part of the festival), Handel in 1973. Finally, in 1974, Stravinsky was added. From then on the festival name could have been changed to "Partially Mozart Festival" or just the "Mozart Festival", where, as indicated above, anything goes.

I cannot confirm that the closing concerts of past seasons have always been all Mozart, but it was this year. The choice of pieces might have been made to appease the casual concertgoer as well as the aficionado: Mozart's most famous piano concerto for the general audience and the lesser-known *Davidde penitente*.

I found the concerto performance problematic from the beginning. The Allegro maestoso, was less Maestoso than Non troppo. The first big dynamic changes at measure 14 and 44 were weaker and flatter than they should have been. Stephen Hough's playing was technically flawless but detached, as if he were on automatic pilot, with little expression to warm the movement up. There was very little pedal use, although Mozart would surely have incorporated it (having at the time of composition just purchased a new pianoforte with an added pedal board). The second movement, an Andante, needed special attention, since it has been so widely heard in elevators and shopping malls as the theme from *Elvira Madigan*. It was played listlessly and indeed did sound like a movie theme instead of the exceptional Mozart that it is. At certain points in the third movement, such as measure 55 where the soloist and orchestra should come in together, Hough was slightly ahead of the conductor and the orchestra. There was very little rapport between the conductor and the pianist who seemed to be rushing a bit. It led one to speculate whether there were differences between the two about tempi? It has happened before, most notably in 1962 when Leonard Bernstein actually announced to the audience before a performance of Brahms' First Piano Concerto that he didn't approve of Glenn Gould's decisions on tempi and dynamics but defended Gould's right to play as he saw fit. Finally, wouldn't you find it puzzling if you wholeheartedly applauded the virtuoso for his performance and he came back to play a deadly slow beginner pianist's chestnut of a piece as an encore? Mr. Hough did so with an encore of Schumann's "Träumerei" from *Kinderscenen*.

The final piece of the Festival was *Davidde penitente*, which has a long and complicated history. This oratorio started out as a Mass that Mozart never finished. At the time of its conception he intended it as celebratory music for his marriage to Constanze and as a thank-you to God for his good fortune. In what sounds like a before-and-after honeymoon comedy, he never got around to finishing what he had started. But this is Mozart: henpecked, yes, but not a slouch. What he did produce was an incomplete masterpiece we now know as the Great Mass in C minor. It would not have been performed as a Mass missing the Credo, Agnus Dei and parts of the Sanctus, so Mozart may have added these sections from other music that he had previously composed. This must have been the case when it was performed in 1783 with Constanze as first soprano.

Two years after the Mass was written he was pressured by a charitable organization into composing an oratorio for its benefit concert. Not having the time to do this he incorporated most of the C-minor Mass into this oratorio, writing only two new arias to complete the libretto. The first of the new arias, "A te, fra tanti affanni," sounds like an aria from *Le nozze di Figaro* written a year later. It is played without strings, accompanied only by horns, flute, clarinet, bassoon and oboe. The other aria, "Tra l'oscure ombre funeste," starts dramatically "through the dark grievous shadows," then suddenly changes in tempo and mood on the words "Aime belle, ah si, godetei!" ("Fair souls, ah yes, rejoice!") from minor to major key. Both new arias are top-notch Mozart.

It was in this work that the orchestra and conductor seemed to come alive. The chorus sang with great enthusiasm and emotion. The soloists handled some of the difficult arias with aplomb; only Carolyn Sampson had some intonation problems at the very high and low ends of the scale. Mozart changed the coda of the last movement to include the soloists in a cadenza of stratospheric heights, the first soprano soaring often to high C and the tenor to second F above middle C.

Now, going out on a high note: that is the best way to end a music festival!

♪Mostly Mozart Festival 6: Freiburg Baroque Orchestra, Alice Tully Hall, Lincoln Center, New York, 19.8.2010

Mozart: Symphony No.16 in C major
Haydn: Concerto for Fortepiano and Violin in F major
Mozart: Bassoon Concerto in B-flat major
Haydn: Symphony No.52 in C minor

What an exceptional concert, delightful in all respects! Here is a group of players each of whom is a virtuoso in his or her own right. Except for Christine Schornsheim, the other soloists are regular members of the orchestra. The musical pieces that were chosen, except for the Bassoon Concerto, are seldom heard in concert. I would rank the pieces in the same order as they were actually played, increasing in both musical craftsmanship and complexity as the evening progressed.

I have always found the early symphonies of Mozart to be very slight works. Even with the advent of early music groups and their application of period standards, they still seem formulaic and superficial. This is true of the Symphony No. 16, although it has several intriguing moments such as the key changes in the development section of the first movement and the closing fuguetta of the second movement. As for the final movement, any theme that can be hummed after only one hearing is not very impressive. Mozart could have used the main theme of the finale as a parody of a lesser contemporary composer's work, as he did with the simple-minded music of other minor composers in his *Ein Musikalischer Spass*. However, the quality or lack of quality thereof had no effect on the performance– it was excellent. Tempos were moderate and as marked in the score. No attempt was made, as is common in other Baroque orchestras (particularly some well-known Italian groups), to see who can most strain the limits of the composer's tempo markings.

The second work on the program was Haydn's Concerto for Fortepiano, Violin, and Strings, a piece I was hearing for the first time. It's a strange situation that most of Haydn's concerti are not well known except for the two cello concerti, the trumpet concerto, and only one out of about 11 piano concerti. All of Mozart's concerti are known, and C. P. E. Bach's 40 or so piano concerti will one day be rediscovered as being of Mozartean quality. I've never been sure that this is the case with Haydn's concerti. The additional 10 piano concerti, three violin concerti, one horn concerto, five concerti for lira organizzate (when infrequently played, flute and oboe are substituted for this extinct hurdy-gurdy-like instrument) have never struck me as particularly interesting pieces. Perhaps I've been wrong. The double concerto performed here was delightful, with a wonderful catchy opening ripieno later bounced back and forth between the two soloists. The second movement (marked Largo but not unpleasantly played as Adagio) is one of those lovely slow movements that are often found in Haydn's piano trios. With an orchestral accompaniment mostly of string pizzicati, the soloists embellished the theme with great élan, ending with a short but heartfelt cadenza. The final movement was less interesting but played energetically by the orchestra and soloists, marred only by a wrong note hit by the violin soloist which kept her slightly off-balance for the rest of the concerto.

Another soloist from the orchestra, virtuoso bassoonist Javier Zafra, played the youthful upbeat Mozart Bassoon Concerto in B-flat major. Not much is certain about this piece's origin, and there are few precedents of concerti for this instrument, certainly none of which Mozart could have been aware. Vivaldi had written 40 or so concerti, but there is no evidence of Mozart having heard any of them. It is Mozart's finest concerto to date, the first he wrote for winds during a period when his earliest masterworks were being written including the Symphony in G Minor, *Exultate Jubilate* and the five violin concerti. Mozart uses the full range of notes available to the bassoon; in the hands of Mr. Zafra, on an original instrument, the bassoon changed from its occasional role as a producer of comic sounds to one capable of singing delicate, silky songs. I heard sounds I never knew this instrument could create, as if the player were disregarding the limitations of the keys and of the early design of the reed. The orchestra sensitively accompanied the somewhat frail output of this historical bassoon, never overpowering or drowning out even its lowest notes.

The concert ended with the last of Haydn's Sturm und Drang symphonies, No. 52. It is not as famous as some of the other Haydn symphonies during this unusual artistic period, perhaps due to the simple fact that it doesn't have an appellation as do most of the others (No. 26, "Lamentatione," No. 39, "The Fist," No. 48, "Maria Therese," No. 59, "Fire," etc.). This marvelous piece of music makes use of dynamic jumps, irregular and unbalanced (at least by period standards) themes, rapid bass passages and pregnant pauses ending in loud orchestral outbursts, qualities that are common to the short musical period between late Baroque and Early Classical. The second movement, although in 3/8 time, sounds like an adulterated minuet filled with sudden volume changes. The third movement, a minuet, often in Haydn the most rigid of forms with the simplest 3/4 time themes, is written here with off-beat syncopation in both the minuet and trio sections. The finale could have been written by C. P. E Bach, so similar is it to his string symphonies with syncopated rhythms, a contrapuntal bass line carrying its own melody and surprising jumps from piano to forte. Although the final movement is scored for strings and winds, winds barely get a workout, not joining in until the 46th measure. The orchestra members played with all stops out, racing to the finish line and being met there by an appreciative audience bursting with bravi.

♫Mostly Mozart Festival 4: Emerson String Quartet, David Shifirin (clarinet), Alice Tully Hall, Lincoln Center, New York, 16.8.2010

Bach: Five fugues for String Quartet from *The Well-Tempered Clavier*, Book II
Mozart: String Quartet in C major, "Dissonance"; Clarinet Quintet in A major

There has certainly been no lack of opinion as to the influence or non-influence of J .S. Bach on composers of subsequent generations. The common belief that Bach was rediscovered by Mendelssohn is only partially true. The story that the *St. Matthew Passion* manuscript disappeared only to resurface sometime in the 1820s in a store as it was about to be to be used as wrapping paper for cheese may or may not be true; but as important as the 1829 performance of the *St. Matthew Passion* was, its sibling, the *St. John Passion*, had already been performed, in part in 1811 and the complete score in 1822. Two of his sons, the eldest, W. F., and second eldest, C. P. E, were proponents of their father's work. The latter, in particular, took pains to maintain his father's manuscripts and reputation, performing the Credo *from* the Mass in B minor in 1786. Martin Geck in his *Johann Sebastian Bach: Life and Work* states: "*The Well-Tempered Clavier* did not need to be rediscovered: Bach's *cantus firmus* remained in continuous use among the cognoscenti."

Every composer worth his salt discovers Bach, and Mozart was no exception. What Mozart supposedly stated about C. P. E. Bach could also be applied to J. S.: "He is the father and we are the children." There is in the performance of these works the certainty that Mozart held Bach in high esteem. Except for some minor technical and transpositional modifications, the fugues are note for note transcriptions of the originals. All five that Mozart chose are written for four voices. If Mozart had wanted to show that he could outdo Bach, he certainly could have chosen more difficult pieces or used one of the two fugues that were written for five voices. The Emerson Quartet played the pieces in a style appropriate to their use as study pieces for Mozart to gain skill in writing contrapuntally, resulting ultimately in his writing of the great fugal finale of Symphony 41.

The second work on the program was Mozart's String Quartet in C major. Without going into the history of dissonance (a word with all kinds of definitions and interpretations, musical and non-musical), the dissonance that Mozart uses in this quartet is unusual for him in this particular period, but not uncommon for composers of earlier periods. The works of Machaut, Gesualdo, Monteverdi and Scarlatti, to name a few, were rife with dissonance, so much so that one wonders why Mozart's use of it was so shocking in its time. Both C. P. E and W. F. Bach used it; W. F. even composed a string symphony called "The Dissonant." As a matter of fact, one would think the collective subconscious of the time would have overtaken the tenets of the Age of

Enlightenment in regard to musical resolution. Understandably, the modern ear has a hard time even recognizing where the dissonance is in this quartet, so harmless is its effect.

The beginning of the first movement of this quartet, one of six dedicated to Haydn, creates such a sensation of ab initio that it seems very likely that Haydn reciprocated the dedication from Mozart in the opening movement of *The Creation*. The approach to this work by the Emerson Quartet, which worked for the earlier piece, did not do so here. The playing was technically faultless but suffered from a mechanical execution. This doesn't have to be the case with music played hundreds of times. If one puts one's heart into it, as Gil Shaham did in an earlier Mostly Mozart performance of the A-major Violin Concerto, the music would express this attitude.

The same cannot be said of the concluding work, the Clarinet Quintet in A major. The addition of David Shifrin to the stage seemed to awaken the Emerson from their sleep. The players warmed up to their instruments and played with flair and feeling. Special mention should be given to violist Lawrence Dutton for his tender and sensitive playing of the second variation in the final movement. Now, if the same attention to the music as Mr. Dutton gave had been given by the other players to the previously performed works, this would have been a truly great evening of music.

Although the Emerson String Quartet performed a pre-concert recital at 6:30, those of us who appeared for the scheduled concert should not have been penalized with a performance of just 40 minutes in the first half, and even less (35 minutes) in the second. Perhaps, based on the audience's applause, an encore was in order?

♫Mostly Mozart Festival 2: Mark Morris Dance Group, Riverside Choral Society Chamber Singers, Orchestra of St. Luke's, Jane Glover (conductor), David H. Koch Theater, Lincoln Center, New York, 5.8.2010

Handel: *L'Allegro, il Penseroso ed il Moderato*

It was good to see Mark Morris's revival of his 1988 production of this Handel ode, if only to be reminded of how incredibly creative and imaginative he can be. His most recent productions have been, at best, moderate successes. Haydn's *L'Isola Disabitata*, performed last year at John Jay College by the Gotham Opera Company, demonstrated some aspects of this decline. Granted, that may not have been a top notch opera, but Morris didn't help by having as the sole stage prop (aside from a blow-up toy of a fawn fondled by the ingenue), a rock representing the island. That set reminded me of the dozens of stock desert islands of dozens of marooned *New Yorker* cartoon characters. The only difference was that the island held the entire cast of four singers: the two females were dressed in diaphanous disarray, and one of the two men solely in a towel as if he had just gotten out of the shower. In his 2008 staging and choreography of Purcell's *King Arthur* for the New York City Opera, silliness met sublime music.

The costumes were designed by Isaac Mizrahi, who previously and successfully collaborated with Morris in Rameau's *Plateé*. Outrageous costumes work in an opera about a self-centered frog but do not work for *King Arthur*, called by Purcell himself a "dramatick opera." I don't think the composer or the librettist, John Dryden, would have liked to see their characters dressed in t-shirts or just their underwear; or the famous aria, *The Cold Song*, sung by the bass baritone from a refrigerator.

I am happy to say that few of these eccentricities marred *L'Allegro, il Penseroso ed il Moderato*. In hindsight one can see some of the above-mentioned defects in this early work: exaggerated vaudevillian gestures, cartoonish mimicking of what is being sung, silly facial expressions. But here there were no inappropriate props, anachronistic costumes or tacky stage sets. The dancers–women in flowing pastel-colored dresses, men in similarly colored shirts and tights–created a magical world of comings and goings, appearings and disappearings. At one moment a solitary figure haunts the stage, the next minute dancers materialize, transformed into a chariot of horses or hunters with their bloodhounds: all this without one single blow-up toy or refrigerator. The stage was enclosed by a series of proscenium arches, one within the other, each one containing scrims of varying transparency and color. This was all that was needed to set the scene. A verdant field was suggested by a green scrim covered (except for a small section touching the stage) by a blue scrim. A darkened transparent scrim served as a mirror for two dancers, revealing their steps from the front and the back. Unfortunately, the physical construction of the stage might also have been the reason why libretto-clarifying supertitles were not available.

In spite of having to give so much of my attention to understanding the text (the libretto handed out with the program was useless during the performance, unless you were wearing night goggles) and focusing on the dancers, I was certainly aware of the music. I could not, though, give much of my attention to the quality of the playing other than to say that I noted no irregularities. Conducted by Jane Glover, the St. Luke's Orchestra performed outstandingly, with special merit given to the key soloists: the oboist in "Come, Thou Goddess Fair and Free" and "As Steals the Morn"; the flutist in "Sweet Bird"; the cellist in "May at Last My Weary Age." (Why was the other heartrending cello obbligato aria, "But O, Sad Virgin, That Thy Pow'r," omitted?) Outside of Handel's *Acis and Galatea*, I can't think of any other work of Handel (including *Messiah*) that is filled with more touchingly sensuous melodies, one right after the other. The vocalists were uniformly excellent. Thankfully, Handel has given us a reprieve in this ode by sparing us from his usual da capo (A-B-A) structure, the basis of so many of his other arias.

I had some trepidation attending this performance. This was the second adaptation that I had seen; the first was at the Paris Opera in 2007. With an all-star roster, starting with William Christie and *Les Arts Florissants* and continuing with soloists Kate Royal, Toby Spence and Roderick Williams, it suffered from the pretentious political agenda of the South African choreographer, Robyn Orlin. *L'Allegro* was set in the mountains of South Africa and *Il Penseroso* in the slums of Johannesburg. Scenes from these locales were, distractingly, projected on a screen at the back of the stage. The dancers spent their time onstage rummaging through piles of clothes and then changing into them. When not doing this, they trotted around the stage holding pocket video cameras aimed at themselves or others; these recordings were displayed in real time on the screen. Was this some political statement about the tyranny of surveillance cameras in South Africa? What does this have to do with Handel? Who knows? The final chorus, ending optimistically in Morris's version by choosing to live with Mirth or ending sensibly in Handel's version by living with Moderation, ends inexplicably in Orlin's version with a video of the destruction of the Twin Towers. I stood up as the Bravi were shouted and walked out.

Thank you, Mark Morris, for enhancing the life affirming music of Handel.

♪Mostly Mozart Festival 1: Gil Shaham (violin), Mostly Mozart Festival Orchestra, Pablo Heras-Cosado (conductor), Avery Fisher Hall, Lincoln Center, New York, 3.8.2010

Stravinsky: "Dumbarton Oaks" Concerto
Mozart: Violin Concerto in A major, "Turkish"
Beethoven: Symphony No. 2 in D major

One can understand why over the years short shrift may have been given to this festival. Surely, the wine cask from which Mozart's music has been poured out for the past 44 years would contain mostly dregs by now. Having been to the first season back in 1966, and having attended regularly for the first 10 years, my reason for not continuing to go was the common complaint that less and less Mozart was being performed. I'm not the purist now that I was, and I could understand that to keep the festival going it would, of necessity, have to broaden its repertory. As a comparison, Seen and Heard International, though granted it's of British origin, receives and publishes dozens of reviews from the London Proms. No Mostly Mozart concert has been reviewed here since 2006, and while no attempt will be made to compete with the Prom's 50 or so concerts reviewed, we will give the Mostly Mozart Festival some of what is due.

This performance was held in a modified Avery Fisher Hall with seating in the back and to the side of the orchestra, in part to increase the number of people attending but also, perhaps, to give the concert hall a stadium-like feeling, *à la* Royal Albert Hall. I'm not sure that this change made for a more congenial space; Royal Albert Hall, which holds twice as many people, still felt warmer and more mellow. I should qualify that by saying the temperature in Avery Fisher Hall rose several degrees with the entrance of young conductor Pablo Heras-Cosado. He and the equally hirsute Gustavo Dudamel share a youthful enthusiasm and a commanding presence. Tall and self-assured, Heras-Cosado conducts baton-less in the tradition of Stokowski, Mitropoulos, Boulez and Leinsdorf ("Why use a stick if I can't promise a carrot'"), with broad and sweeping arm gestures. His only understandable mishap was in the transition between the second and third movement of the Mozart Violin Concerto where he took the upbeat before the orchestra was ready. I suspect he might have done this to avoid being annoyed by the small groups who applauded after every movement.

The "Dumbarton Oaks" Concerto was an ideal starter. If I could summarize the performance in a few words, it would be, to use a borrowed title from a Stravinsky disciple, John Adams, a *Short Ride in a Fast Machine*. The first movement is a stylized Brandenburg Concerto: the opening phrases coming to life in the manner of the opening to the First Brandenburg, the flutes later reflecting the tonal impact of the Fourth Brandenburg. The nearly always present basso continuo and bass instruments are a reminder of the ambiance of the Third and Sixth. The way the instruments individually or in groups take over the orchestra is very much in the style of the concerto grosso. One would not normally think of Stravinsky as comical, but there were outright guffaws during the beginning of the second movement with the unexpected exaggerating tootings of the bassoon. The final movement continues the locomotive sounds of the first movement, the pulsing bass and improvisatory style clearly influenced by jazz of the day. All these complicated goings-on were held together by the taut reins of the conductor. It was totally clear from the conductor's gestures what he wanted to hear, and the orchestra gave him everything he wanted. The final notes, unfortunately, were lost in the hurry of the audience to applaud and cry "Bravo." Unusual as this response is for most of Stravinsky's music, the audience seemed totally, completely caught up in the performance of the music, and of this vibrant conductor.

My feeling is that Gil Shaham knows the score of the Fifth Violin Concerto of Mozart so well that he could play it while reading a book or listening to Hip-Hop music with headphones or both at the same time. The work is clearly a part of him, varied only slightly by the give and take of the conductor and the orchestra. The pacing of the outer movements was slightly faster, more in the style of commonly heard historically informed performances. There was no attempt though to imitate original instruments. There didn't have to be. This was a performance that transcended any parochial protocols. Everything flowed naturally, as if Mozart himself were playing and conducting. The normally hackneyed Turkish interlude in the middle of the third movement had a push and pull that made it sound as if it were a newly discovered revision of the piece by Mozart himself.

I am not sure why some conductors who normally are sticklers about following the score feel they have the freedom to end a piece exactly opposite from the way that the composer specified. The pianist Piotr Anderszewski, for example, whose classic recording of Beethoven's *Diabelli Variations* was praised for its authenticity ("Beethoven as he would have played it himself") ends his recording of the piece with a *piano* when the score clearly marks it as *forte*. Here, Heras-Cosado did the opposite. Instead of ending the piece quietly, he ended it in complete disregard of Mozart's clearly specified *piano* with a *forte*.

The encore performed by Mr. Shaham was an amazing piece of virtuosity:

ten minutes of almost everything a violin can and can't do. Mr. Shaham announced that the piece was "Turkish but not Mozart." I spent the intermission trying to get the name of the piece and the composer from several staff and orchestra members, but all I could find out from them was that it was an improvisation. They ignored the fact (which I kept mentioning) that the orchestra was accompanying him from a score that had to be written and named by someone.

The final piece was Beethoven's Symphony No.2. The performance continued in the punchy, charged style of the conductor with tempi somewhat on the fast side. It was adequate, but I kept wondering if, with the packed agenda of this conductor, he might not have given as much time to rehearsing the piece as it needed. It would be the kind of warhorse that the orchestra should know by heart, and there was not the feeling as in the earlier pieces that Heras-Cosado had thrown <u>his</u> heart and soul into it.

Having broken the ice and rejoined the Festival, I must say I was pleasantly surprised by the high performance level, even though this particular program was, fortunately, Mostly Not Mozart.

Note: After this review was published, it came to my attention that, indeed, the encore Gil Shaham played was an improvisation. According to Alan Kozinn of *The New York Times*, Shaham improvised upon and wrote the orchestral accompaniment for the popular Turkish tune "Nihavent Longa."

♫: The Collegiate Chorale and the American Symphony Orchestra, James Bagwell (conductor), Skirball Center for the Performing Arts, New York University, New York, 12.5.2010

Handel: *Israel in Egypt*

We probably all know at least one story of a composer whose great works were not appreciated in his time. Whether it's Emperor Joseph II's complaint that *The Marriage of Figaro* had "too many notes"; Mark Twain's comment, "I have been told that Wagner's music is better than it sounds"; or Rossini on the same composer, "Wagner has lovely moments but awful quarters of an hour": we often feel superior to those who couldn't hear the "true" music. According to Christopher Hogwood in his biography of Handel, the first performance of *Israel in Egypt* had such "high density of choral writing" and "such scarce opportunities for solo virtuosity" that the audience was numbed. Even with a second performance that Handel billed as "shortened and Intermix'd with Song," it failed.

If I never had heard this oratorio before, I would have had to agree with Handel's audience's complaints about it. Part I in this particular performance has 11 consecutive choruses without a break. To make matters worse, the chorus of 150 so overwhelmed the 25-piece orchestra that you couldn't turn your attention to the instrumental accompaniment for relief from sonic overload. And that was a shame, because the orchestra plays some delightful music, as can be heard in the arias. Note, for example, the trumpet-like oboes in "The Lord is a Man of War." Sir Malcom Sargent in his classic 1955 recording actually substituted trumpets here for the oboes, stating almost convincingly for purists like me that he was sure that if Handel had had our modern-day valved trumpets, which are capable of playing this music, he would have used them.

There are many versions of this oratorio, some with three parts, some with two, some with overtures, some starting out with only a recitative, some with as many as 52 movements or more, some with as few as half that. The real issue here, though, is not which edition is used but how each version produces the most satisfying musical experience given the number of performers involved. It is understandable that if the Collegiate Chorale contains 200 members, you would want as many as possible to perform. You would also want to make sure that the music chosen would be suitable for the size of the chorus and orchestra. I assume some attempt was made to do this, since there were only about 150 singers in this production's chorus. If reducing the chorus by 25 percent doesn't work (which, in this case, it didn't), then the size of the orchestra should be increased. Except for the parts where Handel specified a double chorus, the singers could be split so that that each half of the chorus sings a number in turn.

As for the soloists, the two sopranos were adequate. The countertenor, Brian Asawa, could have controlled his histrionics a bit, but only he and tenor Rufus Müller seemed to be awake and alert enough to attempt (though unsuccessfully) to spark some esprit de corps. At least these singers, in contrast to the two other male singers, were in key. If the rest of the production were even minimally adequate I would have felt that the baritone and bass made some effort, but baritone Ron Loyd had minor intonation problems, and bass-baritone Robert Osborne sang neither as a bass nor as a baritone. I don't remember when I last wished I could turn my ears off, so insufferable was his singing.

To quote from a most intelligent review of a previous performance of *Israel in Egypt* conducted by James Bagwell back in 2007 with a different chorus and orchestra, "Just what went wrong here? I don't believe that the conductor, James Bagwell, is entirely to blame, although his interpretation came across as fussy and lacking in spirit, especially the festive Handelian spirit we all love." I would have to be less kind and say that I'd give him one more strike and he'd be out.

43184488R00212

Made in the USA
Middletown, DE
02 May 2017